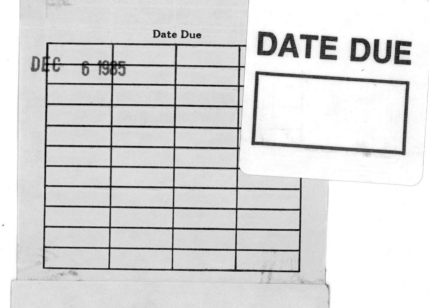

A Source Book for Russian History from Early Times to 1917

A SOURCE BOOK FOR RUSSIAN HISTORY

FROM EARLY TIMES TO 1917

VOLUME 2
Peter the Great to Nicholas I

George Vernadsky, SENIOR EDITOR
Ralph T. Fisher, Jr., MANAGING EDITOR
Alan D. Ferguson
Andrew Lossky
Sergei Pushkarev, COMPILER

New Haven and London: Yale University Press

1972

Copyright © 1972 by Yale University.
All rights reserved. This book may not be
reproduced, in whole or in part, in any form
(except by reviewers for the public press),
without written permission from the publishers.
Library of Congress catalog card number: 70-115369.
ISBN: 0-300-01625-5 (3-volume set); 0-300-01286-1 (vol. 1);
0-300-01602-6 (vol. 2); 0-300-01612-3 (vol. 3).

Designed by John O. C. McCrillis
and set in IBM Press Roman type.
Printed in the United States of America by
The Murray Printing Co., Forge Village, Mass.

Published in Great Britain, Europe, and Africa by
Yale University Press, Ltd., London.
Distributed in Canada by McGill-Queen's University
Press, Montreal; in Latin America by Kaiman & Polon,
Inc., New York City; in Australasia and Southeast
Asia by John Wiley & Sons Australasia Pty. Ltd.,
Sydney; in India by UBS Publishers' Distributors Pvt.,
Ltd., Delhi; in Japan by John Weatherhill, Inc., Tokyo.

CONTENTS VOLUME 2

Preface   vii

Acknowledgments   xi

Guide to Main Topics   xiii

List of Items by Chapters   xvii

List of Abbreviations   xxv

   X. Russia under Peter the Great, 1689-1725   309

  XI. Between Peter I and Catherine II, 1725-1762   375

 XII. The Reign of Catherine II, 1762-1796   393

XIII. Paul, Alexander I, and the Decembrists   471

XIV. Nicholas I, 1825-1855   531

Bibliography   xxvii

Permissions   xliii

CONTENTS VOLUMES 1 AND 3

Volume 1: Early Times to Late Seventeenth Century

    I.   Pre-Kievan Beginnings
   II.   Kievan Russia, Tenth to Twelfth Centuries
  III.   The Russian Lands (except Novgorod and Pskov) from the Late Twelfth through the Fourteenth Century
  IV.   Novgorod the Great and Pskov, Twelfth to Fifteenth Centuries
   V.   The Lithuanian-Russian State (the Grand Duchy of Lithuania) from the Fourteenth to the Mid-Sixteenth Century
  VI.   Muscovy in the Fifteenth Century
 VII.   Muscovy in the Sixteenth Century
VIII.   Muscovite Russia in the Seventeenth Century
  IX.   The Ukraine, Poland-Lithuania, and Russia in the Late Sixteenth and Seventeenth Centuries

Volume 3: Alexander II to the February Revolution

   XV.   Alexander II, 1855-1881
  XVI.   Alexander III and Nicholas II, 1881-1906
 XVII.   The Duma Monarchy, 1906-1914
XVIII.   The War and the Road to Revolution, 1914-1917

PREFACE

Our purpose in this book is to provide, in English, an illustrative sample of the wealth of primary source material that exists for the study of Russia from early times to 1917.

Source books in American and general European history have existed in abundance. They have proved their value as teaching tools to supplement a comprehensive textbook. The need for source books in Russian history has been felt by a great many teachers, to judge from those who offered suggestions to us. It was thanks in large part to their encouragement that we pushed ahead.

As we worked we have had in mind the teacher and especially the purposeful student—the student who is seeking not merely entertainment or native color but solid information as well; the student who does not want to have interpretations handed to him ready-made, but likes to do some evaluating for himself.

Accordingly, in the introductory notes we have avoided either summarizing the document or repeating the background that a text would provide, but we have tried to identify the source and to give enough data to enable the reader to place the document in its historical setting and to figure out what sorts of questions the selection helps to answer.

In the same spirit, we have retained the use of many Russian terms, especially where there is no direct or specific English equivalent, as in the case of territorial divisions, terms of office, and units of measure and money. We believe the hardship this causes to some will work to the net advantage of all of the book's readers—including even the beginner, especially if he is persistent enough in turning to the *Dictionary of Russian Historical Terms* compiled by Mr. Pushkarev.*

In our choice of selections we have sought to achieve a balanced mixture of various types of sources. Along with spirited first-person accounts, there are official documents and other sober fare which require intensive reading. We have included representative samples of the sources that are important enough to be alluded to in the standard textbooks. Often our excerpts are shorter than we would have preferred if expense were no problem, but they are, we think, not too short to convey significant points to the thoughtful reader who is alert to the uses of various kinds of historical evidence.

In response to the wishes of our colleagues, we have emphasized sources not previously published in English translation. About 81 percent of our selections were in that category in 1956 when we began. That proportion is now down to around 75 percent, owing to the new translations that have appeared in recent years. We have cited these new translations in our reference notes for the pertinent items (about 6 percent of our total), so that the reader may locate them easily for further study. About 8 percent of our selections came from publications in English which

---

* A companion volume to this set, the *Dictionary of Russian Historical Terms from the Eleventh Century to 1917* was published by Yale University Press in 1970.

we simply reproduced. Most of these are English in origin, from Richard Chancellor in the sixteenth century to Sir James Buchanan in the twentieth. The remaining selections, about 12 percent, are from sources that had been translated into English but for which we used both the original language and the published translation to produce the version included in this book. In some cases we revised the previous translation only slightly—in other cases, considerably. Our reference notes explain how much.

Scope and coverage. Although our excerpts represent about seven hundred distinct sources (the number could be raised or lowered depending on how one decided to count certain kinds of documents of various dates grouped under one heading), these are of course only a minute fraction of the published sources available. Our original prospectus had to be sharply cut. And although we incorporated about two hundred items from among the additions to our prospectus that were suggested by the letters of our teacher-colleagues, their suggestions totaled around three times that many. It is obvious, then, that much that is worthwhile could not be included here and that many of our choices had to be made on the basis of convenience and availability. At the same time our selections were guided by certain general principles, and these we should explain.

We have felt it necessary to exclude the vast realm of belles lettres, despite its vital importance for the historian. We did not see any way of doing justice to it within the scope of this work. Fortunately that category of source material is widely available in anthologies as well as in translations of individual works.

We have given relatively little space to documents in foreign relations. While we have included some documents bearing on Russia's territorial expansion or on Russian views of certain questions beyond the frontiers, we have generally shunned diplomatic documents which, falling within the scope of general European or world history, are available already in English or are so well summarized in most texts that the marginal gain from an excerpt would be slight.

We have tried to provide sources for political and social history in the broad sense, and have therefore included numerous selections from such fields as intellectual history, church history, economic history, and legal history. We have followed the practice of most textbooks in focusing primarily on the dominant Great Russians, even though by the late nineteenth century they constituted not much over half of the population. We have allotted space to other peoples and areas especially during those periods when they were being brought into the empire. We have not systematically followed the fate of each national element or geographical region thereafter, but have provided occasional illustrations and reminders of the multinational nature of the empire and the problems resulting therefrom.

We have held to a fairly narrow definition of "primary," resisting the temptation to include historical writings that, although "primary" as expressions of the attitudes of their own time, would not generally be classified as such. Our introductions give enough data to enable the student to discern varying degrees of primariness.

In our chronological divisions we have followed the prevailing practice of increasing the coverage as we move closer to the present, but we have given more than the usual emphasis to the 1500s and 1600s, believing, along with many of our colleagues, that we should help to broaden the time span of Russian history beyond that usually taught. On the contemporary end, some of our fellow teachers wanted us to go beyond March 1917. We agree that this would make the book more widely usable in survey courses, but so many sources for Russian history since 1917 had already been translated that we believed such an extension would not be justifiable.

Beyond the problem of achieving a suitable mixture of kinds of sources and a suitable topical and chronological distribution is the at least equally vexing problem of which excerpts to select when, as in most cases, a source is far too long to be included in its entirety. Here, as elsewhere, we have tried not to be unduly influenced by our own preconceptions and have sought to include a wide spectrum of viewpoints from among the voices of the past.

Arrangement, form, style. Our goal in arranging the material has been to make it easy to use this source book along with any textbook in Russian history. Our chapter units thus follow traditional lines. Within them we have arranged the items in a combination of chronological and topical groupings, much as a text might treat them. Particularly where one document touches several topics, our placement has had to be arbitrary. Occasionally—as in the case of the early chronicles—we have broken one source down into separate excerpts by date and topic, but we did not want to overdo this, lest we deemphasize the distinct nature of each source. This means that while it is possible to read the book straight through like a narrative, we have expected, rather, that most users would be reading it by sections or groups of documents, in conjunction with a text or after becoming generally familiar with the period in question. In order to assist both teacher and student in adapting these source readings to any lesson plan, we have provided a Guide to Major Topics.

Our reference notes acknowledge the works we have used as the basis for each item; they are by no means a catalog of all available sources for the same selection. All dates are in the old style or Julian calendar unless labeled N.S. Spaced ellipsis dots indicate that passages in original documents have been omitted in this book; closed-up ellipsis dots represent ellipses contained in the original; double-length dashes represent lacunae—mutilated or otherwise illegible passages—in the original. Unless a selection is identified in our introductory note as a full text, it is an excerpt.

All translators of nonmodern materials understand the compromises required between modern English usage and older expressions which have their counterparts in the Russian of various periods of the past. We felt it unreasonable, in working with so many different kinds of documents, to strive for complete uniformity of style. But even in seeking accuracy we were forced into decisions that will not fully satisfy everyone. Take the example of *tsarskii,* the adjective formed from "tsar." The common rendering, "tsarist," may properly be condemned as now having in English a pejorative connotation that is inappropriate to our uses. But after considering such possibilities as "tsarly" (on the model of "kingly"), "tsarial" (after "imperial"), or "tsarish" (used as "czarish" a few generations back), we returned to "tsarist"—not without dissent in our own ranks. The similar problem of rendering adjectives especially when used as proper names is one familiar to every translator. (Should it be "Resurrection Chronicle" or "Voskresensk Chronicle"? And what about the full adjectival ending and the gender?) We have tried in such cases to follow what seems to be common usage in college textbooks, even though this has led to inconsistencies that may annoy the specialist.

Some of the most frequently used Russian terms have been Anglicized: soft signs have been dropped and plurals have been formed with "s" (for example, "dumas"). In the majority, however, the soft sign and Russian nominative plurals have been retained (*pomest'ia, strel'tsy*). Sometimes this produced results irritating to the Russian speaker, especially when numbers are followed by a nominative case. But the use of genitive forms would have complicated matters unduly for the student who has had no Russian. Where, as an aid to those who have studied Russian, we have added transliterations of Russian words in brackets after the English, we have made some changes toward the modern orthography. But where no confusion would occur we have simply transliterated a term as it stood, thereby preserving changes in spelling, sometimes even within the same document. Our transliterations follow the Library of Congress system with minor modifications.

Family names and patronymics have been simply transliterated. First names have been transliterated except when the English equivalent is very widely used for the person in question (e.g. Tsar Paul). Place names have been transliterated, except where English substitutions are current (Moscow, Archangel). One politically touchy problem is that of rendering place names in the non-Great-Russian parts of the empire. We have in general chosen the solution, favored by English-language texts, of using the Russian form, but we have often added the other names in parentheses.

ACKNOWLEDGMENTS

This book, intended as a service to the teaching profession rather than as a commercial enterprise, owes its existence to many persons and institutions beyond the small group of editors.

Yale University sponsored the project from its very inception. Financial support, working space, materials, and other assistance were provided through the Provost's Office, the Graduate School, and by the Yale Concilium on International and Area Studies and several of its branches: its Council on Russian and East European Studies, its Committee on Faculty Research Grants, and the Henry L. Stimson Fund for Research in World Affairs. We wish to thank the Yale University Press for its continuing interest and support. We depended heavily on Yale's Sterling Memorial Library, and in particular, its reference librarians and its Photographic Division.

The University of Illinois, through its Graduate Research Board, the Russian and East European Center, the James Buchanan Duke Memorial Fund, the Department of History, and the University Library, provided working space and liberal amounts of research assistance, photoduplication, typing, and other clerical support.

A generous grant from the Ford Foundation covered much of the cost of translations, photoduplication, and typing.

The Humanities Fund, thanks to the support of the late Michael Karpovich, contributed toward publication costs. The Rockefeller Foundation, through a half-time fellowship it awarded in 1956-58 to Mr. Fisher for the study of Old Russian and Church Slavic, directly aided his work on documents of the pre-Petrine period for this book.

Assistance came also from many professional colleagues. After we had drawn up a list of the documents we tentatively proposed to include in the sourcebook, we circulated this list to historians and other persons of our acquaintance then active in the Russian field, asking for critical comments. In response, we received helpful suggestions and recommendations of additional documents from over 150 fellow teachers. A mere listing of their names would not indicate the extent of our indebtedness to each of them, and a detailed accounting would be far too lengthy for these pages. As outstanding illustrations we may cite the contributions of Alexander Baltzly, Christopher Becker, Horace William Dewey, Samuel Kucherov, and Dimitri von Mohrenschildt. Mr. Dewey offered us some unpublished translations he had made of early Russian legal documents. Mr. Becker volunteered several translations pertaining to Stolypin. Mr. Mohrenschildt, explaining that he had planned, some years earlier, a handbook of Russian social and political thought, sent us a list of the materials he had assembled, plus microfilms and photostats of untranslated selections, as well as copies of several original and unpublished translations. Messrs Baltzly and Kucherov, who, it turned out, had been working for several years on a project something like ours, placed at our disposal many translations they had completed. The reference notes identify further the materials contributed by the above-mentioned scholars, but we wish to express our appreciation here. They, and the many others who responded with thoughtful suggestions, exhibited a spirit of scholarly generosity that was an inspiration to us.

For initial encouragement and administrative support we are grateful especially to Marian Neal Ash, Radley H. Daly, Norman V. Donaldson, Frederick G. Ludwig, David C. Munford, John H. Ottemiller, and Arthur F. Wright. For assistance with the translations we must first single out for thanks Benjamin P. Uroff. Among the many others who gave translating, editorial, and bibliographic assistance we want to mention especially Norma J. Bruce, Henry L. Eaton, Ida Estrin, J. Gerrit Gantvoort, William G. Gard, Mirra Ginsburg, Judith A. Hill, Peter Hodgson, Stanley Humenuk, Alexandra Kalmykow, Nadezhda S. Kovediaeff, Tamara Kulikauskas, Princess Marie Mestchersky, Vladimir V. Nikouline, Paul L. Roley, and Allen A. Sinel. Our typists included Pauline M. Apperson, Marjorie J. Beauregard, Grey Felstiner, Sandra Swiatowiec Gastineau, Amy Henschen, and Agnes W. Wilson. For the final preparation for printing we are much indebted to our copyeditor, Elizabeth W. Kodama, and to Ellen Graham.

A list of acknowledgments to copyright holders for permission to use selections reprinted in this volume follows the Bibliography.

GUIDE TO MAIN TOPICS, VOLUMES 1-3

This guide is a supplement to both the Contents and the detailed List of Items by Chapters. The reader who wishes to survey the documentary selections for any specific period can locate them through the Contents. The reader who seeks specific documents can locate them through the List of Items by Chapters. The present guide is for the reader who is approaching Russian history topically rather than chronologically, as he might if he were focusing on Russian economic history or on Russian foreign relations. Many of the documents are of course relevant to more than one topic, and the topical categories themselves are so broad that they will serve for general orientation only. Roman numerals indicate chapter numbers; arabic numerals indicate item numbers within each chapter.

POLITICAL, LEGAL, AND ADMINISTRATIVE HISTORY
Including central and local government, armed forces, revolutionary movements

From early times to the late seventeenth century, see:

I:	2, 4, 6, 14, 16	VI:	1-11, 16-21
II:	1, 4-9, 11, 12, 14-21	VII:	1-35, 38-40, 42, 44-47
III:	1-20	VIII:	1-43, 54-59, 61, 62, 65, 67, 71, 77,
IV:	1-28		81, 83-85
V:	1-26	IX:	1-5, 12-18, 20-25

From Peter the Great to Nicholas I, see:

X:	1-29, 33, 35, 40-44, 46-49, 53, 54	XIII:	1, 4, 7, 10-13, 15, 16, 19-48
XI:	1-11, 19	XIV:	1-15, 17, 18, 20, 21, 26-31, 33-35,
XII:	1-28, 31, 34-36, 39-47, 50, 52-55, 57		38, 39, 42

From Alexander II to the February Revolution, see:

XV:	1-22, 24-31, 33, 36-43, 46-63	XVII:	1-25, 27, 28, 30-40, 42, 44-46, 49
XVI:	1-49, 53-66, 78	XVIII:	1-33, 35-47

ECONOMIC HISTORY

From early times to the late seventeenth century, see:

I:	1, 2, 4-6, 14	VII:	2, 5, 7-13, 16, 18, 19, 24, 28, 34,
II:	1-3, 5, 6, 18-21		35, 37-39, 43, 47, 48
III:	3-6, 8-10, 12-14, 17, 19, 20	VIII:	4, 7, 11, 13, 23, 24, 27, 29, 32, 33,
IV:	4-10, 12, 13, 15-19, 22, 27, 28		44-51, 54, 55, 65-71, 77, 83
V:	8, 13, 14, 24-26	IX:	11, 12, 23, 24
VI:	6-8, 10-17		

From Peter the Great to Nicholas I, see:

X:	6-8, 14, 17, 29, 30, 35-44	XIII:	2-6, 8, 14, 18, 24, 25, 34, 38-40
XI:	10-14, 18	XIV:	7, 13, 14, 16-26, 30, 32
XII:	8, 10, 11, 15-19, 21-23, 25-33, 35-		
	38, 40, 46		

From Alexander II to the February Revolution, see:

XV: 5, 6, 12, 14, 20, 25, 26, 30, 32, 33, 38, 45, 46, 48, 52, 58, 59

XVI: 10, 18, 30, 34, 40, 42, 45, 47, 49, 58-62, 67-77, 79, 80

XVII: 3, 7, 8, 13, 17, 18, 20, 22, 24, 26-34, 36, 43, 45-50

XVIII: 4, 6-9, 13, 14, 17, 18, 20-23, 27, 31, 34-37, 42

SOCIAL, CULTURAL, AND INTELLECTUAL HISTORY
Including literature, science, education,
religion, and the press

From early times to the late seventeenth century, see:

I: 1-4, 6-8, 11-15

II: 2, 3, 7-10, 12, 14-16, 18-21

III: 2, 6, 8, 10, 11, 13, 14, 16, 19, 20

IV: 7, 8, 10-13, 15, 16, 19, 21, 27

V: 3-6, 8, 9, 13, 14, 16-26

VI: 6, 7, 9-21

VII: 3-9, 11-13, 15-17, 21-48

VIII: 1-5, 7-24, 26, 27, 29-35, 37-39, 41-48, 52-64, 67, 71, 77, 78, 84, 86, 87

IX: 6-13, 15, 19-28

From Peter the Great to Nicholas I, see:

X: 1, 4-8, 10, 11, 14-16, 19, 25, 31-34, 36-39, 41, 44-54

XI: 3, 5-8, 10, 11, 13, 15-19

XII: 5-11, 14, 16-19, 21-36, 38-57

XIII: 2, 3, 5, 6, 10, 13, 14, 17-19, 22, 24, 25, 31-36, 38-48

XIV: 1-4, 7, 14-21, 24-44

From Alexander II to the February Revolution, see:

XV: 1-18, 21, 23, 26-30, 32-39, 42-59, 62, 63

XVI: 1-4, 6-10, 18, 20, 25-56, 58-60, 62-64, 69, 70, 72, 73, 78-81

XVII: 2, 3, 7, 8, 11-13, 17, 18, 20, 22-24, 26-36, 38-42, 45, 47, 50

XVIII: 3, 6, 7, 9, 12-14, 17, 20, 22, 29, 31, 34, 36, 42, 43

HISTORY OF
LITHUANIAN-RUSSIAN STATE, UKRAINE, BELORUSSIA, SIBERIA, COSSACKS
RUSSIAN EXPANSION
NON-RUSSIAN NATIONALITIES

From early times to the late seventeenth century, see:

I: 1-16

II: 1-11, 13-21

III: 2, 5, 6, 9, 11, 13, 14

IV: 1, 2

V: 1-26

VI: 3, 5, 6, 9, 18-20

VII: 1, 10, 21, 22, 28, 29, 41, 42, 47

VIII: 1, 3, 7, 12, 13, 15-20, 29, 33, 35-39, 53-55, 65-88

IX: 1-28

From Peter the Great to Nicholas I, see:

X: 12, 15, 22-24, 33

XI: 10, 18

XII: 6, 10, 11, 13-15, 18, 20, 22, 24, 35, 40-47

XIII: 2, 8, 9, 19, 21, 30, 31, 34, 38, 39

XIV: 3, 8, 11, 12, 18, 26, 35

From Alexander II to the February Revolution, see:

XV: 21, 22, 24, 25, 30, 41

XVI: 7, 9, 13, 16, 20, 21, 44, 45, 47, 48, 50, 77

XVII: 3, 19, 24, 42, 43

XVIII: 5, 6, 12, 22, 28

DIPLOMATIC HISTORY
HISTORY OF RUSSIAN FOREIGN RELATIONS

From early times to the late seventeenth century, see:

   I: 4, 7, 9, 10
  II: 1-3, 5-7, 11, 13, 14
 III: 3-15, 17-20
  IV: 5-7, 9, 10, 13, 16-19, 21, 22, 24, 26, 28
   V: 1, 2, 4-12, 16, 18

  VI: 1-6, 9, 18-20
 VII: 1, 14-16, 18-20, 22, 27-30, 35, 37-40, 44, 47
VIII: 1-3, 5-22, 28, 29, 33, 34, 37, 49-55, 64, 74-76, 79, 80, 82-85, 88
  IX: 1-5, 7, 13, 14, 17-28

From Peter the Great to Nicholas I, see:

   X: 2-9, 12-17, 22, 32, 45, 48, 51
  XI: 3, 19
 XII: 1, 4-6, 8, 10, 11, 13, 14, 18-21, 35, 50, 56, 57

XIII: 8, 9, 20, 26-31, 36, 44, 46
 XIV: 5, 8-12, 37, 40-44

From Alexander II to the February Revolution, see:

  XV: 19, 21, 22, 31, 39-44, 48, 56, 57
 XVI: 2, 9, 14-17, 75

XVII: 24, 25
XVIII: 1-6, 13, 14, 17-20, 22, 24, 25, 27-29, 32, 44, 47

LIST OF ITEMS BY CHAPTERS, VOLUME 2

Chapter X. Russia under Peter the Great, 1689-1725   309

A. Peter's Personality and Activities

1. Prince B. I. Kurakin on Peter and His Colleagues in the 1680s and 1690s   311
2. Peter's Account of His Sojourn in Holland, 1697-1698   313
3. Electress Sophia of Hanover on Peter's Visit, 1697   313
4. J. G. Korb on Russia in 1698-1699   314
5. Charles Whitworth on Peter, 1710   314
6. John Perry on Life in Russia ca. 1712   314
7. Peter Henry Bruce on Peter the Great, ca. 1711-1715   321
8. J. G. Vockerodt's Memorandum on Russia under Peter the Great in the 1720s   324

B. Political and Military Developments

9. Ivan Pososhkov on the Russian Army, 1701   326
10. Letters of Peter concerning Recruitment for the Army, January 18, 1707, and January 13, 1709   327
11. Documents on Gentry Service and Peter's New Officer Corps, 1708-1722   328
12. Documents concerning Peter and the Ukraine, 1708-1710   330
13. Peter Reports the Victory at Poltava, June 27, 1709   331
14. Otto Pleyer on Peter's Army, 1710   332
15. The Charter of the Esthonian Principality, August 16, 1710   334
16. Documents on Russo-Turkish Relations, 1709-1711   334
17. Decrees Establishing and Defining the Functions of the Senate, 1711 and 1722   336
18. Decrees Establishing the Administrative Colleges, 1717 and 1720   337
19. Correspondence between Peter and Alexis, 1715-1717   338
20. The Manifesto Depriving Alexis of Succession, February 3, 1718   340
21. Peter Henry Bruce on Tsarevich Alexis in 1714 and 1718   341
22. The Peace Treaty of Nystad, August 30, 1721   342
23. Peter's New Title, October-November 1721   342
24. The Table of Ranks, January 24, 1722   343
25. The Statute on Succession to the Throne, February 5, 1722   345
26. The Decree on the Maintenance of Civil Legality, April 17, 1722   345
27. The Decree on the Duties of the Procurator General, April 27, 1722   345

C. Social and Economic Conditions

28. A Decree on Municipal Self-Government, January 30, 1699   346
29. A Decree on Trading Companies, October 27, 1699   346
30. Peter's Decrees on Western Dress and Shaving, 1701 and 1705   347
31. Peter's Manifesto Inviting Foreigners into Russia, April 16, 1702   347
32. Documents Illustrating Popular Reactions to Peter's Measures,
    1701, 1705, and 1708   348
33. Iaguzhinskii on Peter's Attitude toward Foreigners   350
34. Grants of State Factories to Private Individuals, 1709 and 1711   350
35. The Decree on the Inheritance of Real Estate by One Son
    Only, March 23, 1714   351
36. Friedrich Christian Weber Describes the Tax System, ca. 1714-1719   352
37. Peter's Instructions for a General Census and Poll Tax, 1719,
    1720, and 1722   353
38. Peter's Orders Designed to Curb the Growth of Serfdom,
    1719 and 1721   354
39. The Statute of the College of Mining (Berg-Kollegium),
    December 10, 1719   354
40. Decrees on Municipal Administration at the End of Peter's
    Reign, 1721 and 1724   355
41. Peter's Decree on the Development of Factories, November 5,
    1723   357
42. The Statute of the College of Manufactures, December 3, 1723   357
43. Pososhkov's *Book on Poverty and Wealth,* 1724   358

D. Ideology, Education, and Ecclesiastical Affairs

44. The Testament of Patriarch Joachim, March 17, 1690   361
45. The Decree Reestablishing the Monastery Prikaz, January 24,
    1701   363
46. Peter's Memoranda on Printing and Other Interests, 1708-1709   363
47. Peter's Order on the Eve of the Battle of Poltava, June 27, 1709   365
48. A Definition of "Autocracy" in the Military Service Regulations
    of March 30, 1716   365
49. Documents on Education for Sons of the Gentry, 1697-1698
    and 1714   365
50. Leibniz and Peter the Great, 1712-1716   366
51. The Decrees on the Founding of the Academy of Sciences,
    January 28, 1724   368
52. The Manifesto on and the Statute of the Holy Synod, January
    25, 1721   370
53. Theophanes Prokopovich: *The Justice of the Monarch's Will in
    Designating the Heir to His Realm,* 1722   371

Chapter XI. Between Peter I and Catherine II, 1725-1762   375

1. The Decree Establishing the Supreme Privy Council, February
   8, 1726   377

2. The Decree on the Reduction of Administrative Offices, March 14, 1727 — 377
3. The "Conditions" of Anne's Accession to the Throne, 1730 — 378
4. Anne's Manifesto on the Restoration of Autocracy, February 28, 1730 — 378
5. Dispatches of Claudius Rondeau, 1730-1731 — 379
6. The Inheritance Law of March 17, 1731 — 380
7. The Decree Establishing a Military School (Corps of Cadets) for Sons of the Gentry, July 29, 1731 — 380
8. The Manifesto on the Gentry's Service, December 31, 1736 — 381
9. The Dispatches of Edward Finch, 1741 — 381
10. General Manstein's Memoirs, from the 1740s — 382
11. Jonas Hanway on Russia, ca. 1750 — 384
12. The Decree on the Abolition of Internal Customs Duties, December 20, 1753 — 386
13. The Instructions to Cadastral Surveyors, May 13, 1754 — 387
14. The Decree on State Loan Banks, May 13, 1754 — 387
15. The Decree on the Founding of Moscow University, January 24, 1755 — 388
16. The Decree on the First State Theater in Saint Petersburg, August 30, 1756 — 390
17. The Decree Founding the Academy of Arts, November 6, 1757 — 390
18. The Decree Empowering Landlords to Exile their Recalcitrant Serfs to Siberia, December 13, 1760 — 391
19. Peter III's Manifesto Granting Freedom and Liberty to the Russian Gentry, February 18, 1762 — 391

Chapter XII. The Reign of Catherine II, 1762-1796 — 393

A. Political Developments

1. Catherine's Account of Her Girlhood in Russia, ca. 1744 — 395
2. A Letter from Catherine to Potemkin on Her Romantic Attachments, 1774 — 396
3. Catherine's Epitaph, Written by Herself, ca. 1788 — 396
4. The Manifesto on the Accession of Catherine II to the Throne, June 28, 1762 — 396
5. Reports of French Diplomats at Catherine's Court, 1762-1765 — 397
6. Reports of English Diplomats at Catherine's Court, 1762-1768 — 400
7. Catherine's Account of the Legislative Commission, ca. 1765-1768 — 403
8. Catherine's Instructions on a New Code of Laws, 1767 — 403
9. The Decree Establishing the Legislative Commission, December 14, 1766 — 405
10. The Treaty of Kuchuk-Kainardji, July 10, 1774 — 406
11. Catherine's Letters to Grimm, 1774-1795 — 408
12. The Statute on Guberniia Administration, November 7, 1775 — 410

13. Potemkin's Memorandum Urging Annexation of the Crimea,
    ca. 1776-1780   411
14. The Manifesto on the Annexation of the Crimea, April 8, 1783   412
15. A Decree concerning the Inhabitants of the Crimea, July 28, 1783   412
16. The Charter of the Nobility, April 21, 1785   413
17. The Charter of the Cities, April 21, 1785   415
18. The Prince de Ligne concerning Catherine, Her Trip to the
    Crimea, and Potemkin, 1787-1788   418
19. The Decree on the Rupture with France, February 8, 1793   422
20. General Krechetnikov's Manifesto on the Second Polish
    Partition, March 27, 1793   422

B. Social and Economic Conditions

21. William Coxe on Russia in 1778-1779   423
22. Tooke on Russia under Catherine II   428
23. The Records of the Legislative Commission: Views of Nobles
    from Central and Northern Russia, ca. 1767   431
24. The Legislative Commission: Views of Ukrainian Nobles, ca. 1767   432
25. The Legislative Commission: The Discussion of Serfdom by
    Korob'in, Shcherbatov, and Chuprov, May 1768   433
26. The Legislative Commission: Views of Merchants and
    Townspeople, ca. 1767   436
27. The Legislative Commission: Views of State Peasants, ca. 1767   438
28. Estate-Owners' Instructions: P. A. Rumiantsev, 1751 and
    1761-1762   441
29. Estate-Owners' Instructions: P. B. Sheremet'ev, 1764   443
30. Estate-Owners' Instructions: I. I. Shuvalov, ca. 1795   444
31. Estate-Owners' Instructions: V. G. Orlov, ca. 1799   445
32. The Model Instructions of P. I. Rychkov, 1770   447
33. The Model Instructions of A. T. Bolotov, 1770   449
34. Decrees on Peasant Disturbances, 1762   449
35. A Decree Inviting Foreigners to Settle in Russia, July 22,
    1763   450
36. Decrees in Catherine's Campaign against Graft, 1762 and
    1763   451
37. Senate Instructions on Potato Growing, May 31, 1765   452
38. The Decree Enabling Estate Owners to Send Serfs to Forced
    Labor, January 17, 1765   453
39. The Decree Prohibiting Complaints by Serfs, August 22, 1767   453
40. Proclamations and Decrees of Pugachev, 1773-1774   454
41. Correspondence within Pugachev's "Government," 1774   456
42. A Serf's Report on Disturbances near Nizhnii-Novgorod,
    August 1, 1774   456
43. A Government Report on Part of the Pugachev Uprising,
    August 23, 1774   457
44. Testimony of Pugachev's Officers, September-October 1774   458

45. The Manifesto concerning Pugachev's Actions and Capture, December 19, 1774   458
46. The Abolition of the Zaporozhian Sech', August 3, 1775   459
47. The Decree Extending Serfdom to the Ukraine, May 3, 1783   460

C. Intellectual Trends

48. Essays from the Contest of the Free Economic Society, ca. 1766   461
49. An Essay by a Leader of the Free Economic Society, 1770   462
50. Items from Novikov's Satirical Magazines, 1769-1772   462
51. A Statute concerning Public Education, August 5, 1786   464
52. Shcherbatov on the Moral Deterioration of Russia, ca. 1789   465
53. Shcherbatov's "On the Advantages of Poverty," 1780s   466
54. Radishchev's *Journey from Saint Petersburg to Moscow,* 1790   467
55. The Decree Punishing Radishchev, September 4, 1790   468
56. Satirical Pieces by I. A. Krylov, 1792   468
57. A Decree on Censorship, September 16, 1796   469

Chapter XIII. Paul, Alexander I, and the Decembrists   471

A. The Reign of Paul I, 1796-1801

1. The Decree on the Succession to the Imperial Throne, April 5, 1797   473
2. The Decree Forbidding Free Movement of Peasants in Southern Russia, December 12, 1796   473
3. Paul's Manifesto Forbidding Sunday Labor by Serfs, April 5, 1797   474
4. A Report on the Administration of Rural State Properties, August 7, 1797   474
5. Decrees concerning the Allotment of State Lands to Certain State Peasants, November 27, 1797, and July 1800   475
6. Newspaper Advertisements of the Sale of Serfs, 1797   476
7. Alexander's Letter to La Harpe, September 27, 1797   477
8. The Letters Founding the Russian-American Company, July 8 and December 27, 1799   477
9. The Manifesto on the Annexation of the Kingdom of Georgia, January 18, 1801   478

B. The Reign of Alexander I

10. The Memoirs of Prince Adam Czartoryski concerning 1796 and 1801-1802   478
11. The Manifesto Abolishing the Secret Chancery, April 2, 1801   481
12. A Rescript Directing a Commission to Undertake the Drafting of a Code of Laws, June 5, 1801   482
13. A Decree Prohibiting the Use of Torture in the Prosecution of Criminal Trials, September 27, 1801   483

14. The Decree Permitting All Free Persons to Purchase and Own
    Land, December 12, 1801   483
15. The Manifesto Establishing Central Ministries for State
    Administration, September 8, 1802   483
16. The Decree concerning the Rights and Duties of the Senate,
    September 8, 1802   484
17. The Preliminary Directive concerning Public Education,
    January 26, 1803   485
18. The Decree Designating a New Social Class, the Free Farmers,
    February 20, 1803   486
19. A Decree concerning the Jews, December 9, 1804   487
20. The Treaties of Tilsit, June 25, 1807   488
21. The Manifesto on the Political Status of Russia's Newly
    Acquired Finnish Subjects, March 23, 1809   490
22. Speranskii's Plan for a General Reorganization of the
    Administration, October 1809   490
23. The Manifesto Establishing the State Council, January 1,
    1810   493
24. The Manifesto Reorganizing the Ministries and Fixing Their
    Respective Responsibilities, July 25, 1810   494
25. Karamzin and His "Memoir on Ancient and Modern Russia,"
    1811   495
26. Field Marshal Kutuzov's Report to Alexander, September 4,
    1812   497
27. Alexander I's Manifesto on Napoleon's Retreat from Russia,
    November 3, 1812   498
28. Alexander I's Order to the Russian Armies, December 25, 1813   499
29. The Holy Alliance, September 14 (26, N.S.), 1815   499
30. The Constitutional Charter of the Kingdom of Poland,
    November 15, 1815   500
31. Alexander I's Address to the Polish Diet, March 15, 1818   503
32. Alexander I's Orders on the Establishment of the Military
    Settlements, 1817-1818   503
33. N. N. Novosil'tsev's Project for a Constitutional Charter for
    the Russian Empire, 1820   504
34. A Speranskii Statute for the Administrative Organization of
    Siberia, July 22, 1822   506
35. The Decree Prohibiting Masonic Lodges and All Secret
    Societies, August 1, 1822   508
36. Metternich's Comments on Russia and the Greek Revolt
    against Turkey, 1821-1822   508
37. Alexander's Secret Order concerning the Succession to the
    Russian Throne, August 16, 1823   510
38. The Memoirs of F. F. Vigel' on Life in Russia in the Early
    Nineteenth Century   510

C. The Decembrist Movement

39. Writings of P. I. Pestel', ca. 1823-1825 513
40. The Constitution Drafted by Nikita Murav'ev, 1824 516
41. The Decembrist Manifesto of December 13, 1825 518
42. Testimony of Decembrists P. G. Kakhovskii, A. A. Bestuzhev, V. I. Shteingeil', P. I. Pestel', and P. I. Borisov, 1826 518
43. Explaining the Decembrists: Iakushkin on the Military Settlements 522
44. The Memoirs of M. A. Fonvizin on the Decembrist Movement 522
45. The Memoirs of A. E. Rozen on the Decembrist Movement 525
46. The Memoirs of I. I. Gorbachevskii on the Society of United Slavs 527
47. Nicholas I's Own Account of the Events of December 14, 1825 528
48. The Court Report on the Punishment of the Decembrists, July 13, 1826 530

Chapter XIV. Nicholas I, 1825-1855 531

A. Political Developments

1. The Decree Establishing the Third Section, July 3, 1826 533
2. The Statute on Censorship, April 22, 1828 533
3. The Declaration of the Revolution by the Polish Seim, December 20, 1830 534
4. Nicholas's Manifesto Announcing the Code of Laws of the Russian Empire, January 31, 1833 534
5. The Convention of Berlin, October 3 (15, N.S.), 1833 535
6. Nicholas's Directive to the Governors, June 3, 1837 535
7. The Criminal Law Code, August 15, 1845 536
8. The Treaty of Adrianople, September 2 (14, N.S.), 1829 537
9. The Treaty of Unkiar-Skelessi, June 26 (July 8, N.S.), 1833 538
10. The Russian Declaration of War against Turkey, October 20, (November 1, N.S.), 1853 538
11. The Manifesto on War against Great Britain, France, and Turkey, April 11 (23, N.S.), 1854 539
12. The British Parliament Views Russia's Involvement in the Crimean War, March 19 (31, N.S.), 1854 539

B. Social and Economic Developments

13. Two Orders concerning Peasant Disturbances, May 12 and August 9, 1826 541
14. Speranskii's Memorandum of December 1826 542
15. The Manifesto on the Assemblies of the Nobility, December 6, 1831 543
16. Vasil'chikov's Memorandum on the Peasant Question, 1835 544
17. P. D. Kiselev's Report on State Peasants, May 17, 1837 544

18. The Laws Reforming the Administration of the State Peasants,
    December 26, 1837, and April 30, 1838   545
19. Kiselev's Memorandum of 1839   548
20. The Marquis de Custine's Impressions of Russia in 1839   548
21. Zablotskii-Desiatovskii's Memorandum of 1841   550
22. Nicholas's Decree on Railroad Construction, February 1, 1842   551
23. The Decree on the Expansion of Potato Planting, February 16,
    1842   551
24. Nicholas's Speech in the State Council on the Peasant Problem,
    March 30, 1842   552
25. The Law Establishing the Category of "Obligated" Peasants,
    April 2, 1842   553
26. Baron von Haxthausen on Russia in 1843-1844   554
27. Count Kiselev's Circular of November 30, 1843   558
28. The Manifesto on the Holding of Noble Status, June 11, 1845   558
29. The Memorandum of Count L. A. Perovskii, 1846   559
30. Nicholas's Address to a Delegation of Nobles, ca. June 4, 1847   560
31. The Report of the Ministry of Internal Affairs concerning
    Peasant Disturbances, 1847   561
32. Prince Drutskoi-Sokolinskii on the Peasant Question, 1848   561

C. Education and Intellectual Trends

33. The Decree of Nicholas I Limiting Foreign Education, February
    18, 1831   562
34. The Statute for the Russian Universities, July 26, 1835   562
35. S. S. Uvarov's Pronouncements on Autocracy, Orthodoxy, and
    Official Nationality, ca. 1833-1843   564
36. The "First Philosophical Letter" of Peter Chaadaev, 1836   566
37. The Westernizers: Belinskii in the 1840s   567
38. Petrashevskii's Testimony, May–June 1849   571
39. The Directive to Tighten State Control over Higher Education,
    January 23, 1851   573
40. The Westernizers: Granovskii's Writings of ca. 1840-1855   574
41. The Slavophiles: Kireevskii in 1852   576
42. The Slavophiles: Konstantin Aksakov in the 1850s   577
43. The Slavophiles: Khomiakov in the 1840s and 1850s   579
44. Herzen on Russia and Europe in the 1830s and 1840s   582

LIST OF ABBREVIATIONS

AAE

Akty sobrannye v bibliotekakh i arkhivakh Rossiiskoi Imperii arkheograficheskoiu ekspeditsieiu Imperatorskoi Akademii Nauk. 4 vols. St. Petersburg, 1836.

AN BSSR

Akademiia Nauk Belorusskoi Sovetskoi Sotsialisticheskoi Respubliki.

AN SSSR

Akademiia Nauk Soiuza Sovetskikh Sotsialisticheskikh Respublik.

AOIZR

Arkheograficheskaia Komissiia, ed. *Akty otnosiashchiesia k istorii zapadnoi Rossii,* 5 vols. St. Petersburg, 1846-51.

CIOIDRMU

Obshchestvo Istorii i Drevnostei Rossiiskikh. *Chteniia v Imperatorskom Obshchestve Istorii i Drevnostei Rossiiskikh pri Moskovskom Universitete.* 264 vols. Moscow, 1846-1918.

DAI

Arkheograficheskaia Komissiia, ed. *Dopolneniia k aktam istoricheskim.* 12 vols. St. Petersburg, 1846-72.

Gosiurizdat

Gosudarstvennoe Izdatel'stvo Iuridicheskoi Literatury.

Gosizdat

Gosudarstvennoe Izdatel'stvo.

Goslitizdat

Gosudarstvennoe Izdatel'stvo Khudozhestvennoi Literatury.

Gospolitizdat

Gosudarstvennoe Izdatel'stvo Politicheskoi Literatury.

OGIZ

Ob"edinenie Gosudarstvennykh Izdatel'stv.

PBIPV

Pis'ma i bumagi Imperatora Petra Velikogo. 11 vols. Vols. 1-7, St. Petersburg: Gosudarstvennaia Tipografiia, 1887-1918. Vols. 8-11, Moscow: AN SSSR, 1948-64.

PRP

Pamiatniki russkogo prava. 8 vols. Moscow: Gosiurizdat, 1952-61.

PSRL

Arkheograficheskaia Komissiia, ed. *Polnoe Sobranie Russkikh Letopisei.* 31 vols. St. Petersburg, 1841-1968.

PSZRI

Polnoe Sobranie Zakonov Rossiiskoi Imperii . . . 1649-1913. 134 vols. St. Petersburg, 1830-1916 (1st ser., 46 vols., containing laws of 1649-1825; 2d ser., 55 vols., covering 1825-81; 3d ser., 33 vols., covering 1881-1913).

PVL

V. P. Adrianova-Peretts and D. S. Likhachev, eds. *Povest' vremennykh let.* Moscow: AN SSSR, 1950.

RIB

Arkheograficheskaia Komissiia, ed. *Russkaia istoricheskaia biblioteka.* 39 vols. St. Petersburg, 1872-1927.

RPC   Samuel H. Cross and Olgerd P. Sherbowitz-Wetzor, eds. and trans.
               The Russian Primary Chronicle, Laurentian Text. Cambridge, Mass.:
               Mediaeval Academy of America, 1953.

SIRIO   *Sbornik Imperatorskogo Russkogo Istoricheskogo Obshchestva.*
               148 vols. St. Petersburg: Imperatorskoe Russkoe Istoricheskoe
               Obshchestvo, 1867–1916.

Tsentrarkhiv   Tsentral'nyi Gosudarstvennyi Istoricheskii Arkhiv v Moskve.

VOLUME 2

Peter the Great to Nicholas I

CHAPTER X

Russia under
Peter the Great
1689-1725

A. CONTEMPORARY TESTIMONY ABOUT PETER'S PERSONALITY AND ACTIVITIES

Note: The manifold activities of Peter gave rise to a vast body of contemporary literature. The following selections are fairly representative samples.

X:1. PRINCE B. I. KURAKIN ON PETER AND HIS COLLEAGUES IN THE 1680s AND 1690s

Prince Boris Ivanovich Kurakin (1676-1727), an officer of the Guards and Peter's brother-in-law (he was married to a sister of Eudoxia Lopukhina, Peter's first wife), had a distinguished diplomatic career, spending many years in Italy, Vienna, Germany, London, The Hague, and Paris. Being a convinced believer in Westernization, he served Peter loyally and with zeal, though he deprecated some of the social tendencies of the time. In 1723 he began to work on a "History of the Tsar Peter Alekseevich," but never went beyond drafting some notes on the years 1682-94; the following excerpts are taken from these notes. (For excerpts from Kurakin's autobiography see Items X:11 and X:49, below.)

Reference: M. I. Semevskii, ed., *Arkhiv kniazia F. A. Kurakina*, vol. 1 (St. Petersburg, 1890), pp. 64-66, 68-70, 76.

During [Tsar Peter's] administration the beginning of the fall of the first families became evident; particularly was the title of prince mortally hated and disparaged both by His Tsarist Majesty and by the persons in the government who surrounded him; all these people—the Naryshkins, the Streshnevs, the Golovkins—belonged to the lowest and neediest gentry, and, from the tsar's earliest years, they always tried to influence him against the great families. Moreover, His Majesty himself seemed inclined to take away all the power of the great houses by abasing them, and to make himself supreme master in the realm.

The regency of Tsaritsa Natalia Kirillovna [Peter's mother] was very disorderly, unfair, and displeasing to the people. It was then that judges began to hand down unjust decisions, and that much bribery and looting of the treasury, which has continued to increase to this day, first set in; and it is difficult to cure this leprosy. . . .

Upon his return from the expedition to the Trinity Monastery in the year 7197 [1689], His Tsarist Majesty left the administration of his state in the hands of his mother, as we have mentioned before, and spent his time in war games. He started the official levy of two regiments—the Preobrazhenskii and the Semenovskii [i.e. the Guards]. In the Preobrazhenskii Regiment he organized four battalions, in the Semenovskii, three. Over both these regiments he placed commanding general Avtomon Golovin, a very stupid man, though

he was the first chamberlain to master military drill. His Tsarist Majesty was constantly training these regiments [himself], three times a week.

Volunteers for the above-mentioned regiments were enlisted both from the gentry and from other groups. Freedom for boyars' bondmen had its first beginning at this time: they were given the liberty to enlist in these regiments. Every year military maneuvers were held and battles fought between foot regiments. The cavalry composed of the gentry was organized into companies. Encampments were built on the fields of Semenovo [a suburban village], where troops would remain for three days at a time, or longer; advance guards were posted, and sham battles were fought.
. . .

During these exercises foreign officers had occasion to seek their fortune with His Majesty— because they would arrange everything and explain how to conduct the exercises, there being no one among the Russians competent enough to do it. . . .

At that time . . . Franz Iakovlevich Lefort attained extreme favor, and became His Majesty's confidant in amorous intrigues. This Lefort was a gay, prodigal man—in short, a French debauchee. He constantly gave dinners, suppers, and balls in his house; and it was here, in his house, that His Majesty first began to meet foreign ladies and started an amorous affair with a merchant's daughter, Anna Ivanovna Mons. To tell the truth, she was an exceptional and an intelligent maid.

Here, in Lefort's house, [the tsar's companions] began an indescribable debauchery, with much drinking. Locked in for three days at a time, they would remain continually drunk, and it happened that many died therefrom. From that time until this day this immoderate drinking goes on, and it has become fashionable among the first families.

As for the said Lefort, he reached such heights that he was made a general of the infantry, and later an admiral; and he died of drink. . . .

Let us now turn to the recruitment of men for the Preobrazhenskii and the Semenovskii regiments. Many youngsters of low origin became His Majesty's favorites; one should particularly mention a certain Buzheninov, a son of a sexton [*sluzhka*] of the Novodevichii convent, and Lukin, a son of a scribe [*pod'iachii*] from Novgorod; there were many others of this sort, who surrounded His Majesty day and night. Since that time people of low birth have entered all the services of His Majesty's household, while persons of illustrious lineage were removed from them. . . .

At that time His Majesty became a habitual guest in the German [i.e. Foreign] Settlement [Nemetskaia sloboda], and this not by day only; he would spend nights at Lefort's, or in other houses, but most frequently at Anna Mons's.

Many English and Dutch merchants, like Andrew Styles, Christopher Brant, and John Lups, attained His Majesty's extreme favor and confidence and began to have free access [at court]. Not one of the prominent foreign officers or merchants in the German Settlement or at Ganyi [or Ganoi] Prud [perhaps Poganyi Prud, "Foul Pond," a neighborhood where many foreigners lived] could have a wedding without His Majesty and his courtiers being invited to the celebration. They gave special banquets, balls, and soirees; many would also invite him to funerals, where His Majesty would appear with all his household, clad, according to their rank, in black mantles.

Because of his predilection for everything foreign, His Majesty began to study various skills and the Dutch language. His teacher in this language was one of the secretaries [*d'iaki*] of the Foreign Office [Posol'skii Prikaz], Andrew Winius, a man of Dutch

origin, a person of intelligence and good standing; fencing and horsemanship he was taught by a Dane—Butenant, the son of Andrew Butenant [commissioner of the Danish king in Moscow]; mathematics, fortification, and other skills, by Franz Timmerman of Hamburg [a Dutch craftsman]. He had learned military drill, while still a child, from Prisvov, a strelets [musketeer, member of the privileged Moscow garrison] of Obrosim Belyi's regiment; drumming, from Theodore, the chief drummer of the Stremiannyi Regiment; as for Polish dancing, he learned it from one practice in the house of the above-mentioned Lefort.

His Majesty had a great love for artillery and fireworks, and he worked at these crafts with his own hands all the winters.

· · ·

[The tsar's] favor for Lefort continued, but it did not extend beyond parties and feasts; in the affairs of state Lefort had no voice, and he did not meddle in them; though he held the ranks of admiral and general of the infantry, he did not administer anything. Since he was weak in intelligence and incapable of performing the duties pertaining to his rank, his departments had to be managed by others. This Lefort passed his time, day and night, in amusements, supper parties, balls, banquets, card games, debauchery with the ladies, and incessant drinking—from all of which he died before the age of fifty.

At about the same time Alexander Menshikov was becoming a great favorite [with the tsar], and he reached so high a position that one might say he was almost governing the whole state. He was made field marshal; then the [Holy Roman] Emperor made him a count, and shortly thereafter a prince of the [Holy Roman] Empire, and finally His Majesty named him duke of Izhora. He was the only one to be addressed as "Your Serene Highness," both in letters and in speech. He was a favorite of such power that the like of him could perhaps be found only in Roman history. Enormous wealth was bestowed on him, so that the income from his lands alone amounted to 150,000 rubles. He had also amassed great treasures, such as about 1,500,000 rubles' worth of precious stones. One of his jewels—a scarlet ruby of great value—was very famous and was considered to be unique in Europe because of its weight, size, and color.

To describe the character of this prince briefly: he was a mediocrity and quite uneducated; he could barely write, having only learned to sign his name, for he was of very low origin—lower than the gentry.

X:2. PETER'S ACCOUNT OF HIS SOJOURN IN HOLLAND, 1697-1698

The following account of Peter's sojourn in Holland and England in 1697-98 is taken from the preamble to the Naval Service Regulations of 1717. The passages in italics were inserted by Peter himself.

Reference: Nikolai G. Ustrialov, *Istoriia tsarstvovaniia Petra Velikogo*, 5 vols. (St. Petersburg, 1858-63), 2:400-01.

Thus he [Peter] *turned all his thoughts to building a fleet; and when, on account of the Tatar attacks, Azov had been besieged, and later successfully taken,* he could not bear to deliberate long over his unalterable desire but quickly set about the work. A suitable place for shipbuilding was found on the river Voronezh just below the city of that name, skilled shipwrights were called in from England and Holland, and a new enterprise was started in Russia in 1696—the building of ships, galleys, and other boats—at a great expense. So that this work would be established in Russia forever, he decided to introduce this art among his people. For this purpose he sent a large number of noble-born persons to Holland and to other states to study naval architecture and seamanship.

And what is even more remarkable, the monarch, as if ashamed to lag behind his subjects in this art, himself undertook a journey to Holland, and in Amsterdam, *at the East India shipyard,* he devoted himself, together with his other volunteers, to learning naval architecture; in a short time he perfected himself *in what a good ship's carpenter should know,* and with his own labor and skill he built and launched a new ship.

Then he asked Jan Pool, the master shipwright of that shipyard, to teach him the proportions of ships, which he showed him in four days. In Holland, however, this art is not perfected in accordance with the principles of geometry but is guided by a few rules only, and for the rest it is based on practical experience of long standing; the above-mentioned master shipwright also told him this and said that he was incapable of showing him everything on a draft; then he felt disgusted that he had undertaken such a long journey without attaining the desired aim. Several days later His Majesty happened to be at a gathering at the country house of the merchant Jan Tessingh, where he sat very unhappy for the reason mentioned. When, in the midst of the conversation, he was asked why he was so gloomy, he explained the reason. Among those present there was an Englishman who, upon hearing this, said that in England naval architecture had been perfected as much as any other and that it was possible to learn it in a short time. His Majesty was overjoyed at these words, and without delay he went to England, where he mastered this science within four months; and, returning from there, he brought with him two master shipwrights—John Deane and Joseph Ney.

X:3. ELECTRESS SOPHIA OF HANOVER ON PETER'S VISIT, 1697

Electress Sophia of Hanover (1630-1714), wishing to make the acquaintance of Peter the Great, arranged a meeting with him while he was passing through the Hanoverian possessions en route to Holland in 1697. The Electress was accompanied by her daughter, Sophia Charlotte (1668-1705), the wife of Elector Frederick III of Brandenburg-Prussia, and by her three sons, one of whom, Electoral Prince George Lewis of Hanover, was the future George I of Great Britain. The meeting took place on July 27 (August 6, N.S.), 1697; the Electress describes her impressions in a letter to her favorite niece, *Raugraefin* Louise.

Reference: Eduard Bodemann, ed., *Briefe der Kurfuerstin Sophie von Hannover an die Raugraefinnen und Raugrafen zu Pfalz,* Publicationen aus den K. Preussischen Staatsarchiven, vol. 37 (Leipzig, 1888), pp. 160-62 (letter of Aug. 1/11, 1697).

We came [to Coppenbrügge] before the Muscovites, who arrived there only about eight o'clock, and stopped at the house of a peasant. Contrary to our agreement, there assembled such a multitude of people that the tsar did not know what to do to pass by unnoticed. We negotiated for a long time, and finally my son had to disperse the crowd with the help of the guards. While the ambassadors with their retinue were approaching, the tsar sneaked by a hidden staircase into his room, which was next to the diningroom. We all went to the diningroom, and the First Ambassador, Mr. Lefort from Geneva, acted as our interpreter. The tsar is a very tall, fine man, with a handsome face and good posture. His mind is very lively and his retorts are quick and incisive. But with all these great gifts of Nature, he could well have better manners. We went to table without delay. Mr. Koppenstein, who acted as master of ceremonies, offered His Majesty a napkin, which puzzled him, for in Brandenburg they would offer him a fingerbowl after a meal. My daughter and I placed His Majesty between us, with an interpreter on either side of him. He was very gay and quite unconstrained, and we struck up a great friendship with him. My daughter and His Majesty exchanged snuff-

boxes. The tsar's snuffbox is ornamented with His Majesty's initials; my daughter values it very much. We remained at table for a long time, but it did not seem long to us for the tsar never stopped talking and was very gay. My daughter made her Italians sing for him. He liked their singing, though he admitted that he was not a great lover of music. I asked him whether he liked hunting, and he answered, no, but that his father had loved it very much; as for himself, his own real passions, since youth, were sailing and fireworks. He told us that he built ships himself; he showed us his hands and made us feel how hard they were because of work. After supper, His Majesty ordered his violinists to be brought in, and we danced after the Muscovite manner, which is much more graceful than the Polish one. Our dance continued until four in the morning.

... [The tsar] is quite an extraordinary person; one can neither describe nor picture him without having seen him; he has a good heart, full of just and noble sentiments. He did not drink to excess in our presence, but the men of his retinue got drunk after we had left.

X:4. J. G. KORB ON RUSSIA IN 1698-1699

Johann Georg Korb was a secretary to C. von Guarient, the imperial envoy to Moscow in 1698-99, and was thus an eyewitness to the suppression of the strel'tsy rebellion. In 1700, or early in 1701, he published, in Vienna, the diary of his sojourn in Russia, to which he appended a general report on Russian affairs.

Reference: Johann G. Korb, *Diarium itineris in Moscoviam* . . . (Vienna, 1700), pp. 73, 76, 83, 88-89, 108-09, 189; Russian translation: I. G. Korb, *Dnevnik puteshestviia v Moskoviiu (1698-1699 gg.),* trans. and commentary, A. I. Malein (St. Petersburg: A. S. Suvorin, 1906), pp. 79, 82-83, 90, 96-97, 119-20, 217; English translation: *Diary of an Austrian Secretary of Legation at the Court of Peter the Great,* ed. and trans. Count Macdonnell, 2 vols. (London, 1863), 1:154-156, 163, 179-80, 192-93, 241; 2:154-55. The text given here is based on Macdonnell's translation, amended somewhat by the editors. This translation has recently been reprinted (N.Y.: Da Capo, 1968).

September 5 [1698]: The report of the tsar's arrival [from abroad] had spread through the city. The boyars and principal Muscovites flocked in numbers . . . to pay their court.

. . . His Majesty the tsar received all who came, with an alacrity that made it seem as if he wished to be foremost among his subjects in eagerness. Those who, according to the fashion of that country, cast themselves upon the ground to worship majesty, he lifted up graciously from their groveling posture and embraced with a kiss, such as is only due among private friends. If the scissors that were plied promiscuously among the beards

of those present can be forgiven the injury they did, the Muscovites may truly reckon that day among the happiest of their lives. Prince Aleksei Semenovich Shein, field marshal of the tsar's troops, was the first who submitted the encumbrance of his long beard to the scissors. Nor can they consider it any disgrace, as their sovereign is the first to show the example—their sovereign, to whose wish or command they deem it a holy and religious act to devote their lives. Nor was there anybody left to laugh at the rest, for they all shared the same fate. . . .

September 14: . . . The Danish envoy

piqued himself greatly on his victory, vaunting that he had been allowed the precedence because he was the first who had the honor of kissing hands. As these rivals [the Danish and the Polish envoys] were ambitiously contending about precedence, neither willing to be second to the other, the tsar, in indignation, made use of a word familiar to the Muscovites to express a deficiency of the mind, calling them *duraki* [fools]. . . .

October 6-7: . . . Such horrible accounts of the tortures administered daily [to the strel'tsy rebels] reached the patriarch that he thought it his duty to exhort the angered tsar to gentleness. He thought the best thing was to take an image of the most blessed Virgin, the sight of which might remind him of the common lot of man and bring back the common feelings of pity to a mind that was almost degenerating into savagery. But the weights of real justice with which His Majesty the tsar measured the magnitude of this heinous crime were not to be altered by this exhibition of sham piety. For it had come to that pass that Muscovy was to be saved only by cruelty, not by piety. Yet is this severity of chastisement falsely called tyranny; for sometimes even equity itself demands severity: more particularly when disease or obstinate gangrene has taken such firm hold of the members that there remains no other remedy for the general health of the body politic than iron and fire to cut them off. Thus the tsar's invective against the patriarch was not unworthy of his exalted office: "What wilt thou with thy image? Or what duty of thy office brings thee to these places? Hence forthwith, and put back that image in the place where it should be venerated. Know, that I reverence God and honor his most holy Mother more earnestly perhaps than thou dost. It is the duty of my sovereign office, and [a token] of devotion that I owe to God, to save my people from harm and to prosecute with public vengeance crimes that tend to the common ruin." . . .

October 27: . . . All the boyars and magnates who were present at the council that had decreed to fight against the rebel strel'tsy, this day were summoned to a new tribunal. A criminal was set before each, and each had to carry out with the ax the sentence he had passed. Prince Romodanovskii,

who was chief of four regiments of strel'tsy before their revolt, laid four strel'tsy low with the same weapon—His Majesty urging him to it. The more cruel Aleksashka [Alexander Menshikov] went boasting of twenty heads that he had chopped off. Golitsyn was unhappy at having greatly increased the criminal's suffering by striking poorly. Three hundred and thirty that were all led out together to the ax's fatal stroke empurpled the plain far and wide with civil—'tis true—but impious blood. General Lefort and Baron von Blumberg were invited also to this executioner's duty but were excused on alleging that it was foreign from the manners of the countries they came from. The tsar himself, sitting in the judgment seat, looked on with dry eyes at the whole tragedy, at this frightful butchery of such a multitude of men, being only irate that many of the boyars had performed this unaccustomed function with trembling hands; for in his opinion no fatter victim could be immolated to God than a felon.

October 28: Today took place the execution of the priests—that is to say, of such of them as, carrying the images of the blessed Virgin and Saint Nicholas to draw the common people to the side of the mutineers, had, with the customary prayers at the altar, invoked the help of God for the happy success of the impious plot. . . .

February 4 [1699]: [Another mutiny of the strel'tsy had broken out near Moscow.] New tortures awaited the new rebels. Every boyar was made an inquisitor; to torture the guilty was deemed a token of remarkable loyalty. The officials of a certain envoy, whose curiosity for sight-seeing had led them to Preobrazhenskoe, had inspected various prisons of the criminals, hastening to wherever more atrocious howls betokened a tragedy of greater anguish. Already they had passed with horror through three, when howls more appalling and groans more horrible than they had yet heard stimulated them to examine what cruelty was going on in a fourth house. But hardly had they set foot within it than they were about withdrawing again, being startled at the sight of the tsar and the boyars, chief of whom were Naryshkin, Romodanovskii, and Tikhon Nikitich [Streshnev].

· · ·

The tsar's court: The former grand dukes made use of inestimable parade in their apparel and adornment, the majesty of the pontiff being superadded to that of the king. On the head they wore a miter, glittering with pearls and priceless gems; in the left hand they bore an exceedingly rich pastoral staff; their fingers were covered with rings of gold; as they sat upon the throne, on their right there was an image of Christ, and above them, one of the most holy Virgin Mother. The presence and antechambers were thronged with men clad in golden vesture and other precious insignia to the very feet.

But the present tsar, scorning all pomp and ostentation about his own person, rarely makes use of that superfluous multitude of attendants. Nor do the boyars or nobles about the court pride themselves on their ornate garb of old, having learned by the example of the grand duke that luxury in dress is an empty thing and that living in fine houses does not constitute wisdom. The tsar himself, when going through his capital, is often accompanied by only two, and at most three or four, of his more intimate attendants; even in the perilous time of the military revolt he was protected solely by the respect [of his subjects] for majesty.

X:5. CHARLES WHITWORTH ON PETER, 1710

Charles, Baron Whitworth (1675-1725), served as British envoy extraordinary in Russia from 1704 to 1710. His dispatches reveal him as a keen observer and a man of wide interests. During his stay in Russia he had many formal and informal dealings with Peter the Great, who took a liking to him; at the time Whitworth left Russia, Peter presented him with the tsar's portrait set with diamonds. The excerpt printed here is taken from Whitworth's comprehensive report drawn up in 1710.

Reference: Charles Whitworth, *An Account of Russia As It Was in the Year 1710* (London, 1758), pp. 57-60. Many of Whitworth's dispatches from Russia have been published in *SIRIO*, vols. 39, 50.

The present Czar is in his thirty-eighth year, a handsome prince of a strong constitution, but of late much broke by irregular living, and other fatigues. He was very subject to convulsions, said to be the effects of poison from his Sister Sophia in his youth, which made him shy of being seen, but of late they are much mended. He is extremely curious and diligent, and has farther improved his Empire in ten years, than any other ever was in ten times that space; and which is more surprising, without any education, without any foreign help, contrary to the intention of his people, clergy, and chief ministers, but merely by the strength of his own genius, observation and example. He has gradually past [sic] through all the employments of the army, from a Drummer to Lieutenant-General; of the fleet, from a common Seaman to Rear Admiral; and in his shipyards, from an ordinary Carpenter to Master-Builder.

... He is good-natured, but very passionate, though by degrees he has learnt to contain himself, except the heat of wine is added to his natural temper; he is certainly ambitious, though very modest in appearance; suspicious of other people; not over scrupulous in his engagements, or gratitude; violent in the first heat, irresolute on longer deliberation, not rapacious, but near in his temper and expense to extremity; he loves his soldiers, understands navigation, ship-building, fortification, and fire-working. He speaks High-Dutch pretty readily, which is now growing the Court language. He is very particular in his way of living; when at Mosco, he never lodges in the palace, but in a little wooden house built for him in the suburbs as Colonel of his guards. He has neither court, equipage or other distinction from a private officer except when he appears on publick solemnities.

X:6. JOHN PERRY ON LIFE IN RUSSIA, CA. 1712

John Perry (1670-1732), an English civil engineer, came to Russia in 1698 to work on waterways. He built a naval dock at Voronezh, supervised the dredging of the Don, and also occupied himself with the Volga-Don and the Saint Petersburg-Volga canal schemes. After suffering many annoyances, he returned to England in 1712. The excerpts printed here are from the book he wrote shortly thereafter.

Reference: *The State of Russia under the Present Czar: By Captain John Perry* (London, 1716), pp. 227, 244-45, 251-55, 258-62, 264-65, 275-76, 279-80. Cf. Peter Putnam, ed., *Seven Britons in Imperial Russia* (Princeton: Princeton University Press, 1952), pp. 3-20. Perry's book has recently been reprinted (N.Y.: Da Capo, 1967).

I shall conclude this Part of my Discourse, with this Observation of the Russ Way of Life; that notwithstanding their pretended Purity in keeping their Fasts, and abstaining from Flesh, there is nothing more common than to have both the People and the Priest too, go to Church on a Holiday in the Morning, and get drunk in the Afternoon long before Night; especially the greater the Holiday, the more it is excusable, and the Custom, to be drunk. It is very ordinary at such Times, if you ride through *Mosco* in the Evening on a great Holiday, to see the Priests, as well as other Men, lie drunk about the Streets.

. . .

There are two remarkable Times of the Year when the *Russes* express their Joy upon the Alteration of the Seasons; the one is when the Snow first falls on the Ground, and the Winter is so strongly set in, that the Rivers are so frozen up, that they can pass with their Horses and Sleds upon the Ice; which Change, when the Wind shifts about and blows from the Northward, happens so suddenly, that sometimes within 24 Hours there is no Ice to be seen, and the next Day a Horse and Sled may drive over the Rivers; and when the Winter is thus strongly fix'd, they have on all sides across the Land, the Lakes, and the Rivers, wherever the nearest Way lies, an Opportunity of Land-Carriage by Sleds, which is certainly the most commodious and swiftest travelling in the World either for Passengers or for Goods; the Sleds being light and conveniently made, and with little Labour to the Horses, slide smooth and easy over the Snow and the Ice; and the Snow by often passing of the Sleds upon it wherever there is a Way made, becomes smooth and hard like Ice. Against which Season of the Year, great quantities of Goods are laid up in most Places of Russia, for the Easiness and Cheapness of Carriage in the Winter, excepting where there is Opportunity of Water Carriage by their Floats, their Boats and their Vessels. The whole Winter through when once the Sled way

is fix'd, there come several thousand Sleds every Day laden into *Mosco,* drawn usually but with one Horse; and it is remarkable that in *Russia* the price of Land-carriage in the Winter upon sleds, is not above the fourth or fifth part so much as it is in the Summer upon wheels. The *Russes* also usually use but one Horse for their common Carriage by Waggons in the Summer, their Waggons being made light and the Roads thereby preserv'd smooth, and are not cut deep.

The other time of their Rejoycing is in the Spring of the Year, after the Ice has been some Days rotten and dangerous and then breaks away, the River becomes open and free for their Boats and Vessels to pass. On these two Occasions the *Russes* hold a kind of Festival, and are merry with their Neighbours.

The Product or Manufactures of *Russia* with which Commerce is principally maintain'd with foreign Parts, is Pot-ash, Weed-ash, *Russia* Leather, Furs, Linen, Flax, Hemp, Seal-skins, Train-oyl, Rosin, Pitch, Tar, Caviar, Tallow, Honey, Wax, Isinglass of both sorts (the one of which is us'd in Windows for Ships, &c. and the other for making of Glue;) as also Masts, Timber, Plank, and Firr.

. . .

I have before mentioned a new Office that was created by the *Czar,* at his first coming from his Travels; in which Office he impowered some of the principal Merchants to make the Assessments and Collection of Duties, which related to Trade. But not long after this, it was in a great measure laid by, and there were other Projects set on foot; several new Officers were created, called *Prebulshicks* [*pribyl'shchik,* fiscal expert and agent of the government] (or Advancers of Profit to be brought into the *Czar's* Treasury) and these persons had a full power given them, in several Schemes which were laid down (according to the old ways of *Russia*) to manage some one Branch of the Duties and Customs to be paid to the Czar; whereby they proposed to bring more speedy and greater Sums into the Treasury. And the things wherein Trade has been directly injur'd and obstructed have been as follows.

First, by forestalling and monopolizing many of the principal Commodities, the Growth of the *Czar's* Countrey, such as Potash, Tar, &c., by buying up large Quantities of Goods, and then setting an extraordinary Value upon them, and forbidding any *Russ* Merchant to sell the same sort of Goods, until all Goods thus bought for the *Czar* (as they call it) are first sold at the Rate that is set upon them.
. . .

Secondly, When the Czar's Occasions have been declared to require it, and Goods from foreign Markets have arrived at *Archangel,* it has been often order'd that no *Russ* Merchant, or other Person whatsoever, should dare buy any such Goods as are come into Port, until what the *Czar* has occasion for is first bought; whereby foreign Merchants have often been constrained to deliver their Goods at such Prices as have been offer'd them by the Persons who are commission'd to buy them for the *Czar.* . . .

Thirdly, the *Prebulshicks* have been empower'd to go into all Houses to search after Goods, to assess and levy severe Duties in all Inland Markets and Trade, and to trouble and vex the People to the last degree through all the *Czar's* Dominions, beside the general Tax which every House and Family is obliged to pay: So that through these things, the arbitrary Practices, together with the Oppression of the Governors, of the *Diacks,* and petty Officers subordinate to them, the common People have but very little Heart or Desire to any Industry, farther than Necessity drives them. For if at any time by their Ingenuity and endeavours they do get Money, it cannot rightly be said they can call it their own; but with Submission they say, *All that they have belongs to God and the Czar.* Nor do they dare to appear as if they had any Riches, in their Apparel, or in their Houses, it being counted the best way to seem poor, lest there should be any Notice taken of them that they have Money; and they are troubled and harrass'd till they must part with it, and always be making Bribes and Presents to be at rest; of which there are ten thousand Instances. So that every where as you travel through the Villages in *Russia,* for this reason you will see the general part of the common People idle in the Streets, and

in the Houses, especially in the Winter; the chiefest Things which they take Care for, being in the Affairs of their Husbandry, to sow and to reap in their Seasons, and to make a coarse sort of Cloaths to defend themselves from the Cold. What Money the common People get, it is their way often to hide it under the Earth, so that 'tis certain great Sums are thereby wholly lost when Men come to dye.

. . .

All the common People, or Peasants of *Russia,* (who dress and till the Land, &c.) are Slaves, either directly to the *Czar* himself, to the *Boyars,* to the Monasteries, or to the Gentlemen of the Countrey; and when the *Czar* either gives any Person a Village, (which is often forfeited, and taken from one Man and given to another,) or when any Village or Estate is bought and sold in *Russia,* the Way of reckoning the Value of the same, is not according to the Extent of Land that belongs to the same, but according to the Number of Inhabitants or Slaves there are upon it; each House or Family have their Portion of Land allotted to them, and are obliged to pay to their proper Landlord such a Proportion of Money, of Corn, and all manner of Provision in Specie. Besides the common Taxes that are laid on them by the *Czar's* particular Orders for carrying on his Wars, it is the manner of *Russia,* upon Occasion of all Works and Business belonging to the *Czar,* where any Number of common Labourers, Carpenters, Masons, or Smiths, are required, to send an Order into such Provinces and Districts for the respective Governors of the Towns, as is thought fit, to levy them from among such of the Peasants or Slaves, according as the Order directs; which sometimes falls out, that every third, fifth, or tenth House, shall find a Man, whether Carpenter, Smith, or Labourer, sometimes with a Horse, and sometimes without, for so many Months or so much Time as such Order appoints, to be paid at the proper Expense and Charge of the Towns and Villages from whence they are appointed to be levied, till they are order'd to be relieved, and other Numbers of fresh Men, either from the same or some other Districts are sent in their Places. And I have known it sometimes, that even one half of the Men belonging to all the Villages in some particular Districts, have been sent alternately to relieve one another, without having any Wages allowed them. . . .

Upon these Considerations, it is no great wonder that the *Russes* are the most dull and heavy People to attain to any Art or Science of any Nation in the World, and upon every Opportunity are most apt to rebel and to engage in any the most barbarous Cruelties, in hopes of being reliev'd from that Slavery that is hereditary to them.

The *Czar,* where he is present, does indeed give Encouragement to some of those common Artificers and Workmen, who have the Happiness to be under his Eye, and whom he finds deserving, as particularly in the building and equipping of his Ships, where he is daily among the Artificers, and will often take the Tools in hand, and work himself along with them. But his *Boyars* are quite of another Temper, and in all other places and Occasions, through all the Parts of the *Czar's* Dominions, the generality of his Subjects remain still under the same Check and Discouragement to Ingenuity: And this is certain, that if the present *Czar* should happen to die, without the greatest part of his present old *Boyars* go off before him, the generality of Things wherein he has taken so much Pains to reform his Countrey, will for the most part revolve into their old Form. For it is believed that his Son, the present Prince of *Russia,* who is of a Temper very much differing from his Father's, and adheres to Bigottry and Superstition, will easily be prevailed on to come into the old Methods of *Russia,* and quit and lay aside many of those laudable Things that have been begun by the present *Czar.* . . .

. . . Among some other Causes, one of the chief which makes the generality of the Nobility at present uneasy, is, that the *Czar* obliges them against their Will, to come and live at *Petersburgh,* with their Wives and their Families, where they are obliged to build new Houses for themselves, and where all manner of Provisions are usually three or four times as dear, and Forage for their Horses, &c. at least six or eight times as dear as it is at *Mosco;* which happens from the great Expence of it at Petersburgh, and the small quantity which the Countrey thereabouts produces, being more than two thirds Woods and Bogs; and not only the Nobility, but Merchants and Tradesmen of all sorts, are obliged to go and live there, and to trade with

such things as they are order'd, which Crowd of People enhances the Price of Provisions, and makes a Scarcity for those Men who are absolutely necessary to live there, on account of the Land and Sea Service, and in carrying on those Buildings and Works which the *Czar* has already, and farther designs to make there. Whereas in *Mosco,* all the Lords and Men of distinction, have not only very large Buildings within the City, but also their Countrey Seats and Villages, where they have their Fishponds, their Gardens, with plenty of several sorts of Fruit and Places of Pleasure; but *Petersburgh,* which lies in the Latitude of 60 Degrees and 15 Minutes North, is too cold to produce these Things. Besides, *Mosco* is the Native Place which the *Russes* are fond of, and where they have their Friends and Acquaintance about them.

· · ·

Not only in *Mosco,* but generally all the Buildings in every Town and City of *Russia,* being made after the same manner, occasions those often and dreadful Fires, that the like is not to be found in any other Countrey in the World.

Particularly in *Mosco,* it is common when a Fire begins, especially in the Summer Season, when every thing is dry and ready to kindle, to have a Fire spread on all sides, and burn on so furious, that there is no standing before it; and in this extremity, it is the way of the *Russes,* in hopes to put a stop to the Fire, to pull down the Houses and Fences that are made of Wood, tho' they often have not time to carry it off, but as it lies upon the Ground together with the Wood with which the Streets are lined, gives a Train to the Fire; so that I have known it in less than half a Days time, when there has been a Gate of Wind, burn above a *Russ* Mile in length, and destroy many thousand Houses before it has been quench'd, and often without giving the Inhabitants opportunity to carry off the tenth part of their Goods. This has often brought many People to the last degree of Poverty, when all that they have had has been burnt; and it is one great Cause that the Houses appear so poor in *Mosco,* when they cannot raise Money to build them better, and by reason of their being very often, as soon as they are built up, burnt down again to the Ground.

· · ·

As to the common Foot Soldiers, there are some very remarkable Things which render them as fit for Service as any in the World.

First, It is the Manner of all *Russia,* for the common People, (Men and Women) to go at least once, if not twice a Week, into their Bagnio's [*bania,* steam bath] or Sweating Houses; and it is their Manner, even in the Depth of Winter, to come naked out of their Bagnio's, and either jump into the River, or if there be no River open, to pour two or three Pails full of cold Water directly upon their Heads: and by their being thus used from their Infancy to these Extremes of Heat and Cold, it is common for them when they travel in the open *Step* where there are no Houses, to make a Fire in the Night, and to lie round it and sleep in the time of the severest Frosts, and not to catch cold, or known to be troubled with Coughs in that Countrey; and their being thus enured to Hardships, is one thing that renders them fit to be Soldiers. Another is, that a *Russ,* if you give him but *Sucarie* [*sukhar',* biscuit], (which is Rye-Bread first baked and minced in small square Bits, and then dry'd again in the Oven) if they have but Water to drink with it, they will march fourteen Days together, and be very content: But if they get now and then a Dram of Brandy, they think they fare well.

Secondly, the *Russes* do not seem to value or be discouraged at Death; as commonly is observed of them when they go to be executed, they do it with the least Concern in the World. I have seen several of them go together with the Chains on their Legs, and Wax Candles burning in their Hands: and as they pass by the Crowds of People they bow to them, and say, *Prostee Brats* [*Prosti bratets,* forgive me, brother], that is, *Adieu Brothers;* and the People make the like Reply to them, bidding them adieu: And so they lay down their Heads on the Blocks, and with a steady Countenance resign their Lives. On these Accounts it is that the *Russes* are esteem'd by those who are better Judges than I, that if their Officers are good, they will not fail to make good Soldiers: and it has in many Actions been lately proved that those that have been well led on, and used to Action, will stand as firm, and fight as well, as any other Nation.

· · ·

One thing more I will mention, the Places where his [Peter's] Naval Preparations are made, and where his Armies are disposed, being very far distant sometimes one from another, which requires him very often to undertake long and tedious Journeys from Place to Place, he has, I believe (for the Proportion of Time that I was in the Countrey) travell'd twenty times more than ever any Prince in the World did before him, and which in no Countrey, but by Sled Way, could be perform'd; his usual Method of travelling in the Winter, being after the rate of more than a hundred *English* Miles a Day, which he does by fresh Sets of Horses. But though this travelling by Sleds in the Winter be thus commodious in *Russia,* yet there are no Inns or Places of any tolerable Entertainment by the way, excepting in great Towns, which are generally 100 Miles distant one from the other.

Therefore the *Czar* to make his Journeys the more agreeable to him, and his Officers and Lords who travel, has upon the Road to *Veronize* [Voronezh], *Kiow, Smolensky* and *Petersburgh,* order'd convenient Houses of Entertainment to be built at every 20 or 30 Miles distant upon all the said Roads, and has likewise caused handsome Posts to be set up at every Mile, with the distance from Place to Place legibly written, both in *English* Figures and *Russ* Characters, that Travellers as they are upon the Road may easily know how far they have to go. And particularly that *Petersburgh* may be render'd more agreeable, about seven Years since he order'd Mr. *Fergharson* and Mr. *Gwin* to take an exact survey of the Road between *Petersburgh* and *Mosco,* to find the Bearing of one Place from another, in order to make a Road the whole Way, by a straight Line through all the Woods, and over all the Lakes, Morasses and Rivers, by which it will happen about one fifth part nearer than it now is; and a Tract has since been mark'd out through the Woods for making this Way on a direct Line, which was finish'd in the Year 1710. And the *Czar* does design to have a Road accordingly made, when he has Peace, and can better spare Men and Money for it.

X:7. PETER HENRY BRUCE ON PETER THE GREAT, CA. 1711-1715

Peter Henry Bruce (1692-1757), a soldier of fortune of Scottish origin, began his military career in the Prussian army in 1706; from 1711 to 1724 he served in the Russian army, where he enjoyed the protection of his distant relative, Count James ("Iakov Vilimovich") Bruce (1670-1735), Peter the Great's chief of artillery, to whom he refers in his *Memoirs* as "the General" or "General James." Bruce wrote the English version of his *Memoirs,* which had originally been written in German, in 1755.

Reference: *Memoirs of Peter Henry Bruce, Esq.* (Dublin, 1783), pp. 50-53, 136-40, 155-57, 175-77, 179, 180-82. (There is also a 1772 edition, published in London.) The edition of 1783 was recently reprinted (N.Y: Da Capo, 1968).

[The Russian army was marching along the Pruth in 1711] . . . when we discovered the Turkish army crossing the Pruth. Upon this, general James was detached with a body of troops, and twelve pieces of cannon, to dispute their passage; but he was too late, for half their army had passed before he could get up to them, so that he found it prudent to retreat to the army. It was very surprising, that we had not the least intelligence of so numerous an army, which consisted of no less than 200,000 men, till they were within sight of us.

Our army drew up in order of battle, at some distance from the river, in hopes to bring them to an engagement; but they kept out of the reach of our cannon, and extending their numerous army, endeavoured to surround us, and cut us off from the river. We remained under arms till night, and being convinced of their intention, we made a very disorderly retreat to secure the river, our divisions being all separated from each other in the dark, and as we were now greatly deficient in horses, we burnt a number of our baggage waggons, that they should not fall into the enemy's hands; and it was surprising, that from the number of fires that were blazing in the night, the enemy did not perceive our confusion, which afforded them a fine opportunity to have destroyed our whole army, and they might easily have done it with a small part of theirs; but happily for us they seemed to pay greater attention to their own safety than our destruction. . . . At day-break our scattered troops were again put in order, and our army formed into a hollow square, the river serving for the fourth side . . . . and our waggons were formed into an inclosure within, for the protection of the ladies.

On the other side of the river, and opposite to us, the Crim Tartars were placed, where the King of Sweden had pitched his tent to discover the motions of our army. . . . Our army was surrounded by a chevaux de frize, which was the only protection we had.

The Turkish army surrounded us on all sides, with a design to starve us into a surrender, and this they certainly would have done in a short time, had they not been too eager in attacking us, which they did three days and three nights together; but fortunately for us, they attacked only one side of our square at a time, which enabled us to relieve our wearied troops, from time to time, as they became harassed by fatigue, and it also enabled us to use one large train of artillery, which did great execution among them and luckily they had none to annoy us with, as theirs was not yet arrived.

On the fourth day, the czar, being informed that our ammunition was all spent to three charges of cannon and small-arms, ordered all the officers in the army, with a number of select men, to mount on horseback and attend his person; his intention was to force his way through the Turkish army in the night, and to go through Transilvania into Hungary: but the czarina [Catherine] coming to the knowledge of this dangerous resolution, and foreseeing the hazard that would attend the czar, and the loss and disgrace that would fall upon his arms and army, very luckily hit upon a better expedient, which saved us all from destruction. She collected all the money, plate, and jewels which were in the army, for which she gave her own receipt and obligation to pay the respective owners, and with this valuable present she had the address to prevail on the grand vizier to conclude a peace, and the transaction was immediately finished in the name of the field-marshal [Sheremet'ev], without the czar's knowledge who was just going to set out on his very dangerous expedition, which her majesty stopped by telling him that the grand vizier had agreed to conclude a peace on reasonable terms. This piece of consummate female discretion was followed by a most punctual discharge of her obligations for the plate, etc. on her return home. The principal conditions of the peace, on our part, were to deliver up to the Turks Azoph, Taganrog, and Caminiek [Kamenets-Podolsk], and that our troops should evacuate Poland.

· · ·

This city [Saint Petersburg] was now in its infancy, it being yet but barely ten years since its first foundation was laid. When the czar had made himself master of Noteburgh and New Schantz, he went down to the mouth of the river Neva, where it falls into the Baltic by several streams forming so many islands; the situation pleased him so much, that he resolved upon building this city. He found only four fishermen's huts, to which he added a house for himself on an island in the north side of the river, and called it Petersburgh. This house was only a shelter from the weather and to rest in; it is a low hall built of wood, inclosed with a wooden gallery, and the year 1704, in figures, carved over the door. . . . The first thing that was undertaken was the building of two forts; one here, and another at Cronslot, to protect the place from insult from the Swedes by sea; it being naturally guarded against any attempt on the land side, as the country round it is almost one general morass.

Every body now beheld with surprize and admiration such advances toward a city, in so short a time, as many thousand houses were already built. In that part called Petersburgh, stands a large square brick building, with a spacious court within, for merchants and tradesmen, where they have their shops below and store-rooms above, and are shut up every night, being under the same regulations with the grand market-place at Moscow; and the merchants all reside in this part of the town. Here is also a large long brick building, which contains the senate-house, all the supreme courts of the kingdom, chancery court, court of justice, the boards of admiralty and ordnance, the war office, &c, &c. The president

of every court, or board, is a senator. The seat of trade, the courts of justice, all the publick offices, and the grand council of the empire, being combined in such a small space, makes it extremely convenient for the dispatch of business. . . . Below the fort, on the same side of the river, is Wasilio Ostrof (or Island), where prince Menzikoff has built a very grand palace, and a number of fine brick houses for the accommodation of those belonging to his court: this island is large, and well laid out in gardens and parks, and here the grandeur of the Imperial court is displayed, and all foreign ambassadors and ministers have their audiences; on which occasion, the czar always appears as a private gentleman; as indeed, he does every where, attended only by one page and one footman who carries his mathematical instruments and draughts, for he is an excellent draughtsman, and understands all the branches of the mathematics, and is well versed in fortification, architecture, shipbuilding, and the construction of all kinds of engines. . . .

Above the admiralty stands the Inoisemska Slaboda, or Foreign Town, where all European foreigners live, and have several Protestant and one Roman Catholic, meeting-houses: here stands admiral Apraxin's fine palace. This island was also low and marshy, but was drained and raised by digging several canals through it. The czar has both his winter and summer-palace on this island; the former is next the river, and the latter at the east, or upper end of the island, where his yachts and pleasure boats are ranged close up before the door; here are exceeding fine gardens and a large park, inclosed by a large and deep canal. . . . In the garden was a long gallery, or hall, where the czar attended every day from eleven to twelve o'clock at noon, when every body had free access, and he then received petitions from all ranks of his subjects; after that hour none were permitted to address him except upon affairs of consequence. He dined commonly at twelve o'clock, and only with his own family; one dish only was served up at a time, and to have it hot he dined in a room, contiguous to the kitchen, from whence the dish is received through a window from the cook; at one o'clock he lies down and sleeps an hour; he spent the afternoon and evening in some diversions or other till ten o'clock, when he went to bed, and got up again at four in the morning, summer or winter.

. . .

[In 1714] the Czar . . . addressed the following discourse to his senators: "Brethren, who is the man among you, who, twenty years ago, could have conceived the idea of being employed with me in shipbuilding here on the Baltic, and to settle in those countries conquered by our fatigues and bravery? Of living to see so many brave and victorious soldiers and seamen sprung from Russian blood? And to see our sons coming home accomplished men from foreign countries? Historians place the ancient seat of all sciences in Greece; from whence being expelled by the fatality of the times, they spread into Italy, and afterwards dispersed themselves all over Europe; but by the perverseness of our ancestors, they were hindered from penetrating any farther than into Poland; the Poles, as well as the Germans, formerly groped in the same darkness in which we have hitherto lived, but the indefatigable care of their governors at length opened their eyes, and they made themselves masters of those arts, sciences, and social improvements, which formerly Greece boasted of. It is now our turn, if you will seriously second my designs, and add to your obedience voluntary knowledge. I can compare this transmigration of the sciences to nothing better than the circulation of the blood in the human body; and my mind almost prognosticates that they will, some time or other, quit their abodes in Britain, France, and Germany, and come and settle, for some centuries, among us; and afterwards, perhaps, return to their original home in Greece. In the mean time, I earnestly recommend to your practice the Latin saying, *Ora et labora* (pray and work); and in that case be persuaded you may happen, even in your own life-time, to put other civilized nations to the blush, and raise the glory of the Russian name to the highest pitch." The senators heard this harangue of their monarch with a most respectful silence; and answered, that they were all disposed to obey his orders and follow his example. Whether they were sincere in their declaration is another question.

. . .

These rejoicings [after the birth of a son, Petr Petrovich, in 1715] were followed by a kind of carnival; the czar having united the patriarchal dignity, and the great revenues belonging to it, to the crown, and to render the character of the patriarch ridiculous in the eyes of the people, he appointed Sotof [Zotov], his jester, now in the eighty-fourth year of his age, mock-patriarch, who, on this occasion, was married to a buxom widow of thirty-four, and the nuptials of this extraordinary couple were celebrated in masquerade by about four hundred persons of both sexes, every four persons having their proper dress and peculiar musical instruments; the persons appointed to invite the company were four of the greatest stammerers in the kingdom; the four running footmen were the most unwieldy, gouty, fat men, that could be found; the bride-men, stewards, and waiters were very old men; and the priest that joined them in marriage was upwards of one hundred years old. The procession was in the following order . . . then followed Knez Romadanoffski, the farcical czar, who represented King David in his dress, but instead of a harp, had a lyre, covered with a bear-skin, to play upon; and he being the chief character in the show, his sledge was made in imitation of a throne, and he had King David's crown upon his head, and four bears, one at each corner, tied to his sledge, by way of footmen, and one behind, standing and holding the sledge with his two paws; the bears being all the while pricked with goads, which made them roar in a frightful manner; then the bridegroom and bride, on an elevated sledge made on purpose, surrounded with Cupids holding each a large horn in his hand; on the fore-part of the sledge was placed by way of coachman, a ram with very large horns; and behind was a he-goat by way of lacquey; behind them followed a number of other sledges, drawn by different kinds of animals, four to each, as rams, goats, deer, bulls, bears, dogs, wolves, swine, and asses. . . . The procession no sooner began to move, than all the bells of the city began to ring, and all the drums of the fort, toward which they were advancing, began to beat upon the ramparts; the different animals were forced to make a noise; all the company playing upon, or rattling their different instruments, and altogether made such a terrible confused noise, that it is past description. The czar, with his three companions, prince Menzikof, and the counts Apraxin and Bruce, were clad like Friesland boors, each with a drum. . . .

The carnival lasted ten days, the company going every day from one house to another, at each of which were tables spread with all sorts of cold meat, and with such abundance of strong liquors every where, that there scarce was a sober person to be found during that time in Petersburgh.

.   .   .

The czar was all this time indefatigable in the improvements of his country, not only in building ships, forts, and houses, but he provided his new academy with able masters, to teach all the branches of learning necessary for the education of young gentlemen; he also erected printing-houses, well supplied with able translators of all languages, who translated all the most valuable books then in Europe into the Russian language, his agents abroad buying up the most valuable books, and whole libraries at auctions; and it was truly surprising to see such a grand collection already in Petersburgh. . . .

At Moscow he erected large manufactories for woollen and linen cloth, as also glass-works for making window-glass and looking-glass, under the direction of Englishmen. The Russians had formerly only used isinglass for their windows and coaches; for at the building of Petersburgh, they were obliged to take all their glass from England. Although they shipped yearly great quantities of hemp to all parts of Europe, yet they were obliged to bring their sail-cloth and cordage, manufactured abroad, from their own hemp. To remedy this evil, the czar erected manufactories for sail-cloth, and rope-walks at Moscow, Novogrod, and Petersburgh; and that nothing might be wanting for the improvement of his country, skilful miners were got from Hungary and Saxony, who discovered metals of all sorts, gold, silver, copper, lead,

and iron; which last article they were obliged formerly to purchase from Sweden, but they now supply other countries with it.

It was surprising to see so many great things undertaken and put in execution by one single person, without the assistance and help of any one; his own great genius and indefatigable application to things, presiding over all, and seeing every thing with his own eyes, without trusting to the reports of others; so that never monarch was less imposed on than himself. It is to be observed, that the natives, from the highest to the lowest, if they discover any thing of value in their grounds, let it be of what quality it will, keep it a secret, lest their slaves should be employed to work it; so all discoveries of that kind are owing to foreigners. . . .

It was an invariable maxim with the czar to reward merit wherever he found it: after a victory by sea or land, every officer was presented with a gold chain and medal, of a value proportioned to his rank, and every soldier a silver one, or a month's pay in lieu of it; and the officer who had distinguished himself out of the common way had the first promotion: on the other hand, the soldier or officer who had misbehaved, was punished with great severity. The czar took no notice of people on account of their high birth and family, but promoted merit in every station, even in the meanest plebeian, saying, that high birth was only chance, and if not accompanied with merit ought not to be regarded. History scarce affords an example where so many people of low birth have been raised to such dignities as in czar Peter's reign, or where so many of the highest birth and fortune have been levelled to the lowest ranks in life.

X:8. J. G. VOCKERODT'S MEMORANDUM ON RUSSIA UNDER PETER THE GREAT IN THE 1720s

Johann Gotthilf Vockerodt spent many years in Russia as secretary of the Prussian legation. Little is known about him, and even the date of his arrival in Russia is uncertain; but by 1721 the Prussian envoy Mardefeld considered him indispensable, partly because he was quite fluent in Russian. In 1737, at the request of Crown Prince Frederick (the future Frederick the Great), Vockerodt wrote a lengthy memorandum on Russia under Peter the Great; this memorandum, excerpts from which are given here, was intended for the use of Voltaire.

Reference: Ernst Herrmann, ed., *Russland unter Peter dem Grossen: Nach den handschriftlichen Berichten Johann Gotthilf Vockerodt's und Otto Pleyer's* (Leipzig, 1872), pp. 2-3, 48-49, 54, 73-75. There is a Russian translation in *CIOIDRMU,* 1874, bk. 2, sec. 4, pp. 1-120.

If anyone should wonder whether the Russians were an intelligent people prior to the reign of Peter I, then let him look into their history and consider what happened there in

the last century. The Russian state had been torn asunder by innumerable parties owing to the ambition of Godunov and the intrigues of the Poles and was brought to the verge of ruin by internal and external foes, for the Poles had seized Moscow, and the Swedes, Novgorod the Great. Yet, after such calamities, the Russians cleared their country of these two powerful enemies and restored their monarchy; they did this through their intelligent actions and with their own forces, without receiving any aid from abroad, without even consulting any foreign general or minister, and without any knowledge of war but what they had had of old. Moreover, in less than fifty years, they not only took back all the provinces they had had to sacrifice to procure peace, with the exception of Ingria and a part of Karelia, but they also pushed the Poles out of the provinces of Smolensk, Kiev, Chernigov, and Severia [i.e. the former region of the Severiane, in the basin of the Desna]; they even forced the Ottoman Porte, which was then at the height of its power and greatness, to leave them the Cossacks and the whole of the Ukraine. All this they accomplished under the rule of sovereigns who were not noted either for special bravery or for intellectual acumen, and who, moreover, came from such a new family that their first tsar, Michael, would certainly not have been able to prove his rights in any German court.

. . .

If we do not wish to go to the trouble of examining history, then let us take an ordinary Russian townsman or peasant, to whom Peter I's solicitude for the education of his subjects never extended, and try to explore the range of his mental and moral faculties. It will quickly become apparent that, wherever he is not shackled by the prejudices of his country or of his religion, the Russian is usually endowed with very sound natural intelligence and clear judgment, that he also has an unusual capacity to comprehend things and is very quick to invent the right expedients to reach his aim and to turn to his advantage any opportunity that presents itself; most Russians have considerable natural eloquence; they know how to arrange their affairs and astutely discern what is useful or harmful for them; they possess all these qualities to a much greater degree than one usually meets among the common people in Germany or elsewhere. But whoever wishes to undertake such an examination, to get a true idea of the ability of a Russian, must first divest himself completely of all his prejudices and see things as

they are; he must not take the customs and usages of his own country as his yardstick.

. . .

There was no undertaking on which Peter I himself worked with greater zeal and personal care and effort than the establishment of the fleet. In all other affairs he contented himself with examining the general plan and left the details to those whom he charged with its execution; but in anything that concerned the navy he entered into the minutest detail, and nothing ever happened in his admiralties—not a nail would be driven in—without it being referred to him for approval. Not a day went by without his spending several hours at the Admiralty or at the dockyards, and if something had to be attended to there, all other affairs were put aside. No victory [on land] could give him greater pleasure than the smallest advantage gained by his warships or galleys. He celebrated the capture of one poor frigate and six worthless galleys with a solemn triumph and with many other expressions of joy quite out of proportion with the event. When his galleys captured four small Swedish frigates at Grenham, he ordered a big victory monument to be erected in the shape of a pyramid in front of the Senate at Saint Petersburg. [Note: The naval engagement off Grenham in the Åland Islands took place on July 27 (August 7, N.S.), 1720; coming at a time when Peter's allies in the Northern War had abandoned him, it helped to hasten the resumption of direct Russo-Swedish peace negotiations.] At the same time, nothing would cause him more acute distress than the slightest misfortune to his ships, and God have mercy on him to whom it could in any way be imputed!

. . .

In the natural course of things, it is impossible that the Russians would ever be able to build a naval force that could compete with the fleets of the maritime powers. In the first place, their state revenues are quite insufficient for this and would be entirely swallowed up by such a venture. Second, they are short of skilled seamen; and if all the devices of Peter I could not overcome the Russians' aversion to maritime navigation, there is little hope that any of his successors will ever succeed in it. Furthermore, the defense of commerce and navigation—which is the main function of the navies of the other powers—cannot come into consideration in the case of the Russians, for they do not carry on any trade with their own ships, nor do they wish to do so: all the Russian [sea] trade is carried on in foreign bottoms.

. . .

Peter I himself often complained that of all the governmental affairs commerce was the most difficult. . . . Generally speaking, in his mercantile institutions Peter had the following aims in mind: first, to reduce the amount of foreign goods imported into Russia and, at the same time, to increase the export of Russian goods; second, to prevent embezzlement of the customs dues and to introduce better order in their collection; third, to take Russian sea trade out of the hands of foreigners, who had monopolized it, and to encourage his Russian subjects to send their goods abroad in their own bottoms.

To achieve the first aim he chose the most obvious course of developing the mining industry and introducing kinds of manufacturing that are common abroad. Even during his first sojourn in Holland he hired a great many men of liberal professions and craftsmen of all kinds: needle makers, wire drawers, paper millers, gunsmiths, woolen cloth workers, and others; moreover, he offered generous inducements to those among them who were willing to come to Russia on their own and to establish factories there. Though the subsequent outbreak of the Swedish War prevented him from pursuing this aim with the necessary vigor, he never lost sight of it. He not only tried to attract this kind of men into Russia, but sent many of his subjects to England and Holland to study the manufactures practiced in these countries. He

especially tried to improve the Russian linen and woolen manufactures, and, perceiving that Russian wool was very coarse for lack of proper care of the sheep, he brought both sheep and sheep breeders from Saxony and Silesia. Traveling through France, he decided to establish in Russia silk factories like those of Lyons, Orléans, and Tours and entrusted this undertaking to three of the richest and most influential persons in his country, Grand Admiral Apraksin, Baron Shafirov, and Count Tolstoi, to whom he granted very profitable privileges; for instance, they were to enjoy the right to import duty-free rich silk merchandise into Russia; however, this exemption was granted for a few years only, until such time as their factories would be fully developed. These gentlemen sold their privilege to private merchants for 20,000 rubles.

. . .

Nevertheless, even in his lifetime, Peter I put a number of factories on such a footing that they amply supplied Russia's needs in goods like needles, arms, various types of linen, and especially sailcloth, which was sufficient not only for their own fleet, but also to supply other nations with. Finally, during his reign, the mines of Siberia [in the Ural region] also began to be widely exploited, chiefly owing to the efforts of Demidov, a common blacksmith, who made such a fortune out of them that today his son has an income of over 100,000 rubles. As a result, instead of being forced to import iron and copper from Sweden, as was formerly the case, Russia can now send considerable quantities of these metals, especially iron, to foreign countries.

B. POLITICAL AND MILITARY DEVELOPMENTS

X:9. IVAN POSOSHKOV ON THE RUSSIAN ARMY, 1701

Ivan Tikhonovich Pososhkov (1652-1726), son of a minor silversmith, tried his hand at various small business enterprises, prospecting, mechanical inventions, and government service in the Spirits Excise Office. Though not spectacularly successful in his enterprises, at the end of his life he owned several houses, a distillery, and two small villages with seventy-two serfs. He had little, if any, formal education and drew most of his ideas from observation and experience. From 1701 on, he submitted to the government many reports and projects, which show a thorough knowledge of the conditions of life in Russia. Several months after the death of Peter the Great, Pososhkov was arrested, it is not quite clear for what reason, and he died in prison in 1726. The following excerpt is taken from Pososhkov's memorandum "On Military Conduct," which he addressed in 1701 to Boyar F. A. Golovin, head of the Posol'skii Prikaz, who at that time also presided over a committee on recruitment. This memorandum was first published in 1793. (See Item X:43, below, for selections from Pososhkov's *Book on Poverty and Wealth.*)

Reference: I. T. Pososhkov, "Donesenie boiarinu F. A. Golovinu o ratnom povedenii," in *Pamiatniki russkoi istorii,* vol. 8 (Moscow: N. N. Klochkov, 1911), pp. 120, 126. A later edition is available: I. T. Pososhkov, *Kniga o skudosti i bogatstve i drugie sochineniia,* ed. B. B. Kafengauz (Moscow: AN SSSR, 1951), pp. 245-272.

It is dangerous to put complete faith in foreigners [as military experts]: they are not our sincere well-wishers, and we should not believe implicitly in what they teach us. I think that they deceive us in everything and take us for absolute idiots.

But, glory be to God, our great sovereign has all kinds of clever men in his own country. The Germans know much more than we in science, but in acumen, by God's grace, we are no worse than they; yet they disparage us unjustly.

They came here, and have hewed a hole from our realm to all their countries, so that they can clearly see all our affairs of state and of commerce. The postal service is that hole. Of what benefit it is to the great sovereign, God only knows; but how much ruin this postal service causes in the whole realm is beyond calculation. Whatever happens in our state is reported in all countries; only the foreigners are enriched because of it, while the Russians are impoverished.

. . .

If you remember, my Lord, our old methods in military service, you will wonder how on earth they ever managed to carry on at all. Hosts of men would be pressed into service, but if you inspected them carefully you would feel nothing but shame. The infantry had poor firearms and did not know how to use them; they would merely defend themselves with pikes and halberds—dull ones at that. For one enemy's life they would exchange three or four and even more of ours,

while it should have been one of ours to at least three of the enemy. And not only the foreigners, but we ourselves would feel ashamed even to look at the cavalry: they would show up on poor nags, with blunt sabers, ill equipped, ill clad, not knowing how to use any firearms. Upon my word, your Lordship, I have seen some gentry who did not even know how to load a pistol, let alone shoot at a target. So what can one say of all these large regiments? Truly, my Lord, it is frightening what I have to say, but I can only compare them to cattle. Sometimes, when they would kill two or three Tatars, they would gaze upon them in amazement and account it a great achievement, and at the same time consider it as nothing if they had lost a hundred men of ours.

Truly, my Lord, I have heard some of the prominent gentry—not the poorest kind—say that they cared not whether they killed an enemy or not; their only care was how to get back home. And some also pray God to receive a light wound, which would not hurt them unduly but would procure them a reward from the great sovereign; others in the service only seek to hide behind a bush during battle. There are shirkers alive today who would lie low with a whole company in the woods or in a gully and watch for soldiers coming back from battle, then they would join them and return to camp, as if they, too, were returning from battle. I have also heard many of the gentry say: "God grant me to serve the great sovereign, but may I never draw my saber from the scabbard!"

X:10. LETTERS OF PETER CONCERNING RECRUITMENT FOR THE ARMY, JANUARY 18, 1707, AND JANUARY 13, 1709

Recruitment for the new regular army, gradually being organized during the Northern War, raised a number of problems, some of which are illustrated in the following letters written by Peter in 1707 and 1709. By trial and error, Peter had arrived at the practice of conscripting one recruit from every twenty peasant homesteads; this became normal procedure beginning with 1705, each levy of this sort producing 30,000-35,000 recruits.

Reference: *PBIPV,* 5:35, 9:23 (see List of Abbreviations).

[To Vasilii Dimitrievich Korchmin:]

                    Zholkva, January 18, 1707

Honorable Second Lieutenant:

The nobleman Mikhailo Bezobrazov, a resident of the city of Briansk, has reported to us that in the city of Briansk and in its district, as well as in other places in that vicinity, the number of clerks, lay readers, and other petty officials, and especially of all kinds of church attendants, has greatly increased. A great many of them could be recruited for service as dragoons or soldiers. For this purpose you must get in touch with the above-mentioned nobleman, as he is well acquainted with the situation, and, together with him, examine all of these shirkers. Having done so, enroll the men fit for service into the new dragoon regiment of General Prince Menshikov and send the rest, if there remain any, as recruits attached to the same regiment.

                                                                                Peter

[To Avtomon Ivanovich Ivanov, January 13, 1709:]

Mr. Ivanov:

We have received your letter from Moscow, dated December 26, in which you write that recruits are fleeing to the forests. Therefore it is necessary to hold them fast by making them stand surety for each other in groups of twenty men or more and making them responsible for each other; likewise their fathers and kinsmen should be made responsible for them, so that each could be brought to account for his kinsman or comrade. You should send here, as fast as possible, the specified quota of recruits, and if you happen to have any in excess of the quota send them out as well.

X:11. DOCUMENTS ON GENTRY SERVICE AND PETER'S NEW OFFICER CORPS, 1708-1722

The Russian gentry was forced to undergo rigorous retraining before it could provide enough competent junior commanders for the new regular army (see the bitter criticism of the old military establishment in Pososhkov's memorandum "On Military Conduct," 1701, above). The following selections show some of Peter's efforts to draw the gentry into active service through registration, inspections, and "reviews," which continued throughout the Northern War. Increasingly he came to rely on the Guards as a training pool for officers and men to whom he could entrust all kinds of tasks. The Guards were under constant personal supervision of Peter, whose relationship to some of the guardsmen is illustrated in his notes to his sister and to Saltykov.

Reference: Kurakin's autobiography: M. I. Semevskii, ed., *Arkhiv kniazia F. A. Kurakina*, vol. 1 (St. Petersburg, 1890), p. 269; combat instructions: *PBIPV*, 7:101; Peter to Tsarevna Nataliia Alekseevna: ibid., 9:78; Peter to Saltykov: ibid., 9:79; decree on promotion to officer rank, Feb. 26, 1714: *PSZRI*, 1st ser., 5:84-85; decree on registration of nobles: ibid., p. 125; decree on promotion of officers, Jan. 1, 1719: ibid., p. 607; decree on registration and inspection of nobles: ibid., 6:478.

[From the autobiography of Prince B. I. Kurakin:]

That same year [1703-04] His Majesty held an inspection of the service gentry. Some youngsters who seemed capable were assigned to be officers; all other young men were to become cadets and later dragoons. Older men were assigned to collect new taxes, and the rest were left in the service, or available for various tasks; of these there remained about two thousand. Then His Majesty examined the underage sons of the most important persons and selected five or six hundred of them to be enlisted as simple soldiers in the Preobrazhenskii and the Semenovskii regiments; I shall mention the scions of the following illustrious families who are now serving in them: the princes Golitsyn, Cherkasskii, Khovanskii, and Lobanov, the Sheremetevs, and princes Urusov.

[From Peter's Combat Instructions (*Uchrezhdenie k boiu*), March 10, 1708:]

The chief generals should test in the field [the combat efficiency of] each officer and each noncommissioned officer, first individually and then in groups, simulating real battle conditions. If any one of them shows himself unskilled, while a man of lower rank does better, then let the senior man be demoted and the man of lower rank raised. This justice will increase fear and eagerness in everybody. Whoever cheats during these tests, may, in time, pay for it with his head.

[A note from Peter to his sister, Tsarevna Nataliia Alekseevna, February 5, 1709:]

Our major, Mr. Bartenev, has requested me to ask you to speak to the wife [widow] of Mr. Karpov and to persuade her to marry him, since courtship between them has been going on for a long time. Please do your best to bring this affair to successful conclusion. [Note: Major F. O. Bartenev of the Preobrazhenskii Regiment was one of Peter's aides-de-camp.]

[A note from Peter to Peter Samoilovich Saltykov, the voevoda of Smolensk, February 6, 1709:]

Captain Oznobishin of our regiment has leave to go to Smolensk to get married. Please attend the wedding and give the parental blessing on our behalf. [Note: Captain Oznobishin of the Preobrazhenskii Regiment had previously been decorated for his conduct in the Battle of Lesnaia, 1708.]

[Peter's decree on promotion to officer rank, February 26, 1714:]

Since there are many who promote to officer rank their relatives and friends—young men who do not know the fundamentals of soldiering, not having served in the lower ranks—and since even those who serve [in the ranks] do so for a few weeks or months only, as a formality; therefore . . . let a decree be promulgated that henceforth there shall be no promotion [to officer rank] of men of noble extraction or of any others who have not first served as privates in the Guards. This decree does not apply to soldiers of lowly origin who, after long service in the ranks, have received their commissions through honest service or to those who are promoted on the basis of merit, now or in the future; it applies exclusively to those who have remained in the ranks for a short time, only as a formality, as described above.

[Peter's decree on registration of nobles in the Senate, September 26, 1714:]

We hereby announce to all the nobles that they themselves, and their relatives between the ages of ten and thirty, must appear at [the office] established here in Moscow by the Senate for registration in the course of

the coming winter. If anyone disregards this order and fails to appear by March, then all his property and villages shall be [confiscated and] given to him who reports such failure, no matter how lowly his rank may be. . . . [These reports shall be accepted beginning in September 1715.]

[Peter's decree on promotion of officers, January 1, 1719:]

1. No son of an officer or of a noble shall be admitted to any officer rank unless he has first served as a private soldier in the Guards; excepted [from this provision] are men of lowly origin who are promoted to officer rank in the army regiments.

2. No one is to be promoted skipping a rank, but each must follow the regular order from rank to rank.

3. Vacancies are to be filled by ballot, with two or three candidates [presented for each vacancy].

[Peter's decree on registration and inspection of nobles, January 11, 1722:]

[Since many have failed to heed last year's repeated orders on registration and inspection of nobles,] we hereby announce and enjoin by this final decree: Nobles [shliakhetstvo] of every kind and retired officers [as well as half of those on active duty, as specified in previous orders, except those serving in Astrakhan' and Siberia] shall go to Moscow to report to Stol'nik Kolychev not later than January 31 of this year in accordance with previous decrees. All those who fail to report their arrival and appear for inspection shall be disgraced and considered unfit for the society of decent people; if anyone should rob, injure, or deprive such a person of anything, no petition shall be entertained from him, or on his behalf if he is murdered, and no court shall give him redress; his movable and immovable property shall be forfeited to us unconditionally. . . . Lists of all these shirkers shall be printed and posted on the gallows on the square, so that everyone would know them as guilty of contempt of decrees, like traitors. . . . Those who detect and bring such a shirker [to justice] shall receive one half of his movable and immovable property, no matter what their rank, even if they are his own serfs. [A special extension is granted to the old and the infirm.]

X:12. DOCUMENTS CONCERNING PETER AND THE UKRAINE, 1708-1710

The privileges of the Ukrainian Cossacks found a champion in Ivan Stepanovich Mazepa (born between 1629 and 1632, hetman of the Ukraine from 1687 to 1708; died in 1710 in Turkey). Mazepa had originally been a faithful follower of Peter, but, at the end of October 1708, he went over to the side of Charles XII. On October 30, 1708, he wrote to Ivan Skoropadskii, the Cossack colonel of Starodub, that it was necessary "to secede from the hostile power of Moscow which, for many years, has harbored the intention to destroy the last Cossack rights and liberties." But Mazepa represented only a relatively small group of the Cossack upper class, who had been seeking to equate their status to that of the Polish-Lithuanian *szlachta* across the border. He thus recruited only a small following, while the vast majority of the Cossacks, townsmen, and peasants remained firmly attached to Peter. The presence of Menshikov's troops, who destroyed Mazepa's stronghold of Baturin, Peter's speedy arrival on the scene, and his prompt measures to cope with his friend's desertion contributed to this outcome. Given below are excerpts from Peter's correspondence and proclamations at the time.

Reference: Peter to Apraksin, Oct. 24, 1708: *PBIPV*, vol. 8, pt. 1, p. 232; Menshikov to Peter, Oct. 26, 1708: ibid., pt. 2, p. 865; decree of Oct. 28, 1708: ibid., pt. 1, pp. 244-45; proclamation of Nov. 6, 1708: ibid., pp. 282-83; Peter to Apraksin, Nov. 7, 1708: ibid., p. 285; proclamation of Mar. 11, 1710: *PSZRI*, ser. 1, 4:482-83.

[Peter's letter to F. M. Apraksin, October 24, 1708. Admiral General Feodor Matveevich Apraksin (1671-1728), Peter's brother-in-law and close collaborator, was commander in chief of the Russian navy; in 1708-09 he was also in charge of all the forces defending Saint Petersburg.]
Honorable Admiral:

. . . The enemy [the Swedes] has been in the vicinity of Starodub, and has employed his usual enticements in every way; but the Little Russian people, with God's help, remain so steadfast that nothing more could be demanded of them.

[Letter from A. D. Menshikov to Peter, dated Makoshino, October 26, 1708:]

[Menshikov reports on Mazepa's treason, then continues:] . . . P.S. I must also report to Your Grace that I detect no evil effect of the hetman's [Mazepa's] present wicked enterprise either among the military commanders [*starshina*]—except the very highest ones—or among the common people. On the contrary, *sotniki* and other regimental officers from this vicinity come flocking to me, carrying complaints against him, and many entreat me with tears to protect them from ruin should he, the hetman, attempt some enterprise against them. I reassure and encourage them in every way, especially by pointing out that you are due to arrive in the Ukraine shortly, which seems to cheer them up very much.

[Peter's decree to all the people of Little Russia, October 28, 1708:]

[Peter gives a brief account of Mazepa's treason, on the basis of Menshikov's letter of October 26 which he received the night of October 27, then continues: I enjoin] all the [Cossack] supreme military command [*general'naia starshina*] and the regimental command groups [*polkovaia starshina*] to convene without delay in the city of Glukhov in order to elect a new hetman by their free vote and in accordance with their rights and liberties; of this there is extreme need, and the salvation of all Little Russia depends on it. [Note: Within the next two days identical letters were sent to Konstantin Gordeenko and his Zaporozhian Host, and to the bishops and various dignitaries of the Ukraine.]

[Peter's proclamation to all the people of Little Russia, November 6, 1708:]

Our enemy wishes to persuade the people of Little Russia, by his alluring letters, that their former rights and liberties are impaired by us, the great sovereign, and that the cities of Little Russia are taken over by our voevody and our troops; he bids them to be mindful of their former ancient liberties. Every reasonable man among the people of Little Russia will recognize these statements for a most palpable lie, as weeds that the enemy is sowing to raise a rebellion. It is a lie—because our father, of blessed memory, the great sovereign, tsar, and grand duke Aleksei Mikhailovich, autocrat of all Russia, had granted, and confirmed in accordance with the concluded compacts, the privileges and liberties of the people of Little Russia at the time he was accepting them under His Tsarist Majesty's sovereign protection; and they have been sacredly maintained, inviolate and undiminished, to this day by us, the great sovereign. Until the present military emergency arose, not a single place had been occupied by the Great Russian troops in violation [of these agreements]. As for those places that are now occupied for defense against the enemy by our Great Russian troops, the Great Russian men will be evacuated from them as soon as the enemy is repelled to a certain distance, as has already been done at Pochep and at Pagar. Great Russian garrisons will likewise be led out from all other cities where they are now quartered immediately after the retreat of the enemy. We can state without blushing that no people under the sun can boast of such liberties, privileges, and immunities as the Little Russian people, thanks to the grace of Our Tsarist Majesty. Indeed, we have never ordered the collection of a single penny for our treasury from the regions of Little Russia, but, on the contrary, we have graciously taken care of Little Russia by providing our troops and subsidies to protect its holy Orthodox churches, monasteries, cities, and homes from invasion by infidels and heretics. And as for the enemy reminding the Little Russian people of its former ancient liberties, I believe that all the old people know themselves, and the young ones have learned from their parents, what kind of liberty they enjoyed before they came under the most exalted protection of His Tsarist Majesty, our father, of blessed memory. They know what kind of liberty and privileges they had in their secular affairs, in their private lives, and especially in the practice of their pious faith, how grievously oppressed they were under the Polish yoke, with what unendurable injuries and insults the Poles tormented them, and how their holy churches were transformed into Roman and Uniate temples. Thus, by citing these ancient liberties, the king of Sweden has now clearly revealed to the Little Russian people his intention to enslave them once again to the Poles and to Lesczynski, as well as to Mazepa, the traitor.

[Letter from Peter to F. M. Apraksin, Glukhov, November 7, 1708:]
Honorable Admiral:
We inform you that yesterday the people of these parts held an election for a new hetman after the desertion of the felon Mazepa. All, as if speaking with one mouth, elected Skoropadskii, the colonel of Starodub. [Note: Ivan Iliich Skoropadskii (1646-1722), Cossack colonel of Starodub since 1706, had formerly been a friend of Mazepa but remained steadfast in his allegiance to Peter. He was hetman of the Ukraine until his death.] Thus the accursed Mazepa has brought no harm to anybody but himself, for the people here do not even wish to hear his name mentioned—and with [the news of] this momentous affair I greet you.

Peter.

[Peter's proclamation forbidding insults to the Little Russians, March 11, 1710:]
No one shall dare to call "traitors" Our Tsarist Majesty's loyal subjects the Little Russian people. For one who is not guilty of this crime should not suffer such blame vicariously for [the fault of] another person. Indeed, the people of Little Russia and the Zaporozhian Host have faithfully served us, the great sovereign, and took no part in Mazepa's treason; as for those who were traitors, they have suffered the punishment they deserved. . . . Should anyone disobey this injunction of . . . Our Tsarist Majesty and insult, irritate, or reproach any of the Little Russian people, then, if he be an officer or an official, he shall be court-martialed and suffer due punishment accordingly; if he be a private soldier or a man of low rank, he shall be severely punished after an investigation; for very grave offenses capital punishment [shall be meted out] without mercy. For all articles and carts taken without special order the offender shall pay a threefold price to the offended party.

X:13. PETER REPORTS THE VICTORY AT POLTAVA, JUNE 27, 1709

The following is an excerpt from Peter's letter to Admiral Apraksin written immediately after the battle of Poltava.

Reference: *PBIPV*, vol. 9, pt. 1, pp. 227-28, 230-31. Translation based on that of Messrs. Baltzly and Kucherov, revised. This and other documents of this period are reprinted in L. G. Beskrovnyi and B. B. Kafengauz, eds., *Khrestomatiia po istorii SSSR XVIII v.* (Moscow: Izd. Sotsial'no-Ekonomicheskoi Literatury, 1963).

We announce to you a very great and unexpected victory, which the Lord God has vouchsafed to give us through the indescribable bravery of our soldiers and with but light loss to our army, in the following manner:

Early this morning the impetuous enemy attacked our cavalry with all his cavalry and infantry. Our cavalry, although it stood up bravely, was forced to retire, inflicting great loss on the enemy. Then the enemy lined up in front of our camp. At once all our infantry was led out from the fortified camp and brought in sight of the enemy, the cavalry being on both flanks. Seeing this, the enemy at once attacked us, and our forces went to meet him, and they met him in such manner that he was at once driven from the field. A great number of banners and cannon were taken, and likewise Field Marshal General Rehnskiold, as well as four other generals, namely, Schlippenbach, Stackelberg, Hamilton, and Rosen. Also the first minister, Count Piper, and the secretaries Hermelin and Cederhielm were taken prisoner, together with several thousand officers and men, a matter on which we shall supply details soon (we cannot now, for lack of time). In a word, the entire enemy army met the end of Phaeton. (As for the king, we know not yet whether he be with us [among the living] or among our forefathers.) Lieutenant generals Prince Golitsyn and Baur have been sent with the cavalry to pursue the routed enemy. . . .

P.S. And now indeed the final foundation stone of Saint Petersburg has been laid with the help of God. . . .

Peter

X:14. OTTO PLEYER ON PETER'S ARMY, 1710

Otto Anton von Pleyer spent twenty-six years in Russia, first as a minor diplomatic agent (1692-1710) and then as minister resident (1711-18) of the Austrian government. The following selection is taken from Pleyer's "Report on the Present State of the Muscovite Government," drawn up in 1710 for the benefit of his government.

Reference: Ernst Herrmann, ed., *Russland unter Peter dem Grossen. Nach den handschriftlichen Berichten Johann Gotthilf Vockerodt's und Otto Pleyer's* (Leipzig, 1872), pp. 122-26. The Russian translation in *CIOIDRMU*, 1874, bk. 2, sec. 4, pp. 1-21, contains many inaccuracies.

Concerning the Russian military forces, in all fairness, one must admit that they have reached an amazing degree of proficiency thanks to the incessant application and efforts of the tsar and to severe punishments and marks of favor and distinction, as well as to the experience of foreign officers of all ranks drawn from many nations. It is surprising what perfection the soldiers have attained in military movements, how orderly and obedient they are to their superiors' commands, and how bravely they conduct themselves in battle. One hears not a word from anybody—let alone a shout; they are all so eager. The harder and the fiercer the engagement, the closer the tsar is to it. He not only cheers his men with kind words but inspires them with a strong desire to give up their lives for him. He never leaves valiant officers without ample reward, while the cowardly ones he pursues with heavy disgrace, severe penalties, and prolonged displeasure. By these methods the tsar has instilled in the majority of the Russian nobles a feeling of self-respect and emulation. He has done even better: now, when they converse, or drink, or smoke together, they no longer talk of disgusting obscenities, but speak of this or that battle, or of the good or bad conduct of various persons on such occasions, or they discuss military science. All this often sounds ludicrous, for they talk of these matters as if in a dream, or lacking solid knowledge and drawing their information from bits of hearsay.

The artillery is well equipped with all the implements; it is staffed by experienced Germans and other foreigners, as well as by Russians, many of whom were sent to different parts of Germany in order to acquire a thorough knowledge of pyrotechnics; it is also well provided with good horses, though in the cavalry there is a great shortage of them, in spite of the fact that the tsar could have obtained good mounts from the Kalmyks, the Bashkirs, and the Nogai Tatars.

There are many indications that there is no shortage in military materiel for a long war; [in spite of the heavy expenditure of gunpowder] not one powder mill has been working for more than two years because everywhere there is a large ready stock of gunpowder. As soon as the recruits receive a few firearms from the government they conduct all their military exercises with much shooting. Whenever the tsar, or the crown prince, or Prince Menshikov is in Moscow, or in his country house, there is an incessant discharge of firearms during almost every dinner, drinking of healths, ball, or dance, as well as on these persons' birthdays and namedays, or on the occasion of any minor victorious encounter with the enemy. Moreover, an enormous amount of powder is wasted every year for expensive fireworks. In the tsar's absence, any prominent lord in Moscow can easily obtain it for his own private amusement simply by asking the military commandant—so little is powder valued in Russia.

The tsar now gets his iron from Siberia [i.e. from the Urals]. It is so good and soft that a better one could not be found even in Sweden. Of oak and other hard timber there is more than enough, for it is forbidden under heavy penalties to cut it down except for the tsar's service. Sulphur and saltpeter abound in the Ukraine. To make bombs and grenades one could not wish for better iron than that of Tula and of Olonets near Lake Onega; it is hard and brittle and bursts into many fragments. The metal for casting cannon and mortars has been brought from Poland, Livonia, Finland, and Lithuania. In Moscow there is also a considerable store of old ordnance available for recasting, but of this there is no need, for they already have an incredible number of cannon. They no longer need to import firearms from overseas at such great expense, for Siberian iron produces barrels of such excellence that at tryouts they withstand a triple charge of powder without danger. The tsar now obtains all military clothing from his own lands; a large and fine cloth factory has been established and works well. Many hosiers have come from Prussia, and they satisfy all the demand; enough hats are also produced. There is no need to mention

shoes, boots, or broadcloth for shirts, as these wares are exported to Breslau via Kiev. All shipbuilding materials are plentiful, for, indeed, these stores once formed the bulk of the cargo exported from Russia by foreigners; and we have long known by experience how quickly ships can be built here.

There would have been no scarcity of men for the army for a long time to come . . . had conscription (as recruiting should really be called) been conducted less haphazardly and with less damage to the country. The draft always hits only the poor villages and the tillers of the soil, which leads to a considerable shrinking of plowed land and of agriculture. Every year the gentry must supply, in proportion to the size of their estates, a large number of recruits provided with clothes, horses, and sustenance. As a result, peasants are taken away from the soil and often die of hunger in the field for lack of food. Moreover, the fear of future recruitment drives some of them to the forests or makes them run away to the farthest regions, leaving their fields uncultivated. Thus the burden of taxation weighs ever heavier as the number of people bearing it diminishes; food prices rise every year, and grain becomes less plentiful. There is a growing shortage of draft horses which one must use to transport supplies and to travel, for they are used to deliver wagons and army carts to military camps; few of these horses ever come back: many become exhausted on the road and die from lack of care; commerce suffers from this. Furthermore, the Russian nobles have a custom which springs from ostentatious conceit, a custom common among barbarous and pagan peoples of the East, as well as among the Russians of old times: in order to show their high estate, the nobles maintain in their villages a host of useless mouths as countless servants and bondmen, both male and female, whose number may reach five hundred or more; at the beginning of the war the tsar had tried to abolish it, but he finally had to give up the attempt because of insistent and pressing requests by the nobles. . . . These retainers become chummy or related by marriage with their lords' manservants, majordomos, and house stewards, and together with them they fleece and milk the poor peasants even more. . . .

The peasants quickly become good soldiers— as is not uncommon with formerly unskilled people who, once they have mastered some military exercises, are placed among old, well-trained soldiers and are imbued with their discipline. In spite of all the good qualities of the army, many foreigners who have observed it admit that little thought is given in Russia to the preservation of soldiers. Bad organization and inadequate supervision of essential military stores are almost the only, though they are the most serious, defects, and every year this causes more losses in the army than if it had been exposed in the fiercest engagements. Foreign officers and generals still labor almost in vain on this one point, though they have been able to teach the Russians many other military principles and maxims. The tsar has come to realize now that everybody, commoner and great lord alike, is tired of the war which puts to waste and ruin so many fertile lands; but I do not know whether he is aware of the reasons that I have mentioned for desolation and weariness of minds.

X:15. THE CHARTER OF THE ESTHONIAN PRINCIPALITY, AUGUST 16, 1710

The Principalities of Livonia and Esthonia presented a special social problem: since the days of the old Livonian and Teutonic Orders, the nobility was predominantly German, with some Swedish nobles joining its ranks later. The nobility had its quarrels with the German burgesses of the main cities, but, above all, it was determined to hold the local peasantry (mainly Livs, Ests, and so forth) in a state of servitude; nowhere in Europe, not even in the Polish-Lithuanian realm, nor in Muscovy, had the institution of serfdom reached such proportions as in these Baltic provinces. The Swedish administration, especially under Charles XI (1660-97), had taken drastic action against this state of affairs, thereby rousing a violent reaction among the privileged groups, which contributed to the outbreak of the Great Northern War. In conquering the Baltic provinces, Peter had to rely on the groups most hostile to the Swedish administration, whether he liked it or not. This policy found expression in the charter of August 16, 1710, quoted in part below. The annexation of Esthonia and Livonia was to have a marked effect on Russian society in the eighteenth century, particularly under Empress Anne, when Baltic nobles began to flock to Saint Petersburg.

Reference: *PSZRI*, 1st ser., 4:543-45. Cf. similar confirmation of privileges of Livonia and of the city of Riga, July 4, 1710, ibid., pp. 501-19.

We cannot fail to express our special benevolence and favor to the noble gentry and the whole land of the Principality of Esthonia, as well as to the noble city magistrates and all the citizens of the city of Reval. Moreover, as soon as all this land, by God's dispensation, is completely subjected to our power, we intend to leave without any innovation [the free exercise of] the Lutheran religion in the whole land and in the cities that now profess it, and to leave them in the enjoyment of all their ancient privileges, liberties, rights, and advantages, which, as is known to the whole world, were always being violated during the Swedish rule; we promise not only to preserve and maintain them faithfully, according to their letter and spirit, but even, when the occasion presents itself, to augment them by still more extensive and consequential privileges.
... Herewith we also give a specially sacred pledge to the city of Reval and to all the Principality of Esthonia that, if they, by timely action, accept our favor and gracious intention with just and fitting gratitude, we shall permit them to participate in all the advantages and benefits that we have granted to the Principality of Livonia and to its capital city of Riga, which have already manifested their submission and have actually sworn allegiance to us.

X:16. DOCUMENTS ON RUSSO-TURKISH RELATIONS, 1709-1711

Throughout the Great Northern War, Russo-Turkish relations remained tense. As a result of the Russian presence at Azov, continued Russo-Crimean clashes, the flight of Charles XII to Turkey in 1709, and the extension of Russian influence in Poland resulting from military operations against Sweden, the two governments were drawn, more or less against their will, into open war against each other in 1711. As before, the Russian government was being constantly importuned by some of the Eastern Orthodox subjects of the sultan to come to their aid; yet, even more than the old Muscovite government, Peter had been inclined to turn a deaf ear to their supplications. However, eventually he took up their cause against the Ottomans, first as a diplomatic bargaining point in his relations with Constantinople, and then as a weapon in the war against the Turks. In the peace treaty that followed the failure of Peter's Pruth campaign, both governments willingly abandoned their unstable or inconvenient allies, vassals, and clients to settle the real issues in dispute between them. In the subsequent negotiations with Turkey, right down to the final confirmation of the Pruth settlement in 1720, Peter made no effort to champion the cause of the Orthodox. Given below are excerpts from some of the documents illustrating Russo-Turkish relations in 1709-11.

Reference: Peter's letter to Ahmed III, June 26, 1709: *PBIPV*, 9:223-25. Peter's diploma to Dimitri Kantemir, April 13, 1711: *PSZRI*, 1st ser., 4:659-62. Peace treaty on the river Pruth, July 12, 1711: Jean Dumont, *Corps universel diplomatique du droit des gens*, 8 vols. (Amsterdam, 1726-31), vol. 8, pt. 1, pp. 225-26 (giving both the Russian and Turkish versions of the treaty); Russian version in *PSZRI*, 1st ser., 4:715-16.

[Letter from Peter the Great to Sultan Ahmed III, June 26, 1709:]

We hope that, as a token of your equal inclination and desire to maintain peace, you will show us some benevolence. That is why we, the great sovereign, suggest to you a measure that would be most pleasing to us and not only harmless, but most glorious to Your Sultanic Majesty: namely, to restore to the custody of the clergy of your own Greek subjects the Holy Sepulchre of our Lord Jesus Christ and other holy places in Jerusalem, in conformity with ancient customs. At present, to the detriment of your own subjects, these holy places are held by the Roman clergy, who are subjects not of Your Majesty, but of foreign states [Note: In 1690, the Ottoman government, at the instigation of Louis XIV, had handed over the custody of the Holy Sepulchre to the Roman Catholic (mainly French) clergy, much to the disgust of the Eastern Orthodox. Peter's diplomats, however, did not press the request contained in this letter, and, in fact, withdrew it in 1709 in order to promote better relations with the Turks.]

[The diploma (charter) to the Moldavian Prince Dimitri Kantemir, April 13, 1711:]

We, the great sovereign, Our Tsarist Majesty, having invoked the aid of the Lord, and trusting in the justice of our arms, have likewise declared war against the above-mentioned [sultan], and have ordered our armies to invade the Turkish lands under our personal leadership, in the hope that God will give us victory over this perjurious and hereditary enemy not only of ourselves but of all Christendom . . . and that he will vouchsafe to liberate with the help of our Christian arms many other Christian nations now

groaning under his barbarous yoke. For this goal, we, as a pious Christian monarch, are ready to toil for the glory of the Lord's name, without sparing our personal well-being. And whereas, seeing the approach of our troops, the most serene sovereign and prince of the Wallachian land, Dimitri Kantemir, being a pious Christian and zealous in the cause of Jesus Christ, has seen fit to offer to collaborate with us toward the liberation of the glorious Wallachian people, which is under his rule, as well as of other Christian nations now suffering under the barbarous yoke . . . [and whereas the said prince] for this purpose has declared through his letters his inclination and desire to place himself, all his land, and the Wallachian people under the protection of Our Tsarist Majesty; therefore, we, observing his Christian zeal, do most graciously accept this prince under our protection.

[The peace treaty on the river Pruth, July 12 (23, N.S.), 1711:]

ARTICLE 1: . . . [It has been agreed] to conclude a permanent peace on the following conditions: Let the towns conquered from the Turks be restored to them [Note: This included Azov]; and let the towns recently built [by the Russians in the border region] be razed and left unoccupied by both parties.

ART. 2: Neither party shall be allowed to interfere in Polish affairs or to claim possession of any [Polish] subjects or lands. . . .

ART. 4: Since the king of Sweden has put himself under the protection of His Sultanic Majesty, His Tsarist Majesty promises, in token of his friendship for His Sultanic Majesty, to allow the [king of Sweden] free and safe passage and return to his lands, and to make peace with him, if they can reach mutual agreement.

ART. 5: In the future let no harm or damage be inflicted by anybody on the subjects
of either party, whether Russian or Turkish.

[Note: This meant that raids of the Crimean
Tatars and of the Cossacks must be stopped.]

X:17. DECREES ESTABLISHING AND DEFINING THE FUNCTIONS OF THE SENATE, 1711 AND 1722

Peter's constant travels and many measures upsetting the old order produced chaos in the administration of the state. During his reign the old Boyar Duma had died a natural death, and, to
supply the need for a central administrative body, Peter experimented with many types of ad
hoc committees of chief officials functioning in his absence. The establishment of the "Governing Senate" in 1711 was an attempt to find a more permanent solution to the problem. Nevertheless, the two decrees of 1711 quoted here show that originally the Senate was not unlike one of
the former temporary ministerial committees. It was only with the decree of 1722 that the Senate
received its final form as a permanent institution. However, some of Peter's favorites, like Menshikov or Admiral Apraksin, were not subordinated to the Senate, and could even issue instructions
to it "by His Majesty's Order." For explanations of the various ranks and titles mentioned in
these and other documents, see the *Dictionary of Russian Historical Terms*, including especially
the article on the *Tabel' o Rangakh* (Table of Ranks). See also, for an abridged version of the
Table, Item X:24, below.

Reference: *PSZRI*, 1st ser., 4:627, 643; 6:660-61. This and many other documents pertaining
to this section are also included in V. I. Lebedev, comp., and N. Rubinshtein, ed., *Reformy Petra I.
Sbornik dokumentov* (Moscow: Gosudarstvennoe Sotsial'no-Ekonomicheskoe Izdatel'stvo, 1937);
and N. A. Voskresenskii, comp., and B. I. Syromiatnikov, ed., *Zakonodatel'nye akty Petra I.
Redaktsii i proekty zakonov, zametki, doklady, doneseniia, chelobit'ia, i inostrannye istochniki*
(Moscow: AN SSSR, 1945). See also *PRP*, vol. 8 (1961), ed. by K. A. Sofronenko.

[The decree establishing the Senate, February
22, 1711:]

Because of our absences, we establish the
Governing Senate to carry on the administra-
tion; [it shall consist of:] Count Musin-
Pushkin, Mr. Streshnev, Prince Peter Golitsyn,
Prince Michael Dolgorukii, Mr. Plemiannikov,
Prince Gregory Volkonskii, Mr. Samarin, Mr.
Basil Opukhtin, and Mr. Mel'nitskii. Anisim
Shchukin shall be the chief secretary of this
Senate. . . . Instead of the Military Service
Prikaz, let there be a Military Service Office
attached to the above-mentioned Senate.
Also, in the above-described court, let there
be two commissioners from each guberniia
[large administrative unit, province] to give
information and to receive decrees.

[The decree on the powers and duties of the
Senate, March 2, 1711:]

A directive [to the Senate] on what to do
during our absence:

1. Maintain an impartial court and punish
unjust judges by depriving them of honor and
of all their possessions; the same punishment
applies to false denunciators.

2. Watch over [government] expenditures
in the whole country, and prevent all unnecessary, and especially all useless, expenses.

3. Collect as much money as possible, for
money is the sinews of war.

4. Enroll young nobles as officer replace-
ments, and especially seek out those who try
to conceal themselves. For the same purpose,
draft one thousand men among the literate
boyars' servants.

5. Check letters of credit, and keep them
in one place.

6. Inspect and make an inventory of the
goods leased out or stored in government
offices and in the provinces.

7. Try to farm out the salt monopoly and
to make it profitable.

8. Farm out the trade with China to a sound
company to be founded for this purpose.

9. Increase the trade with Persia, and favor
the Armenians as far as possible by giving them
appropriate privileges, in order to attract more
of them to this country. Set up controllers
[*fiskaly*] in all departments; of their functions
we shall give further notice.

[The decree on the functions of the Senate,
April 27, 1722:]

1. The Senate shall consist of right privy
councillors [*deistvitel'nye tainye sovetniki*]
and privy councillors [*tainye sovetniki*], whom
we have assigned or shall assign to it in the

future. They shall sit according to their rank. During their deliberations no [outside] person shall be admitted without a special invitation, apart from the procurator general [*general prokuror*], the high procurators [*ober-prokurory*], the chief secretary [*ober-sekretar'*], the secretary, and the minute clerk [*protokolist*]. . . .

2. Whenever a matter comes up that cannot be decided in a college [department], the president of the college must report it to the procurator general, who shall present it to the Senate, and it shall be resolved in the Senate; if the Senate cannot resolve an affair, let it report [to us], appending its recommendation.

3. All governors and voevody must report to the Senate those affairs that do not belong to the colleges, such as an outbreak of war or of a plague, or various disorders, or unusual occurrences.

4. Whenever any petitions are presented to the master of requests [*Reketmeister*] concerning unjust verdicts of the colleges or of offices not under the direction of a college, the master of requests shall receive them and report them to us. . . . The Senate shall then investigate all these affairs, and when it comes to the point of passing judgment, before doing so, its members shall take an oath to maintain justice before God; having taken this oath, they shall render judgment in accordance with the truth and pursuant to regulations and to their oath, never acting through malice or bias because of friendship or kinship; should anyone transgress in this point, let the procurator general intervene in accordance with his duty.

5. [The Senate shall] elect by ballot those to be promoted to the higher ranks—from college councillor [the sixth rank, equivalent to a colonel] and on up. . . .

7. The master herald [*Gerol'dmeister*] shall be ordered to present two or three worthy candidates for every vacancy to be filled in the above-mentioned [higher] ranks that should be held by nobles, pursuant to requests from colleges and from other offices; as for vacancies to be filled by non-nobles, let each college present under the signature of all its members . . . two or three worthy candidates for each place; the Senate shall then determine the candidate most fit for the post.

X:18. DECREES ESTABLISHING THE ADMINISTRATIVE COLLEGES, 1717 AND 1720

As departments of the central government, the numerous and overlapping prikazy were unable to cope adequately with the tasks imposed by Peter. In the new administrative "colleges" Peter retained the collegiate or committee principle of the old prikazy but tried to introduce a more rational, functional distribution of work between central government departments, whose number was to remain relatively small. Peter began to experiment with new colleges as early as 1713; the general plan of collegiate administration was later drawn up, at Peter's request, by Heinrich Fick, a Holsteiner who entered Russian service in 1715; Fick took the Swedish colleges for his model and later helped to hire some hundred and fifty officials in Germany for the college staffs. Ten colleges were established during the period 1717-20; throughout the eighteenth century their number varied slightly. Here are some of the key passages from the decrees of 1717 and 1720.

Reference: *PSZRI,* 1st ser., 5:525; 6:141.

[The decree on college personnel, December 11, 1717:]

The following officials shall sit in each college [*kollegiia*]: president, vice-president (Russian or foreigner), four college councillors [*sovetniki*], four college assessors [*assessory,* advisers], one secretary, one notary, one actuary, one registrar, one interpreter; clerks of three grades. Foreigners: one councillor or assessor, one secretary, one clerk. Starting with the New Year the presidents should begin to organize their colleges and to gather the necessary information everywhere; however, they are not to transact any business until the year 1719, and in the following year [1720] they are to assume full administration of their colleges.

[The decree on the appointment of councillors and assessors December 11, 1717:]

The presidents shall select councillors and assessors in the following manner:

1. They must not be either the president's relatives or his clients.

2. They shall select two or three candidates for each position and then present them at a general meeting of all the colleges; the final selection for the central colleges shall be by ballot.

[The General Statute (*General'nyi Reglament*) for the colleges, February 28, 1720:]

PREAMBLE. To provide for an orderly direction of his affairs of state, an accurate assessment and accounting of his revenues, the proper functioning of justice and police (that is, of judicial and civil administration), and also for the greatest possible protection of his loyal subjects, for the maintenance of his sea and land forces in a good condition, as well as for [the encouragement of] commerce, arts, and manufactures, for a sound organization of collection of his customs on sea and on land, for an increase and expansion of the mining industries, and for diverse other needs of the state, His Tsarist Majesty, our most gracious sovereign, following the example of other Christian countries, has conceived a most gracious intention to set up the following state colleges necessary [to these ends], and pertaining to these needs; to wit: Foreign Affairs, Revenues, Justice, Accounting, Army, Admiralty, Commerce, Disbursements, Mining, and Manufactures.

In these colleges [he has decided] to appoint presidents, vice-presidents, as well as other necessary members and office personnel; most of the appointees shall be from among his own subjects; likewise, the necessary central and provincial offices shall be established in connection with [these colleges].

X:19. CORRESPONDENCE BETWEEN PETER AND ALEXIS, 1715-1717

Succession to the throne presents the most difficult problem that an "enlightened despot" must face, as Peter found out in his dealings with his lawful heir, Alexis. These excerpts are taken from Peter's correspondence with his son in 1715-17. (See also the next item, below.)

Reference: Nikolai G. Ustrialov, *Istoriia tsarstvovaniia Petra Velikogo*, 6:346-49, 388-89, 411. Translations based on those of Messrs. Baltzly and Kucherov, to whom the editors are indebted.

[Peter to Alexis, October 11, 1715:]

Declaration to my son:

Everyone knows how, before the beginning of this war, our people were hemmed in by the Swedes, who not only stole the essential ports of our fatherland . . . but cut us off from communication with the whole world. And also later, in the beginning of this war (which enterprise was and is directed by God alone), oh, what great persecution we had to endure from those eternal enemies of ours because of our incompetence in the art of war, and with what sorrow and endurance we went to this school and, with the help of the above-mentioned guide, achieved a creditable degree [of effectiveness]. We were thus found worthy of looking on this enemy now trembling before us, trembling, perhaps, even more than we did before him. All this has been accomplished with the help of God through my modest labors and through those of other equally zealous and faithful sons of Russia.

However, when, considering this great blessing given by God to our fatherland, I think of my successor, a grief perhaps as strong as my joy gnaws me, when I see you, my heir, unfit for the management of state affairs (for it is not the fault of God, who has not deprived you of mind or health; for although not of a very strong constitution, you are not very weak either). But, above all, you have no wish to hear anything about military affairs, which opened to us the way from darkness to light, so that we who were unknown before are now honored. I do not teach you to be inclined to wage war without a just cause, but to love this art and to endow and learn it by all means, for it is one of the two activities necessary for government: order and defense.

I have no wish to give you many examples, but I will mention only the Greeks, who are of the same religion as we. Did they not perish because they laid their arms aside, and were they not vanquished because of their peaceableness? Desirous of tranquil living, they always gave way to their enemy, who changed their tranquillity into endless servitude to tyrants. Perhaps you think that it can all be left to the generals; but this is really not so, for everyone looks up to his chief, to comply with his desires, which is an obvious fact. Thus, in the days of my brother's reign [Theodore, 1676-82], everyone liked clothes and horses above all things, and now they like arms. They may not be really interested in one or the other; but in what the chief is interested all take an interest, and to what he is indifferent, all are indifferent. And if they turn away so lightly from the frivolous pastimes, which are only a pleasure to man, how much more easily will they abandon so burdensome a game as war!

Furthermore, you do not learn anything because you have no desire to learn it, and you have no knowledge of military affairs. Lacking all knowledge, how can you direct these affairs? How can you reward the diligent and punish the negligent when you yourself do not understand their work? You will be forced to look into people's mouths like a young bird. Do you pretend to be unfit for military work because of weak health? But that is no reason. I ask of you not work, but good will, which no malady can destroy. Ask anyone who remembers my brother whom I spoke of but now, who was, beyond comparison, sicklier than you and could not ride spirited horses, but he had a great liking for them and was always looking at them and kept them before his eyes. . . . So you see, not everything is done by great labor, but also by a strong desire. You say to yourself, perhaps, that many rulers do not themselves go to war, and yet campaigns are still carried on. This is true when, although not going themselves, they have a desire for it, as had the late French king [Louis XIV], who went to war himself but little, and who yet had a great taste for it and showed such magnificent deeds in war that his wars were called the theater and school for the whole world. But he had a taste not only for war, but also for other affairs and for manufactures, through all of which he procured glory for his state more than anybody else.

Now that I have gone into all this, I return again to my original point, thinking of you. I am a man, and subject to death. To whom shall I leave all this sowing, done with God's help, and that harvest which has already grown? To one who, like the idle slave in the Gospel, buried his talent in the ground (which means that he threw away everything that God had given him)? I also keep thinking of your wicked and stubborn disposition; for how many times I used to scold you for that, and not only scold but beat you, and also how

many years I have now gone without speaking to you, and all without success! . . .

I have pondered this with much grief, and, seeing that I can in no wise dispose you toward good, I have deemed it appropriate to write to you this last admonition, and to wait a short time for you to mend your ways, and that *not hypocritically* [Peter's emphasis]. If you do not, know that I shall totally disinherit you like a gangrenous member; and do not imagine that, because you are my only son, I write this only to frighten you; I will do it indeed (with God's consent), because I have never spared my own life for my fatherland and people, nor do I now; therefore how can I spare you, unworthy one? Better a good stranger than an unworthy kinsman.

                                                        Peter

October 11, 1715
Saint Petersburg

[Alexis to Peter, October 31, 1715:]
    Most gracious sovereign and father:
    I have read [the letter] that was given me on your behalf on October 27, 1715, after the funeral of my wife. I have nothing to say about it, except that if you wish to disinherit me of the Russian crown because of my worthlessness, let it be as you will. Most humbly I ask you for this very thing, Sire, for I consider myself unqualified and unfit for this task, being most deficient in memory (without which it is impossible to accomplish anything). All my mental and physical capacities are weakened by various illnesses, and I have become unfit to rule such a people, which task requires a man less rotten than I. Therefore, I do not make a claim, nor will I make claim in the future, to the inheritance of the Russian throne after you—God give you health for many years—even if I did not have a brother (but now, thank God, I have one [note: Prince Peter, born to Peter and Catherine on October 29, 1715], God give him health); let God be my witness [in this matter], and to show that I testify truthfully I write this with my own hand.

    I entrust my children to your will and ask only for maintenance for myself to the end of my life. This is submitted to your decision and merciful will.

    Your most humble slave and son Alexis
Saint Petersburg
October 31, 1715

[Peter to Alexis, in Naples, July 10, 1717:]
My son:

The whole world knows how you have disobeyed me and shown contempt for my will; how you have not followed my directions, spurning my words and admonition. Finally, deceiving me, and invoking God as witness at the time of our parting, what did you do? You went away [from the country] and put yourself under foreign protection like a traitor, a thing unheard of, not only among our children but even among common subjects. What offense and grief you have thus inflicted on your father and shame on your country! That is why I am sending to you this final message to bring you to conform to my will, of which the lords Tolstoi and Rumiantsev will inform you. Should you fear me, I reassure you and promise you by God and his judgment that no punishment shall be inflicted upon you, but that I will show you my full love if you obey me and return. However, if you do not do [as I commanded], I, as your father, by virtue of the power given me by God, will damn you forever, and, as your sovereign, I will declare you a traitor, and shall leave no means unemployed to punish you as a traitor and abuser of your

father; and God will support me in my just cause. Remember, furthermore, that I have not used force with you. If I had wished to do so, why should I have relied on your [good] will? I would have done as I pleased.

                                                                    Peter
Spa
July 10, 1717

[Alexis to Peter, October 4, 1717:]
Most gracious sovereign and father:

I have received your most gracious letter through the lords Tolstoi and Rumiantsev, in which is contained, Sire, your pardon to me, unworthy one, for my self-willed departure, on condition that I return, and this they have also expressed to me verbally. Thanking you with tears and throwing myself at the feet of your clemency, I beg you to pardon my crimes, though they are worthy of every punishment. Relying upon your gracious promise, I submit myself to your will, and shall presently go from Naples to you, Sire, at Saint Petersburg. Your most humble and worthless slave, unworthy of the name of son,

                                                                    Alexis
Naples
October 4, 1717

X:20. THE MANIFESTO DEPRIVING ALEXIS OF SUCCESSION, FEBRUARY 3, 1718

In this manifesto Peter sought a provisional solution to the problem discussed in the preceding item.
Reference: *PSZRI*, 1st ser., 5:535, 538.

We saw that all our exertions for the upbringing and education of our son were vain, for he was never forthright in his obedience to us, paid no regard to what is appropriate for a good heir [to the throne], did not apply himself to study, and did not listen to the teachers we had appointed for him. . . . Later we sent him abroad, in the hope that the sight of well-ordered states would awaken his fervor and induce him to be upright and diligent. But all these efforts of ours availed nothing. The seeds of learning had fallen on stony ground: for not only did he fail to follow [good precepts], but he hated them and showed no inclination either for military or for civil affairs; instead, he constantly consorted with worthless and base people whose habits were coarse and disgusting. . . . [There follows a lengthy account of Alexis's misdeeds, culminating in his flight to the Habsburg lands, intrigues against

Peter abroad, and of his return from Naples to Saint Petersburg. Although Alexis deserves to be put to death, the manifesto declares, Peter grants him full pardon and remission from all punishment.]

                                                 . . .

Nevertheless, in view of his unworthiness and his disreputable behavior described above, we cannot, in good conscience, leave him as our successor on the Russian throne, knowing that through his disgraceful actions he would forfeit all the glory of our people acquired by God's grace and our tireless toil and squander all the benefits we have gained for the state with so much labor—not only in restoring provinces torn away from our state by the enemy, but also in adding to it many notable cities and lands; it is also well known that we instructed our people in many military and civil sciences to the profit and glory of the state. Therefore, out of apprehension for our state and faithful subjects—lest they be brought by such a ruler into a worse condition than they had been in before—we, in virtue of our paternal power . . . and as an autocratic sovereign, do, for the good of the state, deprive our son Alexis of the inheritance of our throne of all Russia on account of his faults and crimes, even if there be no person of our family left [to rule] after us. We proclaim as heir to the said throne our other son, Peter [Note: born in 1715, died in 1719], though he is still a minor, for we have no other heir who is of age.

X:21. PETER HENRY BRUCE ON TSAREVICH ALEXIS IN 1714 AND 1718

These glimpses of Tsarevich Alexis are from the memoirs of Peter Henry Bruce (concerning whom see Item X:7, above).
Reference: *Memoirs of Peter Henry Bruce*, pp. 118-19, 220-21.

The czarowitz [Alexis] arrived in Moscow this winter [1713-14], where I saw him for the first time. He kept a mean Finlandish girl for his mistress. I went often with the general [James Bruce], to wait on him, and he came frequently to the general's house, commonly attended by very mean and low persons. He was very slovenly in his dress; his person was tall, well made, of a brown complexion, black hair and eyes, of a stern countenance, and strong voice. He frequently did me the honour to talk with me in German, being fully master of that language: he was adored by the populace, but little respected by the superior ranks, for whom he never showed the least regard; he was always surrounded by a number of debauched ignorant priests, and other mean persons of bad character, in whose company he always reflected on his father's conduct for abolishing the ancient customs of the country, declaring, that as soon as he came to succeed, he should soon restore Russia to its former state; and threatening to destroy, without reserve, all his father's favourites. This he did so often, and with so little reserve, that it could not miss reaching the emperor's ears; and it was generally thought he now laid the foundation of that ruin he afterwards met with.

. . .

On the next day [7 July (N.S.), 1718], his majesty, attended by all the senators and bishops, with several others of high rank, went to the fort, and entered the apartments where the czarowitz was kept prisoner. Some little time thereafter marshal Weyde came out, and ordered me to go to Mr. Bear's the druggist, whose shop was hard by, and tell him to make the potion strong which he had bespoke, as the prince was then very ill: when I delivered this message to Mr. Bear, he turned quite pale, and fell a shaking and trembling, and appeared in the utmost confusion, which surprised me so much, that I asked him what was the matter with him, but he was unable to return me any answer; in the mean time the marshal himself came in, much in the same condition with the druggist, saying, he ought to have been more expeditious, as the prince was very ill of an apoplectic fit; upon this the druggist delivered him a silver cup with a cover, which the marshal himself carried into the prince's apartments, staggering all the way as he went, like one drunk. About half an hour after, the czar with all his attendants withdrew with very dismal countenances, and when they went, the marshal ordered me to attend at the prince's apartment, and in case of any alteration, to inform him immediately thereof: there were at that time two physicians and two surgeons in waiting, with whom, and the officer on guard, I dined on what had been dressed for the prince's dinner. The physicians were called in immediately after to attend the prince, who was struggling out of one convulsion into another, and after great agonies, expired at five o'clock in the afternoon. . . . Various were the reports that were spread concerning his death: it was given out publicly, that on hearing his sentence of death pronounced, the dread thereof threw him into an apoplectic fit, of which he died; very few believed he died a natural death, but it was dangerous for people to speak as they thought.

X:22. THE PEACE TREATY OF NYSTAD, AUGUST 30, 1721

The Great Northern War (1700-21) not only established Russia as a great European power but also occasioned many internal measures of Peter the Great which had far-reaching social and administrative consequences. Here are some of the provisions of the peace treaty that ended it.

Reference: Dumont, *Droit des gens,* vol. 8, pt. 2, pp. 36-39. Also in Jean Rousset de Missy, *Recueil historique d'actes . . . et traitez de paix depuis la Paix d'Utrecht,* 21 vols. (The Hague, 1728-55), 1:327-44. The Russian version of the treaty is in *PSZRI,* 1st ser., 6:420-31.

ARTICLE 4: His Majesty the king of Sweden hereby cedes, for himself and for his successors to the throne and realm of Sweden, to His Tsarist Majesty, and to his successors in the Russian Empire, in full, irrevocable, and perpetual possession, the provinces conquered and taken in this war by His Tsarist Majesty's arms from the Swedish crown, to wit: Livonia, Esthonia, Ingria, a part of Karelia, as well as the district of the Vyborg Fief, as specified hereunder . . . the cities and fortresses of Riga, Duenamuende [a fort just west of Riga], Pernau [Pernov], Reval, Dorpat, Narva, Vyborg, Kexholm [on Lake Ladoga], and all the other cities, fortresses, havens, places, districts, banks, and shores belonging to the said provinces; as well as the islands of Oesel, Dagoe, Moen, and all the other islands lying along the coasts of Livonia, Esthonia, and Ingria, beginning with the frontier of Courland; and, east of Reval, the islands lying to the south and east of the line [Russian version: "the deep-water passage"] from Reval to Vyborg. . . .

ART. 5: In exchange, His Tsarist Majesty undertakes and promises to evacuate and restore to His Royal Majesty and the crown of Sweden, within four weeks after the exchange of ratifications of the present peace treaty, or earlier if possible, the Grand Duchy of Finland, with the exception of the part that is excluded below in the . . . delimitation, which part shall belong to His Tsarist Majesty, so that His Tsarist Majesty and his successors shall not have and shall not raise any pretensions to the said duchy on any pretext whatsoever. Moreover, His Tsarist Majesty undertakes and promises to pay [to the king of Sweden] the sum of two million talers [*écus*] promptly, without fail, and in full. . . .

ART. 6: His Majesty the king of Sweden also reserves for himself . . . a perpetual right to buy grain for fifty thousand rubles annually in Riga, Reval, and Arensburg [on the Isle of Oesel]; which grain shall [be allowed to] leave these places freely, without payment of duty or any other impost, to be transported to Sweden. . . .

ART. 9: His Tsarist Majesty moreover promises that all the inhabitants, whether nobles or commoners, of the provinces of Livonia and Esthonia, and of the Isle of Oesel, as well as the cities, magistrates, guilds, and trade corporations, shall be maintained in [Russian version: "shall permanently retain and shall be unswervingly sustained in"] the full enjoyment of the privileges, customs, and rights that they had enjoyed under the dominion of the king of Sweden [Russian version: "under the Swedish administration"]. [Cf. the Charter of the Esthonian Principality, 1710, Item X:15, above.]

ART. 10: Likewise, no constraint on conscience shall be introduced in the ceded lands, but the Evangelical [Lutheran] religion, together with its churches, schools, and whatever appertains to them, shall be left and maintained on the same footing as under the last administration of the king of Sweden [Russian version: "as under the former Swedish administration"]; on the condition however, that the Greek Orthodox religion shall also be exercised freely [Russian version: "freely and without any interference"] in these lands.

X:23. PETER'S NEW TITLE, OCTOBER-NOVEMBER 1721

The conclusion of peace with Sweden was followed by a change in the title of the Russian sovereign. But in spite of Peter's tendency to establish a unified and centralized state, the official title of the sovereign continued to reflect the historical growth of the Muscovite state. The first excerpt is taken from an official account of the "Proclamation of the Empire of All Russia" on October 22, 1721. The second is taken from a decree of November 11, 1721, fixing the sovereign's title to be used in formal correspondence with foreign courts.

Reference: *PSZRI,* 1st ser., 6:444-48, 453.

[Proclamation of October 22, 1721:]

On this twentieth day of October, the Senate, in consultation with the Ecclesiastical Synod [*dukhovnyi sinod*], resolved: In order to show their due gratitude to His Majesty for his gracious and paternal care and exertions for the welfare of the state during the whole of his glorious reign, and especially during the late Swedish War; and [since] through his own guidance only, as is well known to all, he has brought the state of all Russia into such a strong and prosperous condition and [procured for] his subjects such glory in the whole world: to beg His Majesty, in the name of the whole Russian people, to accept from them, following the example of other [rulers], the title of "Father of the Fatherland, Emperor of All Russia, Peter the Great."

[There follows an account of negotiations with Peter over this new title. After mass, on October 22—the day set aside for the celebration of peace with Sweden—the Treaty of Nystad was read aloud in church, whereupon Count Golovkin, the chancellor, delivered a speech in which he said that Peter had "taken us . . . from the darkness of ignorance onto the stage of glory before the whole world, and, so to speak, out of nonbeing into being, and has brought us into the society of political nations." He then offered Peter the new title.] After this speech, all the senators shouted "Vivat!" three times. This acclamation was taken up loudly and joyfully by all the people both in the church and outside, and was accompanied by the sound of drums and kettledrums; then the guns of the fortress of Saint Petersburg and of the admiralty fired a salute, and then the Guards, drawn up on the square, and the 125 galleys [on the river] . . . kept up a running fire with their musketry. After this, His Imperial Majesty deigned to answer the senators' speech in a few, but very forceful, words:

After salutation: "I wish very much that all our people should clearly perceive what the Lord God has done for us in the last war and through the conclusion of this peace.

"We must thank God with all our strength. But, hoping for peace, we should not slacken in the military field, lest we suffer the same fate as the Greek monarchy.

"We must work for the welfare and profit of the whole community, both inside and outside, as God lays it before our eyes; this will bring relief to the people."

[There followed a *Te Deum* service, and more congratulations and firing of salutes; then dinner was served for 1,000 guests, followed by a ball, fireworks, and distribution of wine to the populace.]

[The decree of November 11, 1721:]

We, Peter I, by the grace of God emperor and autocrat [*Imperator i Samoderzhets*] of all Russia, of Moscow, Kiev, Vladimir, Novgorod; tsar of Kazan', tsar of Astrakhan', tsar of Siberia; sovereign of Pskov, and grand duke of Smolensk; prince of Esthonia, Livonia, Karelia, Tver', Ugra [former Novgorod possessions in the Arctic region], Perm', Viatka, Bulgaria [on the Volga], and of other [principalities]; sovereign and grand duke of Novgorod of the Nizovian land [i.e. Nizhnii Novgorod], of Chernigov, Riazan', Rostov, Iaroslavl', Beloozero, Udoria, Obdoria, Kondia [the last three names designate the former Novgorod possessions in northwestern Siberia], and overlord of all the Northern land; sovereign of the Iverian land [part of Georgia], and of the Kartalinian and Georgian tsars; and hereditary sovereign and suzerain of the Kabardinian land and of the Circassian and mountain princes [*Cherkasskikh i gorskikh kniazei,* i.e. in the northern Caucasus].

X:24. THE TABLE OF RANKS, JANUARY 24, 1722

The Table of Ranks was promulgated January 24, 1722, in order to regularize the status of government officials, courtiers, officers of the army, the navy, the artillery, and the Guards by dividing each category into fourteen classes. In the table printed here the artillery officers and the courtiers have been omitted altogether, and the list of civil and military officers has been considerably shortened. (For a subsequent amendment by Nicholas I to the provisions of articles 11 and 15, concerning entrance into the *dvorianstvo,* see the manifesto of June 11, 1845, Item XIV:28; for the Table of Ranks in 1901, see Item XVI:78.) See also the entry *Tabel' o Rangakh* in the *Dictionary of Russian Historical Terms.*

Reference: *PSZRI,* 1st ser., 6:486-92.

CLASS	ARMY	GUARDS	NAVY	CIVIL SERVICE
1.	Field Marshal General	—	Admiral General	Chancellor [Kantsler]
2.	Generals of the Cavalry and of the Infantry	—	Admirals	Right Privy Councillors [Deistvitel'nye Tainye Sovetniki]
3.	Lieutenant Generals	—	Vice-Admirals	Procurator General [General-Prokuror]
4.	Major Generals	Colonel	Rear Admirals [Schout-bij-nacht]	Presidents of Colleges; Privy Councillors [Tainye Sovet-niki]; High Procurator [Ober-Prokuror]
5.	Brigadier	Lieutenant Colonels	Commodore-Captains	Vice-Presidents of Colleges
6.	Colonels [Polkovniki]	Majors	Captains, 1st Grade	College Councillors [Sovet-niki v Kollegiiakh]; Presi-dents of Superior Courts [Prezidenty v Nadvornykh Sudakh] [i.e. in nine guberniia capitals]
7.	Lieutenant Colonels	Captains	Captains, 2d Grade	Vice-Presidents and Procura-tors in Superior Courts
8.	Majors	Lieutenant Captains	Captains, 3d Grade	Assistant College Councillors [Asesory v Kollegiiakh]; Senate Secretaries; Superior Court Councillors [Nadvornye Sovetniki]
9.	Captains	Lieutenants	Lieutenant Captains	Titular Councillors [Titu-liarnye Sovetniki]; Doctors of all faculties in state service
10.	Lieutenant Captains	Sub-Lieutenants	Lieutenants	College Secretaries [Sekretari Kollegii]
11.	—	—	Ship Secretaries (Pursers)	—
12.	Lieutenants [Leitenanty]	Ensigns [Fendriki]	Sub-Lieutenants	Secretaries in Superior Courts, in special offices, and in guberniia administration
13.	Sub-Lieutenants [Unter-leitenanty]	—	—	Secretaries in provintsiia administration
14.	Ensigns [Fendriki]	—	Ship Commissaries	Assistant Councillors [Ase-sory] in Provintsiia Courts; Registrars and Bookkeepers in Colleges

.   .   .

All state officials, Russian or foreign, who now belong, or have formerly belonged, to the first eight classes, and their legitimate children and descendants in perpetuity, must be considered equal in all dignities and advantages to the best and oldest nobility, even if they are of humble origin.

.   .   .

Any military man who is not [himself a hereditary] noble and who attains the rank of a company-grade officer becomes a nobleman; all his children born after the promotion are also nobles; but if no children are born to him after the promotion, but he had them previously, then, upon the father's request, nobility shall be conferred upon one of his sons only, at the father's choice. [Note: This is a clarification of the decree of January 16, 1721 (PSZRI, 1st ser., 6:290), conferring the status of hereditary noblemen on all company-grade officers.]

X:25. THE STATUTE ON SUCCESSION TO THE THRONE, FEBRUARY 5, 1722

This statute was Peter's drastic solution to the vexing problem of succession (see above). In theory, this statute remained in force until 1797.
    Reference: *PSZRI*, 1st ser., 6:496-97.

[Recalling the misdeeds of Alexis and citing some biblical and historical precedents] we have deemed it good to establish the principle that the ruling sovereign should always have the power to designate his successor, and, after having designated him, to set him aside, if he notices that he is in any way unfit, so that our children and descendants, feeling this restraint, would not fall into evil ways. . . . Wherefore we command all our faithful subjects, both clerical and lay, without exception, to swear before God and his Gospel to [maintain] this law of ours, so that anyone who contravenes it or misrepresents it should be considered a traitor liable to capital punishment and ecclesiastical excommunication.

X:26. THE DECREE ON THE MAINTENANCE OF CIVIL LEGALITY, APRIL 17, 1722

This decree (*Ukaz o Khranenii Prav Grazhdanskikh*) embodies Peter's ideas on the functioning of the state apparatus in what he called a "regular state."
    Reference: *PSZRI*, 1st ser., 6:656-57.

Nothing is more important for the administration of the state than firm observance of civil legality, for it is useless to compose laws if they are not respected, or are sorted out at will, like cards, suit by suit; nowhere in the world were such practices more rampant than in our country, and they still continue to some extent, for there are people who strive by every means to undermine the fortress of justice. For these reasons this decree is promulgated to set the seal of confirmation on all the existing statutes and regulations, so that no one would ever dare to hand down decisions or administer any affairs not in accordance with the statutes. . . . Should anything appear obscure in these statutes, or should the affair be such that there is no clear provision for it, then no decision should be rendered, but a written report must be submitted to the Senate. . . . The Senate [shall consult the colleges; however, it] shall not decide the matter, but shall set down its opinion and report it to us; after we render the decision and sign it, then let it be published and added to the statutes. . . .

If anyone, under any pretext whatsoever, acts in Gagarin-like fashion [Note: Prince Matvei Petrovich Gagarin, governor of Siberia, was executed in 1721 for malfeasance in office] contrary to this decree, he shall be put to death as a lawbreaker and enemy of the state, and let no one expect any mercy on account of his former merits if he is guilty of this crime. Therefore let this decree be printed and incorporated into the code of laws and brought to public notice. It shall be posted on a special board in the Senate; and let it always be displayed, like a mirror before the eyes of the judges in all [court] rooms, from the Senate down to the lowest court. Each time that this decree is not displayed on the desk, a fine of one hundred rubles shall be paid for the benefit of the hospital.

X:27. THE DECREE ON THE DUTIES OF THE PROCURATOR GENERAL, APRIL 27, 1722

The chief duties of the procurator general (*general prokuror*: attorney general) as an intermediary between the emperor and the Senate were set forth in this decree.
    Reference: *PSZRI*, 1st ser., 6:662-64.

1. The procurator general shall have a seat in the Senate and shall keep strict watch that the Senate performs its duties and that all matters coming up for the Senate's consideration and decision are dealt with truthfully, diligently, and honestly, without loss of time, and according to regulations. . . . Also he must keep a sharp lookout that decisions not be merely reached on paper in the Senate, but that [the Senate's] orders be actually executed. . . .

2. He must also watch strictly that the Senate carries out its functions with justice and impartiality. . . .

3. He must supervise all other state attorneys [procurators], so that they perform their duties honestly and diligently. . . .

4. He shall receive reports from the in-

vestigators [*fiskaly*] . . . transmit them to the Senate, and instigate proceedings; he must also keep an eye upon [these] investigators and report to the Senate without delay if he notices anything amiss. . . .

10. He must bring to the Senate's attention matters that are not clearly explained in decrees, so that they may resolve them in clear decisions. . . .

11. Since this magistrate can be likened to our eye and our proxy in affairs of state, he must act loyally, for he will be the first to be brought to account. If he practices any deceit, or in any other way knowingly and willfully transgresses against his duties, he shall be punished as a breaker of the law and as a flagrant criminal of state.

C. SOCIAL AND ECONOMIC CONDITIONS

X:28. A DECREE ON MUNICIPAL SELF-GOVERNMENT, JANUARY 30, 1699

The decree excerpted below reflects Peter's first attempt at introducing municipal self-government. However, only eleven out of approximately seventy eligible cities availed themselves of the opportunity offered them; the rest declined on various pretexts, chief of which was their inability to pay higher taxes. Only in Moscow did the Chamber of Burgomasters (*Burmisterskaia palata*), or Ratusha (town hall), established in 1699, function with some degree of success. In addition to its local duties, the Moscow Chamber of Burgomasters supervised the land chambers mentioned in the text below, and soon it developed into an agency of the central government, administering the collection of excise and customs revenue. However, with the establishment of the guberniias (each guberniia comprising a group of provintsii under the administration of one governor) in 1708, many of its functions were curtailed: it became, in fact, a local institution serving the city and the guberniia of Moscow until the municipal reform of 1721.

Reference: *PSZRI,* 1st ser., 3:600. See also the decree on the Chamber of Burgomasters in Moscow, Jan. 30, 1699, ibid., pp. 598-600.

The great sovereign has decreed as follows: To announce this, the great sovereign's, decree in all the cities to the townsmen and to merchants of all ranks, and in the great sovereign's volosti and villages to all the craftsmen and suburban people [*uezdnye liudi*]: If they— the townsmen and all manner of merchants, craftsmen, and suburban people—desire to be freed from the control of the voevody [provincial governors] and government officials in the cities over their . . . civil and judicial affairs, petitions, and other affairs, on account of the many impositions, exactions, and bribes [extorted by these officials], then let their various civil and judicial affairs, petitions, and collection of the great sovereign's revenues be controlled by men of their own

communes [*mirskie liudi*] elected to sit in the land chambers [or communal offices— *zemskie izby*]. And they—the townsmen, merchants, craftsmen, and suburban people— must elect among themselves good and honest people, whomsoever they will, to the land chambers to take care of their civil and judicial affairs, petitions, and collection of revenue. For this gracious protection of the great sovereign, which will free them from the offenses, impositions, exactions, and bribery of the voevody and government officials, they—the townsmen, merchants, craftsmen, and suburban people—will pay to the great sovereign's treasury double the amount of all kinds of the great sovereign's annual taxes assessed upon them heretofore.

X:29. A DECREE ON TRADING COMPANIES, OCTOBER 27, 1699

Like many of Peter's measures, the decree quoted in part below was inspired by his experience in Holland. It had little immediate effect, chiefly because Russian merchants were too weak and inexperienced to compete with the Dutch and later the English merchants, who virtually monopolized Russian trade with western Europe and the colonial world. Moreover, like the attempted municipal reform of 1699, this measure was too obviously influenced by the fiscal needs of the treasury to evoke much response.

Reference: *PSZRI,* 1st ser., 3:653.

The Moscow and provincial merchants of all ranks shall trade [with foreign countries] as the merchants of other states do, that is, they shall form trading companies and shall deliver their merchandise for the account of their company to the city of Archangel, to Astrakhan', and a smaller amount to Novgorod. Let all the merchants establish, in a general council among themselves, fitting rules in order to expand their trade—which will result in increased revenue for the great sovereign's treasury.

X:30. PETER'S DECREES ON WESTERN DRESS AND SHAVING, 1701 AND 1705

Compulsory shaving and wearing of Western dress began, for the limited circle of the tsar's immediate entourage, soon after Peter's return from abroad in 1698. In the next two years these measures were spread to other strata of society, though they came to be somewhat modified by the fiscal needs of the treasury. These innovations, more than any others, had an immediate impact on the man in the street.

Reference: *PSZRI,* 1st ser., 4:182, 282-83.

[The decree on "German" dress, 1701:]

Western ["German"] dress shall be worn by all the boyars, okol'nichie, members of our councils and of our court . . . gentry of Moscow, secretaries . . . provincial gentry, deti boiarskie, gosti, government officials, strel'tsy, members of the guilds purveying for our household, citizens of Moscow of all ranks, and residents of provincial cities . . . excepting the clergy (priests, deacons, and church attendants) and peasant tillers of the soil. The upper dress shall be of French or Saxon cut, and the lower dress and underwear—[including] waistcoat, trousers, boots, shoes, and hats—shall be of the German type. They shall also ride German saddles. [Likewise] the women-folk of all ranks, including the priests', deacons', and church attendants' wives, the wives of the dragoons, the soldiers, and the strel'tsy, and their children, shall wear Western ["German"] dresses, hats, jackets, and underwear—undervests and petticoats—and shoes. From now on no one [of the above-mentioned] is to wear Russian dress or Circassian coats, sheepskin coats, or Russian peasant coats, trousers, boots, and shoes. It is also forbidden to ride Russian saddles, and the craftsmen shall not manufacture them or sell them at the marketplaces. [Note: For a breach of this decree a fine was to be collected at the town gates: forty copecks from a pedestrian and two rubles from a mounted person.]

[The decree on the shaving of beards and moustaches, January 16, 1705:]

A decree to be published in Moscow and in all the provincial cities: Henceforth, in accordance with this, His Majesty's decree, all court attendants . . . provincial service men, government officials of all ranks, military men, all the gosti, members of the wholesale merchants' guild, and members of the guilds purveying for our household must shave their beards and moustaches. But, if it happens that some of them do not wish to shave their beards and moustaches, let a yearly tax be collected from such persons: from court attendants . . . provincial service men, military men, and government officials of all ranks—60 rubles per person; from the gosti and members of the whole-sale merchants' guild of the first class—100 rubles per person; from members of the whole-sale merchants' guild of the middle and the lower class [and] . . . from [other] merchants and townsfolk—60 rubles per person; . . . from townsfolk [of the lower rank], boyars' servants, stagecoachmen, waggoners, church attendants (with the exception of priests and deacons), and from Moscow residents of all ranks—30 rubles per person. Special badges shall be issued to them from the Prikaz of Land Affairs [of Public Order] . . . which they must wear. . . . As for the peasants, let a toll of two half-copecks per beard be collected at the town gates each time they enter or leave a town; and do not let the peasants pass the town gates, into or out of town, without paying this toll.

X:31. PETER'S MANIFESTO INVITING FOREIGNERS INTO RUSSIA, APRIL 16, 1702

Though foreign military men and craftsmen had been living in Russia long before Peter the Great, Peter's concerted efforts to attract more of them into Russia were unprecedented. His attempts

to hire foreigners for Russian service in 1697-98 are well known, and the manifesto quoted here
was not the only document of its kind.
    Reference: *PBIPV*, 2:47-49.

1. ... Effective this date, we shall cause
our renewed orders and instructions to be
sent to all our vicegerents [namestniki],
governors, and officials, both at the border
and between here and Kiev, Smolensk, and
Pskov, so that the arriving officers may suffer
no hindrance or inconvenience, but, on the
contrary, that they be met with every kind
of assistance and benevolence. We order that
the same gracious favor that is to be shown
to the military men be shown to all the
merchants and practitioners of the arts who
may intend to come here, that they be given
free and unrestricted passage and treated
with due honor.
    2. We have already introduced here, in our
capital, the free exercise of faith for all Christian religious sects, even though they are
separated from our church; nevertheless, by
these presents, we do confirm it anew, that
since we, deriving our power from the All-
Highest, do not pretend to compel any
human conscience but readily allow each
Christian to work for his own salvation at his
own risk, so we shall strictly enjoin that, in

accordance with established usage, no one is
to suffer any hindrance in practising his religion
in public or in private.
    3. In order that the aliens and foreigners be
not deterred from coming here by fear of finding themselves under [unfamiliar] institutions,
courts, and administration, and liable to types
of punishment not usual in their own countries,
it is our pleasure to establish, in pursuance of
this decree, a regular commission of the Military Privy Council, or a [special] committee
with a president, councillors, secretaries, and
other clerical assistants; this [commission] will
consist of foreigners skilled in military affairs
and will have jurisdiction and cognizance over
all the foreign military men, of whatever nature
and rank, over their servants, as well as over
the foreign military commissariat, and over
treasury matters [affecting them] ...
    4. To assure those entering our service that
their liberty to leave our service will in no
way be impaired, we do hereby promise that
the manner of leaving our service will in all
respects follow the practices usually adhered
to by the other sovereigns of Europe.

X:32. DOCUMENTS ILLUSTRATING POPULAR REACTIONS TO PETER'S MEASURES, 1701, 1705, AND 1708

Peter's measures evoked much opposition among many different groups; however, being very
diverse in their outlook, these groups could never unite in a concerted movement. The excerpt
from an inquest of August 1701 offers an example of some of the more moderate views expressed about Peter by many monks; the conversation allegedly took place between two regular
priests. The Astrakhan' rebels who sent the letter of July 31, 1705, to the Don Cossacks had a
considerable leavening of the Old Believers among them, as well as people concerned with the
preservation of their status and old customs. The commotion in the Don region in 1708, which
prompted the Don ataman's letter to the Zaporozhians, was an echo of the Bulavin movement,
and was inspired largely by fear that the modern state would encroach on the old liberties of the
Don Cossacks; this movement also had a sprinkling of the Old Believers in its ranks.
    Reference: Ustrialov, *Istoriia tsarstvovaniia Petra Velikogo*, vol. 4, pt. 2, pp. 204 [inquest of
1701], 352-53 [letter of July 31, 1705]; *PBIPV*, vol. 7, pt. 2, p. 698 [letter of 1708].

[From "An inquest concerning indecent
words about the sovereign," August 1701:]
    At the inquest the regular priest Paul said
... that in August of this year, 1701 ...
while visiting the Semilutsk hermitage, he
had asked Tarasii, the builder [also a regular
priest], during vespers: "Did the great sovereign pass here on his way from Moscow?" to
which Tarasii replied: "What's the good of
asking? When, during this year's Lent, the

great sovereign deigned to travel from Moscow
to Voronezh and deigned to come to the village of Khlevnoe, that same day they bought
some eggs for him." He, Paul, then asked
Tarasii, the builder: "What did they buy these
eggs for?" To which Tarasii answered: "Well,
he, the great sovereign, eats eggs even during
Lent." Whereupon the priest Paul argued with
Tarasii, saying, "Why do you utter such indecent words about the great sovereign?" and

proceeded to scold him for it; but he, Tarasii, the builder, said: "Not only does the great sovereign partake of eggs, but he even eats meat during Lent." To which Paul retorted: "Only the Germans [i.e. foreigners] do that; our great sovereign would never do a thing like that—eat meat during Lent." And Tarasii, the builder, then reportedly said: "But he, the great sovereign, is himself a son of a German."

[A letter from the Astrakhan' rebels to the Don Cossacks, July 31, 1705:]

To Ataman Iakim Filipovich and to all the Don Cossack Host, we . . . [there follows a list of names], and all the city folk of Astrakhan' and of the up-river towns, and all who are now in Astrakhan', send our greetings. We wish to inform you of what has happened in Astrakhan' on account of our Christian faith, because of beard-shaving, German dress, and tobacco; how we, our wives, and our children were not admitted into churches in our old Russian dress; how men and women who entered the holy church had their clothes shorn and were expelled and thrown out; how all kinds of insults were heaped upon us, our wives, and our children; and how we were ordered to worship idolatrous manikins [i.e. wigs]. We have thrown these manikin idols out of the houses of the men in authority. Moreover, in the last year, 1704, they imposed on us, and collected, a [new] tax: one ruble "bath money" apiece; and they also ordered us to pay a grivna [ten copecks] per sazhen' [seven feet] of cellar space. The voevoda Timothy Rzhevskii, together with other men in authority, colonels and captains, took away all our firearms and wanted to kill us: of this plan we were informed by soldiers doing guard duty. They also took away from us, without orders, our bread allowance and forbade that it be issued to us. We endured all this for a long time. [At last,] after taking counsel among ourselves, in order not to forsake our Christian faith, not to worship idolatrously the manikin gods, not to have our souls and those of our wives and children destroyed in vain, and also moved by our great distress—for we could endure it no more to be in danger of losing our Christian faith—we resisted: we killed some of them and have put some others in prison. You, the Cossack atamans, and all

the Host of the Don, please deliberate among yourselves, and stand up together with us to defend the Christian faith, and send a message [about your decision] to us at Astrakhan'. We are awaiting you, Cossack atamans, and we rely upon you. We have been informed by traders and by various other people that in Kazan' and in other cities foreigners ["Germans"] are being billeted by twos and threes in people's houses; they oppress and molest the inhabitants, their wives and children in the same way as they did with us at Astrakhan', oppressing and murdering service men.

[A letter from an ataman of the Don Host (probably Semen Alekseevich Dranoi) to Ataman Gordeenko of the Zaporozhian Host, 1708:]

To Kostiantii [Konstantin Gordeenko], *koshevoi ataman* [military commander in chief of the Zaporozhian Cossacks] of His Most Serene Tsarist Majesty's very brave Zaporozhian Military Host beyond the Dnieper, and to all the friendly brotherhood of the great Zaporozhian Host;

From Semen Alekseev, Ataman of the great Field Host of the Don, and from all the Don Field Host—greetings:

On the twenty-sixth day of May of this year, 1708, in accordance with the instructions of the great Host of the Don, we, the [Cossack] army, settled on the rivers Don, Khoper, Medveditsa, Buzuluk, and Northern Donets, and on their tributaries wherever our Cossack organization exists, have been ordered to take the field against the Moscow regiments approaching our land in order to destroy our Cossack towns. . . . Prince Vasilii Volodimerovich Dolgorukii is said to be marching at the head of these Russian regiments with the goal of annihilating our Cossack towns and laying waste the whole region of the [Don] river. Having taken the field, we are now encamped near the town of Iampol'. We expect you to show your Cossack brotherly devotion and are awaiting your aid, so that we may preserve our Cossack rivers in their pristine state and our Cossackhood as it always was; let there be unanimity and brotherhood among us, Cossacks. And so we ask you, the doughty atamans of all the great Zaporozhian Host, to bring speedy aid to our field forces, so that you and we should not lose our common and true Cossack glory and our reputation for bravery. If, some day, you happen to be in need, we, too, will be happy to die by your side, so that we do not fall under the domination of Russia, and that our common Cossack

glory be not held to derision. [Note: Gordeenko remained faithful to Peter at that time; in 1709 he joined Mazepa.]

X:33. IAGUZHINSKII ON PETER'S ATTITUDE TOWARD FOREIGNERS

The passage below is taken from some of the reminiscences that Count Pavel Ivanovich Iaguzhinskii (1683-1736), Peter's procurator general, communicated to the German historian Jacob von Staehlin, who joined the Russian Academy of Sciences in 1735.

Reference: Jacob von Staehlin-Storcksburg, *Original Anecdotes of Peter the Great* (London, 1788), pp. 71-75.

The monarch, however, soon perceived that several Russian noblemen censured, in secret, the favour he showed to foreigners in general. . . . One day, when he saw himself surrounded by a great number of these noblemen, all Russians, he availed himself of the opportunity, and turned the conversation on the foreigners— "I well know," said he, "that the favour I am obliged to grant them publicly does not please all my subjects: but I have two kinds of subjects; I have intelligent and well-meaning ones, who see very plainly that if I endeavour to retain foreigners in my dominions, it is only for the instruction of my people, and consequently the good of the empire: I have others

who have neither sufficient discernment to perceive my good intentions, nor candour to acknowledge, and cheerfully to comply with them; who, in short, from want of reflection, despise all that appears new, feel regret on seeing us emerge from our ancient state of sloth and barbarism, and would hold us down, if it were in their power. Let them reflect a little what we were before I had acquired knowledge in foreign countries, and had invited well-informed men to my dominions: let them consider how I should have succeeded in my enterprises, and made head against the powerful enemies I have had to encounter, without their assistance!"

X:34. GRANTS OF STATE FACTORIES TO PRIVATE INDIVIDUALS, 1709 AND 1711

Many factories founded at the very beginning of the eighteenth century were directly administered by various government departments; for instance, the glass factory near Vorob'evo, founded in 1705, was run first by the Foreign Office (Posol'skii Prikaz), and then by the Siberian Prikaz. Peter's favorite method of reviving such enterprises when their production was unsatisfactory is shown in these two selections.

Reference: *PBIPV*, 9:347-48 [Peter's letter to Gagarin]; Nikolai V. Kalachev, ed., *Doklady i prigovory v . . . Senate v tsarstvovanie Petra Velikogo*, 6 vols. (St. Petersburg, 1880-1901), 1:26 [Peter's order in the Senate].

[Letter from Peter to Prince Matvei Petrovich Gagarin, Commandant of Moscow and head of the Siberian Prikaz, August 16, 1709:] Honorable Colonel and Commandant:

The Englishman William Lloyd [a merchant settled in Russia] has requested us to grant him the Moscow glass factories situated near the village of Vorob'evo (in which all kinds of glassware, except mirrors, have been manufactured), with all their buildings, for ten years, beginning with the next year, 1710, free of taxes. We have granted this request, and have ordered that he be given these factories, in consideration of his, William's, promise to expand the said glass factories in these [ten] years and to instruct, at his own expense, twelve Russians in the manufacture of glass,

so that they would fully master this craft, no worse then the masters overseas. At these factories he must use the purest glass, which he shall procure at his own expense, to manufacture all kinds of glassware and windowpanes. He will also be permitted to build, at his own expense, similar factories in other places, wherever it is convenient, and to sell glassware and windowpanes from these factories in all the cities of the Russian state at a free price. Meanwhile, during these [ten] years no other Russians or foreigners are to establish or lease any glass factories (excepting those that are in existence already or will be built by our treasury); nor shall they bring any other skilled glass masters from overseas or entice any workers away from the said

William. Nevertheless, anyone is still permitted to trade in glassware imported from overseas or manufactured at the factories already established at home, or in glassware of local production brought from the Ukrainian cities. Accordingly, you must hand over these factories [at Vorob'evo] to the said foreigner Lloyd. Inform me about all the factory buildings and their appurtenances given to the said William. But if the said William declines to take over these factories at the present time, you must order the craftsmen left at the factories to continue the manufacture of glassware as before, until he, William, takes them over.

Peter

[Note: The Vorob'evo glass factory burned down in 1713 and was not rebuilt.]

[Peter's order registered in the Senate, February 20, 1711:]

On the twentieth of February, 1711, Privy Councillor Count Ivan Alekseevich Musin-Pushkin ordered the registration of the following personal decree of His Majesty: "The great sovereign, tsar, and grand duke Petr Alekseevich, during his visit to the Foreign Office, issued the following personal order: To grant to the Moscow merchants who trade in Moscow only and do not move to any other localities—that is, to Andrew Turok, Stepan Tsynbalshchikov, and others—the linen, tablecloth, and napkin factories, and the yard acquired in the New German Settlement, which were formerly under the administration of the Foreign Office (having first made a full inventory of the said factories and yard); [they shall] likewise [take over] the foreign master craftsmen invited from overseas for this purpose, in accordance with their contracts, and the Russians who have learned this craft. They, the merchants, must expand these factories at their own expense and show profit; they shall sell the articles manufactured at these factories at a free price and for their own profit. If, through their efforts, they expand this enterprise, and show profit, they shall receive a token of the great sovereign's favor; but if they fail to expand their business, or let it decline through their negligence, then they and their associates shall each pay a fine of one thousand rubles."

X:35. THE DECREE ON THE INHERITANCE OF REAL ESTATE BY ONE SON ONLY, MARCH 23, 1714

The chief purpose of this measure was to prevent the impoverishment of the gentry, in order to enable them to serve more effectively. Like the decree on schools for the gentry (see Item X:49) the new inheritance law was inspired by Theodore Saltykov, Peter's maritime agent in England, who had drawn up, in 1712, a comprehensive plan of reform of Russian society and institutions. The inheritance law of 1714 proved to be hard to enforce, for it was very unpopular; it was repealed in 1731 (see Item XI:6).

Reference: *PSZRI,* 1st ser., 5:91-94.

First, if the real estate would always pass to one son, and only the movables to the others, the state revenue would be more regular, since a master can always be more easily satisfied from a larger estate, even if his intake is at a lower rate. There would be one household and not five (as described above); he could then more easily alleviate the burdens of his subjects and not impoverish them. Second, families would not decline but would stand serene and unshaken in the glory and greatness of their houses. Third, the other sons would not remain idle, for they would have to earn their living through service, or education, or trade, or some such thing. Whatever they do for their livelihood will be profitable for the state.

Therefore we have judged it right to set up the following practice:

1. All immovable property, such as patrimonies and pomest'ia, whether inherited, obtained by service, or bought, as well as homesteads and shops, shall not be sold or mortgaged but shall be retained in the family in the following manner:

2. Whoever has sons shall bequeath his real-estate property to one of them only, at his choice. All other children of both sexes shall be endowed with movable property, which their father or mother must divide themselves, as they wish, between all the sons and daughters to the exclusion of the one who will be heir to the landed property. If a man has no sons, but only daughters, he shall follow the same procedure. If he fails to apportion his property in his lifetime, then the real-estate property shall be assigned by decree as the inheritance of the

eldest son, and the movables shall be divided equally among the others; the same procedure also applies to daughters.

3. A childless person shall be free to leave his real estate property to any family member of his choice and to apportion the movables in any way he pleases among his relatives or even strangers, as he may wish.

X:36. FRIEDRICH CHRISTIAN WEBER DESCRIBES THE TAX SYSTEM, CA. 1714-1719

Friedrich Christian Weber remained in Russia from 1714 to 1719, first as secretary of the Hanoverian Legation and later as minister-resident. In 1721 he began to publish his account of Russia, under the title *Das veraenderte Russland;* an English translation of the first part of this work, an excerpt from which is given here, appeared in 1722-23.

Reference: Friedrich Christian Weber, *The Present State of Russia*, 2 vols. (London, 1722-23), 1:70-72. A reprint has recently become available (N.Y.: Da Capo, 1968).

Excepting the above-mentioned Taxes, neither the Townsmen nor Peasants are charged with any Contributions on Account of their Possessions or Trade, so that if they knew how to make the best Advantage of those Blessings which Nature has bestowed upon them, those Imposts would appear easy enough. . . . [But conservative methods of agriculture used by the peasants impoverish the country.] The same Unthriftiness is the Reason that many Country Families run away from their Habitations, when they find themselves insolvent, being apprehensive of the Execution [i.e. seizure of goods for default in tax payment], which in these Parts falls little short of Torture. Some of those fugitives run into the Forrests, and join the Party of *Roskolnikes,* who are a sort of Zealots that stickle for the ancient liturgy . . . others take their Refuge in some Nobleman's House in another Province; however at present hardly anybody will harbour them, it being enacted by the Provincial Law, that if one finds his Peasant in another man's Estate, the latter is bound not only to deliver up the Fugitive, but also to pay to his right Master twenty-five Rubels for every Year, during which he shall have entertained him, so that no Body would be a great Gainer by such a Bargain, seeing a Peasant seldom pays half that Sum to his Lord. But they who suffer most by such a Runaway, are his Neighbours, for as they are under an Incapacity of manuring his Land, which, as it is easy to imagine, is commonly quite out of Heart, and yet are forced to make up the full Sum of the Czar's Taxes, as though there was no Deficiency in the Number of Inhabitants; it follows of Course, that being at length quite ruined themselves, they follow the Example of their Brethren, and fly from their Habitations to the Forrests. Yet even these Disorders are not so prejudicial to the Country as the Mismanagement of the Provincial Commissioners, Chancellors, and Clerks, who are entrusted with the Collection of Taxes. These Cormorants no sooner enter upon their Offices, but they make it their sole Study how to build their Fortunes upon the Ruin of the Country People, and he that came among them having hardly clothes to his Back, is often known in four or five Years time, to have scraped so much together as to be able to build large Stone-Houses, when at the same Time the poor Subjects are forced to run away from their Cottages. It is certain they cannot clear so much by their Salaries, which some time ago hardly amounted to six Rubels a Year, but were lately augmented to fifteen or twenty, by a new Order from the Czar, to the intent, that no pretext be left for the like Extortions. But as the superior Officers are no less greedy of unlawful Gains than their Inferiors, and consequently connive at their vile Practices, the Country is exhausted to that Degree, that though in the most difficult Times a House is hardly taxed above six or seven Rubels a Year, yet the Inhabitants by the Extortions of those Officers of the Finances, are forced to pay every Year no less than thirteen, or even fifteen; and a certain Russian, who has been conversant in these Affairs, was once heard to say, that of one hundred Rubels collected in the Country, he was positively assured not thirty ever came into the Czar's Coffers, the Remainder being divided among the Officers for the Trouble of gathering them in. The Artifices which they make use of are innumerable, and though a Stop is put to some by the Czar's Regulations, yet they are surprisingly dexterous in finding out new ones.

X:37. PETER'S INSTRUCTIONS FOR A GENERAL CENSUS AND POLL TAX, 1719, 1720, AND 1722

The Northern War imposed a heavy financial burden on the state. During Peter's reign many attempts were made to count the population for the purposes of taxation and recruitment. Prior to 1718 it was normal to count "hearths" or "homesteads" as fiscal units; the practice gave rise to many frauds and led to much crowding in each homestead. The idea of a head count of all the taxable population was launched in 1717 and adopted by Peter in 1718. Some of the difficulties of carrying out such a census are apparent from the selections given here, and the practice of demanding "revised lists" (*revizskie skazki*) from time to time began almost immediately after the first census. Peter first tried to have the poll tax collected by the voevody (governors of provintsii, subordinate to governors of guberniias) and their commissioners and councillors; but this apparatus soon proved inadequate, and, by the force of circumstances, the pomeshchiki found themselves charged with collecting taxes from the peasants, until, in 1731, they were made fully responsible for it. This tended to increase the power of the landlord over the peasants, and thus contributed to the strengthening of serfdom.

Reference: *PSZRI,* 1st ser., 5:618 [decree of Jan. 22, 1719]; 6:1 [order of Jan. 5, 1720], 506 [instructions of Feb. 5. 1722.]

[Peter's decree on the general census, January 22, 1719:]

In order to provide for a distribution of [the tax burden for] the army among the peasantry of the whole state, the great sovereign has ordained, by a personal decree, to compile new census lists in every guberniia of the peasants living in the villages belonging to the [sovereign's] household and in other villages belonging to the sovereign, to the bishops, the monasteries, the churches, and the pomest'e and the patrimony owners; the *odnodvortsy* [one-homesteaders, descendants of service men with very small holdings], the Tatars, and the *iasak*-payers [iasak: tax in furs paid by the natives, mainly in the Ural region and in Siberia] must also submit a report. . . . These lists shall be compiled without any concealment, and regardless of any old or recent census lists of the homesteads or of the inhabitants. Let them themselves [the landlords?] compile truthful lists showing the number of peasants, landless single peasants [*bobyli*], [the gentry's] household and landed peasants in each village of every volost'. All the peasants of the male sex, from the old men down to the last infant, without exception, must be entered by name, and their age must be indicated. These census lists must be submitted to the guberniia administrations. [Note: In February 1722 the number of peasant homesteads was reported as 888,284 in 10 guberniias and 48 provintsii; see *PSZRI,* 1st ser., 6:510.]

[Peter's supplementary order on the general census, January 5, 1720:]

I hear that in the census lists that are now being compiled only the [landed] peasants are counted, and the [gentry's] household peasants and the other kinds [of peasants] are omitted. Since this practice can allow the same kind of fraud as was common in counting homesteads, you must now issue a confirming directive that the gentry must list all their subjects, whatever their status. Likewise, all church attendants must be included, with the exception of priests and deacons, who must submit a special list. Give them all half a year to compile their lists.

[Peter's instructions to Major General Chernyshev, who was in charge of the census in the Moscow guberniia, February 5, 1722:]

You must inform the gentry that they must pay at the rate of eighty copecks for every soul of the male sex of the peasants, whether of their households, or landed, or of any other status, who live in their villages. . . . They must make these payments not in kind but in money; they may make the payment in two, three, or four installments a year, as is most convenient for them; for the purposes of this collection they must elect, in December of every year, a land commissioner among themselves [in every district]. At the same time, you are to inform them that there will be no other taxes, transport services, and so forth, imposed on them. [Note: In 1725 the poll tax was definitely fixed at seventy-four copecks for each male peasant.]

X:38. PETER'S ORDERS DESIGNED TO CURB THE GROWTH OF SERFDOM, 1719 AND 1721

The development of serfdom did not square with Peter's intentions. His attempts to check at least some of the worst practices that had grown up are seen in these two selections.
Reference: *PSZRI*, 1st ser., 5:628-29; 6:377.

[From Peter's instructions to voevody, January 1719:]

31. Since there are some wretched people who wantonly despoil their own villages and who, on account of their drunkenness or loose living, not only fail to stock [with supplies] or to protect their patrimonial estates [*votchiny*] but also ruin them by imposing all kinds of unbearable burdens on the peasants, and beat and torment their peasants; and since this makes the peasants run away, abandoning their tax communes, all of which depopulates the countryside and causes the sovereign's revenue to fall in arrears; therefore the voevoda and the land commissioners must be on the watch not to allow such ruinous practices. . . . Should they detect such despoilers of their estates—through census lists and witness accounts—let them order such persons' close relatives, whether by blood or by marriage, to correct them and to manage their villages until they mend their ways.

[From Peter's decree prohibiting the sale of serfs separately from their families, April 15, 1721:]

There was a custom in Russia which still exists: petty gentry sell their peasants, laborers, and domestic servants to any bidder singly, like cattle—something that is not done anywhere else in the world; a pomeshchik sells [his serf's] son or daughter, taking them away from their family, from their father or mother—a custom that gives rise to much lamentation. Therefore His Majesty has ordered that this sale of serfs shall cease. But if it proves impossible to eradicate it altogether, they should at least be sold, in cases of dire necessity, by entire families, and not separately. This decree is to be included and further explained in the code of laws that is now being written in the manner the high-governing lord senators may deem right.

X:39. THE STATUTE OF THE COLLEGE OF MINING (BERG-KOLLEGIUM), DECEMBER 10, 1719

Peter the Great came to rely more and more on chartered private enterprise for the development of mining, industry, manufacturing, and trade, the central government providing the general direction—and prodding—through the Colleges or Departments of Mining, Manufactures, and Commerce.
Reference: *PSZRI*, 1st ser., 5:760-62.

PREAMBLE. . . . Careful management of the mining establishments will make the country grow rich and flourish, and, as the experience of many lands abundantly shows, uninhabited and barren lands will become populous.

Our Russian state, more than many other countries, abounds in useful metals and is blessed with minerals, which, until now, have not been explored with due application; and especially, since they were improperly exploited, many benefits and profits that could have accrued to us and to our subjects were neglected. . . .

1. Permission and liberty are granted to all and sundry, of whatever rank or condition, whether working on their own lands or on those belonging to others, to prospect for, smelt, found, and refine all kinds of metals, namely gold, silver, copper, tin, lead, iron;

all minerals, such as saltpeter, sulphur, vitriol, and alums, and all kinds of useful colored clay and stones; for this purpose each may employ as many metal workers as the mine can use and he can afford. . . .

7. If a landowner has no desire to engage in mining either by himself or in a company, or if he lacks the necessary funds, he must allow others to prospect for metal ores and minerals on his land, to mine and to refine them, so that God's blessing shall not remain buried in the earth in vain. However, in this case, the industrialists must pay, without any withholding, to the owner of the land on which their installations are built one-thirty-second part of the profit realized from the metal ores or finished mineral products drawn from his land; they shall pay in cash for any additional sites that may be needed for the establishment, as well as for the necessary wood and timber. If the

owner demands an exorbitant price for these sites, or for timber, wood, or coal, the matter shall be referred to the college. . . .

10. The working men of these establishments who learn their trade properly shall not only be freed from monetary taxes, army or navy service, and all extra imposts but shall also receive full pay for their work at regular times.

11. Moved by these considerations and by love for our loyal subjects, we do thus graciously concede to all and sundry who may desire it the ownership and exploitation of mining establishments, which by right belong exclusively to us as monarch. For this privilege we demand no more than is customary in other states—one-tenth of the profit—to provide for the salaries of the Mining College personnel and for other necessary expenses. . . .

12. Moreover, we reserve to ourselves the preemption on gold, silver, copper, and saltpeter in preference to other buyers. Thus no one shall presume to sell even the smallest amount of the above-designated materials to anyone but the mining directors assigned in the vicinity of that province or to a member of the Mining College accredited for this purpose.

13. The price for the above-designated metals shall be established by our Mining College in accordance with the location and cost of production, in such a way that our loyal subjects receive a net and sufficient profit and that we sustain no loss in our mints and other enterprises. . . .

15. As for other metals, like iron, tin, lead, and various other minerals, every prospector is free to sell them to whomever he wishes.

X:40. DECREES ON MUNICIPAL ADMINISTRATION AT THE END OF PETER'S REIGN, 1721 AND 1724

Peter never abandoned his dream of making Russian cities flourish like those of Holland. The general scheme of municipal reform, for which the cities of Riga and Reval served as main models, was approved by Peter in 1718, but many difficulties delayed its promulgation for several years. The Supreme Municipal Administration (Glavnyi Magistrat) was to be an administrative college and a department of the central government.

Reference: *PSZRI*, 1st ser., 6:291-309; 7:388-97.

[The Statute for the Supreme Municipal Administration, January 16, 1721:]

Whereas His Tsarist Majesty has ordered . . . the appointment of Brigadier and Captain of the Life-Guards Prince Trubetskoi as chief president [*ober-prezident*] over the administration [*magistrat*] of this city [Saint Petersburg] and over other city administrations, he is to exercise jurisdiction over all mercantile people and to report on their affairs to the Senate; he must rebuild the dilapidated edifice of Russian commerce. President Il'ia Isaev is appointed to serve as his associate in the administration of this city.

. . .

CHAPTER II: The main functions of the Supreme Municipal Administration:

. . . [1.] To establish adequate municipal administration in all cities.

2. To provide good statutes and protective regulations.

3. To supervise the administration of justice.

4. To set up a good police force.

5. To increase and improve commerce and manufactures (by the latter we mean not only the big enterprises, such as cloth or brocade manufactures, iron and copper works, and the like, but also the equally necessary enterprises, like those of shoemakers, carpenters, smiths, silversmiths, and so forth; it must also use discretion in introducing good order and improvement, wherever possible, in all matters pertaining to municipal welfare. . . .

CHAP. VI: . . . [The Supreme Municipal Administration must] begin to make adequate provisions for city governing bodies; for this purpose it must select in every city good, prosperous, and clever men from among the gosti, members of the merchant guild [*gostinaia sotnia*], junior gosti [*gostinye deti*], and citizens of the first order, and form municipalities [magistraty] from them in cities where there are large settlements of townsmen. Within these municipalities it must designate some as presidents—for administrative and appellate jurisdiction—and others as burgomasters. . . . Let city councillors [*ratmany*] be associated with each burgomaster (in large cities—two per burgomaster), and should the welfare of the city demand the holding of a [special] council, let [the magistrates] call in good and clever men chosen from citizens of the first order and from those of the middling condition. . . . All members of municipal administration, i.e. presidents, burgomasters, and councillors, shall be exempt from all [other] civil service. . . . The Supreme Municipal Administration must diligently strive that the newly established city governments be everywhere held in such renown and respect as is usual in other states, that they be regarded by the citizens as their true authorities, so that they may be clothed with certain rank commensurate with [the importance of] the city.

CHAP. VII: Division of the citizenry:

. . . Citizens of the first order [*pervoi gil'dii*] are distinguished from the rest of the citizens . . . by their privileges and advantages. [Note: For orders of citizenry, see below, Instructions for Municipal Governments, 1724.] In accordance with the size of the city and the number of craftsmen, each profession and trade is to have its special guild or assembly of craftsmen, with aldermen (or elders) set above it. Each craft and profession must also maintain its books containing its statutes, regulations, and the rights and privileges of its members. Should any of the aldermen of the said guilds distinguish themselves by meritorious actions, they may be selected to fill the above-mentioned municipal posts, where they are to aid the city government by word and deed, and the best of them may be elected city councillors and, later, even burgomasters. . . .

CHAP. XIV: The powers of city administrations:

Since municipal government is the head of the citizenry and exercises authority over it, its duties are to judge the citizens, to control the police, to collect the revenue due from the citizens and to transmit it as the College of Revenues [Kammer-Kollegium] may direct, to organize the whole economy of the city, its commerce, all kinds of trades and professions, and to make appropriate representations to the Supreme Municipal Administration on all the needs [of the city] and on whatever may concern its welfare. Consequently, the municipalities must not be subject to the governors and voevody in any matter pertaining to municipal law courts and economy. Neither the civil nor the military governor is to summon a citizen before his

court, but he should carry his complaint against such a citizen before the municipal administration.

[From the Instructions for Municipal Governments, 1724:]

2. A municipal administration [gorodovoi magistrat] shall consist of the following persons: one president, two burgomasters, and four councillors.

The following office personnel shall be attached to them: one secretary, one clerk, two assistant clerks, four copyists, and four watchmen; however, they must try to appoint fewer men, if they can manage. . . .

15. The citizenry shall be divided into three categories, excluding the gosti and the merchant guild [gostinaia sotnia]:

The first order [gil'diia] shall comprise rich merchants who have a large export business and wholesale dealers, town doctors, apothecaries and medical practitioners, and shipbuilders. [Note: Chapter VII of the Statute for the Supreme Municipal Administration also mentions bankers, skippers of merchant ships, goldsmiths, silversmiths, icon painters, and painters as belonging to the first order.]

The second order shall comprise retail traders, craftsmen of all kinds, and the like.

All the rest, that is, people of mean condition—hired men, those employed on drudging toil, and the like—though they are citizens, and must be entered as such on the rolls, are, nevertheless, not considered as substantial, regular citizens.

16. When all the citizens are thus divided and enrolled, each order is to elect several elders from among their prominent men. These elders, especially those from the first order, must aid the municipal administration by their counsel in all civic matters. One of these elders shall be elected a superintendent, and another shall serve as his associate: they must interest and exert themselves in all matters pertaining to civic welfare, and make fitting proposals to the municipal administration. The municipal administration must likewise call in the superintendents and elders for consultation in matters concerning the citizens, and especially their welfare.

17. Even though the above-mentioned people of mean condition are not accounted among the substantial, regular citizens, still, they are within the purview of the municipal

administration as citizens and are obliged to pay appropriate moderate taxes according to their means and capacity; [therefore] they too must elect elders and *desiatskie* [i.e. an agent with responsibility for ten households or thereabouts], who must report on their needs to the municipal magistrates, and these latter must take due care of them, help them in every way they can, and watch that they be not overburdened beyond their means.

X:41. PETER'S DECREE ON THE DEVELOPMENT OF FACTORIES, NOVEMBER 5, 1723

The excerpt given below expresses Peter's ideas on the role of the government in directing the economy of the country.
Reference: *PSZRI*, 1st ser., 7:150-51.

This directive [to the College of Manufactures, July 13, 1722] has been sufficiently explained but seems to have had little effect for the following reasons: either it is disregarded and not applied properly, or there are few men willing [to found new factories], or both. Moreover, it appears that [some] manufacturers who had expanded [their production] have been ruined by the importation of similar goods. . . .

That there are few men willing [to start new factories] is a fact: for our people are like untutored children, who would never begin to study the alphabet unless they are constrained by the master; at first they resent it, but once having learned it, they are grateful. We see this clearly from the present state of our affairs—has not everything been accomplished by constraint? Yet, we already hear many thanks, and [our labors] have borne fruit. For in promoting manufacturing we should not limit ourselves to making suggestions (as is done in countries where such enterprises are common) . . . but we must also press people and help them with advice, with procuring machinery, and in other ways; and we must teach them how to become good businessmen.

X:42. THE STATUTE OF THE COLLEGE OF MANUFACTURES, DECEMBER 3, 1723

The College of Manufactures had begun to function as a subdivision of the College of Mining before it was established as a separate institution in 1722. Its statute was issued the next year. Unlike the other colleges, it had its main office in Moscow, the industrial center of Russia.
Reference: *PSZRI*, 1st ser., 7:167-74.

6. His Imperial Majesty is diligently striving to establish and develop in the Russian Empire such manufacturing plants and factories as are found in other states, for the general welfare and prosperity of his subjects. He [therefore] most graciously charges the College of Manufactures to exert itself in devising the means to introduce, with the least expense, and to spread in the Russian Empire these and other ingenious arts, and especially those for which materials can be found within the empire; [the College of Manufactures] must also consider the privileges that should be granted to those who might wish to found manufacturing plants and factories.

7. His Imperial Majesty gives permission to everyone, without distinction of rank or condition, to open factories wherever he may find suitable. This provision must be made public everywhere. . . .

8. In granting a privilege to establish a factory, the college must take care not to debar others who might later wish to establish similar factories. For competition between manufacturers may not only help industrial growth but also ameliorate the quality of goods and keep prices at a reasonable level, thereby benefiting all His Majesty's subjects. At the same time, in cases where existing factories are sufficient for the general needs, the college must see to it that the creation of new ones does not lead to a deterioration of original manufactures, especially through the production of inferior goods, even though they may sell at a low price. . . .

10. Factory owners must be closely supervised, in order that they have at their plants good and experienced [foreign] master craftsmen, who are able to train Russians in such a way that these, in turn, may themselves become masters, so that their produce may bring glory to the Russian manufactures. . . .

15. The factories and plants that have been built or will be built at His Majesty's expense should be turned over to private individuals as soon as they are put into good condition;

let the college exert itself to this end. . . .

17. By the former decrees of His Majesty commercial people were forbidden to buy villages [i.e. to own serfs], the reason being that they were not engaged in any other activity beneficial for the state save commerce; but since it is now clear to all that many of them have started to found manufacturing establishments and build plants, both in companies and individually, which tend to increase the welfare of the state—and many of them have already started production; therefore permission is granted both to the gentry and to men of commerce to acquire villages for these factories without hindrance, [but] with the permission of the College of Manufactures, on the condition, however, that such villages remain permanently attached to the said factories. Therefore neither the gentry nor the merchants are allowed to sell or mortgage such villages separately from the factories . . . unless, for reasons of pressing personal need, they wish to sell these villages together with the factories, which they may do with the permission of the College of Manufactures. . . . [Note: Paragraph 17 reproduces almost verbatim the decree of January 18, 1721 (*PSZRI,* 1st ser., 6:311-12), which had specified the Colleges of Mining and of Manufactures as having to approve all purchases and sales of villages connected with the factories within their respective jurisdictions.]

23. In order to stimulate voluntary immigration of various craftsmen from other countries into the Russian Empire, and to encourage them to establish factories and manufacturing plants freely and at their own expense, the College of Manufactures must send appropriate announcements to the Russian envoys accredited at foreign courts. The envoys should then, in an appropriate way, bring these announcements to the attention of men of various professions, urge them to come to settle in Russia, and help them to move.

X:43. POSOSHKOV'S BOOK ON POVERTY AND WEALTH, *1724*

Pososhkov (see Item X:9, above) summed up his experience, criticism of the social and economic order, and recommendations in *A Book on Poverty and Wealth* (*Kniga o skudosti i bogatstve*), which he completed in 1724. It was first published only in 1842.

Reference: I. T. Pososhkov, *Kniga o skudosti i bogatstve* (Moscow: AN SSSR, 1937), pp. 100, 101, 118, 161-63, 171, 173, 179, 192, 200-01, 215, 253-54. A later edition is also available, ed. by B. B. Kafengauz (Moscow: AN SSSR, 1951).

Preface

The wealth of the realm consists not in the amount of money stored in the tsar's treasury, nor in the gold-embroidered attire of His Majesty's courtiers. The real wealth of the realm consists in the entire people being rich in household goods that it needs rather than in external garb with lace trimmings. For these trimmings enrich not us but the states from which they are imported, while they drain our wealth. . . .

It seems to me that it would be no great achievement and would, in fact, be quite easy to fill the tsar's coffers with riches; for, within his sphere, the tsar, like God, can do as he pleases. But it is a great and very difficult task to make the whole people rich, for no measures to enrich the people will suffice unless justice is instilled, and oppressors, thieves, robbers, and all kinds of open and hidden despoilers are exterminated.

. . .

Chapter 1: The Clergy

I do not know how village priests in other Christian lands make their living, but I do know quite well that in Russia the village priest lives by the labor of his hands and is in no way different from the peasant who tills the land. When the peasant begins to plough, the priest does likewise; the peasant starts to mow—so does the priest; and in the meantime, he neglects the holy church and his flock. Because of this husbandry [of the priests] many Christians die not only without communion, but even without the sacrament of penance, like cattle. . . .

Here is my humble opinion: if possible, a tithe should be assessed upon all the parishioners of every church. Let each of them give a tenth or a twentieth part of his food to the clerics, as the tsar and the bishops may decide. Thus the priests would be fed without having to till the fields. And it is right that they should have no fields, for they are servants of God and,

according to the injunction of the Lord,
should live on the church, not on agriculture.

. . .

Chapter III: Justice

. . . It seems to me that above all else we must
seek [to establish] justice in the law courts;
for if justice is established among us, all
people will shy away from wrongdoing. All
that is honorable is based upon fair and impartial administration of justice; [if we
achieve it,] even the tsar's revenue will be
doubled. For this purpose a [new] code of
laws must be drawn up, with provisions for
all kinds of cases. . . .

To our Russian provisions, past and present,
we should add some from the German code-
books; and, in general, any laws out of foreign
codes that are suitable for us should be incorporated into our code. Even the Turkish
code should be translated into the Slavic language, as well as their regulations on judicial
and civil procedures. We should adopt those
of their practices that suit us, for it appears
that their administrative proceedings are clear
and fair—even better than the German ones—
so that their courts render quick and just
decisions; they do not waste as much paper
as we do, nor are they used to feeding useless
mouths; but above all they give just protection to their businessmen [kupechestvo].

Two or three men from [each of the following groups] should be selected to draft
this code of laws: the clergy—those who are
the wisest, the most learned, and well versed
in the Scriptures; civil administrators familiar
with court and administrative procedures;
dignitaries of high rank—those who are not
proud but well disposed to all men; officials
of low rank—those who are not conceited;
officials of government departments [pri-
kaznye liudi] who understand administration;
the gentry—those who are wise and truth-
loving; merchants who have had experience
in all sorts of transactions; soldiers—who are
intelligent and truth-loving and who have
lived through many hardships in the course
of their service; boyars' retainers [liudi
boiarskie]—those who are used to responsibility; and government inspectors [fiskaly]. It
also seems to me that it would not be bad to
select a few peasants too—among those who
have been village elders and sotskie [centurions],
who have handled various affairs and are

sharp-witted. I have seen clever men even
among the Mordvins [Finno-Ugric natives in
the Middle Volga region, near Simbirsk], so
why would there not be intelligent men
among the peasants?

After the articles of this new code are
drafted, the whole people should approve
them by a completely free vote, without
compulsion of any sort. In this way no one—
neither of high nor of low birth, neither rich
nor poor, neither of high nor of low rank,
nor even the peasant—would find himself
abused or oppressed by these new provisions
as a result of ignorance of the problems of his
group.

After the code has been drafted in full
consultation with all, let it be presented for
consideration by His Majesty's sharp mind.
Those articles that His Majesty approves
shall remain, and those [that he finds] unsuitable shall be stricken out or amended as
appropriate. Many will object to my proposal,
saying that I am limiting His Majesty's autocratic power by the advice of the people. But
I do not seek to limit His Majesty's autocracy;
my suggestion amounts to this: that to establish true justice, each man should inspect the
newly drafted articles insofar as they concern
his group, to see whether they contain any
unsuitable or oppressive provisions contrary
to justice. . . .

The establishment of just laws is a most
sublime achievement and one should go about
it with such circumspection that no group of
men would ever be able to shake it. It cannot
be accomplished without much consultation
and free advice from many people. For God
has not given perfect understanding to any
one person, but has divided it into small
particles which he has given to each man according to his capacity: to some—more; to
others—less. However, there is no person to
whom God has given nothing.

. . .

To our great shame, just courts of law
exist not only in foreign countries that profess Christianity but even among the infidels.
We, on the contrary, profess the holy and
pious faith, which is glorious in all the
universe, yet our courts of law are not worth
anything; and whatever decrees His Majesty
may issue are all brought to naught, everybody carrying on after his own manner, as
before.

. . .

It is very difficult to turn the magistrates away from iniquity and to inculcate the principles of justice in them, for iniquity has struck deep roots in them and has become inveterate. From the lowest to the highest they have all become susceptible to temptation: some are open to bribes; others fear powerful persons; still others are afraid of calumny; and there is also the official who expects the same preferential treatment, if the person concerned should later have the same power as he now enjoys. As a result, state affairs suffer, investigations are rigged, and His Majesty's decrees remain inoperative. All administrators from the nobility connive with their brethren, the noble-born; they are powerful and fearless only with the weakest people but do not dare even to utter a prohibitory word to an illustrious nobleman; they do as he desires. This is why everything is in disorder.

How many decrees concerning the young sons of the nobility have been sent to all the cities? Even when a nobleman is summoned [to service] by name, they are in no hurry to send him out, but tarry, following the custom laid down in the old code, awaiting the third call. Only then, if they can find no further excuse, do they send him out [to serve]. Some nobles have grown old in such disobedience and contempt of His Majesty's orders, living all the time on their estates, never having set one foot in the service.

· · ·

We all see how hard our great monarch works; but he cannot accomplish anything, for he has not many helpers, such as he would wish to have. How can he succeed, pulling uphill alone—be it with the force of ten men—while there are millions pulling downhill? Even when he punishes someone severely, immediately there are a hundred men ready to take [the culprit's] place. Therefore, however hard he tries, he will always be let down, unless the ancient customs are changed.

· · ·

Chapter IV: The Merchants
The merchants should not be brought low, for no realm, large or small, can subsist without them. Merchants are comrades even to men at arms: while the latter fight, merchants aid them and provide them with various necessities. For this reason one must take unflagging care of them. Just as the soul cannot subsist

without a body, so the men at arms cannot do without merchants; nor can the merchants live without men at arms.

The realm is extended by the men at arms and ornamented by the merchants. Therefore it is necessary to defend them against offenders, so that they be not in the least molested by the military men. There are many stupid people who despise the merchants and scorn and offend them without reason. In fact, in the whole world there is no station in life that would not require the services of a merchant.

Merchants should not only be protected from outside offenders but must also be prevented from doing harm to one another. Men of other classes should not [be permitted to] engage in trade and interfere with their business transactions in any way; but merchants should be allowed to trade freely, so that they would prosper by their trade and thereby further His Majesty's profit.

· · ·

If [the foreigners] should stop bringing their goods to us altogether, we could survive even without their goods, whereas they cannot survive even ten years without ours. Thus it behooves us to adopt the tone of masters with them, while they should assume a humble, servile mien before us, not a haughty one.

It is strange that, coming to us with their trinkets, they set a low price on our substantial merchandise, while putting a double price, and sometimes even more, on their own wares.

Why, they even evaluate the money of our great tsar, which should be none of their business. They should rather evaluate the money of their own sovereigns, for they have power over their overlords [literally, "over their proprietors," (vladel'tsy)]. As for our great emperor, he is a master unto himself, and if, within his state, he should ordain that a copeck be taken for a grivna [ten copecks], it will be so accounted.

In our realm, with the permission of our monarch, we are free to set any price we want on the goods brought to us; and if [the foreigner] does not like it, let him not deliver the goods: for he is free to deliver or not to deliver them; we shall certainly not take them from him by force. But we can be firm in our refusal to allow ashore any unconsigned goods or goods of inferior quality; they may take them back with them or keep them aboard ship.

It is time they laid aside their former conceit. They used to mock us in the days when our monarchs would not themselves intervene in mercantile matters, and when the boyars governed. In those days, the foreigners, upon arrival, would pass a hundred or two-hundred-rubles' worth of gifts to some influential persons, and then make a profit of a million for every hundred rubles thus distributed—all because the boyars considered our merchants as not worth a broken eggshell; they would sell them all out for a penny.

Now, thank God, our monarch has taken good care of all this.

. . .

In my opinion, it is better to throw money away into the water than to give it away overseas for drink. . . . To promote the prosperity of the realm, even the other overseas goods must be bought after careful consideration, for we should buy only those we cannot do without. As for their foreign [literally: "German"] novelties and luxuries, we could just as well forbid their entry, so as to stop the draining of wealth from Russia. Let us pay no heed to their sweet and flattering tales and bragging.

Let us keep our wits about us: we should buy from them whatever we need for the welfare of the realm and what is profitable for us. We must refuse to buy their articles that bring us no profit or are of inferior quality.

. . .

Chapter VII: The Peasants
It does not seem to be just that the pomeshchiki should overburden their peasants. There are some inhuman gentry who, in the busiest seasons, never let their peasants have a single free day so that they can work for themselves, and thus the peasants lose all their ploughing and harvesting time. There are also those who, after receiving quitrent [obrok]

or food rent due from their peasants, demand more from them and, by these excessive exactions, drive the peasants to poverty; or, if a peasant becomes a little better off, they impose higher money dues on him. Subjected to such treatment, no peasant of theirs can ever become rich. Many of the gentry say: "Do not let a peasant get shaggy; shear him naked like a sheep." Following this precept, they despoil the realm, for they rob their peasants, not leaving a single goat to some of them. From this misery, the peasants run away, leaving their homesteads: some, for the Middle or Lower Volga region [ponizovye mesta]; others, to the borderlands [ukraennye mesta]; still others, abroad, thereby helping to settle foreign lands and leaving their own deserted.

. . .

The pomeshchiki are not permanent proprietors of the peasants; that is why they do not take good care of them. The true proprietor of the peasants is the autocrat of all Russia, while the pomeshchiki have them only temporarily.

Thus the pomeshchiki must not be allowed to ruin their peasants, who should be protected by a decree of the tsar, so that they be true peasants, not beggars; for peasant wealth is the wealth of the realm.

Therefore, it seems to me that it would be best to fix by a decree the amount of quitrent and other dues a pomeshchik can claim from his peasants, the number of days per week that they must work for him, and the other payments in kind due from them. [All this must be calculated] at such a rate that the peasants would be able to pay the sovereign's tax and the rent of the pomeshchiki and still live without privation. Judges must watch carefully that the pomeshchiki do not impose any burdens on the peasants over and above what is specified by law, and that they do not drive them to misery.

D. IDEOLOGY, EDUCATION, AND ECCLESIASTICAL AFFAIRS

X:44. THE TESTAMENT OF PATRIARCH JOACHIM, MARCH 17, 1690

Peter's activity brought him into conflict with some of the prelates of the established church. Patriarch Joachim (1620-90), who had occupied the patriarchal see since 1674, was a capable administrator and an implacable enemy of the Old Believers. Although a foe of Patriarch Nikon during the latter's disgrace and trial, Joachim continued Nikon's policies of defending the church's rights and domains against the encroachments of the civil authorities. He looked with disfavor on the new tendencies apparent in the last years of the reign of Alexis and during the regency of

Sophia. His testament (dated March 17, 1690), excerpts from which are given below, was addressed to the co-tsars Ivan V and Peter. It is quite revealing of the mentality of the more conservative wing of Russian prelates of his time; it also helps to explain why Peter, a man of sincere religious belief, pursued an anticlerical policy in administration. (On the church in this period, see also Chapter VIII, Section D.)

Reference: Ustrialov, *Istoriia tsarstvovaniia Petra Velikogo,* vol. 2, app. 9, pp. 467-77.

Another thing: may our sovereign never allow any Orthodox Christians in their realm to entertain any close friendly relations with heretics and dissenters—with the Latins [Roman Catholics], Lutherans, Calvinists, and godless Tatars (whom our Lord abominates and the church of God damns for their God-abhorred guiles); but let them be avoided as enemies of God and defamers of the church. May they command by their tsarist decree that men of foreign creeds who come here to this pious realm shall under no circumstances preach their religion, disparage our faith in any conversations, or introduce their alien customs derived from their heresies for the temptation of Christians; they should be strictly forbidden to do all this on pain of severe punishment.

. . .

I again implore Their Most Serene Tsarist Majesties, the pious tsars, and call upon them before God, our savior, that they prohibit in the whole realm all accursed foreign heretics and dissenters from exercising any kind of command in their regiments; but let them order that these enemies of Christendom be completely removed from such positions. For these dissenters do not agree in faith with us, Christians, who are in possession of true Orthodoxy; they are completely at variance with us in interpreting the tradition of the [holy] fathers; they are alien to our mother, the Orthodox church. Of what help could such accursed heretics be to the Orthodox host? They only bring on the wrath of God. The Orthodox pray to God according to the rules and customs of the church, while they, the heretics, sleep, and perform their abominable deeds, despising Christian prayer. The Christians honor the most pure Mother of God, the Virgin Mary, and invoke in every way her aid and that of all the saints; but the heretics—the military commanders—being ungodly, revile it and blaspheme; in no way do they respect the most holy Mother of God and all the saints; they do not honor the holy icons; they scoff at all Christian piety. Christians observe the fasts; heretics—never. As

the Apostle said, their belly is their God. Even if they stay with our regiments, God will not be there on account of their profaneness; [thus] there is no benefit from them. . . .

In [our] Christian regiments [we have] these God-abhorred living idols, the heretics, who malign our holy faith and piety: these Lutherans, Calvinists, and Latins, who dispense injustice; yea, more—as superiors, they are wolves set over hapless Christian lambs, on whom they heap every insult. No good can come from allowing a heretic—a non-Orthodox man—to hold in bondage, to command, or to judge the Orthodox Christians in the pious tsarist realm. Are there no Orthodox men fit to fill these positions and to perform in them capably? Indeed, by God's grace, the Russian tsardom abounds in pious men among the subjects of the tsarist realm, who are well versed in military science and skilled in leading troops. . . .

It is true that both in olden times and within our memory foreigners have served in Russian regiments. But what good came of it? Very little. This is natural, for they are enemies of God, of the most pure Mother of God, of the holy church, and of us, Christians. For all Orthodox Christians in the army lay down their lives in battles, unsparingly and with fervor, much more for their faith and for the church of God than for their fatherland and their homes. But the heretics who are in command care nothing for it.

Likewise, [Their Majesties] must not put any Christians into subjection or bondage to the godless Tatars who, though they are Their Majesties' subjects, continue to live in misbelief. If they do not want to be baptized and live in piety, the Christians should be taken away from them: Christian souls should not be left under the power of impious unbelievers, to be insulted by them.

With all my soul I implore and beg of you, our great and most pious Sovereigns and Tsars, to follow these precepts, and, by my episcopal power, I lay down this testament of mine for the guidance of all [future] pious autocrats.

. . .

Postscript: Let me remind you again not to allow, under any circumstances, the heretic dissenters to build Roman [Catholic] temples, Lutheran kirks, or Tatar mosques anywhere in your realm or dominions, nor to bring in any new Latin and alien customs, nor to introduce the wearing of foreign dress: for it is not through such practices that piety will spread in a Christian realm or faith in our Lord will grow.

I am amazed at the councillors and statesmen in the tsar's council who have been on embassies to other lands and realms: [surely, they must have observed] how all states hold on to their manners and customs, in dress as well as in actions, and do not accept any others; in their dominions they do not bestow any dignities upon men of other creeds; they do not permit foreigners of other faiths to build their own churches; such is the situation in all the heretic realms that surround us. Is there in any Western ["German"] land a single church of pious faith where a Christian could find haven? No, nowhere! But here, heretics are now permitted to do what was never allowed before: they have built temples for their accursed heretical assemblies, where they viciously curse and malign the pious people, scorn our faith, trample the holy icons, revile us, Christians, and call us ungodly idolaters. This is not good, but evil in every way.

This situation should be dealt with resolutely, both now and later, by pious men and especially by the most autocratic tsars and sovereigns, whom it behooves to provide wise direction to their realm, for its welfare and advantage, but most of all for the glory of God.

X:45: THE DECREE REESTABLISHING THE MONASTERY PRIKAZ, JANUARY 24, 1701

The Monastery Prikaz was first instituted by the Code of Laws of 1649. It had judicial authority over litigation among the clergy, and controlled the management of the church and monastery lands. Only the patriarch and his eparchy were exempt from its jurisdiction. In 1677, upon the insistence of Patriarch Joachim, it was abolished. After Patriarch Hadrian's death in 1700, Peter was strong enough to block the nomination of any candidate likely to prove uncooperative, and the patriarchal see thus remained vacant. By a decree of January 24, 1701, whose opening lines are given here, the Monastery Prikaz was reestablished as a branch of the secular government to control some of the matters formerly under ecclesiastical jurisdiction, now including the patriarchal eparchy and domains. Supervision of the possessions of monastic establishments was especially important, not only for fiscal reasons, but because monasteries were the chief breeding ground of conservative ecclesiastical opposition to Peter's measures. In 1721 the Monastery Prikaz was again abolished. It was eventually replaced by the Kollegiia Ekonomii.

Reference: *PSZRI*, 1st ser., 4:133.

The chancery of the most holy patriarch and the chanceries of the bishops and all affairs pertaining to the monasteries shall be placed under the administration of Boyar Ivan Alekseevich Musin-Pushkin; Secretary Efim Zotov is to be his assistant. They shall set up their offices on the premises of the former Office of Landed Estates [Pomestnyi Prikaz] in the patriarch's chancery; their office is to be known as the Monastery Prikaz.

X:46. PETER'S MEMORANDA ON PRINTING AND OTHER INTERESTS, 1708-1709

Throughout his reign Peter was a man of many interests. The selections given here from Peter's letters and memoranda illustrate a few of his preoccupations during even so busy a time as the critical phase of the Great Northern War.

Reference: *PBIPV*, vol. 8, pt. 1, p. 289 [letter of Nov. 8, 1708]; 9:12-13 [letter of Jan. 4, 1709], 31-32 [Jan. 19, 1709], 79 [Feb. 6, 1709], 101 [Feb. 21, 1709], 166 [May 2, 1709].

[Peter to Prince Matvei Petrovich Gagarin, November 8, 1708:]

You must print a complete alphabet with letters made in Moscow and not with those of Amsterdam. Take from the Amsterdam font only such letters as are lacking in the Moscow type. However, you must print the *d* and the *t* with characters appropriate for book printing and not for penmanship, as is shown here: " Т ," "Т." Also, print some prayer, like "Our Father," with this type, and send it to me with the alphabet. At the same time, have the book sent to you herewith printed with the Amsterdam type in octavo, and have the sketches pasted onto sheets of white paper. Also tell Pickaerdt [Note: Pieter Pickaerdt (1668-1737), an Amsterdam engraver who worked in Russia in 1702-32] to etch the sketches properly and to print them.

[Peter to Ivan Alekseevich Musin-Pushkin, January 4, 1709:]
Mr. Musin-Pushkin:

Your letter arrived here together with Rimpler's and Borgsdorff's book and the alphabet. [Note: Georg Rimpler (1636-83) and Baron Ernst Friedrich von Borgsdorff (active in the 1690s and early 1700s) were military engineers in the army of Emperor Leopold I and authors of several treatises on fortification.] But, compared with the previous books, their print is very bad, indistinct, and too thick. You should supervise the printing thoroughly in order to have the books printed as carefully as the previous ones, that is, as the ones on etiquette and on sluices. Also, let them be bound in the same manner as these last two books, for the binding of the newly arrived books is poor, chiefly because the backs are too tight, which causes the pages to come open: the backs of books should be much looser and wider. . . . Send me here about fifteen hundred or two thousand calendars, and let a third of them be printed in the same manner as the ones that have now arrived; the other two-thirds should be printed in quarto, so that officers could note their agenda on them. Also, send me a man to sell the calendars (for they will buy them very willingly). Give the necessary orders to sell the calendars in Moscow and in other cities. Order that there be sent to me one newly revised alphabet font (in accordance with the pattern enclosed here); but have the letters *b* and *p* recast, for they are very poorly designed and the type is too thick. Have something short printed with the new alphabet and send it to me. . . .
                                                                    Peter

[Peter to Ivan Alekseevich Musin-Pushkin, January 19, 1709:]

Upon the receipt of this letter you must order a diligent search to be made in all the government offices [prikazy] and in old houses of note for old charters dating from the time before Tsar Ivan Vasilievich [Ivan the Terrible]; let the Moscow seals of that

time be examined and a report on them be made to us.

I am sending you by this post the book on Swedish military law, which you should order to be printed in octavo. But first it should be revised, for in some places the translation is obscure and in other places the language is most crude. For this purpose you should employ the same translator who translated it in the first place—Schilling [Note: Benedict Schilling, a Swedish prisoner of war working as a translator in the Foreign Office]; after amending the text, have it printed. We are also sending you a history of Troy, which should likewise be printed (there is no need to amend the text) in the same size, but in medium-sized type, such as was used for the books on sluices and on epistolary etiquette. The book that Golovkin was translating should be printed with the same medium-sized type. Take good care of the bindings, so that they bind them as well as your book of geometry.

P.S. When the book on geometry is ready, have about two hundred copies of it printed; don't let it be sold until you are ordered to do so, but have ten or fifteen copies of it sent here. It is also necessary to print three or four hundred copies of the book on architecture, like the one that has been sent to Mr. Gagarin for correction; they are also not to be sold until the receipt of orders, and let ten or fifteen copies of them be sent here.

[Peter to Fedor Matveevich Apraksin, Akhtyrki, February 6, 1709:]
Honorable Admiral:

On the twenty-eighth day of this month there will be a visible eclipse of the sun, but it is not yet known to what extent it will be eclipsed. Please write about it to the mathematics teachers in Moscow, and tell them to calculate the extent of the eclipse at Voronezh; let them make a diagram of the eclipse and send it to you.
                                                                    Peter

[Peter to General James Bruce ("Iakov Vilimovich Brius"), chief of artillery, Voronezh, February 21, 1709:]
Honorable Lieutenant General:

We are sending to you, herewith, Coehoorn's sketches. [Note: Baron Menno van Coehoorn (1634-1704) was a renowned Dutch military engineer and author of several treatises on military architecture.] When the translation of Coehoorn's book that you have is finally corrected, and a clean copy of it made, then have these sketches taken out of the present binding, attach them to the clean copy, and send them to us for printing. We are also sending you a book on mechanics together with its translation into the Slavic language. Later on, when you have time, correct it, for this translation was made by Andrew Winius, and in many places it is inaccurate and obscure. [Note: Andrei Andreevich Winius (1641-1717), son of a Dutch merchant who had settled in Russia, began his service in the Foreign Office in 1664, where he rose

to fairly high rank, and later occupied a number of diplomatic and administrative positions.] Also, please send us the two books that are called *The Commandant's Mirror*, and the third— a small one—about politics.

Peter

[Peter to Jan ("Ivan") Lups, a prominent Dutch merchant settled in Russia, May 2, 1709:]
Mr. Lups:
Upon the receipt of this letter, please write to Amsterdam, asking that they find there a good binder, who binds books, and send him to Archangel without delay.

X:47. PETER'S ORDER ON THE EVE OF THE BATTLE OF POLTAVA, JUNE 27, 1709

Many histories cite an order supposedly issued by Peter to his troops just before the battle of Poltava. Quite possibly the reported text (given here in full) is Theophanes Prokopovich's or someone else's synthesis of ideas expressed less formally by Peter as he was inspecting his troops.
Reference: *PBIPV*, 9:226.

Let the Russian soldiers know that the hour has come in which the very existence of the whole fatherland is placed in their hands: either Russia will perish completely, or she will be reborn for the better. They must think that they have been armed and drawn up in battle array, not for the sake of Peter, but for the sake of the state entrusted to Peter, for the sake of their kin and of the whole of the Russian people, which, until now, has been protected by their arms, and which today is awaiting from them the final decision of its fortune. Neither let them be

disturbed by the glory of the enemy reputed to be invincible, for they themselves have repeatedly given the lie to this report. In the action to come let them keep only this before their mental eye—that God himself and Justice are fighting with us, of which fact, the Lord, who gives strength in battles, has already given them testimony by his aid in many combats: let them rely upon him alone. And as for Peter, let them know for certain that his life is not dear to him, if only Russia and Russian piety, glory, and prosperity survive.

X:48. A DEFINITION OF "AUTOCRACY" IN THE MILITARY SERVICE REGULATIONS OF MARCH 30, 1716

Reference: *PSZRI*, 1st ser., 5:325.

CHAPTER III, ARTICLE 20:
Comment: His Majesty is an autocratic [*samoderzhavnyi*] monarch who is not obliged to answer for his acts to anyone in the world;

but he holds the might and the power to administer his states and lands as a Christian monarch, in accordance with his wishes and best opinions.

X:49. DOCUMENTS ON EDUCATION FOR SONS OF THE GENTRY, 1697-1698 AND 1714

Very few were willing, or could afford, to send their sons abroad, even for the kind of superficial training that Prince Boris Ivanovich Kurakin had in Venice in 1697-98. The decree of February 28, 1714, aimed at providing the sons of the gentry with a few rudiments of knowledge indispensable for their future military service.
Reference: Semevskii, *Arkhiv kniazia F. A. Kurakina*, 1:255; *PSZRI*, 1st ser., 5:86.

[From the autobiography of Prince B. I. Kurakin:]
While I was in Venice [in 1697-98] . . . I

studied mathematical sciences, and I learned arithmetic, theoretical geometry (the five books of Euclid), practical geometry, trigonometry, cartography, astronomy (the part before navigation), navigation, mechanics, and defensive and offensive fortification. As proof of all these studies I have a certificate from my teacher, signed by the prince of Venice [the doge], with his seal affixed. I also learned, to my own satisfaction, to speak a little, to read, and to write Italian.

[A decree on compulsory education for sons of nobles, February 28, 1714:]

The great sovereign has ordained: In all the provinces the children of nobles (excepting the *odnodvortsy* [here exempted because as lesser service men their status in the eighteenth century came close to that of state peasants]) and of state officials (secretaries and scribes) between the ages of ten and fifteen shall be taught arithmetic and some

geometry. For this purpose students from mathematics schools shall be sent—several to each province—[and shall report] to the bishops and to the renowned monasteries; rooms for their schools shall be assigned in the bishops' households and in the monasteries. While they are teaching, these teachers are to receive for their subsistence ten copecks [*po 3 altyna po 2 den'gi*] per day out of the revenues of the province . . . and they must not accept anything from their pupils; but when their pupils have thoroughly mastered the subject, the teachers shall issue to them certificates under their own signature and, when releasing them, shall receive the tuition fee of one ruble from each of their students. Without such certificates these students are forbidden to marry, and marriage licenses are not to be issued to them.

X:50. LEIBNIZ AND PETER THE GREAT, 1712-1716

Leibniz's correspondence bears witness to his interest in the activities of Peter the Great and to the possibilities of scientific exploration in Russia. The two men met at Torgau in October 1711, and from that time until his death in 1716, Leibniz penned many memoranda to the tsar; excerpts from two of them are given below. One of Leibniz's favorite schemes was the establishment of academies of science all over the world for the advancement of "universal science"; there is not much doubt that he contributed to Peter's desire to found such an academy in Russia and that he strengthened Peter's interest in the creation of an extensive library and museum (or "chamber of curiosities"), which were finally organized in 1714 from several public and private collections and were later attached to the Academy of Sciences.

Reference: W. Guerrier, *Leibniz in seinen Beziehungen zu Russland und Peter dem Grossen* (Leipzig, 1873), pt. 2, and a Russian version of part 2 of this work: Vladimir Ger'e, *Sbornik pisem i memorialov Leibnitsa otnosiashchikhsia k Rossii i Petru Velikomu* (St. Petersburg, 1873); in both editions the pagination is the same and the documents are given in the original language—French, German, Latin, or Russian. Draft of Jan. 16, 1712: pp. 207-08; decree of Nov. 1, 1712: pp. 269-70; draft of 1716: pp. 349-51, 359-60.

[Draft of Leibniz's letter or oral memorandum to Peter the Great, January 16, 1712:]

P.S. . . . It appears to be the will of God that science should encompass the globe and should now come to Scythia, and that for this purpose its instrument should be Your Majesty; for you are so situated that you can take the best from Europe on the one side and from China on the other and, through good institutions, improve upon the achievements of both. Indeed, since in most parts of your empire all the studies are as yet in a large measure new and resemble, so to speak, a *tabula rasa,* it is possible for you to avoid countless errors which have crept in gradually and imperceptibly in Europe. It is generally known that a palace built altogether anew

comes out better than one that is rebuilt, improved upon, and much altered through many centuries.

This new and great development of the arts entails the building of libraries, museums or collections of rarities, workshops for models and objects of art, chemical laboratories, and astronomical observatories. However, it is not necessary to have all these things at once; one should proceed step by step and entertain suggestions on the quickest means of obtaining the most essential of them without excessive cost.

But the more important task is to procure men suitable for this great purpose; they should be sought out in different parts [and persuaded] to settle in Your Majesty's empire in order to teach your young people conscientiously. Since food is cheap in Russia, it would not require a great deal of money to maintain these settlers.

I would deem it the greatest honor, pleasure, and privilege to be able to serve Your Great Tsarist Majesty in an undertaking so praiseworthy and pleasing to God. For I am not one of those who have an exclusive passion for their country or for any particular nation but concern myself with the interest of all mankind. Indeed, I hold Heaven for my fatherland and all right-thinking men for my compatriots. I would rather do much good for the Russians than little good for the Germans or other Europeans, even though, in remaining among them, I may enjoy ever so great honor, wealth, and tranquillity; but if, in so doing, I cannot be of great service to others, then my natural inclination and desire move me to prefer the general good.

[Peter's decree on the acceptance of Leibniz into Russian service, November 1, 1712:]

We, Peter I, tsar and autocrat of all Russia, etcetera, etcetera, etcetera.

We have most graciously judged it right that Gottfried Wilhelm von Leibniz, privy councillor in the judicature of the elector and duke of Brunswick-Lueneburg, be also appointed and confirmed as our privy councillor in the judicature, on account of his outstanding good qualities which have been praised to us and which we ourselves have found in him. Since we know that he can be of great help in the development of mathematics and of other arts, in historical research, and in the growth of learning in general, it is our intention to employ him, so that sciences and arts may flourish more and more in our realm. In consideration of the said rank of our privy councillor in the judicature it pleases us to appoint his yearly salary at one thousand Albertus-talers, which are to be paid out to him punctually every year on our behalf; for this we shall issue the necessary orders; his service begins from the date indicated below.

In confirmation whereof we issue these letters under our own signature and with our seal of state affixed.

Given at Karlsbad, November 1, 1712.

(Signed) Peter

(Countersigned) Count Golovkin

[Draft of Leibniz's memorandum on the improvement of arts and sciences in Russia, 1716:]

The improvement of arts and sciences in a great empire involves:

1. Procurement of necessary equipment.
2. Training of men in sciences already established.
3. Discovery of new knowledge.

Equipment consists of books, museums ["curiosity collections"], instruments, and exhibits of works of nature and of human contrivance.

Under the heading of books one should consider libraries, bookshops, and printing presses. As for libraries, it seems to me that a great monarch like the tsar must always strive to set up as complete a library as possible, especially because there will be but few libraries in his realm for a long time to come. At the other extremity of Europe, the king of Portugal, in whose country there was also a great lack of foreign books, is now likewise setting up an expensive library.

Such a library should contain both manuscripts and printed books, and I do not doubt that His Tsarist Majesty can acquire from Greece, Turkey, and Persia many manuscripts as yet unknown in Europe. . . .

A central library of this kind should be so constituted that one could find in it the fullest possible information on all the histories, lands, languages, objects of nature and of art, business, science, professions, and trades; it should also contain the entire treasure of man's knowledge in so far as it is stored in writing.

Next to the library comes the museum ["collection of curiosities"], where one should find old and new medals, serving as a source and confirmation of history; remains of Roman, Greek, Hebrew, Chinese, and other antiquity; all kinds of rare objects from the three realms of nature, namely all sorts of mineral stones, ores, plants, insects, and strange animals; also all kinds of works of art—paintings and sculptures; as well as optical, astonomical, architectural, military, nautical, mechanical, and other inventions. To all these I would add all kinds of tools that a builder, an engineer, a mechanic, or an astronomer may need; they do not take up much space, and can be exhibited in a room. . . .

So much for the equipment for sciences and arts. Let us now consider the ways and means of bringing them to the people. These include schools for the children, universities and academies for the young people, and finally scientific and learned societies and other [associations] for those who are advanced in their studies and are concerned with the improvement [of knowledge].

. . .

Lastly we must consider the institutions for new discoveries by which sciences are advanced; here the extensive lands of the Russian Empire, with so many possessions in Europe and others adjoining Asia, offer excellent opportunities; for Russia is almost virgin soil and is still insufficiently explored; thus it should yield many plants, animals, minerals, and other natural objects that have not yet been described.

At Your Tsarist Majesty's command it could be found out whether Asia can be circumnavigated on the north, or whether the edge of the ice cap is attached to America, which is something that the English and the Dutch have tried in vain to discover during their dangerous sea explorations.

Finally, Your Tsarist Majesty can render a great service to navigation by conducting assiduous observations of magnetic variations in your far-flung empire and in the neighboring lands in order to come closer to solving this mystery. This will be of great help in determining longitude at sea, i.e. how far east or west one is—in short, the exact spot on the sea one finds oneself at—even if it does not fully solve this problem.

X:51. THE DECREE ON THE FOUNDING OF THE ACADEMY OF SCIENCES, JANUARY 28, 1724

The problem of higher education and scientific research in Russia presented many difficulties, chiefly because of the deficiency of primary and secondary education, although progress had been made in this field during Peter's reign. In 1698 Peter's project to transform the Greco-Slavo-Latin Academy into a university met with a cool reception on the part of Patriarch Hadrian. Gradually Peter was won over to the idea of setting up an academy of sciences as the highest institution of learning; he thought that this would later force his successors to develop its educational base. The final order to establish the academy was given in 1718, but it took several years to work out the particulars. Finally one of the court physicians, Laurentius Blumentrost (1692-1755), who was in charge of the tsar's library and museum, presented a detailed project, which Peter approved on January 22, 1724, and which was incorporated into the decree establishing the Academy of Sciences. The first session of this academy was held after Peter's death, on November 12, 1725. Most of its members had been recruited abroad. Laurentius Blumentrost was its first president and retained this position until he fell into disgrace in 1733 under Empress Anne.

Reference: *PSZRI*, 1st ser., 7:220-24.

His Imperial Majesty has ordained the establishment of an academy where [it would be possible] to study languages as well as other sciences and fine arts, and where books would be translated. On January 22 [1724] His Majesty, after examining in his winter house the project for the establishment of this academy, wrote the following resolution on it with his own hand: "Assign for the maintenance of this [academy] the customs and export license revenues collected in the cities of Narva, Dorpat, Pernau, and Arensburg—24,912 rubles [yearly]." . . .

Project for the Establishment of an
Academy
Two types of establishments are normally used for the development of arts and sciences:

one is called a university, and the other, an academy, or society of arts and sciences.

1. A university is an association of learned men who teach the young men high sciences, like theology, jurisprudence, medicine, and philosophy up to the limit to which these sciences have been developed. An academy is an association of learned and skilled men who not only know their respective sciences to the extent to which they are developed but also seek to perfect and to develop them further through new discoveries (and publications), while taking no pains to teach others.

2. Though academy and university both comprise the same sciences and the same [type of] members, there is no connection between them in some countries, where the large number of learned men makes it possible

to set up several [learned] assemblies. This is done so that teaching duties would not interfere with the speculations and research of the academy, whose sole purpose is to improve arts and sciences—from which both university professors and students benefit; at the same time the university should not be distracted from teaching by various ingenious investigations and speculations, which would leave the young men unattended to.

3. Since it is now necessary to create in Russia an establishment for the development of arts and sciences, it is impossible to adopt the pattern followed in the other states, for we must consider the conditions existing in this country. . . .

5. Thus the most appropriate type of an association [for Russia] would be one consisting of the very best men of learning who would:

a. develop and perfect the sciences, but in such a way that they would at the same time

b. teach young men publicly (those who are found fit for it) and

c. give special instruction to several men who would then be able to teach the fundamentals of all the sciences to young men. . . .

7. . . . The sciences to be represented in this academy can generally be divided into three classes: the first class to comprise the mathematical sciences and all that depends on them; the second class—all parts of physics; and the third class—the humanities, history, and law. . . .

11. The duties of the academicians are as follows:

a. To seek out everything that has already been achieved in the sciences; to perform the tasks necessary for their correction and expansion; to make reports on all their discoveries in this connection, and to give them to the secretary, who must then edit [and publish] them at the appropriate time.

b. Every academician must read the good authors in his field who publish their works abroad; it will thus be easy for him to draw up a summary of such works; these summaries shall be published by the academy at designated times, together with [the academy's] other findings and deliberations.

c. Since the academy is nothing but a society of persons who must cooperate with one another in the development of sciences, it is highly important that they should meet together for several hours every week. Each member could then present his own opinions, benefit from the advice and opinions of others, and check in the presence of all the members experiments that he had performed alone; this last feature is especially necessary, for very often in the conduct of such experiments one member will hold another to a perfect demonstration [of his discovery]—for instance, the anatomist might do it with the mechanist, and so forth.

d. The academy must also:

i. Examine all the discoveries that will be made from time to time in the abovementioned sciences, and give its candid appraisal as to whether they are correct.

ii. Determine whether [these discoveries] are of great or of little use.

iii. Determine whether they were known before or not.

e. Should His Imperial Majesty demand from an academician an investigation of some matter within the sphere of his science, he must perform it with the utmost application and report on it after a reasonable lapse of time (for there are many matters that appear to be simple, but demand time-consuming research).

f. Each academician must draw up a system or an exposition of his science for the benefit of students, which shall then be published in Latin at the expense of the imperial government. And since it would redound not only to the great benefit but also to the glory of the Russian people to have such books published in Russian [as well], let each class of the academy have a translator attached to it; likewise, one translator shall be attached to the secretary.

h. It is necessary to organize a library and a natural science collection, so that the academicians will not suffer from any lack of materials they need. The librarian shall have control over this [collection] and shall be empowered to order the books and instruments needed by the academy [from abroad] or to have [the instruments] made here . . . the treasury shall pay for the things that an academician needs for his experiments, both private and public.

X:52. THE MANIFESTO ON AND THE STATUTE OF THE HOLY SYNOD, JANUARY 25, 1721

With the establishment of the Holy Synod, at first known as the Ecclesiastical College (Dukhovnaia Kollegiia), on January 25, 1721, the Russian patriarchate was officially abolished and the collegiate principle was introduced into the administration of the Russian Orthodox church. The synod remained the supreme administrative organ of the Russian church until the restoration of the patriarchate in 1917. This reform brought the Russian church under closer control of the state and relieved Peter of the fear that a powerful church leader might arise to oppose his work. The secular government exerted its influence mainly through the *ober-prokuror* (high procurator or high attorney), a lay official sitting in the synod; his instructions were substantially the same as those of the procurator general (see Section B of this chapter). The manifesto on and the statute of the Holy Synod, excerpts from both of which are given below, were drawn up by Theophanes Prokopovich (see below); yet Stephen Iavorskii, Theophanes' rival and a convinced opponent of this reform, was to be the first president of the Ecclesiastical College.

Reference: *PSZRI,* 1st ser., 6:314–18. See also the decree on the duties of the ober-prokuror, June 13, 1722: ibid., pp. 721-22.

[Manifesto on the establishment of the Holy Synod, January 25, 1721:]

Having looked into the situation of the clerical estate, we found it full of disorder and quite lacking in direction, and our conscience became troubled with unfeigned fear lest we appear ungrateful in the eyes of the Almighty, if, after receiving so much help from him in reforming both our military and our civil orders, we were to neglect to do the same for the clerical estate.... Therefore, following the example of the pious tsars of antiquity, both in the Old Testament and in the New, we have conceived a care for the improvement of the clerical estate, for which end we can see no better means than to set up a conciliar administration. For a single person is seldom unbiased, and, since his power is not hereditary, he often takes poor care of his office. [Hereby] we establish an Ecclesiastical College, that is, a conciliar ecclesiastical administration, which shall administer all manner of ecclesiastical affairs in the Church of All Russia in accordance with the statute laid down below. We command all our faithful subjects of all the estates, both clerical and temporal, to consider this [council] as an exalted and plenipotentiary administration, to which they must apply for final decision, resolution, and direction in all cases pertaining to church administration; they shall consider its judgments final and shall obey its decrees in all matters, in preference to those of the other colleges, on pain of severe punishment for resistance and disobedience.

[The statute of the Holy Synod, January 25, 1721:]

PART I.

What is an Ecclesiastical College, and what are the chief advantages of such an administration?

A government college is nothing but a governing council wherein certain appropriate matters are administered not by a single person but by several suitable persons appointed by the supreme power.... We present here important considerations showing that this conciliar administration is an ancient institution; and, like the synod or sanhedrin of old, it is more perfect and better than government by a single person, especially in a monarchy, such as our Russian state.

1. First of all, truth is more likely to be found by a conciliar assembly than by one person....

2. ... A council's decision carries greater persuasion and induces more obedience than a personal decree. The power of the monarchs is autocratic, and God himself commands scrupulous obedience to them; yet they have their advisers, not only the better to find the truth, but also to prevent unruly people from vilifying this or that order of the monarch as despotic or capricious rather than prompted by considerations of justice and truth. How much more is this true of the church, whose government is not monarchic, and whose governors are forbidden to dominate over the clergy....

5. But what is most beneficial is that in a

college of this kind there is no room for favoritism, chicanery, or bribery to influence its judgments. . . .

6. Moreover, a college has more spiritual freedom to render justice than an individual administrator, who may fear the wrath of the mighty. . . .

7. Of great importance also is the fact that with a conciliar [church] administration the country need not fear as many riots and turmoils as are occasioned when there is a single spiritual director for the whole country. For the common people do not perceive the distinction between the spiritual power and the [temporal] autocratic one; overawed by the great honor and glory of the highest spiritual pastor, they imagine him to be [so exalted] a ruler that he is like a second sovereign, of equal power with the autocrat, or even greater than he, and they regard the clerical estate as a separate and a better state; this kind of thinking is ingrained among the common people. What happens when vain words of ambitious ecclesiastics are added thereto, acting like a fire lit under dry brushwood? Thus simple hearts are led astray and look to the supreme religious pastor [for guidance] in all affairs rather than to their sovereign. And when they hear of any rift between these two, they blindly and foolishly obey their religious pastor rather than their secular ruler, and they have the temerity to take up the cudgels and mutiny on his behalf; these reprobates delude themselves that they are laboring for God himself and that they are not defiling but sanctifying their hands even when they turn them to bloodshed. There are some crafty individuals, who are not themselves of the common people, who are delighted to see such opinions held among the populace. . . . What would happen if the chief pastor, puffed up with such an opinion of himself, were to be devoured by a craving for power? It is hard to describe the great calamities that arise out of such situations.

This is not just an imaginary hypothetical situation, for it has in fact occurred a number of times in many states. It is enough to examine the history of Constantinople after the time of Justinian to see many examples of it. It was precisely in this way that the pope has had so much success: not only did he put a full end to the Roman state and arrogate to himself a large part thereof, but on a number of occasions he shook even the other states almost to their utter ruin. And let us not mention the similar turmoils that we have had [in Russia]. . . .

8. There is another advantage both for the church and for the state from such a conciliar administration: in cases of serious misdemeanor, not only each member, but even the president, or chairman, himself will be subject to the judgment of his peers, that is, of the college itself—which is not the procedure followed when a single autocratic pastor exercises dominion, for he would not wish to be judged by his subordinate bishops. . . . The result is that to deal with such a wicked monocrat an ecumenical council must be convened, which entails great difficulties for the country and is quite costly. Moreover, under the present circumstances, with the Eastern patriarchs living under the Turkish yoke, and the Turks being more than ever apprehensive of our state, it would seem virtually impossible [to convene such a council].

9. Finally, such a governing assembly will be like a school of church administration.

X:53. THEOPHANES PROKOPOVICH: THE JUSTICE OF THE MONARCH'S WILL IN DESIGNATING THE HEIR TO HIS REALM, *1722*

Theophanes (Feofan) Prokopovich (1681-1736; appointed bishop of Pskov in 1718 and archbishop of Novgorod in 1720) was one of Peter's closest collaborators in ecclesiastical and other affairs (see above). The treatise from which excerpts are given here was written on the occasion of the promulgation of the statute on succession to the throne, in 1722, and was first published in the same year. *The Justice of the Monarch's Will (Pravda voli Monarshei . . .)* can be taken as a fairly faithful representation of Peter's views and became a classic statement of the ideology of Russian "enlightened despotism." In 1727, under Catherine I, it was prescribed that this treatise be read in churches, after mass, on Sundays and holidays.

Reference: *PSZRI,* 1st ser., 7:604-05, 614, 619, 622-25.

Foreword

... [Prokopovich declares that this book is
not written for the benefit of those versed in
political philosophy. Nor is it meant to lend
force to the monarch's statute on succession
to the throne.] For the monarch's statutes
and laws are perfectly confirmed by the
Power Above and require no aid from the
reasoning of the teachers. Moreover, anyone
who would claim to second the determinations
of the sovereign would be guilty of no small
transgression against the unconditional sovereignty of the autocrats, for he would thereby cast doubt upon [the validity of] these
determinations, as if they were of uncertain
force unless confirmed by the reasonings of
the teachers.

The only reason for writing this book is
that among our people there are a number of
hotheads, consumed with the itch of contradiction, who do not wish to praise any decision emanating from the sovereign power. In
their stubborn and malicious hearts—and
sometimes with their spiteful tongues—they
decry the very things they themselves had
approved and honored, if only they see them
laid down in the monarch's edict. These villains seduce and confuse the simple souls, to
their temporal and eternal undoing; they sow
the weeds of riot in our country and bring
the Russian people into disrepute among
foreigners, making it appear as though its
manners were barbarous, its loyalty to its
sovereigns a mere pretense, and its obedience
not filial but slavish, given only because of
the [ruler's] wrath and not for conscience's
sake.... Therefore we have judged it proper
to write this booklet, with the consent of
both the spiritual and the lay authorities, and
with the gracious approbation of His Imperial
Majesty. For though the monarch's statute
mentioned above contains sufficient demonstration of its justice, [my booklet] will treat
this subject somewhat more clearly and at
greater length....

The Justice of the Monarch's Will
in Designating the Heir to His Realm

... Every father has the right to cast his
son out of the state of primogeniture, to deprive him of a part or of the whole of the inheritance, if he sees that his son is ungrateful,
rejects his father's advice, and shows no hope
of repentance.

Knowing this, who can doubt that fathers
who are at the same time autocratic sovereigns
[have the same right]? ... For an autocratic
sovereign is sovereign not only over his subject
people, but over his children as well.

· · ·

All the nations, Slavic and others, use the
title of "majesty" to designate the highest and
unsurpassable honor; it is applied to supreme
rulers only. This title points not only to their
very high dignity, than which, under God,
there is none higher in the world, but it also
implies the supreme legislative power, the
power to judge without appeal and to issue
incontrovertible orders, while [this power]
itself is not subject to any laws. It is thus that
the most eminent jurists define "majesty";
for instance, Hugo Grotius says: "sovereign
power (termed majesty) is one whose actions
are not subject to control of another power,
so that they cannot be rendered void by another human will." [Note: Cf. H. Grotius, *De
jure belli ac pacis*, bk. 1, chap. 3, par. 7; the
words "(termed majesty)" were inserted by
Prokopovich.]

· · ·

If we consider the heavy duty laid upon
the tsars by God himself, we shall understand
not only that it is not a sin for them to choose
their successor according to their will but also
that it would be a sin for them not to do so.
It is the duty of a tsar ... to keep affliction
away from his subjects and to procure them
the best possible instruction, both for their
godliness and for honorable living. To preserve
his subjects from affliction the tsar must strive
[to uphold] true justice in the state, so as to
protect his [weaker] subjects from offenders,
and also to maintain a strong and efficient
armed force to defend the whole country
against its enemies. As for providing the best
possible instruction, the tsar must see to it
that there be a sufficient number of skilled
teachers, both clerical and lay. On all these
duties the sovereign can find much instruction
in the Holy Scriptures....

If the autocrat must take so much care of
the common good of his subjects, then how
can he fail to see to it that his successor be
good, vigorous, and skillful? Such a one as
would not only preserve intact the good condition of the country, but would confirm and
strengthen it, and strive to bring to perfect
completion whatever he may find unfinished?

Of what benefit will be his good administration of the state if he leaves it to an unskilled and lazy heir, more likely to fritter away than to strengthen the general welfare? Would not he himself be the author of all the confusion and ruin wrought by his heir? Of what profit would it be that he has done much good for his country, if he himself destroys it all through his incompetent successor? . . .

If a monarch is so unfortunate in his sons that he does not think any of them capable and fit to govern, then it is his duty before God, to whom he must render account for his stewardship, to find a capable and virtuous [person], if need be outside his family, and to designate him his successor. This duty derives from the obligations that we have discussed above, which are imposed upon the tsars by God himself.

[There follows a brief discussion of democracy, aristocracy, monarchy, and mixed forms of government.] . . . This diversity of government clearly shows that every form of rule, including hereditary monarchy, has its inception from the original consensus of the people, always and in all places wisely [directed] by the Divine Providence. . . .

The will of the people at the founding of an elective monarchy can be expressed in the following words: "We all desire unanimously," say the people to the first monarch, "that you govern us for our common good as long as you live. We all divest ourselves of our will and shall obey you without reserving for ourselves any right of general direction—but this only until your death. After you die, however, we shall again resume our will [and the

right] to give the supreme power over us to whomsoever we deem worthy of it and on whom we agree."

In a hereditary monarchy, the will of the people was thus expressed to the first monarch, if not in words, then in deeds: "We all desire unanimously that you govern us for our common good forever: that is, since you are mortal, you must yourself leave after you a hereditary ruler for us. We, for our part, having once divested ourselves of our will, shall never exercise it again, not even after you die; but we bind ourselves and our posterity by an oath to obey you and your heirs after you."
. . .

It must be understood that the will of the people, be it in an elective or in a hereditary monarchy, or in other forms of government, does not act without special intervention of God. . . . It acts moved by God's decision, for, as the Holy Scripture clearly teaches, and as we have amply shown above, there is no power but of God. Therefore all the duties of the subjects to their sovereign and of the sovereign to the common good of his subjects derive not only from the will of the people, but also from the will of God. . . .

The duties of the subjects are as follows:

The people must obey all the orders of the autocrat without contradiction or murmur . . . for since the people have divested themselves of their general will and have given it up to the monarch, they must obey his orders, laws, and statutes without raising any objection. . . .

[Further down, the author discusses at length the advantages of hereditary over elective monarchy.]

CHAPTER XI

Between Peter I
and Catherine II,
1725-1762

The Supreme Privy Council (Verkhovnyi Tainyi Sovet) was set up under Catherine I as the chief policy-making body. Its membership reflected an uneasy compromise between the old aristocracy, led by Prince Dimitri Golitsyn, and the upstarts who had reached high rank under Peter the Great, like Prince Menshikov. The latter had the upper hand under Catherine I, while the old aristocratic group predominated during the reign of Peter II (1727-30). With the establishment of the Supreme Privy Council, the Senate lost its attribute of "Governing" and became simply "the High Senate," thus being officially relegated to a subordinate position.

Reference: *PSZRI*, 1st ser., 7:568-69.

We have deemed it beneficial and have [accordingly] ordered that there be established at our court, from now on, a Supreme Privy Council for important external and internal affairs of state, in which we ourselves shall be present. Those of the first senators who are thus to attend our person shall be replaced in the Senate by other persons chosen for it, who will occupy themselves with senatorial duties exclusively. The following persons shall attend us in the Supreme Privy Council: Field Marshal General and Right Privy Councillor Most Serene Prince Menshikov; Admiral General and Right Privy Councillor Count Apraksin; State Chancellor and Right Privy Councillor Count Golovkin; Right Privy Councillor Count Tolstoi; Right Privy Councillor Prince Golitsyn; Vice-Chancellor and Right Privy Councillor Baron Osterman. . . .

In pursuance of the above decree of Her Imperial Majesty on the Supreme Privy Council it was decided as follows: (1) Decrees that are to be sent to the Senate, to all the colleges, and to other offices shall have the heading: "A Decree of Her Imperial Majesty decreed in the Supreme Privy Council." . . . (2) Reports submitted by the Senate and all the colleges on the most important affairs shall have the heading: "A Report to the Supreme Privy Council."

XI:2. THE DECREE ON THE REDUCTION OF ADMINISTRATIVE OFFICES, MARCH 14, 1727

The Supreme Privy Council had to deal with the aftermath of some of Peter the Great's half-digested reforms and with the overburdening of the population with service obligations and taxes. Its general tendency was toward leniency in tax collection, greater freedom of trade, and, above all, simplification of Peter's government apparatus which was too complex to function smoothly, especially in the provinces. Prince Dimitri Mikhailovich Golitsyn (1663-1737) was the chief advocate of these measures. Given below is an excerpt from one of the decrees worked out by the Supreme Privy Council.

Reference: *PSZRI*, 1st ser., 7:760-61.

4. Whereas the growing number of administrators and offices in the realm not only tends to swell the number of officials but also greatly increases the burden of the people; for where previously they would have recourse to one judge to petition about their affairs, they now have to appear before ten or more, each of whom has his own office, clerks, and particular court, where he drags out proceedings concerning the affairs of poor people—not to mention various other disorderly practices daily indulged in by shameless men to the greater overburdening of the populace: we have therefore ordained the complete abolition of the superior provincial courts [*nadvornyi sud*] and the elimination of all superfluous administrators and their offices and bureaus of accounting, [such as] *kameriry* [local collectors of customs and excise revenue], land commissioners [see Item X:38, above], and the like. All the administrative and judicial power shall be vested in the governors and voevody, as was the case before; appeals from [the judgment of] the governors are to be sent to the College of Justice. This will bring relief to the subjects, who will henceforth deal with one office instead of many different offices and judges; however, this decree notwithstanding, the conquered provinces of Livonia and Esthonia shall continue to be administered in accordance with their privileges.

XI:3. THE "CONDITIONS" OF ANNE'S ACCESSION TO THE THRONE, 1730

After the death of Peter II, during the night of January 18-19, 1730, the Supreme Privy Council, then consisting of five members, invited three other dignitaries to join it in deliberating on succession to the throne. The resulting assembly consisted of four of the princes Dolgorukii, two Princes Golitsyn, Count Golovkin, and Baron Osterman. This group decided to offer the crown to Anne, the dowager duchess of Courland, daughter of Ivan V and niece of Peter the Great; the offer, however, was hedged with certain conditions, which Anne signed in Courland. Set down below is most of the final text of these *konditsii,* rather hastily drawn up on January 19, mainly under the influence of Prince Dimitri Golitsyn, an admirer of the Swedish constitutional developments of 1719-20 which had put the aristocracy in the saddle in that country. (The document uses the first person singular and plural forms interchangeably.)

Reference: Dimitri A. Korsakov, *Votsarenie Imperatritsy Anny Ioannovny* (Kazan', 1880), pp. 17-18. This document is included in Marc Raeff, *Plans for Political Reform in Imperial Russia, 1730-1905* (Englewood Cliffs, N.J.: Prentice-Hall, 1966), pp. 41-52.

We hereby give a most binding promise that my main concern and effort shall be not only to maintain but to spread, as far as possible and in every way, our Orthodox faith of the Greek confession. Moreover, after accepting the Russian crown, I will not enter into wedlock so long as I live; nor will I designate a successor, either in my lifetime or after. We also promise that, since the safety and welfare of every state depends upon good counsel, we will always maintain the Supreme Privy Council as it is at present established with its membership of eight persons. Without the consent of this Supreme Privy Council:

1. We will not start a war with anybody.

2. We will not conclude peace.

3. We will not burden our faithful subjects with any new taxes.

4. We will not promote anybody to high rank—above that of a colonel—either in the civil or in the military service, be it on land or on the sea; nor will we assign any important affair to anybody; the Guards and the other regiments are to remain under the control of the Supreme Privy Council.

5. We will not deprive members of the gentry [*shliakhetstvo*] of life, possessions, or honor without [due proceedings in] a court of law.

6. We will not grant any patrimonies [*votchiny*] or villages.

7. We will not promote anyone, whether Russian or foreigner, to an office at court without the advice of the Supreme Privy Council.

8. We will not spend any revenues of the state.

And [we also promise] to maintain an unalterably gracious disposition toward all our faithful subjects.

Should I not carry out or fail to live up to any part of this promise, I shall be deprived of the Russian crown.

XI:4. ANNE'S MANIFESTO ON THE RESTORATION OF AUTOCRACY, FEBRUARY 28, 1730

The Supreme Privy Council tried to keep the conditions imposed on Anne secret at least until her arrival in Moscow for the coronation ceremony. However, rumors of the council's proceedings soon leaked out, and the conditions were read to the Senate and the Holy Synod on February 2; they met with an icy reception. The lower nobility and the Guards were especially disturbed by the oligarchic nature of the proposed form of government. The next few weeks witnessed much agitation: many constitutional projects were drawn up, most of them hostile to the Supreme Privy Council. Some professed to prefer autocracy to oligarchy. In the confusion that followed, Anne, who had arrived from Courland on February 10, found it easy to tear up publicly, on February 25, the conditions she had signed. Given below is an excerpt from Anne's manifesto on the restoration of autocracy. A few days later, on March 4, the Supreme Privy Council was abolished, while the "Governing Senate" was restored in its functions.

Reference: *PSZRI,* 1st ser., 8:253. See also Korsakov, *Votsarenie Imperatritsy Anny Ioannovny,* pp. 240-78. Cf. the manifesto on the suppression of the Supreme Privy Council and restoration of the Governing Senate, *PSZRI,* 1st ser., 8:253-54.

After our safe and happy arrival in Moscow and accession to the Russian throne, our faithful subjects, both clerical and lay, have taken an oath of allegiance and loyalty to us and to the state. But since our same faithful subjects, thereafter, have all unanimously begged us to deign to assume the autocratic power in our Russian Empire as it had been held of old by our forefathers, we have, in consideration of their humble plea, deigned to assume the said autocratic power.

XI:5. DISPATCHES OF CLAUDIUS RONDEAU, 1730-1731

Claudius Rondeau served in Saint Petersburg first as secretary to the British consul (1728-31) and later as British minister-resident (1731-40). Given below are excerpts from two of his dispatches sent to the secretaries of state for the Northern Department. The dispatch of February 2, 1730 reports on one of the many constitutional schemes rife at that time; it happens to be an outline of Prince Dimitri Golitsyn's project for a final constitutional settlement.

Reference: *SIRIO*, 66:133-34, 271-73. Cf. Korsakov, *Votsarenie Imperatritsy Anny Ioannovny*, pp. 179-82.

[Rondeau to Viscount Townshend, Moscow, February 2, 1730:]

If the russ mind to make use of the present juncture, they may perhaps be so happy as to get themselves freed from their ancient slavery. Since His Czarish Majesty's death, field-marshal prince Dolgoruky and Galitzin have taken place in the high council.

I cannot yet acquaint your lordship with certainty what form of government the russ design to settle, but it is generally whispered:

1. that the empress is to have a fixed sum allowed for her household and she is to command no part of the army but the guard that will be actually on duty in her pallace;

2. there is to be a high council composed of 12 of the most considerable of the nobility, who are to manage all the affairs of great consequence, as peace and war, or making alliances. A treasurer of the crown is to be named who is to give account to the high council how he disposes of the government money;

3. there is to be a senate of 36 persons, who are to examine the affairs before they are brought to the high council;

4. there is to be an assembly of 200 of the little nobility to maintain their rights in case those of the high council should encroach upon them.

5. there is to be an assembly of gentlemen or merchants, who are to take care that the people are not oppressed.

This in general is the scheme they are working upon. As yet they are not very well agreed amongst themselves how to settle it, but they have gone too far to go back, which obliges most people to think they certainly will make some considerable alterations.

[Rondeau to Lord Harrington, Moscow, January 4, 1731:]

I beg leave to begin this new year by informing your excellency of the miserable condition this court is now in.

The old russ nobility are very uneasy to see how the affairs of this country are managed and that they find themselves entirely excluded from Her Majesty's confidence, who is wholly and absolutely governed by her favourite count Biron, the two counts Levenwolde, Paul Iwanitsch Jaguginsky [Iaguzhinskii], and baron Osterman, who seems a little more in favour than he was some time ago. As all [?] those gentlemen are foreigners and continually about Her Majesty, she grants no favours but through them, at which the russ are enraged, and even the Czarinna's nearest relations have hardly anything to say.

The two regiments of guards grumble very loudly that the Czarinna or some of her favourites seem to have a greater confidence in the third regiment, called Ismailowsky, than in the others, which are composed of the best families in the country, and what yet adds to their uneasiness is that a regiment of horse-guards is also raising, which is to be called life-guards. . . .

Your excellency cannot imagine how magnificent this court is since the present reign, though they have not a shilling in the treasury, and, of course, nobody is paid, which contributes very much to the general complaints. Notwithstanding this want of money, great sums are laid out by all courtiers to get magnificent habits for the mascarade, which we are soon to have, and a fine troop of comedians is daily expected from Warsaw, which are sent by the king of Poland to divert Her Majesty, who thinks of nothing else, and to heap up riches and honour on count Biron, and to enrich his brother also.

XI:6. THE INHERITANCE LAW OF MARCH 17, 1731

During the agitation of February 1730, the lower nobility voiced a number of political and social desires. The latter included repeal of the inheritance law of 1714 (see Item X:36) and of the obligation to serve in the ranks prior to receiving a commission in the army (see Item X:11), as well as a limitation of the required term of service. The next three documents reflect the attempts of Anne's government to satisfy at least some of the social desires of the lower nobility. The present excerpt is from the decree on inheritance. (During this period, reflecting Peter's introduction of foreign terms, the nobility or gentry were referred to in official documents as the *shliakhetstvo*. In the latter part of the century the traditional term *dvorianstvo* came back into official use.)
    Reference: *PSZRI,* 1st ser., 8:396.

Following the decrees of our forefathers, and in accordance with the law of God and the precepts of the holy apostles, the Conciliar Code of Laws [of 1649] declared that fathers must divide their movable and immovable property in equal shares among their children, while widows were to be assigned for their sustenance a certain income from the pomest'ia of their deceased husbands as well as the patrimonial estates bought during their married life. However, in the year 1714 . . . Peter the Great deigned to promulgate a special law which did away with these divisions [of property] and provided for settlement of the estate on one heir [only] in accordance with primogeniture; his most gracious intention was to prevent the impoverishment of families and illustrious houses ensuing from subdivision of landed property. Nevertheless, fathers, moved by natural tenderness for their children, endeavored by every means, regardless of cost and ruinous expense, to divide their estates in equal parcels between their children; they would do it through [fictitious] sales and mortgages to various people, and those who were unable to complete such transactions in their lifetime would seek various other means, such as exacting a heavy oath from their children to divide the inheritance remaining after their death equally among themselves. These practices gave rise to hatred and squabbles between children and between relatives, and some have gone so far as to commit murder. Therefore we, Our Imperial Majesty, moved by zeal to [restore] the law of God, and taking pity on our loyal subjects, have most graciously ordained that henceforth, in pursuance of this present decree of ours, both the pomest'ia and the patrimonial estates shall be classed alike as patrimonial [votchina] immovable property; fathers and mothers are to divide them equally among all their children in accordance with the Code [of 1649]; likewise let them settle dowries on their daughters as of old.

XI:7. THE DECREE ESTABLISHING A MILITARY SCHOOL (CORPS OF CADETS) FOR SONS OF THE GENTRY, JULY 29, 1731

Attendance at the special Corps of Cadets (Kadetskii Korpus, or military academy), which was set up in 1731, counted as service in the ranks; thus, a son of a nobleman, on leaving this school, could immediately receive his commission in the army or an equivalent rank in the civil service. The school was organized by Field Marshal Count Münnich (1683-1767), who had entered Russian service in 1721 as a military and civil engineer. Prince B. G. Iusupov, the superintendent of this school during the reign of Elizabeth, was a great lover of the theater; with his encouragement the cadets staged many plays, both Russian and foreign, and their amateur troupe played an important role in the development of the Russian theater (see Item XI:16, below).
    Reference: *PSZRI,* 1st ser., 8:519. Cf. statute of the Corps of Cadets, Nov. 18, 1731: ibid., pp. 557-59.

[During the reign of Peter the Great] good order [was introduced and] has been maintained to this day in our military affairs. However, to foster the highest possible proficiency in this glorious art, so necessary for the state, it is essential that the gentry should be taught its theory from an early age, so that they would be prepared to practice it later. Therefore we have ordained the establishment of a Cadet School for two hundred sons of the gentry between the ages of thirteen and eighteen, both of the Russian and of the Esthonian and Livonian provinces. They are to be taught arithmetic, geometry, drawing, fortification, artillery, fencing, horsemanship, and other sciences and skills needed in the military art.

However, since nature does not predispose everyone to the military profession exclusively, and since the state needs political and civil education no less, let this school also have teachers of foreign languages, history, geography, law, dancing, music, and other useful subjects, which students would be made to study in accordance with their natural abilities.

XI:8. THE MANIFESTO ON THE GENTRY'S SERVICE, DECEMBER 31, 1736

In 1731 a committee was set up under the chairmanship of Field Marshal Münnich to study the conditions of the gentry's service. The new provisions that the committee worked out, some of which are set forth in the manifesto below, were to go into effect after the termination of hostilities with Turkey. But as soon as the Turkish war had ended in 1739 there was such a rush to get out of the service that the government had to retract some of its concessions: a nobleman could leave the armed forces only after twenty-five years of genuine, active service; the procurator general had to examine each application for retirement; and no civil servant was to retire under the age of fifty-five (cf. Item XI:10). It was only during the reign of Peter III that the gentry's desire to escape from service was fully satisfied (see Item XI:19, below).

Reference: *PSZRI*, 1st ser., 9:1022.

Moved by motherly compassion, we have most graciously ordained to establish the following rules for the good of the state and for the better maintenance of noble families and of their estates: (1) A father who has two or more sons should appoint one of them—whomsoever he chooses—to remain at home to manage the estate; likewise, if there are two or three brothers remaining without parents who would wish to leave one of themselves to look after their villages and estates, they may do so at their discretion. However, those who remain at home must be sufficiently instructed in reading, writing, and at least in arithmetic, to be suitable for civil service. (2) All the other brothers, whatever their number, must enter military service as soon as they are ready for it. However, until now, there has been no provision fixing the length

of military service so that at present [many] are retired from it so old and decrepit that, on returning home, they are incapable of properly looking after their estates. Henceforth, all nobles from the age of seven to twenty must attend to their studies; at the age of twenty they must enter military service and must remain in military service for twenty-five years counting from the time they attain the age of twenty. After [serving] twenty-five years they should all be promoted to the next rank and retired from military or civil service, with permission to go home, even though they may be fit to be retained in the service; however, those who volunteer to continue to serve may do so. . . . (4) Those who remain at home in the manner described above and do not enter military service must supply recruits in their stead from among their serfs . . . at the rate of one recruit for every hundred serfs.

XI:9. THE DISPATCHES OF EDWARD FINCH, 1741

Edward Finch was British minister plenipotentiary at the Russian court from June 1740 to February 1742. His report on Elizabeth's coup d'état is all the more interesting because he had been instrumental in warning the government of the regent Anne of the danger that Princess Elizabeth and her entourage presented to it. This circumstance, which was known to Elizabeth, brought an end to Finch's usefulness as a diplomatic representative at the Russian court. Here are excerpts from two of Finch's dispatches to Lord Harrington, secretary of state for the Northern Department.

Reference: *SIRIO*, 91:111-12, 338-40.

[Saint Petersburg, June 2, 1741:]

After all the pains which have been taken to bring this country into its present shape,

by which it is so nearly connected with the rest of Europe, and has so great a weight in the affairs of it, I must confess that I can yet see it in no other light, than as a rough model of something meant to be perfected hereafter, in which the several parts do neither fit nor join, nor are well glewed together, but have been only kept so first by one great peg and now by another driven through the whole, which peg pulled out, the whole machine immediately falls to pieces. The first peg was Peter the great, the present is count Osterman; let him drop, whose age and infirmities cannot set it at a great distance, and what will follow must soon be seen.

[Saint Petersburg, November 26, 1741:]

The princess Elizabeth, universally beloved and adored in this country, went yesterday morning about one o'clock to the barracks of the Preobrazensky guards, accompanied only by one of her chambellans, m-r Vorontzoff, m-r Lestock, her surgeon, and m-r Swartz, who, I think, is her secretary, and, putting herself at the head of the 300 grenadiers with their bayonets screwed and granadoes in their pockets, she marched directly to court, where, after having made the proper dispositions and possessed herself of the different avenues, she seized the young monarch [Ivan VI] and the little princess, his sister, in their cradles, the great-duchess regent [Anne, Duchess of Brunswick-Wolfenbüttel]

and the duke generalissimo [Anthony Ulric, Duke of Brunswick-Wolfenbüttel] in their beds, and sent them all with the favourite, Julia Mengden, to her house. The princess immediately after ordered the field-marshal Munich, count Osterman, count Golofkin, young count Munich, master of the household to the great-duchess, and the president of the college of commerce, Mengden, with their wives to be seized in their beds and carried likewise to her own house or those joining to it. The prince Lewis [Anthony Ulric's brother] is under arrest in the palace, the grand-marshal count Lowenwold, m-r Lapokin [Lopukhin], count Golofkin's lady, and his sister, countess Jagozinsky [Iaguzhinskii] are so in their houses; the duke's two adjutants also: Haimbourg at court, and Gramatin in his lodgings.

After all these orders had been executed with the greatest expedition, the princess returned to her own house, whither almost everybody in town immediately resorted, and before which the regiment of horse guards and the three of foot were drawn up, and she was unanimously declared sovereign of Russia, and the oath of fidelity taken to her. About two Her Majesty took possession of the winter palace, upon which the cannons of the citadel and admiralty were fired between two and three.

XI:10. GENERAL MANSTEIN'S MEMOIRS, FROM THE 1740s

Christoph Hermann von Manstein (1711-57), whose father had entered Russian service under Peter the Great, served as a colonel in the Russian army from 1736 to 1744; in 1739 he was made chief aide-de-camp to Field Marshal Münnich. The hostility of Elizabeth's chancellor, Bestuzhev-Riumin, made him leave Russia; he entered the army of Frederick the Great and ended his days as a Prussian general. Manstein wrote his *Memoirs of Russia from the Year 1727 to 1744* in French for the benefit of Frederick the Great, and the final text was polished by Voltaire. A manuscript copy of these memoirs came into the hands of David Hume, who published an English translation of it in 1770. The original text of Manstein's memoirs was first published in Paris in 1860, the French editions of 1771 and 1772 being retranslations from the English version.

Reference: Christopher Hermann von Manstein, *Memoirs of Russia from the Year 1727 to 1744*, ed. David Hume (London, 1770), pp. 255, 279-83, 321, 395-97, 407-08, 416. Cf. Christopher Hermann von Manstein, *Mémoires historiques, politiques et militaires sur la Russie depuis l'Année 1727 jusqu'à 1744, par le Général de Manstein*, 2 vols. (Paris, 1860), 2:103-04, 232, 323-26, 328, 349-50, 352-53, 368-69, 382-83. Russian translation: *Zapiski Manshteina o Rossii, 1727-1744* (St. Petersburg, 1875; supplement to *Russkaia starina*), pp. 186, 248, 294-96, 306-08, 316, 322-23. An English edition of 1856 has recently been reprinted (New York: Da Capo, 1968).

[1740:] The Empress [Anne] . . . caused an edict to be published, in which permission was given to every gentleman who had been twenty years in the army, and had made

campaigns, to petition for leave to lay down the service; but no sooner was this ordinance published than the number of petitioners was excessive. Half, at least, of the officers presented petitions for leave to resign; each pretending to have served above twenty years. There were seen young men who were scarce past thirty, that insisted on their discharge; for having, at the age of ten or twelve years, had their names inrolled in some regiment, they reckoned from that date the time of their service. Several even who had not a copeck at home, preferred, however, retiring to their respective countries, there to cultivate their fields with their own hands, to the military service. This made it necessary, some months after, to repeal the ordinance.

. . .

[1741:] . . . It was reckoned that since the commencement of the Empress Anne's reign, there had been above twenty thousand sent to Siberia. There were five thousand of them, of which the habitation could never be discovered, nor any of the least news learnt of what was become of them. But as the Empress [Elizabeth] had recalled all that could be found, there was not a day passed but there were seen at court some new faces of persons who had passed several years successively in the most horrid prisons.

. . .

Supplement to the Memoirs of Russia . . . But then this vast empire is far from being so well cultivated and peopled as most of the other nations in Europe. There are several deserts from 80 to 120, and even to 200 English miles, in which there is not a living soul to be found, though some parts of these deserts are situated in a very good climate, and have the best soil that could be wished.
. . .

According to the last numbering in the years 1744 and 1745 of the people of those provinces which properly constitute Russia, there were seven millions of males from the age of four years to that of sixty, who pay the capitation or poll-tax. Seven millions might be allowed for women, children, and old men. The Russian nobility, with their families, might be computed at five hundred thousand. The officers of the revenue and clerks of the chancery, who form a class apart, are, with their wives and children, reckoned about two hundred thousand. For Livonia, Ingwa [Ingria], and Finland provinces, which are not comprehended in the capitation, there are allowed six hundred thousand souls: as for the Cossacks of the Ukrain, of the Don,

of the Jaick [Iaik], as well as for the different nations of heathens that inhabit Siberia and the frontiers of Auria [China] and Japan, they are computed at a million eight hundred thousand: the total making about eighteen millions four hundred thousand individuals.

Neither is the revenue which the sovereign draws from these vast dominions proportioned to their extent; they amount at most to twelve or thirteen millions of rubles, which makes pretty near sixty-five millions of French livres, reckoning five livres to the ruble (not three millions sterling). I have been at a great deal of pains to come at the knowledge of the specific sums of all the different branches of receipt, in order to give a more satisfactory account on this head, without being able to get at any thing authentic, as the several colleges which administer the revenue keep a profound secret upon it.

The capitation is levied on none but the males, from the age of four to sixty. The inhabitants of town and country are comprehended in it. Every citizen pays a hundred and twenty copecks a year, and every peasant seventy-four. [Note: The English translation in Hume's edition gives the figure twenty-four, which is a misprint.] . . . Though these revenues appear so little in proportion to the greatness of the empire, they are, nevertheless, sufficient, not only for the common expenses of the state, but for extraordinary exigencies.
. . .

It must also be granted that the Russian army cannot make, for any series of years together, campaigns at a distance from their frontiers, especially in countries where the provisions and necessaries for the maintenance of troops are dearer than in Russia, for their pay, which is sufficient for the army when it remains within the Russian territories, where every thing is comparatively cheap, is too little on its coming into parts where every thing is at a higher price. . . .

It may, in general, be demonstrably averred, that there is a scarcity of money in Russia, nothing being more common than to pay twelve, fifteen, and even twenty per cent. interest for it.

Under the ancient Czars, the revenues were yet smaller than they are at present. It is only since Peter I that they have augmented.

. . .

At length, in 1724, he [Peter the Great]

was resolved to found an academy at Petersburgh, taking that of Paris for his model in every thing; and, at the outset of it, to give a lustre to this new establishment, he engaged several men of literature, of the highest reputation, such as Wolff, Bernouilli, Hermann, de l'Isle, etc. to become members. He gave them great stipends; and assigned for the support of the academy an annual fund of twenty-five thousand rubles (above 5,000 pounds) on the customs of Narva, Pernow [Piarnu, Pärnu, Pernau, Pernov], and Dorpat.

The Emperor did not live long enough to have the satisfaction of seeing this work finished; but his first physician, Bluckmentrost [Blumentrost], whom he had made president of the academy, with a stipend of three thousand rubles a year (600 pounds) preserved influence enough to have the inauguration of it solemnised in the reign of Catherine. And though a great part of the ministry were against this establishment, which they considered as useless to the state, Blumentrost, however, found means to keep his ground even in the reign of Peter II.

When the Empress Anne came to the throne, Blumentrost was disgraced; but as the academy was an establishment founded by Peter I Anne was induced to preserve it. . . .

. . . This academy is not managed or ordered in such a manner that Russia can ever hope to have the least advantage from it. For the languages, morality, the civil law, history, and practical geometry, which are the only sciences that are the most eminently useful to Russia, are not the greatest objects of their application. It is to algebra, to speculative geometry, and to the other points of sublime mathematics; to critical solutions and researches on the habitations and languages of some ancient people; to anatomical observations on the structure of man, and of other animals, that all the attention is given. Now, as the Russians consider all these sciences as

frivolous, and even useless, it is not at all astonishing, that they should not care to send their children to study at the academy, though all the lessons are given gratis. This is so far true, that the number of professors in it has very often exceeded that of the students, and that they have been obliged to bring youth there from Moscow, to whom pensions were given to excite them to study, that the professors might have at least the appearance of some to attend their lessons.

· · ·

[James] Bruce . . . was the person that in the reign of Peter I made the first good orders and establishment in the board of ordnance, so that it may now be confidently averred that the Russian artillery is in as good condition and as well served as most in Europe. Few are equal to it, and fewer yet surpass it, for it is the only branch of the art of war to which the Russians apply themselves with great assiduity, and in which there are very able officers of the nation itself.

The number of cannon in this empire is infinite. In 1714, it was reckoned at thirteen thousand pieces, and has, since that time, been considerably augmented, as they have kept constantly casting new guns at six different foundries, of brass at those of Moscow and Petersburgh, and of iron at those of Woronitz [Voronezh], Olonetz, Seisterburgh [apparently Sestroretsk], and Catherinenburgh. . . .

When Peter I died, he left his marine in very good condition; his magazines well stored; in short, a great abundance of every thing necessary for completing the naval armaments. For, as it was his ruling passion, he had spared neither pains nor money to put every thing into the best order possible. He had, especially, expended immense sums in bringing to his country able ship-builders and other artists necessary for the formation of a navy. In the reign of Catherine, the marine began to decline; and under that of Peter II it was totally neglected.

XI:11. JONAS HANWAY ON RUSSIA, CA. 1750

Jonas Hanway (1712-86), an English merchant of the Russia Company, had had some experience in foreign trade in Lisbon before he entered into partnership, in 1743, with Dingley, an English merchant settled in Saint Petersburg. In 1743-44 he encountered many adventures during a trip to Persia with a wool caravan. Hanway returned from Russia to England in 1750 and devoted the rest of his life to philanthropy and writing. He published an account of his sojourn and travels in Russia and Persia in 1753.

Reference: Jonas Hanway, *An Historical Account of the British Trade over the Caspian Sea, with a Journal of Travels from London through Russia into Persia and Back,* 2 vols. (London, 1753), 1:92-94; 2:123-27, 131, 136-38.

Mosco . . . is built in some measure after the eastern manner, having not many regular streets, but a great number of houses with gardens. Its circumference is about 16 English miles. . . .

The number of churches and chapels in Mosco, is hardly within belief: they are estimated above 1800, but many of them are very mean: most of the paintings were done when this art was in its infancy.

The most remarkable thing I saw, is the great bell, which is indeed stupendous, and surprizes equally on account of its size, and the folly of those who caused it to be made: but the Russians, for time immemorial have had a strange ambition of this kind. . . .

. . . Being in the heart of the empire it is the grand residence of that part of the nobility which is not obliged to follow the court; and it is particularly inhabited by the chief merchants and manufacturers. This city having for many ages frequently suffered by dreadful fires, which have swept away several thousand houses at a time, it would be amazing that they should still continue to build with wood, were it not that the cheapness of this kind of building, and the poverty of many of the inhabitants render it necessary. . . . It is the custom in Russia to build very fast, and without proper attention to the quality of the materials. Mosco has been more than once ravaged by the TARTARS and POLES; it yet shows many antient works of defence, but the present pacific state of this country renders the fortifications less an object of regard.

. . .

I shall now make a few general remarks in regard to the commercial interest of Russia. The productions of the earth, and foreign trade are acknowledged to be the great sources from whence the riches of every nation proceed: Russia has made great strides in the improvement of her commerce for several years past, enjoying some advantages beyond any other nation: the number and greatness of her rivers open a communication almost to every part of the globe, but particularly within her own extended dominions. As to timber, hemp, and iron, which are the instrumental causes of trade, no country in the world produces a greater quantity, which is

a natural consequence of the cheapness of land and labour. . . .

. . . Iron is a very improveable article; they have both wood, hands and oar [ore] in Siberia sufficient to make a quantity, which would depreciate the value of the Swedish iron, raise their rivalship and competition with the Swedes in this important article of the revenues of that nation, and at the same time greatly augment those of the Russian empire. . . . It is not 40 years since the Russians began to open iron mines, and yet in the year 1750 they exported 20,000 tons: the ordinary annual export may now be called 12 or 15,000 tons, which is so much more in favour of the Russians, as the Swedish forges, for these few years past, have not produced so much by one third as formerly.

. . .

The ordinary computation of the Russian general export from St. Petersburg is three millions (in 1750, the exports were four millions of rubles, or 880,000 pounds value), of which the British subjects in Russia take off two, consisting chiefly in hemp, flax, iron, hog's bristles, hare skins, hempen and flaxen manufactures, Russia leather, and other articles. The ordinary imports of the Russians were two millions, consisting in indigo, cochineal, lead, pewter, tin, wrought silks, gold and silver lace, toys, cotton and linnen manufactures, woollens and wines. The Russians receive the ballance in their favour in silver and gold. . . .

The interior trade of Russia is certainly very much augmented, and the commerce they carry on with the Tartars and other frontier nations, is a considerable object, as Russia sometimes receives a large quantity of foreign silver and gold from those nations, in exchange either for her own or foreign productions.

. . .

The empress Elizabeth Petrowna . . . is one of the most accomplished ladies of her rank, nor was her person less amiable: time, which wears off the charms of youth, has rendered her corpulent, but she is yet very active, dances, hunts, and rides on horseback: on certain days she appears in men's cloaths, particularly on the day of her accession to the throne, when she treats her life-company of granadiers at supper in the grand saloon of the palace, and sits at table with her officers, in regimentals as their colonel, in which she makes an agreeable figure. . . . The Empress is in every instance gracious to an extreme: the great tenderness of her heart, or some other cause, has even forbid the execution of malefactors of whatever denomination, so that it is said there have been in different parts of the empire near 30,000 criminals in prison at one and the same time; but this, among many good actions, is a species of mercy which neither her subjects nor foreigners pretend to understand.

. . .

The revenues of the Russian empire, which were formerly of five millions only, are now encreased to 15 millions of rubles, and are yet improvable without distressing the subject. These may be computed to arise from the pole tax of 75 copecks a head, on 8,750,000 male subjects. The boyar, or lord, receives of his boors about 120 copecks each head male, according to the goodness of the estate: some bring in yet more considerably, and others cannot support themselves. The lord has also a certain number of them to work for him, but he pays the tax due to the crown on all his vassals, and after a revision

is made, the same tax continues whatever mortality may succeed till a further revision takes place. . . .

The pay of a major-general in Russia is not above 3,600 rubles a year, a commandant or brigadier 1,800, a colonel 800, a major 400, a captain 180, a lieutenant 120, and a common soldier 6. They are said to have at least 250,000 regulars, including garrisons of 70,000; and supposing a third part of them cloathed annually, and giving them their allowance of salt, croop, and bread, their pay will hardly exceed 30 rubles a man, officers included; and consequently this formidable force costs only 7,500,000 rubles, which does not take up half the national income.

. . .

The number of souls in St. Petersburg are generally computed at 250,000, including the garrison, which is numerous; but in reckoning the subjects throughout the whole empire, they lay it down as a rule, that the hundred and seventy fifth male raises an army of near 50,000 men, and consequently supposing an equal number of females, the whole may be reckoned 17,500,000 souls: the tributary Tartars, the Russian Ukrain, and the conquered provinces, are not included in this account; if we consider the vast extent of that empire, though many parts are not inhabited, it is probable this number is near the truth.

XI:12. THE DECREE ON THE ABOLITION OF INTERNAL CUSTOMS DUTIES, DECEMBER 20, 1753

This measure was worked out by Count Petr Ivanovich Shuvalov (1710-62), one of the most influential persons in Elizabeth's government. By their origin the Shuvalovs belonged to the poor gentry, but, being attached to Elizabeth's household, they made their fortune after her accession to the throne. Peter Shuvalov became a senator, a minister of state ("conference minister"), head of the Cadastral Office, and chief of artillery, to mention only a few of the posts he held. Few dared to contradict him in the Senate. His own industrial enterprises, fisheries, and various monopolies were spread all over Russia. His detractors alleged that he promoted the abolition of internal customs mainly for his personal profit and convenience. Nevertheless, the many projects and reports that Peter Shuvalov drew up, dealing chiefly with economic and military affairs, show a thorough insight into the economic conditions and needs of the country. Among the many other measures authored by Peter Shuvalov are the cadastral survey and the foundation of state banks in 1754 (see below).

Reference: *PSZRI*, 1st ser., 13:947-48.

We have . . . observed that the collectors of customs duties and tolls inside the state cause great hardships to those who are liable to these imposts. Though after due investigation the malefactors do not go unpunished, these malpractices—surcharges, extortions, and pilfering—seem to continue; they give rise to many in-

vestigations and special commissions which interrupt the normal course of current business in government offices and courts, while merchants incur many losses: their trade is interrupted and their competitors gain an unfair advantage over them. For these reasons, and especially in order to increase the

welfare of the people and their strength . . .
we [hereby] free our faithful subjects from
internal customs duties and retail taxes inside
the state. . . . [There follows a list of seven-
teen categories of internal customs and tolls
to be abolished.] We therefore most graciously command the closing of all customhouses
within the state, with the exception of those
at the seaports and at the frontiers. These
customhouses being abolished, the collection
of duties enumerated above will cease. Instead
of the abolished customs and tolls, the customhouses at the seaports and at the frontiers
shall collect a single internal customs duty
for all goods imported and exported at the
rate of thirteen copecks per ruble ad valorem.
No further internal duty shall be imposed on
goods for which this customs duty has been
paid. [This customs duty] for imported goods

shall be paid by both foreign and Russian
merchants, while for exported goods it shall
be paid by our subjects [only], since the
Russian merchants, our subjects, will henceforth buy and sell all goods within our state
duty free. The current practice is to impose
a sales tax of one grivna [ten copecks] per
ruble on every sales transaction, which sometimes results in the same article being taxed
three times or more if it is resold. From now
on these merchants, our subjects, will be
free of all such impositions; they shall pay
internal customs only at the seaport and
border customhouses, as explained above, at
the rate of five copecks per ruble as before,
plus an additional eight copecks per ruble.
. . . The present decree is to take effect on
the first day of April, 1754.

XI:13. THE INSTRUCTIONS TO CADASTRAL SURVEYORS, MAY 13, 1754

The alienation of taxable lands, especially in favor of the church, presented a problem in the
eighteenth century as it had in the fifteenth. The excerpt given below is taken from the "Instructions to the Cadastral Surveyors" drawn up by Peter Shuvalov in 1752 and promulgated May 13,
1754, in the section, "On the lands of the Viatka and Ustiug Provintsii and other districts containing state peasants." The same rule, making the alienation of state peasants' lands by private
individuals null and void, was later repeated in the cadastral survey instructions of 1766 (*PSZRI,*
1st ser., 17:769).
Reference: *PSZRI,* 1st ser., 14:147.

6. During this land survey it may become
apparent that, since the promulgation of the
Code [of 1649], some state peasants in the
Viatka provintsiia and in other districts have
given part of their taxable lands, village allotments, and various other holdings to the
diocese or to monasteries and churches for
requiem services or as donations; or . . . that
they have sold, mortgaged, or otherwise given
away [such possessions] . . . to men of different conditions who are not registered as
poll-tax payers in these districts . . . or that

such lands were adjudged to others by the
[local] authorities in settlement of claims
against [their possessors]. All such lands,
village allotments, and various other holdings
mortgaged, sold, donated, or given away for
requiem services or in settlement of claims
shall be confiscated without monetary recom-
pense from the said diocesan, monastic, and
church estates [votchiny] and from the men
of different conditions described above; they
shall revert to their former status of state
lands held by state peasants [chernososhnye
krest'iane].

XI:14. THE DECREE ON STATE LOAN BANKS, MAY 13, 1754

The foundation of the state banks in 1754 was prompted mainly by the government's desire to
prevent the impoverishment of the gentry and to strengthen Russian foreign trade; the latter was
apt to be adversely affected by the increase in export and import tariffs in 1754. According to
Peter Shuvalov's project, the initial capital for these credit establishments (750,000 rubles for the
nobles' bank and 500,000 rubles for the merchants' bank) was to come from the spirits monopoly.
The decree on state banks contained, in addition to the provisions illustrated in these excerpts,
other provisions for the punishment of usurers.
Reference: *PSZRI,* 1st ser., 14:87.

The following announcement is to be brought to public notice: Many of our Russian subjects—especially the gentry—who need money are forced to borrow it at usurious interest and on securities whose value sometimes exceeds the loan by 50 or 100 percent; those who cannot manage to redeem them within the time specified are thereby brought to poverty and ruin; some are forced to pay, not just 12, but 15 or even 20 percent interest [on loans], which is not done anywhere in the world; and there are also some shameless robbers who refuse to return the security if the borrower repays his debt but a few days late . . . thus making him lose a valuable asset on account of a small sum of money. We have therefore most graciously directed our Senate to establish state banks, with large funds to be deposited by our treasury, for the purpose of lowering interest rates on loans in the whole country: the first such bank—with branches in Moscow and Saint Petersburg—shall be for the gentry; the second—for the merchants, in order to improve commerce at the port of Saint Petersburg. The first bank shall make loans to Russian gentry exclusively . . . the second, exclusively to the Russian merchants trading in the port of Saint Petersburg. . . . Branches of these banks shall be run in exactly the same manner as foreign commercial banks, maintaining their ledgers and books. . . . These branches of the bank shall loan money to the Russian gentry at the rate of 6 percent annual interest, and no more; and the amount loaned to each applicant shall be from 500 to 10,000 rubles. [The rate of 6 percent also applied to loans to the merchants of Saint Petersburg.]

XI:15. THE DECREE ON THE FOUNDING OF MOSCOW UNIVERSITY, JANUARY 24, 1755

The founding of a university was a logical, though a belated, step after the establishment of the Academy of Sciences (see Item X:52, above). The person mainly responsible for it was Ivan Ivanovich Shuvalov (1727-97, a cousin of Peter Shuvalov), who was chiefly interested in the arts, science, and education. Together with his friend and protégé Lomonosov (1711-65), the famous scientist, Ivan Shuvalov worked out the detailed plan for Moscow University, and when it was established he was appointed its chancellor ("first curator"). The university subsequently celebrated its birthday not on January 24 but on January 12, the day the "project" received the empress's approval.

Reference: *PSZRI*, 1st ser., 14:284-90.

Our . . . glorious, beloved father and sovereign, Peter the Great, emperor and reformer of his fatherland, did his utmost to bring the enfeebled Russia, sunk in the depths of ignorance, to an understanding of the true welfare of mankind. Not only does Russia feel [the effects of] his labors . . . but the greater part of the world has witnessed them. His most useful enterprises were not brought to perfection . . . in his lifetime; however, by the benevolence of the Almighty, we have constantly applied ourselves since our accession to the throne of all Russia to bring to completion all his glorious enterprises, as well as to promote [new ones] for the benefit and welfare of our whole country. . . . All that is good proceeds from an enlightened mind, which also serves to eradicate evil; for this reason it is a matter of urgent necessity to strive to increase every kind of useful knowledge in our extensive empire through fostering appropriate sciences. Consequently, our Senate . . . has submitted to us . . . the following report presented [to it] by our right honorable chamberlain and cavalier Shuvalov, to which was appended a project . . . for the establishment in Moscow of one university and two secondary schools [*gimnazii*]. Sciences are both necessary and useful everywhere: it is through them that educated nations are raised and glorified above those that live in the darkness of ignorance. In our lifetime we have had visible proof of this, inasmuch as the divinely inspired undertakings of our father and sovereign, Emperor Peter the Great, for the good of our empire, owe their success to [the application of] science. To his undying glory . . . his deeds, which surpass imagination, brought about in a short time a change of long-established habits, customs, and prejudices. . . . Though the Saint Petersburg Academy . . . bears useful fruit through its international reputation and the benefits it bestows on this country, this learned body alone does not suffice . . . for our far-flung empire. . . . Our said right honorable chamberlain and cavalier Shuvalov [therefore] recommends that there be established for the education of nobles who may desire it . . . and for the general education of commoners [*raznochintsy:* men of no specific estate] in higher learning, a university in Moscow . . . following the pattern of European universities, in which men of all conditions have free access to sciences. [He also recommends that there be established] two secondary schools: one for nobles, and one for commoners, with the exception of serfs. . . . He gives the following reasons for choosing Moscow as the seat of this university: (1) the large number of nobles and commoners residing there; (2) its geographical position near the middle of the Russian state makes it easily accessible; (3) the cost of living is relatively low; (4) nearly everybody has relatives or friends living there with whom he can find lodging and board; (5) the large number of tutors whom the landlords [pomeshchiki] maintain at great expense in their Moscow residences; most of these tutors are incapable of teaching anything, never having mastered the rudiments of knowledge themselves; thus they only waste the young years of their charges—the best time to receive instruction—while drawing high pay and serving no useful purpose. . . . [Shuvalov believes] that the institutions described above will help to overcome these shortcomings in instruction . . . especially when they start to produce enough Russians competent in sciences, who are needed in our extensive empire to explore its hidden resources, to complete the undertakings that have been started, and to set up schools in important Russian towns staffed by Russian teachers. Even among the common people in the remote regions such schools would eventually help to eradicate superstition, schisms, and heresies stemming from ignorance.

For the above reasons we have most graciously confirmed the project of the said chamberlain and cavalier Shuvalov . . . and are confident that all our loyal subjects will strive to give their children a decent upbringing and education which would make them fit to serve us and to enhance the glory of the country.

. . .

Project for a University in Moscow

2. The following measures are considered essential for the encouragement of learning:

(1) Her Imperial Majesty should herself assume the high protectorship over the university and should . . . appoint one or two of the most illustrious persons to be its chancellors ["curators"], as is usually done in other countries; they would supervise this entire body and report on its needs to Her Imperial Majesty. (2) This institution must not be subject to any office other than the Governing Senate and must not be forced to receive any orders from anybody else. (3) Without the knowledge and [express] permission of the chancellors and of the director of the university, no court other than that of the university itself must be empowered to cite the professors, teachers, or any other persons enjoying the protection of the university. . . .

5. The total number of professors in the three faculties of the university shall be ten:

In the Faculty of Law:

1. The professor of general jurisprudence, who shall teach natural law and the law of nations, as well as the law of the Roman Empire, both ancient and modern.

2. The professor of Russian jurisprudence, who must also be versed in internal constitutional law and teach it as a separate subject.

3. The professor of politics should lecture on international relations, alliances, and policies of states and sovereigns, both past and present.

In the Faculty of Medicine:

1. The professor of chemistry—a doctor—shall teach physical chemistry and pharmacology as two separate subjects.

2. The professor of natural history—a doctor—shall lecture on various types of minerals, plants, and animals.

3. The professor of anatomy—a doctor—shall teach the structure of the human body; he shall demonstrate it in the anatomic theater and shall also train students in medical practice.

In the Faculty of Philosophy:

1. The professor of philosophy shall teach logic, metaphysics, and ethics.

2. The professor of physics shall teach both experimental and theoretical physics.

3. The professor of eloquence shall teach rhetoric and prosody.

4. The professor of history shall expound universal and Russian history, as well as archaeology and heraldry.

XI:16. THE DECREE ON THE FIRST STATE THEATER IN SAINT PETERSBURG, AUGUST 30, 1756

The theater had had a more or less continuous history in Russia since the reign of Tsar Alexis. In the first half of the eighteenth century there were a number of more or less permanent troupes, both professional and amateur, at court, in the cadet academy (see Item XI:7, above), and in the households of individual noblemen and even merchants. A young merchant from Iaroslavl', Fedor Grigorievich Volkov (1729-63), became an enthusiast of the theater during his visit to Saint Petersburg in 1746, when he frequented the Italian opera and some of the performances at the Cadet Academy. Upon returning to Iaroslavl', Volkov founded a troupe of his own, which soon became so famous that, at Empress Elizabeth's bidding, it was brought to Saint Petersburg to give command performances at court. Many of Volkov's actors were lodged, and some were even enrolled, in the Corps of Cadets. Volkov's troupe was the kernel around which the first permanent Russian state theater was built in 1756. Its director, Aleksandr Petrovich Sumarokov (1718-77) was himself a writer of tragedies in the classical style; he was an alumnus of the Corps of Cadets, where his tragedy *Khorev* was first produced in 1747. Moscow did not lag far behind Saint Petersburg: in 1757, Mikhail Matveevich Kheraskov (1733-1807), an epic poet, founded the Moscow Public Theater.

Reference: *PSZRI*, 1st ser., 14:613.

We have ordered that there be established a Russian Theater for the presentation of tragedies and comedies; we assign for its use Golovin's stone house on the Vasilii Isle (Vasilievskii Ostrov] near the House of the Cadets. Actors and actresses are to be engaged for this theater: actors, from among the student singers and members of the Iaroslavl' troupe, who are now at the Corps of Cadets, as well as others who are not in the service—as many as are needed; likewise, let a sufficient number of actresses be engaged. For the maintenance of the said theater . . . the sum of 5,000 rubles [shall be] paid yearly from this day on.
. . . We appoint Brigadier Alexander Sumarokov director of this Russian Theater. . . .

XI:17. THE DECREE FOUNDING THE ACADEMY OF ARTS, NOVEMBER 6, 1757

The project for the Academy of Arts was worked out by Ivan Shuvalov (see Item XI:15, above), who was himself an art collector and a Maecenas. At the time of its opening, the academy offered drawing, sculpture, and architecture as its main subjects; painting and etching were soon added.

Reference: *PSZRI*, 1st ser., 14:806-07.

Moscow University reports to the Governing Senate that it is essential to establish an academy of arts in order to bring to perfect completion the development of sciences that has had its beginning in Moscow thanks to the generosity and under the protection of Her Imperial Majesty. . . . The fruits of such an institution, when they ripen, are expected not only to enhance the glory of this empire but also to have a very good effect on works of art commissioned by the state and by private individuals. Heretofore such works have been performed by foreign artists of mediocre talent who, having grown rich on enormous fees, return home; so far, they have not left behind a single Russian sufficiently trained in any art. The reason for this is that many young men who have a great desire and even greater natural talent for artistic work are not versed in foreign languages that would enable them to understand the instruction of their masters; they have even less grounding in the fundamentals of sciences that are necessary for the arts. Should the Governing Senate accept and approve this proposal—just as it has approved the proposal on the establishment of the university—then it would be possible to select several gifted students at the university who have already been put to study the languages and sciences connected with the arts; with such students, good results and success will not be long in coming. This academy should be established here, in Saint Petersburg, since the best foreign artists do not wish to go to Moscow, both because they hope to receive orders from the court, and because foreigners generally find life here more to their liking. . . .

[The Governing Senate] has decreed: To establish the said academy here, in Saint Petersburg. Lieutenant General and Cavalier [Ivan] Shuvalov, chancellor of Moscow University, must work out a [detailed] project of the said [institution] and present it to the Governing Senate.

XI:18. THE DECREE EMPOWERING LANDLORDS TO EXILE THEIR RECALCITRANT SERFS TO SIBERIA, DECEMBER 13, 1760

With the promulgation of this measure the legal status of the serfs reached its nadir. What prevented this measure from being widely applied was the reluctance of the landlords to part with cheap labor, for the serfs transported to Siberia escaped from personal dependence on the landlord and eventually acquired a status not unlike that of state peasants.

Reference: *PSZRI*, 1st ser., 15:582-84.

The following decree is brought to public notice:

Whereas there are very good lands that are suitable for settlement and agriculture in the Siberia guberniia, in the Irkutsk provintsiia and in the Nerchinsk uezd, and whereas the interest of the state demands that they be settled, therefore the Governing Senate has decreed to publish the following decree in the whole state: (1) Some of the landlords [pomeshchiki] may wish to send away their serfs and peasants, male or female, who, instead of rendering the services appropriate to their condition, cause much harm, destruction, loss, and turmoil by their thievery, drunkenness, and other unbecoming and insolent actions, and who, moreover, set a bad example to others like them. For the said bad conduct such peasants may be delivered up for settlement on the above-mentioned lands, provided that they are fit for peasant and other labor and are not over forty-five years of age. They are to be accepted for transportation to Siberia pursuant to personal attestations of the landlords themselves or of their agents.

. . . [Upon delivery of these men] the landlords or their agents shall be given appropriate recruit receipts, without delay or expense to themselves, which they shall present at future recruit levies [to acquit themselves of their obligation]. The married men shall be delivered with their wives; if they have small children whom the landlord may wish to leave with their parents, the treasury shall pay the landlord . . . ten rubles for each male child under five years of age and twenty rubles for each [male] child between the ages of five and fifteen; for each [male] child of fifteen or more no money shall be paid, but a recruit receipt shall be issued; for female children [the rate] shall be half of the above. . . . [The receiving agents] must make certain that the delivered serfs are in good health and without physical defects. . . . [The landlords had to provide these serfs with clothing and pay for their upkeep until their actual departure for Siberia at the rate of twenty rubles per single man, fifteen rubles for a married couple, and ten rubles for a family with one or more children.]

XI:19. PETER III'S MANIFESTO GRANTING FREEDOM AND LIBERTY TO THE RUSSIAN GENTRY, FEBRUARY 18, 1762

Earlier documents have shown the attempts of the nobility to escape from, or at least to limit, the heavy service obligations imposed upon it by Peter the Great. Peter III's enactment of 1762 gave virtually full satisfaction to this desire. It represents a reversal of the trend that had been apparent in Russia since the fifteenth century to tie more and more groups to the service of the state. Logically, the charter of the gentry should have been immediately followed by a charter freeing the serfs from the power of the landlords, since previously the justification invoked for the growing dependence of the serfs on their masters had been the unlimited service obligations of the nobility. That it took the Russian government ninety-nine years to complete this step is one of the anomalies of Russian legal and social history.

This "Charter of Liberty" turned the Russian nobility into a truly privileged order, a situation that persisted until about the middle of the nineteenth century. The gentry who went to live on their estates contributed toward raising the intellectual level in the provinces and gave Russian cultural life a leisurely, rural imprint for the next several generations. With their obligatory tie to the government severed, many of the gentry went their own way and eventually began to develop various tendencies in opposition to the government. From a purely constitutional point of view, the charter of 1762 purports to be a step toward a restoration of the concept of fundamental law and away from the unlimited sovereignty of Peter the Great.

Reference: *PSZRI,* 1st ser., 15:912-15. A translation of this document is included in Basil Dmytryshyn, ed., *Imperial Russia: A Source Boqk, 1700-1917* (New York: Holt, Rinehart and Winston, 1967), pp. 57-60. Dmytryshyn also contains translations from several other eighteenth-century sources. In addition to that work and others already cited in the reference notes, students may consult Marthe Blinoff's *Life and Thought in Old Russia.* It includes quite a few excerpts from eighteenth- and nineteenth-century documents grouped under topical headings.

In virtue of the power vested in us by the All Highest, we, by our imperial benevolence, do hereby grant freedom and liberty to all the noble Russian gentry [dvorianstvo] and their descendants from now on in perpetuity: they may continue their service in our empire as well as in other European states allied with us on the basis of the following enactment:

1. All gentry now employed in our various services may continue to serve for as long as they desire or their condition permits; however, no military man shall be so bold as to ask for release or retirement from service in the course of a campaign or within three months prior to the opening of a campaign. . . .

4. Our College of Foreign Affairs shall issue appropriate passports without any hindrance to those who, after release from our service, may wish to go abroad to other European countries. However, the gentry sojourning abroad shall be obliged to return to their country if need arises, in which case a special proclamation shall be issued; in such [emergencies] everybody must carry out our command with all possible speed, on pain of fine and sequestration of his estates. . . .

7. Though in virtue of this present enactment . . . all the noble Russian gentry . . . shall be forever free [from service obliga-tions] . . . let no one be so bold as to raise his children without giving them an education appropriate to their noble standing, on pain of our grave displeasure. . . .

9. . . . We establish this . . . enactment in favor of all the noble gentry as a fundamental and unalterable law in perpetuity, and, in conclusion, we most solemnly confirm it, pledging our imperial word always to maintain it sacred and inviolate; and our lawful successors are not to infringe upon it in any way, for the preservation of this law shall serve them as an unshakable foundation of the autocratic throne of all Russia. At the same time we hope that all the noble Russian gentry, feeling the effects of our bounty toward them and their descendants, will be moved by their zeal and loyalty to us not to relinquish or shun our service but to enter it willingly and with eagerness. . . . We command all our faithful subjects and true sons of the fatherland to despise and to scorn as neglectful of the common good all those who have never served anywhere, who pass all their time in sloth and fail to instruct their children in the arts and sciences beneficial to their country; such persons shall be denied access to our court; nor shall they be tolerated at public assemblies and ceremonies.

CHAPTER XII

The Reign of Catherine II,
1762-1796

A. POLITICAL DEVELOPMENTS

XII:1. CATHERINE'S ACCOUNT OF HER GIRLHOOD IN RUSSIA, CA. 1744

In an autocracy the personality of the ruler assumes special importance. In Catherine's case many of the most revealing documents come from her own pen. She never wrote a comprehensive autobiography, but she did write several memoir-style accounts of portions of her life. Most of these papers were found after her death in a package addressed to her son Paul. Though copied privately and read at first by a few trusted persons, these papers were rigorously suppressed by Nicholas I, who hated the memory of his romantically energetic grandmother. After Nicholas's death some of Catherine's writings which had come into the hands of Alexander Herzen were published by him abroad, but Catherine's intimate papers remained inaccessible until 1907, when they were published by the Russian Academy of Sciences. Among them was a memoir dedicated to Countess Bruce (born Rumiantsev), excerpted here. It was begun April 21, 1771, and was written in French.

Reference: First three excerpts: *Memoirs of Catherine the Great*, trans. Katharine Anthony (New York: Knopf, 1927), pp. 45, 58, 60. Last excerpt: *The Memoirs of Catherine the Great*, trans. Moura Budberg (New York: Macmillan, 1955), pp. 62-63.

April 21, 1744, my birthday; I was fifteen years old.

After this day, the Empress and the Grand Duke wished to have Bishop Simon Todorsky of Plescau [Pskov] visit me and speak with me about the dogmas of the Greek Church. The Grand Duke thought he would convince me of what I had been firmly convinced since my first entrance in the empire—that the heavenly could not be separated from the earthly crown. I listened humbly to the Bishop of Plescau without contradicting him. I had besides been instructed in the Lutheran religion by a Churchman by the name of Wagner, a clergyman in my father's regiment, who had often told me that every Christian up to the day of his first communion might choose the religion that seemed the most convincing to him. I had not yet been to communion, and so I found that the Bishop was right in every respect. He caused my faith to grow no less, strengthened me in dogma, and had no trouble in converting me. He often asked me whether I had an objection to make or doubts to utter; but my answer was always brief and satisfactory to him, because my decision stood firm.

· · ·

When [ca. 1744] I felt that I had gained a firm foothold in Russia, I came to the following conclusion or rather made the following resolution, which I have never lost sight of for one moment:

1) to please the Grand Duke.
2) to please the Empress.
3) to please the Nation.

I would have gladly fulfilled all three points, and if I was not successful, the reason was that the matter was not of such a nature or that Providence had not so decreed it. For in truth I neglected nothing in order to achieve it; obligingness, humility, respect, the effort to please, the effort to do good, sincere affection,—everything was employed on my part from the year 1744 to 1761. I confess that when I gave up hope with regard to the first point, I redoubled my efforts and strove all the more eagerly to fulfill the other two.

· · ·

[Speaking of the year 1744, when she was 15:] Since I tried on principle to please the people with whom I had to live, I adopted their habits and customs. I wished to be a Russian in order to be liked by the Russians.

· · ·

[Speaking again of 1744:] I already had three teachers; one, Simon Theodorski [Todorskii], to instruct me in Greek religion, another, Basil Adadurov, for the Russian language, and Landé, ballet master, for the dance.

To make more rapid progress in the Russian language I jumped out of bed in the middle of the night and while everyone was still asleep I learnt by heart all the lessons set by Adadurov; as my room was warm and I had no experience of the climate, I remained barefoot and went on with my studies without slipping anything on over my nightdress. On the thirteenth day after our arrival in Moscow I caught a pleurisy from which I nearly died.

XII:2. A LETTER FROM CATHERINE TO POTEMKIN ON HER ROMANTIC ATTACHMENTS, 1774

The romantic side of Catherine's activities attracted so much attention in her own lifetime, as well as later, that it would not be hard to fill most of this volume with primary sources devoted to that topic. But the interests of scholarship dictate restraint. The following passage is taken from Catherine's letter written (in Russian) to Potemkin in 1774, before their secret marriage of that year.

Reference: *Memoirs of Catherine the Great,* trans. Anthony, pp. 324-25.

[After mentioning her years of unhappiness with Peter and her liaisons with Saltykov and Poniatowski, Catherine continues:] After 1758, and since Prince Gregory Gregorievich [Orlov] was taking so much trouble, to whom again good people called attention, my way of thinking changed! He might have stayed forever, if he had not grown tired! I learned this . . . and simply drew from this the conclusion that with this knowledge I could have no more confidence. This thought cruelly tormented me and forced me from desperation to make a choice at random [Alexander Vasil'chikov]. . . . Then came a certain hero [i.e. Potemkin himself]. . . .

Now, Sir Hero, can I hope after this confession to receive forgiveness for my sins? You will deign to see that there were not fifteen but only one-third of that. The first [Peter], against my will, and the fourth taken out of desperation, can not at all be set down to frivolity. Of the other three only think rightly. God is my judge that I did not take them out of looseness, to which I have no inclination. If fate had given me in youth a husband whom I could have loved, I should have remained always true to him. The trouble is that my heart would not willingly remain one hour without love. It is said that we strive by this to cover up our human vices, as if this had its foundation in kindness of heart. But it can happen that such a condition of the heart is more a vice than it is a virtue. But I write this to you needlessly, for according to this you will love or will not wish to go away to the army for fear I might forget you. But really I do not think that I could commit such a blunder; if you wish to fetter me to yourself eternally, then show me as much friendship as love, and above all love and speak the truth!

XII:3. CATHERINE'S EPITAPH, WRITTEN BY HERSELF, CA. 1788

Among the papers Catherine left behind was this epitaph which she composed in French, apparently in 1788 (full text).

Reference: *Memoirs of Catherine the Great,* trans. Anthony, p. 326.

EPITAPH
Here lies
Catherine the Second
born in Stettin April 21/May 2, 1729
In the year 1744 she went to Russia to marry Peter III.
At the age of fourteen she made the threefold resolution, to please her Consort, Elisabeth, and the Nation.
She neglected nothing in order to succeed in this.
Eighteen years of tediousness and solitude caused her to read many books. When she had ascended the throne of Russia, she wished to do good and tried to bring happiness, freedom, and prosperity to her subjects.
She forgave easily and hated no one.
She was good-natured and easy-going; she had a cheerful temperament, republican sentiments, and a kind heart.
She had friends.
Work was easy for her; she loved sociability and the arts.

XII:4. THE MANIFESTO ON THE ACCESSION OF CATHERINE II TO THE THRONE, JUNE 28, 1762

The opening paragraphs of the manifesto Catherine issued upon ascending the throne show how she sought to justify her usurpation.

Reference: *PSZRI*, 1st ser., 16:3; translation based on William Tooke, *The Life of Catharine II, Empress of Russia*, 4th ed., 3 vols. (London, 1800), 1:489-90, slightly revised.

It has become obvious to all true sons of the Russian fatherland what great danger has been facing the whole Russian state. First, the foundations of our Orthodox Greek religion were shaken and its traditions destroyed to such a point that the Orthodoxy established in Russia from the earliest times was in critical danger of being supplanted by an alien faith. Second, the glory of Russia, brought to a high pitch by her victorious arms at the expense of much blood, has now been trampled underfoot by the conclusion of peace with her most villainous enemy. Meanwhile, the internal regulations which are the basis of our fatherland's welfare have been entirely overturned.

Therefore, being convinced of the perils that threatened our faithful subjects, and especially seeing how obvious and sincere were their desires, we, with the help of the Almighty and his divine justice, have been obliged to ascend the sovereign imperial throne of all Russia, and have received a solemn oath of fidelity from all our loving subjects.

XII:5. REPORTS OF FRENCH DIPLOMATS AT CATHERINE'S COURT, 1762-1765

One valuable source on developments early in Catherine's reign is the reports of French diplomats. The authors of these excerpts from the period 1762-65 are: Laurent Bérenger, chargé d'affaires of the French embassy in Saint Petersburg and hence the chief French representative during the absence of the ambassador; Louis Charles August Le Tonnelier, Baron de Breteuil, French ambassador to Russia 1760-63; and Mattia Nicolas, Marquis de B(e)ausset, French ambassador to Russia 1765-67. Their reports are addressed either to Louis XV or to César Gabriel Comte de Choiseul, designated Duc de Praslin in 1763, who was French minister of foreign affairs from 1761 to 1766.

Reference: *SIRIO*, 140:1 [letter of July 2, 1762]; 646-48 [Sept. 3, 1762]; 85, 91 [Oct. 9, 1762]; 102, 117, 134, 164, 199-200, 203, 413, 542.

[From Bérenger, July 2, 1762:]

Sire: The Russian nation, highly dissatisfied with the government of Peter III, deposed him on the ninth of this month and raised to supreme power the empress, his spouse, under the name of Catherine II.

This princess already held sway over all hearts. The crown that has been bestowed upon her by unanimous and general consent will only add another title to her empire.

[From Bérenger, September 3, 1762:]

If Russian ambition is not checked, its effects may be fatal to the neighboring powers.

. . .

I know that the degree of Russian power should not be measured by its expanse and that its domination of eastern territories is more an imposing phantom than a source of real strength. But I also suspect that a nation which is capable of braving the intemperance of the seasons better than any other because of the rigor of its native climate, which is accustomed to servile obedience, which needs little to live and is therefore able to wage war at little cost, especially if the war is on its borders, which occupies only swamps or largely uncultivated terrain while the fortunes of war are uncertain, with fertile and abundant lands lying before it: such a nation, I suspect, is likely to conquer; and the history of past centuries confirms me only too well in this opinion.

It is futile to seek reassurance in the alleged laziness and inertia of the Muscovites. It is true, to be sure, that the character of this nation inclines to indolence; the excessive cold here seems to produce the same effect as the excessive heat does in Asia; one has to use force to drag a Russian away from his stove in winter; but once out-of-doors, the icicles that whiten his beard do not affect him, and he sleeps in the snow without feeling discomfort. Perhaps the prime cause of his laziness is that he has no interest whatever in the fruits of his industry; it is inconceivable how little attachment to life a Russian seems to have. When the rivers freeze and thaw, one sees people crossing them regardless of the evident danger; and if one tries to hold them back, warning them that they are risking death, they answer coolly, "Bog znaet" ("The Lord knows"), and continue on their way. A very great number of people perish in this way every year. One should not delude oneself: this contempt for life is very favorable to the plans of an ambitious ruler who will know how to put such a disposition skillfully to account.

It is still impossible to forecast what use Catherine will make of it; this princess seems to combine every kind of ambition in her person. Everything that may add luster to her reign will have some attraction for her. Science and the arts will be encouraged to flourish in the empire; projects useful for the domestic economy will be undertaken. She will endeavor to reform the administration of justice and to invigorate the laws; but her policies will be based on Machiavellianism; and I should not be surprised if in this field she rivals the king of Prussia. She will adopt the prejudices of her entourage regarding the superiority of her power and will endeavor to win respect not by the sincerity and probity of her actions but also by an ostentatious display of her strength. Haughty as she is, she will stubbornly pursue her undertakings and will rarely retrace a false step. Cunning and falsity appear to be vices in her character; woe to him who puts too much trust in her. Love affairs may become a stumbling block to her ambition and prove fatal for her peace of mind. This passionate princess, still held in check by the fear and consciousness of internal troubles, will know no restraint once she believes herself firmly established.

[From Baron de Breteuil, Moscow, October 9, 1762:]

Sire: The coronation has taken place in a most orderly and peaceful way. Public rejoicing has not been very hearty, and the measures the government took to make it appear more brilliant were visible wherever the acclaim of the populace needed to be heard. It happened at one such moment that instead of shouting "Long live the Empress Catherine II," the soldiers and the populace gathered in the inner court of the palace began to shout: "Long live our Emperor Paul Peter [Petrovich]," meaning the grand duke. The court, informed of this mistake, forthwith dispatched officers who stopped the shouting, explaining to the soldiery in a friendly way that the empress did not doubt their joy, and asked them to restrain it for the day. This little incident caused some alarm at court, but it had no consequences at all. Although the

satisfaction, Sire, is far from general, the coronation is sure to impress the malcontents greatly; and if the tsaritsa behaves moderately it is probable that she will no longer have anything to fear from plots and factions, at least not for a time. So far she has been very careful in handling everyone and has taken great pains to seduce her subjects and the court with every kind of cajolery. I have no doubt, Sire, that she will abandon this solicitude before long; her character does not allow for such assiduity, and it may be very dangerous to push it too far. The Russians are accustomed to feel the yoke and wish to be governed with some harshness.

[From Baron de Breteuil, Moscow, October 9, 1762:]

The tsaritsa plans, a few days from now, to go on a pilgrimage to the Trinity Monastery, some twenty leagues from here. She does not overlook anything to give the people a great impression of her profound piety and devotion to the Greek Orthodox faith.

[From Baron de Breteuil, October 17, 1762:]

However it be, the resentment of the yoke is remarkable; all Russians talk heatedly about their bondage. But the tsaritsa has gained everything in gaining time, and all those who are most outspoken in favor of liberty will take up their chains again and will bear them without daring, possibly without even thinking, to complain.

[From Baron de Breteuil, Moscow, October 18, 1762:]

At this moment, Sire, everything here is very quiet. This does not mean, however, that the majority of the people are contented, albeit the empress is lavish with cajoleries toward all. The Guards conduct themselves with as much license as ever, and nobody dares restrain them; no doubt the empress endures them with impatience, but her position does not allow her to lose her temper, nor even to take vigorous measures to curb the soldiery.

[From Baron de Breteuil, Moscow, December 20, 1762:]

Everything here is quiet, Sire; the malcontents keep silent, and the authority of the empress imperceptibly gains stability. . . . Monsieur Panin, who is the soul of liberty, told me a few days ago that his nation was not yet sufficiently enlightened to use absolute freedom in a moderate way and needed a reign or two more of good rulers, who would imperceptibly yield their excessive authority, so as to share it in time with the nation. Such discourse is proof of the turmoil of minds on this point. In general the nation has a taste for extremes, which are in keeping with its gross ignorance; so that one may expect a revolution some day.

[Copy of a letter from Baron de Breteuil to the empress, January 14, 1763:]

You did me the favor, Madam, of talking to me two days ago of the great love and respect of your subjects; you described these feelings as "enthusiasm" and "fanaticism." They are not the only ones who carry their admiration this far. Those who, like myself, have the privilege of knowing personally what graciousness and what amiable qualities you bring to the power of the throne will add to the homage paid to you by Europe all that is owed to you by your own subjects.

[Baron de Breteuil's copy of a letter from the empress to him, ca. January 15, 1763:]

All the pleasant and flattering things you tell me in your letter I regard as politesse. The same things, more or less, were said to Nero. Yet I know that you like me a little more than you do him.

[From Bérenger, Moscow, May 30, 1763:]

From the diversity of Russian loyalties and prejudices there have emerged three parties, more or less opposed to each other, which I divide into three groups.

The first is composed in part of persons attached to the present government because of the favors it bestows on them daily, and in part of prudent or timid persons who see the happiness of the empire in tranquillity and believe that nothing is to be gained by revolutions. This group is rather important by virtue of its numbers and the influence it derives from the positions it occupies; and only among this group can the empress expect to find the support she needs to maintain herself on the throne.

The second group consists of malcontents. They regard the accession of Catherine to the throne as altogether illegal and a usurpation

of the rights of the grand duke [Paul], sole legitimate heir to the empire. They would welcome the voluntary or enforced abdication of the empress and, for the preservation of order, would be in favor of a regency council to govern the empire in the name of the grand duke during his minority. Very important men belong to this group—generals of the army with troops at their disposal, ambitious men jealous of the favor enjoyed by the Orlovs, who are secretly or openly hostile to them, and who hope for a share in the administration of affairs in case of a change of regime.

The third group is composed of those who believe that neither the empress nor the grand duke has any right to the throne. There are some among them who would like to recall the senior line of the old Russian tsars, reestablishing Prince Ivan [Ivan VI, then imprisoned in Schlüsselburg] or, if he is not available, one of his brothers.

[From Bérenger, Saint Petersburg, June 28, 1763:]

The calm which, at the end of my stay in Moscow, followed the storm I had seen brewing in that city was a deceptive calm. Angry feelings rose so high that people were prepared to wrest the Russian scepter from Catherine's hands. The portrait of that princess, placed above a triumphal arch in the city of Moscow, was taken down and torn to pieces. But since the conspiracy had been hatched in haste and had not sufficiently matured, the plots were discovered, and the unfortunate men who had threatened the throne were detained. Sixty persons have been arrested, among them some men with titles, gentlemen of the chamber, and several Guards officers. [Note: Apparently this report of a conspiracy was based on false rumors.]

[From Bérenger, September 18, 1764 (after the election of Stanislaw Poniatowski as king of Poland):]

This proud princess will no longer doubt that she is in a position to dare anything.

[From the Marquis de Bausset, October 4, 1765:]

Discontent persists among the nobility, the clergy, and the common people, but Catherine's genius and courage still hold all classes within the bounds of respect and obedience.

XII:6. REPORTS OF ENGLISH DIPLOMATS AT CATHERINE'S COURT, 1762-1768

Another foreign perspective on Catherine's first years as empress is obtained through the dispatches of the English diplomats assigned to her court. Robert Keith was ambassador till the autumn of 1762, when he was replaced by the earl of Buckingham. Early in 1765 George Macartney assumed the post. Upon his departure two years later, Henry Shirley remained as chargé d'affaires in the interim until the arrival in the summer of 1768 of the new ambassador, Lord Cathcart. The persons to whom the letters are addressed were the successive secretaries of state.

Reference: *SIRIO,* 12:3, 9, 48, 232, 248-50, 292-93, 304-05, 309-10, 315-16, 334-35, 348, 356-57, 385. Here as elsewhere, all dates are given in the old style or Gregorian calendar unless otherwise noted.

[Robert Keith to Mr. Grenville, Saint Petersburg, July 1, 1762:]

This surprising revolution [i.e. Catherine's coup] was brought about and completed in little more than two hours, without one drop of blood being spilt, or any act of violence committed, and all the quarters of this city, at any distance from the palace, especially the street where I and most part of his Majesty's subjects reside, were as quiet as if nothing had happened; the only novelty to be seen, were some *Picquets* placed at the bridges, and some of the Horse-Guards patrolling through the streets in order to preserve the public tranquillity.

As soon as the Guards assembled in the morning, several detachments were sent to the Peterhoff road, to hinder any intelligence from being sent to the Emperor, and this piece of duty was performed with so much diligence and exactness, that no person got through except the Master of the Horse Mr. Nariskin.

About ten o'clock in the evening the Empress marched out of town, on horseback at the head of 12 or 14 thousand men, and a great train of Artillery, and took the road toward Peterhoff in order to attack the Emperor at that place or Oranienbaum or wherever they should meet him, and next day, in the afternoon we received the account of his Imperial Majesty having surrendered his person, and resigned his crown, without one stroke being struck.

· · ·

With regard to the motives of this revolution, it is plain that the taking away the Church Lands was the principal joined to his neglect of the clergy; the next was the severe discipline which the Emperor endeavoured to introduce amongst the troops especially the Guards, who had been accustomed to great idleness and licence, and the discontent among them was heightened by the resolution his Imperial Majesty had taken of carrying a great part of that corps into Germany with him, in his expedition against Denmark, which was a measure disagreeable to the whole nation, who stomached greatly their being drawn into new expenses and new dangers for recovering the Dutchy of Sleswick, which they consider as a trifling object in itself, and entirely indifferent to Russia, and this after the Emperor had just sacrificed the conquests made by the Russian arms, and which might have been of great importance to this Empire, to his friendship for the King of Prussia, which however their desires for peace would have made them not only put up with, but approve. Several other little circumstances greatly exaggerated, artfully represented and improved contributed to the fall of this unhappy Prince.

[The earl of Buckingham to the Right Honorable George Grenville, Moscow, October 24, 1762:]

The most distinguished manner in which the Empress has received me, would induce me to hope that She Herself, divested from every other consideration, sees England as a great, a glorious, and a powerful Kingdom, the natural Ally of Russia, and the natural enemy of France.

[Sir George Macartney to His Grace the duke of Grafton, Saint Petersburg, November 5, 1765:]

It is my duty to inform Your Grace, that I think it impossible to obtain any farther concession from this Court [in the matter of a trade treaty with England]. . . .

This Court rises hourly higher and higher in her pride, and dazzled by her present prosperity looks with less deference upon other powers and with more admiration on herself. Strengthened as they are by the alliance of Denmark and Prussia, proud of having imposed a Monarch upon Poland and elated by their recent success in Sweden, I am persuaded that we shall every day find them less moderate in their pretensions and more difficult in negotiation.

[Sir George Macartney to the duke of Grafton, Saint Petersburg, February 11, 1766:]

And here I must observe that the two powers [England and Russia] are under mutual mistakes with regard to each other. At Petersburg they imagine that the Court of London can make the British nation adopt her ideas as easily as the Empress of Russia can enforce to Her subjects the obedience of an edict or the Execution of a Command. And though I have taken uncommon pains to represent the difference of the Two Constitutions, they either are incapable or unwilling to understand it. Our error with regard to them is in looking upon this nation as a civilized one and treating them as such. It by no means merits that title, and notwithstanding the opinion that persons unacquainted with it may have conceived, I will venture to say that the Kingdom of Thibet, or the Dominions of Prester John, might as justly be honored with the same appellation. There is not one of the Ministry here that even understands Latin, and few that can be said to possess the common rudiments of literature. Pride is the offspring of ignorance and of consequence Your Grace will not be surprised if the proceedings of this Court sometimes appear tinctured with haughtiness and vanity. I might as well talk of Clark and Tillotson, to the Divan of Constantinople, as quote Grotius and Puffendorff to the Ministers of Petersburg. . . . You may imagine the Law of Nations cannot have made any great progress in a country where there is no such thing as a university.

Barbarous as they are and ignorant of those arts which improve the understanding, enlighten the mind or promote discovery, I have little apprehension either from their experiments in commerce or their efforts in navigation. Like children they are allured by every new idea, pursue it for a moment and then abandon it when another starts up in their imaginations. That this has always been the case with them, a very slight knowledge of their history is sufficient to evince. The Edicts of Peter the First in the year 1718 are found on Our Act of Navigation, yet I believe none of the Maritime Powers ever felt any ill effects from them, nay so soon and so strangely did their ardour for sea-affairs abate, that in Peter the seconds time, The Prince Dolgorouky had an Ukase issued by which, even ship-building was discountenanced. Upon his disgrace at the Empress Anne's accession to the Throne, they again changed their opinions and renewed their former system, but so little progress have they made in it, that all their late attempts in commercial enterprizes have been attended with loss, disappointment and shame. Their obstinacy in refusing to grant the declaration arises at bottom merely from haughtiness, and it is harder to beat a Russian out of his pride than even out of his interest. For my own part according to the best of my judgment and information I think it absolutely impossible to persuade them to comply with our demands. Therefore my humble opinion is that at all events we should ratify the Treaty [of commerce] as by that means we shall secure what is already stipulated and obtained, but which we shall certainly lose perhaps for ever if once it be annulled.

[Sir George Macartney to the Right Honorable Mr. Secretary Conway, Saint Petersburg, January 26, 1767:]

The Empress (of Russia) seems of late to give much less attention to foreign politics than formerly. . . . Another grand object will claim Her attention; I mean the convening of the States of the Empire, in order to compose and establish a new code of laws. Now as these States are to consist of a number of deputies, perhaps eleven or twelve hundred, chosen out of all ranks of people, and out of all nations whatsoever under the Russian dominion, whether Christian, Pagan, or Mahometan, it is not to be supposed that the proceedings of so tumultious [sic] an assembly should be very regular, or their decisions very speedy. These circumstances together with many others, too tedious to be here enumerated, will probably blunt the edge of every appetite for foreign politics, and during a considerable time totally engross the attention of the Empress, of Her Ministers, and of Her people.

[Henry Shirley to the Right Honorable Henry Seymour Conway, Moscow, August 13, 1767:]

The assembly of the deputies is become at present the favourite occupation of the Empress, and excludes, at least in appearance, all other business from her Cabinet. The Russians think and talk of nothing else, and in seeing the representatives of several Nations, so very different both as to dress, customs, and religion, such as the Samoiedes, Cossacks, Bulgarians, Tartars etc., and whom they suppose to be (perhaps not without foundation) entirely dependants of the Russian Empire, assemble in their capital, they are apt to conclude, that they are now the wisest, the happiest, and the most powerful nation in the universe; and it would be the most useless attempt, to endeavour to persuade them, that this assembly is far from being a check to the despotic power of their Sovereign. A man however, who will consider with attention their manner of proceeding, what they are permitted to deliberate upon, and how far they are allowed to extend their reformations, and will compare it with what is practised in those countries blest with a mixt Government, will soon perceive that this is nothing more than a certain number of men sent by every province of the Empire, and by those Nations under the protection of Russia, to be in some respect the Empress's councillors in the drawing up of the laws of this country, and that these men are endowed with privileges, which no citizen in any well governed state ought ever to enjoy.

[Henry Shirley to the Right Honorable Henry Seymour Conway, Moscow, September 3, 1767:]

Give me leave to observe to you, Sir, that the credit of the French Court and the reputation of the French Nation in Russia, are very different from what they were formerly, though she may easily recover, in case of another administration, considering that almost all the nobles in this country are educated by Frenchmen, who from their tenderest infancy inspire them with the highest idea of France, and with a kind of contempt for every other Nation. They now seem to grow very fond of any thing that is English, and they have already adopted several of our customs, forming their taste to ours.

[The Right Honorable H. S. Conway to Mr. Shirley, Saint James's, October 9, 1767:]

I grant, that if any powers in Europe could remain absolutely independent of all others, it would be Russia and England: the remote situation of the one, and the insular position of the other, along with the great power of each in its own element, seem to give them sufficient security, without any external assistance. But it is still evident that while they can never have any reason to interfere with each other, these two Crowns are invited by many circumstances to renew and corroborate their ancient alliance. The commerce between them is very useful to England, very profitable to Russia; the naval power of the former is great, and may, on occasion, give assistance to the latter; the land forces of Russia, may, on occasion, be equally serviceable to England: this country abounds with money, that with men: thus each State seems calculated by nature to supply the defects of the other, and were their union once established and generally known, it would add consideration to both, and enable them not to gain advantage of their neighbours, which the Empress has declared is not her view, but to pursue, without impediment, those arts of peace and cultivation which form the real grandeur and happiness of a people, and which now appear so much the object of that great and wise Princess.

[Henry Shirley to the Right Honorable Lord Viscount Weymouth, Saint Petersburg, July 20, 1768:]

It must be confessed that the Empress of Russia understands the proper manner of governing Her subjects, much better than could have been expected from a foreign Princess; She is so well acquainted with their genius and character, and She makes so good a use of this knowledge, that their happiness seems to the nation in general to depend on the duration of her reign. It is surprising what difficulties She has had to conquer, and how unaffectedly assiduous She has been in removing every object that could give her the least uneasiness. The Crown is now so firmly settled on her head, that I cannot foresee any accident capable of obliging her to place it on that of her son.

[Lord Cathcart to the Right Honorable Lord Viscount Weymouth, Saint Petersburg, August 12, 1768:]

The Empress is perhaps the woman in the world the most able to conduct so complicated a machine [i.e. the Russian Empire].
. . .

She is carrying on great public works, and magnificent institutions; the army of Russia never was on such a footing, her finances are reckoned to be in good order, and the ballance of her trade higher than ever.

[Lord Cathcart to the Right Honorable Lord Viscount Weymouth, Saint Petersburg, August 19, 1768:]

[I have learned] that She is every day settled at business before five in the morning, that She is at the head of every work and looks into every detail Herself, and that all

Her conversation turns upon subjects of improvement which She manages in a manner void not only of affectation, but even of the appearance of seriousness or gravity.

[Lord Cathcart to the Right Honorable Lord Viscount Weymouth, Saint Petersburg, October 7, 1768:]

The Empress exteriorly has more dignity than can be expressed, a dignity superior to all form; is cheerful, calm and of an attention and benevolence that extends to all. I must not suffer myself to go too deep in this dispatch on a subject so interesting, but will just beg leave to assure you that, as far as I can judge, Her Imperial Majesty's measures for her own security, the happiness of her subjects and the grandeur and improvement of Her Empire are wise and well directed.

XII:7. CATHERINE'S ACCOUNT OF THE LEGISLATIVE COMMISSION, CA. 1765-1768

This account is from one of Catherine's private memoir-style papers that remained unpublished until 1907. It dates from sometime in the period 1794-96 and, unlike most of her memoirs, was written in Russian.

Reference: *Memoirs of Catherine the Great,* trans. Anthony, pp. 306-07.

I decided in my own mind [ca. 1765] that the general attitude and the civil law could only be improved by the adoption of useful rules, which would have to be written and ratified by me, for all the inhabitants of the Empire and for all circumstances.

And to this end I began to read and then to write the Instruction for the law-making Commission.

I read and wrote two years and said not a word for a year and a half, but followed my own judgment and feelings, with a sincere striving for the service, the honor, and the happiness of the empire, and with the desire to bring about in all respects the highest welfare of people and of things, of all in general and each individual in particular. When in my opinion I had pretty well arrived at my goal, I began to show parts of the subjects I had worked out to different persons, laying before each that which would be of interest to him, among others Prince Orlov and Count Nikita Panin. The latter said to me: "Those

are principles to cast down walls." Prince Orlov thought very highly of my work and often wished to show it to this person or that; but I never showed more than one or two pages at a time. At last I composed the manifesto concerning the calling of delegates from the whole empire, in order to learn more about the conditions of each district. The delegates then assembled in Moscow in the year 1767. I summoned several persons of quite different ways of thinking to the Kolomensky Palace, where I was living at the time, in order to have them listen to the finished Instruction for the Commission on Laws. At every section there was a difference of opinion. I permitted them to cross out and efface whatever they liked. They crossed out more than a half of what I had written, and the Instruction remained as it was printed. . . .

The Commission on Laws assembled and brought me light and knowledge from the whole empire, with which we had to deal and which we had to care for.

XII:8. CATHERINE'S INSTRUCTIONS ON A NEW CODE OF LAWS, 1767

For the guidance of the deputies who were to assemble in the Legislative Commission and to draw up a new code of laws, Catherine strove to commit to paper a set of principles. After her advisers had eliminated the more radical statements, the rest were published in 1767 as a nakaz or set of instructions containing over five hundred points. Here are a few of them.

Reference: Nikolai D. Chechulin, ed., *Nakaz Imperatritsy Ekateriny II, dannyi Komissii o sochinenii proekta novogo Ulozheniia* (St. Petersburg: Izd. Imper. Akademii Nauk, 1907), pp. 2-4, 30, 41-42, 57, 76, 78, 86, 107, 134-35, 141. The present translation borrows somewhat from the English translation of 1768, as given in W. F. Reddaway, ed., *Documents of Catherine the Great: The Correspondence with Voltaire and the Instructions of 1767* (Cambridge: At the University Press, 1931), pp. 216-93, but incorporates extensive revisions both to modernize the English and to bring it closer to the Russian version. This document and many others of this period are also found in L. T. Beskrovnyi and B. B. Kafengauz, eds., *Khrestomatiia po istorii SSSR XVIII v.* (Moscow: Izd. Sotsial'no-Ekonomicheskoi Literatury, 1963).

6. Russia is a European power.

7. This is proven by the following observations: The changes that Peter the Great undertook in Russia succeeded all the more easily because the then prevalent customs, which had been introduced among us by a mixture of different peoples and the conquest of foreign territories, were quite unsuitable to the climate. Peter I, in introducing the manners and customs of Europe among a European people, found the process even easier in his time than he himself expected....

9. The sovereign is absolute; for no other authority except that which is concentrated in his person can act appropriately in a state whose expanse is so vast.

10. The expanse of the state requires that absolute power be vested in that person who rules over it....

12. Another reason is that it is better to obey the laws under one master than to please several.

13. What is the purpose of autocracy? Not to deprive people of their natural freedom, but to guide their actions so as to attain the maximum good....

15. The intention and the aim of autocracies is the glory of the citizens, the state, and the sovereign....

123. The use of torture is repugnant to a healthy and natural mind. Humanity itself cries out against it and demands that it be totally abolished....

158. Laws ought to be written in the common tongue; and the code that contains all the laws ought to be a book of utmost usefulness and ought to be sold as cheaply as a book of *ABCs*....

200. In order that a punishment should not seem like violence on the part of one or many rising up against a citizen, it ought to be public, as speedy as is appropriate, necessary to the public, as moderate as possible

under the circumstances, proportionate to the crime, and precisely specified in the laws.
. . .

260. It would be improper suddenly or by means of a general law to liberate a large number [of slaves or serfs].

261. Laws may accomplish something useful by enabling slaves to own private property.
. . .

269. It seems, too, that the method the nobles have newly introduced to collect their revenues diminishes both the population and agriculture in Russia. Almost all the villages are on an obrok basis [i.e. must pay in cash or kind rather than in labor]. The nobles, who seldom or never reside in their villages, impose a payment of one, two, and even five rubles per head without having any concern for the means by which their peasants may be able to raise this money.

270. It is highly necessary that the law should direct the nobles to collect their revenues more judiciously and to exact such payments as will tend least to separate the peasant from his house and family. In this way agriculture will expand and the country's population will increase....

295. Agriculture cannot flourish where no one has any property of his own....

299. It would not be bad to give rewards to those farmers who bring their fields into better condition than others....

365. There are few ways that lead more directly to the attainment of honor than military service. To defend their fatherland and to conquer its enemies are the first right and the proper job of the nobles....

367. Yet still the proper dispensing of justice is no less required in time of peace than in war, and the state would be destroyed without it.

368. From this it follows that noble status may be acquired by civil as well as by military virtues....

494. In such a great state, which extends its rule over so many different peoples, the mistake of forbidding or discriminating against various faiths would greatly endanger the tranquillity and security of its citizens. . . .

496. Human minds are irritated by persecution, while permission to believe according to one's own faith softens even the hardest hearts and leads them away from even the most inveterate obstinacy, stifling those disputes detrimental to the tranquillity of the state and the unity of the citizens.

497. One ought to be extremely cautious in the examination of cases concerning witchcraft and heresy. Accusations of these two crimes may excessively disturb the tranquillity, freedom, and welfare of the citizens and may be the source of innumerable torments unless the laws set proper bounds. . . .

520. All this will never please those flatterers who daily tell all the rulers on earth that their people were created for them. But we think, and esteem it our glory to declare, that we were created for our people, and for this reason we are obliged to speak of things just as they ought to be. For God forbid that after this legislation is finished any nation on earth should be more just and, consequently, more flourishing; otherwise the intention of our laws would not have been fulfilled—an unhappiness I do not wish to survive.

XII:9. THE DECREE ESTABLISHING THE LEGISLATIVE COMMISSION, DECEMBER 14, 1766

In this decree Catherine both explained why she was establishing the commission and laid down certain rules governing its composition and procedures. (For the records of the commission, see Items XII:23 through XII:27.)

Reference: *PSZRI*, 1st ser., 17:1092-95, 1101.

By the grace of God, we, Catherine II, empress and autocrat of all Russia, etcetera, etcetera, proclaim to all the people:

It is now going on five years since God and the beloved fatherland through its chosen men have entrusted to us the scepter of this realm for the salvation of the empire from manifest ruin. From the day of our accession to the throne to this day, we have pursued a single aim and have considered it our duty toward God himself to fulfill what we had most solemnly promised on our imperial word in our manifesto of the sixth of July 1762 . . . to raise the scepter high in upholding our Orthodox faith, in strengthening and defending our beloved fatherland, in preserving justice, in eradicating evil and every kind of iniquity and oppression.

· · ·

In the course of the first three years we learned that great confusion in the trial and punishment of crime and consequently in the dispensation of justice is caused in many cases by the lack of laws and in other cases by an excessive number of them issued at different times, and also by an imperfect distinction between permanent and temporary enactments; and in particular that after the lapse of a long time and frequent changes, the sense in which the old civil laws were conceived is now completely unknown to many persons in our day. Moreover, passionate argument has often obscured the direct sense of many laws, and the difficulties have been increased by the difference between past times and customs and those of our own day.

· · ·

And inasmuch as it is our primary aim to see our people happy and contented, so far as human happiness and contentment can be extended on this earth, and in order that we may better learn of the needs and the sorely felt wants of our people, we command that, half a year after the proclamation of this manifesto in each locality, deputies be sent to our old capital city of Moscow. . . . After having elected the deputies, each locality shall give them instructions and a mandate, as described in the accompanying explanation of election procedures. . . .

We summon these deputies . . . not only to hear from them about the needs and deficiencies of each locality, but also to include them in the commission for the drafting of a new code of laws [*ulozhenie*] to be submitted to us for confirmation. This commission shall receive from us instructions and rules of procedure. In establishing it we offer our nation a test of our sincerity, our great trust in the nation, and our real maternal love.

· · ·

[A.] 1. One deputy each shall be sent from the Senate and the [Holy] Synod, from the three first and from all other colleges as well as chancelleries (which will receive special directions from the Senate) except those of the guberniias and *voevodstva* [large territorial units].

2. One deputy from each uezd ... where there are nobles [*dvorianstvo*].

3. One deputy from the inhabitants of each town.

4. One deputy from the small landholders [*odnodvortsy*] of each provintsiia.

5. One deputy from the military settlers [*pakhatnye soldaty*], military service men [*sluzhilye liudi*] in various branches, and others constituting the land-militia in each provintsiia.

6. One deputy from the state peasants—both those paying taxes on land [*chernososhnye*] and those paying tribute in furs [*iasachnye*]—in each provintsiia.

7. One deputy from each of the various non-nomadic nationalities dwelling on our territory, whatever their faith, baptized or nonbaptized, in each provintsiia.

8. From the Cossack troops and from the Zaporozhian Host, the supreme command to which they are subordinate shall send an appropriate number of deputies, in conformity with the present regulation.

9. All such deputies must be no less than twenty-five years of age.

10. The deputies thus elected shall receive an annual salary from the treasury—nobles [dvoriane] 400 rubles each, townsmen 122 rubles each, and all others 37 rubles each.

11. The deputies shall have the following privileges:

For the duration of his life each deputy, whatever offense he may commit, shall be immune from (1) the death penalty, (2) torture, and (3) corporal punishment. . . .

And whoever, while the law code is in preparation, attacks a deputy, robs him, beats him, or kills him, shall be punished twice as heavily as is usual in such cases.

In order that a member of the Legislative Commission be recognizable, all deputies shall wear identical badges, which they may keep all their lives. . . .

13. Deputies from our subject peoples who lack sufficient knowledge of the Russian language must bring interpreters with them. . . .

[B. 5.] In the election of a deputy from the nobility, any noble may take part who is the actual owner of an estate in that uezd. . . .

[C.] Election procedures to be followed by the inhabitants of towns for the purpose of sending deputies to the commission charged with drafting a new code of laws. . . .

2. The inhabitants of each town shall elect one deputy. . . .

5. Those entitled to elect the town deputy are all those householders who actually have a house, a house and a shop, a house and a trade, or a house and a business in the town concerned.

XII:10. THE TREATY OF KUCHUK-KAINARDJI, JULY 10, 1774

Russia's victory in the war of 1768-74 against Turkey was marked by the signing of a peace treaty in the village of Kuchuk-Kainardji (Kainardzhi) in Bulgaria just south of the Danube. The terms excerpted here were crucial not only for Russia's immediate territorial expansion but also for her future relations with Turkey.

Reference: *PSZRI*, 1st ser., 19:959-64.

ARTICLE 3. All the Tatar peoples without exception—Crimean, Budzhat, Kuban' ... will be acknowledged by both empires to be free and completely independent of any foreign authority, remaining under the autocratic power of their own khan of the line of Genghis, chosen and elevated by the entire Tatar community [*obshchestvo*]; and may he govern them according to their ancient laws and customs, in no way answerable to any foreign power; and for this neither the Russian court nor the Ottoman Porte will in any way interfere either in the choice and elevation of the said khan or in their household, political, civil, and internal affairs, but will acknowledge and respect the political and civil status of this Tatar nation as they do other selfgoverning powers dependent on no one save God alone; in religious rites, being of one faith with the Moslems, and thus under the jurisdiction of His Majesty the sultan as supreme caliph of the Mohammedan faith, they will conform to the rules prescribed by their faith, without the least prejudice, however, to the political and civil freedom confirmed for them. . . .

ART. 7. The Sublime Porte promises to give its firm protection to the Christian faith and its churches, and likewise to allow ministers of the Russian imperial court to make various representations in all affairs in behalf of the church erected in Constantinople . . . and of its servitors, and promises to take them into consideration as made by an authorized representative of a neighboring and sincerely friendly power. . . .

ART. 11. For the profit and benefit of both empires, there will be free and unhindered navigation for merchant vessels belonging to the two contracting powers in all seas washing their lands; and the Sublime Porte will permit exactly the same kinds of Russian merchant vessels as other states use for commerce in its ports and elsewhere to have free passage from the Black Sea to the White [i.e. the Mediterranean] and from the White Sea to the Black, and also to anchor in all harbors and ports on the coasts of these seas and in the straits or canals connecting them. . . .

ART. 16. The Russian Empire returns to the Sublime Porte all of Bessarabia with the cities of Akkerman, Kilia, Izmail, and others, with the suburbs and villages and everything this province contains; likewise it returns the fortress of Bendery. The Russian Empire also returns to the Sublime Porte the two principalities of Wallachia and Moldavia with all the fortresses, cities, suburbs, and villages, and everything that is found therein; while the Sublime Porte shall receive them on the following conditions, with a solemn promise to observe them strictly: (1) In regard to all the inhabitants of these principalities, whatever be their dignity, rank, station, calling, and origin, to observe a full amnesty without the slightest exception. . . . (2) Not to hinder in any manner whatsoever the absolutely free profession of the Christian faith, or the erection of new churches and the repair of old ones. . . . (4) To recognize and respect the clergy with the honor due this class. . . . (6) Not to demand or exact any monetary or other payments for old accounts, whatever they may be. (7) Not to demand from them any contributions or payments accrued either during the war or for the next two years, in view of the great suffering and destruction they have undergone during this war. . . .

(8) Upon the expiration of the said time, the Sublime Porte promises to observe the greatest humanity and magnanimity in imposing monetary taxes upon them and to receive the same through deputies sent every two years; if the taxes imposed upon them are paid punctually, no pasha or governor or any other personage whosoever shall oppress them or demand from them any other payment or [additional] taxes under any name or pretext whatsoever. . . . (10) [The Sublime Porte] likewise agrees that in the affairs of both these principalities the ministers of the Russian imperial court present at the Sublime Porte can speak in behalf of these two principalities, and promises to listen to them with the respect befitting friendly and deferential powers.

ART. 17. The Russian Empire returns all the islands it holds in the Aegean Sea to the Sublime Porte, while the Sublime Porte agrees on its part: (1) To observe strictly, in respect to the inhabitants of these islands, the conditions stated in the first article concerning a general amnesty. . . . (2) That the Christian faith will not be subjected to the slightest oppression, and that there will be no hindrances to the rebuilding or repair of its churches; similarly, those who serve in them will not be insulted or oppressed. (3) That, because of their great sufferings in the course of the present war, they shall not be required to pay any of their yearly taxes for the time that they were under the dependence of the Russian Empire and for two years to come, counting from the time of the return of these islands to the Sublime Porte.

ART. 18. The castle of Kinburn at the mouth of the Dnieper River, and a sufficient area [*dovol'nyi okrug*] along the left bank of the Dnieper, together with the corner formed by the steppes lying between the Bug and Dnieper rivers, remains in the complete, eternal, and unquestioned possession of the Russian Empire.

ART. 19. The fortresses of Enikale and Kerch in the Crimean Peninsula, with their docks and all that is found within them, including also their uezdy . . . remain in the complete, eternal, and unquestioned possession of the Russian Empire.

ART. 20. The city of Azov with its uezd . . . shall belong eternally to the Russian Empire.

XII:11. CATHERINE'S LETTERS TO GRIMM, 1774-1795

Catherine carried on an active correspondence with her fellow monarchs and other prominent Europeans. Much of it is useful as evidence of her skills as a propagandist and as a demonstration of how far some people were led by her persuasiveness and her monetary and other rewards to support her cause in important places. (See, for example, her exchanges with Voltaire, published in English under Reddaway's editorship.) At the same time, her letters are important sources for her appraisals of contemporary events and personalities. Among the most valuable are her letters to Baron Friedrich Melchior von Grimm, a German literary critic who lived in France and served Catherine well among the encyclopedists and other opinion leaders there. Here are a few samples from that correspondence, which lasted from 1774 until her death.

Reference: *SIRIO*, 23:12, 93-94, 116, 410-11, 412, 561, 581-82, 620-21, 647.

[December 21, 1774:] I avow that I cannot be a single day without the *Encyclopedia;* with all its shortcomings, it is still an indispensable and excellent work.

[June 21, 1778:] The month of May has been an ill-fated one for me: I lost two men whom I have never seen, who loved me and whom I honored—Voltaire and Lord Chatham [William Pitt]; not for a long time, if ever, will men of equal merit be found to replace them, particularly the former, and never men superior to them; and for me they are an irreparable loss: I feel like crying. . . . Upon my return to the city in the autumn, I am going to collect the letters that great man [Voltaire] wrote to me and send them to you. I have a great many of them, but if it is possible, please purchase his library and whatever is left of his papers, including my letters. For my part, I shall gladly pay a high price to his heirs, who probably do not know the value of all this.

[December 7, 1778:] Today I am going to read the eulogy of Voltaire they have just sent me from Berlin; I share the opinion of Frederick [the Great]: his fame will last throughout the ages like that of Homer and Virgil.

[At Kherson, May 15, 1787:] The next day we had a better dinner, and the day after that we proceeded to Ekaterinograd, where the first stone was laid for the construction of that town. Then it took us three days to reach this place, where we have been staying these four days. Today we launched three warships; they are the seventh, eighth, and ninth built here; but how can I tell you of all we have been doing and seeing here?

Kherson is not yet eight years old, and it can claim to be one of the finest military as well as commercial towns of the empire. All the houses are of hewn stone; the town is at least six versts long; its location, its soil, its climate are admirable; there are at least ten to twelve thousand inhabitants of every nationality; one can obtain anything one wants just as in Saint Petersburg; in a word, the efforts of Prince Potemkin have transformed this town and this region, where at the time of the peace treaty there was hardly a hut, into a flourishing town and countryside; and it will become even more so from year to year.

[At Bakhchisarai, May 21:]
We passed the Isthmus of Perekop the day before yesterday; and yesterday toward six in the afternoon we arrived here all in good health and high spirits; all along the way we were escorted by Tatars, and at a few versts from here we were met by all the notables of Taurida [the Crimea] on horseback. It was a superb spectacle; in an open carriage that contained eight persons, preceded, surrounded, and followed in this manner, we entered Bakhchisarai and went straight to the palace of the khans; and we are here now, lodged between minarets and mosques where people shout, pray, chant, and turn round and round on one foot five times in the course of twenty-four hours.

[At Sevastopol, May 23, 1787:] Confound it, all this is so much like the fantasies of the *Arabian Nights* that one does not know whether one is asleep or awake. Here, where three years ago there was nothing, I have found a rather pretty town and a small fleet, rather lively and sprightly; the port, the anchorage, and the moorings are naturally good; and one has to give credit to Prince Potemkin for having shown in all this a formidable activity and intelligence.

[October 13, 1791:] Yesterday a terrible blow once again descended upon my head. Toward six in the afternoon a courier brought me the sad news that my pupil, my friend, and almost my idol, Prince Potemkin of Taurida, had died in Moldavia after about a month's illness. You can have no idea of my affliction. With an excellent heart he combined rare understanding and an extraordinary range of mind; his views were always lofty and magnanimous; he was very humane, knowledgeable, singularly amiable, and his ideas were always new; nobody ever possessed such a gift for the witty saying and the apt phrase; during this war [with Turkey] he displayed striking military qualities, for he suffered not a single defeat either on land or on sea. No man has ever been so little commanded by others, while he himself had a particular ability for directing his subordinates. In a word, he was a statesman, great both in counsel and in execution; he was attached to me with passion and zeal; scolding and grumbling whenever he thought that things could be done better; with growing age he corrected his own defects. . . . But the rarest quality he possessed was a courage of heart, mind, and soul that distinguished him entirely from other human beings; and because of this we understood each other perfectly, leaving those of lesser understanding to babble to their heart's content. I regard Prince Potemkin as a very great man, who did not accomplish half of what was within his power to achieve.

[April 13, 1793:] Hitherto one has seen kingdoms given over into the hands of women, but never yet, so far as I know, given over into infamy. This special treat has been reserved to the eighteenth century which once prided itself on being the gentlest, the most enlightened of ages, and yet has generated the most wicked beings in the midst of the most famous of cities. Fie upon the abominable creatures! . . . Do you know what you are witnessing in France? It is the Gauls trying to drive out the Franks; yet you will see the Franks come back, and the wild beasts thirsting for human blood will either be exterminated

or driven into hiding. As for myself, I made all those [French émigrés] who did not want to be expelled from Russia take an oath; now please imagine for yourself what happened: all those who took the oath have become zealous royalists; I call to witness the Count d'Artois [the future Charles X] who has been here these five weeks, treated as befits a prince of the French royal house. He leaves tomorrow, pleased, I hope, with his sojourn here; at least he could see that the greatest pains were taken to alleviate his misfortune, without any mixture of that bitter ingredient to which many have had the cruel desire to accustom them [the émigrés]. Well, I hope he will say that our conduct toward him has been frank and loyal. I found this prince such as I hoped to find him—of facile understanding, of noble soul, of a kind and generous heart.

[April 5, 1795:] That dolt Hertzberg [a Prussian statesman] deserves a thorough thrashing all by himself; he has no more knowledge of history than my parrot. He has had the impudence to say that Russia, in taking possession of Polotsk, could produce no title to it; he should have said that Russia did not attach any importance to outdated titles. For Polotsk was given by Vladimir I to his eldest son Iziaslav. . . . The fifth son of Olgerd, Iagailo or Jacob, in 1386 became king of Poland and a convert to the Latin faith under the name of Wladyslaw, when he married Jadwiga, queen and heiress of Poland. Thus it was he who joined Lithuania to Poland, but the stupid, ignorant minister of state [Hertzberg] does not know this; arrogance makes him ignorant, stupid, and coarse like a Pomeranian ox. The underfed creature (the late king starved him, by his own admission) does not know that not only in Polotsk but in all of Lithuania up to the seventeenth century all governmental affairs were transacted in the Russian language; that all the Lithuanian archives are written in Russian; that all state documents were written with Russian characters in the Russian language; that all events since the creation of the world were dated according to the usage of our Greek church and that in this matter even the Greek ecclesiastical indictions were used as the authority—all this being proof that up to the seventeenth century the Greek religion was dominant not only in Polotsk but in all of

Lithuania and had been the faith of the princes and grand dukes; that all the churches there, notably the cathedrals, have the altars placed eastward, according to the custom of the Eastern church. If you need still more evidence you have only to ask for it; it is not difficult to prove what is true. Moreover, Polotsk and Lithuania have been taken and retaken about twenty times, and no treaty was ever concluded without one side or the other claiming part or all of it, depending on circumstances. That fool of a minister of state deserves an even sounder thrashing for his ignorance regarding the peoples he lays claim to on behalf of his stupid master state [*Herresstaat*]. The silly ass!

[September 16, 1795:] Now listen to the historical gospel on Poland which I shall expound in black and white. Poland, from its beginnings and up to 1386, was composed of the palatinates of Cracow, Sandomir, Mazovia, and, beyond the Vistula, what is called Great Poland. In 1386 Jadwiga, queen of Poland, married Iagailo, grand duke of Lithuania, a direct descendant of Vladimir I, grand prince of Russia, who had given Polotsk to his eldest son Iziaslav, and [had given] to another son Lithuania, which fell to the line of Iziaslav by right of inheritance. Now, in the partitions, I did not take for myself a single inch of Poland but only what the Poles themselves continued to call Red Russia: the palatinates of Kiev, Podolia, [and] Volynia with its capital of Vladimir, a town built by Vladimir I in 992; for Lithuania had never been a part of Poland proper, nor had Samogitia. Thus, not having taken an inch of Poland, I cannot assume the title of queen of Poland. Besides, if that nation has lost even its name, it seems to me that it has well deserved its fate, having itself broken all the treaties that assured its existence, having never listened to reason, and having lost any principle of unity, with no two individuals ever able to agree on anything. Venal, corrupt, frivolous, garrulous, given to oppression and fanciful projects, entrusting their private estates to Jews who suck their subjects dry and give very little to them: here you have the exact image of the Poles. They don't even know that I have not a single inch of Poland in my possession and propose that I become queen of Poland!

XII:12. THE STATUTE ON GUBERNIIA ADMINISTRATION, NOVEMBER 7, 1775

Some of the aims and methods of the guberniia reform of Catherine II are explained in these excerpts from the preamble to her statute "for the administration of the guberniias of the All-Russian Empire," which set a pattern that persisted in general until the end of the empire. The basis for Catherine's divisions—the principle of the number of inhabitants rather than simply historical tradition—was in keeping with the reforming spirit of the enlightened despots.

Reference: *PSZRI*, 1st ser., 20:230-31. This document and many others of this period have also been republished in M. T. Beliavskii, comp., *Dvorianskaia imperiia XVIII veka (osnovnye zakonodatel'nye akty). Sbornik dokumentov* (Moscow: Izd. Moskovskogo Universiteta, 1960).

We have found, first, that because of the great size of certain guberniias these same are insufficiently provided with organs of government and with the necessary men for administrative work, so that the administration of a guberniia is carried out in the same office in which are handled government revenues and accounts, as well as provost or police matters including even criminal cases and civil trials. The administrations of provintsii and uezdy are no less subject to such inconveniences, since affairs of all categories and types are handled in the same voevoda's chancery [*voevodskaia kantseliariia*].

The results of this disorganization are obvious. On the one hand, sluggishness, neglect, and procrastination are natural consequences of such an inconvenient and unsatisfactory state of affairs, where one task delays another, and where again the impossibility of discharging in the same voevoda's chancery all the affairs of various kinds with which it is charged may sometimes serve as a perennial excuse, cover up neglect of duty, and give occasion to partiality in the performance of duties. On the other hand, slow execution of duty gives rise to arbitrariness and chicanery, and to many vices in general, since retribution for crimes and vices is not meted out with such speed as would be necessary to restrain and intimidate the guilty. In other offices the multitude of authorized appeals delay justice not a little. . . .

To abolish all these and many other inconveniences, which it would take up too much space to enumerate, and above all to establish better order and the unhindered flow of justice, we have now thought it fit to issue a statute for the administration of the guberniias and to furnish each of them, as component parts of the Russian Empire, with an administration, so as to prepare and assist the better and more exact execution of the highly beneficial legislation to be issued in the future.

This, our decree, as all can perceive, separates the courts from the guberniia administrations, prescribes for each office its duties and rules, and makes it possible for them to carry out instructions. Not only does it correspond in its form to the present internal conditions of our empire, but it also strengthens and secures the general tranquillity and safety, particularly as compared to the state of affairs previously existing.

XII:13. POTEMKIN'S MEMORANDUM URGING THE ANNEXATION OF THE CRIMEA, CA. 1776-1780

This note addressed by Potemkin (1739-91; see above, Item XII:11) to Catherine II ca. 1776-80 sets forth his arguments for annexing the Crimean Khanate, until 1774 a vassal of Turkey. It also gives us another glimpse of the capable statesman who, even after Catherine had resumed her practice of taking a succession of lovers, continued not only as her morganatic husband but also as her chief adviser and friend and as the developer of the "New Russia" on the Black Sea.

Reference: Sergei M. Solov'ev, "Istoriia padeniia Pol'shi," *Sobranie sochinenii S. M. Solov'eva* (St. Petersburg: Obshchestvennaia Pol'za, 1900), cols. 102-03.

The Crimea, by its position, creates a breach in our borders. Whether the Turks have to be watched along the Bug or on the Kuban' side, we always have to worry about the Crimea. Here we can clearly see why the present khan [of the Crimea] does not please the Turks: it is because he will not let them enter through the Crimea into our very heart, so to speak. Now, just imagine that the Crimea is yours and no longer a thorn in your side; suddenly our frontier situation becomes splendid: along the Bug the Turks adjoin us directly and therefore have to deal with us themselves and not use others as a cover. Here we can see every step they take. And as for the Kuban' side, in addition to a dense series of forts, manned with garrisons, the numerous Don [Cossack] Host is always in readiness. The security of the population of the Novorossiia guberniia will then be beyond doubt; navigation on the Black Sea will be free; as it is now, your ships have difficulty in leaving port and find it still harder to enter. In addition, we shall rid ourselves of the difficulties of maintaining the forts we now have in remote outposts in the Crimea. Most Gracious Sovereign! My unbounded devotion to you compels me to speak out: disregard envy, which is powerless to hinder you. It is your duty to exalt the glory of Russia. Look what others have acquired without opposition: France took Corsica; the Austrians [*tsesartsy*], without

war, took more from the Turks in Moldavia than we did. There are no powers in Europe that would not divide Asia, Africa, and America among themselves. The acquisition of the Crimea can neither strengthen nor enrich you, but it will give you security. It will be a heavy blow, to be sure, but to whom? To the Turks! a still more compelling reason for you to act. Believe me, you will acquire immortal fame such as no other sovereign of Russia ever had. This glory will open the way to still further and greater glory: with the Crimea will come domination of the Black Sea; it will be in your power to blockade the Turks, to feed them or to starve them. To the [Crimean] khan you may grant anything you choose in Persia; it will keep him happy. He will offer you the Crimea this winter; the population will gladly submit a petition to this effect. Just as the annexation will bring you glory, so will posterity shame and reproach you if continued disturbances lead it to say: "She had the power to act but would not or let the moment slip by." If gentle is thy rule, then Russia needs a paradise. Kherson of Taurida [Crimea]! You were the source of piety for us; now behold how Catherine II shall again bring you the peace of a Christian rule. [Potemkin refers here to the legend that the Kievan prince Vladimir was baptized at the Crimean town of Khersones (Korsun'), an ancient town in the extreme southern Crimea, about where Sevastopol' stands today. The new Kherson developed by Potemkin was and is not in the Crimea, but over 150 miles to the north, on the lower Dnieper.]

XII:14. THE MANIFESTO ON THE ANNEXATION OF THE CRIMEA, APRIL 8, 1783

These excerpts from the manifesto proclaiming the annexation of the Crimea, Taman', and the Kuban' region, give both Catherine's justification for this act and her promises for the future.
    Reference: *PSZRI,* 1st ser., 21:897-98.

The active experience of many years has given abundant proof that just as the former submission [of the Tatar peoples of the Crimea and Kuban'] to the [Ottoman] Porte led to coolness and disputes between the two powers [Russia and Turkey], similarly their reorganization into a free territory, given their inability to enjoy the fruits of this freedom, serves as a constant source of disturbances, losses, and difficulties for our troops.

. . .

But now, on the one hand, we must take into consideration the great expenditures consumed on the Tatars and for the Tatars, totaling, by accurate calculation, over twenty million rubles, without counting the loss in human lives which cannot be measured in money; and on the other hand, it has become known to us that the Ottoman Porte is beginning to exercise supreme authority in Tatar territory, to wit, on the island [actually a peninsula] of Taman', where an [Ottoman] official, who had come with troops, ordered to be publicly beheaded an envoy sent to him by the khan Shagin-Girei to inquire as to the reason for his arrival, and proclaimed the local inhabitants to be Turkish subjects. This act has nullified our former mutual obligations concerning the freedom and independence of the Tatar peoples; it makes us all the more certain that our assumption at the time of the peace treaty, in making the Tatars independent, is not enough to eliminate all occasions that might arise for disputes over the Tatars; and it restores to us all those rights which we acquired by our victories in the last war and which existed in full force up to the conclusion of peace. And therefore, in keeping with the solicitude incumbent upon us for the welfare and majesty of our fatherland, striving to assure its welfare and security, and likewise looking upon this as a means of eliminating forever the unpleasant causes that disturb the eternal peace concluded between the Russian and Ottoman empires, which we sincerely wish to maintain forever, and no less as compensation and satisfaction for the losses we have suffered, we have decided to take under our dominion the Crimean Peninsula, the island of Taman', and the entire Kuban' region [the right bank of the Kuban' River].

In proclaiming to the inhabitants of these regions, through this our imperial manifesto, this change in their way of life, we make a sacred and unshakable promise on behalf of ourselves and our successors upon the throne to maintain them on a basis of equality with our hereditary subjects [and] to preserve and defend their persons, property, temples, and ancestral faith, and may the unhindered practice of this faith, with all its lawful ceremonies, remain inviolable; [and we promise] finally, to allow each class [*sostoianie*] among them all those rights and privileges enjoyed by the corresponding [classes] in Russia; in return for which we require and expect from the gratitude of our new subjects that, in their happy change from unrest and confusion to peace, tranquillity, and lawful rule, they will make every effort to liken themselves to our ancient subjects in loyalty, zeal, and moral conduct and to merit alongside of them our monarchical favor and bounty.

XII:15. A DECREE CONCERNING THE INHABITANTS OF THE CRIMEA, JULY 28, 1783

This is the burden of a decree issued by Catherine to Prince Potemkin, then governor-general of "New Russia" (Novorossiia), concerning the Tatar and other inhabitants of his domain.
    Reference: *PSZRI,* 1st ser., 21:985-86.

We instruct you to make arrangements regarding revenues in such a manner that in those newly annexed territories the regular taxes should be collected into the treasury, to be expended on the needs of that area, to wit: customs duties, the tax on salt sold from the lakes, the taxes on land replacing the poll tax, and the tithe imposed on produce; yet care is to be taken that they not be a burden on the people. Out of these revenues we order that an appropriate and adequate subsidy should be assigned for the support of the mosques and their servitors, their schools, and for similar beneficent works; also for various necessary public buildings, and in particular for fountains for the benefit of the population—one of which should be erected in a suitable place at your discretion, to commemorate such a glorious event as the annexation of the Crimea and all the Tatar territories to the Russian Empire. None of these, our new subjects, is to be pressed into military service against his own free will and desire.

XII:16. THE CHARTER OF THE NOBILITY, APRIL 21, 1785

The following articles from Catherine's lengthy Charter of the Nobility (*Gramota na prava, vol'nosti i preimushchestva blagorodnogo Rossiiskogo Dvorianstva*) spell out some of the blessings of the privileged and carry certain implications concerning the status of the mass of village dwellers.

Reference: *PSZRI*, 1st ser., 22:347-51. A recent translation of this document is included in Dmytryshyn, *Imperial Russia*, pp. 98-102.

With the new gains and the enlargement of our empire, at a time when we enjoy complete internal and external tranquillity everywhere, we are directing our efforts increasingly to the ceaseless task of securing for our faithful subjects firm and stable institutions in all necessary areas of the internal administration of the state, so that order and well-being may increase in times to come. And therefore we have seen fit, first, to extend our solicitude to our loyal and gracious subjects, the Russian nobility, mindful of its . . . merits, ardor, zeal, and unshakable loyalty to the autocrats of all Russia, which they have displayed toward ourselves and toward our throne in the most turbulent times, in war as in the midst of peace. And, following the examples of justice, clemency, and mercy set by our late predecessors who adorned and glorified the Russian throne, and being moved by our own maternal love and particular gratitude toward the Russian nobility, by our imperial judgment and will, for the remembrance of [future] generations [and] for the benefit of the Russian nobility, our [state] service, and the empire, we do ordain, proclaim, institute, and confirm the following articles, immutably and for all time to come:

A. Concerning the personal privileges of nobles.

1. The title of nobleman [*dvorianskoe nazvanie*] is a consequence that proceeds from the qualities and virtues of men who were leaders in times long past, who distinguished themselves by their merits, through which, deriving [noble] dignity from their service, they obtained the designation of nobles [*naritsanie blagorodnoe*] for their descendants.

2. It is not only beneficial for the empire and the throne but likewise just for the esteemed status of the honorable nobility to be preserved and confirmed immutably and inviolably; therefore, as it was of old and as it is today, let the honorable dignity of nobles be imprescriptible, hereditary, and inheritable in those worthy families who enjoy the same; and consequently:

3. A nobleman shall transmit his noble dignity to his wife.

4. A nobleman shall transmit his honorable noble dignity to his children by inheritance.

5. A nobleman or noblewoman shall not be deprived of noble dignity unless he should deprive himself of the same through a crime that is incompatible with the basic dignity of a nobleman.

6. The crimes that violate and are incompatible with the basic dignity of a nobleman are the following: (1) breaking an oath, (2) treason, (3) brigandage, (4) thievery of any kind, (5) fraud, (6) crimes that by law are punished by deprivation of honor and corporal punishment, (7) if it be proved that he tried to persuade or instruct others to commit such crimes. [Note: The "if proved" in no. 7 seems superfluous and it throws the syntax off, but it is there.]

7. But since noble dignity shall not be

taken away except for a crime; [and since] marriage is a worthy [institution], established by divine law: therefore a noblewoman who marries a non-noble shall not be deprived of her status; but she shall not transmit noble rank to her husband and children.

8. A nobleman [*blagorodnyi*] shall not be deprived of his honorable noble dignity without trial.

9. A nobleman shall not be deprived of his honor without trial.

10. A nobleman shall not be deprived of life without trial.

11. A nobleman shall not be deprived of his property without trial.

12. A nobleman shall not be tried except by his peers.

13. The judicial case of a nobleman who has perpetrated a criminal offense, and deserves by law to be deprived of his noble dignity or his honor or his life, shall not be concluded without bringing it before the Senate and without confirmation by the Imperial Majesty.

14. If ten years have passed since the commission of a crime (by a nobleman), and in the course of so long a time it has not come to light and no proceedings have been instituted, we order all such cases to be consigned to eternal oblivion henceforth, [even] if any claimants, plaintiffs, or accusers should appear. [Note: This was a general principle of Russian justice.]

15. Corporal punishment shall not be inflicted upon a nobleman.

16. Nobles serving as enlisted men in our army shall be treated, in cases of punishment, in the same way as prescribed by our military regulation for officer ranks.

17. We confirm for all time to come [and] for future generations the freedom and liberty of the honorable Russian nobility.

18. We confirm permission for all nobles who are in service [either] to remain in service [or] to request discharge from service according to the rules set forth for this.

19. We confirm permission for nobles to enter the service of other European powers allied with us and to travel abroad.

20. But since the honorable title and dignity of a noble shall in the future be acquired, just as it was in times past and is today, by service and efforts beneficial to the empire and the throne, and since the essential condition of the Russian nobility depends upon the security of the fatherland and the throne, therefore at any time needful for the Russian autocracy, when the service of the nobility is necessary and needful for the common welfare, every honorable nobleman is obligated to respond to the first summons from the autocratic power [and] to spare neither his efforts nor his very life in serving the state. . . .

26. Noblemen are confirmed in their right to buy villages.

27. Noblemen are confirmed in their right to sell wholesale whatever is produced in their villages or is manufactured by hand.

28. Noblemen are permitted to maintain mills and factories in their villages.

29. Noblemen are permitted to organize trading centers [*mestechki*] on their patrimonial estates and to hold markets and fairs in them, in conformity with the legislation of the state, [and] with the knowledge of the governor general and the administration of the guberniia, seeing to it that the dates for a fair in a trading center shall not conflict with the dates [for fairs] in other neighboring towns.

30. Noblemen are confirmed in their right to own or build or buy houses in the cities and to maintain workshops in them. . . .

32. Noblemen are permitted to sell wholesale, or to ship by sea from indicated ports, whatever goods each shall have or shall manufacture in conformity with the law; for they are not forbidden to maintain or establish mills, workshops, and factories of every kind.

33. Noblemen are confirmed in the rights of private ownership granted by the gracious decree of June 28, 1782, not only over the surface of the land that belongs to each of them, but also over the bowels of that land and over the waters belonging to it, over all hidden minerals and vegetation, and over all metals produced therefrom, as explained in that decree in its full strength and meaning. . . .

35. In the villages the landowner's house shall be free from billeting [by soldiers].

36. A nobleman shall be personally exempt from personal taxes.

B. Concerning assemblies of nobles, the establishment of noble corporations [*dvorianskie obshchestva*] in each guberniia, and the privileges of the noble corporations.

37. We grant to our faithful subjects, the nobles, permission to assemble in the guberniia in which they live and to form a noble corporation in each vicegerency [*namestnichestvo*]. [Note: The statute on provincial administration of 1775 employs two equivalent names for the same administrative unit: namestnichestvo and guberniia. In each of these a vicegerent (namestnik), also called the governor general (*general-gubernator*), was to head the administration; the governor [gubernator] was subordinated to him. Sometimes a vicegerent was given jurisdiction over several guberniias.]. . .

39. The assembly of nobles in each vicegerency [i.e. guberniia] is permitted to elect a guberniia marshal of the nobility [*predvoditel' dvorianstva*] for that guberniia; and for this purpose every three years the assembly of nobles should present two of the uezd marshals of the nobility before the sovereign's vicegerent or administrator [*pravitel'*], and whoever of these is appointed by the governor general or governor shall be the guberniia marshal of the nobility for that guberniia.

40. . . . The uezd marshal of the nobility is elected by the nobility of that uezd every three years by ballot.

41. . . . The ten assessors [*zasedateli*] of the higher land court [*verkhnii zemskii sud*, which had jurisdiction on the guberniia level over criminal and civil cases involving nobles] and two [out of six] assessors of the court of conscience [*sovestnyi sud*, which was a court for mediation and the protection of civil rights] are to be elected every three years by the nobility of those uezdy that are under the legal jurisdiction of that higher land court and they are to be presented to the administrator or governor, in the absence of the governor general; if they have no evident vices, then the sovereign's vicegerent, or in his absence the administrator of the vicegerent, shall confirm the nobility's election. . . .

43. . . . Uezd or okrug [district] judges

and the police chief or captain [*zemskii ispravnik ili kapitan*] are to be chosen by the nobility every three years and presented by the same to the administrator; if they have no evident vices, the governor shall confirm the nobility's election.

44. . . . The assessors of the uezd court [*uezdnyi sud*, which handled criminal and civil cases involving nobles on the uezd level, as the higher land court did on the guberniia level] and the noble assessors of the lower court [*nizhnii zemskii sud*, which was instituted on the uezd level to deal with violations of public order and tranquillity] shall be elected every three years by the nobility and presented to the administrator; if they have no evident vices, the governor shall confirm the nobility's choice. . . .

47. The assembly of the nobility shall be permitted to make representations to the governor general or governor concerning its corporate needs and welfare.

48. The assembly of the nobility is confirmed in its permission to make representations and complaints through its deputies both to the Senate and to the Imperial Majesty, in accordance with the laws. . . .

62. The assembly of the nobility is forbidden to elect, to those posts which by virtue of the statutes shall be filled by election, any nobleman whose [yearly] income from his villages consists of less than one hundred rubles or who is under twenty-five years of age.

63. A nobleman who does not own a village himself or who is under twenty-five years of age may be present at assemblies of the nobility but may not vote.

64. A nobleman who has never been in service or who, having served, did not attain officer's rank (even if officer's rank was given to him upon retirement) may be present at assemblies of the nobility; but he may not sit with the meritorious, may not vote in the assemblies of the nobility, and may not be elected to those posts filled by election of the assembly of the nobility.

XII:17. THE CHARTER OF THE CITIES, APRIL 21, 1785

In her eagerness to have a thriving bourgeoisie, Catherine issued, along with her Charter of the Nobility, a Charter of the Cities. Although much of this lengthy document remained on paper only—especially as concerns urban self-government (which had to await the decree of 1870)—it contains some useful descriptions of the categories and posts that existed in the Russian towns of the time. (Note: In the excerpts below, the term *meshchane* is used in two senses. Sometimes it refers broadly to the entire commercial-artisan class in the towns and has thus been translated "townsmen." Sometimes it is used in the limited nineteenth-century sense, designating only those craftsmen and petty tradesmen who lacked the capital to enroll in a guild as merchants; used in this sense the term has been left untranslated.)

Reference: *PSZRI,* 1st ser., 22:361–83.

B. Concerning city dwellers [*gorodovye obyvateli*]; [concerning] the establishment of city corporations [*gradskie obshchestva*] and concerning the privileges of city corporations.

29. In each city the city dwellers are granted permission to hold assemblies in that city, to form a city corporation, and to enjoy the rights and benefits stated below.

30. The city dwellers shall hold an assembly in winter every three years, by order and permission of the governor general or governor, to hold the elections permitted city dwellers and to hear the recommendations of the governor general or governor.

31. . . . The mayor [*gorodskoi golova*], burgomasters [*burgomistry*], and aldermen [*ratmany*] shall be elected by the city corporation every three years by ballot; judges [*starosty*] and assessors [*zasedateli*] of the verbal court [*slovesnyi sud,* instituted for mediation and the settlement of small civil suits] shall be elected by the same corporation each year by ballot.

32. . . . Assessors of the guberniia magistracy [*gubernskii magistrat,* which served as a court of appeal from decisions of the city courts, and handled cases concerning the entire city] and of the court of conscience [sovestnyi sud, a court for arbitration and the protection of civil rights] shall be elected by the capital city of the guberniia from among the merchants and meshchane of that capital city every three years by ballot and shall be presented to the administrator [pravitel'] or governor for confirmation; if they have no evident vices, the governor shall permit them to take office.

33. Court assessors [in the city courts: zasedateli v sudu] shall be elected by the townsmen from among the townsmen who live in that city. . . .

34. . . . Two city aldermen [ratmany gorodovye] shall sit in session in the police office [*uprava blagochiniia*] together with the police commissioner [*gorodnichii*] and the bailiffs [*pristavy*] for criminal and civil cases. . . .

36. The city corporation is permitted to make representations to the governor concerning its corporate needs and interests. . . .

49. The city corporation is forbidden to elect, to those offices which by virtue of the statutes [of 1775 for the administration of the guberniias] are filled by election, any townsman whose capital yields him an income of less than fifty rubles or who is under twenty-five years of age.

50. A townsman whose capital yields him an income of less than fifty rubles or who is under twenty-five years of age may attend the assemblies of the city corporation but may not vote.

Note: The prohibition in articles 49 and 50 forbidding townsmen whose capital yields an income of less than fifty rubles to vote or to be elected to office applies to those cities in which [men with] this much capital can be found in the guilds; if such is not the case, those who have less capital are permitted to vote and to be elected to office. . . .

53. In each city a register of city dwellers [*gorodovaia obyvatel'skaia kniga*] shall be compiled, in which the residents of that city shall be listed, so that each citizen may pass on his legal status [*dostoianie*] from father to son, grandson, great-grandson, and their descendants. . . .

C. Instructions for the compilation and continuation of a register of city dwellers.

61. The mayor of each city, together with deputies elected by the city from each city category [*chast'*], shall compile a register of city dwellers from the lists of the elder [starosta, elected by each category for this purpose].

62. The register of city dwellers shall be divided into six categories.

63. In the first category of the register of city dwellers shall be entered the legal status [sostoianie] and names of the true city dwellers [*nastoiashchie gorodovye obyvateli*], in alphabetical order.

Definition: True city dwellers are those who own a house or other building in that city, or an empty lot or land in the city.

64. In the second category of the register of city dwellers shall be entered those who are enrolled in the first, second, and third guilds [of merchants], in alphabetical order.

Definition: Enrolled in guilds are all those (whatever their origin, descent, family, legal status, business, occupation, handicraft, or trade) who declare that they own a certain capital, to wit: (1) those who declare a capital of from 10,000 rubles to 50,000 rubles shall be enrolled in the first guild; (2) those who declare a capital of from 5,000 rubles to 10,000 rubles shall be enrolled in the second guild; (3) those who declare a capital of from 1,000 rubles to 5,000 rubles shall be enrolled in the third guild.

65. In the third category of the register of city dwellers shall be entered those who are enrolled in trade corporations [tsekhi], in alphabetical order.

Definition: Enrolled in trade corporations are those masters, journeymen, and apprentices of various trades who have enrolled in their respective trade corporation.

66. In the fourth category of the register of city dwellers shall be entered the temporary residents [gosti] from other cities and foreign countries, in alphabetical order. . . .

67. In the fifth category of the register of city dwellers shall be entered the distinguished citizens [imenitye grazhdane], in alphabetical order.

Definition: Distinguished citizens are: (1) those . . . who, elected from the townspeople, have performed the duties of assessors of the court of conscience or the guberniia magistracy, or burgomaster or mayor, in a praiseworthy manner; (2) learned men who can present a diploma from an academy or university, or written testimony of their knowledge or ability, and who are acknowledged as such through examination by the Russian higher schools [glavnye uchilishcha, the future gymnasiums]; (3) artists practising the three [sic] fine arts, namely: architects, painters, sculptors, and composers who are members of an academy or have a certificate from an academy of their knowledge or ability and are acknowledged as such through examination by the Russian higher schools; (4) capitalists of any occupation or legal status who declare a capital of over 50,000 rubles; (5) bankers who transfer money and for this occupation declare a capital of from 100,000 to 200,000; (6) those who engage in wholesale trade and do not keep shops; (7) ship-masters who send their own ships beyond the seas.

68. In the sixth category of the register of city dwellers shall be entered the posad men, in alphabetical order.

Definition: Posad men are those old inhabitants [starozhily] of that city, or those who have settled or been born there, who are not entered in other categories of the register of city dwellers and who make their living by trade, handicraft, or labor in that city. . . .

D. Concerning the personal benefits of middle-class city dwellers, or townsmen in general.

80. The title of middle-class city dwellers, or townsmen, is a consequence of the industry and virtue through which they have acquired this special legal status. . . .

82. A townsman shall transmit his status as a townsman to his wife, whether she be of equal or of inferior descent.

83. Children of townsmen shall inherit their father's status.

84. A townsman may not be deprived of his good name, or his life or property, without trial.

85. A townsman shall be tried by a court of townsmen.

86. A townsman shall be deprived of his good name for the following deeds: (1) violation of his oath; (2) treason; (3) brigandage; (4) theft of any kind; (5) fraud; (6) crimes for which the law prescribes corporal punishment; (7) if it is proved that [sic] he taught or persuaded others to commit such crimes.

87. It is reiterated that it is strictly prohibited for any one to dare arbitrarily to confiscate a townsman's property or to inflict damages upon it without legal trial and sentence by the appropriate courts. . . .

123. "The statute on artisans" [remeslennoe polozhenie]. . . .

i. Masters engaged in the same trade shall assemble each year and elect by ballot, from among the practicing masters enrolled in their corporation [uprava], one corporation elder [upravnoi starshina] and two assistants to the elder and shall present them to the municipal magistracy [gorodovoi magistrat] or ratusha for confirmation; if they are free of any evident vices the municipal magistracy or ratusha shall permit them to take office. . . .

k. All the corporations [of artisans] shall jointly elect each year a prefect of artisans [*remeslennyi glava*] by ballot and present him to the municipal magistracy or ratusha for confirmation; if he is free of any evident vices the municipal magistracy or ratusha shall permit him to take office. . . .

O. Concerning the general municipal council [*gorodskaia obshchaia duma*] and the six-member municipal council [*gorodskaia shesti-glasnaia duma*].

156. City dwellers are permitted to organize a general municipal council.

157. The general municipal council shall be composed of the mayor and representatives from the true city dwellers, from the guilds, from the trade corporations, from the temporary residents from other cities and foreign countries, from the distinguished citizens, and from the posad men. Each of these groups shall have one vote in the city community [i.e. in the general municipal council]. . . .

164. The general municipal council shall elect from among its members a six-member municipal council. . . .

168. The municipal council is forbidden to interfere in lawsuits between inhabitants of that city, since the statutes place such matters under the jurisdiction of the magistracies or ratushy.

XII:18. THE PRINCE DE LIGNE CONCERNING CATHERINE, HER TRIP TO THE CRIMEA, AND POTEMKIN, 1787-1788

Charles Joseph, prince de Ligne (1735-1814), was a high officer in the Austrian army, a writer, and a friend and adviser of the emperor Joseph II. In his letters and memoirs the prince provides an eyewitness account of Catherine's triumphal journey of 1787 to New Russia and the Crimea. Perhaps more perceptive and certainly more honest than the Saxon envoy Helbig, chief author and disseminator of the crude tales about "Potemkin villages," De Ligne enables his readers to see both the surface display and the real achievements that lay behind it. He also provides precious glimpses of late-eighteenth-century monarchs and their aides at work.

Reference: Katharine Prescott Wormeley, ed. and trans., *Prince de Ligne: His Memoirs, Letters and Miscellaneous Papers,* 2 vols. (Boston: Hardy, Pratt, 1899), 2:13-15, 18-20, 46-50, 81-82. The editors are indebted to Messrs. Baltzly and Kucherov for the selection of these passages.

[From a letter to Mme la Marquise de Coigny, in Paris, from Kherson, 1787:]

Cleopatra's fleet left Kiev as soon as a general cannonading informed us that the ice in the Borysthenes [the Dnieper] had broken up. If any one had asked, on seeing us embark in our great and little vessels to the number of eighty, with three thousand men in their crews, "what the devil we were going to do in those galleys," we should have answered, "Amuse ourselves, and—*Vogue la galère!*" for never was there a voyage so brilliant and so agreeable. Our chambers are furnished with chiné silk and divans; and when any of those who, like myself, accompany the empress, leaves or returns to his galley, at least twelve musicians whom we have on board celebrate the event. Sometimes there is a little danger in returning at night after supping with her Majesty on her galley, because we have to ascend the Borysthenes, often against the wind, in a small boat. In fact, one night there was a tempest, in order that we might have all experiences, and two or three galleys went ashore on a sand-bank.

Our Cleopatra does not travel to seduce Mark Antonys and Caesars. The Emperor Joseph was already seduced into admiration of her genius and power. Cleopatra does not swallow pearls, but she gives them away plentifully. She resembles her prototype of antiquity only in a liking for costly navigation, magnificence, and study. She has given more than two hundred thousand volumes to the libraries of her empire. That is the boasted number of the library of Pergamos, with which the Queen of Egypt restored that of Alexandria; and as for fêtes, Kherson is indeed another Alexandria.

After those [fêtes] at Krementczuck [Kremenchug] given by Prince Potemkin, who caused to be transplanted into a really magical English garden exotic trees as big round as himself, we disembarked at the cataracts of Keydac [presumably Kodak], former capital of the Zaporoguas, aquatic brigands. Here the Emperor Joseph II came to meet us, and the fêtes were renewed on his arrival. . . .

I forgot to tell you that the King of Poland awaited us at Kaniève [Kanev] on the Borysthenes. He spent three months and three millions in waiting to see the empress for three hours. I went in a little Zaporogian canoe to tell him of our arrival. An hour later the grandees of the empire came to fetch him in a brilliant barge. As he set foot upon it he said, with the inexpressible charm of his beautiful face and the soft tones of his voice: "Messieurs, the King of Poland has charged me to present to you the Comte Poniatowski." The dinner was very gay; we drank the king's health to a triple salute of all the artillery of the fleet. On leaving the table, the king looked about for his hat, and could not find it. The empress, more adroit, saw where it was and gave it to him. "Twice to cover my head!" said the king, gallantly, alluding to his crown; "ah, madame! that is heaping too many benefits, too much gratitude upon me."

The empress has never before known so well the charms of social intercourse; and, as there are two or three of us who do not play cards, she has sacrificed the little game she usually plays in Russia. . . .

The empress said at table yesterday: "It is very singular that *you,* which is plural, should have come to be the rule. Why have they banished *thou?*" "It is not banished, Madame," I replied, "for Jean-Jacques Rousseau says to God: 'Lord, in thine adorable glory;' and God is thee'd and thou'd in our prayers; for instance: *Nunc dimittis servum tuum, Domine.*" "Well, then," said the empress, "why do you treat me with more ceremony? Come, I will set you the example. Wilt thou give me some of that?" she said to the grand equerry. "Yes," he replied, "if thou wilt hand me something else." And thereupon a deluge of thee-ings and thou-ings, each more funny than the others. I mingled mine with "Majesty," and *Ta Majesté* seemed to me the right thing. . . . But in spite of it all, her thee-ing and thou-ing and thee'd and thou'd Majesty still wore the air of the autocratress of all the Russias, and of nearly all the rest of the world.

[From a letter to Mme la Marquise de Coigny, in Paris, from Bakhchisarai, June 1, 1787:]

After leaving Kherson, we found marvellous camps of Asiatic magnificence in the middle of the desert. I no longer know where I am, or in what age I live. . . . Again I dream, methinks, when I meet the young princes of the Caucasus, almost covered with silver, on their dazzling white horses. When I see them armed with bows and arrows I fancy I am back in the days of the old and the young Cyrus. . . . When I meet detachments of Circassians, handsome as the day, with their waists more tightly nipped into their corselets than that of Madame de L— ; when I see Mourzas more daintily dressed than the Duchesse de Choiseul at the queen's ball, Cossack officers with better taste in draping their scarfs than Mlle. Bertin, and furniture and garments of more harmonious coloring than Mme. Le Brun can put into her paintings, I am lost in amazement. At Stare Krim [Staryi Krym, in the eastern Crimea] (where a palace was raised in which to sleep one night) I could descry from my bed all that is most interesting in two quarters of the world as far, almost, as the Caspian Sea. I think it was a part of Satan's temptation, for nothing finer could have been shown to our Lord. I could see from the same point on leaving my chamber, the Black Sea, the Sea of Azov, the Sea of Zabache [Sivash, the stagnant bay along the northeastern shore of the Crimea], and the Caucasus. . . .

Again I think I dream when, in a coach of six places (a triumphal car adorned with jewelled monograms), being seated between two persons on whose shoulders the extreme heat makes me often drop asleep, I hear, as I waken, one of them say to the other: "I have thirty millions of subjects, so they tell me, counting only males." "And I," says the other, "twenty-two, counting all." "I require," adds the first, "an army of six hundred thousand men, at least, from Riga to Kamtschatka." "With half that number," replies the other, "I have just as many as I want."

· · ·

All nations and their greatest personages have been reviewed in that coach, and God knows how they were served. "Rather than sign the separation of thirteen States, as my brother George has done," said Catherine II, softly, "I would have shot myself." "Rather than throw up my power, as my brother-in-law has done by convoking and assembling the nation to talk of abuses," says Joseph II, "I don't know what I would have done." They were quite agreed about the King of Sweden [Gustavus III], whom neither of them liked, and against whom the emperor had taken a prejudice in Italy on account, so he said, of a blue and silver dressing-gown with a diamond badge that the king wore. They both agreed, however, that he had energy, talent, and intellect. . . .

Their imperial Majesties felt each other [out] now and then about these poor devils of Turks. They threw out suggestions and glanced at each other.

[From the prince the Ligne's memoirs:]

The enemies of Prince Potemkin had assured his sovereign that her army was only on paper; they even denied the existence of the light-horse cavalry. So that when, on the Borysthenes, fifty or sixty squadrons galloped to meet her all glittering with silver and steel, she was amazed at the sight. She said to me: "Those wicked people! how they tried to deceive me! Why, *there* is enough to snap our fingers at the Turks." Then, looking at the portrait of Peter I as usual, she said, with an air that dictated my answer, "What would he say? what would he do?" It will not be doubted that my desire to please and to make war inspired my reply. "But the French?" she said. "They have just made their public confession," I answered, "in that Deficit which Necker has announced to the Notables. Poor devils! they may perhaps have a revolution. Besides, M. de Vergennes is dead, and the Archbishop of Toulouse, whom they talk of as the next prime minister, has no house of business of his own in Constantinople." "But the Prussians?" she said. "Let us make haste," I replied; "the emperor can take Belgrade, and your Majesty Oczakow, Bender, and Akermann before King William knows that there is any question of war."

Prince Potemkin, who was dying to command an army in order to get the grand cordon of Saint George, talked to me incessantly about the war. The emperor arrived at Kherson in my carriage, which I had sent for him, and said to me the next day: "It seems to me these people want war. Are they ready? I don't think they are; and, in any case, I am not. And what do they expect to get? I have just seen their fleets and their fortresses, and they are only sketched out to throw dust in one's eyes. Nothing is solid; it has all been done in a hurry, and very expensively, to humbug the empress." I, who did not see so accurately as he, and was dazzled by the passing of so much artillery and such superb

regiments and by what I was told of magazines and munitions, assured him that I thought the Russians were ready. What was singular is that the emperor was seduced himself by the same sights, of which he was not the dupe when he saw them alone. The cleverness of showing them again in presence of the empress, the quantity and importance of the military objects presented daily before him, the magic of this journey of six thousand versts, seemed to proclaim a power he blamed himself for having misjudged.

Potemkin thought that the moment had come to explain matters to the emperor. He went to see him one morning and told him about the pretended wrongs the Court of Russia had received from the Porte—which was being insulted constantly by M. de Bulgakoff [ambassador to Constantinople] and a crowd of little scamps of consuls, of whom the Porte complained quite mildly. The emperor answered with generalities, personal attachment to the empress, fidelity to his engagements, and so forth. Prince Potemkin is timid, and easily embarrassed. He did not say all that he wanted to say, so he begged me to speak to the emperor and complete that which he had only begun.

I did not fail to do so. "I don't see exactly what he wants," said his Majesty. "It seems to me that when I do as much as I did in helping them to get the Crimea, that ought to be enough. What would they do for me if I should have war with Prussia some day or other?" "Everything, Sire," I said; "at least they promise it; they even say everything your Majesty may want in this affair." "What I want is Silesia, and war with Turkey will not give me that," he replied. "Well, we'll see; we'll see."

I have related elsewhere all that was done to intoxicate the empress. A cloud of Cossacks from the Don arrived like a whirlwind and enveloped our carriage in the deserts of Perekop. The empress supposed them eight hundred leagues distant. An armament of Tartar guards, all young Mourzas, with splendid figures superbly dressed, appeared as suddenly to escort the empress on her approach to Taurica. And when, close to Inkermann [just east of Sevastopol'] they parted, as if by a fairy wand, into two columns and revealed the fleet of Sevastopol, this final draught of champagne went to her head. She rose suddenly, during dinner, looked at us with fire in her eyes, and said: "I drink to the health of my best friend," motioning to the emperor. Kissing of hand on his part. Embrace on hers. Great hopes of war in me and the Prince of Nassau. Embarrassment in Ségur, fearing to play a poor *rôle* in it all; philosophic indifference in Fitz-Herbert, one of the most amiable of Englishmen; uncertainty in Comte Cobenzl, trying to read in the eyes of the emperor; and great curiosity in all the courtiers.

Prince Potemkin, who had kissed hands also, and made believe weep with joy and gratitude, kept up the salvos of the fleet incessantly, in order to keep our heads turned.

[From a letter to the comte de Ségur, August 10, 1788, after de Ligne's extended visit to New Russia and its governor general, Potemkin:]

I see the commander of an army, who seems to be lazy and works without ceasing; who has no desk but his knees, no comb but his fingers; always in bed and never sleeping day or night because his ardour for his sovereign, whom he adores, incessantly agitates him; while a single cannon-shot, which does not come nigh him, makes him wretched with the thought that it costs the lives of some of his soldiers; timid for others, brave for himself, pausing under the fierce fire of a battery to give orders; more Ulysses, nevertheless, than Achilles; uneasy before danger, gay when in it, sad in pleasures. Unhappy because so fortunate; *blasé* about everything, easily disgusted; morose, inconstant; a profound philosopher, able minister, splendid politician, child of ten years old; never vindictive, asking pardon for a pain he may have caused, quick to repair an injustice; believing that he loves God, fearing the devil, whom he imagines the greater and more powerful of the two; with one hand giving proofs of his liking for women, with the other making signs of the Cross; his arms in crucifix at the feet of the Virgin, or round the necks of those who, thanks to him, have ceased to be so; receiving benefits innumerable from his great sovereign, sharing them instantly with others; accepting estates, returning them to the giver, or paying her for them without ever letting her know it;

gambling incessantly or else never touching a card; preferring to give than to pay his debts; enormously rich, yet without a penny; distrusting or confiding; jealous or grateful; ill-humoured or jovial; easily prejudiced for and against, returning as quickly from either extreme; talking theology to his generals and war to his archbishops; never reading, but sifting those with whom he talks, and contradicting them in order to learn more; presenting the most brutal or the most pleasing aspect, manners the most repulsive or the most attractive; with the mien of the proudest satrap of the Orient, or the cringing air of Louis XIV's courtiers; a great appearance of harshness, very soft in reality at the bottom of his heart; fantastic as to his hours, his meals, his sleep, his tastes; wanting all things like a child, able to go without everything like a great man; sober with the air of a gourmand; biting his nails, or apples, or turnips, scolding or laughing, dissembling or swearing, playing or praying, singing or meditating; calling, dismissing, and recalling twenty aides-de-camp without anything to say to them; bearing heat as if he thought only of a luxurious bath, laughing at cold, apparently able to do without furs; always in a shirt and no drawers, or else in a uniform embroidered on every seam, feet bare or in spangled slippers, without cap or hat (as I saw him once under fire); in a shabby dressing-gown or a splendid tunic, with his three stars, ribbons, and diamonds as big as my thumb round the portrait of the empress which always attracts the bullets; bent double, huddled up, stunted when in his own room; tall, his nose in the air, proud, handsome, noble, majestic, or seductive when he shows himself to his army with the air of an Agamemnon amid the kings of Greece.

What is his magic? Genius, and then genius, and again genius; natural intelligence, an excellent memory, elevation of soul, malice without malignity, craft without cunning, a happy mixture of caprices, of which the good when they are uppermost win him all hearts; great generosity, grace, and justice in his rewards, much tact, the talent of divining that which he does not know, and great knowledge of men.

XII:19. THE DECREE ON THE RUPTURE WITH FRANCE, FEBRUARY 8, 1793

The news of the execution of King Louis XVI on January 10 (21, N.S.), 1793, reached Catherine on January 31. According to the diary of an eyewitness (State Secretary A. V. Khrapovitskii), Catherine, upon receiving the news, "went to bed sick and mournful." By February 8 she had recovered from her shock sufficiently to sign the decree of which portions follow.
   Reference: *PSZRI*, 1st ser., 23:402-04.

The disturbances that have occurred in France since 1789 could not fail to arouse concern in every rightly ordered state. So long as there still remained the hope that time and circumstances would bring to reason those who had gone astray, and that order and the power of the legitimate authority would be restored, we permitted the unhindered presence of Frenchmen in our empire and maintained all kinds of relations with them. Having witnessed subsequently their violence and ever growing spirit of rebellion against their sovereign, combined with a frenzied determination, not only to establish in their own country the principles of godlessness, insubordination to the supreme authority, and alienation from every good moral doctrine, but also to spread this disease throughout the world, we broke off political relations with France. . . . Today, when, to the horror of all, violence in that unhappy country has exceeded all bounds, and more than seven hundred monsters have come forth to put their wrongfully usurped power to evil use by raising their hands against the Lord's anointed, their legitimate sovereign, and putting him to death, on the tenth of January of the current year, in a cruel and most painful manner, we deem it our duty before God and our conscience no longer to tolerate any relations between our empire and France, such as can exist only between rightly ordered countries.
. . .
   In consideration whereof we ordain that:
(1) The operation of the commercial treaty

concluded between us and the deceased king of France, Louis XVI, on the thirty-first day of January 1786 shall be terminated until the restoration of order and legitimate authority in France. (2) Until such time, all vessels navigating the seas under the French national flag shall be forbidden to enter our ports; conversely, our merchants and shipowners shall be forbidden to send their merchant ships to French ports. . . . (5) All Frenchmen . . . who recognize the present government of their country and pay obedience to it shall not be tolerated in our empire and shall be deported from all localities where they reside. . . . (6) Exemptions from this [rule] shall be made for French persons of both sexes . . . who shall manifest a sincere intent and desire to renounce the godless and subversive principles professed in their native country by the usurpers of governmental power, by taking an oath in accordance with the model attached hereto . . . and who will give proof of their sincere determination, based on the Christian faith which they profess and into which they were born, to be loyal and obedient to the king who will assume the crown by right of succession. . . . (10) All our subjects shall be prohibited from journeying to France and from maintaining any communication with Frenchmen residing in their country or enrolled in the French armies. . . . (11) It shall be forbidden to import into Russia newspapers, journals, and other periodicals published in France.

XII:20. GENERAL KRECHETNIKOV'S MANIFESTO ON THE SECOND POLISH PARTITION, MARCH 27, 1793

Russian troops having invaded Poland-Lithuania in mid-1792, agreement was reached between Russia and Prussia in January 1793 concerning the second partition of the commonwealth. Russia's ostensible reasons for this partition, as well as her promises to the annexed population (numbering some three million), were set forth in a manifesto issued March 27, 1793, upon imperial authorization, by General in Chief Krechetnikov, commander of the Russian army of occupation.
   Reference: *PSZRI*, 1st ser., 23:410-12.

The participation of Her Majesty the empress of all Russia in Polish affairs has always based itself on the immediate, fundamental, and mutual advantage of both states. That all her efforts to preserve peace, tranquillity, and freedom in this neighboring region not only were in vain but turned into a fruitless burden and a source of untold detriment is indisputable and has been palpably demonstrated by thirty years of experience. Amidst the disorders and violence resulting from the turmoil and dissension that ceaselessly torment the Polish republic, Her Imperial Majesty has always looked with particular compassion upon that oppression to which have been subjected the lands and cities adjoining the Russian Empire, which once were truly its possessions and which are inhabited and were founded by men of the same nationality, who were instructed in the Orthodox Christian faith and continue to profess it to this day. At present certain unworthy Poles, enemies of their fatherland, are shamelessly inciting a government of godless rebels in the French kingdom and asking their assistance, so that they might unite with them involving Poland in a bloody civil war. . . .

In view of these considerations, to provide satisfaction and compensation for the great losses she has suffered, as well as to safeguard the interests and safety of the Russian Empire and of the Polish regions themselves, and to ward off and cut short once and for all any instability or frequent and various changes of government, Her Imperial Majesty now resolves to take under her power and incorporate into her empire for all time to come all lands enclosed within the line described below [western Belorussia, Volynia, Podolia, and the entire province of Kiev] and their inhabitants.

          ·   ·   ·

Through the solemn assurance of the free exercise of religion and the inviolable integrity of property, extended . . . to one and all, it is understood that the Jewish communities living in the towns and lands incorporated within the Russian Empire will be maintained and preserved with all those liberties they now enjoy with regard to the law and to their property. . . . May justice continue to be dispensed by the present courts in the name and by the authority of Her Imperial Majesty, with the observance of the strictest order and justice.

B. SOCIAL AND ECONOMIC CONDITIONS

XII:21. WILLIAM COXE ON RUSSIA IN 1778-1779

William Coxe (1747-1828), historian, writer, and an archdeacon of the Anglican church, spent about seven months in Russia in 1778-79 as the traveling tutor of a young English aristocrat, George, Lord Herbert (later earl of Pembroke). Despite the relative shortness of his stay, his observations—of which these excerpts are only a small sample—were more accurate than those of many who made greater claims to expertise.

    Reference: William Coxe, *Travels into Poland, Russia, Sweden, and Denmark,* 3 vols. (London, 1784-90), 1:263-66, 273, 288, 291, 294 [all on Moscow]; 435-38, 441-42 [peasants]; 491-92, 503-05 [the nobles]; 2:19 [Catherine's accession], 94-99 [customs], 104 [clergy], 110-11, 113-14 [peasants]; vol. 3 (1802 ed.), pp. 316-17 [artels]. Coxe has recently been reprinted (New York: Da Capo, 1968).

Notwithstanding the predilection which Peter conceived for Petersburgh, in which all the succeeding sovereigns, excepting Peter II, have fixed their residence, Moscow is still the most populous city of the Russian empire. Here the chief nobles who do not belong to the court of the empress reside; they here support a larger number of retainers; they love to gratify their taste for a ruder and more expensive magnificence in the antient style of

feudal grandeur; and are not, as at Petersburgh, eclipsed by the superior splendour of the court.

          ·   ·   ·

If I was struck with the singularity of Smolensko, I was all astonishment at the immensity and variety of Moscow. Something so irregular, so uncommon, so extraordinary, and so contrasted, never before fell under my observation. The streets are in general exceedingly long and broad: some of them are paved; others, particularly those in the suburbs, are formed with trunks of trees, or are boarded with planks like the floor of a room; wretched hovels are blended with large palaces; cottages of one story stand next to the most superb and stately mansions. Many brick structures are covered with wooden tops; some of the wooden houses are painted, others have iron doors and roofs. Numerous churches presented themselves in every quarter built in a peculiar style of architecture; some with domes of copper, others of tin, gilt or painted green, and many roofed with wood. In a word, some parts of this vast city have the look of a sequestered desert, other quarters of a populous town, some of a contemptible village, others of a great capital.

Moscow may be considered as a town built upon the Asiatic model, but gradually becoming more and more European; and exhibiting in its present state a motley mixture of discordant architecture. It is distributed into the following divisions: 1. Kremlin. 2. Khitaigorod. 3. Bielgorod. 4. Semlainogorod. 5. Sloboda; which, for want of a more precise term, I shall call the suburbs.

· · ·

Nothing can exceed the hospitality of the Russians. We could never pay a morning visit to any nobleman without being detained to dinner; we also constantly received several general invitations; but as we considered them in the light of mere compliments, we were unwilling to intrude ourselves without further notice. We soon found, however, that the principal persons of distinction kept open tables, and were highly obliged at our resorting to them without ceremony.

· · ·

The Russian nobles display a great degree of grandeur and magnificence in their houses, domestics, and way of living. Their palaces at and near Moscow are stupendous piles of buildings; and I am informed that their mansions, at a distance from Moscow and Petersburgh, are upon a still greater scale, where they reside as independent princes, like the feudal barons in early times; have their separate courts of justice, and govern their vassals with an almost unlimited sway.

· · ·

The places of divine worship at Moscow are exceedingly numerous; including chapels, they amount to above a thousand: there are 484 public churches, of which 199 are of brick,

and the others of wood; the former are commonly stuccoed or white-washed, the latter painted of a red colour.

· · ·

Before I close the general description of the Russian churches, I must not forget their bells, which form, I may almost say, no inconsiderable part of divine worship in this country, as the length or shortness of their peals ascertains the greater or lesser sanctity of the day. They are hung in belfreys detached from the church: they do not swing like our bells, but are fixed immoveably to the beams, are rung by a rope tied to the clapper, and pulled sideways. Some of these bells are of a stupendous size: one in the tower of St. Ivan's church weighs 3551 Russian poods, or 127,836 English pounds. It has always been esteemed a meritorious act of religion to present a church with bells; and the piety of the donor has been measured by their magnitude.

· · ·

The villages which occasionally line this route [from Moscow to Saint Petersburg] are extremely similar to each other; they usually consist of a single street, with wooden cottages; a few only being distinguished by brick houses. . . . [Each house] contains one, or at most two rooms, one whereof is occupied by the whole family.

I have frequently had occasion to observe, that beds are by no means usual in this country. . . . The family slept generally upon the benches, on the ground, or over the stove [Coxe's footnote: "The stove is a kind of brick oven; it occupies almost a quarter of the room, and is flat at top"]; occasionally men, women, and children, promiscuously, without any discrimination of sex or condition, and frequently almost in a state of nature. In some cottages I observed a kind of shelf, about six or seven feet from the ground, carried from one end of the room to the other; to which were fastened several transverse planks, and upon these some of the family slept with their heads and feet occasionally hanging down, and appearing to us, who were not accustomed to such places of repose, as if they were upon the point of falling to the ground.

The number of persons thus crouded into a small space, and which sometimes amounted to twenty, added to the heat of the stove, rendered the room intolerably warm, and

produced a suffocating smell, which nothing
but use enabled us to support.

. . .

The peasants, in their common intercourse,
are remarkably polite to each other: they take
off their cap at meeting; bow ceremoniously
and frequently, and usually exchange a salute.
They accompany their ordinary discourse
with much action and innumerable gestures,
and are exceedingly servile in their expressions
of deference to their superiors.

. . .

The peasants are well clothed, comfortably
lodged, and seem to enjoy plenty of wholesome food. Their rye-bread, whose blackness
at first disgusts the eye, and whose sourness
the taste of a delicate traveller, agrees very
well with the appetite; as I became reconciled
to it from use, I found it at all times no unpleasant morsel, and, when seasoned with
hunger, it was quite delicious: they render
this bread more palatable by stuffing it with
onions and groats, carrots or green corn, and
seasoning it with sweet oil. . . .

The backwardness of the Russian peasants
in all the mechanical arts, when compared
with those of the other nations of Europe, is
visible to the most superficial observer.

. . .

In our route through Russia I was greatly
surprized at the propensity of the natives to
singing. Even the peasants, who acted in the
capacity of coachmen and postilions, were no
sooner mounted than they began to warble an
air, and continued it, without the least inter-
mission, for several hours. But what still more
astonished me was, that they performed occasionally in parts; and I have frequently
observed them engaged in a kind of musical
dialogue, making reciprocal questions and
responses, as if they were chanting, (if I may
so express myself), their ordinary conversation.

The postilions *sing*, as I have just observed,
from the beginning to the end of a stage; the
soldiers *sing* continually during their march;
the countrymen *sing* during the most laborious
occupations: the public-houses re-echo with
their carols; and in a still evening I have frequently heard the air vibrate with the notes
from the surrounding villages.

. . .

The richness and splendour of the Russian
court surpasses all the ideas which the most
elaborate descriptions can suggest. It retains
many traces of its antient Asiatick pomp,
blended with European refinements. An immense retinue of courtiers always preceded
and followed the empress; the costliness and
glare of their apparel, and a profusion of
precious stones, created a splendour, of which
the magnificence of other courts can give us
only a faint idea. The court-dress of the men
is in the French fashion: that of the ladies is
a gown and petticoat, with a small hoop; the
gown has long hanging-sleeves and a short
train, and is of a different colour from the
petticoat. The ladies wore, according to the
fashion of the winter of 1777 at Paris and
London, very lofty headdresses, and were
not sparing in the use of rouge. Amid the
several articles of sumptuousness which
distinguish the Russian nobility, there is none
perhaps more calculated to strike a foreigner
than the profusion of diamonds and other
precious stones, which sparkle in every part
of their dress. In most other European countries these costly ornaments are (excepting
among a few of the richest and principal
nobles) almost entirely appropriated to the
ladies; but in this the men vie with the fair
sex in the use of them. Many of the nobility
were almost covered with diamonds; their
buttons, buckles, hilts of swords, and epaulets,
were composed of this valuable material.

. . .

The Russian nobility of Petersburgh are no
less than those of Moscow distinguished for
their hospitality towards foreigners. We were
no sooner presented to a person of rank and
fortune, than we were regarded in the light of
domestick visitants. Many of the nobility
keep an open table, to which one invitation
was considered as a standing passport of admission. The only ceremony necessary to be
observed on this occasion was to make inquiry
in the morning if the master of the house dined
at home; and if he did, we, without further
ceremony, presented ourselves at his table.
The oftener we appeared at these hospitable
boards, the more acceptable guests we were
esteemed; and we always seemed to confer,
instead of receiving, an obligation.

The tables were served with great profusion
and taste. Though the Russians have adopted
the delicacies of French cookery, yet they
neither affect to despise their native dishes,
nor squeamishly reject the solid joints which
characterize our repasts. The plainest, as well

as the choicest viands, were collected from the most distant quarters: I have frequently seen at the same time sterlet from the Volga, veal from Archangel, mutton from Astrachan, beef from the Ukraine, and pheasants from Hungary and Bohemia. Their common wines are chiefly claret, Burgundy, and Champaigne, and I never tasted English beer and porter in greater perfection and abundance.

. . .

The houses of the nobility are furnished with great elegance, and the suite of apartments in which they receive company is uncommonly splendid. They are fitted up in the style of London and Paris, and the new fashions make their appearance as soon as in those two capitals.

. . .

Peter III had by some part of his conduct rendered himself so odious, and, by others, so contemptible to his subjects, that the first account of his dethronement, and of Catharine's accession . . . was received with universal joy.

. . .

Much has been written concerning the great civilization which Peter I introduced into this country; that he obliged the people to relinquish their beards, and their national dress; that he naturalized the arts and sciences; that he disciplined his army, and created a navy; and that he made a total change throughout each part of his extensive empire. We may readily allow the truth of this eulogium with respect to his improvements in the discipline of his army and the creation of a navy, for these were objects within the reach of the persevering genius of a despotick sovereign; but the pompous accounts of the total change which he effected in the national manners, seem to have been the mere echos of foreigners, who have never visited the country, and who have collected the history of Peter from the most partial information. . . . I was astonished at the barbarism in which the bulk of the people still continue. I am ready to allow that the principal nobles are perfectly civilized, and as refined in their entertainments, mode of living, and social intercourse, as those of other European countries. But there is a wide difference between polishing a nation, and polishing a few individuals. The merchants and peasants still universally retain their beards, their national

dress, their original manners; and, what is most remarkable, the greatest part of the merchants and burghers of the large towns, even the citizens of Petersburgh and Moscow, resemble, in their external appearance and general mode of living, the inhabitants of the smallest village: and, notwithstanding the rigorous edicts issued by Peter I, I can venture to assert, that of the 11,500,000 males, which form the population of the Russian empire, at least nine millions wear their beards. . . .

The greatest part of the peasants, who form the bulk of the nation, are still almost as deficient in the arts as they were before Peter's time, although the sciences have flourished in the capital. But the civilization of a numerous and widely dispersed people cannot be the work of a moment, and can only be effected by a gradual and almost insensible progress.

. . .

In Russia, as in the Oriental governments, there is scarcely any distinction of ranks among the nobility, excepting what is derived from the service of the sovereign. Even the eldest sons of those persons, who have been raised to the most considerable honours and the highest employments, excepting the advantages which they undoubtedly retain of facilitating their promotion by a ready access to court, do not derive any solid benefits from their birth like those which the peers of England, the grandees of Spain, or the dukes, who are peers of France, enjoy from their hereditary descent. The importance of a noble family of immense property and official honours is almost annihilated upon the death of the chief; because his property is equally divided among his sons; and because titles, though allowed to be hereditary, do not, independent of the sovereign's favour, contribute much to aggrandize the possessors; that of a prince, a count, or a baron, conveying in themselves little personal distinction, unless accompanied with a civil or military employment.

. . .

According to the system introduced by Peter I, but which has gradually been corrupted as it has receded from its source, every person takes precedence from his military station; he must rise in regular gradation, and, before he can be an officer, must have served as a corporal or serjeant: but this ordinance is easily eluded; as frequently infants are made serjeants and corporals; and it is not necessary to have served even one campaign in order to attain precedence, as it may be conferred by civil offices.

And although the law of Peter I, which compelled each nobleman or gentleman, under pain of degradation, to serve in the army, was abolished by Peter III, yet its effects still subsist. No one under the rank of a major, let his fortune be ever so considerable, is permitted to drive more than two horses; under that of brigadier more than four; a nobleman of the highest fortune and distinction, who has never been in the army, is not allowed, excepting by the special permission of the crown, to use in the capital a carriage drawn by more than one horse; while a merchant may have two.

. . .

I cannot omit mentioning, that, during the five months we passed at Petersburgh, and the almost constant intercourse in which we were daily engaged with the nobility and gentry, I never once saw in company a single person of the sacred profession. It must be allowed indeed, that the parish-priests are for the most part too low and ignorant to be qualified for admission into genteel societies; while the dignitaries, being a separate order and restrained by several strict regulations, reside chiefly in their palaces within the monasteries; and contract an aversion, perhaps an unfitness, for social intercourse. This general character of the Russian hierarchy does by no means comprehend all the individuals; as some of them with whom I occasionally conversed were men of liberal manners and enlightened understandings.

. . .

The peasants of Russia . . . may be divided into, 1. peasants of the crown; 2. peasants belonging to individuals.

1. The former inhabit the imperial demesnes, and probably comprehend, including those belonging to the church lands which are now annexed to the crown, about the sixth part of the Russian peasants. [According to the Fifth Revision or census, in 1796, the state peasants constituted about two-fifth of the peasantry.] They are immediately under the jurisdiction of the imperial officers or bailiffs. Although liable to great exactions by the tenure of their subjection from these petty tyrants, yet they

are much more secure of their property; and being under the protection of the sovereign, any flagrant instances of oppression are more easily made known and redressed. Many of these vassals in particular districts have been franchised, and permitted to enrol themselves among the merchants and burghers; the whole body will gradually receive more and more privileges, as the spirit of humanity and policy penetrates further into these regions; and as the empress can venture to realize the generous system of diffusing a more equal freedom among the subjects of her vast empire.

2. Peasants belonging to individuals are the private property of the landholders, as much as implements of agriculture, or herds of cattle; and the value of an estate is estimated, as in Poland, by the number of boors, and not by the number of acres.

. . .

In regard to the lord's authority over their persons, according to the ancient laws, he might try them in his own courts of justice, or banish them without any process; he could inflict every species of penalty excepting the knoot, order them to be whipped, or confined in dungeons; he might send them to houses of correction, or banish them into Siberia; or, in short, take cognizance of every misdemeanor which was not a publick offence. He had, indeed, no power over their lives; for, if a slave was beat by order of his master, and died within the space of three days, the latter [the master] was guilty of murder, unless other reasons could be assigned for his demise. But was not this almost a mockery of justice? . . .

I am far from asserting, that inhumanity is the general characteristick of the Russian nobility; or that there are not many persons who treat their vassals with the utmost benevolence and justice. I am also well aware, that several peasants are in such a flourishing condition as to have formed very considerable capitals without dread of exaction; and that some even possess landed estates under their masters' name. But if we consider the unhappy pleasure which too many feel in tyrannizing over their inferiors, we have every reason to conclude, that the generality of boors must still be cruelly oppressed.

. . .

An Artel consists of a certain number of

labourers, who voluntarily become responsible, as a body, for the honesty of each individual. The separate earnings of each man are put into the common stock, a monthly allowance is made for his support, and at the end of the year the surplus is equally divided. The number varies in different associations from 50 to 100; and so advantageous is it considered to belong to one of these societies, that 500,

and even 1000 roubles are paid for admission. These societies are not bound by any law of the empire, or even written agreement; nor does the merchant restrain them under any legal obligation; yet there has been no instance of their objecting to any just claim, or of protecting an individual whose conduct had brought a demand on the society.

XII:22. TOOKE ON RUSSIA UNDER CATHERINE II

William Tooke was one of England's earliest Russian specialists in the modern sense. He spent many years in Russia during Catherine's reign, made extensive use of libraries there, interviewed eyewitnesses to important events, read widely in the accounts of other foreign visitors to Russia, and then in 1799 published his findings in three substantial volumes—with occasional citations to other sources. His work is thus a combination of primary and secondary material. The following excerpts present some of his observations and conclusions, particularly on matters social and economic.

Reference: Tooke, *View of the Russian Empire,* 1:260; 2:4-5, 21, 25, 37, 51, 58-59, 133, 144-45, 146, 256, 388-89; 3:151, 316-17, 461-63, 472-75.

No other country throughout the globe contains such a mixture and diversity of inhabitants. Russians and Tartars, Germans and Mongoles, Finns and Tonguses, live here at immense distances, and in the most different climates, as fellow-citizens of one state, amalgamated by their political constitution, but by bodily frame, language, religion, manners, and mode of life, diversified to the most extraordinary contrasts. It is true, there are some european countries in which we find more than one nation living under the same civil constitution, or where we still perceive evident traces of the former difference between the primitive and modern inhabitants; but in almost all these countries the dominant nation has in a manner swallowed up the conquered people; and the individuality of the latter has, in the course of some centuries, by insensible degrees, been almost entirely lost. Whereas in Russia dwell not only some, but a whole multitude of distinct nations; each of them having its own language . . . each retaining its religion and manners.

· · ·

The bodily frame of the Russians is excellent. Their happy organization, their cheerful and blithe temper, that hardness which they oppose to every inconveniency, the natural simplicity of their manner of living, and their rude, but dry and wholesome climate, procure to the great mass of the people a degree of physical complacency of which few other

nations can boast. The Russians are endowed with a vitality, of which an instance has scarcely ever yet been found in any other country. . . . If the Englishman or the Spaniard excels the Russian in bodily strength, the latter is superior to them by far in the endurance, or in the patient suffering of severer hardships. Hunger and thirst, want of accomodation and repose the Russian can bear longer than any other nation.

· · ·

Noble boors, as they are called, are the vassals of their lord, on whose arbitrary disposal they entirely depend, and according to the temper and disposition of whom, they are either treated with harshness or humanity; such as are so happy as to belong to benevolent and generous masters generally live comfortably enough, and some of them frequently get rich. From all of them such as are fit to be made soldiers are taken by lot as recruits. The peasantry are not bound to follow agriculture, the breeding of cattle, and the other employments of husbandry, but may strike into trade and pursue it either alone or in conjunction with their rural concerns, as they find it most beneficial or convenient.

The kozaks form a particular class originating from the peasantry. They live, exempt from taxes, in villages, forts, and petty towns, on the produce of their fields and pastures or the labour of their hands, furnish no recruits, are not given away as serfs, and enjoy other privileges. But they all serve as light horsemen, as early and as long as they are fit for it, providing themselves with horses, clothes, and accoutrements, and only receive pay when they are in actual service.

. . .

The vassal-boors are employed, at the pleasure of their lord, either in country or city occupations, in manufactories and fabrics, the handicraft trades, or the mines. Agriculture, therefore, is not so generally the business of the peasantry in Russia as in other countries. However, on the whole it is carried on to so great an extent, as not only to furnish the nations of the empire that eat bread with that article, and the prodigious quantities of corn, at a very moderate price, consumed by the brandy distilleries; but also can export a great superfluity to foreign countries.

. . .

The mixture of town and country professions: . . . In the different villages all over the empire we see the mechanical businesses of towns carried on; but more especially in the parts adjacent to the Volga, and in the vicinity of the Governments of Mosco, Nishney-Novgorod, and Kazan. It is scarcely possible to come to a village where there is not a smith, a taylor, a shoemaker, a tanner, a soap-boiler, a builder, a joiner, a house-painter, &c. and many of the boors follow these professions as their main business. In numbers of villages almost all the boors are either boat and ship builders, wire-drawers, braziers, cotton-printers, comb-makers, coopers, dyers, turners, &c.

. . .

The Russians are a race much hardened by climate, education, and habits of life, having their own peculiar usages, which have a greater affinity with the asiatic than the european, only without the effeminacy. They sleep on the floor, the hard benches, or the boards placed shelf-wise for that purpose; in the summer contentedly lying down in the open air, in the field, or the yard of the house, as they do in the winter on the top of the oven, without beds, or merely on a piece of felt, sometimes with and often without any pillow, either under a thin covering or in their clothes.

. . .

On the whole globe we shall scarcely meet with a country where the song is more jovial and universal than in Russia. They all sing from the child to the hoary head of age, and on all occasions, old women excepted, even while at the most laborious and toilsome work, and generally with all their might; the country-roads re-echo with the songs of the drivers, the village-streets with the merry voices of the girls, and the drinking-houses are never without a concert. Their songs are simple recitations, antient or modern; on the subject of love, nature, and tales of chivalry, giants, and heroes, frequently lewd, and their melodies uniform and monotonous, but sometimes pleasing enough.

. . .

Vassal boors . . . are usually called simply boors; but here this addition is necessary as a distinction between them and the . . . free boors. They have no civil liberty; their children belong not to them, but to their manorial lord, on whose will they depend; they also, with their children, singly or in families, may be alienated, sold, and exchanged; they possess no immovable property, but they themselves are treated, sometimes as the movable, sometimes as the immovable property of another.

. . .

Noble, or private boors. Several authors, and among them our countryman Perry, give a lamentable account of their condition. It is, however, not only exaggerated, but almost always represented in too general a manner. There are indeed lords who strain their exactions too far, and oppress their vassals; yet this can only be said of those who require too great and too various tributes, or of some of the country-nobles, particularly the poorer of them, who carry on the farming business themselves, or leave it to the management of some merciless upravitel, or overseer, who by birth is only a vassal himself. Their condition, indeed, depends entirely on the humour or caprice of their lord; yet it is not to be denied that a great part of them, especially such as belong to wealthy lords, who require neither task-service nor deliveries of products, but only take a moderate obrok, live happily, grow rich, and would hardly be persuaded to change their condition for what passes under the name of freedom, but is commonly nothing more than a brilliant conceit.

. . .

The dues to their lord are settled by no laws; some pay the obrok, others perform task-service, or, in lieu of it, deliver certain portions of their natural products; from others again all these are demanded: however, the obrok alone, especially where the lord is rich, is the most usual. Many take, for every male head only three, others five, and some, from the most opulent of their boors, twenty-five rubles, or even more. Those who fare the worst are the private boors who are obliged to perform task-service, in lieu of the obrok, at the mineworks of their lord, which may lie at a great distance; and perhaps the length of the way is not at all considered.

· · ·

The russian soldier will not fall back one step, while his commander bravely keeps his ground; he contents himself with an extremely little pay, and with very slender diet, and is always cheerful; hungry and thirsty, he traverses the heavy sands of the deserts under the load of his accoutrements, without murmur or complaint; executes every command; reckons nothing impossible or too difficult; does every thing that he is ordered without shunning any danger; and is inventive of a thousand means for accomplishing his design.

· · ·

Foreign gentlemen coming to Russia have perhaps entered a peasant's house by the road, and at the sight of some objects have been led to think the condition of the russian boors to be extremely wretched and miserable.

They found, for example, no feather-beds; as the russian boor sleeps on a hard bench, his coat or a sort of rug serving him both for coverlet and pillow. But the common russian, who is inured to this from his very infancy, and generally has nothing at all to cover him, requires no feather-bed; otherwise he could soon provide himself with one, since he is neither in want of tame poultry nor wild fowl.

· · ·

There is certainly no country in Europe where agriculture on the whole is conducted with so much negligence, and yet at the same time yields so great and important a produce; but with few countries has Nature dealt so liberally as this in most of the provinces of middle and southern Russia.

· · ·

An important article of foreign commerce is the *Iron,* of which annually about five millions of pood are obtained . . . Russia exports every year so great a quantity of this metal, that, next to hemp, it forms the most important article of exportation. In the year 1793 this export in bar and soft-iron, as well as in cast-iron goods, amounted to 3,033,249 pood, or in value of money as given in the custom-house books, 5,204,125 rubles.

· · ·

The whole account of the commerce in 1775 [as presented on pp. 461-63 of vol. 3, condensed:]

At the Sea-portes	Imports Rubles	Exports Rubles	Duties Rubles
St. Petersburg	6,892,834	8,299,585	1,696,830
Archangel	281,748	1,367,926	144,962
Astrakhan	237,224	561,327	24,308
Riga	1,950,803	4,619,798	588,496
Reval	556,994	420,380	42,667
Kiachta, towards China	1,427,450	1,294,581	462,559
Total	12,469,373	18,557,279	3,326,182

· · ·

The aggregate national wealth of Russia, in its annually arising products, may be reckoned with tolerable accuracy in the following manner:

Thirty millions of inhabitants of both sexes, making about 6 millions of families (each at five persons) consume monthly at least 48 millions, in the whole therefore 576 millions of poods of all kinds of meal, grits, &c. each pood, on an average, at 25 kopecks, makes a sum of rubles 144,000,000.

Brandy is made yearly, and its consumption is about five millions
of eymers, each at three rubles 15,000,000
Salt, 12 millions of poods, at 35 kopecks 4,200,000
Gold, silver, lead, copper, iron, &c. 8,750,000
Fine and coarse furs, at least amounting to 5,000,000
Hemp, flax, tobacco, linens, hemp-oil, linseed-oil &c. 30,000,000
Fire-wood, timber, charcoal, ship-timber, tar, pitch &c. 20,000,000
Cattle, leather, wool, milk, pulse, garden-vegetables &c. 58,050,000
Product of the fisheries 15,000,000

Total   300,000,000

Consequently of this capital comes to each inhabitant an annual share of ten rubles.
By commerce, every year is exported of these products, namely,

In metal-wares to about 3,000,000
In hemp, flax, and all articles prepared from them 10,000,000
In leather, tallow, furs, and all other products from the
animal kingdom 8,000,000
In corn, wood, and other petty articles 4,500,000

Total   25,500,000

To this the transport-article, at−2,000,000.
Which together make out the . . . sum of 27½ millions of rubles.

XII:23. THE RECORDS OF THE LEGISLATIVE COMMISSION: VIEWS OF NOBLES FROM CENTRAL AND NORTHERN RUSSIA, CA. 1767

An exceptionally valuable survey of the opinions and desires of many elements of the population in the 1760s is provided by the records of Catherine's Legislative Commission of 1767-68. These records include both the instructions various segments of the populace gave to their elected representatives and the speeches and declarations made by these representatives in the commission. The student may here compare the views of the state peasants, the townspeople, and the nobles from various regions.

This first group of excerpts presents the statements of some of the nobles from central and northern Russia.

Reference: *SIRIO*, 4:226 [Moscow], 298-300 [Iaroslavl']; 363 [Kaluga]. The records (*Materialy* or, earlier, *Istoricheskie svedeniia*) of the Commission were published in 14 volumes of *SIRIO* (vols. 4, 8, 14, 32, 36, 43, 68, 93, 107, 115, 123, 134, 144, and 147).

[Instructions of the Moscow nobility to their representative, General in Chief Count P. I. Panin:]

In considering the general needs of the entire Russian nobility [dvorianstvo], it should be remembered that from time immemorial it has been a body that, on the one hand, has assured the strength, defense, and independence of the state and consequently also the stability of the rule of its sovereigns and, on the other hand, has linked its own privileges and security to the integrity and unshakable solidity of the realm; and by virtue of this natural interdependence it has at all times left the preservation of its rights to the will and the benevolent discretion of its autocratic sovereigns. It would appear that, following that very praiseworthy example of our forebears, we today, under the beneficent rule of the great Catherine . . . should, with redoubled and unlimited confidence, leave the new legislation regarding us and the entire nobility to the wise, sagacious, and maternal judgment and decision of Her Imperial Majesty.

[Instructions of the nobles of the uezd of Iaroslavl' to their representative, Prince Mikhail Mikhailovich Shcherbatov:]

1. The nobles of Russia, constituting the foremost class [*chin*] of this empire, by virtue of their services have been honored with the

special trust of their monarchs, so that from time immemorial all the highest offices, both military and civilian, have been filled by them, and still are. They alone (apart from especially worthy and deserving members of other classes) are entitled to occupy the same. They are free to serve the state for as long as they please, to travel to foreign countries and take service there, and to own villages [landed estates], which in ancient times were divided into pomest'ia [estates held on the basis of service] and votchiny [patrimonies] but now are equally the property of the nobles. They have also many other rights that have fallen into oblivion through a change in customs or as a result of encroachments by other classes, or else have been obliterated through the undermining of the laws. Therefore your aim must be that the noble class, being the most loyal and devoted to the sovereign and the fatherland, be restored to the former plenitude of its privileges, both for the benefit of the whole state and for the well-being of the nobles. . . .

4. . . . The proposal should be made that a census be taken of all the nobles in the towns, that annual assemblies of the nobility be established in every provintsiia, and that to this end lists be made of all the nobles of each uezd concerned. . . .

5. By the decree of Emperor Peter the Great of eternally glorious memory, which was designed to encourage the Russian merchants to establish factories, they were allowed to purchase villages for the needs of their factories and plants. They have not only made use of this right but have stretched it beyond what was proper and have bought villages in places remote from their factories. Thus they not only disregard but even violate the intentions of Peter the Great, since, upon becoming the owners of numerous villages, these manufacturers no longer apply themselves with the necessary zeal to the management of their factories, which they no longer

regard as the sole source of their livelihood and wealth, but begin to concern themselves with the income from their landed estates. Those who actually bought the villages for the needs of their factories and employ the people to work therein do harm by taking everybody away to work for them and pay them so little that it hardly suffices for their daily subsistence. This prevents the increase of the population and results in the decline of agriculture, and the peasants themselves are so overworked that they often break out in riots. Therefore may it not be provided that, after investigation, the villages bought by the manufacturers in violation of the law shall be taken away from them, in an orderly way so that, for the sake of mercy, they may not suffer losses; and that the factories to be established in the future should be subject to proper regulation: a certain number of workers and craftsmen being retained, according to the amount of work and the size of the factory, and all other workers being hired.

[Instructions from the nobility of the Serpukhov, Tarusa, and Obolensk uezdy (later in the guberniia of Kaluga) to their deputy, Major General Prince A. N. Volkonskii:]

Any nobleman who finds it expedient to establish a factory or plant on his estates should be allowed to proceed without petitioning the College of Mines and Manufactures [Berg i Manufaktur-Kollegiia] and should be allowed to sell the goods and merchandise produced in said factories at ports both on the borders and within the state, and in towns and at fairs, without prohibition; and when such a factory or plant functions perfectly, only then shall it be reported to the college what the factory produces; and if the nobleman does not choose to keep it for himself, he should be free to sell the factory to whomever he pleases, without asking permission of the college.

XII:24. THE LEGISLATIVE COMMISSION: VIEWS OF UKRAINIAN NOBLES, CA. 1767

Reference: *SIRIO,* 68:174-75 [Kiev], 217 [Gadiach, Mirgorod, and Poltava].

[Instructions from the nobles of Kiev:]

The Ukrainian [Malorossiiskii—"Little Russian"] people and we, your humble servants, among them, ever since we came into the all-Russian realm by our own will

and with our fervent desire to become its subjects, have been honored by the ancestors of Your Imperial Majesty with grants of privileges and with charters to our hetmans [getmanskie stat'i] establishing and confirming our privileges and freedoms, so that they would continue to be enjoyed by us without violation. And Your Imperial Majesty, our most gracious sovereign, in the year 1763 and later, in 1765, has deigned to confirm by her own hand that Ukrainian justice and punishment should be dispensed in exact observance of Ukrainian rights. That the same be most graciously reaffirmed for all time and that, by virtue of said privileges, all administrative offices in the Ukraine be given solely to commanders and other elders from among native Ukrainians, we most humbly entreat Your Imperial Majesty. . . .

When the Ukraine [Malaia Rossiia] entered the all-Russian realm, the nobles [*shliakhet-stvo*], at the request of the hetman Bogdan Khmel'nitskii, were granted the following charter by the sovereign of blessed memory, Tsar Aleksei Mikhailovich, in the year 7162 from the creation of the world [i.e. A.D. 1654], on the twenty-seventh of March: "The nobles [*shliakhta*] inhabiting the Ukraine shall enjoy the ancient rights and privileges of their class freely, without any constraint; and they shall elect their elders [starshina] among themselves, for judicial, rural [zemskii], and municipal offices"; which rights we, your humble servants, enjoy as nobles to this day. Moreover, the privileges of the nobility [dvorianstvo ili shliakhetstvo] were received and are still enjoyed by many Ukrainians, thanks to both the Polish kings and the august ancestors of Your Imperial Majesty, the all-Russian sovereigns; yet more than a few of those privileges enjoyed by our ancestors have been lost. . . . We therefore most humbly beg Your Imperial Majesty most graciously to ordain—in order to strengthen the honor of the nobility and its appropriately high station and to dispel the harmful uncertain-

ties to which it has been hitherto exposed— that all those who themselves or whose ancestors have faithfully served in military and civilian offices, and who still do serve and will do so in the future, be listed in a register of the nobles [shliakhetstvo] and be admitted as equals into the Russian nobility [dvorianstvo]; and that the special rights and privileges inviolably enjoyed by our ancestors and by ourselves in the past and the present be assured to us in perpetuity, through inclusion in the new laws now being drafted.

[Instructions from the gentry of Gadiach, Mirgorod, and Poltava:]

First of all, we most humbly entreat Your Imperial Majesty to reaffirm the rights, old customs, privileges, freedoms, and benefits that were granted by the Polish kings and the Lithuanian grand dukes [*kniaz'ia*—princes or dukes] and confirmed by the ancestors of Your Imperial Majesty, the august all-Russian sovereigns resting in the Lord, and in particular the tsar and grand prince Aleksei Mikhailovich, autocrat of all the Russias, when Hetman Khmel'nitskii became a subject, and which were bestowed on the Ukrainian hetman, nobles, clergy, army, townsfolk, and the whole people, to be kept and preserved inviolate for all time . . . so that one and all may enjoy their rights, customs, freedoms, and privileges, may make use of them on every occasion, and may in this manner protect themselves. May it therefore be most graciously ordained . . . that the charters and privileges granted to Bogdan Khmel'nitskii, on the basis of which he and the Ukrainian people accepted the sovereignty of the all-Russian realm, be entered and printed in the general code, to be known and unfailingly preserved in perpetuity.

XII:25. THE LEGISLATIVE COMMISSION: THE DISCUSSION OF SERFDOM BY KOROB'IN, SHCHERBATOV, AND CHUPROV, MAY 1768

Some of the most radical criticisms of serfdom were made by Grigorii Korob'in, at the instigation of Catherine herself. Here are excerpts from, first, the official minutes of Korob'in's speech, then a transcript of the speech itself, and finally the comments of Prince Shcherbatov and state peasant Chuprov, two of the many who participated in the heated discussion of Korob'in's proposals— which, incidentally, were not put to a vote.

Reference: *SIRIO*, 32:54-55 [minutes regarding Korob'in], 406-09 [text of Korob'in's address], 489-90 [Shcherbatov], 504 [Chuprov].

[From the minutes of the session of May 5, 1768:]

The deputy of the nobility of Kozlov [in Tambov guberniia], Grigorii Korob'in, following the reading of the laws regarding fugitive people [serfs], states that there are in the world many proprietors who exact more taxes [podat'] from their peasants than is customary and that there are also some who, having gone heavily into debt, take their people [serfs] away from the land and hire them out to someone else in order to earn at least enough so that the proprietors can make the yearly interest payments on their debts; but what is still worse, there are also some among them who, when they notice that one of their peasants has accumulated some small resources through the work of his hands, suddenly deprive him of all the fruits of his endeavor and in this way seriously endanger the whole state. . . . The peasants, unable any longer to bear the heavy burden, are driven to abandon their homes and their landlords [pomeshchiki, estate owners]. To put an end to such abuses, the aforesaid deputy considers it necessary to limit the power of the landlords over the property of their peasants. To this end he proposes, on the basis of articles 295 and 261 of the Grand Nakaz [Instructions], that some kind of law be passed regarding the property of the slaves [raby]. The amount of the tribute paid annually by the peasant to the landlord should be defined by law, and, according to article 277 of the said Nakaz, it should be moderate. In his opinion, based on article 270 of the Nakaz, it may be paid either in produce or in money. Finally, the aforesaid deputy Korob'in answers the possible argument that this measure would lead to the peasants becoming so insubordinate that it would be impossible to rule them; in the matter of administration he leaves to the landlords the same authority over peasants that they now possess.

[From the appendix giving the text of Korob'in's address of May 5, 1768:]

Often I have reflected upon what it is that compels a peasant to leave his land, from which he considers departure unthinkable, to abandon his kin, his wife and children, whose presence to him is an ineffable comfort, so that in parting with them he sheds a fountain of tears—to leave all that and to wander to strange places, encountering innumerable woes and sometimes death itself. . . . I assume, honorable deputies, that many of you are aware that there are enough proprietors in this world who exact from their peasants heavier taxes than is customary; that there are also some who, having squandered their fortune and incurred many debts, tear their serfs away from agriculture and hire them out to someone else in order to earn at least enough so that the proprietors can meet the yearly interest payments on their debts; and there are others who, when the income they receive from their peasants does not suffice to satisfy their idle whims, separate the peasants from their families and use them solely for their [the landlords'] own profit; but what is still worse, there are also some among them who, when they notice that one of their peasants has accumulated some small resources through the work of his hands, suddenly deprive him of all the fruits of his endeavor. . . . If all this is considered dispassionately, it becomes clear that it threatens the whole state with ruin, inasmuch as a society is only flourishing and strong when all its members are contented: this assures tranquillity and also generates a spirit that is readily aroused for the defense of the fatherland. As is well known, the tillers of the soil are the soul of society. It follows that when the soul of society is in a state of exhaustion society itself is weakened; thus, the decline of the soul of society renders its members ineffectual. This means that the ruin of the peasantry brings ruin to all the others within the state. . . . It is therefore necessary that the power of the landlords over the property of their peasants be defined by law. . . . If the peasant knows that he may keep some share of property for himself, he will apply greater efforts to his labors. No longer will he bury his money in the ground or wander away from his birthplace; no longer will he have cause to become a fugitive; and agriculture, in consequence, will achieve its full measure of abundance.

Yet in order to attain this highly desirable condition, and to see farming strong and the farmer affluent and enjoying his own property, it is necessary to prescribe by law that the peasant should pay his landlord a definite tribute, which, according to article 277 of

the Nakaz given to us, should be a moderate
one.

[From the text of the address given on May
22, 1768, by Prince Mikhailo Shcherbatov,
deputy representing the nobles of Iaroslavl':]

They [the peasants] have full freedom to
dispose of what they have earned [i.e. their
movable property]. . . . As for deputy
Korob'in's proposal that the peasants should
have full ownership of a part of the landed
estate and be able to sell it, mortgage it, give
it away, and so forth . . . certain questions
arise: (1) Out of which lands should this
property be given to them, and (2) would not
this be ruinous for the state? To the first of
these questions I answer as follows. A great
deal of land since ancient times has been
given to the nobles by their sovereigns, first
on a temporary basis and later as patrimonies
in perpetuity [votchiny], in return for their
faithful service to the fatherland, such as the
resistance to the Tatars and the Poles, the
repeated liberation of Moscow, and the like;
and these grants, if not fully deserved in the
beginning, since then have been deserved over
and over again through incessant shedding of
blood on many occasions. . . . Would it be
just to deprive that class [the nobility] of
those very lands that oblige it to serve its
country and which it regards as its patrimony,
and to take away the estates bought by them
not only with blood but also with money?
As a reward for having liberated Russia from
the Tatar yoke, for having preserved inviolable
fidelity, for having, during riots, sealed their
devotion to their sovereigns with violent and
agonizing death, for having acquired many
provinces for Russia—in return for all that, to
have their very reward taken away and given
over to subjects who never had any right to
it or who only followed the commanders who
led them? No! Merely to imagine this is enough,
I believe, to horrify the most unjust! . . .
Surely, honorable deputies, surely you have
heard from your fathers what great services
the noble class has rendered to all Russia? In
many places where you live you can still see
the ruins of churches destroyed and settlements laid waste by the fury of peoples of
alien faith! Who has preserved the Orthodox
faith for you? Who has freed you from the
yoke and tyranny of barbarians and foreigners—
who if not the nobles? When our fathers had

the honor of leading their servants against the
common foe and of defending the Orthodox
faith and the state, they hardly expected that
as a reward their descendants today would be
likened to tyrants! Is this our reward from
you for having saved you and your souls? . . .
And in answer to the second question I shall
say even more: that this is harmful to the
whole state. How is it possible to allow the
peasants to sell real estate by giving them full
rights of ownership? Is an orderly economy
possible if every peasant, who has been given
the right to sell his lands or to give them away,
should sell them to others and split them not
only into parts but into shreds? . . . Those
who have not enough concern for farming,
or who have been driven to it by adversity,
will sell their land to strangers. Within the
lands of one village there will be pieces owned
by peasants from a hundred other villages.
And those who have sold their sole property,
which could have fed them, . . . will have exchanged a real possession for an illusory one,
and will be compelled either to abandon farming or to become hired laborers, and then,
actually no longer possessing anything, will
come to real grief. . . .

It is my opinion, therefore, in view of the
arguments I have had the honor to present,
that it should be plain to all how harmful are
the measures recommended by Deputy
Korob'in.

[From the text of the address given on May
23, 1768, by Ivan Chuprov, the deputy
representing the state (chernososhnye) peasants of Arkhangel'sk provintsiia:]

To the address of the deputy of the
Iaroslavl' nobility, Prince Mikhailo Shcherbatov, read yesterday, May 22, in which he
disputes the views of Korob'in . . . and,
among other things, praises the services of
the nobles to the Russian state since ancient
times, I have this to answer. It is true that
service always deserves recognition, and the
honor of the nobility must be given its due;
however, people of every rank and calling
are assigned various tasks within the state,
and, whatever any man's duty, I trust that
each fulfills it as best he can. But this is not
in question today, and the honorable deputies
are here foregathered not to claim honor for
themselves, but to make laws, for all in general
and for every one in particular, as the Grand

Nakaz given us by Her Imperial Majesty directs us . . . in order that not a single matter may remain undefined by law. It is apparent therefore that the peasants on the landlords' estates should not be left without a definite

law, lest they remain, after the new code has been drafted, in the same state of poverty and unrest as they are today under some proprietors, deprived of care and protection.

XII:26. THE LEGISLATIVE COMMISSION: VIEWS OF MERCHANTS AND TOWNSPEOPLE, CA. 1767

Reference: *SIRIO*, 93:164-65, 168 [Kostroma], 336-37, 343 [Iaroslavl']; 107:18-19 [Suzdal'], 33 [Mosal'sk]; 123:424-25 [Vologda]; 144:438 [Kursk].

[Instructions from the townspeople of Kostroma:]

Noblemen should not be allowed to engage in trade, nor to own mills and factories, nor to acquire merchants' rights, inasmuch as the nobility has its own rights which endow it with great advantages; and they should be allowed to sell only what is produced on their estates and be forbidden to buy other goods for profit from anyone. . . . Should any nobleman engage in such an occupation, unbefitting his noble rank, that is to say, should he buy merchandise for profit and trade in it, or else should he, under the pretense of laying up supplies, engage in the transportation of various goods, and should this be proven, then all such goods bought for profit or transported without a certificate [from the city magistrates] should be confiscated by the treasury of Her Imperial Majesty.

. . .

Both merchants and government clerks [*prikaznye sluzhiteli*] are greatly in need of servants for necessary household tasks and for police duties; for, not having their own domestic serfs [*dvorovye liudi*], the merchants are compelled to abandon their commercial pursuits and the clerks the duties entrusted to them, so as to manage all the necessary household tasks and police duties themselves; and in particular, when [a merchant] has to go on a journey on commercial business he has the utmost need of a trusted man [to leave behind]. The merchants therefore should be most graciously allowed to purchase male serfs without land: up to five souls for [merchants] of the first guild, [and] up to three [souls] for [merchants] of the second [guild], with the same number of female serfs; while government clerks [should be allowed to purchase] as many as the commission shall decree. And serfs bought heretofore by men of the aforesaid ranks should be left in their possession inalienably.

[Instructions from the townspeople of Iaroslavl':]

The sovereign emperor Peter the Great, of blessed and eternally revered memory, vouchsafed to make laws to rebuild the shattered edifice, that is to say, to raise the Russian merchants and craftsmen to the position occupied today by the merchants of European states, to which end he issued many laws for the benefit and protection of the merchant class. Yet in the course of time the merchant class has been falling into decline and disruption as a result of various circumstances harmful to the Russian merchants; for many peasants, not content with their agricultural pursuits, hayfields, forests, and other related resources [*ugod'ia*], have been engaging in commerce, trade, and handicrafts, in violation of the law; while other peasants have abandoned agriculture altogether to engage in commerce and trade, which results in a lack of bread, while the commerce of the merchants is undermined and disrupted by their trading. The merchants, moreover, are obliged to perform services to the state; and if a merchant is elected to a particular post, he has to abandon his business for a year, and spend [another] half a year rendering account [to the government]; and particularly when the man is single, and has to be absent [i.e. serve in another town], this naturally interferes with his commerce; meanwhile the peasant carries on his commerce or trade without any hindrance and becomes more and more strongly established.

. . .

Although by decrees of the Governing Senate in the years 1744 and 1746 merchants are forbidden to buy male and female serfs to serve them, nevertheless we beg that this be graciously reconsidered; and let it be ordered that, instead of hiring serfs and peasants, merchants of the first and second guilds be allowed to buy as many as would be permitted, to perform household and [other] tasks and errands for the merchants, and likewise to carry on in rotation the municipal police duties as watchmen, and as *sotskie* and *desiatskie,* so that all may carry out their duties more conveniently.

[Instructions from the merchant corporation (*kupecheskoe obshchestvo*) of the town of Suzdal':]

We, the merchants, suffer intolerable and grievous ruin through our service as [tax] collectors for the treasury, since [each merchant elected to a post] is obliged to spend one year in constant service and [another] two or three years rendering accounts. In such cases he is forced to abandon his merchant's pursuits and lose all his commercial business. And especially ruinous for the merchants are their annual elections [as assistants] to the crown [liquor] agents [*koronnye poverennye*], formerly [called] the franchise holders [*otkupshchiki,* who bought from the government the monopoly on the sale of liquor in a given area], for receiving the liquor from the contractors [*podriadchiki,* i.e. the individual distillers] and distributing it to taverns [*piteinye doma*]; and it sometimes happens that because of an inadequate supply [of liquor] from the contractors the elected [merchants] are sent by order to the Kamennomoskovskii liquor warehouse [*piteinyi dvor*] in Moscow, to take the [necessary amount of] liquor and transport it back at their own risk; and as a result they may incur exceedingly long and ruinous investigations if any liquor has leaked away, or often the hoops break on the barrels, not to speak of false records which may be kept by the [government] chanceries or the franchise holders. All these services [to the state] may simply result in the utter ruin of the merchant, with society deprived of a prosperous merchant and the treasury of its taxes, which he could have paid if he had not been impoverished by [state] service; and consequently neither the interests of Her Majesty nor the welfare of the state profit at all therefrom; [the sole result is that] the merchant class is imperceptibly falling into ruin, to which several thousand merchants who have been utterly ruined therefrom can truthfully testify. In general the excessive hindrances to merchant commerce prevent any [of the merchants] from improving their condition. And should Her Imperial Majesty

display her maternal charity in regard to this, our most humble petition, then one of the best ways to improve our condition might be to appoint, to all these [tax] collections and services, retired officers and other ranks whose salaries could be paid out of the revenues collected, and to relieve the merchants of the prescribed elections.

[Instructions from the merchant corporation of the town of Mosal'sk, just west of Kaluga:]

People of all ranks, and in particular the peasantry, do great injury to the merchant class in the pursuit of commerce, the more so since many peasants have abandoned their agricultural pursuits and are engaged in merchants' business, and their landowners not only do not forbid this but even encourage them by allowing them to buy and sell in their name; and through this the small merchants have suffered great losses, so that they are barely able to pay the state taxes, and particularly after the poor grain harvest this year, many are almost starving to death. And if the peasants were prohibited from doing this, then surely they would apply themselves more diligently to agriculture. To this end the merchants of Mosal'sk find it necessary most humbly to petition Her Imperial Majesty that she most graciously vouchsafe to forbid people of other rank, and especially the peasantry, to engage in commerce either under their own or under someone else's name, both in the towns and in markets and villages throughout the countryside.

[Instructions from the townspeople of Vologda:]

The merchants of Vologda, in their zealous devotion to commerce, apply themselves with great diligence both to domestic and to foreign commerce, not so much for their own benefit as for the benefit of the whole people and the treasury, and for the glory of their beloved fatherland. . . . And thus by our strenuous labors we bring great benefit to the whole people, and likewise to the treasury through the payment of duties at the customhouses in the harbors and at the borders. Yet we are hindered in earning profits from our commercial endeavors by the following, to wit: the municipal services, whereto a great many are elected each year, from among both the prominent [*pervostateinye*] and the lowly people, in rotation, to serve in the local town and uezd [as government tax collectors] at the sale of liquor, salt, and gunpowder, and as accountants for conveying to Moscow the taxes collected from the sale of liquor and other items, and also [to collect] upon oath [*na vere*] the tax on [the sale of] horses. And sometimes by order of the chief magistrate they are chosen to collect various taxes in other towns and uezdy, and if extreme necessity makes it impossible for someone to serve himself, he must pay a large sum to the agent [poverennyi] who will serve in his place. And all this puts a heavy burden on the merchants and disrupts their commercial affairs, since they cannot manage their affairs so efficiently during their term of office and do not have enough time; for [a merchant] always runs the great risk of overlooking the interests [of the state] and subjecting himself to investigation. And thus he serves for a year and spends much of the next year rendering account; meanwhile he neglects his own affairs and thus suffers losses and is removed from commercial affairs; and especially when he is elected [to serve] in another town, his commercial affairs often fall into complete decay; and this brings harm, not only to him, but to the treasury and the nation as a whole. We therefore petition Her Imperial Majesty to issue a decree freeing us from collecting taxes on the sale of liquor, salt, gunpowder,

and horses, and from being elected as accountants, and from service in other towns, leaving only service in the municipal administration and the collection of municipal taxes; so that, cognizant of the maternal clemency of Her Imperial Majesty toward us, her faithful subjects, we may work and strive more zealously, and make our commerce flourish, and vie with each other in bringing benefits to all the people and to the treasury.

[Instructions from the townspeople of Kursk:]

A good many *odnodvortsy* [petty service men whose status in the eighteenth century approached that of state peasants] and other people of various ranks [*raznochintsy*] from the Kursk uezd and other uezdy, having abandoned their former habitations and agricultural pursuits, have settled in our town among the merchants, and without having the rights of merchants they engage on their own in trade and various crafts, thereby causing great injury to the merchants, both in commerce and in handicrafts; wherefore may legislation be decreed, by the all-sovereign will of Her Imperial Majesty, that such people be deported from dwelling-places of merchants to their former domiciles, and be confined to their rightful occupations, such as agriculture and other kinds of domestic economy; and that strict orders be issued to that end.

XII:27. THE LEGISLATIVE COMMISSION: VIEWS OF STATE PEASANTS, CA. 1767

In the instructions sent by the state peasants of the northern provinces one may see something of the nature of their life, their attitude toward landed property, and the specific ways they hoped Catherine's government would help them. Note: The term "soul tax" (*podushnaia podat'* or *podushnye den'gi*) is used in these documents by the peasants to refer to all their financial obligations to the state. Actually there were two different taxes, both collected in the same way: the soul tax proper and the obrok, or rent for the use of the peasants' land allotments. Before 1761, the soul tax was seventy copecks per year per male peasant, and the obrok was forty copecks; in 1761 the obrok was increased by sixty copecks.

Reference: *SIRIO*, 123:267 [Kortkeroskaia volost'], 177 [Strilenskaia volost'], 315 [Kochenskaia slobodka], 292 [Spasskii pogost], 310-13 [Molskaia volost'], 324 [Tot'ma volost'], 63-64 [Khimanevskaia volost'], 217 [Pacheozerskaia volost'], 222 [Aleksinskii stan], 129 [Iagryshskaia volost']; 115:147-48 [Kargopol' uezd].

[Instructions from the peasants of the Kortkeroskaia volost', Iarensk uezd:]

Our Kortkeroskaia volost' is located on the upper Vychegda River, on densely wooded and marshy ground, and in each hamlet [some grain] suffers from frost every year and does not ripen properly because of the local climate;

and the hunting and trapping of squirrels and other animals and also the fish in the lakes and rivers have greatly decreased as compared with former years, so that now there is less than a third of the [former] hunting and fishing; and in some years, because of a poor harvest of grain, the peasants feed on fir bark and chaff and beet tops; and the peasantry has [likewise] become impoverished . . . by the [obrok] payments imposed in 1762 of sixty copecks per soul above the former payments; and in many cases they feed themselves, as described above, on fir bark and chaff and beet tops; thus many are leaving their homes and their plowlands, taking out passports, and going to work at various jobs and in various industries, thereby to provide a livelihood for themselves and their families and to pay the soul tax.

[Instructions from the peasants of the Strilenskaia volost', Ustiug uezd:]

The best hamlets have been taken by merchants from the towns [posadskie kupecheskie liudi], yet in the payment of the soul tax, as apportioned by the commune, they make no contribution at all to the commune.

Unwilling to displease Her Imperial Majesty, we yet fearfully make bold to mention the burdensome increase in the soul tax of sixty copecks above the former assessment of seven grivny [one grivna equals ten copecks]. The circumstances described above have caused great misery and hardship; which we do confirm by our signature.

The instructions are signed, at the request of the peasants of Strilenskaia volost', by the priest of the Church of Saint Nicholas, Iakov Ivanov.

[Instructions from the peasants of the Kochenskaia settlement (slobodka) in the Tot'ma uezd:]

We pay the soul tax as formerly assessed plus an increase. Formerly there was an annual assessment of one ruble and ten copecks per soul, and now sixty copecks have been added, and this makes one ruble and seventy copecks per soul each year. And we peasants have to keep moving to make our living; in winter we go out to work for hire, and in summer we work on ships, while some go into the forest to trap squirrels, and others hew logs and take them to the town of Ustiug to sell. And because of the poor, infertile plowland, and the meager hayfields, and the heavy tax payments, the peasants of our Kochenskaia settlement have fallen into great want and misery; which we do confirm with our signatures.

[Instructions from the peasants of the Spasskii pogost of the Shiksneiskaia volost', Tot'ma uezd:]

According to the registry books [pistsovye knigi] and the title deeds [kreposti] and other agreements, the plowlands and their appanages in the hamlets and wastelands are not distributed among the peasantry in an equitable manner, in relation to the number of registered souls of the male sex. Some [families] with one soul own [enough land] for two or three; and in the settlement of the soul tax those who have little land or no land, [but] receive no contribution [toward the tax] for their souls from those who possess much land, are greatly burdened and wronged, in the absence of any reallotment of the land; while others with similar plots of land have no registered souls at all, and when the soul tax is assessed they pay very little on such holdings to help the poor ones, and some do not pay at all.

[Instructions from the peasants of the Nikolaevskii pogost of the Molskaia volost', Tot'ma uezd:]

Holdings of plowlands and hayfields, both in inhabited hamlets and lying waste, are now apportioned without regard to the number of souls registered in the latest census [and] not measured off in desiatinas, as prescribed by the land-surveying regulations [mezhevaia instruktsiia]; instead [they are apportioned] in accordance with the old registry books . . . [and] whatever [land] was registered and allotted [by the registry books] to each [peasant] is still held by him and his heirs after him. . . . And there are many such landholders, almost a third of the volost' [peasants], who have everything in abundance, yet are registered for only a few souls, many having [only] one or two or three souls each.

And, on the other hand, almost two thirds of the volost' [peasants] are land poor and needy; some of them have no land at all because their fathers sold it before them; or even if they have land, it is such a small amount that there is hardly anything to take possession of; yet these land-poor peasants have three or four or five or six [registered] souls apiece, many of whom are dead; and they have to pay the soul tax out of their [side] earnings.

By virtue of the decree issued in 1761 regarding the census, the soul tax is now assessed on the number of souls and not on the amount of land owned; and this is to the advantage of those who own much land; but those who own little land are falling into complete ruin because of the inequitable allotment of land, whereby they cannot sow enough grain.

· · ·

And should the Governing Senate, in response to this representation, decree that the land be conveniently reapportioned, measured off equally in desiatinas in accordance with the number of registered souls, then there would be enough land in our Molskaia volosti for the 1,381 registered souls, including the hamlets and wastelands, and the obrok-bearing [i.e. cultivated] and forested lands; which we, the sotskii and the elected peasant officials [*vybornye liudi*], do confirm with our signatures. March 29, 1767.

[Instructions from the peasants of the upper half (*verkhniaia polovina*) of the Tolshemskaia volost', Tot'ma uezd:]

In our volost', according to the records of the third census [1762-66], many peasant [families] have eight or seven or six souls each yet have the very smallest amount of arable land; and there are other peasant [families], with one or two or three souls, who own a full measure of arable land; and this brings ruin and poverty to those who have many souls.

[Instructions from the peasants of the Khimanevskaia volost' of the Letskii stan, Vaga uezd, near the lower course of the Northern Dvina:]

On February 28, 1767, the undersigned elected officials and peasants of the Khimanevskaia crown [*dvortsovaia*] volost' of the Rozhdestvenskii pogost, in the Letskii stan of the Vaga uezd have given this written mandate to the elected deputy [to the Legislative Commission] of the pogost, Savva, son of Prokofii Zhdanov, concerning our needs and wants, as stated in the following representation from us.

Although our locality is on the seashore and infertile, and our lands are difficult to plow and of poor quality, being hilly, clayey, and sandy, nonetheless, by divine favor, the number of souls, according to the current third census, has greatly increased since the first census; wherefore, in view of the shortage of

land and resources, those who are zealous husbandmen put manure on their plots every year and in addition make unceasing efforts to enlarge the arable lands; and in this manner they have added, and continue to add, much new plowland and meadowland reclaimed from forests and swamps. But various other idlers not only lack any zeal and industry but are given to laziness and wastefulness and as a result have squandered away their plots and left them waste, and have become impoverished and unable to pay their taxes; and now they petition that those tilled and manured lands be reapportioned according to the number of souls. And if those manured lands, cultivated with such great labor and at such expense, should be divided with those wasters and idlers according to the number of souls, each male soul would receive a little over one desiatina, which is not enough for subsistence. And henceforth no one would be willing to apply such efforts and zeal to the increase and cultivation of arable land, and there would be no sense in incurring any expenses; inasmuch as the industrious would till the land and the idlers would take possession of the fruits of their labor, to squander and neglect them again.

[Instructions from the peasants of the Pacheozerskaia volost' of the Dvina quarter (*chetvert'*), Ust'-Sysol'sk uezd, about 150 miles east of Sol'vychegodsk:]

Village plots containing the best plowland and sufficient amounts of meadowland . . . have been taken away from many peasants of the Pacheozerskaia volost' . . . and through various machinations have been appropriated by merchants and townspeople not of merchant rank in the towns of Ustiug the Great and Sol'vychegodsk, and also by servitors of the barons Stroganov.

[Instructions from the peasants of the Aleksinskii stan, Ust'-Sysol'sk uezd:]

Our former ancestral patrimonial lands [*votchiny*] are now in the possession of various urban merchants—namely, from the towns of Archangel, Ustiug the Great, Sol'vychegodsk, [and] Tot'ma—and of other inhabitants of those towns, yet the two earlier censuses and likewise the third, current [census] list us by name as owners of those patrimonial lands; and whether our fathers and grandfathers and great-grandfathers had sold them, mortgaged them, or, because of some urgent need, had given them to those merchants and townspeople, this we do not know; and now we live on those patrimonial lands as sharecroppers [*polovniki*, who received half the harvest] of the merchants and townsmen, doing the hardest work. In the summertime [we work] in the hayfields and at other tasks, together with all the members of our households and with our horses, with some providing their own bread and food. And after the harvest [the landholders] divide all the grain with us by halves, and we transport their half wherever they order us, using our own horses and providing our own bread, food, and hay. And in the wintertime we again take the hay, both what we supplied and what they bought in addition, to their houses, wherever they may order, to feed their livestock, using our own horses and without respite; and in this manner we work for them all year round, with all the members of our households and with our horses.

[Instructions from the peasants of the Iagryshskaia volost' of the Dvina third (*tret'*), Ustiug uezd:]

In our locality many [peasants] become impoverished for the following [reason]: they have no children, yet because of ill health or old age are unable themselves to manage their households and economy, and work their plowland; yet they are forbidden to sell it; wherefore their hamlets become completely impoverished and neglected, and the souls registered in those hamlets are distributed [for purposes of taxation] among the other peasants of the volost', which causes general misery and hardship.

If, however, the buying and selling of land among the tax-paying [chernososhnye] state peasants were allowed, society would benefit; inasmuch as it has actually been demonstrated in the past that those who buy land from others regard it just as ancestral land which is inherited through [earlier] title-deeds; and in the hope of leaving it to their descendants, the owners have labored with zeal and industry, [thereby] benefiting the state; they have cleared and improved both plowlands and hay-

fields, with consequent great public benefit.

The instructions are signed by the priest Mikhail Ivanov of the Church of Saint Nicholas; he likewise wrote the whole of the instructions.

[Instructions from the peasants of the tax-paying state volosti of the Kargopol' uezd, on the Onega River:]

In our uezd the tax-paying state peasants, on the strength of previous decrees and the earlier land-surveying regulations of 1754, used to sell and mortgage their land plots in the hamlets, according to their needs, not only to each other but also to the merchants of the local town; and this was to the general advantage, inasmuch as those who had too much land and those who were unable to make use of their property would sell an appropriate part of their plots on the condition that the soul tax assessed on the seller of the plot should be paid proportionately or in full [by the new owner], thereby assuring a more punctual payment of the soul tax. However, ever since the regulations of 1765, issued to all the land-surveying chanceries and bureaus in the guberniias and provintsii, which prohibit (in art. 20, no. 107) . . . the sale and mortgage [of land] to [other] peasants and to outsiders, the peasants of our uezd no longer engage in selling or mortgaging their plots either to each other or to the posad men of the local town. And since many peasants are unable to make use of their plots of land and are unable therefore to pay the soul tax assessed upon them, the collection of the soul tax from them is greatly hampered by delay and arrears. . . . So, if it is impossible to collect the soul tax from the poor peasants, it becomes necessary to collect it from those peasants who are better off; and inasmuch as these already pay a large part of the soul tax assessment, the added payments in place of the poor will begin to impoverish them and will soon bring them down to the level of the poor. And in order to avoid this, in consideration of the above-mentioned circumstances, all the peasants most fervently desire that the state peasants be allowed to sell and exchange their land plots among themselves as before.

XII:28. ESTATE-OWNERS' INSTRUCTIONS: P. A. RUMIANTSEV, 1751 AND 1761-1762

An especially rich source on the Russian peasantry is the instructions of estate owners concerning the administration of their estates. Written instructions, normally addressed to a steward or bailiff, were not necessary on estates where the pomeshchik lived and supervised the work himself; hence these sources refer primarily to estates that were relatively large. The following several excerpts, suggesting some of the economic and sociological data available, are selected from an assortment of instructions ranging from the middle to the end of the eighteenth century. The first three were issued by Count Petr Aleksandrovich Rumiantsev (1725-96), prominent general of the third quarter of the eighteenth century, for the regulation of his numerous holdings.

Reference: Mitrofan V. Dovnar-Zapol'skii, ed., "Materialy dlia istorii votchinnogo upravleniia v Rossii" (Kiev: *Kievskie Universitetskie Izvestiia,* 1903), no. 12, pp. 2-3 [first document], 7, 12 [second document]; ibid., 1904, no. 6, pp. 37-38, 43, 44, 47-48, 68 [third document].

[From his "rules by which the managers, stewards, and elders in all our patrimonial estates in the Volga-Oka basin (*nizovye votchiny*) shall punish peasants for various offenses," January 17, 1751:]

1. For using abusive language, if the complaint is found to be true, fine the guilty one ten copecks.

2. For assault, if no scars are left, fine [the guilty one] thirty copecks and put him in chains for three days, or even flog him, depending on the seriousness of the beating.

3. If someone wounds another, exact a monetary fine of fifty copecks, punish him severely with rods besides, and put him in chains for seven days on bread and water.

4. For stealing something, whether large or small, sell the possessions [of the guilty one] and make compensation for the stolen article, and flog him publicly with lashes. Then send him away to work as soon as the occasion arises or enroll him as a recruit, taking away his property and giving it over to us, without making any representations.
. . .

7. If anyone ventures to steal anything belonging to us, no matter how small, confiscate all the property [of the guilty one], put him in irons, and bring him before us with an exact description of the matter.

8. If on a feast day anyone fails to attend church services without legitimate cause, he should be fined ten copecks without indulgence, and the money shall be given to the church.

[From his "instructions according to which all the affairs of our manorial administration, from all our patrimonial estates in the Volga-Oka basin, shall be conducted in the administration office (*prikaznaia izba*) in the village of Cheberchino" (near Nizhnii-Novgorod), also 1751:]

5. Under pain of severe punishment, do not in any circumstances and under any

pretence or pretext interfere with marriages between peasants, nor forcibly compel anyone to marry; these marriages must be performed according to their own desires and agreements, nor is it necessary to report them.
. . .

33. In selecting men for the recruiting levies do not act arbitrarily, as was formerly the custom. Instead the commune should select ten of the most worthy peasants, empower them, and have them take an oath; then these chosen peasants should appoint men from the various families, sparing no one regardless of his wealth and acting with the strictest justice; lots should be cast, and whomever the lots may fall upon, these must themselves bring their own children or brothers without contradicting. And if anyone is prosperous enough to wish to buy a substitute, he may be allowed to do so, and his entire tiaglo [here meaning the peasant labor unit (usually a man and wife or a family) and its land; it also was used to mean the obligations levied on that unit] shall be freed for two years from paying taxes to the state and to us, and from performing labor for us.

[From his "Household Regulations" (*uchrezhdenie domovoe*), 1761-62:]

[PART V, SECTION 3.] 13. Do not, under pain of the most severe punishment, interfere in communal affairs: that is, in selecting people to perform various duties for me, or in recruiting levies, or in marriages. Trials, the dispensation of justice, and the appropriate punishment of the guilty shall always be carried out in the presence of the first-ranking peasants [pervostateinye]; at the end of each month a certificate shall be demanded of these first-ranking peasants, with the assent of the entire commune, testifying that these matters have been dealt with justly and that no oppression or injury has been inflicted. . . .

SEC. 6. Concerning the appointment of

peasants as elders [starosty], sworn assistants [tseloval'niki], and merchants [kupchiny].

1. These should be chosen at the beginning of each year in all my estates by the first-ranking peasants with the consent of the entire commune, and the duties of each should be designated exactly. The certificates of election should be sent to my manor office, with the priests of those villages affixing their signatures in place of those peasants, and these certificates should contain a testimonial that [the elected peasants] are of good character and sufficiently prosperous and that, if they cause me to suffer any losses through the negligent performance of their duties, the entire commune is obliged to make compensation for them in every case. . . .

[PT. VI.] 10. Collect money for communal expenses as the communal council decrees; the receipts and the name of the person chosen to collect them must be written down; money shall likewise be spent [only] with the consent of the commune. . . .

14. The first-ranking peasants, *sotskie, piatidesiatskie,* and *desiatskie* [peasants selected to perform police functions, with the sotskii being responsible for one hundred households and the piatidesiatskii and desiatskii, acting as his assistants, responsible for fifty and ten households respectively] must look after negligent peasants strictly, lest they leave their land unsown, sow another landowner's land for a half share of the harvest, or otherwise impoverish their households; in such cases, if they fail to pay their obligations to the state or to me, the first-ranking peasants, sotskie, piatidesiatskie, and desiatskie will be held responsible. . . .

15. My own office, rather than the communal council, shall arrange the distribution of peasant tiagla; everyone who has reached the age of fifteen or sixteen shall be counted as a worker. . . .

23. . . . Select the worthiest and most prosperous men to be merchants, to transport and sell my grain and provisions, to receive and expend money and [other] articles, and to act as field elders and stackyard elders [polevye i gumennye starosty]; the entire

commune must issue a written resolution [of election], with the obligation to compensate for any losses I may suffer or any missing receipts and expenditures. . . .

25. Trials of household serfs must take place in the office of the estate; the entire matter must be recorded in the registry book [registratura], and the appropriate punishment must be inflicted accordingly. The same is to be done with the peasants, only in the presence of the first-ranking peasants, and the judgment of each case is to be read to them; if this [judgment] violates my instructions, they [the first-ranking peasants] must declare to the steward that they will not act as witnesses in the matter and must report the injustice of his action [to me, the landlord], as is their duty. They must do this without delay, in view of the fact that I have instituted them solely to protect the peasants against oppression by the stewards, and they have been appointed to observe this precept. The entire commune must choose the first-ranking peasants [pervostateinye] from among the most worthy and conscientious men: one first-ranking peasant for one hundred souls; four, for two hundred; six, for three hundred; and ten, for a thousand or more. . . .

PT. IX. 1. All unmarried peasants assigned to my service [i.e. as domestic serfs] are to be fed at my expense, reckoning three chetverti [one chetvert' equalled about 250 pounds] of rye flour per man each year, one and a half *chetverik* [one chetverik equalled one-eighth of a chetvert'] of groats, one chetverik of dried oatmeal and peas for fast-days, and on meat-eating days half a pound of meat from my cattle, choosing those unsuited for breeding, and from my provisions. All these things must be stored up, and the necessary dishes, knives, and spoons provided, and [the peasants] must be fed in one place and at a single table. Married men should receive bread and provisions as prescribed, each month, except for meat, instead of which each family should be given one cow, two sheep, and one pig; these will be maintained on my fodder, which shall be distributed each month in the same quantity as allotted to my own cattle.

XII:29. ESTATE-OWNERS' INSTRUCTIONS: P. B. SHEREMET'EV, 1764

The serfs of Count (and General) Petr Borisovich Sheremet'ev, one of the largest landowners in eighteenth-century Russia, had a reputation for prosperity due largely to the successful manufacturing enterprises they owned and operated under his protection. That fact lends special interest to some features of these instructions to the steward of his votchina in the Murom region, village of Karacharovo, particularly as concerns the less prosperous of his serfs.

Reference: Dovnar-Zapol'skii, *Kievskie Universitetskie Izvestiia,* 1904, no. 7, pp. 84-85, 86, 87, 94, 95.

[22.] If any of my peasants need to buy men as laborers from some landowner, they are ordered to obtain the permission and attestation of the stewards and peasant deputies [vybornye] and to buy them in my name, obtaining purchase-deeds from the bureau for serf affairs; these purchase-deeds should be sent along with a report to my house chancery [*domovaia kantseliariia*] in Moscow, leaving copies on the estate [votchina]. Under no circumstances must they be bought without permission and without certification. . . .

[27. Passports] may be issued to peasants to carry on trade, but for one year only and never for a longer period. Obtain a surety when issuing passports. And if someone fails to return within the allotted time, or if his family fails to pay its taxes, [this] should be exacted from his guarantors. . . .

[33.] No peasant should be without land [*bobyl'*] or outside a tiaglo; all peasants must bear tiaglo. . . .

[34.] Peasants should redistribute the tiagla among themselves according to the disposition of the commune, so that the poor should not bear an excessive tiaglo; the stewards and peasant deputies should not

interfere in this redistribution, which shall be made yearly. . . .

[64.] If some peasants should be reduced to poverty through the theft of their property, or if by the will of God they should lose their horses and cattle, or if for some other reason they should become impoverished, as certified by the testimony of all the peasants, and if their land remains unplowed through poverty: then order all the peasants of that hamlet in which these poverty-stricken peasants live to plow and harvest from this same hamlet as much grain as is necessary for seed and to sow the land of the poor, lest the latter become utter beggars and scatter in every direction. The land must not lie uncultivated [*pusta,* empty]. Therefore, order it to be strictly observed that no tiaglo-bearing land lie unsown anywhere on the estate. If there should be such unsown land, those peasants who are responsible must be punished in front of the assembly. . . .

[69.] Tiaglo-bearing uncultivated land should be distributed among the tiagla according to the disposition of the commune; no land should remain uncultivated.

XII:30. ESTATE-OWNERS' INSTRUCTIONS: I. I. SHUVALOV, CA. 1795

Some significant features of estate management appear in these instructions of Ober-Kamerger Ivan Ivanovich Shuvalov on the administration of his votchina, the village of Myt with its hamlets, on the Kliazma River in the Vladimir guberniia. As a young man in the 1750s, Ivan Shuvalov had been a favorite of the already aging Empress Elizabeth, and it was she who gave him this estate (and one other). A patron of the arts and the first president ("curator") of Moscow University (see Item XI:15) Ivan Shuvalov was not a large landowner, but these instructions bespeak long experience. They date from the period 1795-97, shortly before his death (November 14, 1797).

Reference: Dovnar-Zapol'skii, *Kievskie Universitetskie Izvestiia,* 1909, no. 7, pp. 222-23, 224, 227, 231.

Rules Established for My Votchina, Which
Must Always Be Followed Precisely
I.
Concerning the Bailiff [*Burmistr*]
The bailiff must be chosen for his post with the prior approval of the commune [*po odobreniiu mirskomu*] and with my consent; he will be fully entrusted by me to administer the entire estate and to administer justice to

the peasants without prejudice or oppression, and he must give a good account of himself in all respects before me.
Concerning the Deputy [*Vybornyi*]
The deputy, who is at the same time the bursar [*raskhodchik*], must be elected yearly by the peasants and must be a worthy man, so that he can assist the bailiff in administration. . . .

Concerning the Elder [Starosta]

The elder must likewise be chosen yearly by the bailiff together with the peasants; he must be a man who can assist the bailiff in the collection of my money on the estate without arrears, and upon collecting it he must hand it over to the bailiff in full.

Concerning the Clerks [*Zemskie*]

There should be two clerks, selected by the bailiff; they should be accurate in keeping records and not be drunkards; they must attend to every document and must keep accurate accounts in the proper manner. And they must be obedient in all matters to the bailiff, as their superior. . . .

Concerning the Peasant Representatives
[*Pripisnye Krest'iane*]

There must be one peasant representative from every small hamlet, and two from a large hamlet, or as many as are assigned by the commune. They must gather in the administration office [prikaznaia izba] at the order of the bailiff whenever any matters are being judged or sentences passed, instead of always burdening the people by calling them all together. . . .

Concerning the Church Elder
[*Tserkovnyi Starosta*]

The church elder must be chosen by the commune; he must be a man of good conduct. He is entrusted with the church money, of which he must keep a record and give an account to the administration of the estate and to the commune. This money must then be used for decorating the church, and the church elder will be entrusted with looking after the granary, the receipt of grain, and its disbursement to the poor; each year he must

send me accurate information about all these things: the church money as well as the condition of the granary.

IV.
Concerning the Equal Distribution of Land

The land must be distributed so that one village will not have an excess of land while another has too little; in order that each village can pay taxes on it without falling into arrears. . . .

[VI.]
Concerning Fugitive Peasants

Fugitive and passportless peasants must not be kept anywhere on my estate under any circumstances; and if such should be found with any [of my peasants], the latter must answer for it himself in the proper place, without expecting any help from me.

Concerning Those Who Absent Themselves
without Permission

A peasant who absents himself without the permission of the bailiff and goes to the city without having a pass from him is to be fined in money, depending on the amount of property he has: from traders of the first rank—fifty [rubles?]; of the second rank—thirty; of the third rank—twenty; from nontraders—ten. In issuing passes the bailiff should oppress no one, lest the trader should lose his profit and the nontrader his benefits.

Concerning Unmarried Girls

Girls who have reached the age of twenty should not be kept at home by their fathers but should be given away in marriage, without waiting for me to force them into a marriage which would run counter to the will of the father and of the bride.

XII:31. ESTATE-OWNERS' INSTRUCTIONS: V. G. ORLOV, CA. 1799

These statutes (*ulozhenie*) for the village of Porech'e in the Rostov uezd of the Iaroslav guberniia were issued by Count Vladimir Grigor'evich Orlov at the end of the 1790s. Among their significant points are some concerning the role of the mir or commune, the policy on marriage, and the regulations on buying workers—which permitted some serfs, like those of the Sheremet'ev family, to become wealthy entrepreneurs.

Reference: Dovnar-Zapol'skii, *Kievskie Universitetskie Izvestiia*, 1910, no. 11, pp. 253-57, 259, 266-67.

CHAPTER I. Concerning the bailiff [burmistr], his assistants and their duties.

ARTICLE 1. Chief authority on the estate belongs to the bailiff; therefore all peasants must be in complete obedience to him.

ART. 2. Each year two men should be

chosen to assist the bailiff, or more if the commune [mir] deems it necessary; this is left to its discretion.

ART. 3. For these duties the commune should choose men who are capable, trustworthy, intelligent, and conscientious; the commune should draw up a written resolution of their election and keep it in the administration office.

ART. 4. In all the more important affairs the bailiff should counsel with the deputies [vybornye] and other worthy peasants, and if necessary, with the entire commune....

ART. 15. Guilty persons should be punished on the — with rods and cudgels, but not with whips....

ART. 17. The bailiff is not to be replaced without my consent.

ART. 18. If the bailiff complains that he is unable to carry out his duties, the worthiest of the peasants and deputies should write to me about this, explaining exactly why he is incapable, and await my decision.

ART. 19. The bailiff receives his salary from the commune; its amount depends upon the commune's wishes.

ART. 20. The commune shall decide if the deputies are to receive a salary, and its amount....

CHAP. III. Concerning the communal assemblies.

ART. 1. The bailiff shall announce when the communal assembly is to take place; all the peasants must attend....

ART. 3. When the commune agrees to settle a matter in one way or another, a communal resolution must be drawn up and signed....

CHAP. V. Concerning obrok....

ART. 8. To assist the poor and weak the following practice is to be observed: an appropriate number of souls [*dusha,* here meaning the sum of payments imposed on a single tiaglo-bearing peasant] shall be removed from the family, but in no case should land be taken away on account of the removal of souls; thus they can use land without paying for it and thereby improve their resources. ... And these removed souls [i.e. the obligations falling upon each soul] shall be imposed upon the more prosperous....

ART. 10. For this purpose assessors [*okladchiki*] should be chosen each year; the commune shall decide how many are needed. They should be the most conscientious, intelligent, and just people, so that this distribution might be carried out with all fairness.

ART. 11. This relief should be extended to the poor not only in the amount of obrok they pay me but in all state taxes and in all

necessary and extraordinary communal expenses....

ART. 13. The commune should pay the soul tax and other state taxes for the household serfs registered on the estate....

CHAP. VI. Concerning the collection of money for communal expenses and the rational utilization of the same.

ART. 1. There are necessary and extraordinary communal expenses. The will of the commune shall decide when the money should be collected for these expenses and how much should be collected. The commune should draw up resolutions for these collections, to which all must consent....

CHAP. XIII. Concerning permission to give maidens and widows away to outsiders in marriage, and concerning those who do not marry....

ART. 5. It is highly necessary for all girls of marriageable age and bachelors who have attained manhood to enter into marriage. This is an act pleasing to God; it safeguards morality and wards off many vices. Thus the authorities, and especially the bailiff, are enjoined to incline such people, by means of admonishments and other measures, to enter into marriage.

ART. 6. When a girl reaches the age of twenty, the eldest in the family should give her away in marriage; a period of half a year should be allowed to find a bridegroom.

ART. 7. If upon the expiration of the allotted time the girl is not married, penalties should be exacted yearly: twenty-five rubles from a household of moderate means and fifty rubles from a wealthy family; the poor, who are unable to pay, should be punished at the discretion of the authorities.

ART. 8. Then the chief [*nachal'nik,* presumably the bailiff], inviting the deputies and the worthiest of the old men to assist him, must find bridegrooms for these girls at his discretion and unite them in a legal marriage; he must see to it carefully that they be worthy of each other and of their families.

ART. 9. Bachelors twenty-five years of age and older who are not yet married should be dealt with in the same way as unmarried girls, as described in the seventh article of this chapter. Widows are likewise subject to this rule....

CHAP. XV. Concerning the buying of men.

ART. 1. Peasants who wish to buy workers,

male or female, to serve them, must ask the permission of the bailiff.

ART. 2. The bailiff is ordered to ascertain closely and precisely if those who wish to buy men to work for them are worthy of this favor, i.e. whether they are kindly and of good morals, whether they can be depended upon to maintain their workers decently, or whether they would burden them with excessive work or punish them without cause.

ART. 3. Thus, those who deserve this favor should be allowed to buy workers, but first written testimony of their good qualities must be sent and [my] decision awaited.

ART. 4. Those who do not deserve this favor are to be denied it; there is no need to report this.

ART. 5. It is forbidden to buy people of dissolute morals, lest disturbances be caused me and my administration thereby; only people who lead a good and decent life may be bought.

XII:32. THE MODEL INSTRUCTIONS OF P. I. RYCHKOV, 1770

Petr Ivanovich Rychkov, geographer and historian of Orenburg krai (territory), drew up a set of instructions which were awarded one of two gold medals (worth thirty-five *chervonnye* or 350 rubles) by the Free Economic Society (see Section C of this chapter), which published the instructions in 1770. They represent, then, a model approved by a relatively enlightened element among the large landlords of the day.

Reference: Vol'noe Ekonomicheskoe Obshchestvo, *Trudy Vol'nogo Ekonomicheskogo Obshchestva k pooshchreniiu v Rossii zemledeliia i domostroitel'stva*, vol. 16 (St. Petersburg, 1770), pp. 13, 15-17, 23-27, 30-31, 33-34, 53-55, 57-59.

Instructions
For a manager or steward, concerning the proper maintenance and administration of villages in the absence of the owner

1. Every manager or steward, when entering upon the administration of the villages and hamlets entrusted to him, must first obtain an exact knowledge of the rights of his master in respect to his land with all its appurtenances [*ugod'ia,* including pastures, forests, waters, and so forth], and to the household serfs and peasants belonging to those estates; and particularly he must know what belongs to the land and the various ugod'ia of the village. . . .

2. . . . It is a well-known fact that in our country there are small and even very large hamlets in which no one knows how to read and write. In this respect almost all peoples living in Europe who practice the Christian faith excel us. Even the Tatars of Mohammedan faith living within our empire put us to shame. . . . It is very necessary and mandatory for the managers and stewards to have at least one person in each village and hamlet who is able to read and write. They should select from among the best peasants male children six to eight years of age and order them to be taught reading and the prayers most necessary for a Christian to know. Those who show the greatest aptitude and reliability should also be taught to write; however, in such numbers that in a village containing one hundred souls there will be not more than two or three who know how to write, since it has been observed that such people often turn their knowledge to evil ends, such as the making of false passports, and so forth. But the more people able simply to read, the better, both for their own enlightenment and for society as a whole. . . .

5. It is an ancient custom among us to distribute peasants capable of working into tiagla, counting a man and wife as one tiaglo (the crippled and the aged being excluded from the tiagla), and to divide the land among them. . . .

6. Among us, tiaglo-bearing peasants are employed to work for the landowner at the latter's discretion. Some are so strict that they do not leave the peasants even a single day to work for themselves; they give each family a monthly supply of food and make them work for the master every day without exception. Others make the peasants work for the landowner four days a week and leave them three days including Sunday. Those who treat their peasants with moderation make them work for the landowner three days and for themselves three days, leaving Sunday as a day of rest; but in most cases plowland is cultivated on the basis of the area to be farmed [*urokami*]. In some cases each tiaglo cultivates a little over two desiatinas, in other cases—

two, one and a half, or one desiatina in each
field. The working days are divided equally
between the landowner and the peasants, but
some make the peasants finish tilling the plowland of the landowner without leaving it for
a single day and only then permit them to
begin working their own. A humane master
who truly loves his fatherland will never order
his managers and stewards to make each tiaglo
plow, sow, and harvest more than one desiatina of land, and certainly not more than one
and a half desiatinas. This is enough to provide
him with a sufficient profit. . . .

8. As for the assignment of peasants as
elders and deputies [vybornye], sworn assistants [tseloval'niki] for receipts and expenditures, and to other functions in the volost',
village, and hamlet, on large estates this may
be left to the choice and discretion of the
stewards and peasant deputies, unless the
landowner has enough knowledge and confidence to wish to appoint one of his peasants
to some duty; this he is always free to do.
But when such people are assigned their duties
through the choice of the commune and at
the discretion of the managers and steward,
then in case of negligence the latter will be
held responsible. In medium-sized or small
villages the elder and deputies are chosen by
the communal peasants, who are likewise
held responsible for them. . . .

10. . . . Prudent managers and stewards
must strive . . . that no young peasants who
are over eighteen or at most twenty years of
age should run around unmarried. When such
are found, they should be encouraged to
marry and their fathers should be prevailed
upon; girls should be found for them in the
same village, of the same age or even two or
three years younger. But since it often happens that in one village there are more young
men, and in another more young girls, the
landowners should give the managers and
stewards permission to remove marriageable
girls into another village [presumably belonging to another landowner], deciding upon a
sum of removal money [vyvodnye den'gi]
which shall be agreeable to both sides. . . .
As far as the removal money is concerned, it
seems sufficient for the landowner to be paid
from ten to fifteen rubles for a girl who is

removed from one village to another; but this
must be done with the permission of the
managers and stewards. If their elder and
deputies are absent, make a written record
and obtain the consent of the father and
mother of both parties, without attempting
to do anything against their will. But if such
a young man refuses to marry, or if some
inclination makes his mother and father unwilling, then they ought to be compelled in a
decorous way. . . .

21. Among us it is customary in many
places for each tiaglo-bearing peasant woman
to spin and weave twelve *arshiny* [an arshin
equalled 28 inches] each of cloth and linen a
year, while on some estates they are given
still more to do; all this is called obrok. The
landowner distributes his own sheep's wool,
flax, and hemp for this work. If the estate
does not produce its own, then it is bought
elsewhere and distributed. When cloth is not
woven, then the obrok in linen is doubled. . . .

22. Good managers and stewards see to it
that peasant children who have reached the
age of ten are used to work from time to
time for the benefit both of the master and
the peasants, rather than letting them be idle
and become accustomed to indolence. . . .

24. . . . The managers and stewards must
ascertain through the elder and peasant
deputies in what condition each peasant
maintains his household. . . . If there be peasants who, in spite of every admonishment
and effort, fail to apply themselves to agriculture and retain their bent for idleness,
brawling, and other intemperances, such
people, if they are young and healthy, should
be ordered into the first recruiting levy; those
who are older, in order to restrain and frighten
the others, should be exiled as the law prescribes for settlement in a distant place, and
a certificate should be obtained to count them
as recruits for the next recruiting levy. In this
way such parasites and brawlers will not set
a bad example for others. However, it is necessary to write in advance to the landowner
about this and obtain his permission; if the
latter is too far away, act with the consent of
the elder and deputies and the best peasants,
and not on your own.

XII:33. THE MODEL INSTRUCTIONS OF A. T. BOLOTOV, 1770

The second gold medal of the Free Economic Society went to a writer who specialized in agronomy, Andrei Timofeevich Bolotov. Here are three short excerpts from his lengthy *Instructions for a Village Administrator*, published in 1770 by the Free Economic Society.

Reference: Vol'noe Ekonomicheskoe Obshchestvo, *Trudy Vol'nogo Ekonomicheskogo Obshchestva*, 16:76, 169, 183.

8. . . . The reasons for which villages are reduced to a bad state and to impoverishment are of three types: the first is by their master or by his own administration of them: as, for example, if the inhabitants are burdened with excessive labor, heavy requisitions, numerous cartage duties [*podvody*], and other such things; or similarly when the administration of the estate is disorderly and ruinous. . . .

66. The requisitions usually collected from the peasants consist of supplies of food and other articles, such as pork meat, sheep, butter, hens, eggs, and sometimes wool, mushrooms, berries, linen, and similar things, while in some provintsii they consist of the so-called *piatina*, or every fifth sheaf of the peasants' grain. They provide no small source of income, and moreover, a certain one. . . .

75. . . . For the most part the rule is followed that the peasant should plow as much land for the master as he can for himself, or as much as he has for his own use. Therefore that amount of land the peasants are able to cultivate with their own labor and harvest in the proper manner ought to be divided in half: one half should go to the peasant and the other half to the master. Nothing can be easier and more suitable for the peasants.

XII:34. DECREES ON PEASANT DISTURBANCES, 1762

When Peter III released the nobles from obligatory service to the state (see Item XI:19, above), some people thought the next step would be the releasing of serfs from the obligation to serve their estate owners. These excerpts from decrees of 1762 show how Catherine's government responded to these "false rumors," as she called them.

Reference: *PSZRI*, 1st ser., 16:10-11, 75-76.

[Decree of July 3, 1762:]

Upon our accession to the imperial throne of all Russia, we learned, to our great displeasure, that the peasants of some landlords, seduced and deluded by false rumors spread by unscrupulous people, had departed from the obedience due to their landlords and had proceeded to commit many unruly and defiant acts. We are firmly convinced that such false rumors will presently die away by themselves; the deluded peasants will recognize that from thoughtlessness they have fallen into grievous crime and will forthwith repent, endeavoring thereafter to earn forgiveness through mute submission to their masters. Nevertheless, in order to check the spread of such evil and to prevent any false rumors from being disseminated again and credulous peasants being corrupted thereby, we deem it right to make known herewith that (1) inasmuch as the welfare of the state, in accordance with divine and public laws, requires that each and every person be protected in the enjoyment of his well-earned property and his rights, and, conversely, that no one step beyond the bounds of his rank and his office, we therefore intend to protect the landlords in their estates and possessions inviolably and to keep the peasants in their proper submission to them.

[Decree of October 8, 1762:]

With great concern the Governing Senate notes that the peasants of the Princes Dolgorukov, of Voskresenskii village, uezd of Viaz'ma, not heeding any admonitions, remained in their ignorance so recalcitrant and insubordinate that when Major General Prince Viazemskii was assigned to restore order, about 2,000 of them foregathered, carrying boar spears and other weapons, and in a plainly criminal manner not only offered resistance to the military unit but also rang the alarm bell and attacked the unit, throwing stones and sticks, in consequence of which the unit was compelled to use armed force against them and fired a cannonade by which up to twenty rioters were killed and no fewer wounded. Thereupon the worst ringleaders were seized and turned over to the town chancelleries to be punished according to the laws. Observing such severity applied to them, the others chose to submit and were returned to their landlords. Grieved by this occurrence caused by the brutality and ignorance of the insubordinate peasants, and in order that other peasants, deterred by the cruel punishment of the rioters, may not venture upon similar ungodly actions and thereby expose themselves to severe military measures, and that unnecessary bloodshed may be avoided, the Governing Senate, by order of Her Imperial Majesty, has decreed: In all guberniias and provintsii, notably those where there still are recalcitrant peasants, the contents of the present publication are to be published in the form of printed edicts, with the explanation that if the still rebellious peasants, even after the publication of the present decree of Her Imperial Majesty, fail to repent and voluntarily to resume the

obedience they owe to their landlords and to the authorities, and if they, or other peasants following their lead, dare to commit similar acts of resistance and disobedience against their landlords and the authorities, or against the estate stewards, village elders, and elected village officials [vybornye] or whatever other person has been placed in charge of them by their landlords and the authorities, such peasants shall be punished like criminals and disturbers of the public tranquillity, with the same severity as the aforementioned peasants of the Princes Dolgorukov, without fail. And in order that the present decree may be forever remembered and that no one may pretend ignorance of it, it shall be read on Sundays and holy days, in villages, in parish churches, and at markets, for the information of all the people.

XII:35. A DECREE INVITING FOREIGNERS TO SETTLE IN RUSSIA, JULY 22, 1763

This decree had importance for the economic growth of Russia as well as for the racial composition of the empire. Among the results were prosperous German settlements just north of the Black Sea and along the Middle Volga.

Reference: *PSZRI*, 1st ser., 16:313-16.

As we administer the expanse of the lands of our empire, we note among other things some especially useful regions, most advantageous for the settlement and habitation of humankind, which remain vacant to this day, and many of which regions conceal in their bowels an inexhaustible wealth of various metals; and having a sufficiency of forests, rivers, lakes, and trade-carrying seas, they are also superbly adapted for the multiplication of manufactures, factories, and other works of many kinds. This prompted us to issue a manifesto for the benefit of all our faithful subjects, on the fourth of December of the past year, 1762; but inasmuch as in the same [manifesto] our permission to foreigners desiring to settle in our empire was proclaimed in a brief manner, so now, to complete the same, we command to make known to all the following ordinance, which we most solemnly ordain and command to be executed:

1. We grant permission to all foreigners to enter our empire and to settle wherever each chooses, in all our guberniias. . . .

3. Among the foreigners wishing to migrate to Russia, there may be some who will not have sufficient means for the journey. Such persons may present themselves before our

ministers and residents at foreign courts, who not only will dispatch them immediately to Russia at our expense, but will also provide them with money for expenses on the way.

4. As soon as foreigners arrive at our residence [in Saint Petersburg] and present themselves at the Chancery of Guardianship [Kantseliariia Opekunstva] or reach any other of our border towns, they have to declare their definite intent: whether it is their desire to enroll in the merchantry or the guilds and to become townsfolk, and in which town; or else to establish colonies and settlements on unoccupied lands appropriate for agriculture and many other profitable pursuits. All such persons will receive assignments in accordance with their wishes without delay; and where and in which places in our empire unoccupied lands suitable for settlement are to be found can be seen from the following list, although there are spacious lands with all kinds of resources in incomparably greater number than those listed, and on these also we allow anyone to settle wherever he chooses in his own interest. . . .

6. And in order that all foreigners wishing to settle in our empire may see how great, for their benefit and advantage, is our benevolence,

we grant: (1) To all foreigners settling in our empire the freedom to practice their faith according to their rules and rites without hindrance. . . . (2) Such foreigners who settle in Russia are not obliged to pay any taxes into our treasury, or to perform ordinary and extraordinary [state] services, or to quarter soldiers. To conclude, they are exempt from all taxes and burdens in the following way: for thirty years, those who have settled in vacant areas in groups of families and whole colonies; for five years, those who choose to dwell in cities, enrolling in the guilds and merchantry in our residence, Saint Petersburg, or in the vicinity thereof, in the towns of Livonia, Estonia, Ingermanland, Karelia, and Finland, as well as in the capital city of Moscow; for ten years, those who settle in the capitals of guberniias and provintsii and in other towns. Over and above this, anyone who has come to Russia not for a temporary stay but for permanent settlement will be given free lodgings for half a year. (3) All foreigners settling in Russia will be given every assistance and satisfaction. Those who are inclined to farming or any other manual labor, or to the establishment of mills, factories, and workshops, will not only be provided with an adequate quantity of profitable lands suitable for their purpose but will also be given every needed assistance, according to the condition of each, with special regard to

the necessity and utility of new industries, in particular those that have not hitherto been established in Russia. (4) For the building of houses, the acquisition of livestock, the purchase of tools, supplies, and materials for agriculture and manual crafts, the required amounts of money will be supplied by our treasury without any interest, to be repaid after the passage of ten years in three equal and annual payments. (5) Those settlers who establish separate colonies and settlements shall have jurisdiction over the managing of their internal affairs, and our officials shall play no part whatsoever in their internal arrangements; yet in everything else they shall obey our civil law. . . . (9) To those foreigners settling in Russia who establish factories or plants and produce goods therein such as hitherto did not exist in Russia, we grant permission for ten years to sell said goods and to export them from our empire without any payment of domestic harbor dues and customs duties. (10) Should any foreign capitalist set up factories or plants in Russia at his own expense, to him we grant permission to purchase the necessary number of serfs and peasants for the needs of said industries. (11) To foreigners who have established colonies and settlements in our empire, we grant permission to establish markets and fairs, at their own discretion, without any levies or payment of taxes into our treasury.

XII:36. DECREES IN CATHERINE'S CAMPAIGN AGAINST GRAFT, 1762 AND 1763

While these decrees hardly accomplished Catherine's aims, they do provide eloquent testimony concerning conditions within the bureaucracy.
Reference: *PSZRI*, 1st ser., 16:22-23, 457-62.

[Decree of July 18, 1762:]

We consider it our unquestionable and imperative duty to announce to the people, with genuine contrition of our heart, that we have long heard much and now have actually seen to what extent extortion has increased in our state, so that there hardly exists the smallest domain of government where justice, that divine function, is administered without the contamination of this plague: he who seeks office, pays; he who defends himself against slander uses money as his shield; he who slanders another strengthens his crafty machinations with gifts. Conversely, many judges convert their sacred post, where it is their duty to dispense justice in our name,

into a marketplace, regarding the office of disinterested and impartial judge, which we have entrusted to them, as a revenue granted them for the improvement of their own affairs and not as a service to God, to us, and to the country. . . . Our heart shuddered when we learned from our Life[-Guards] Cuirassier Lieutenant Colonel Prince Mikhail Dashkov, reporting on his recent journey from Moscow to Saint Petersburg, how a certain Iakov Renber, registrar of the Novgorod Guberniia Chancery, while administering the oath of fidelity to us to some poor people recently, exacted money for himself from each who took the oath; and it was only because of our maternal clemency that we commanded that the said Renber be deported to Siberia for lifelong penal labor, inasmuch as for such an odious though hardly profitable crime he ought by rights to have been deprived of his life.

. . . No one accused of extortion (provided a just complaint reaches us), as one who has incurred the wrath of God, will escape our own wrath, inasmuch as we have promised God and the people that there shall be mercy and justice throughout the blameless course of our reign.

[Decree of December 15, 1763:]

To our exceeding sorrow and regret we have been forced by frequently recurring incidents to perceive that many of our faithful subjects not only fail to obtain quick and just decisions, consistent with the laws, from various judicial establishments, notably in places remote from our residence, but even are brought to ultimate ruin and destitution through coercion and extortion, or in plain words, outright robbery.

It is true that, to put an end to this evil, certain decrees were issued, in conformity with the conditions of the time, as early as the period of Tsar Peter the Great, and that the full severity of the laws was applied; yet not enough of the desired success has been achieved. This has been so partly because magistrates were appointed to office not always upon properly thorough scrutiny—magistrates who had neither standing nor ability, and whose authority therefore was assumed by their subordinates—and partly because men who not only lacked a modest private income but did not have enough for their daily subsistence were assigned to judicial posts yet were not given any salary. . . . And in truth it appeared that everyone lived for himself alone, without giving a thought to the public good.

The consequence of this was great harm—the oppression and ruination of our subjects through various devices. Indigent magistrates

were driven by dire poverty to commit extortion, and ignoramuses, leading the way for their subordinates, boldly engaged in any enterprise to acquire some gain for themselves: be it inspection tours on the felling of timber under the instruction of the forest supervisor; or the repairing of roads; or the issuing of passports; or the reassessing of rents on various government properties; or the issuing of receipts; or [the policing of] the wearing of the prescribed dress by Old Believers; or the forwarding of the prescribed payments to the chancery. In a word, they invented every device one can possibly imagine in order to secure, under any pretext, a livelihood and revenue for themselves. They thereby placed an unbearable burden on our subjects, especially the poor country people who had no one to defend them and were thus reduced to utter exhaustion.

After a close study of the above-mentioned abuses, we have decided upon a most equitable and most direct measure to eliminate the aforesaid scourge.

All judicial posts shall be filled by worthy, informed, and honest men. To secure such persons immediately, it is necessary to give them appropriate salaries to assure to each a decent livelihood according to his condition. Accordingly we have determined and approved the necessary staffs of magistrates, office workers, and other personnel—not only for the colleges [i.e. administrative departments] and chancelleries, but also for the guberniias, provintsii, and municipalities—in numbers appropriate to the status of each place and the business transacted therein; and to each man, from the highest to the lowest, we have allocated a sufficient salary. . . .

Should anyone, in contempt of this, our imperial generosity, dare to practice extortion and to touch bribes and gifts, or to oppress petitioners, such a one, dishonest and ungrateful, like an infected member of society, will be obliterated not only from the number of honest people, but from all humankind.

XII:37. SENATE INSTRUCTIONS ON POTATO GROWING, MAY 31, 1765

Reference: *PSZRI*, 1st ser., 17:141–42.

Of all the American fruits and vegetables brought over to Europe none thrives so well in any climate and in respect to its great usefulness is so different from sown grain as this

species of earth apples, also called earth pears, and in some localities tartufels or kartufels. They are all the more important in the household and among villagers—especially where rye, wheat, buckwheat, and other kinds of known cereals grow poorly or not at all—because they grow freely in any soil with a minimum of soil improvement and multiply in such a manner that no bad weather can impede their growth.

All the treatises on economy published in various languages testify that, ever since earth apples have been intensively cultivated, especially in non-grain-producing areas, and ever since people have begun to bake bread from them in addition to using them in other ways, the scarcity and high prices formerly frequent in such areas have disappeared. . . .

And although this vegetable has been grown for some time in Russia, notably in Saint Petersburg and in the palace and manorial gardens in that vicinity, and also in market-gardens, still to this day it is little used by the common people. . . .

It was considered right, therefore, to select from various books on economy the passages dealing with the methods of cultivation and the uses of the aforesaid earth apples and to have them published as follows for the information of the general public.

[Several pages of instructions follow.]

XII:38. THE DECREE ENABLING ESTATE OWNERS TO SEND SERFS TO FORCED LABOR, JANUARY 17, 1765

Empress Elizabeth, in a decree of December 13, 1760 (see Item XI:18, above), had given estate owners the right to send recalcitrant serfs to exile in Siberia. Catherine II, in this decree of January 17, 1765, extended the nobles' privileges still further. (Complete text.)
Reference: *PSZRI,* 1st ser., 17:10.

To be announced for the information of the whole populace: In consequence of the confirmation given by Her Imperial Majesty, on the eighth of January [1765], to a report submitted by the Senate, it has been ordained that, should an estate owner desire to commit any of his people [i.e. serfs] who deserve just punishment for recalcitrance to penal servitude in Siberia, for the sake of stricter discipline, the College of the Admiralty shall take the same in charge and employ them at hard labor for as long as their estate owners wish; and during the time such people remain at hard labor they shall be provided with food and clothing from the treasury on the same basis as convicts; and whenever their estate owners desire to take them back, they shall be returned without argument, with the sole reservation that if such people during their stay have not worn their clothes and footwear for the full prescribed term, these shall be taken away from them and returned to the treasury.

XII:39. THE DECREE PROHIBITING COMPLAINTS BY SERFS, AUGUST 22, 1767

At the same time as Catherine was soliciting criticism of her liberal-sounding instructions to the Legislative Commission (Item XII:8, above), her Senate issued the decree of August 22, 1767, which is generally considered to mark the apogee of serfdom.
Reference: *PSZRI,* 1st ser., 18:335-36.

The Governing Senate . . . has deemed it necessary to make known that the landlords' serfs and peasants . . . owe their landlords proper submission and absolute obedience in all matters, according to the laws that have been enacted from time immemorial by the autocratic forefathers of Her Imperial Majesty and which have not been repealed, and which provide that all persons who dare to incite serfs and peasants to disobey their landlords shall be arrested and taken to the nearest government office, there to be punished forthwith as disturbers of the public tranquillity, according to the laws and without leniency. And should it so happen that even after the publi-cation of the present decree of Her Imperial Majesty any serfs and peasants should cease to give the proper obedience to their landlords . . . and should make bold to submit unlawful petitions complaining of their landlords, and especially to petition Her Imperial Majesty personally, then both those who make the complaints and those who write up the petitions shall be punished by the knout and forthwith deported to Nerchinsk to penal servitude for life and shall be counted as part of the quota of recruits which their landlords must furnish to the army. And in order that people everywhere may know of the present decree, it shall be read in all the

churches on Sundays and holy days for one
month after it is received and thereafter once

every year during the great church festivals,
lest anyone pretend ignorance.

XII:40. PROCLAMATIONS AND DECREES OF PUGACHEV, 1773-1774

Russia's highly combustible domestic situation burst into flames in September 1773, the spark
being provided by Emel'ian Ivanovich Pugachev. Pugachev (1726-75), a Don Cossack and former
soldier in the Russian army, followed the practice—rather common in the previous decade—of
pretending to be the real Peter III. The nature of his appeal to various discontented elements is
suggested by his decrees and proclamations, like those excerpted here.

Reference: Tsentrarkhiv, *Pugachevshchina,* 2 vols. (Moscow: Gosizdat, 1926-29), 1:25 [decree
of Sept. 17, 1773], 31-32 [October 1773], 40-41 [July 31, 1774], 41-42 [August 1774]. For
the manifesto of July 31, 1774, the editors have used with some revisions a translation contributed
by Messrs. Baltzly and Kucherov.

[Decree of September 17, 1773, complete
text:]

From the autocratic emperor, our great
sovereign Petr Feodorovich of all Russia,
etcetera, etcetera, etcetera.

Through this, my sovereign decree, be it
expressed to the Iaik [Ural] Cossacks: Just
as you, my friends, and your grandfathers
and fathers served former tsars to the last
drop of blood, now should you serve me, the
great sovereign and emperor Petr Feodorovich, for the good of your fatherland. For as
you stand up for your fatherland, your Cossack glory and that of your children shall not
pass away now or ever. And I, the great sovereign, shall bestow my bounty upon you:
Cossacks and Kalmyks and Tatars. As for
those of you who have been at fault before
me, the sovereign and imperial majesty Petr
Feodorovich, I, the sovereign Petr Feodorovich, forgive you these faults and confer
upon you: the [Iaik, renamed "Ural" as an
aftermath of the rebellion] river from its
source to its mouth, and land, and meadows,
and a monetary wage, and lead, and powder,
and grain provisions.

I, the great sovereign and emperor Petr
Feodorovich, bestow my bounty upon you.

The seventeenth day of September 1773.

[Decree of October 1773, complete text:]

From our autocratic emperor, the great
sovereign of all Russia Petr Feodorovich,
etcetera, etcetera, etcetera.

Through this, my sovereign decree, I issue
this command to my regular army:

As you, my faithful slaves, soldiers of the
regular army, both privates and officers, have
in the past served me and my ancestors, the
great sovereigns and emperors of all Russia,

faithfully and invariably, now likewise must
you serve me, your lawful great sovereign Petr
Feodorovich, to the last drop of your blood.
Cast off the obedience you were forced to
show your false commanders, who corrupt
you and deprive you, along with themselves,
of my good graces; and come to me in obedience and, placing your weapons beneath
my banners, display the loyalty of faithful
subjects to me, the great sovereign. For this
I shall reward you and bestow upon you wages
in money and grain and confer ranks upon
you; and you and your descendants shall be
granted the greatest privileges in my state and
shall be enlisted in glorious service, attached
to my own person. But if anyone should forget his duty to his hereditary [*prirodnyi,*
natural] sovereign Petr Feodorovich, should
dare to disobey this, my sovereign decree, and
by force of arms should fall into the hands of
my faithful army, he shall feel my righteous
wrath upon himself and then suffer the death
penalty.

The great sovereign and emperor of all
Russia Petr Feodorovich.

["Manifesto" of Pugachev, July 31, 1774,
complete text:]

By the grace of God we, Petr III, emperor
and autocrat of all Russia, etcetera, etcetera,
etcetera, announce the following tidings to
all the world:

Through this sovereign decree we declare,
in our monarchical and fatherly mercy, that
all who were formerly peasants and subjected
to landowners shall be faithful subjects and
slaves of our own crown; we grant you your
ancient cross and prayers [referring to the
Old Believers], your heads and your beards,
and bestow upon you freedom and liberty

and the eternal rights of Cossacks, including freedom from recruiting levies, the soul tax, and other monetary taxes; we confer likewise the ownership of lands, forests, hayfields, fisheries, and salt lakes without purchase or rent; and we free the peasants and all the people from the taxes and oppression formerly imposed by the villainous nobles and the venal city judges. And we desire the salvation of your souls and a peaceful life on this earth, for which we have tasted and endured many wanderings and many hardships from the above-mentioned villainous nobles. But since our name now flourishes in Russia by the power of Almighty God, we therefore command through this, our sovereign decree: those who formerly were nobles on their estates and patrimonies, opposing our power, disturbing the empire, and despoiling the peasantry shall be caught, executed, and hanged, and treated just in the same fashion as they, lacking any Christian feeling, dealt with you, the peasants. After the extermination of which enemies and villainous nobles, every man may experience peace and a tranquil life, which shall forever endure.

Given the thirty-first day of July 1774.

Petr

[Decree to the Don Cossacks, August 1774:]

By the grace of God we, Petr III, emperor and autocrat of all Russia, etcetera, etcetera, etcetera.

A proclamation to the ataman of the Berezov *stanitsa* [Cossack settlement] and to all the Don Cossacks living in it, and to all the world.

Long enough has Russia been filled with the credible rumor of our concealment from the villains (chief senators and nobles); nor was this unknown to foreign states. This resulted from nothing other than the fact that during our reign we beheld that the Christian faith as laid down by the ancient tradition of the holy fathers had been entirely violated and dishonored by the said villainous nobles; instead they introduced into Russia another faith of pernicious invention taken from German customs, and introduced likewise the most godless shaving of beards, and they have done violence to the Christian

faith in the cross and in other matters. And they put in subjugation to themselves all of Russia, in defiance of our monarchical power; they imposed the greatest oppressions, and through this brought Russia to the verge of ruin, so that the Iaik, Don, and Volga Cossacks came to expect their total ruin and extermination. Looking upon all that has been described above with fatherly compassion, we took pity and intended to free you from their villainous tyranny and to establish liberty throughout Russia. For this we were suddenly deprived of our throne over all Russia and imputed to be dead through the publication of ill-intentioned decrees. But now, by the Providence of Almighty God and his holy will, instead of complete oblivion our name flourishes. And carrying out the oath they had previously pledged, having acknowledged our name and convinced themselves of its truth, the inhabitants of the Orenburg, Kazan', and Orenburg [sic] guberniias with their subordinate [*pripisnye*] towns and uezdy, and likewise the Bashkir and Kalmyk hordes, the Saxons [Germans] living along the Volga River, and the Volga Cossacks have accepted and bowed down before our scepter and crown; and they display ardor and zeal in our service, willingly and without any constraint on our part. We have therefore thought it fit to vouchsafe to inform the said Berezov stanitsa as well as all the hereditary Don Cossacks of our approach with our victorious army. If you come to feel our fatherly solicitude and wish to declare yourselves for your hereditary sovereign, who for the sake of the general tranquillity and peace has endured long wanderings and many hardships, then should those willing to display their ardor and zeal for the extermination of the nobles who harm society appear before our main army, where we ourselves are present; for which our monarchical mercy shall not forsake them, and they shall straightway be rewarded with a bonus payment of ten rubles apiece. And to make this known to all the Don Cossacks we order: to dispatch this decree from stanitsa to stanitsa downstream along the Don River, to transcribe copies from it, and to leave a copy in each stanitsa for its proper execution.

XII:41. CORRESPONDENCE WITHIN PUGACHEV'S "GOVERNMENT," 1774

Something of the operational methods of Pugachev's army, which at one time numbered perhaps more than twenty thousand troops, is seen in excerpts from instructions and reports such as these.

Reference: Tsentrarhkiv, *Pugachevshchina*, 1:82, 207.

[Instructions of "Count Chernyshev," the head of Pugachev's State Military Collegium, to Ataman Semen Volkov, February 13, 1774:]

From His Most Exalted Serenity Count Ivan Nikiforovich Chernyshev to Ataman Semen Volkov and *Esaul* [captain] Vasilii Zav'ialov.

Instructions

From a signed letter sent to me by the communal men [*mirskie liudi*] of the Rozh[d]estvenskii factory and the villages of Pristanichnaia and Zobachevka, I have perceived that with the consent of the commune you, Volkov and Zav'ialov, have been elected: you, Volkov, as ataman, and Zav'ialov as esaul. It is therefore incumbent upon you to maintain your detachment in good order and to permit no insubordination and plundering; and if someone shows himself an enemy of His Imperial Majesty and disobedient to you, it is your duty to inflict corporal punishment upon him according to your will and the guilt involved. On the contrary, you must not risk any bad conduct yourselves, and at all times you must heed the manifestos and decrees of His Majesty and execute them immediately, for which you may receive special praise for yourselves. But do not inflict any wrongs, extortions, and desolation upon your detachment, and touch not bribes, being mindful of the inescapable death penalty for any such delinquency. And furthermore, direct your efforts to the immediate execution of the orders and other instructions I send you.

[Report of "Colonel" Bakhtiar Kankeev, July 14, 1774:]

To the most serene and regal emperor Petr Feodorovich, the great autocrat of all Russia, our all-merciful sovereign.

From Colonel Bakhtiar Kankeev to the State Military Collegium [Gosudarstvennaia Voennaia Kollegiia]—a most humble report.

At present, during my march along this side of the Kama and Viatka rivers in the Kazan' region, [I find that] people of all callings, young and old alike, wholeheartedly and very willingly desire to serve Your Imperial Majesty and make haste to come to me; from every Russian and Tatar settlement they come out a verst ahead to meet us, and besides offering us bread and salt weep tears of joy that God has elevated you as tsar; they rejoice in Your Majesty and pray that God grant you a long life, so that they may obtain relief from heavy factory labor and taxes. At present we have more than six hundred people, Russians and Tatars, in our military force; each day more people eagerly hasten with promises to serve, and some who are eager to serve come without horses and without weapons. I most humbly beg you to issue to me your imperial decree as to where they can get horses and weapons; for there are noble estates along my route which have horses left in them, and these we can seize for the crown and give to the people.

XII:42. A SERF'S REPORT ON DISTURBANCES NEAR NIZHNII-NOVGOROD, AUGUST 1, 1774

As the successful conclusion of the Russo-Turkish War freed regular troops for action against Pugachev's motley army, increasing numbers of his sympathizers were captured and interrogated. Here is a report, dated August 1, 1774, of the testimony of one Vasilii, son of Fedor Chernov, a fifty-year-old serf on the estate of Count Aleksandr Nikolaevich Golovin, from the village of Vorotynets in Nizhnii-Novgorod uezd.

Reference: Tsentrarkhiv, *Pugachevshchina*, 2:361–63.

And therefore on the twentieth day of the month [of July 1774], by order of the *sotskii* [elected peasant police official] Andrei Anan'in . . . all the peasants and factory workers assembled at a meeting, at which meeting

. . . all shouted unanimously that they would leave their master and become the subjects of the said impostor and scoundrel [*zlodei*] Pugachev, considering him to be their sovereign Peter III; and all who were at the meeting, the peasant deputy [*vybornyi*], the starosta, and the sotskii Urusov, together with the peasants and factory workers, were asked to agree to this. And on their advice all consented to seize and put in chains and confine in the master's house the manager [of the estate and factory], Aleksei Teteev, his wife, Nastas'ia Nikolaevna, his brother Ivan Teteev; his nephew Vasilii Ivanov, a Frenchman, a German, and the Vorotynets peasant Andrei Kireev, with this intention: if the scoundrel Pugachev or someone sent by him should come to their village, they would hand the prisoners over to him, so that he might order them to be hanged for the wrongs they had perpetrated.

[On July 22 other peasants from the same estate arrived.]. . . They announced that in the town of Kurmysh they had been admitted into the presence of the said imposter and scoundrel Pugachev, who ordered them to bring all the estate ravagers to Kurmysh. To this the entire commune agreed, and they handed over the above-mentioned manager Teteev and the others to these peasants from [the villages of] Sem'iano and Berezov, and sent some Vorotynets peasants along with them. . . . They returned alone and announced to all the peasants and factory workers that they had stopped in the village of Sem'iano; there a colonel of the said scoundrel Pugachev had hanged the manager with his wife, the Frenchman, the German, and the peasant Kireev because of the complaint of injury the peasants of Sem'iano and Berezov had brought against them; and the colonel promised that he would come to them in the village of Vorotynets soon.

Therefore, on the morning of the following day, that is, the twenty-third day of July, the priests Ivan Fedorov and Grigorii Timofeev and their sextons, holding icons in their hands, and the peasants with the sotskii and *desiatskii* [assistant to the sotskii], as well as

the peasant deputy Stepanov and the elder Chuev . . . and the factory workers, all gathered together with bread and salt, and waited for the said so-called colonel; nor did the priests make them any admonishment; and they all greeted him together when he rode into the settlement. And upon his arrival this so-called colonel went into the tavern, where the factory worker Aleksei . . . had brought the manager's brother Ivan Teteev and his son Vasilii. And the said so-called colonel, inquiring only of their position, ordered them to be hanged on the peasants' gates as had been done with the manager and the others. This was carried out by the peasants Nikita Denisov, Grigorii Krivenkov, and who else hanged them I don't remember any more. After all this had taken place, this so-called colonel first called forth those willing to enter the service of the scoundrel Pugachev, with the announcement that each man who wished to come with him would receive a wage of twenty rubles a month; seduced by this promise, the peasants of Vorotynets along with the sotskii Andrei Anan'in and the factory workers agreed. Then they performed still further villainies, until finally the factory workers were stirred up and, by order of that so-called colonel and accompanied also by the peasants living in the village of Vorotynets, destroyed the entire linen factory, leaving nothing standing, and divided the cloth up among themselves; they burned the tannery and wrecked the master's house; the belongings of those who were hanged were locked up and sealed in a closet by the elder.

[The investigator adds:] . . . During this interrogation, and under cruel torture, the above-mentioned Chernov long refused in his stubbornness to call Pugachev a scoundrel, honoring him with the name of the sovereign Peter III; at length, however, not from the pangs of his conscience but from his unbearable torments, he called him a scoundrel.

XII:43. A GOVERNMENT REPORT ON PART OF THE PUGACHEV UPRISING, AUGUST 23, 1774

How the "Peasant War" looked to a provincial government official is illustrated in this copy of a report from the Tambov provintsiia office (complete text).

Reference: Tsentrarkhiv, *Pugachevshchina*, 2:363.

On August 21 of this year a villainous mob of three hundred mounted men and a thousand of the rabble [*chern'*] arrived at the crown village [*dvortsovoe selo*] Raskazovo, which is

thirty versts from Tambov. Calling together the rabble they gave them wine to drink and themselves drank the health of Petr Feodorovich. The crown peasants met them with bread and salt and helped these scoundrels in their assault on the factories of the manufacturers Tulinov and Olisov: they carried cannon and set fire to the factories. And at four o'clock in the afternoon the two sides, that is, the manufacturers and the scoundrels, engaged in a battle marked by continuing cannon and rifle fire. After a prolonged battle three of the villainous mob's cast-iron cannon were captured and three scoundrels were killed, and nine men were taken prisoner; these men have been sent here by the said manufacturers along with a report. In the interrogations, the captured scoundrels testify that their real intention, after demolishing the factories and taking the factory workers along to help them and seizing the cannon and so forth, was to proceed to Tambov and the settlements along the Savala River.

Along the rivers Vorona and Khoper there are many such villainous parties organized in various bands and totaling two thousand people; and they all agree they should join forces. These same scoundrels testify that in the course of the looting many nobles and other people, the common people excepted, were barbarously tortured and hanged.

The twenty-third day of August 1774.

XII:44. TESTIMONY OF PUGACHEV'S OFFICERS, SEPTEMBER-OCTOBER 1774

Between the time of Pugachev's capture (September 15, 1774) and his gruesome execution (January 10, 1775), Catherine's government energetically investigated the Peasant War, questioning Pugachev's cohorts wherever possible. Here are excerpts from two of the many pieces of testimony that were gathered.

Reference: Tsentrarkhiv, *Pugachevshchina*, 2:218 [Sept. 26], 162 [Oct. 27].

[Testimony of Second Major (*sekund-maior*) Andrei, son of Mikhail Salmanov, who had been taken prisoner by Pugachev's men and had served with them, September 26, 1774:]

On the march from Saratov to Tsaritsyn, not only did the settlements along the road itself willingly submit to [Pugachev's] will, but from all sides as well priests came forth with the peasants to greet him with bread and salt; they knelt and bowed to the ground, and begged his protection as the sovereign, which people he dismissed to their homes; while his bands raided and despoiled everyone alike. In the town of Dmitrievsk [Kamyshin], which is on the Kamyshenka [River], a certain defense was effected, but soon the firing ceased: the landless Little Russian peasants met them and the soldiers were taken prisoner; Sergeant Abyzov was selected from their number and on the following day was appointed colonel and given a detachment. From the Kamyshenka they went through the territory of the Volga Cossacks, through four of their towns; in each place they were greeted with crosses and joyful congratulations by a large gathering which included priests; and in their chief town of Dubovka even by a whole assembly, elders and Cossacks, all dressed in their best garments, carrying banners and presenting a joyful appearance.

[Testimony of Pugachev's "colonel" Ivan, son of Aleksandr Tvorogov, October 27, 1774:]

I considered the scoundrel to be the true sovereign Peter III because, first, the Iaik Cossacks accepted and considered him as such; second, the old soldiers as well as the people of other classes who through various circumstances happened to be with us made assurances that the scoundrel was the true sovereign; and third, all the rabble, namely the factory and landowners' peasants, bowed down before him joyfully, and zealously furnished us with men and all else that might be demanded of them, without protest. And therefore, although we did hear the decrees issued about him which made him out to be a Don Cossack, we had little belief in them and considered them to be false until such time as we came to Tsaritsyn; and here, finally, for [certain] reasons—namely, his illiteracy and his recognition by the Don Cossacks— our eyes were opened and we recognized our mistake.

XII:45. THE MANIFESTO CONCERNING PUGACHEV'S ACTIONS AND CAPTURE, DECEMBER 19, 1774

Shortly before proceeding not only to destroy Pugachev himself but to erase all memory of his existence (going so far as to move and rename his native village, and to rechristen as "Ural" the

Iaik River that had been his home base), Catherine issued a manifesto "concerning the crimes of the Cossack Pugachev." Here is part of it.

Reference: *PSZRI*, 1st ser., 19:1064, 1067.

Realizing that our sole aspiration is to bring the empire to the highest degree of prosperity . . . who can help but feel righteous indignation at these internal foes of the tranquillity of the fatherland: these men who, casting aside all manner of obedience, have first dared to raise arms against the legal authority and join that notorious rebel and imposter, the Don Cossack of the Zimoveisk stanitsa Emel'ka [contemptuous form for Emel'ian] Pugachev, and have then for a whole year perpetrated together with him the most ferocious barbarities in the Orenburg, Kazan', Nizhnii-Novgorod, and Astrakhan' guberniias; who have set aflame the churches of God, towns, and settlements, who have pillaged the holy places [*sviatye mesta*, i.e. churches and monasteries] and every sort of property, who with the sword and with various tortures they have devised have smitten and put to death clergymen and persons of high and low estate and of both sexes, including even innocent children.

. . .

After looting Saratov and killing all who did not please their fancy, the scoundrels proceeded to Tsaritsyn. This fortress put up a stouter resistance to them than many cities and forced them to retreat and flee onward;

but on the way to Chernoiarsk, forty versts from Tsaritsyn, along the Astrakhan' road, the scoundrels were again overtaken by the corps of Colonel Mikhel'son, who had continually surmounted all difficulties and obstacles. Then the Don Cossacks arrived in time to aid this colonel, and with their help Emel'ka and his whole mob were irrevocably and finally crushed; but the scoundrel himself escaped, crossed the Volga River to the lower [left] bank with a small number of Iaik Cossacks, and made his way to the Uzeni [rivers, i.e. the Bol'shaia Uzen' and Malaia Uzen'] in the steppes between the Volga and Iaik rivers. Here God willed that this enemy of humanity and of the empire be brought to justice. And his own accomplices and favorites, the Iletsk Cossack Tvorogov and the Iaik Cossacks Chumakov and Fedulev, repenting of the villainies in which they had participated, and learning of the pardon promised by the manifestos of Her Imperial Majesty to all those who exhibit sincere repentance, agreed among themselves to put Emel'ka Pugachev in chains and to bring him to Iaitskii Gorodok [later renamed Ural'sk]; they induced some other Cossacks, about twenty-five in number, to aid them in this deed, and carried it out.

XII:46. THE ABOLITION OF THE ZAPOROZHIAN SECH', AUGUST 3, 1775

These excerpts are from the manifesto of August 3, 1775, abolishing the Zaporozhian Sech' (the fortified encampment of the Cossacks below the Dnieper rapids). The reader will wish to evaluate the government's arguments in justification of this act. Apropos of the closing passage, it may be noted that many of the Zaporozhians moved to the Kuban' area.

Reference: *PSZRI*, 1st ser., 20:191-93.

Through this we wish to proclaim throughout our empire to the general knowledge of all our faithful subjects that the Zaporozhian Sech' has been permanently dissolved, and the very name of Zaporozhian Cossacks abolished for all time to come, for no less a reason than the offenses committed against Our Imperial Majesty by the behavior and insolence displayed by these Cossacks in disobedience to our sovereign commands.

. . . The offenses that have compelled us to take stern measures are headed by the following:

1. Let us leave in oblivion their earlier serious and pernicious crimes, their treacherous violation of fealty and the duties of subjects. Beginning over ten years ago and continuing to the present day, they have exceeded all their earlier insolence in appropriating and finally demanding for themselves, as if it were their own property, not only all the lands we acquired in our last war with the Ottoman Porte [in 1768-74] but even settled lands in the Novorossiia guberniia, claiming that all these lands belonged to them in former times. . . .

4. Nor did they hesitate to seize summarily

for their own winter quarters the new lands between the Dnieper and Bug rivers acquired by the peace treaty [of Kuchuk-Kainardzhi].
. . .

5. Despite frequent prohibitions by our government, they not only accepted single fugitives who enrolled as Cossacks but even employed various enticements to persuade men with wives and families to flee from Little Russia, in order to bring them under subjection and provide themselves with agricultural resources, in which they have had considerable success; since at present within the regions formerly belonging to the Zaporozhians there are around 50,000 settlers engaged in agriculture.

6. At length these same Zaporozhians began to extend their lawless usurpations even to lands belonging from ancient times to the host of our Don [Cossacks], who are unshakable in their loyalty to us, who have always displayed excellence and courage in our service, and who have legitimately and through their good conduct obtained for all time our special sovereign and monarchical benevolence. They tried to prohibit these Don Cossacks from using these lands, which for a long time have been in their possession. . . . Trade with the lands of the Ottoman Porte . . . cannot by itself achieve the results that are visible in prospect for it, to the envy of all Europe, unless the harmful mob of Zaporozhian Cossacks which has made rapine and pillage its chief occupations is first excluded from those regions through which part of this trade must

necessarily pass and be conducted. Nor is there likewise any reason to conceal the fact that at the very beginning of the last war with the Ottoman Porte many of the Zaporozhian Cossacks, fearing not God and forgetting the loyalty due us and the fatherland, plotted to desert to the side of the enemy. . . .

True, we take pleasure in rendering all due praise in one matter, that no small part of the Zaporozhian force serving in our armies provided splendid examples of courage and bravery during the above-mentioned war with the Ottoman Porte, as glorious as it was successful. . . .

And thus, in due consideration of all that has been expressed above, we now judge ourselves obligated before God, before our empire, and before all mankind to abolish the Zaporozhian Sech' and the Cossack name derived from it.

· · ·

In determining the future destiny of all individuals who formerly were Zaporozhian Cossacks, we order all those who do not wish to remain in permanent residence in their own regions [i.e. the sech' itself, on the lower Dnieper, and the adjoining steppes] to be dismissed to their homelands [rodina], and those who wish to settle here to be given land for their permanent domiciles; while all the officers [starshiny] who served faithfully and have the approval of our military commanders shall be informed of our imperial favor and shall be given ranks corresponding to their service and calling [zvanie].

XII:47. THE DECREE EXTENDING SERFDOM TO THE UKRAINE, MAY 3, 1783

The provision for extending serfdom to the peasants of the Ukraine was included in a decree of May 3, 1783, concerned with the collection of taxes in the western guberniias. By these harmless-sounding phrases Catherine satisfied the demands of the Ukrainian Cossack army officers who for some two score years had desired the enserfment of the peasants on their estates.

Reference: *PSZRI,* 1st ser., 15:907-11.

I. . . . 8. In order to ensure the certain and exact receipt of state revenues in the vicegerencies [namestnichestva] of Kiev, Chernigov, and Novgorod-Seversk, and to prevent the flight of peasants, which burdens the landowners and the inhabitants who remain in the settlements, every villager is to remain in the locality and calling in which he is enrolled according to the last, currently conducted, census.

· · ·

II. . . . Because of the proximity and similarity of their lands and inhabitants, we have found it necessary to make similar arrangements for those uezdy that formerly comprised the Sloboda Ukraine guberniia, and which now form the Khar'kov and part of the Kursk and Voronezh vicegerencies.

C. INTELLECTUAL TRENDS

XII:48. ESSAYS FROM THE CONTEST OF THE FREE ECONOMIC SOCIETY, CA. 1766

Upon Catherine's initiative and under her patronage, the Free Economic Society (Vol'noe Eko-nomicheskoe Obshchestvo) was established in 1765 "for the improvement of agriculture and the domestic economy" in Russia. Bringing together men of learning as well as men of wealth (its membership was 179 in 1781), it continued to play an important role in Russian intellectual life down to 1917. It met weekly, collected and published much information on the condition of various branches of the economy, and sponsored essay contests with prizes for the best papers. In 1766, on the initiative of an "anonymous person" (Catherine), the society announced the following essay topic: "Whether it is more beneficial to society for the peasant to own land, or only movable property, and the degree to which his rights should extend over either type of property." The very formulation of this question caused some serf owners to respond in indignation. On the other hand, there were some liberal responses. Here are excerpts from two of the replies: the first from Actual State Councillor (also translatable as "Right State Councillor") A. Sumarokov (not a member of the society), and the other from Béardé de l'Abbaye, a member of the Academy of Dijon. Béardé's essay, one of 160 responses from various European countries outside of Russia, was judged best and was awarded the prize in 1768. It was published by the society both in French and in a Russian translation. (See also the series of estate-owners' instructions and related documents in Section B of this chapter.)

Reference: Vol'noe Ekonomicheskoe Obshchestvo, *Istoriia Imperatorskogo Vol'nogo Ekonomicheskogo Obshchestva s 1765 do 1865,* comp. A. I. Khodnev (St. Petersburg, 1865), pp. 24-25, 30-31. The editors wish to thank Messrs. Baltzly and Kucherov for suggesting the Sumarokov excerpt.

[From the statement of Sumarokov:]

The question to be answered, whether it is more beneficial to society for the peasant to have property rights over only his personal belongings, or over land as well, cannot be solved without further clarification. . . . First of all one must ask: Does the general welfare require that the serfs be free? To this I shall answer: Does a canary that brings me amusement need freedom, or does it need a cage; or, does the dog that guards my house need a chain? The canary is better off without a cage, and the dog without a chain. But then the canary will fly away and the dog will bite passersby; thus the peasant needs one thing and the nobleman needs another. It now remains to be decided what is most useful for the general welfare; and if the freedom of the peasants is better than serfdom, only then can we answer the announced question. To this not only all sons of our society but its slaves as well will say that it is the lesser of two evils for the peasant not to own land: nor can they, for all the land is owned by the nobility. The further question arises whether the nobles are obligated to transfer to the peasants, against their will, the land that is theirs by purchase, grant, inheritance, and

other means; and whether the peasants can own land in Russia; for this is the right of the nobility. What will become of the nobleman when the peasants and the land are no longer his; what will be left to him? Indeed, peasant emancipation would be not only harmful but fatal to society, fatal for reasons it is hardly necessary to discuss.

[From the prize-winning essay of Béardé de l'Abbaye:]

There can be no question of any peasant property if the person of the peasant himself is not free and belongs to another. The slave who is not his own master can own property only in a fictitious sense, for there can be no property rights without freedom. Clearly, before granting property of any kind to a slave, it is necessary to set him free. . . . The glory of a sovereign, which constitutes the glory of his realm, attains its greatest splendor through the grant of freedom. The praise of that priceless treasure resounds throughout the world. The personal interest of sovereigns compels them to restore to the peasants the blessings they have received from God.

· · ·

Beyond all doubt, the best way to attract,

arouse, and encourage the tillers of the soil is to give them ownership of the land they cultivate. Then each one will toil for himself, for his children, for his descendants; in a word, he will enrich the state while increasing his property.

But what limits should be assigned to this property? If he owns only movable goods, this can hardly be called property; it holds no attraction for the peasant; he should be given land. But he must be free; freedom and property rights are united in an indissoluble bond. Two thousand peasants doing forced labor will be of less benefit to the state than one hundred husbandmen who see a sure path open to their own enrichment; for the former labor under duress and always seek ways of avoiding hard work.

XII:49. AN ESSAY BY A LEADER OF THE FREE ECONOMIC SOCIETY, 1770

Another approach to the same question is illustrated in these observations by Timofei fon Klingshtet (von Klingstaedt), one of the leading members of the Free Economic Society, published in 1770 in the Society's *Works,* under the title "Exposition of a Method to Encourage Agriculturists to Be Hardworking."

Reference: Vol'noe Ekonomicheskoe Obshchestvo, *Trudy Vol'nogo Ekonomicheskogo Obshchestva k pooshchreniiu v Rossii zemledeliia i domostroitel'stva,* 16:240–41, 247–48.

To overcome man's innate indolence, it is essential to impart to him, step by step, not only an awareness of new satisfactions but also a sense of their necessity and a desire to enjoy them.

The Russian agriculturist . . . is little aware of the possibilities of human life. Despite the natural abundance of fertile soil to reward his labor, his food is usually so poor that it barely serves to sustain his life. He eats meat only on rare occasions in the course of the year. His dwelling and his household goods are no better than his food. A shabby sheepskin and a loose overall [*balakhon*] comprise his entire wardrobe; only in a few localities is he acquainted with the use of boots or leather footwear; usually he wears only bast shoes [*lapti*]. He hardly knows of any entertainment outside of taverns; and under these circumstances he has so little thought of attempting to rise above his brethren that ambition is a thoroughly incomprehensible word for him.

. . .

Freedom and ownership of property should no doubt be regarded as the strongest incentives to human industry. But at the same time, when one observes the miserable condition of so many Finnish and Ukrainian inhabitants, even though they are all free men, one has to admit that freedom does more harm than good to those who do not know how to make proper use of it and that freedom alone cannot eliminate indolence and the poverty it breeds. It may be further argued that our peasant is generally accustomed to conceal and hide from view in every way any indication of prosperity, and instead he takes pains to appear poorer than he really is, prompted by the fear that his stern master, or the even more dreaded steward, might take away every last bit of what he has gained. . . . [Yet] in this our enlightened age, there are few noblemen who would not seek to increase their property by improving the condition of their peasants, or who would deprive them arbitrarily of the fruits of their labor. Anyone shameless enough to do this would immediately earn for himself not only a bad reputation but also the justified contempt of his associates. It may be that more examples can be found among the stewards, but since most of them are serfs, their masters in the course of time might be able to put an end to this evil without much difficulty.

XII:50. ITEMS FROM NOVIKOV'S SATIRICAL MAGAZINES, 1769-1772

Among the early enterprises of Nikolai Ivanovich Novikov (1744-1818) was the editing of satirical weekly magazines. Below are excerpts from the two principal ones, *Truten'* (The drone, 1769-70) and *Zhivopisets* (The painter, 1772-73). Some of his sallies were aimed directly at the Empress, and caused her to react against his journals in ways that shortened their life span. Nevertheless, Novikov was able to carry on an extensive and vigorous career of writing, publishing, and philanthropic service until 1792, when Catherine, frightened by the French Revolution, had him imprisoned.

Reference: P. N. Berkov, ed., *Satiricheskie zhurnaly N. I. Novikova* (Moscow: AN SSSR, 1951), pp. 63, 64, 75, 106, 125 [*Truten'*], 295, 299-300 [*Zhivopisets*]. Translated excerpts of the lively debates carried on between Novikov and Catherine in the pages of these magazines and *Vsiakaia vsiachina,* which she patronized, have recently appeared in Harold B. Segel, ed., *The Literature of Eighteenth-Century Russia,* 2 vols. (N.Y.: E. P. Dutton, 1967), 1:255-300.

[From *Truten'*, 1769, selections from a series of short notices in the style of the *New Yorker:*]

Those who wish to see a young Russian pig who has traveled in foreign lands to improve his mind and who, having profited thereby, has returned a complete swine may look at him free of charge along many streets of this city.

· · ·

Sale

A recently appointed voevoda [governor of a province] is leaving for his assigned post and, to lighten the journey, wishes to sell his conscience; those who wish to buy it may find him in this city.

The judge of a certain court has bent the scales of justice. He is not to blame, but rather a contractor who placed so many bags of flour on the judge's side that justice could not withstand such a weight. Those who wish to repair these scales using their own materials may appear in that court.

[Again from *Truten'*, 1769:]

Several days ago a ship from Bordeaux arrived at the local port [Kronstadt] carrying, along with the most fashionable wares, twenty-four Frenchmen who say that they are all barons, chevaliers, marquises, and counts, and that, being unlucky in their own fatherland in various matters concerning their honor, they were driven to such extremities that they were compelled to go to Russia, rather than America, to acquire gold. In their stories they lied very little, since trustworthy sources indicate that they are all native Frenchmen who have engaged in various trades and occupations of the humbler sort. Many of them lived in the greatest disharmony with the Paris police, which as a result of its hatred toward them extended an invitation which did not appeal to them at all. It consisted of this: to get out of Paris immediately, unless they wanted to dine, sup, and sleep in the Bastille. Although this invitation was quite sincerely meant, it did not appeal to these French gentlemen, and so they have come here planning to occupy the positions of teachers and house stewards to our young noblemen. They soon will leave here for [Saint] Petersburg. Gracious fellow countrymen, make haste to hire these foreigners for the education of your children! Lose no time in entrusting the future mainstay of the state to these vagabonds, and rest assured that you have fulfilled your parental obligations by hiring Frenchmen as teachers, without previously inquiring as to their learning and behavior.

[Another excerpt from *Truten'*, 1769:]

Bezrassud ["Imprudent"] suffers from the opinion that peasants are not human beings, but peasants; as to what peasants are, he knows only that they are his enserfed slaves. This is just how he acts toward them, collecting from them the burdensome tribute called obrok. He not only never says a word to any of them, but does not even deign to nod his head when, following the oriental custom, they prostrate themselves on the ground before him. At such times he thinks: "I am the master [*gospodin*]; they are my slaves; they have been created so that, lacking everything themselves, they might work day and night and fulfill my wish by paying obrok punctually; remembering my position and their own, they should tremble before my gaze." . . . The poor peasants dare not love him as a father; rather do they tremble, honoring him as their tyrant. They work day and night, but withal they can barely obtain their daily subsistence, since only with difficulty can they pay the master's requisitions. They say: "This is not mine, but God's and the master's." The Almighty blesses and rewards their labors, while Bezrassud reaps their fruits. Imprudent one! Have you forgotten that you were created a human being? How can you despise yourself so in the image of the peasants, your slaves? Do you not know that your slaves are more like human beings than you are yourself?

[From *Zhivopisets*, 1772. A note in *Satiricheskie zhurnaly N. I. Novikova,* pp. 560-61, says the author of this work, "An Excerpt from the Trip of V. I. T." (*Otryvok puteshestviia V . . . I . . . T . . .*), may be either Novikov or A. N. Radishchev:]

Upon my departure from this city I stopped in almost every village and hamlet, since they all attracted my curiosity equally, but in the three days of my journey I found nothing worthy of praise. Everywhere I encountered poverty and slavery in the person of the peasants. Unplowed fields and poor grain harvests informed me of the zeal with which the local landowners applied themselves to agriculture. Tiny huts made of thin wooden planks and covered with straw; yards enclosed by wattle fences; small stacks of grain; the very small number of horses and cattle—all this confirmed for me the gross poverty of those miserable creatures who ought to compose the wealth and majesty of the entire state.

Nor did I pass by a single settlement without asking the reasons for the poverty of the peasants. And listening to their answers I always found, to my great disappointment, that the landowners themselves were at fault. O humanity! You are unknown in these settlements. O masters! You tyrannize over human beings like yourselves. O love for one's neigh-

bor—blessed virtue—you are misused: the stupid owners of these poor slaves display you more toward horses and dogs, rather than toward men!

[Also from *Zhivopisets*, 1772:]

From Moscow

The infectious disease [the plague] raging in our city has been halted by the all-wise institutions of our dearest mother of all Russia [Catherine], and by the indefatigable efforts of certain true sons of the fatherland. . . . O would that another disease, which has taken root in Moscow and Petersburg, could be wiped out as quickly. By this disease we mean the blind infatuation of certain eminent Russian boyars and young noblemen for all foreigners. To our shame this infatuation extends exceedingly far. Russian learned men, artists, and craftsmen are despised by them, while foreigners, although many lack all merit, are willingly received and defended by them and always receive their patronage. May this infatuation, harmful and unnatural to any nation, be extirpated; may foreign merits be given their just due, but may the sons of the fatherland take heart, and learning, art, and craftsmanship flourish in Russia; and may all those who hate the fatherland be despised!

XII:51. A STATUTE CONCERNING PUBLIC EDUCATION, AUGUST 5, 1786

Catherine shared with her early collaborator on educational matters, Ivan Ivanovich Betskoi (ca. 1703-95), a keen interest in rearing a "new breed" of people (see Betskoi's report of March 22, 1764, in *PSZRI*, 1st ser., 16:669). Her early efforts in this direction were on a small scale. In 1782, however, the Serbian educator Theodor Iankovich-de-Mirievo (1741-1814), who had helped reorganize the Austrian schools, came to Russia and was appointed to Catherine's school commission. It was largely he who developed the statute on public schools that Catherine approved on August 5, 1786. The following excerpts give some idea of this program, which encountered difficulties in part because its curriculum was so ambitious.

Reference: *PSZRI*, 1st ser., 22:646-48, 654.

The education of the young has been so highly esteemed by all enlightened nations that it has been regarded as the only means of assuring the welfare of civil society. This cannot be disputed, inasmuch as the chief supports of the general welfare of the state lie in those pedagogical subjects that comprehend a pure and rational concept of the Creator and his sacred law, as well as the fundamental principles of unshakable loyalty to the sovereign and of true devotion to one's fatherland and fellow citizens. Education adorns man's soul by enlightening his mind through various kinds

of knowledge; it serves as a guide to a virtuous life by bending the will toward doing good; and finally, it imparts concepts to man that are absolutely essential to him in social intercourse. It follows that the seeds of such necessary and useful knowledge should be implanted from childhood in youthful hearts, that they may sprout in adolescence and bear fruit in manhood, for the benefit of society. But inasmuch as the fruits can be multiplied solely through the spread of education itself, institutions are now being established for this purpose, in which instruction shall be given to the young in their native tongue, in accordance with general prescripts. Such institutions must be established in all the guberniias and vice-gerencies [namestnichestva] under the name of public schools [narodnye uchilishcha], which shall be divided into upper [glavnye] and lower [malye].

· · ·

1. In the capital city of every guberniia there shall be one upper-level public school, consisting of four grades or classes. . . .

[Article 5 states that one of the subjects of study in the second grade shall be a book "on the duties of a man and a citizen."]

8. The fourth grade shall review Russian geography and continue with drawing, world history, and Russian grammar, and the young pupils shall be given practice in writing compositions of a sort that are used in everyday life. . . . Instruction shall be given in Russian history, world and mathematical geography, with problems to be solved on a globe; also in the principles of geometry, mechanics, physics, natural history, and civil architecture. Of the mathematical sciences, geometry and architecture shall be taught in the first year;

in the second year, mathematics and physics [shall be taught], and architecture, including the drawing of plans, shall be continued. . . .

11. In all upper-level public schools, in addition to the rules of the native Russian language, instruction shall further be given in the fundamentals of Latin for those who intend to continue their studies in higher schools, such as gymnasiums or universities; moreover, instruction shall be given in whatever foreign language would be most useful for social intercourse in the neighborhood of the vicegerency in which the upper school is located. . . .

24. Lower schools [in the uezd seats] shall be those institutions in which the young are instructed, in their native language, in the subjects that are also taught in the first and second grade of the upper-level public schools.

· · ·

69. The director of the public schools shall be selected and appointed by the governor general. He must be a lover of scholarship, order, and virtue, who is well disposed toward the young and knows the value of education.

XII:52. SHCHERBATOV ON MORAL DETERIORATION IN RUSSIA, CA. 1789

Prince Mikhail Mikhailovich Shcherbatov (1733-90), of ancient boyar lineage and a prominent defender of the old aristocracy, produced a six-volume history of Russia which, published between 1770 and 1791, was the outstanding historical work of Catherine's time. Perhaps Shcherbatov's views were most clearly expressed in his O povrezhdenii nravov v Rossii (On the corruption of morals in Russia), which was written in 1786-89 but remained unpublished until 1858 (when it appeared in London). Why Shcherbatov declined to rush it into print in his lifetime will be clear from these short excerpts.

Reference: I. P. Khrushchov and A. G. Voronov, eds., Sochineniia kniazia M. M. Shcherbatova, vol. 2 (St. Petersburg, 1898), cols. 159, 202, 225-26, 243. Recently there has appeared a translation of the whole work, with the Russian text on facing pages and with a comprehensive introduction and notes: M. M. Shcherbatov, On the Corruption of Morals in Russia, ed. and trans. A. Lentin (Cambridge: At the University Press, 1969).

[As a result of the changes brought about by Peter the Great] manners have become less coarse, but flattery and self-seeking have come to the fore instead. Hence the servility, the contempt for truth, the seducements directed toward the sovereign, and all the other evils that are now rampant at court and which have installed themselves in the homes of the magnates.

· · ·

[Under the Empress Elizabeth] luxury and voluptuousness found their way down from above, bringing ruin on those below;

and since voluptuousness knows no limit to its excesses, the magnates themselves sought ways to indulge in it in their own homes. The court, to imitate the empress, or rather to ingratiate itself with her, arrayed itself in gold-brocaded garments; the magnates sought in dress whatever was richest, in drink whatever was rarest. As for their domestics, they restored the ancient custom of having innumerable servants, decking them out in costly attire. The carriages were resplendent with gold; expensive horses became necessary to draw the gilded coaches, not so much for convenience as for display. The houses were being adorned with gilt, with silken tapestries in every room, with costly furniture, mirrors, and the like.

. . .

A spouse [Catherine II], not of the blood of our sovereigns by birth, who had overthrown her husband in an armed revolt, was rewarded for this virtuous deed with the crown and scepter of Russia, together with the title of "pious sovereign," which is used when we pray for our sovereigns in church.

It cannot be said that in personal qualities she is unworthy to rule such a great empire, if indeed any woman is able to assume such a burden, and if personal qualities alone suffice for such high office. She is endowed with considerable beauty, is intelligent, affable, magnanimous and compassionate in principle, ambitious and hard-working in her ambition, frugal, enterprising, and quite well read. Her morals, however, are based on the modern philosophers, which means that they are not firmly established on the rock of divine law; and since they are founded on shaky worldly principles they are apt to be unsteady. Conversely, these are her vices: she is lascivious and relies wholly on her favorites; she is full of pompousness in all matters and has infinite

self-esteem; she takes everything upon herself, but being unable to force herself to do things that may bore her, she lacks concern for their execution; finally, she is so changeable that she rarely adheres to any system in the matter of government for as long as a month.

. . .

Intoxicated by her thoughtless reading of modern writers, she sets the Christian faith at naught (albeit pretending to be quite pious). However she may try to conceal her thoughts, they are often revealed in her discourse and even more so in her deeds; many of Voltaire's books which subvert religion have been translated by her order, such as *Candide, The Princess of Babylon,* and others; and not only was the *Bélisaire* by Marmontel, which makes no distinction between the virtue of the heathen and the Christian virtue, translated by her order, but she herself took part in the translation. And her toleration or rather permissiveness toward marriages contrary to [church] law . . . proves this more than anything else; and thus it can be said that under her rule even this immutable mainstay of conscience and virtue has been destroyed.

In this way, by degrees, the deterioration of good morals in Russia has taken place.

XII:53. SHCHERBATOV'S "ON THE ADVANTAGES OF POVERTY"

Shcherbatov's concern over what his cherished Russian aristocrats were coming to is revealed in this sketch, written during the 1780s.

Reference: Khrushchov and Voronov, *Sochineniia kniazia M. M. Shcherbatova,* vol. 2, cols. 398–400.

I call up the image of a gorgeous wealthy magnate, toward whom a blissful stream of money and precious things abundantly flows, to be swallowed by his luxury and voluptuousness as by a yawning gulf.

I behold him in his coach. His coach is gilded, resting on many springs, so that in the bumpy street hardly a jolt is felt; it is closed in with costly chiseled glass panes so that not the slightest breeze or speck of dust may importune him; curtains protect him against the rays of the sun; the thick frame and the glass panes keep the cold of winter out. It is upholstered in velvet, with pillows, filled either with down or with air, providing softness and gentle rest. It is drawn by six splendid steeds, bedecked with gilt harnesses made of morocco leather . . . the reins are silken and

trimmed with gold; and as he rides he is surrounded and followed by a multitude of mounted servants waiting for him to make a sign. . . .

I behold him stepping out of the coach. His clothes are resplendent with gold and precious stones. His fur coat is made from the best Siberian sables, his muff from black foxes; both are like black velvet in color. And the total cost of all his clothes is very high.

I follow him into his house, the facade of which extends a considerable distance along the street. Marble pillars support an ornate gilded balcony. Marble bas-reliefs adorn the top of the windows. I step into the entrance hall—marble and porphyry glitter everywhere. The steps of the stairs are of the best black marble, and pillars of porphyry support the vault. Handrails of white marble rest on gilded copper grille. The walls and ceiling are decorated with fine paintings. In a word, everything here is such that not only does the whole charm the eye, but every separate part evokes admiration. Then I enter his rooms; I behold silk, gold, crystal, marble—in short, all the most precious materials used by craftsmen, treated so artfully that material and skill vie with each other in arousing admiration. All the arts seem to have achieved the impossible just to adorn this house. Huge mirrors reflect the light of numberless burning candles; pendant chandeliers with glittering prisms sparkle like diamonds. Floors of the most varied wood attract the eye; or else they are covered with rich carpets. Wealth and taste are here united. The best craftsmen of the most learned nations have applied all their skill to beautify this house, worthy to be the abode of a god. In the bedroom, in the study, I behold restful armchairs, sofas, couches, and the like, made to pamper the flesh of the voluptuous magnate.

Numerous servants are in attendance, awaiting a glance from him; a great many retainers and sycophants, with utter servility, endeavor to humor him and to enliven his gloomy countenance. And his mistress, neither by birth nor still less by conduct worthy of the company of noblemen, is treated with respect by many, to please the magnate.

But it is time for the evening meal, and the magnate and all his guests proceed to the dining room. Heavens! What decoration! Gold and silver sparkle on every plate. . . . And when at last the viands are uncovered and the potations are served, I suddenly behold all the finest products from the four corners of the earth.

XII:54. RADISHCHEV'S JOURNEY FROM SAINT PETERSBURG TO MOSCOW, 1790

Aleksandr Nikolaevich Radishchev (1749-1802) began to write his famous *Journey from Saint Petersburg to Moscow* in 1780 and published it in 1790. These excerpts, in view of the fact that the French Revolution was then in progress, make his subsequent fate explainable if not excusable.

Reference: A. N. Radishchev, *Puteshestvie iz Peterburga v Moskvu* (Moscow: AN SSSR, 1935, photographic reproduction of the original edition of 1790), pp. 76, 244, 290, 362, 387, 413. Translation based, with some changes, on Roderick Page Thaler, ed., *A Journey from Saint Petersburg to Moscow, by A. N. Radishchev,* trans. Leo Wiener (Cambridge: Harvard University Press, 1958), pp. 45, 143-44, 168-69, 213-14, 229-30, 245.

[In a dream the author sees himself as the tsar, to whom Truth has appeared in the guise of a pilgrim, saying] "Know that you have it in your power to be the greatest murderer in the commonweal, the greatest robber, the greatest traitor, the greatest violator of the public tranquillity, the most savage of enemies in directing your ferocity against the lives of the weak. You will be to blame if a mother weeps over her son, or a wife over her husband, slain on the field of battle. . . . You will be to blame if the fields lie fallow, if the plowman's fledgelings starve at their mother's breast, withered from lack of healthy food."

· · ·

But who amongst us is bound in fetters? Who feels the burden of slavery? The plowman! The man who feeds us in our leanness and satisfies our hunger, who gives us health and prolongs our life, without having the right to dispose of what he cultivates or of what he produces. But who has a greater right to a field than the man who cultivates it? . . . In primitive society he who could cultivate his field had a proprietary right to it and, by virtue of cultivating it, reaped the sole benefits thereof. But how far removed are we from the primitive social conditions of ownership. Amongst us, he who has a natural right to the land not only is completely excluded from this right but, while working another's field, sees his sustenance dependent upon another's power!

· · ·

The censorship has become the nursemaid of reason, wit, and imagination, of everything lofty and graceful. But where there are nursemaids, it follows that there must be children who are tied to their apron strings, which often leads to crooked legs; where there are guardians, it follows that there are minors who have not yet reached the age of reason and are unable to take care of themselves. If there are always to be nursemaids and guardians, the child will long be tied to their apron strings, and will grow up to be a cripple.

· · ·

[From the "Ode to Liberty":]

> An armed host shall arise everywhere,
> Hope shall arm everyone;
> In the blood of the crowned tyrant
> Everyone hastens to wash out his shame.
> Everywhere glistens a sharp sword—
>   I see it,
> Death flies about in various guises
> Soaring above the prideful head.
> Rejoice, O peoples fettered together!
> The avenging law of nature
> Has brought the tsar to the scaffold.
>   . . .

O, if the slaves oppressed by heavy fetters, raging in their own despair, would seize the iron that binds their freedom and crush our heads, the heads of their inhuman masters, and redden their fields with our blood! How would the state suffer thereby? Soon great men would spring from their ranks to replace the murdered generation; but they would be of another mind and without the right to oppress others. This is no dream; my vision penetrates the thick curtain of time which veils the future from our eyes; I see ahead through a whole century.

          . . .

Here may be seen the greed of the nobility, our rapaciousness and tyranny, and the helplessness of the poor. Avaricious beasts, insatiable leeches, what do we leave for the peasants? That which we cannot take away—the air. Yes, and nothing but the air! Often we take away from them not only the gifts of the earth, bread and water, but also the very light. The law forbids us to take their life— that is, to take it suddenly. But there are so many ways to take it from them by degrees! On the one side there is almost unlimited power; on the other, helpless impotence. For the landlord is to the peasant at once legislator, judge, executor of his own judgments, and, if he so desires, a plaintiff against whom the defendant dares not say a word. It is the lot of one cast into fetters, of one thrown into a dismal dungeon: the lot of the ox under the yoke.

XII:55. THE DECREE PUNISHING RADISHCHEV, SEPTEMBER 4, 1790

Catherine, having read Radishchev's *Journey*—"every page of it," she said—concluded that he was advocating "the immoral example of contemporary France." Radishchev was brought to trial. Here is the crucial portion of the resultant decree.

Reference: *PSZRI*, 1st ser., 23:168. For Catherine's own observations, see *CIOIDRMU*, 1865, bk. 3, pp. 67-76.

Aleksandr Radishchev, collegiate councillor [*kollezhskii sovetnik*] and chevalier of the Order of Saint Vladimir, has been found guilty of a crime violating his oath and the duties of a subject, by the publication of a book entitled *A Journey from Saint Petersburg to Moscow*, filled with the most harmful reasonings which disturb the public tranquillity, lessen the respect due the authorities, strive to arouse among the people resentment against authority and against their superiors, and filled, finally, with insulting and violent expressions against the tsarist dignity and power; he has committed, moreover, a deceitful act by adding, after censorship, many pages to this book, published by his own printing shop, which fact he did freely acknowledge. For this crime he has been sentenced to death by the criminal court of the Saint Petersburg guberniia, and then by our Senate, on the basis of the state laws; and although he deserves this sentence of death by the enormity of his crime and the strict application of the law, as designated above, we, nevertheless, following our principle of tempering justice with mercy . . . free him from forfeiting his life and command instead that he be deprived of his rank, the insignia of the Order of Saint Vladimir, and of the dignity of a nobleman, and that he be exiled to Siberia to the frontier settlement of Ilimsk [north of Irkutsk] for a continuous term of ten years.

XII:56. SATIRICAL PIECES BY I. A. KRYLOV, 1792

These two brief excerpts from the monthly *Zritel'* (Spectator), edited by Ivan Andreevich Krylov (1768-1844), illustrate characteristic targets of this talented satirist.

Reference: Nikolai K. Gudzii, ed., and L. B. Lekhtblau, comp., *Russkie satiricheskie zhurnaly XVIII veka* (Moscow: Uchpedgiz, 1940), 277-78, 296.

[From "A Speech Delivered by a Rake at an Assembly of Fools":]

For some time now fashion has seen, with justifiable envy, how science draws to itself the attention of our fellow countrymen and threatens to make the entire state an academy. Taking pity on perishing humanity, and taking pity most of all on the poor women who would be bored to death, sitting alongside their husbands or lovers and listening to their learned deliberations, fashion has been forced to enter among us by stealth, and to bring in, as its first devotees, Frenchmen who have done us the honor of forsaking in their fatherland the dignity of French water-carriers and peddlers, in order to refine our manners and customs. They are the ones who have turned us from bears into men; they are the ones who have shown us the necessity of changing our tunics fifty times a year; they have furnished us with a key: that one may be more successful in seeking happiness with the help of a tailor, a barber, and a carriage maker than with the help of a professor of philosophy; they are the ones, at length, who by teaching us how to dance have disclosed to us a secret every man of the world must know: that in high society educated feet are more useful than an educated head.

[From "A Eulogy in Memory of My Grandpa, Delivered by His Friend, in the Presence of His Pals, over a Bowl of Punch":]

To have an ancestor who was intelligent and virtuous and who brought benefit to his fatherland—this is what makes one a nobleman, this is what distinguishes him from the rabble and from the common people, whose ancestors were neither intelligent nor virtuous, and brought no benefit to the fatherland. The more ancient and remote from us this ancestor, the more splendid is our nobility; and this is what distinguishes the hero whose worthy praises I venture to sing; inasmuch as more than three hundred years have passed since there appeared in his family a virtuous and intelligent man, who did so many fine deeds that his posterity had no more need of such phenomena, and has lived on to the present day without any wise and virtuous men, not losing a trifle of its dignity.

XII:57. A DECREE ON CENSORSHIP, SEPTEMBER 16, 1796

Some of Catherine's responses to the spreading of subversive publications were embodied in this decree.

Reference: *PSZRI*, 1st ser., 23:933-34.

In order to put an end to various inconveniences resulting from the free and unrestrained printing of books, we have deemed it necessary to issue the following orders: (1) Censorship boards, composed of one ecclesiastic and two laymen, shall be established in both our capital cities, Saint Petersburg and Moscow, under the jurisdiction of the Senate; and in the guberniia capital and maritime town of Riga, in the maritime town of Odessa in the Voznesensk vicegerency [*namestnichestvo*], and in the Radzivilov customs office in the Podolia vicegerency—the only places where under the new tariff rules the importation of foreign books is allowed—under the supervision of the guberniia authorities. (2) Printing houses operated by private persons, except for those established by our special permission on the strength of agreements concluded with one of the central organs of government, shall be abolished because of the abuses resulting therefrom; the more so since for the printing of useful and necessary books there is a sufficient number of printing shops attached to various schools. (3) No books written or translated within our state may be printed in any printing house whatsoever without examination by one of the censorship boards established in our [two] capital cities, which must certify that these writings or translations contain nothing contrary to religion, the laws of the state, or good morals. (4) The established . . . censorship boards shall observe the same rules with regard to books brought from foreign countries, so that no book may enter without such examination; those books that will be found contrary to religion or the supreme authority, or apt to corrupt morals, shall be burned. (5) Permission is given to establish printing houses attached to the vicegerent's administrative office in the capital city of each guberniia. . . . (7) By a decree of our Senate the postmaster general shall be instructed to apply the same rules to journals and other periodicals ordered through the mails.

CHAPTER XIII

Paul, Alexander I,
and the Decembrists

A. THE REIGN OF PAUL I, 1796-1801

XIII:1. THE DECREE ON THE SUCCESSION TO THE IMPERIAL THRONE, APRIL 5, 1797

On the day of his coronation in the Cathedral of the Dormition, Paul I moved to clarify many things about the status of the imperial family, including the succession. The decree on succession had been signed by Paul and his wife Maria on January 4, 1788, when he was still heir, but it was formally confirmed only upon his coronation.

Reference: *PSZRI*, 1st ser., 24:587-88.

We, Paul, heir to the throne, *tsesarevich* and grand duke, and we, his consort, Maria, grand duchess.

In the name of the Father, the Son, and the Holy Ghost.

Having come, after careful consideration and in a tranquil state of mind, to a voluntary and common understanding, we herewith state our joint decree whereby, in consideration of our love for our fatherland, we appoint as heir, in conformity with natural law, after my death, our eldest son, Alexander, and after him all his male issue. With the surcease of the eldest male issue, the succession rests with the family of my second son, following the order set down for the descendants of my eldest son, and so forth, in the event of my having more sons. *This is what is known as primogeniture.*

With the surcease of the last male descendants of my sons, the succession will remain in our family but will pass to the female issue of the last reigning sovereign as being the closest to the throne. In order to avoid the difficulties in the passing of succession from one family to another, [the succession] will follow in the same order as above, priority always being given to a male descendant over a female one. Let it be here noted, however, once and forever, that the female descendant from whom the right of succession is directly transmitted never loses her right of inheritance. Should our family become extinct, the right of succession will pass to the female issue of my eldest son, and the nearest female relative of the last reigning sovereign from the family of my above-mentioned son will succeed to the throne. Failing this, the succession will pass to such male or female person as may stand in her place, always seeing to it that priority is given to a male over a female. *This is what is known as substitution [zastuplenie].*

With the surcease of these lines, the succession will pass to the female line of my other sons, following the same order, and then to the family of my eldest daughter, to her male descendants and, with their surcease, to her female issue following the order observed for the female issue of my sons. With the surcease of the female issue of my eldest daughter, the succession will rest with the male and then with the female descendants of my second daughter, and so forth. It must be stipulated here as a rule that the younger daughter, even though she has sons, cannot usurp the rights of her older sister, though the latter be single; for she could marry and bear children. A younger brother inherits before his elder sisters.

Having established the rules of succession, I deem it essential to explain the reasons thereof. They are as follow: that the state never be without an heir to the throne, that the heir to the throne always be designated by the law itself, that there be not the slightest doubt as to who should succeed to the throne, that the rights of succession of several lines be maintained without transgressing the natural law, and that the difficulties inherent in the passing of the right of succession from one family to another be avoided.

XIII:2. THE DECREE FORBIDDING FREE MOVEMENT OF PEASANTS IN SOUTHERN RUSSIA, DECEMBER 12, 1796

Late in 1796 Paul effected what turned out to be the last territorial extension of Russian serfdom.

Reference: *PSZRI*, 1st ser., 24:233-34.

It is known to us that, in the southern regions of our state, including the Ekaterinoslav, Voznesensk, and Caucasian guberniias and the Taurida oblast', the free movement of peasants from place to place has brought to many of the local inhabitants great economic disorder and even ruin. . . . There was no way, without applying the most severe measures, that we could put an end to it, so widespread had it become in those areas. Meanwhile, the prevailing state of affairs gave the occasion to some seekers after personal gain who, oblivious of their oath of allegiance, ventured to incite serfs from even the central guberniias to flee to those southern regions, depriving many landowners in central Russia of their serfs. In order to put a stop to such practices, to establish order once and for all . . . and to confirm forever the rights of each owner [*vladelets*], we have deemed it expedient to decree that:

1. All peasants in the guberniias of Eka-terinoslav, Voznesensk, and Caucasia, and in the Taurida oblast' must remain in the place and vocation under which they will be registered in the present census; the same to apply in the region of the Don and on the island [peninsula] of Taman'. . . .

2. Compensation shall be paid to those owners who, due to the unstable situation which has existed up to the present in those areas, have suffered losses and who, prior to this decree, have discovered the whereabouts of their runaway serfs and with whom they are staying and have submitted claims to the proper authorities. . . . This money is to be given to the owners to whom the serfs belong. If the new owners do not wish to pay the money, the serfs shall be returned to their former pomeshchiki [estate owners].

3. The permanent location of peasants on the land they inhabit is to be maintained, and their transit is henceforth to be forbidden. If after this date the villages belonging to po-meshchiki take in runaway serfs and keep them, these owners [pomeshchiki] shall be liable to punishment in accordance with the decree of May 13, 1754, without the least leniency.

XIII:3. PAUL'S MANIFESTO FORBIDDING SUNDAY LABOR BY SERFS, APRIL 5, 1797

In this manifesto Paul made a feeble gesture toward reducing the *barshchina* labor generally required of serfs.
   Reference: *PSZRI*, 1st ser., 24:587.

We proclaim to all our loyal subjects. The law of God given to us in the Ten Commandments teaches us to devote the seventh day of the week to him. Therefore, on this day, made famous by the triumph of the Christian faith and on which we were honored to receive the holy anointing and were crowned tsar on the throne of our forefathers, we deem it our duty before our Maker and the Bearer of All Blessings to confirm that this law must be observed, exactly and without fail, throughout our empire, and we command one and all to see that no one under any pretext dares to force serfs to work on Sundays; all the more so because for agricultural production the six remaining days in the week, which are in general distributed equally between serfs' labor for themselves and their labor due the pomeshchiki, should with good management be sufficient to satisfy all economic needs.

XIII:4. A REPORT ON THE ADMINISTRATION OF RURAL STATE PROPERTIES, AUGUST 7, 1797

This report, approved by Paul and designed to improve the administration of state properties and to set a standard for general rural administrative machinery, provides information on rural local government in Russia at the end of the eighteenth century.
   Reference: *PSZRI*, 1st ser., 24:673-77.

Report of the Branch [*Ekspeditsiia*] of State Economy approved by His Majesty: Concerning the Grouping of State Villages into Volosti and the Ordering of Their Internal Administration
. . . The branch begs, on the basis of Your Imperial Majesty's decree concerning crown [*udel'nye*] lands, to submit the following regulations for the grouping of state villages into volosti and for the ordering of their internal administration. . . .

1. In view of the diversity of the guberniias that constitute the Russian Empire and the inequality among state villages in number of

inhabitants and size of landholdings, no fixed number of persons shall be assigned to each volost', this being left to the executive charge of the civil governor together with the fiscal board [*kazennaia palata*, established in each guberniia]. It must be borne in mind, however, that for the best ordering of rural administration no volost' should have more than 3,000 registered persons. . . .

2. Each volost' shall be known by the name of its principal village. In this village, or in another more suitable, the volost' board [*pravlenie*] shall be established, consisting of the volost' head [*volostnoi golova*], one elder or elected representative [*vybornyi*] from the village, and one clerk [*pisar'*]. . . .

4. Besides the volost' board there will be in each village or hamlet one village or hamlet headman . . . and one household police officer [*desiatskii*] for every ten households. . . .

5. The volost' head and the clerk shall be elected for a two-year term by the entire community of villages and hamlets in the given volost'; inspectors [*smotriteli*] . . . shall be elected yearly by every village from among peasants of good behavior who are excellent farmers and particularly skillful in land cultivation and animal husbandry so that they may serve as examples for others. The household police officers are to be changed each month. . . .

7. At appointed times the volost' head must exact from the peasants of his volost' all direct and indirect taxes and duties. . . . At the end of each year the volost' head must account to the peasants themselves for all the money collected from them during the year for various needs; in case of deficit or error, the peasants must exact the deficient sums from the volost' head. In such matters the peasants may ask the aid of the rural district police officer [*ispravnik*]. If, however, the accounts are found to be in order, those of the peasants who are literate, or the parish priest, must append to the books listing income and expenditures a signed statement to the effect that the expenses have been verified by the mir. . . .

9. The volost' head must: (1) administer justice and seek a reconciliation in all minor disputes and claims, but in case of dissatisfaction or disagreement he must allow them to settle their accounts in court. . . .

15. The inhabitants in each village must, without fail, hasten to the meeting place in accordance with the summons of the volost' head or elected representative . . . and there, in a quiet and orderly manner, must heed and carry out exactly what was ordered of them. The fine for disobedience or failure to appear after being summoned to a meeting shall be fifty copecks, and four times that amount for outrageous and noisy behavior. . . .

25. No peasant registered in a volost' may absent himself from his home without the permission of the volost' board and the consent of the mir and without a special passport which is issued by the uezd treasurer to the volost' head. The reasons for such absences must be investigated and, if there are no reasons, delivery of the passport must be withheld. The volost' head, together with the peasants, is held responsible for the punctual return of those who have been given a leave of absence and for the payment of state taxes on their behalf at the time due.

26. Finally, the volost' head, clerks, and elected representatives of the villages, having been distinguished from and esteemed above all other peasants, must, by common effort, promote in every way the welfare of the peasants and must forewarn and caution all concerning this. They must be strict but orderly in the enforcement of their duties, without treating the peasants in a condescending and indulgent manner. They must receive patiently all petitions, heed all needs, act as direct agents, and on no account accept any bribes; for they shall be subject to punishment and questioning according to law just as much for neglect of their duties as for oppression of their subordinates.

XIII:5. DECREES CONCERNING THE ALLOTMENT OF STATE LANDS TO CERTAIN STATE PEASANTS, NOVEMBER 27, 1797, AND JULY 1800

These decrees illustrate one of the many means by which the government sought to ensure fiscal stability.

Reference: *PSZRI*, 1st ser., 24:807-08; 26:247-50.

[From the decree of November 27, 1797:]
Inasmuch as Her Majesty's decree of May 3, 1783, to the heads of guberniias expressed approval of compensating peasants having

meager landholdings, the Senate has deemed it expedient that peasants whose holdings fall below the norm of fifteen desiatinas per male . . . should be given enough land from the state obrok land to bring the total amount owned by them up to the said norm. Where obrok lands are so few that even with the distribution of all these lands the norm would not be reached, then whatever land there is is to be distributed, for the compensation of peasants having meager landholdings would raise their material welfare and make them punctual in the payment of state taxes.

[From the decree of July (n.d.) 1800:]

In short, the fiscal board [kazennaia palata] must in this instance maintain as far as possible the rule that all state peasants, since they have equal obligations, are to be treated equally as concerns amount of land and quality of soil. . . . *It has been ordered:* Inasmuch as His Majesty's decree of November . . . [27] 1797 . . . commands the allocation, to state peasants whose landholdings fall short of the norm of fifteen desiatinas per male, of enough of the state obrok lands

to bring the insufficient holdings up to the said norm . . . the Senate, on August 12, [1]798, accordingly ordered all fiscal boards, in every guberniia, once and for all and in general, to make an apportionment of land among state peasants which is perfectly equitable and in accord with the capacities of the village. But neither the personal decree of His Imperial Majesty nor the Senate's decrees order that land should be taken from those villages whose landholdings fall below the required norm and given to others for the purpose of equalization. Wherefore, all fiscal boards must be instructed that in cases where there is not enough state land to fulfill the fifteen-desiatina norm, all [other] available state land shall be allocated. . . . Concerning the transfer of state peasants, excepting those under the jurisdiction of the Department of Crown Properties, to villages where land is plentiful, all fiscal boards must be instructed to make such transfers only at the wish of the peasants themselves and in such a manner as to avoid any interruption in the payment of state taxes and to incur the least expenditure of public funds.

XIII:6. NEWSPAPER ADVERTISEMENTS OF THE SALE OF SERFS, 1797

These advertisements are from *Moskovskie vedomosti* (Moscow news) of 1797.

Reference: A. K. Dzhivelegov, S. P. Mel'gunov, and V. I. Picheta, eds., *Velikaia reforma* (Moscow: Sytin, 1911), 1:258. The editors are indebted to Messrs. Baltzly and Kucherov for the selection and the translation. The items are reproduced photographically from clippings, apparently from several different issues of *Moskovskie vedomosti.*

For sale: a waiter, 25 years old, with his wife and a minor son. A very good weaver; can also shave and draw blood. The wife can look after the mistress and is capable of any work. Also for sale in the same place: a dormeuse [traveling carriage], not much used, of the best workmanship. Those interested may obtain all details at no. 138, 2d block, 7th ward, in the parish of Afanasii and Kirill.

At house no. 352, 4th block, 6th ward, there are for sale: a good hairdresser for men and women; height above average, of fairly good figure, also useful as a valet de chambre, waiter, or footman, 27 years old; his wife, 24 years old, a laundress and needlewoman, with a daughter over 2 years old; both of good conduct. Lowest price for the lot, 1,000 rubles.

For sale: a peasant, 35 years old, with wife

of same age and three minor children. Inquire about price at owner's in the 10th ward in the parish of Nikola, on the Bolvanovka, house no. 529.

In the 12th ward, in the former old-age asylum, an officer living there offers for sale a girl, 16 years old, who knows how to knit lace, to sew linen, and to iron, starch, and dress her mistress. She also has an agreeable face and figure.

For sale: 3 horses: 2 bay stallions, 4 years old, of English breed, well matched, of good size; and a dark bay gelding, 3 years old, also of English breed. They can be seen, and inquiry made about the price, at house no. 260, block 1, ward 8. In the same house there is for sale a musician who plays the bassoon and is beginning to sing in a bass voice. Very well trained in reading and writing. 15 years old.

XIII:7. ALEXANDER'S LETTER TO LA HARPE, SEPTEMBER 27, 1797

Alexander's correspondence with his tutor and friend La Harpe sheds valuable light on the attitudes of the future monarch. Here is a brief sample.

Reference: N. K. Shil'der, *Imperator Aleksandr Pervyi, ego zhizn' i tsarstvovanie*, 4 vols. (St. Petersburg: A. S. Suvorin, 1897-98), 1:280-81. The editors are indebted to Messrs. Baltzly and Kucherov for the selection and much of the translation.

You are acquainted with the various abuses that prevailed in the time of the late empress; they merely increased as her health and her mental and physical powers became enfeebled. Finally, last November, she ended her career. I shall not give you the details of the tribulation and general grief her death brought to everyone, a grief which, unfortunately, increases every day. My father, on ascending the throne, wanted to reform everything. His beginning, it is true, was brilliant enough, but the results have not been in keeping with it. Everything has been turned upside-down at the same time, and this has only served to increase the confusion, even now too great, which already prevailed in affairs.

The military wastes almost all its time, especially in parades. Elsewhere no plan is followed. What is ordered one day is countermanded a month later. Suggestions are permitted only when the harm has already been done. Finally, to speak plainly, the well-being of the state is not in the least considered in the administration of affairs; there is only absolute power which does everything wrong and at cross purposes. It would be impossible to enumerate to you all the follies that have been committed; add to this a severity quite devoid of justice, much favoritism, and the greatest inexperience in all affairs. The choice of officials is entirely a matter of favoritism; merit counts for nothing. In sum, my poor country is in an indescribable state. The farmer is plagued; commerce is hindered; personal liberty and well-being are reduced to nothing. There you have the picture of Russia; judge how my heart must suffer. As for myself, engaged in military trivialities, wasting all my time in the duties of a subaltern, with not even a moment to give to my studies, which were my favorite pursuit before the change, I have become the most unhappy of men.

XIII:8. THE LETTERS FOUNDING THE RUSSIAN-AMERICAN COMPANY, JULY 8 AND DECEMBER 27, 1799

Indicative of Paul's efforts to expand Russian commercial facilities was the founding of the Russian-American Company in 1799. This act opened an important chapter in Russo-American relations.

Reference: *PSZRI*, 1st ser., 25:700, 923.

[From the "Rules for the Company," July 8, 1799:]

1. The company that is hereby being founded for trading on the mainland of northeastern America [northeastern, that is, from the standpoint of the Pacific Ocean] and the Aleutian and Kurile Islands, as well as throughout the entire area of the Northeastern Sea belonging to Russia by right of discovery, is to be known, under the high patronage of His Imperial Majesty, as the Russian-American Company.

2. This company is not new but is composed of the two already existing private companies of Golikov and Shelekhov, and Myl'nikov and Company. Its initial joint capital consists of 724,000 rubles and is divided into 724 shares. However, inasmuch as participation in it is open not only to others engaged in such trading, in addition to the above, but also to all other Russian subjects desiring to enter this company, 1,000 new shares shall be added.

[From the decree of December 27, 1799:]

The Russian-American Company is graciously granted the following privileges for twenty years from this time:

1. Insofar as Russian navigators had from olden times discovered the coast of the northeastern part of America, from 55° northern latitude, and the chain of islands extending

from Kamchatka northward to America and southward to Japan, and by virtue of Russia's right of possession of same, the company is granted the privilege of using all the businesses and establishments existing today along the northeastern coast of America from the above-mentioned 55° to Bering Strait and beyond it, as well as the Aleutians, Kuriles, and other islands lying along the northeastern coast.

2. It is to make new discoveries not only above 55° northern latitude but also beyond it further south and is to occupy the lands discovered by it as Russian possessions according to the rules defined above, if such lands have not been previously claimed and occupied by other nations and have not become their dependents.

3. It may have the exclusive right to exploit everything in these regions, both on the surface and underground, that has been or will henceforth be discovered by it, regardless of claims from anyone else.

4. The company is permitted in the future to found settlements and establish fortifications for safe residence wherever needed and according to its best understanding, dispatching to this territory ships with goods and traders without any hindrance in this matter.

XIII:9. THE MANIFESTO ON THE ANNEXATION OF THE KINGDOM OF GEORGIA, JANUARY 18, 1801

This manifesto was one of the few actions taken by Paul that was approved by Alexander I.
Reference: *PSZRI*, 1st ser., 26:502.

Since ancient times the Georgian kingdom, oppressed by neighbors of an alien creed, has been exhausting its strength in perpetual self-defense, thus bearing the inevitable consequences of an almost continuously unfortunate war. Disagreements within the royal house have complicated this situation, threatening to complete the ruin of the kingdom by reviving internecine war. Tsar Georgii Iraklievich, seeing the end of his days approaching, and high-ranking officials, and the Georgian people themselves have now appealed for our protection and, seeing no other salvation from ultimate disaster and subjugation by their foes, have petitioned through plenipotentiary delegates concerning the admission of territories in the possession of the Georgian kingdom into the direct dominion of the imperial throne of all the Russias.

Heeding this petition on account of our merciful relationship with all co-religionists and from our constant concern for the welfare of the Georgian people, we have determined to fulfill the desire of Tsar Georgii Iraklievich and of the Georgian people and have therefore ordered our troops into Georgian territories, as much for the preservation of internal order in the land as for its protection against outside attacks. And, with the publication of this, our imperial decree, we declare that, upon the annexation of the Georgian kingdom under our rule forever, not only will there be left and kept intact to our beloved new subjects of the Georgian kingdom all of its dependent territories, all rights, privileges, and properties lawfully belonging to each, but also that henceforth every class of people in the aforementioned territories will enjoy all those rights, liberties, advantages, and privileges enjoyed by hereditary Russian subjects.

B. THE REIGN OF ALEXANDER I

XIII:10. THE MEMOIRS OF PRINCE ADAM CZARTORYSKI, CONCERNING 1796 AND 1801-1802

The memoirs of Czartoryski, written in the 1830s, shed much light on the attitudes of Alexander I's "unofficial committee" and on the tsar himself in the years around the turn of the century. (See also Alexander's letter to La Harpe, Item XIII:7, above.)

Reference: *Memoirs of Prince Adam Czartoryski and His Correspondence with Alexander I*, ed. Adam Gielgud, 2d ed., 2 vols. (London, 1888), 1:109-14, 127-30, 256-58, 260-61. For translated excerpts from the papers of another of Alexander's associates of this period, Count Paul Stroganov, see Warren B. Walsh, ed., *Readings in Russian History*, 3 vols., 4th ed. (Syracuse, N.Y.: Syracuse University Press, 1963), 2:275-82.

[Under the date 1796:]

Before the break-up of the ice on Lake Ladoga, which generally occurs towards the end of April, St. Petersburg has a few days of fine weather, with bright sun and a moderate temperature; and the quays are then full of gaily dressed people walking and driving. The Grand-Duke Alexander was often there alone or with his wife; and this was an additional incentive for high society to assemble. I used also to come with my brother, and whenever the Grand-Duke met one of us, he stopped to talk, and showed us particular attention.

These morning meetings were, so to say, a continuation of the Court soirees, and our relations with the Prince daily became more intimate. In the spring the Court moved as usual to the Tauris [Tauride] Palace, where the Empress Catherine professed to live in greater retirement. . . . The Grand-Duke still came occasionally to the quay; he told me he was sorry to see me so seldom, and asked me to come to [visit] him to the Tauris Palace for a walk in the garden, which he wished to show me. Spring had already begun, and as generally happens in this climate, nature had made up for lost time, and vegetation had rapidly developed itself in a few days; the trees and fields were green and covered with flowers. . . .

As soon as I came in, the Grand-Duke took me by the hand, and proposed that we should go into the garden, in order, he said, that he might enable me to judge of the skill of his English gardener. We walked about in every direction for three hours, keeping up an animated conversation all the time. . . . He added that he did not in any way share the ideas and doctrines of the Cabinet and the Court [concerning Poland]; and that he was far from approving the policy and conduct of his grandmother, whose principles he condemned. He had wished for the success of Poland in her glorious struggle and had deplored her fall. Kosciuszko, he said, was in his eyes a man who was great by his virtues and the cause which he had defended, which was the cause of humanity and justice. He added that he detested despotism everywhere, no matter in what way it was exercised; that he loved liberty, to which all men had a right; that he had taken the strongest interest in the French Revolution, and that while condemning

its terrible excesses, he wished the French Republic success and rejoiced at its establishment. He spoke to me with veneration of his tutor, M. de la Harpe.

. . .

This conversation was, as may be imagined, occasionally interrupted by demonstrations of friendship on his part, and of astonishment, gratitude, and devotion on mine. He bade me farewell, saying that he would try to see me as often as possible, and urging on me the greatest circumspection and secrecy. . . .

I was deeply moved, and could hardly believe my ears. That a Russian Prince, Catherine's successor, her grandson and her favourite child, whom she would have seen reigning after her instead of her son . . . should disavow and detest his grandmother's principles—should repel the odious policy of Russia—should be a passionate lover of justice and liberty—should pity Poland and wish to see her happy—seemed incredible. . . .

. . . I was subjugated by a charm which it is easy to understand: there was so much candour, innocence, resolution which seemed unshakable, and elevation of soul in the words and countenance of this young prince. . . . My attachment to him was boundless, and the feeling with which he inspired me at that moment lasted even after the illusions which had given birth to it successively disappeared; it resisted the attacks which Alexander himself made upon it, and it never died in spite of the many events and sad misunderstandings which might have destroyed it. . . . It should be remembered that at that time so-called liberal opinions were much less prevalent than they are now, and had not yet penetrated into all the classes of society and even into the Cabinets of sovereigns. . . .

. . . Now that I look back, forty years afterwards, upon the events which have taken place since that conversation, I see only too well how little they have realised the picture that our youthful imaginations had drawn. Liberal ideas were at that time in our eyes still surrounded by an aureole which has paled since they have been tested by experience; their realisation had not yet produced the cruel deceptions which have so often disheartened us. That period, in the years 1796 and 1797, was the most brilliant one of the dawn of liberal ideas: the cycle of the French Empire had not yet chilled and dispersed the warmest partisans of the Revolution.

. . .

It is certainly astonishing that Catherine, who took pleasure in the thought that Alexander would continue her reign and her glory, did not think of preparing him for this task by familiarising him in his early youth with the various branches of government. Nothing of the sort was attempted. Perhaps he would not have acquired very correct information on many things, but he would have been saved from the want of occupation. . . . Alexander's education remained incomplete at the time of his marriage, in consequence of the departure of M. de la Harpe. He was then eighteen years old; he had no regular occupation, he was not even advised to work, and in the absence of any more practical task he was not given any plan of reading which might have helped him in the difficult career for which he was destined. I often spoke to him on this subject, both then and later. I proposed that he should read various books on history, legislation, and politics. He saw that they would do him good, and really wished to read them; but a Court life makes any continued occupation impossible. While he was Grand-Duke, Alexander did not read to the end a single serious book. I do not think he could have done so when he became Emperor, and the whole burden of a despotic government was cast upon him. The life of a Court is fatiguing and yet idle. . . . He read by fits and starts. . . . The passion of acquiring knowledge was not sufficiently strong in him; he was married too young, and he did not perceive that he still knew very little. . . . The few years of his early youth thus passed away, and he lost precious opportunities which he had in abundance so long as Catherine was alive. . . .

. . . It must be concluded that nature had endowed him with rare qualities, as notwithstanding the education he had received he became the most amiable sovereign of his age and the cause of Napoleon's fall. After having reigned for some years, and acquired the experience entailed by the necessity of at once taking the management of important affairs of State and by constant intercourse with men in office, people were surprised to find him not only an accomplished man of the world, but an able politician, with a penetrating and subtle mind, writing without assistance excellent letters on complicated and difficult subjects, and always amiable, even in the most serious conversations. What would he have become had his education been less neglected and more adapted to the duties which were to occupy his life? . . .

M. de la Harpe does not seem to have directed Alexander into any serious course of study, though he had acquired so much influence over the Grand-Duke's mind and heart that I believe he could have made him do anything. Alexander derived from his teaching only some superficial knowledge; his information was neither positive nor complete. M. de la Harpe inspired him with the love of humanity, of justice, and even of equality and liberty for all; he prevented the prejudices of flatteries which surrounded him from stifling his noble instincts. It was a great merit in M. de la Harpe to have inspired and developed these generous sentiments in a Russian Grand-Duke, but Alexander's mind was not penetrated by them; it was filled with vague phrases, and M. de la Harpe did not sufficiently make him reflect on the immense difficulty of realising these ideas.

. . .

[Under the date 1801-02:]

The opinions and sentiments which had seemed to me so admirable in Alexander when he was Grand-Duke did not change when he became Emperor; they were somewhat modified by the possession of absolute power, but they remained the foundation of all his principles and thoughts. . . .

There was no longer any question of the old reveries of extreme liberalism; the Emperor ceased to speak to me of his plan of giving up the throne. . . . But he was constantly thinking of more practical matters, such as the administration of justice, the emancipation of the masses, equitable reforms and liberal institutions; this was his diversion when he was alone with me. He understood the often insurmountable obstacles which the most elementary reforms would meet with in Russia; but he wished to prove to those with whom he was intimate that the sentiments he had expressed to them were still the same, notwithstanding the change in his position. . . . It was necessary, however, not to disclose them, and still less to take a pride in them, in the presence of a public which was at that time so little prepared to appreciate them, and would have regarded them with surprise and horror. Meanwhile the government machine continued to work according to the old routine, and the Emperor was obliged to take part in its management. . . . In order to remedy the discrepancy between Alexander's opinions and his acts, he established a Secret Council composed of persons whom he regarded as his friends and believed to be animated by sentiments and opinions in conformity with his own. The first nucleus of this Council was formed by the young Count Paul Strogonoff, M. de Novosiltzoff, and myself. We had long been in near relations with each other, and these now became more serious. The necessity of rallying around the Emperor and not leaving him alone in his desire of reform drew us more closely together. We were regarded for some years as models of intimate and unshakable friendship. To be superior to every personal interest, and not to accept either presents or distinctions, was the principle of our alliance. . . . It was not always liked by my companions, and the Emperor himself afterwards grew tired of servants who wished to distinguish themselves by refusing to accept rewards which were so eagerly sought by everyone else.

. . . The fourth member admitted by the Emperor to the Secret Council was Count Kotchoubey. . . .

We were privileged to dine with the Emperor without a previous invitation, and we used to meet two or three times a week. After coffee and a little conversation, the Emperor used to retire, and while the other guests left the palace, the four members of the Secret Council entered through a corridor into a little dressing-room of their Majesties, and there met the Emperor. Various plans of reform were debated; each member brought his ideas, and sometimes his work, and information which he had obtained as to what was passing [happening] in the existing administration and the abuses which he had observed. The Emperor freely expressed his thoughts and sentiments, and although the discussion at these meetings for a long time had no practical result, no useful reform was tried or

carried out during Alexander's reign which did not originate in them. Meanwhile the Official Council, namely, the Senate and the Ministers, governed the country in the old way. Directly the Emperor left his dressing-room he came under the influence of the old Ministers, and could do nothing of what had been decided upon in the Secret Council; it was like a masonic lodge from which one entered the practical world.

This mysterious Council, which was not long concealed from the suspicions, or ultimately from the knowledge, of the Court, and was designated "the young men's party," grew impatient at not obtaining any result whatever from its deliberations; it pressed the Emperor to carry out the views he had expressed to us. . . . Once or twice an attempt was made to induce him to adopt energetic resolutions, to give orders and make himself obeyed, to dismiss certain superannuated officials who were a constant obstacle to every reform and to put young men in their place. But the Emperor's character inclined him to attain his end by compromises and concessions, and moreover he did not yet feel sufficiently master of the position to risk measures which he thought too violent. In our council Strogonoff was the most ardent, Novosiltzoff the most prudent, Kotchoubey the most time-serving, and I the most disinterested, always striving to curb undue impatience. Those who urged the Emperor to take immediate and severe measures did not know him. Such a proposal always made him draw back, and was of a nature to diminish his confidence. But as he complained of his Ministers and did not like any of them, an attempt was made in the Council, before inducing him to change them, to discuss the matter in a practical spirit, apart from the abstract considerations of reform which had previously occupied us. Strogonoff accepted the post of Procurator of the First Department of the Senate; and Novosiltzoff was appointed one of the Emperor's secretaries, a place which gave him many advantages, as every letter addressed to the Emperor passed through his hands.

XIII:11. THE MANIFESTO ABOLISHING THE SECRET CHANCERY, APRIL 2, 1801

Although the reform was short-lived, Alexander early in his reign issued this command concerning the police practices of the government.
    Reference: *PSZRI*, 1st ser., 26:603–04.

The customs of the age and circumstances peculiar to past times prompted our imperial forebears to establish, among other temporary institutions, a Secret Chancery for Investigation which, under various names and regulations, existed even before the time of our most gracious grandmother, Empress Catherine II. Recognizing that this was inconsistent with the established order of government in Russia and that it strongly contradicted her own principles, she solemnly abolished and repudiated it in a manifesto issued in 1762. Meanwhile, however, in view of existing circumstances, it was felt essential to continue its activities under the title of the Secret Branch [Ekspeditsiia], with every possible moderation in the application of its regulations through the personal wisdom and examination of all cases by the sovereign. But since, on the one hand, it later became apparent that personal principles, being by their very nature subject to change, could not establish a reliable bulwark against abuses and that the authority of law was needed to endow these regulations with the necessary firmness, and, on the other hand, reasoning that in a well-organized state all offenses should be encompassed, tried, and punished through a common process of law: we have deemed it wise to abolish and eliminate forever not only the name but all the activities of the Secret Branch and hereby decree that all affairs being handled by it be consigned to eternal oblivion in the State Archives. In the future all such business is to be under the jurisdiction of the First and Fifth Departments of the Senate and in all those government offices that have jurisdiction over criminal cases.

XIII:12. A RESCRIPT DIRECTING A COMMISSION TO UNDERTAKE THE DRAFTING OF A CODE OF LAWS, JUNE 5, 1801

As one of the first of his official acts, Alexander I sought to deal with the chaotic state of Russia's body of law. His goal was outlined in this excerpt from the preamble to his directive to Count Petr Vasil'evich Zavadovskii, appointed by him to head the drafting commission.
Reference: *PSZRI*, 1st ser., 26:683.

Imperial Rescript. Finding in the law alone the basis as well as the source of the people's welfare, and being convinced of the fact that, while all other measures may bring felicitous times to the state, the law alone can assure their permanence, I have deemed it necessary in the very first days of my reign, and upon an initial survey of the state administration, to ascertain the actual state of affairs prevailing in this sphere.

I have always known that ever since the time of the code [the Ulozhenie of Tsar Aleksei Mikhailovich, 1649], i.e. for almost one and a half centuries, the laws that issued forth from the legislative authority in various and often contradictory directions, designed more often for particular occasions than in accordance with any general consideration of national interests, could have had neither cohesiveness, nor unity of purpose, nor uniformity in their application. Hence stems the general confusion of every man's rights and obligations, as well as the uncertainty that envelops equally the judge and the defendant, the ineffectiveness of laws in their application, and the facility with which they can be changed upon the first impulse of whim or despotism.

I have always known that Tsar Aleksei Mikhailovich's code, issued more for Moscow than for Russia, and more for the Russians of that time than for Russians in general, could not have a complete and unalterable effect, either in our time, or even during the period immediately following its adoption. Subsequent to its adoption, cases were encountered at every step that either were left undefined by the code or were not within its scope. The so-called newly decreed articles with their supplementary provisions proved its incompleteness, on the one hand, and, on the other, by contradicting its provisions on many points and undermining its strength, rendered it even more obscure; and having subjected its application to uncertainty they engendered numerous arbitrary interpretations more harmful even than this uncertainty.

Peter the Great pointed out all these deficiencies at the very beginning of his reforms and proposed to correct them with a new code.

You are all aware of the efforts that have been exerted from that time on in almost every reign toward the improvement of the laws. Commissions created for this purpose have existed in various forms and have been more or less active intensively almost without interruption for over eighty years. As a result of this activity plans have been developed in various areas, projects prepared, statutes actually composed, important improvements proposed for old divisions of jurisprudence, and new divisions devised.

XIII:13. A DECREE PROHIBITING THE USE OF TORTURE IN THE PROSECUTION OF CRIMINAL TRIALS, SEPTEMBER 27, 1801

In November of 1801, the Senate issued orders implementing this command from the tsar. Although the tsar's attempt constituted a significant landmark in Russian judicial history, the complete reform of ancient practice was not quickly realized.
  Reference: *PSZRI*, 1st ser., 26:797-98.

It is extremely distressing that it has come to our attention that in connection with frequent fires in the city of Kazan' a local citizen was arrested on the suspicion of arson, that he was questioned and did not confess. But with torture and torment a confession was wrung from him and he was tried. . . . Throughout the trial, wherever possible, he reiterated his innocence, denying his coerced confession. But cruelty and prejudice did not heed his voice; he was condemned to death. . . .

  The Governing Senate, fully realizing the importance of this abuse, as well as the degree to which it is contradictory to the most basic principles of justice and oppressive to all civil rights, is not to fail to issue . . . throughout the empire, the strictest injunction that nowhere, in any guise whatsoever, neither in the highest nor in the lowest levels of the administration and the courts, may anyone, under the threat of certain and severe punishment, dare to apply or allow others to apply or perform any kind of torture. Offices to which review of criminal cases is assigned by law must, in their judgments and sentences, proceed from the personal testimony of the defendants given before the court that, in the course of the investigation, they were not subjected to interrogation under torture. And, finally, the very designation torture, that shame and reproach to mankind, is to be erased forever from the memory of the people.

XIII:14. THE DECREE PERMITTING ALL FREE PERSONS TO PURCHASE AND OWN LAND, DECEMBER 12, 1801

An ancient privilege of the Russian nobility was modified in this decree, which Alexander emphasized by publishing it on his birthday. It should be noted, however, that while serfdom was in existence, "lands without serfs" tended to be of relatively little value.
  Reference: *PSZRI*, 1st ser., 26:863.

Desiring to give a new incentive to agriculture and to the national industry commensurate with the potential Russia possesses by virtue of her size and location, we have recognized the need of extending to all Russian subjects, except those who are attached to pomest'ia, the right of acquiring, under any of their various designations, lands without serfs and of possessing everything on or below their surfaces. Consequently, we grant not only to merchants, small tradesmen [*meshchane*], and all who enjoy municipal rights, but also to state peasants regardless of the department in whose jurisdiction they belong, as well as to those persons who have been set free by pomeshchiki, the right to purchase land from any persons who have the legal right to sell it and to confirm their ownership of such acquisitions by concluding a purchase agreement, each in his own name, in government offices established for that purpose according to lawful procedure for inviolably protecting their ownership rights.

XIII:15. THE MANIFESTO ESTABLISHING CENTRAL MINISTRIES FOR STATE ADMINISTRATION, SEPTEMBER 8, 1802

Alexander I, seeking to modernize his administrative machinery, moved early in his reign to replace the antiquated collegiate system started by Peter I.
  Reference: *PSZRI*, 1st ser., 27:243-47.

We have thought it fit to divide governmental affairs, according to their natural connections, into several parts and, for their most successful operation, to entrust them to the jurisdiction of our selected ministers after establishing the main principles by which they shall be guided in the accomplishment of everything their office shall demand of them and of that which we expect from their loyalty, efforts, and devotion to the general welfare. To the Governing Senate, whose duties and basic powers we have confirmed by our decree of this date, we assign the authority, most important and fitting for this high institution, to oversee the activities of the ministers in all subdivisions entrusted to their administration and, after duly comparing and coordinating these activities with the laws of the state and with the reports received by the Senate directly from lower administrative offices, to state its own conclusions and to submit them to us in reports. . . .

. . . Accordingly the following clauses will serve to designate all these departments in their natural interrelation, as well as all matters pertaining to them and the main duties of the ministers to whose administration we entrust them.

1. The administration of the affairs of the government is divided into eight departments, each of which, comprising those areas which by their nature belong to it, constitutes a separate ministry and is under the direct control of a minister to be named by us today or whom we shall deem fit to name later.

These departments are the following: (1) of the Army; (2) of the Navy; (3) of Foreign Affairs; . . . (4) of Justice; (5) of Internal Affairs; (6) of Finance; (7) of Commerce, and (8) of Public Education.

XIII:16. THE DECREE CONCERNING THE RIGHTS AND DUTIES OF THE SENATE, SEPTEMBER 8, 1802

Another effort at administrative reform in the early years of Alexander's reign was the ambitious decree whose main provisions are given here.

Reference: *PSZRI*, 1st ser., 27:241-43.

1. The Senate is the highest administrative organ of our empire; having authority over all the government offices, and as guardian of the laws, it sees that justice prevails everywhere; it supervises the collection of taxes and governmental expenditures; it is concerned with the means of easing the needs of the people, the preservation of the general peace and order, and the termination of all unlawful actions in all those places subordinate to it. The right of civil, criminal, and agrarian law belongs to its unbiased and sincere judgment.

2. The Senate's power is limited only by the power of His Imperial Majesty; otherwise, it is under no higher power. . . .

4. The decrees of the Senate are obeyed by all as if they were imperial decrees. Only the emperor, or an imperial decree, can countermand the Senate's orders.

5. All decrees signed by His Majesty, except those subject to special secrecy, must be communicated to the Senate by all offices and individuals to whom they may be issued. . . .

7. All collegiate boards [*kollegii*] and those heads of guberniias and of government offices who are directly subordinate to the Senate will, in all doubtful or difficult cases, as well as in all important matters referring to cases subject to examination by the Senate, refer to the Senate by means of reports or communications, in the same way that attorneys refer to the attorney general [*general-prokuror*]. . . .

9. Should there exist a decree concerning general government affairs whose execution would entail great difficulty, or be contradictory in its particulars to other laws, or be unclear in its meaning, the Senate is permitted to make a report of this to His Imperial Majesty; however, if, following such a report, no changes are made, said decree will remain in force. . . .

11. It is a senator's duty, on the basis of the decree of August 16, 1760, to report those lawbreakers who are known to him as well as any acts detrimental to the state. If, in the course of government proceedings, he observes an infraction of lawful procedure, be it even in the Senate chancellery itself, he is bound by duty to expose it to the Senate, so as to direct the force and penalty of the law against the culprit.

12. We neither presuppose nor expect that any gentleman belonging to the honorable

membership of the Senate might be convicted of violating a senator's duty but, if against expectation it were found to be so, a senator would be tried for such offense in no other place but in the general assembly of the Senate.

13. The final decision on affairs before the Senate's general assembly will be by majority vote, the majority being two thirds of the votes; decisions in the departments must be taken unanimously. . . .

14. Should there be disagreement within a department . . . the case in question is to be transferred to the Senate's general assembly.

XIII:17. THE PRELIMINARY DIRECTIVE CONCERNING PUBLIC EDUCATION, JANUARY 26, 1803

This blueprint for a nationwide system of public education at all levels was based on Condorcet's plan presented to the French Legislative Assembly in 1792. The results of this directive (and those of 1804 which implemented it) were much more significant for higher and secondary education than for primary schooling. By the end of Alexander's reign Russia had 6 universities, 48 gymnasiums, and 337 uezd schools.

Reference: *PSZRI,* 1st ser., 27:438-41.

CHAPTER I. The establishment of schools.

1. Public education in the Russian Empire is to constitute a separate branch of the state administration, entrusted to a minister for that department and administered under his supervision by a Central School Board.

2. For the sound education of citizens which accords with the duties and interests of each legal class, four types of schools are to be established, namely: (1) parish schools, (2) uezd schools, (3) guberniia schools or gymnasiums, and (4) universities.

3. Each church parish, or two parishes combined, depending upon the number of parishioners and the distances between their residences, must have at least one parish school.

4. In state villages [*kazennye seleniia*] the parish schools are to be entrusted to the care of the parish priest and a highly respected local resident. In villages belonging to private landowners the [parish] schools are to be left to the enlightened and well-intentioned care of the landowners themselves.

5. In parish schools the instructional procedure is to be supervised by the school inspector of the uezd to which the schools belong.

6. In the chief town of each uezd there must be at least one uezd school.

7. The inspectors of uezd schools are to be appointed directly by the university, or upon the recommendation of the guberniia director of schools. The inspectors belong to the ninth rank unless holding higher rank. . . .

9. In the capital city of each guberniia, besides the lower schools of the first two classes, there is to be a gymnasium under the direct authority and administration of the guberniia director of schools.

10. The guberniia directors of schools are to be appointed by the Central School Board upon the recommendation of the university of the okrug [region] to which they belong. They belong to the seventh rank, unless holding a higher rank. . . .

13. . . . Universities are to be established in okrugi for teaching the arts and sciences on the highest level. At the present time six of these universities are designated. Besides those already existing in Moscow, Vil'no, and Dorpat, new ones are to be established in Saint Petersburg, Kazan', and Khar'kov in acknowledgment of the patriotic offering proffered by the nobility and citizenry of these guberniias. The cities next destined for [the establishment of] universities are: Kiev, Tobol'sk, Ustiug Velikii, and others as means become available for this. . . .

15. Each university is to have its own administrative board. Its chairman is the rector of the university. He is elected by the general assembly of the university and presented for His Majesty's approval by the Central School Board through the minister of public education.

16. Professors are elected to this status by the general assembly of the university and, upon recommendation of the superintendent [*popechitel'*], are confirmed by the minister of [public] education. For the teaching of theology, however, members of the clergy are appointed to each university by the Most Holy Synod. Full [*ordinarnye*] professors belong to the seventh rank, and rectors, during their terms of office, to the fifth.

17. Each year the university sends one or several of its members for a personal survey

of the schools within its jurisdiction and an investigation of their progress.

18. The rector, in his capacity as head of the university, receives reports from the gymnasiums on all matters pertaining to the instructional and economic administration of [those] schools within the university's okrug. He reports on this to the member of the Central School Board who has been designated by His Imperial Majesty as the superintendent of that university and its okrug.

19. The Central School Board consists of the superintendents of the universities and their okrugi, and other members appointed by His Imperial Majesty. . . .

30. Censorship of all books published within a guberniia will rest solely with the universities as soon as they are established in the okrugi. . . .

CHAP. II. The instructional organization of schools.

32. In parish schools the teacher is to teach reading, writing, and the fundamental elements of arithmetic. He is to give instruction in the basic principles of religious study, good conduct, and obligations to the emperor, to the authorities, and to one's neighbors; and, in a simple, clear manner consistent with the students' abilities, to give them a proper understanding of the world. Instruction is to continue from the time work in the fields stops until it begins again the next year. . . .

34. In the uezd schools, pupils entering from the parish schools are to be taught Russian grammar and the grammar of one local language, such as Polish, German, and so forth, a short course in geography and history, and the basic principles of geometry and the natural sciences. They are also to be given instruction in their duties as men and citizens and practical knowledge useful to local commerce and the needs of the region.

35. At the gymnasium level, belles lettres,

Latin, French, German, logic, the basic principles of pure mathematics as well as of mechanics, hydraulics, and those other parts of physics that are most useful in everyday life, a short course in natural history, world geography, and history, and the fundamentals of political economy and commerce are to be taught. Moreover, such works will be read and translated as will further one's spiritual development and implant a clear understanding of God's law and one's civic duties. Teachers of gymnastic exercises may be added as supernumeraries.

36. At the universities, students entering from the gymnasiums, or [students] admitted to this status after examination, are to be taught, in their broadest scope, those arts and sciences that may be necessary for any profession or for various kinds of government service.

37. At the universities the professors, for purposes of administrative order and academic counseling, are to organize themselves into separate departments or faculties, according to the subjects they teach, each of which departments is to elect, by a majority vote and for a fixed term, its own dean. These deans together with the rector constitute the university board. The professors of all departments together constitute the general assembly of the university. [Note: By regulations issued November 5, 1804, for the universities in Moscow, Khar'kov, and Kazan', the departments or faculties were to be (1) moral and political sciences, (2) physical and mathematical sciences, (3) medicine, and (4) philology—the latter including languages, literature, and history.]

38. In the parish and uezd schools, and in the gymnasiums, standardized books and rules will be used in instruction, but in each university the method of instruction and the subjects will be prescribed by the General Assembly and submitted to the superintendent for approval.

XIII:18. THE DECREE DESIGNATING A NEW SOCIAL CLASS, THE FREE FARMERS, FEBRUARY 20, 1803

Count S. P. Rumiantsov said of this decree, "Now, without anxiety and without fear, it is possible to begin the gradual destruction of serfdom." In the ensuing half century, however, very few estate owners actually took advantage of the possibility.

Reference: *PSZRI*, 1st ser., 27:462-63.

Actual Privy Councillor Count Sergei Rumiantsov, having expressed to certain of his serfs

the desire to secure for them, upon their liberation, property rights to parcels of his land, either through sale or through some other voluntary agreement, petitions that such agreements, voluntarily concluded, have the same legal force and effect as pertain to other serf obligations and that peasants freed in this manner be able to retain the status of free farmers, being under no compulsion to adopt a new way of living.

Having found that, on the one hand, the freeing of peasants and the ownership of landed property by these freed peasants is permitted by existing laws, i.e. the manifesto of 1775 and the decree of December 12, 1801, and that, on the other hand, such ownership of land may in many cases offer various advantages to the landowners [pomeshchiki] and have an encouraging effect on promoting agriculture and other areas of the national economy: we consider it just and advantageous to permit such a disposition to Count Rumiantsov as well as to all such landowners as wish to follow his example; and in order that this have legal force we deem it necessary to decree the following:

1. A landowner who desires to set free some of his serfs, acquired or inherited [by him], singly or as a whole settlement, and simultaneously to secure for them the possession of a parcel of land or even of the landed estate as a whole, must, after concluding with them an agreement mutually satisfactory to both parties, submit such agreement together with his petition, through the marshal of nobility of his guberniia to the minister of internal affairs to consider and submit to us; and if there follows from us a decision favorable to his desire, then this agreement will be presented in the civil court and registered in [the Department of] Serf Affairs [which handled all such real-estate transactions—eds.] together with the remittance of fees established by law. . . .

3. In the case of infraction of the terms of such an agreement by one or another of the parties, the courts will investigate complaints and administer penalties in accordance with the general provisions of the laws concerning contracts and title-deeds with the understanding that if peasants or even entire settlements do not fulfill their obligations, they are to be returned, their lands and families included, to the estate of the landowner, as before.

4. Peasants or settlements released, with land, by the landowners, under such conditions, if they do not choose to enter into any other legal class, may continue as land tillers on their own lands and thereby constitute a special legal class of free farmers. . . .

7. For purposes of trial and punishment they are liable to the same courts as the state peasants; but, regarding the possession of their land, they are to be treated as owners of real estate, and action is to be taken on the basis of their title-deeds [krepost', a written document certifying the ownership of landed property].

8. As soon as peasants, having fulfilled the terms of their agreement, receive land, they will have the right to sell or mortgage it or to bequeath it to their heirs, without, however, breaking it into plots of less than eight desiatinas; they likewise have the right to purchase new land and, in consequence, to move from one guberniia to another—however, not without notifying the kazennaia palata [the office of the Ministry of Finance in each guberniia] for purposes of transferring their poll tax and military service obligations.

XIII:19. A DECREE CONCERNING THE JEWS, DECEMBER 9, 1804

Prior to the reign of Catherine II, there were very few Jews in Russia. As a result of the Polish partitions about 900,000 Jews in Lithuania, the western Ukraine, and Belorussia became Russian subjects. They were ordered to remain in the areas where they lived, and thus the Pale of Settlement was established. It remained in force after the decree of 1804, which was characterized by the Russian-Jewish historian S. M. Dubnow as a "mixture of liberties and disabilities."

Reference: PSZRI, 1st ser., 28:731-36.

Imperial Decree issued to the Senate. Acting upon repeated complaints submitted to us and to the governing Senate concerning various existing abuses and disorders detrimental to the agricultural and commercial pursuits of the inhabitants of those guberniias where Jews reside, we have deemed it necessary to form, by a decree issued to the governing Senate on November 9, 1802, a special committee to consider questions pertaining to this matter and to select means of correcting the present condition of the Jews.

REGULATIONS FOR THE JEWS
I. Education

1. All Jewish children may be admitted to and educated in any Russian public school, gymnasium, or university without any distinction from other children.

2. No Jewish child, while being educated at a school, should under any circumstances be diverted in his religious beliefs or compelled to study anything that might be offensive to these beliefs or even in disagreement with them. . . .

5. Those Jews who, through their ability, may attain at the universities certain degrees of distinction in medicine, surgery, physics, mathematics, or other branches of knowledge will be given recognition, and university degrees will be conferred upon them on equal terms with other Russian subjects.

6. If, despite all these inducements, Jews should not wish to enroll their children in the ordinary public schools, then separate schools are to be established at their cost, wherein their children are to be educated; the assessment necessary for this is to be established by the government. One of the following languages—Russian, Polish, or German—must be included among the subjects taught there. . . .

8. All Jews residing in the Russian Empire, while enjoying complete freedom in the use of their language in all their affairs, whether pertaining to their religion or to their domestic pursuits, are obligated to use, beginning January 1, 1807, the Russian, Polish, or German language in all public documents, contracts, promissory notes, and title-deeds of all kinds. Otherwise, none of their acts may be registered or recognized as legally valid. . . .

II. The Various Legal Classes and Trades of the Jews, and Their Privileges

11. All Jews are divided into four legal classes: (a) farmers, (b) manufacturers and artisans, (c) merchants, (d) tradesmen [meshchane]. . . .

12. Jewish farmers are all free and can under no circumstances be bound into serfdom or given over to anyone in ownership.

13. Jewish farmers, as well as manufacturers, artisans, merchants, and tradesmen, may, within the guberniias of Lithuania, White Russia, Little Russia, Kiev, Minsk, Volynia, Podol'sk, Astrakhan', the Caucasus, Ekaterinoslav, Kherson, and Taurida, acquire by purchase unsettled lands, sell them, mortgage them, give them as gifts, and bequeath them to their heirs, within the entire scope of the decree of December 12, 1802. . . .

16. Jews are permitted to receive lands for use from landowners and to conclude agreements with them, which agreements, upon their registration in government offices, are to be held sacred and inviolable; it is understood, however, that they are under no circumstances to sell liquor. . . .

42. All Jews residing in Russia . . . [or] arriving from other countries are free and remain under explicit protection of the laws on equal terms with all other Russian subjects. . . .

50. In the guberniia capitals and uezd towns [uezd capitals or main towns] they have the right to elect one rabbi and several elders of the kagal [Jewish community] who are to be presented to the guberniia board and, after its approval, are to assume their offices, and who are to be replaced every three years, unless returned to office by new elections. In settlements belonging to private landowners, Jews also may elect rabbis and elders, without any participation on the part of the landowners, who are furthermore forbidden on these occasions to collect any levies from the rabbi.

XIII:20. THE TREATIES OF TILSIT, JUNE 25, 1807

These two treaties, one of peace after Russia's defeat by Napoleon at Friedland, the other a secret alliance between Russia and France, portended great events. Count Speranskii (see below), expressing a view widely held among the actors in this drama, observed that the treaties contained every possible ingredient for war between the two nations.

Reference: Fedor F. Martens, *Recueil des traités et conventions conclus par la Russie avec les puissances étrangères*, 15 vols. in 8 (St. Petersburg: A. Böhnke, 1874-1909), 13:309-21 and 322-25. A recent reprinting of this treaty is in *Vneshniaia politika Rossii XIX i nachala XX v. Dokumenty Rossiiskogo Ministerstva inostrannykh del*, Series 1 (1801-15), 7 vols. (Moscow: Gospolitizdat, 1960—), vol. 3 (Jan. 1806-July 1807, pp. 631-50. See other volumes of this series, still in progress, for additional documents.

[The treaty of peace with France, June 25 (July 7, N.S.), 1807:]

ARTICLE I. There will be, from the date of the exchange of ratifications of the present treaty, peace and perfect friendship between His Majesty the emperor of all the Russias and His Majesty the emperor of the French, king of Italy. . . .

ART. V. The provinces [provintsii] that on January 1, 1772, were part of the ancient Kingdom of Poland, and which at varying times since have passed under Prussian domination, will be, with the exception of the territories named or designated in the preceding article [those territories Napoleon was willing to restore to Prussia] and those that will be specified in article IX below [the Belostok region which Napoleon gave to Russia], held in full ownership and sovereignty by His Majesty the king of Saxony, under the title of the Duchy of Warsaw. . . .

ART. XXII. Russian forces will retire from the principalities of Wallachia and Moldavia, but these provinces [provintsii] will not be occupied by the forces of His Highness [the Turkish sultan] until the exchange of ratifications of the future and final treaty of peace between Russia and the Ottoman Porte.

ART. XXIII. His Majesty the emperor of all the Russias accepts the mediation of His Majesty the emperor of the French, king of Italy, for the purpose of negotiating and concluding a favorable and honorable peace between the two empires [i.e. Russian and Ottoman]. . . .

Separate and secret articles:

ART. I. Russian forces will relinquish to French forces the territory known under the name of Cattaro.

ART. II. The Ionian Islands will be held in full ownership and sovereignty by His Majesty the emperor Napoleon.

ART. III. His Majesty the emperor of the French, king of Italy, agrees neither to disturb nor to investigate, either directly or indirectly, any subject of the Sublime Porte, and especially the Montenegrins, for any part they may have taken or wished to take in hostilities against French forces, provided that henceforth they live quietly.

[The secret treaty of alliance with France, June 25 (July 7, N.S.), 1807:]

His Majesty the emperor of all the Russias

and His Majesty the emperor of the French, king of Italy, and protector of the Rhenish Confederation, desiring especially to re-establish the general peace in Europe on firm and, as far as possible, lasting foundations, have for this purpose concluded an offensive and defensive alliance. . . .

ART. II. In the event of the activation of the alliance, and each time it may be activated, the High Contracting Parties will establish, by a special convention, the forces each must employ against the common enemy and the places where these forces must be used; but henceforth they agree to employ, if circumstances so dictate, the totality of their forces on land and sea. . . .

ART. IV. Should England not accept the mediation of Russia or, if accepting, she does not agree, by next November 1, to conclude a peace recognizing that the flags of all nations must enjoy equal and complete independence on the high seas and restoring the properties she has taken from France and from France's allies since 1805, when Russia made common cause with [England], then, in the course of the said month of November, a note will be delivered to the Cabinet of Saint James's by the ambassador of His Majesty the emperor of all the Russias. This note, expressing the interest His Imperial Majesty takes in the peace of the world and his intention to use all the power of his empire to secure for humanity the benefits of peace, will set forth a positive and precise statement to the effect that, upon the refusal of England to conclude a peace on the stated terms, His Majesty the emperor of all the Russias will make common cause with France. In the event that the Cabinet of Saint James's has not given a categorical and satisfying response by December 1, the Russian ambassador will be given orders to request his passports on the specified date and to leave England at once.

ART. V. Should events develop as outlined in the preceding article, the High Contracting Parties will, together and at the same time, call upon the three courts at Copenhagen, Stockholm, and Lisbon to close their ports to the English, to recall their ambassadors from London, and to declare war on England. Any of these three courts that shall refuse will be considered an enemy of the High Contracting Parties and, if Sweden refuses, then Denmark will be obliged to declare war on her. . . .

ART. VII. If, on the contrary, England in the period specified above makes peace on the stated terms . . . Hanover will be restored to the king of England as compensation for the French, Spanish, and Dutch colonies.

ART. VIII. Equally, if the Porte, as a consequence of the changes taking place in Constantinople, does not accept the mediation of France or if, after having accepted such mediation, a satisfactory result is not reached with-

in three months from the beginning of negotiations, France will make common cause with Russia against the Ottoman Porte, and the two High Contracting Parties will come to an agreement to free from the yoke and molestation of the Turks all the provinces of the Ottoman Empire in Europe, with the city of Constantinople and the province of Roumelia excepted.

ART. IX. The present Treaty shall remain secret.

XIII:21. THE MANIFESTO ON THE POLITICAL STATUS OF RUSSIA'S NEWLY ACQUIRED FINNISH SUBJECTS, MARCH 23, 1809

Upon seizing the Finnish provinces from Sweden in the Russo-Swedish War of 1808-09, Alexander I moved immediately to win the loyalty of his new subjects. The political status he accorded the Finns was in striking contrast to that prevalent in Russia.

Reference: Petr P. Shilovskii, *Akty otnosiashchiesia k politicheskomu polozheniiu Finliandii* (St. Petersburg: Stasiulevich, 1903), p. 136.

We, Alexander I, tsar and sovereign of all Russia, etcetera, etcetera, etcetera, grand duke of Finland, etcetera, etcetera, etcetera, herewith declare: After having assembled the estates of Finland at a general diet and accepted their oath of allegiance, we desired on this occasion to confirm and ensure by a solemn act, prepared in their presence and proclaimed in our Lord's sanctuary, the preservation of their religion and fundamental law [*grundlagar*], together with the liberties and rights enjoyed by each estate separately and by all inhabi-

tants of Finland conjointly. Simultaneously with the communication of this act to our loyal subjects in Finland, we desire to let them know that, since we adhere and conform to the ancient customs of this land, we consider the oath of allegiance given freely and without compulsion by all estates in general, and in particular by the representatives of the peasant estate, for themselves and on behalf of their brethren left at home, effective and binding upon every inhabitant of Finland without exception.

XIII:22. SPERANSKII'S PLAN FOR A GENERAL REORGANIZATION OF THE ADMINISTRATION, OCTOBER 1809

With the support of Alexander I, Michael M. Speranskii (1772-1839) developed a detailed plan for the reorganization of Russia's state machinery. His suggestions provoked extreme criticism from the conservative gentry and were instrumental (along with his pro-French sympathies) in his being sent into exile in 1812.

Reference: Mikhail M. Speranskii, *Plan gosudarstvennogo preobrazovaniia, vvedenie k "Ulozheniiu Gosudarstvennykh Zakonov" 1809 g.* (Moscow: Izd. Russkoi Mysli, 1905), pp. 4, 15, 16, 19, 30, 31, 33, 54, 55, 63, 66-68, 73-79. A translation of somewhat lengthier excerpts from the same document has recently been published in Raeff, *Plans for Political Reform*, pp. 92-120.

[In] every well-organized state there must be some positive, permanent, and fixed legislative principles with which all the other laws may be correlated.

These positive principles are the fundamental state laws.

Three powers move and govern the state: the legislative, executive, and judicial.

The origin and source of these powers is in the people, for they are nothing else but the

moral and physical powers of men in relation to social life.

· · ·

In almost all states, constitutions were established at various times, piecemeal, and most often in the midst of harsh political transformations.

The Russian constitution will owe its existence, not to inflamed passions and extreme situations, but to the beneficial inspiration of the supreme authority which, in organizing the political life of its people, can give the most correct forms and has every means for doing so.

Earthly kingdoms have their epochs of greatness and of decline, and in each epoch the form of government must be consistent with the level of civic enlightenment of the state.

Whenever the form of government lags behind or exceeds this level it is overthrown with a more or less violent shock.

· · ·

And so, time is the first principle and source of all political renovations. No government out of harmony with the spirit of the time can withstand its all-powerful action.

Therefore, the first and main question that must be answered at the threshold of all political changes is that of their timeliness.

· · ·

How many misfortunes, how much bloodshed could have been averted if the rulers of states, observing more closely the development of the public spirit, had conformed with it in the principles governing their political systems and, instead of compelling the people to adapt to the government, had adapted the government to the condition of the people. [Speranskii's footnote: "What a contradiction this is: to desire science, commerce, and industry and yet to forbid their most natural consequences; to want reason to be free but the will enchained; to want passions to move and change but their objects, the longing for freedom, to remain static; to want the people to grow in wealth but not to enjoy the best fruits of its enrichment—freedom. History knows of no instance when an educated and commercially advanced people was able to remain long in a state of slavery."]

· · ·

The present system of government is no longer in accord with the nature of the public spirit, and . . . the time has come to change it and found a new order.

I. On the General Principle of the Transformation

The general object of the transformation is that the government, which has until now been autocratic, be founded and established on the basis of immutable law.

The government cannot be based on law if the sovereign alone both makes the law and carries it out. Hence arises the necessity for institutions active in formulating and executing the law.

· · ·

1. The legislative body should be so constituted that it could not promulgate its laws without the sovereign, but its opinions should be free and should express the views of the people.

2. The judicial body should be so formed that its existence depends on free election, and only the supervision of judicial forms and the preservation of general security should be in the hands of the government.

3. The executive power should all in its entirety be entrusted to the government. But inasmuch as this power could, under the guise of executing the laws, not only distort them but even entirely destroy them by its regulations, it should also be made responsible to the legislative power.

· · ·

Civil freedom has two main aspects: personal freedom and material freedom.

The former consists of the following two principles:

1. No one may be punished without trial.

2. No one is obligated to render personal services except according to the law, and not at the arbitrary will of another. [Speranskii's footnote: "The first of these principles gives serfs the right of trial and, taking that right away from the landowners, makes them [the serfs] equal before the law with everyone else. The second principle abolishes the right to send people into the army out of their proper turn. Personal freedom rests on these two foundations."]

The nature of freedom of the second kind, i.e. material freedom, is based on the following principles:

1. Everyone may dispose of his property as he wishes, in accordance with the general law; no one may be deprived of property without trial.

2. No one is obligated to render material service or to pay taxes and duties except according to law or contract, and not at the arbitrary will of another.

· · ·

From this review of civil and political

rights, it becomes clear that they may properly be divided into three classes:

1. General civil rights, belonging to all subjects.

2. Particular civil rights, which must belong only to those who are prepared for them by their way of life and education.

3. Political rights, belonging to those who own property.

This leads to the following division of estates:

1. The gentry
2. Persons of the middle estate
3. Working people

. . .

The middle estate consists of merchants, townspeople, odnodvortsy [one-homesteaders], and all villagers who own a certain amount of real estate.

The Rights of the Working People

1. The working people enjoy the general civil rights but have no political rights.

. . .

3. The class of the working people consists of all the landowners' peasants, artisans and their workmen, and domestic servants.

Organic Laws

The organic, fundamental laws should determine the order of institutions through which the government powers are exercised.

These institutions are: the council, the legislative body, the senate, and the ministries.

. . .

Each of these institutions, uniting to form the sovereign authority and constituting the leading governmental bodies, should extend through the entire empire and, gradually dividing, descend to the very last villages.

. . .

The Legislative System
First Level

Every three years an assembly called the volost' duma is brought together in each volost' town or principal volost' village [i.e. in the administrative center of each volost']; this assembly is composed of all owners of real estate. . . .

The first action of the volost' duma is to elect a chairman and a secretary.

All votes are equal in the volost' duma. No one can delegate his vote to another by proxy.

The functions of the volost' duma are:

1. Election of members of the volost' administration.

2. Accounting for the collection and the expenditure of the funds entrusted to the volost' administration.

3. Election of deputies to the okrug duma; their number may not exceed two-thirds of the total number of property owners.

4. Compiling a list of twenty of the most distinguished residents of the volost', including those who are not present.

5. Submitting statements to the okrug duma concerning the public needs of the volost'.

When these activities are completed the duma is disbanded, and its place is taken by the administration elected by it.

. . .

Second Level

Every three years a body called the okrug duma, consisting of deputies of the volost' dumas, is brought together in the okrug city [i.e. okrug administrative center].

The okrug duma elects a chairman and a chief secretary.

All voices are equal in the okrug duma.

The functions of the okrug duma are:

1. Election of members of the okrug council [sovet].

2. Election of members of the okrug court.

3. Election of deputies of the guberniia duma. Their number may not exceed two-thirds of the membership of the okrug duma.

4. Making up a list of twenty of the most distinguished residents of the okrug from the lists presented by the volost' dumas. Those who are not present are not to be excluded from the list.

5. Accounting to the okrug authorities for the funds collected for public expenditures.

6. Statements to the okrug [meant to say guberniia—eds.] duma . . . concerning public needs, based on consideration of the statements of the volost' dumas.

On completion of these tasks, the duma is disbanded.

. . .

Third Level

Every three years an assembly called the guberniia duma, consisting of deputies of the okrug dumas, is brought together in the guberniia capital.

The guberniia duma's first action is to elect a chairman and a secretary.

All the votes in the guberniia duma are equal, and those who are absent cannot delegate their votes to others.

The functions of the guberniia duma are:

1. Election of members of the guberniia council.

2. Election of members of the guberniia court.

3. Election of members to the State Duma from both estates possessing political rights. Their number in each guberniia is fixed by law.

4. Compilation of a list of twenty of the most distinguished residents of the guberniia on the basis of the okrug lists, not excluding those who are not present.

5. Accounting to the guberniia administration for the funds collected for public expenditures.

6. Statement of public needs, in accordance with the statements of the okrug dumas.

The duma sets up special commissions from among its members to consider the accounts and the statements concerning public needs.

When these tasks are completed, the chairman transmits the following, signed by all members of the assembly, to the State Council [*sovet*], addressed to the Chancellor of Justice: lists of all members elected to the volost' administrations, okrug courts, and guberniia court; also, addressed to the Chancellor of the State Duma: (1) lists of members elected to okrug councils and the guberniia council; (2) lists of members elected to the legislative body; (3) lists of the most distinguished residents of the guberniias; (4) statements concerning the needs of each guberniia.

This completes the activity of the guber-niia duma and its place is then taken by the guberniia council.

. . .

Fourth Level

The deputies sent by the guberniia dumas constitute a legislative body called the State Duma.

The State Duma has a status equal to that of the Senate and of a Ministry.

The State Duma assembles under the fundamental law, and without any special convocation, annually in the month of September.

Its term is determined by the amount of business brought before it.

The activity of the State Duma is ended in two ways: (1) by its adjournment to the following year; (2) by the complete dismissal of all its members.

Adjournment is accomplished by an act of the sovereign authority in the State Council. [See Item XIII:23, below.]

The dismissal is accomplished by a similar act but includes the naming of the new members, [from among those] named in the most recent elections of the guberniia dumas.

. . .

The matters to be taken up by the State Duma are brought before it in the name of the sovereign authority by one of the ministers or members of the State Council.

Excepted from this rule are:

1. Proposals concerning state needs

2. Proposals concerning neglect of responsibility

3. Proposals concerning measures violating fundamental state laws

In these three cases . . . the members of the Duma may take the initiative.

XIII:23. THE MANIFESTO ESTABLISHING THE STATE COUNCIL, JANUARY 1, 1810

In a sense the establishment of the State Council was the height of Speranskii's achievement, even though it constituted only one part of his grand design for organizing Russia's legal and legislative machinery. It was bitterly attacked by such conservatives as Karamzin.

Reference: *PSZRI*, 1st ser., 31:3-6.

For the strengthening and extending of unity and order in state administration, we have deemed it necessary to institute a State Council [Gosudarstvennyi Sovet] to give proper organization to the expanse and greatness of our empire.

. . .

The civic codes, no matter how perfect they may be, cannot be made stable without permanent state institutions.

Among these institutions, the Council has for a long time occupied an important position. In its beginning it was temporary and impermanent. But with our ascent to the throne, having named it a State Council, we have determined at the same time to give it a formation compatible with the public institutions.

Now, with God's help, we have decided to complete this formation.

. . .

VII. The president of this Council is ourself.

. . .

Formation of the State Council

PART I. Basic laws of the state council.

A. Among state institutions the State Council constitutes a body in which all parts of the government, in their main relationships toward legislation, are united, and through which they have access to the supreme imperial power.

B. Accordingly, all laws, statutes, and regulations in their original drafts are propounded and examined in the State Council and then, through the action of the sovereign power, are executed in accord with predetermined objectives.

C. No law, statute, or regulation can be issued from the Council or can become effective without confirmation by the supreme power.

PT. II. Special regulations of the State Council.

A. Organization of the departments.

1. The Council is divided into four departments:

    a. The Department of Laws.

    b. The Department of Military Affairs.

    c. The Department of Civilian and Ecclesiastical Affairs.

    d. The Department of State Economy.

2. Everything that, by its very nature, falls under the subject of laws goes to the Department of Law. The Commission of Laws shall present to this department all the first drafts of laws drawn up by them.

3. The affairs of the Ministries of War and Navy fall under the consideration of the Department of Military Affairs.

4. The affairs of justice and the administration of religion and of police fall under the Department of Civilian and Ecclesiastical Affairs.

5. Those matters pertaining to general industry, sciences, commerce, finance, the treasury, and accounting fall under the Department of State Economy. . . .

PT. III. Designation of matters to be considered by the State Council.

29. Among the state affairs requiring the deliberation and confirmation of the supreme power, the following matters are presented to the State Council for preliminary consideration:

    a. All subjects requiring new laws, statutes or regulations.

    b. All subjects of internal administration requiring repeal, restriction, or supplementation of former regulations. . . .

    f. The declaration of war, conclusion of peace, and other important foreign measures, when in view of the circumstances they are subject to preliminary general consideration.

    g. Annual estimates of general state income and expenses, ways of balancing them, allocation of new expenses that may occur in the course of the year, and extraordinary financial measures.

XIII:24. THE MANIFESTO REORGANIZING THE MINISTRIES AND FIXING THEIR RESPECTIVE RESPONSIBILITIES, JULY 25, 1810

This document, whose author was Speranskii, has been termed the "organic charter" of Russia's bureaucracy, since it established lines of responsibility for state business which remained in effect until 1917.

Reference: *PSZRI*, 1st ser., 31:278-80. See also ibid., pp. 686-719.

In the manifesto on the establishment of the State Council, published on the first day of January of this year [1810], it was resolved to complete the present organization of the ministries by a certain modification which, in view of the experience of past years, was considered necessary.

The basic reason for this modification is to introduce a more equal division of state affairs and more uniformity in their execution, and to simplify and make easier their function-ing in order that the limits of authority and responsibility may be precisely defined and that thereby the executive branch [of the government] may obtain more means for the speedy and precise execution of the laws.

. . .

Part I. The Formation of the Ministries

CHAPTER I. The general division of state affairs.

1. The executive affairs of the state are [to be] divided into five main categories:

a. Foreign relations
b. Maintenance of defense
c. State economy
d. Maintenance of civil and criminal courts
e. Maintenance of internal security

2. The number of ministries and central administrative agencies in each is determined by the scope of the particular category of its affairs.

3. State affairs are, thereby, divided as follows:

a. Foreign relations: Ministry of Foreign Affairs [Inostrannykh Del]
b. Defense (external security): Ministry of War [Voennoe]; Ministry of the Navy [Morskoe]
c. State economy: Ministry of Internal Affairs [Vnutrennikh Del]; Ministry of Public Education [Narodnogo Prosveshcheniia]; Ministry of Finance [Finansov]; the State Treasury [Gosudarstvennoe Kaznacheistvo]; Department of Control of State Accounts [Reviziia Gosudarstvennykh Schetov]; Central Administrative Agency for Transportation [Glavnoe Upravlenie Putei Soobshcheniia]
d. The courts: Ministry of Justice [Iustitsii]
e. Internal security: For the overall co-ordination and central administration of those matters that are the concern of the state police, and which until now have been under the jurisdiction of the Ministry of Internal Affairs, the former post of Policemaster General [General-Politsmeister] is to be reestablished under the title minister of police.

4. In the realm of state affairs, those mat-ters concerning the clergy of the Greco-Russian Orthodox faith are centered in the Holy Synod and there is no necessity to supplement the form of their central administration. But the affairs of the clergy of various other faiths, now scattered throughout various departments, require unification. Accordingly, a Central Administrative Agency for the Clerical Affairs of Sundry Religions is to be added to the above-mentioned ministries. . . .

6. The main object of the Ministry of Internal Affairs is to encourage and foster the expansion of agriculture and industry. In consequence, the following categories of affairs belong within the jurisdiction of this ministry:

a. Affairs concerning the encouragement of agriculture and colonization, re-settlement within the country, and those various branches of the economy pertaining to this question.
b. Factories
c. Internal trade
d. The mails
e. Public buildings

. . .

12. The affairs of the Ministry of Police are divided into two categories, the first of which includes the administration of all agencies entrusted with the general welfare or connected with the Protective Police, such as: medical matters and quarantine, food supplies, emergency stores in towns and villages, the safe-guarding of transportation, matters of censorship, matters pertaining to the government Charity Offices, and so on. In the second category are all the affairs of the Executive Police, such as: the execution of the verdicts of the courts, the collection of tax arrears, and the maintenance of local police, corrective institutions, workhouses, prison guards, and the like.

XIII:25. KARAMZIN AND HIS "MEMOIR ON ANCIENT AND MODERN RUSSIA," 1811

Nikolai Mikhailovich Karamzin (1766-1826), friend of the royal family and historian of Russia, spoke in this document for the conservative and reactionary gentry. Although subsequent events might suggest that the memoir was influential during the later years of Alexander's reign, actually it had a much greater influence on Nicholas I than on his older brother. The memoir was presented to Alexander in 1811 but came to public knowledge only after 1834.

Reference: N. M. Karamzin, *Zapiska o drevnei i novoi Rossii*, ed. Richard Pipes (Cambridge: Harvard University Press, 1959), pp. 22-23, 38-40, 43, 52-63, 73-74, 113. Translation based largely on Richard Pipes, *Karamzin's Memoir on Ancient and Modern Russia: A Translation and Analysis* (Cambridge: Harvard University Press, 1959), pp. 121-22, 135-36, 139, 147-56, 165-66, 200. For some of Karamzin's earlier writings, see Karamzin, *Letters of a Russian Traveler 1789-90*, trans. Florence Jonas (New York: Columbia University Press, 1957).

Peter [I] was unable to realize that national spirit constitutes the moral strength of states. This national spirit, together with the faith, had saved Russia in the days of the pretenders. It is nothing other than respect for our national dignity. By uprooting ancient customs . . . the sovereign of the Russians humbled Russian hearts. Does humiliation predispose a man and a citizen to great deeds? . . . Enlightenment is commendable, but what does it consist of? The knowledge of things that bring prosperity: arts, crafts, and sciences have no other value. . . . Two states may stand on the same level of civil enlightenment even though their customs differ.

· · ·

Paul ascended the throne at the time, so propitious for autocracy, when the horrors of the French Revolution had cured Europe of its dreams of civil freedom and equality. But what the Jacobins did to the republican system, Paul did to autocracy; he created a hatred for its abuses. . . . The Russians . . . knew that the sovereign, no less than his subjects, must fulfill his sacred obligation. . . . The son of Catherine could have been stern yet have earned the gratitude of the fatherland. To the perplexed amazement of the Russians, however, he began to rule by general terror, following no law save his whim. . . . He casually destroyed the time-honored fruits of political wisdom, hating in them the work of his mother. . . . Let us note a curious feature. It was thought by foreigners that during that reign of terror Russians were afraid even to think. This was not so! They talked even daringly; they were silent only because of the boredom of frequent repetition. . . . A certain spirit of sincere brotherhood prevailed in the capitals; common calamity brought hearts together and selfless rage against the abuses of authority smothered the voice of personal caution. The consequences of Catherine's humane reign could not be destroyed in four years of Paul's. They proved that we were worthy of having a wise and lawful government founded on justice.

· · ·

The true, virtuous citizen of Russia would say [to you, Alexander]: ". . . Russia, taught by a long history of calamities, handed over autocratic power to your ancestor before the sacred altar and demanded that he rule her supremely and indivisibly. This covenant is the basis of your power; you have no other. You may do anything, but you may not limit your authority by law."

· · ·

Instead of reverting at once to the order established by Catherine [II] . . . the counselors of Alexander developed a fancy for introducing novelties into the principal organs of royal authority.

· · ·

Alexander . . . in accord with the ideas of Field Marshal Münnich and the political system of foreign countries, established ministries.

· · ·

Russia is governed by ministers, that is, within his own department every minister may act at will. . . .

"Patience," reply the royal counselors, "we shall yet devise a method of curbing ministerial authority." And they issue the act establishing the [State] Council.

· · ·

The Council, it is said, will curb the ministers. The emperor is going to submit to the Council for its consideration the most important ministerial proposals. In the meantime, however, the ministers will continue to govern the country in the sovereign's name. . . .

. . . On the whole, Russia's new legislators are distinguished more for the art of clerkship than for that of statemanship. . . .

. . . The reforms accomplished so far give us no reason to believe that future reforms will prove useful. We anticipate them more with dread than with hope; for it is dangerous to tamper with ancient political structures.

. . .

Let us reiterate that one of the main reasons for the dissatisfaction of Russians with the present government is its excessive fondness for political changes, changes that shake the foundations of the empire, and the advantages of which are still an open question.

· · ·

What does it mean to enfranchise the serfs? It means to give them the liberty of living where they please, to deprive the master of all power over them, to subordinate them exclusively to the authority of the government. Very well! But these cultivators of the soil will have no land, for the land—this is incontrovertible—is the property of the nobility. The serfs will either remain with their landowners on the condition of paying rent, cultivating the master's fields, delivering grain where it is needed, in a word, working for them as before; or, dissatisfied with their lot, they will go to that landowner who is most moderate in his demands. . . . Greedy landowners will try to get out of them the maximum physical effort. Contracts will be signed and the serfs will fail to fulfill them. As a result, litigation, endless litigation! In the second place, if the serf is to be one day here and the next day there, will not the treasury suffer losses in poll taxes and other dues? Will not many fields remain uncultivated, many granaries empty? . . . Another evil: no longer depending on the decisive jurisdiction of landowners, the serfs will begin to quarrel amongst themselves and will apply to the law court in the town. What a catastrophe! Freed from the supervision of masters who have their own police [zemskaia isprava] . . . serfs will begin to drink and to commit crimes. What a rich harvest for taverns and venal district police officers! But what a blow to morals and public order! In a word, as things are now, the noblemen scattered all over the state cooperate with the monarch in keeping peace and order. By depriving the nobility of these functions, the monarch will lift the load of Russia onto his own shoulders like a second Atlas. . . . Will he be able to bear it? The crash would be terrific. . . . Would it not be better, in some informal fashion, to take measures to curb cruel masters? They are known to the provincial governors. If the latter perform their duty faithfully, cruel masters will soon disappear. If there are no intelligent and honest governors in Russia, however, then neither can there be prosperity for the free peasants.

. . .

Autocracy is the Palladium of Russia. Its integrity is indispensable for Russia's happiness. Yet there is no reason why the emperor, who is the sole source of power, should humiliate the nobility, which is as ancient as Russia itself. The nobility has never been anything other than a brotherhood of distinguished servants of the grand prince or the tsars. It is bad if servants secure control over a weak master, but a reasonable master, on the other hand, holds in esteem his chosen servants and, in honoring them, casts luster on himself. The rights of the nobility are not a part of the monarchical authority but are rather its principal and indispensable instrumentality for keeping the body politic in motion.

XIII:26. FIELD MARSHAL KUTUZOV'S REPORT TO ALEXANDER, SEPTEMBER 4, 1812

Kutuzov, in full command of Russia's armies opposing Napoleon's invading forces, explains his reasons for not defending Moscow to the last man.

Reference: Nikolai M. Korobkov, ed., *Fel'dmarshal Kutuzov, Sbornik dokumentov i materialov* (Moscow: OGIZ, 1947), pp. 177-78.

September 4(16, N.S), 1812, Zhilino After the bloody battle of August 26, victorious for our side, I was obliged to withdraw from our position at Borodino for reasons I had the pleasure of reporting to Your Imperial Majesty. After this battle the army was reduced to a state of extreme disorganization; the second [supporting] army was considerably weakened. With our forces in this condition we approached Moscow, making major daily encounters with the enemy vanguard. At this close distance there was no position where I could safely engage the enemy. The other troops with which we hoped to join had not yet been able to arrive, while the enemy sent out two new columns, one along the Borovsk road, the other along the Zvenigorod road, attempting to attack my rear from the direction of Moscow. There-

fore I could not venture into a battle which, if lost, might have resulted in not only the destruction of the army but also the bloody ruin and reduction to cinders of Moscow itself. In such an extremely dubious position, and after conferring with our leading generals, some of whom held a contrary opinion, I had to decide to allow the enemy to enter Moscow, from which all treasures, arsenals, and almost all possessions, both state and private, had been evacuated, and where virtually no residents remained.

I venture most obediently to suggest to you, our most gracious sovereign, that the entry of the enemy into Moscow does not signify his subjugation of Russia. . . . I do not deny that the occupation of the capital is a most grievous wound. But, choosing without hesitation between this event and the developments that may follow in our favor with the preservation of our army, I am now launching an operation with all our forces in a line, by means of which, beginning from the Tula and Kaluga roads, my units will break into the entire enemy line, stretched from Smolensk to Moscow. Thus, preventing all aid that the enemy army might receive from its rear, and drawing the enemy's attention, I hope to compel him to leave Moscow and to alter his entire operational line. . . .

Now, having gathered my troops, I can firmly await the enemy at this short distance from Moscow. As long as Your Imperial Majesty's army is intact and moved by its well-known courage and our zeal, the still recoverable loss of Moscow is not the loss of our fatherland. Furthermore, I beg Your Imperial Majesty graciously to agree that these consequences are indissolubly bound with the loss of Smolensk.

General of the Infantry,
Prince G. Kutuzov

XIII:27. ALEXANDER I'S MANIFESTO ON NAPOLEON'S RETREAT FROM RUSSIA, NOVEMBER 3, 1812

In this manifesto Alexander I characterized Russia's response to Napoleon's devastating invasion. Reference: *PSZRI,* 1st ser., 32:450-51.

We make this declaration to all the people: The entire world knows in what manner the enemy entered the boundaries of our empire. None of our efforts to observe carefully our peace treaties with him, nor our constant endeavors in every possible way to avoid a bloody and ruinous war, availed to halt his stubborn intention which could not be deflected by any effort. With peaceful promises on his lips he never ceased to think of war. Finally, having prepared a strong army . . . the enemy moved with all these multitudinous forces and great quantities of arms into our land. Murders, fire, and devastation followed in his wake. Looted possessions, burned cities and villages, flaming Moscow, a blasted Kremlin, defiled churches and altars of the Lord, in short, all these unprecedented atrocities and outrages finally revealed in action what he had hidden so long in his thoughts. The mighty, rich, and prospering Russian realm has always caused fear and envy in the heart of the enemy. Possession of the entire world could not appease him as long as Russia flourished and remained prosperous. Filled with this fear and deep hatred of her, he devised, planned, and arranged in his mind every treacherous means by which he might deal a terrible blow to her forces, wreak boundless ruin upon her wealth, and devastate her abundance. By cunning and false promises, he hoped to shake loyalty to the throne; by desecration of sacred objects and the churches of God, he hoped to shake the people's faith and contaminate the people with violence and evil. On these hopes he built his pernicious plans, and with them he rushed into the heart of Russia like a baleful and deadly storm. The whole world turned its eyes to our suffering fatherland and despondently thought to see the last day of its freedom and independence in the flaming skies of Moscow. . . . The triumph of the enemy did not last long. Soon, hemmed in on all sides by our brave troops and militia, he realized that he had carried his insolent steps too far and that neither his dread forces, nor his cunning blandishments, nor the terrors of his villainies could frighten the valiant and loyal Russians. And he saw that he could not escape his ruin. After all vain attempts, seeing his multitudinous armies crushed and beaten everywhere, he sought his own personal salvation in speedy flight with the small remnants of his forces. He fled from Moscow with humiliation and fear equal only to the pride and vanity with which he had approached it. . . . Thus is God's righteous wrath visiting chastisement upon the profaners of the holy! Mindful, with fatherly love and a joyous heart, of these great and glorious feats of our beloved subjects, we turn first to bring our warm and fervent thanks to the Source and Giver of all blessings, the Almighty God. Then solemnly, in the name of the fatherland, we wish to express our thanks and gratitude to all our loyal subjects, true sons of Russia. By their concerted zeal and ardor, the enemy forces have been reduced to extreme exhaustion and have, for the most part, been either annihilated or taken prisoner. Everyone has helped in this. . . . This great spirit and the unshakable steadfastness of the entire people have won it undying glory, worthy of preservation in the memory of our descendants! . . . In the meantime we deem it our duty and obligation by this, our proclamation, before the face of the entire world, to express our gratitude and render their just due to the courageous, loyal, and pious people of Russia.

XIII:28. ALEXANDER I'S ORDER TO THE RUSSIAN ARMIES, DECEMBER 25, 1813

As Russian troops were about to enter French territory for the first time in history, the tsar addressed them in these words.

Reference: Nikolai F. Dubrovin, *Sbornik istoricheskikh materialov izvlechennykh iz arkhiva Pervogo Otdeleniia Sobstvennoi Ego Imperatorskogo Velichestva Kantselarii*, 16 vols. (St. Petersburg: Pervoe Otd. S. E. I. V. Kantseliarii, 1876-1917), 3:167-68.

Order to the Russian Armies
December 25, No. 414, Karlsruhe
Soldiers!

Your courage and valor have brought you from the Oka River to the Rhine. They are now taking us further. We are crossing the Rhine, to enter the boundaries of the land with which we are engaged in bloody and cruel war. We have already saved our fatherland and covered it with glory, and we have restored to Europe her freedom and independence. It remains to crown this great accomplishment with the much-desired peace. May calm and tranquillity be established over the whole globe! May every kingdom live in prosperity under the sole power of its own government and laws! May faith, language, sciences, arts, and trade flourish in every country, for the general weal of the peoples! Such is our intention, and not the continuation of war and ruin. Entering into the heart of our country the enemies have done us much harm, but they have also suffered dire punishment. They were scourged by the wrath of God. Let us not be like them: inhumanity and brutality cannot please God, who loves mankind. Let us forget their deeds; let us carry to them, not anger and vengeance, but friendliness and a hand stretched out for reconciliation. It is the glory of the Russian to overthrow the armed enemy and, after wresting the arms from his hand, to be charitable to him and his peaceful brothers. This we are taught by the Orthodox faith which we cherish in our hearts; with divine words it speaks to us: love your enemies, and do kindness to those who hate you.

Soldiers! I am fully confident that, through your gentle conduct in the land of the enemy, you will conquer it with your generosity as you have with your arms, and, combining within yourselves the courage of the warrior against armed enemies with the kindness of the Christian toward those who are unarmed, you will crown your heroic accomplishments by preserving your renown as a courageous and kind people, thus hastening the coming of the goal of our desires—a general peace.

I am also confident that your superior officers will not hesitate to take the necessary and stern measures to this end, so that the actions of some of you, which may be at variance with it, shall not darken, to your general sorrow, the good name you have heretofore justly enjoyed.

XIII:29. THE HOLY ALLIANCE, SEPTEMBER 14 (26, N.S.), 1815

An act of faith rather than a treaty in the usual sense, this statement, concocted by Alexander I and agreed to initially by the rulers of Austria and Prussia, was as much of an enigma in its own time as it would be if announced today (complete text).

Reference: Edward Hertslet, ed., *The Map of Europe by Treaty since the General Peace of 1814*, 4 vols. (London, 1875-91), 1:317-19, translation slightly altered. Russian text in *PSZRI*, 1st ser., 33:279-80.

In the name of the most holy and indivisible Trinity.

Their Majesties the emperor of Austria, the king of Prussia, and the emperor of Russia, having, in consequence of the great events that have marked the course of the last three years in Europe, and especially in consequence of the blessings it has pleased divine Providence to shower down upon those states that place their confidence and their hope in him alone, become convinced of the necessity of subjecting the policies to be observed by the powers, in their reciprocal relations, to the sublime truths taught by the divine law of God, our Savior:

Solemnly declare that the present act has no other object than to publish, in the face of the whole world, their fixed resolution to take for their sole guide in the administration of their respective states, and in their political relations with every other government, the precepts of the holy religion, namely, the precepts of justice, Christian charity, and peace, which, far from being applicable only to private life, must have an immediate influence on the will of monarchs and guide all their steps, being the only means of consolidating human institutions and remedying their imperfections.

In consequence, Their Majesties have agreed on the following articles:

ARTICLE I. Consistent with the words of the Holy Scriptures, which command all men to consider each other as brethren, the three contracting monarchs will remain united by the bonds of a true and indissoluble fraternity, and, considering each other as fellow countrymen, they will, on all occasions and in all places, lend each other aid, assistance, and support and, regarding themselves as fathers of families in respect to their subjects and armies, will lead them, in the same spirit of fraternity with which they themselves are animated, in preserving religion, peace, and justice.

ART. II. In consequence, the sole predominant principle, whether between the said governments or between their subjects, shall be to do each other reciprocal service, to display mutual goodwill and affection, to consider themselves all as members of one and the same Christian nation; inasmuch as the three allied princes look upon themselves as merely delegated by Providence to govern three branches of the same family, namely, Austria, Prussia, and Russia, thus confessing that the Christian world, of which they and their people form a part, has in reality no other sovereign than him to whom alone power really belongs, inasmuch as in him alone are found all the treasures of love, knowledge, and infinite wisdom, that is to say, God, our divine Savior, Jesus Christ, the Word of the Most High, the Word of Life. Their Majesties consequently entreat their subjects, with the most tender solicitude, to strengthen themselves every day more and more in the principles and conscientious exercise of the duties which the divine Savior has taught mankind, as the sole means of enjoying that peace which arises from a good conscience and which alone is durable.

ART. III. All the powers who shall choose solemnly to avow the sacred principles set out in the present act and shall acknowledge how important it is for the happiness of nations, too long agitated, that henceforth these truths should promote the welfare of the destinies of mankind may be received with ardor and affection into this holy alliance.

Done in triplicate, and signed at Paris, the year of grace 1815, September 14/26.

(l.s.) Francis
(l.s.) Frederick William
(l.s.) Alexander

XIII:30. THE CONSTITUTIONAL CHARTER OF THE KINGDOM OF POLAND, NOVEMBER 15, 1815

A result of the settlement of the Congress of Vienna, this charter provided a brief honeymoon period of constitutional government for Poland under Alexander I's rule. Since the charter was published in both French and Russian, and since many of the French terms passed into general use in British and American works on Poland, the translation below makes liberal use of the French words for the various institutions mentioned. In some cases the terms used in the Russian text have been inserted for the sake of comparison.

Reference: Nikolai D. Sergeevskii, ed., *Konstitutsionnaia khartiia 1815 g. i nekotorye drugie akty byvshego Tsarstva Pol'skogo (1814-1881),* Biblioteka Okrain Rossii no. 5 (St. Petersburg: Izd. Sergeevskogo, 1907), pp. 41-63.

SECTION I. The political relations of the kingdom [*tsarstvo*].

ARTICLE 1. The Kingdom of Poland is forever united with the Russian Empire. . . .

ART. 3. The crown of the Kingdom of Poland is hereditary in our person and in that of our descendants, heirs, and successors, according to the order of succession established for the imperial throne of Russia. . . .

ART. 5. The king [*tsar'*], in case of his absence, names a viceroy [namestnik] who must reside in the kingdom. The viceroy is recallable at will. . . .

ART. 8. The external political relations of our empire are applicable to the Kingdom of Poland. . . .

ART. 9. The sovereign alone has the right to determine the participation of the Kingdom of Poland in the wars of Russia, as well as the treaties of peace or commerce which that power may conclude. . . .

SEC. II. General guarantees.

ART. 11. The Roman Catholic religion, professed by the greater part of the inhabitants of the Kingdom of Poland, will be the object of the particular attention of the government, without thereby impairing at all the liberty of the other faiths, which, without exception, will be able to be exercised fully and publicly and will enjoy the protection of the government. The difference in the Christian faiths plays no role in the enjoyment of civil and political rights. . . .

ART. 16. The liberty of the press is guaranteed. The law shall regulate the means of limiting abuses. . . .

ART. 19. A person may not be arrested except according to the forms and in the cases determined by the law. . . .

ART. 23. No one may be punished except according to the existing laws and under a sentence rendered by a competent magistrate. . . .

ART. 31. The Polish nation shall for all time to come have a national representation [représentation nationale; narodnoe predstavitel'stvo]. It shall consist of the Diet [Seim], composed of the king [tsar'] and of two chambers. The first [chamber] shall consist of the Senate; the second, of the nuncios [posly] and deputies of the communes [gminy]. . . .

SEC. III. Concerning the government.

CHAP. I. Concerning the king.

ART. 35. The government resides in the person of the king. He exercises the functions of executive power in all their scope. . . .

ART. 41. The king names the senators, ministers, members of the State Council [see Art. 63, below], their reporters, presidents of palatinal [*voevodskie*] commissions, presidents and judges of the various tribunals reserved for his nomination, the diplomatic and commercial agents, and all the other functionaries of the administration, either directly or through the authorities to whom he has delegated the power. . . .

ART. 45. All of our successors to the Kingdom of Poland are required to be crowned king of Poland in the capital, following the form we will establish, and they will swear the oath: "I swear and promise before God and on the Gospels to maintain and execute the Constitutional Charter with all my power." . . .

CHAP. III. Concerning the viceroy and the State Council.

ART. 63. The State Council, presided over by the king or his viceroy, is composed of the ministers, the councillors of state, and their reporters, as well as those people whom it shall please the king to appoint specially.

ART. 64. The viceroy and the State Council shall, in the absence of the king and in his name, administer the public affairs of the kingdom. . . .

SEC. IV. Concerning the national representation. . . .

ART. 86. The legislative power resides in the person of the king and in the two houses of the Diet, consistent with the provisions of article 31.

ART. 87. The Diet is ordinarily convened every two years in Warsaw, at a time determined by the act of convocation issued by the king. The session shall last thirty days. The king alone shall be able to prolong, adjourn, or dissolve it.

ART. 88. The king may convene the Diet under extraordinary circumstances when he judges it necessary. . . .

ART. 90. The Diet deliberates over all the proposed laws—civil, criminal, or administrative—which are referred to it on the part of the king by the State Council. . . .

ART. 91. The Diet deliberates according to the proposal of the sovereign on the increase or decrease of tariffs, taxes, levies, and government fees, on those changes it can effect in the best and most just manner of assessment, in the compiling of the budget of income and expenditures, in the regulation of the monetary system, in the selection of recruits, and in all other matters that may be entrusted to it by the sovereign. . . .

CHAP. II. Concerning the Senate.

ART. 108. The Senate is composed of:

princes of imperial and royal blood; bishops; palatines [*voevody*]; and castellans [*kastelliany*]. . . .

ART. 110. The king names the senators. They serve for life. The Senate presents to the king through the viceroy [namestnik] two candidates for each vacant office of senator, palatine, or castellan. . . .

CHAP. III. Concerning the Chamber of Nuncios [Palata Poslov].

ART. 118. The Chamber of Nuncios is composed of:

1. Seventy-seven nuncios named by the dietines [seimiki] or assemblies of nobles, at one nuncio per district [*povet*].

2. Fifty-one deputies of the communes [gminy]. The chamber is presided over by a marshal chosen among its members and named by the king. . . .

ART. 121. In order to be elected a member of the Chamber of Nuncios, one must be at least thirty years old, enjoy civil rights, and pay a tax of one hundred Polish florins. . . .

CHAP. IV. Concerning the dietines [seimiki].

ART. 125. The noble property holders of each district assembled in the dietine choose one nuncio and two members for the council of the palatinate [sovet voevodstva] and make up a list of candidates for administrative positions.

ART. 126. The dietines can assemble only upon the call of the king, which fixes the day, the duration, and the subjects of the deliberations of the assembly.

ART. 127. No noble can be admitted to vote in a dietine if he is not registered in the civic book of the nobles of the district, if he does not enjoy civil rights, if he is not twenty-one years of age, and if he is not an owner of real estate. . . .

CHAP. V. Concerning the communal assemblies [gminnye sobraniia]. . . .

ART. 131. The following are admitted into the communal assemblies:

1. Any non-noble, property-owning citizen who pays a real-estate tax.

2. Any manufacturer or atelier manager; any merchant whose shop or store is valued at no less than ten thousand Polish florins.

3. All curés and vicars.

4. Professors, teachers, and other persons charged with public education.

5. Any artist distinguished by his talents, knowledge, or service rendered to commerce or to the arts. . . .

CHAP. VI. Concerning the council of the palatinate [sovet voevodstva].

ART. 135. In each palatinate there will be a council of the palatinate composed of councillors chosen by the dietines and the communal assemblies. . . .

ART. 137. The principal function of the council of the palatinate will be:

1. To choose the judges for the first two echelons of courts.

2. To cooperate in compiling and revising the list of candidates for administrative positions.

3. To attend to the interests of the palatinate. . . .

[From Sec. V, concerning the judiciary:]

ART. 140. The courts are composed of judges named by the king and judges chosen according to the Organic Statute.

ART. 141. The judges named by the king are unimpeachable for life. The elected judges are also unimpeachable for the duration of the term of their service. . . .

[From Sec. VI. concerning the armed forces:]

ART. 156. The army shall preserve the colors of its uniform, its special dress and everything that concerns its nationality. . . .

[From Sec. VII, general regulations:]

ART. 159. The punishment of confiscation is abolished and may not be reestablished in any case.

ART. 160. The civil and military orders of Poland, namely, that of the White Eagle, that of Saint Stanislas and that of the Military Cross, are maintained. . . .

Believing in our conscience that the present Constitutional Charter answers our paternal wishes to maintain in all the classes of our subjects of the Kingdom of Poland the peace, harmony, and union so necessary for their well-being, and to strengthen the happiness we desire for them, we have given and give them the present Constitutional Charter which we adopt for ourselves and our successors.

XIII:31. ALEXANDER I'S ADDRESS TO THE POLISH DIET, MARCH 15, 1818

Clearly delighted with his new role as a constitutional monarch, Alexander delivered to the Polish Diet an address (in French) which represented one of the high points of his idealism. The address was welcomed by all liberals of the day and did much to foster Polish nationalism.

Reference: Shil'der, *Imperator Aleksandr Pervyi,* 4:86-88. The translation is based on the Russian text but includes in brackets the French expressions that were included in parentheses in the Russian version.

Representatives of the Polish Kingdom! Your hopes and my desires are being realized. The nation you have been called upon to represent enjoys, at last, that autonomous existence which is implicit in your nature and time-honored institutions. Only in forgetting the past could your restoration have been brought about. This question has been firmly resolved in my mind ever since I was first able to hope for a way to implement my decision.

Zealous for the glory of my country, I wished it to obtain yet another measure of glory. And indeed, after the end of a terrible war, Russia, in accordance with the tenets of Christian morality, repaid evil with good, opened to you her fraternal embrace, and preferred, from among all the privileges brought by victory, solely the honor of bringing restoration to a brave and deserving people. Furthering this great step, I obeyed an inner conviction, strongly facilitated by events. I have acquitted myself of a duty dictated solely by conscience and therefore most precious to my heart.

The political structure [*organisation*] already existing in your land allowed me to establish without delay the system I have granted you, guided by the principles of these legally free institutions [*en mettant en pratique les principes de ces institutions libérales*] which had been constantly present in my thought and whose salutary influence I hope to spread, with the Lord's help, over all the regions entrusted by Providence to my care.

Thus you gave me the means to present before my country that which I have long since been preparing for her, and which she will possess when the beginnings of this most important undertaking reach appropriate maturity.

Poles! Casting aside those perilous prejudices which have brought such disaster upon you, it is now within your power alone to provide a solid foundation for your restoration. Your existence is irrevocably bound to the fate of Russia. All your efforts should be bent toward strengthening this alliance, an alliance both salutary and protective. Your restoration is defined in solemn agreements. It is sanctified by a constitutional charter [*charte constitutionnelle*]. The inviolability of these external obligations and of this basic law assigns henceforth to Poland a fitting place among European nations: a precious attainment which she has long sought in vain amidst most cruel trials.

XIII:32. ALEXANDER I'S ORDERS ON THE ESTABLISHMENT OF THE MILITARY SETTLEMENTS, 1817-1818

Few chapters in Russia's social and military history have left less satisfactory impressions than this effort to help solve both the military and financial needs of the state. (See the comments of Vigel', Item 38, and of Iakushkin, Item 43, below.)

Reference: *PSZRI,* 1st ser., 34:220-21, 944; 35:549.

[From an order to the civil governor in the Novgorod guberniia, April 18, 1817:]

In order to eliminate the existing burden accompanying the recruiting obligation, according to which those entering military service must be located far from their home area, separated from their families and kin, which naturally frightens them at their very entrance into service and weakens their strength with longing for their home area, making their new position unbearable to them, we, with a paternal desire to make the transfer of these people into a military situation painless and the service itself less burdensome, have adopted the basic rule that, in peacetime, a soldier serving the fatherland is not to be separated from his home area; and therefore we have adopted the unalterable intention of settling each regiment in a specified district and of manning the regiment exclusively with residents of that district.

Consistent with this aim, and designating for the settlement of the Count Arakcheev Grenadier Regiment the Vysotskaia volost', we command you immediately to set out for this volost' and, traveling through all its towns and villages, to read and display in the original this, our decree, to all the peasants, and then to declare that they all are appointed to military settlements [*voennye poseleniia*] in order to form the Count Arakcheev Grenadier Regiment on the following principles, especially advantageous for them: (1) they are freed now and forever from all state requisitions and from all local obligations, of whatever designation they are; (2) they are freed from the general recruitment levy, and all those fit for military service will constitute the Count Arakcheev Grenadier Regiment, on the model of the Cossack troops; (3) the government takes upon itself the maintenance of their children and their preparation for service, providing them with food and uniforms without any burden on the parents; (4) the Count Arakcheev Grenadier Regiment will, in peacetime, always remain quartered in the Vysotskaia volost'; consequently, those of its inhabitants entering service in this regiment will remain in their own homes with their families and kin with all their domestic occupations, not being subjected to those discomforts of constant separation from their home area to which they have been subjected heretofore upon entering service in accordance with the general recruitment levies.

[From a charter for the inhabitants of the Chuguev district, near Khar'kov, December 19, 1817:]

We command . . . [that our agent], upon the assembling of all the inhabitants, read through and display in the original this, our

document, and then inform them that they are all under the general designation of military settlers, designated for the composition of the Chuguev Ulan Regiment . . . with new benefits and privileges of which the major are the following:

1. All those settlers who have unsuitable installations will be resettled at government expense for increased comfort in working the fields, and likewise new homes, more suitable to the location and befitting people who are distinguished from peasants by title and obligation, will be erected to replace their old buildings.

2. All to whom such an allotment is necessary will be supplied with agricultural implements as well as domestic and draft livestock.

3. The government takes upon itself the support of the children of these military settlers and their preparation for service, providing them with food and uniforms without any burden on the parents. . . .

5. The Chuguev Ulan Regiment will always be quartered in its own district in peacetime, and the squadrons settled there will never be required to leave it on a march and, in accordance with this new arrangement, will be able more easily to work their fields with the aid of those in the reserve and the active squadrons. . . .

6. The personal property of every military settler, current and future, will remain inviolable.

7. The district of the settlement of the Chuguev Ulan Regiment, dependent solely and directly on the military administration, is forever freed from all state requisitions, from all local obligations of whatever designation they are and from the general recruitment levies.

[From the closing portion of a decree of Alexander's, August 26, 1818:]

When, with God's help, these settlements take their final form and are established in conformity with our purpose, then in times of peace there will be no need for general recruitment anywhere in the entire empire.

XIII:33. N. N. NOVOSIL'TSEV'S PROJECT FOR A CONSTITUTIONAL CHARTER FOR THE RUSSIAN EMPIRE, 1820

Drawing heavily upon the example of Michael Speranskii's plan for the organization of the Russian state (see above, Item 22), as well as the Polish charter of 1815, Nikolai Nikolaevich Novosil'tsev (1761-1836) undertook his project in 1818-19 at the request of Alexander I. The draft copies were found in Warsaw in 1830. Although the project was not carried out, it serves to illustrate the influence of England, France, and the United States on contemporary political thinking in Russia.

Reference: An English translation edited by David Urquhart from the original French is in the English journal *The Portfolio*, 5 (1837): 511-22, 610-39; 6 (1837): 72-83. The excerpts included here are taken from that source, slightly modified. A few key words have been inserted from the Russian text, which is found in Shil'der, *Imperator Aleksandr Pervyi*, 4:499-526. For a French text and analysis, see George Vernadsky, *La Charte Constitutionelle de l'Empire russe de l'an 1820* (Paris: Librairie du Recueil Sirey, 1933). For a partial translation from Russian to English see Raeff, *Plans*, pp. 110-20.

Title II.
Section I. On the Sovereign and His Power.

Article 9. The crown of the Imperial Russian throne is hereditary, passing on according to the order of succession established by Our late father, the emperor Paul. . . .

Article 12. The Sovereign is the sole source of all the civil, political, legislative, and military power in the Empire.

He administers the executive branch with all of its ramifications.

All authority—executive, administrative, and judicial—can emanate only from him.

Article 13. Nevertheless, legislative power is exercised by the Sovereign in concurrence with the State Diet [Seim] . . . on the basis of the Constitutional Charter and special regulations. . . .

Article 26. In order to define the legislative power of the Sovereign, the basic scheme of jurisprudence in the Empire is divided into three categories:

The first contains the *laws*.

The second contains the *statutes* and *regulations*.

The third contains the *decrees, injunctions, rescripts*, and *resolutions*. . . .

Article 30. The laws are divided into general laws of the Empire and the particular laws of the provinces. The general laws constitute the common law of the State and are applicable in all cases in which the particular laws do not pronounce judgement.

Article 31. The general laws are issued by the consent of the Sovereign and of the General Diet. . . .

Article 32. The particular laws of the provinces are issued by the consent of the Sovereign and the diets of the vicegerencies.

Article 33. The right of issuing ordinances, statutes, regulations, ukases, decrees, orders, and rescripts is exclusively vested in the Sovereign, who may delegate it in whole or in part. . . .

Section II. The Council of State.

Article 35. The Council of State, at which the Sovereign presides, is composed of the Ministers, the State Councillors, the State Reporters or State Secretaries, and any other persons whom the Sovereign may please to summon to it.

Article 36. The Council of State is divided into a General Assembly and an Administrative Council, or Council of Ministers. . . .

Article 42. The General Assembly of the Council of State . . . shall be composed of the members designated in Article 35.

The functions of the Council of State, independently of those which it at present exercises according to the Regulation of 1809, are:

1. To discuss and draw up all projects of laws and regulations concerning the general administration of the Empire.

2. To legislate in cases of conflicting jurisdiction.

3. To pronounce on [the basis of] the reports of the Council of Administration or the Council of Ministers, on the prosecution of the [highest] administrative functionaries appointed by the Sovereign or by the Council of Ministers [the Russian text omits the phrase "or . . . Ministers"] in cases of abuses in the exercise of their functions. . . .

4. To examine and verify, annually, the accounts delivered by each principal branch of the administration.

5. To make observations on all the abuses which exist or are introduced into the administration, as well as upon all attempts against, and all violations of, the fundamental principles of the State or of the Laws, and to make a general report on them to the Sovereign. . . .

Title III. GENERAL REGULATIONS GUARANTEED BY STATE AUTHORITY

Article 78. The Orthodox Greek-Russian religion shall always be the prevailing religion of the State. . . .

Article 80. The Law protects equally all citizens, without any distinction.

Article 81. The Russian Fundamental Law that "no one shall be punished without having been judged," and the principle established by the Regulation on the Administration of Guberniias [1775], #401, which states that "no one shall be imprisoned or deprived of liberty without the crime of which he is accused being made known to him, and without his having been questioned within three days after his arrest," apply to all inhabitants. . . .

Article 89. The liberty of the press is guarenteed; the Laws shall determine the means of repressing its abuses.

Article 90. Every Russian subject is free to establish himself in a foreign country and to carry there his personal fortune. . . .

Article 91. The Russian nation shall enjoy in perpetuity a national representation. It shall consist of a Diet [in the Russian version: seim, duma] composed of the Sovereign and of the two chambers. The first, called the Upper Chamber, shall be formed from the Senate; the second, named the Chamber of the Nuncios [posol'skaia palata], shall be composed of the nuncios [zemskie posly] and the deputies of the communes [deputaty okruzhnykh gorodskikh obshchestv]. . . .

Article 100. The Diet of the Empire is divided into the diets of the vicegerencies [chastnye seimy (dumy) namestnicheskikh oblastei], which are to assemble every three years, and a General Diet [obshchaia gosudarstvennaia duma ili seim], which shall assemble every five years.

XIII:34. A SPERANSKII STATUTE FOR THE ADMINISTRATIVE ORGANIZATION OF SIBERIA, JULY 22, 1822

Disgraced on the eve of Napoleon's invasion of 1812, Speranskii was rehabilitated in 1816 and in 1819 was appointed governor general of Siberia. He sought to reorganize the administration of the area. In 1822 he got approval for the fundamental statutes, of which the present document is one. Of particular interest is his use of native non-Russian customs and organization. These laws remained in force until 1917. Note: The noun rendered here as "natives" is *inorodtsy*, meaning "aliens" or "people of another kind." In this document it refers to the native tribes of Siberia, although in other contexts it was also applied to many of the non-Russian peoples who had long inhabited the northern, eastern, and southern parts of European Russia.

Reference: *PSZRI,* 1st ser., 38:394-410.

PART I. The rights of natives.

CHAPTER I. Division.

1. All the native tribes inhabiting Siberia, heretofore referred to as *iasachnye* [subject to the *iasak* or tax], are to be divided into three main categories according to their different degrees of social development and their present manner of life. The first category shall include the settled tribes, i.e. those living in towns and settlements; the second, the nomads, occupying definite locations, within which they shift with the seasons; the third, migrants or trappers, who move from place to place, following rivers and other landmarks. . . .

CHAP. II. General rights of the settled natives. . . .

13. All settled natives are on an equal footing, with regard to rights and obligations, with Russians, according to the legal class into which they are incorporated. They are to be governed in accordance with the general laws and regulations. . . .

CHAP. V. The general rights of the nomadic natives. . . .

24. The nomadic natives constitute a special legal class on an equal footing with the peasant class but different from the latter in the way they are governed.

25. The nomadic natives retain all their former rights. They must be made to understand that, the [proposed] increase in agriculture notwithstanding, they are never to be forced against their will to be incorporated into the peasant class, and in general they will not be included in any other legal class, unless they so desire.

26. Nomadic natives are to have, for each generation, lands assigned to their ownership.

27. The particulars of the distribution of these lands into [individual] parts will depend on the nomads themselves, according to the drawing of lots or any other of their customs.

28. The nomads are to be reaffirmed in the ownership of those lands they now occupy,

with the provision that the area owned by each tribe be defined in detail by order of the local authorities.

29. Each native tribe has complete freedom to engage in agriculture, breed cattle, or follow local trades on the lands and waters assigned to them.

30. Natives are to be protected from any mutual encroachments which might occur as one tribe enters, without mutual agreement, upon the lands belonging to another tribe, for the purpose of practicing a trade.

31. Russians are strictly forbidden to settle willfully on lands assigned to the ownership of natives.

32. Russians may lease land from natives, but always subject to agreement with [native] communities.

33. Hiring of natives for private labor may be done with the knowledge of tribal authorities, and in accordance with the special rulings concerning the duties and obligations of peasants and natives.

34. Natives are to be governed by their own tribal headmen and elders, who constitute their "Steppe Administration."

35. The nomads are to be governed according to those laws, peculiar to each tribe, that exist in the steppes.

36. Only for criminal offenses are the nomads to be tried in the government offices and in accordance with the general laws of the empire.

37. In the case of natives, the following are to be regarded as criminal offenses: (1) insurrection, (2) premeditated murder, (3) robbery and violence, (4) the manufacture of counterfeit money and, in general, any theft of government or public property. All other offenses, not excepting stealing, are to be considered as infractions of civil law, until such time as their moral standards become tempered by education.

38. For misdeeds [committed] in Russian towns and settlements, they are to be prosecuted by the local police in accordance with general regulations.

39. Natives are to pay a per capita tax regulated by special edict, the number of taxable individuals to be established by a general census.

40. Nomadic natives participate in the general duties [and obligations] of their guberniias, as established by special decree.

41. The support of the Steppe Administration is an internal responsibility of the nomads.

42. All native nomads are exempt from military obligation. . . .

45. Natives have the right to dispose of their products and of their catch through sale or barter in towns and settlements and at established fairs.

46. Free trade with the nomads, of all produce and manufactures except intoxicating beverages, is permitted at all times.

47. The importation and sale of intoxicating beverages in the camps and at the fairs of the nomads is most strictly forbidden.

48. It is forbidden to the government officials serving in a given province to trade with its nomads in any form or under any pretext whatsoever. . . .

58. Natives have the right to enroll their children in government-established schools for the purpose of education. They also have the right to establish their own schools, but only with the permission of their civilian governors or oblast' *nachal'niki* [chiefs].

[PART II.] CHAP. II. Structure of the administration of nomadic natives. . . .

94. Every nomad camp, or *ulus,* numbering not less than fifteen families is to have its own administration.

95. Encampments, or ulusy, having less than fifteen families are to be attached to those others that are closest to them.

96. The administration is to consist of one elder and one or two assistants from among the best and most honored members of the clan.

97. The elder is either elected or inherits his rank, according to custom. Among his own clan he may bear the title of princeling, *zaisan,* and so forth, but in his relations with the government he must in all tribes be termed elder. . . .

103. Several encampments, or ulusy, of the same clan are subordinated to a native board.

104. Such a native board is to consist of a chief, two elected members, and, if it is possible to introduce written recording, a scribe.

105. The clan administrations are in all respects subordinated to the native board.

106. The chiefs of the boards receive their titles either by inheritance or upon election, in accordance with the local customs of each tribe.

107. Elected board members and scribes are always to be elected by the clan members for a definite or indefinite period of time. . . .
CHAP. XII. Worship. . . .
286. Natives who do not profess Christianity have the freedom to conduct religious services in accordance with their own law and ritual.
287. In converting them the Russian clergy is to follow the dictates of mildness, using only persuasion without the least coercion.

XIII:35. THE DECREE PROHIBITING MASONIC LODGES AND ALL SECRET SOCIETIES, AUGUST 1, 1822

This decree reflected not only Alexander I's growing conservatism in social and political affairs but also the general uneasiness felt by Europe's monarchs over the liberalism sweeping their lands and disturbing the status quo.
Reference: *PSZRI*, 1st ser., 38:579-80.

Count Viktor Pavlovich [Kochubei, minister of internal affairs]: Disorders and subversion arising in other states due to the existence of various secret societies, some of which are called Masonic lodges, originally dedicated to charitable activities—certain ones secretly engaged in political pursuits which turned out later to be harmful to the peace of those states—have forced some of the states to prohibit these secret societies.

Watching always vigilantly that a firm barrier be opposed to anything that might prove harmful to [our] state, especially at a time when, unfortunately, in some other lands, such grievous consequences result from contemporary thinking there, we have deemed it beneficial to decree the following regarding the above-mentioned societies:

1. All secret societies, regardless of the names under which they may be existing, whether Masonic lodges or any other, are to be closed, and in the future no permission is to be given for their establishment.

2. After this has been announced to all members of those societies, a signed declaration is to be obtained from them that in the future they will not form, within the empire or outside of it, any Masonic or other secret societies, under any guise whatsoever, no matter under what plausible title these might be projected. . . .

5. To the heads of guberniias and civilian governors is assigned the duty of strictly observing that, first, no lodges or secret societies be established anywhere under any pretext and that, second, all government officials entering the service be required to give . . . a signed declaration that they will not belong to any in the future; without such declarations they cannot be appointed to positions or be allowed to enter the service.

XIII:36. METTERNICH'S COMMENTS ON RUSSIA AND THE GREEK REVOLT AGAINST TURKEY, 1821-1822

Striving for independence from Turkey, the Greeks appealed to Russia for help as co-religionists against the Moslems. This issue, in view of Alexander I's support of the Metternichean defense of all legitimate monarchies, placed the tsar in a quandary. His decision was not the end of the affair. How it all looked to Metternich may be seen in these excerpts from his letters and dispatches.
Reference: Prince Richard Metternich, ed., *Memoirs of Prince Metternich*, trans. Mrs. Alexander Napier, 5 vols. (New York, 1880-82), 3:522-23 [Mar. 25, 1821], 525-26 [Mar. 26], 529, 533 [Apr. 21-22], 501-02 [July 23], 613 [Apr. 19], 626 [May 31], 627 [June 3].

[From a letter to Rechberg; Laibach, March 25 (N.S.), 1821:]

A new event which must at this time of general commotion powerfully contribute to agitate men's minds is the insurrection of the Greeks in the Ottoman Empire. The Emperor Alexander received all the particulars by a courier. . . .

Prince Ypsilanti, major-general of the Russian service, has put himself at the head of this insurrection . . . it is the work of a secret society, which has been preparing the material for two years. . . .

In this fresh emergency, the Emperor Alexander has given proof of his noble and loyal character; his views and principles entirely agree with those of the Emperor my august master. . . . The Emperor Alexander cashiers and removes from his army all the military Greeks who take part in this insurrection; and refuses all support and help to the Greek insurgents.

The two monarchs have simultaneously declared at Constantinople that, faithful to the principles which they have publicly announced, they will never support the enemies of public order. . . .

[From a letter to Stadion (Austrian minister of finance); Laibach, March 26 (N.S.), 1821:]

As for the Greek revolution—let it alone. I answer for it that the Emperor Alexander has as little to do with that now as with the revolution in Piedmont. . . . This affair must be looked upon as placed beyond the pale of civilization; it will end, I believe, badly for the Greeks, who depended on a support which failed them the very day they took up arms. It is the same with the Neapolitans, who believed that Russia would be, if not for them, at least against us.

[From a letter to Stadion; Laibach, April 21 and 22 (N.S.), 1821:]

Facts alone speak in 1821. All the promises, all the speeches of the Emperor of Russia would have been valueless; but his setting in motion some hundred thousand men, their effective march, the expenditure on them of ten million—these are facts. The command to halt is another fact not less important; and a hundred and twenty thousand men placed in the Russian provinces nearest our frontiers, with orders to march at the first request of Austria, is certainly a third fact which will prevent these disturbers from counting so readily on the Emperor Alexander in future.

.   .   .

Do you know the true, the only reason why the Emperor Alexander objects to an army, even of ten thousand men, being stationed beyond his frontiers? Because he is convinced that this body would pass over to the enemy. So much have the liberal efforts of the good people who surround this Prince liberalised the whole army.

[From a private letter of Metternich's, July 23 (N.S.), 1821:]

The Emperor Alexander and I took the same views of the present affair [the Greek revolt]. But he has changed his place of residence, and hence it is uncertain whether he will remain true to the point of view which is easy for me, but difficult for him, to take. The setting in which a man finds himself has immense influence on him; it requires great strength of mind to withstand surrounding influence, and still greater to break through it. The Emperor remains firm, but he stands alone. Some wish the contrary of what he wishes, and have pointed it out; others have not the strength to wish anything at all. To keep him right, the Emperor must be separated from his surrounding. He wills what I will, but those about him will the contrary.

With this feeling, the Emperor Alexander has taken the only resolution that could be taken; he has withdrawn from all positive action and thrown himself morally upon me. This explains my cobweb. Such webs are pretty to look at, cleverly spun, and will bear a light touch, but not a gale of wind.

[From a letter to Alexander I, April 19 (N.S), 1822:]

His Imperial Majesty of All the Russias, applying those principles of justice, moderation, and benevolence of which the Cabinet of Austria is so deeply sensible, to an affair [the Greek rebellion in Moldavia and Wallachia] which offers such grave considerations for the personal dignity of the Sovereign of Russia and for the interests of his Empire, has invariably announced his resolution of not separating these considerations [the ill-treatment of the Christian Greeks in the Ottoman Empire], however grave they may be, from those which concern the preserving intact of the political system which is at present the only foundation and condition of the tranquillity of Europe and the preservation of social order.

[From a note to the emperor Francis; Vienna, May 31 (N.S.), 1822?]

By the courier who arrived an hour ago from St. Petersburg, I have a despatch from Lebzeltern on the 22nd inst. [instant, i.e. of the current month], giving the details of perhaps the greatest victory that one Cabinet [the Austrian] has ever gained over another.

The Emperor has adopted all our Reports. Tatishchev will return here in ten or twelve days in order to place the rest of the negotiations in our hands. The Emperor goes further. . . . His Majesty is ready to re-establish diplomatic relations with the Divan immediately. Count Capo d'Istria is quite beaten, and is, for the present, silent.

I feel myself very fortunate that I may venture to believe that the whole position of things in Europe can now take a definite and decided turn.

[From a note to the emperor Francis; Vienna, June 3 (N.S.), 1822:]

Since politics have been carried on in an enlightened manner, never has a Cabinet compromised itself like the Russian Cabinet.

All the remarks which your Majesty will find used by Count Nesselrode himself on the loss of Russian influence on the Turkish kingdom are correct. The present Russian Cabinet has with one blow destroyed the work of Peter the Great and all his successors. Everything is here on a new basis, and what Russia loses in moral strength the Porte gains. We have done them [the Turks] here a service which they can never sufficiently reward, and it will maintain ours as well as the English influence.

XIII:37. ALEXANDER'S SECRET ORDER CONCERNING THE SUCCESSION TO THE RUSSIAN THRONE, AUGUST 16, 1823

Alexander I's insistence on preserving the utmost secrecy about this arrangement helps to explain his reputation as the "Enigmatic Tsar."
Reference: *PSZRI*, 2d ser., 1:3, 5.

[Quoting Tsesarevich Constantine's letter of January 14, 1822:]
Most Gracious Sire!

Encouraged by the repeated displays of Your Imperial Majesty's boundless benevolent disposition toward me, I presume to appeal to it once more and to lay at your feet, Most Gracious Sire, my most humble plea.

Since I do not feel within me either those gifts or that strength or that spirit necessary to be, at any time, elevated to that eminence to which, by birth, I may have the right, I venture to beg Your Imperial Majesty to transfer that right to the one who is entitled to it next after myself, and by this act to affirm forever the unshakable position of our empire.

[Alexander's secret order of August 16, 1823:]

Our beloved brother, the tsesarevich and grand duke Konstantin Pavlovich, directed by his own inner urge, addressed to us his plea that his right to the eminence to which he might sometime be elevated due to his

birth be transferred to the one who is entitled to it next to him.

. . .

We have determined: First, that the voluntary renouncement of his right to the throne of all the Russias, by our first brother, the tsesarevich and grand duke Konstantin Pavlovich, be considered firm and unalterable; and that the record of his abdication, for the sake of complete authenticity, be preserved in the great Cathedral of the Dormition in Moscow, and in the three highest governmental offices of our empire: the Holy Synod, the State Council and the Governing Senate. Second, in consequence of this, and in precise agreement with the act concerning the succession to the throne, our second brother, the grand duke Nikolai Pavlovich is to be our heir.

. . .

Issued at Tsarskoe Selo, on August 16 of the year A.D. 1823, the twenty-third year of our reign.

The original signed in His Imperial Majesty's own hand:

Aleksandr

XIII:38. THE MEMOIRS OF F. F. VIGEL' ON LIFE IN RUSSIA IN THE EARLY NINETEENTH CENTURY

A civil servant who worked in the Ministry of Foreign Affairs, Filipp Filippovich Vigel' (1786-1856) had a wide acquaintanceship with people in high political and literary circles. His memoirs are useful not only because he was a keen observer and mirror of his times, but also because he represents a viewpoint quite different from those of Speranskii (see above) or the Decembrists (see Section D, below).
Reference: Filipp F. Vigel', *Vospominaniia F. F. Vigelia,* 7 vols. in 3 (Moscow, 1864-65), 1:73, 181; 2:26-27; 4:77. Filipp F. Vigel', *Zapiski,* ed. S. Ia. Shtraikh, 2 vols. (Moscow: Artel' Pisatelei

Krug, 1928), 1:154, 176, 289; 2:119-20, 276-77. (The first five paragraphs are from the 1864 edition; the rest are from that of 1928.)

There were strange customs at that time [the end of the eighteenth century], which was, albeit, a very happy one for Russia. The education of boys usually ended at the age of fifteen. People held that they had now learned everything and hastened to enter them into military service, so that they might advance in rank as rapidly as possible. . . .

There was another strange thing, which might even be termed an abuse: every Guards regiment had on its rosters hundreds of sergeants, cavalry sergeant majors . . . quartermaster sergeants, and corporals; all of them were minors, living at home and awaiting promotion in rank. For each of these lower ranks in the Guards regiment, there was a corresponding higher officer's position in the army, and therefore the children received their rank at the time of enlistment according to their parents' connections with the commanding officers, according to the patronage they were able to secure, and occasionally according to their merits and deserts.

. . .

Only their services, the largesse of sovereigns, and thrift could increase the wealth of nobles. This venerable prejudice was followed even more carefully in the West, until the duke of Orleans turned his dwelling into a marketplace, and the royal palace became known as the center of Paris trade. Nowadays, in order to get rich, our princes and counts, even the wealthiest, employ the same means as the *meshchane;* they build breweries and sell drinks in taverns, and yet they parade before the meshchane with their famous names. But can they be respected? Worship of the golden calf levels all classes and conditions. It was not so under Paul, some forty years ago.

. . .

To describe the bureaucratic type. . . . As soon as a bureaucrat obtains a place of any prominence, he begins to think of becoming a minister. He becomes proud, cold in his demeanor, and at the same time talkative, but only with those who are willing to listen silently for hours. He dresses elegantly, has a good chef, a stylish wife, and a piano in his drawing room. But he does not live very hospitably, receiving only those who need him, or those whom he needs. He knows

foreign languages and has read enough to discourse with a learned air on topics that interest him least of all. But he says little in society about matters relating to his official duties: these are reserved for his office and department. The welfare of the state or the good of mankind never enters into his thoughts; he will not humble himself even to mention them and regards those who are concerned with such matters as childishly weak-minded. Apart from the passion for power and enrichment, he has no weaknesses or vices, but he encourages and loves to see them in others, for to respect others is to him unbearable, but to despise is sweet and comforting. No matter how petty his office, he compels petitioners to wait in the ante-room, treats them with condescension, and even takes bribes as if he were collecting tribute from the vanquished. He has never known compassion, and there was never anything sacred to him in the world. He is an educated robber, but not bold enough for the highway. I have depicted here one example of bureaucratic perfection; not all can vie with him, but all approach him more or less closely.

. . .

People still talk of "General Frost," forgetting that our autumn that year [1812] was warmer than in France, that the first defeats near Tarutino and Maloiaroslavets occurred in the early days of October, and that, over the distance of almost four hundred versts from Moscow to Smolensk, when this "general" had not yet even ventured an appearance, entire brigades and divisions had already begun to disappear from the enemy army.

. . .

Since the time of Peter the Great fate has commanded Russia to submit to one or another European state or people and to worship it like an idol. To please Peter, it was necessary to become a Dutchman; Germany dominated us under Anna Ioannovna and Biron; under Elisaveta Petrovna, La Chetardie appeared on the scene, with the temptations of France; they were increased and multiplied by the passion of Catherine II for French literature and by her friendship with the eighteenth-century philosophers. Peter III and Paul I wanted to turn us into Prussians; England was our patroness during the first years of Alexander's reign. Can it be that Poland is now becoming our idol?

. . .

Under Peter the Great, Europe began to teach us; under Anna Ivanovna [Ioannovna] it tormented us; but the reign of Alexander is an era of our total subjugation to it. His persistent efforts over the course of twenty-five years have succeeded, if not throughout Russia then at least in Petersburg, in driving our national feeling down to the last, the very lowest class.

. . .

It would seem that there is not a single nation in Europe or Asia whose representatives were not to be found serving in Russia and finally becoming Russian nobles, which is the reason why this class is so different from our other, purely Russian classes and is becoming a mixture of all peoples.

. . .

Why are military settlements [voennye poseleniia] needed inside a country, and against what internal enemies can they protect it? Such were the questions many people asked one another. It would seem that, observing the rebellious attitude of the Western peoples toward their governments during his latest visit abroad, and foreseeing new troubles in the future, our sovereign felt that in order to curb them it was necessary to preserve the large army he needed during the general war. He considered methods of accomplishing this without burdening the state, and the unfortunate idea of the military settlements occurred to him. He had probably divulged this to Arakcheev, who, chosen as the instrument for the planning and execution of this important undertaking, did not dare or—more likely— did not wish to dispute it. At first, approaching the matter slowly, the sovereign intended, apparently, to colonize the entire army, which would thus be tripled in numbers and would become self-supporting. The first experiment was made with state peasants bought up from landowners for this purpose. They were established in settlements in the Novgorod guberniia, in the neighborhood of Count Arakcheev's estates. The frightful order he instituted in his henceforth memorable village of Gruzino, transforming human beings into insensible machines, began to spread

itself to the hapless peasants in nearby areas and to the soldiers settled amongst them. During the ensuing years, military settlements of this type were established in Belorussia, along the Bug River, and finally in Chuguev, in the Khar'kov guberniia. It seems that the future economy in the maintenance of troops, however, proved too costly in the present and was ruinous to the treasury. And this halted the spread of the evil which would have led to countless unfortunate consequences.

. . .

The example of the Cossacks, who came into being without any assistance, subsidy, or supervision, must have prompted the initial idea of this monstrous institution. . . . The Cossacks were a special, spontaneous element. . . . Everything about them was as free as the air of the steppes which they breathed; the flame of courage never dimmed in their hearts and eyes, and their movements were as rapid as the flow of the rivers along which they settled. At the same time, just as their land obeyed the laws of nature, so they freely obeyed the authorities placed over them. But here the poor settlers were doomed to a lifetime of forced labor. Two conditions entirely different from one another were harnessed under the same yoke; the tiller of the soil was forced to take up a gun, and the soldier was compelled to walk behind the plow. The Russian, who is both industrious and carefree, likes to enjoy himself freely after work, instead of resting. What matter if his house is not too clean, as long as there are cakes to grace the table, as the folk proverb puts it. But the unfortunates were compelled to give up everything; for all was now organized in the German, the Prussian manner. Everything was counted, weighed, and measured. Exhausted by the day's labor in the fields, the military settler had to stand at attention and march; when he came home, he found no peace: he was compelled to scrub and clean his house and sweep the street. He had to report every egg laid by his hen.

. . .

[Concerning the corps of gendarmes established by Nicholas I in 1826:]

This entire observation corps was formed by the end of the year, although it was difficult at first to persuade any fairly decent men to join it. The blue uniform, different in color from all the other military uniforms, as if it were the clothing of informers, aroused repugnance even in those who finally decided to don it.

The organization of this new type of police apparently had a dual purpose. The gendarmes were to uncover all evil designs against the government and prevent the spread of any bold political ideas of freedom, should they appear anywhere. This was somewhat difficult, for the number of people infected with liberalism and unconnected with the affair of December 14 [1825] was small, and, what is more, these kept quieter than ever and were extremely circumspect in communicating their opinions. Further, every field officer of this corps was to see to it that the courts of the guberniia where he was stationed were just in their decisions. He was also expected to bring to the governor's attention all wrongs and irregularities, the extortion of bribes by civil officials and cruel treatment by landowners, and to report all this to his own superiors. The intention, of course, seemed to be of the best; but where were to be found the men capable of carrying it out, men who were conscientious, impartial, informed, and clear-sighted? Were there no governors, city and rural police, and, finally, public prosecutors charged with enforcing the legal conduct of affairs? Was there no order at all in Russia before this? Had lawlessness, indeed, prevailed throughout the country? And, if so, could everything be rectified by a handful of army officers recruited at random and with considerable difficulty?

To invest such men with complete power meant to withdraw this power from all the local authorities, from the highest to the lowest. Many of the field officers who had joined the gendarme corps enjoyed living in the provinces, entirely independent, without any definite permanent occupation, and feared by everyone. They accepted information from the most ill-intentioned men—men expelled from decent society—and forwarded it to Petersburg with their own added comments. If investigation should prove their reports false, what would it matter? They might have erred from excess of zeal and they were in no way answerable for it. And where were the guberniia authorities, let alone private individuals, to seek protection against them when their chief, Benkendorf, was himself in a manner of speaking placed in surveillance of the other ministers? Our entire quiet, provincial, rural life was shaken by this development. It can well be imagined what . . . demoralization must have set in as a result.

In September this black cloud rose over Russia and darkened its horizon for many years to come. . . . And I would say under oath that I have not met a single man who would approve this institution, or who would speak of it without extreme displeasure.

C. THE DECEMBRIST MOVEMENT

XIII:39. WRITINGS OF P. I. PESTEL', CA. 1823-1825

Pavel Ivanovich Pestel' (1793-1826), a fast-rising young army officer and leader of the Southern Society, expressed most of his political ideas in his *Russkaia Pravda* (Russian law), begun around 1814 and completed in 1823-25. These excerpts are from that document and his *Konstitutsiia* (Constitution) which represented in part a condensation of the longer work. (Incidentally, the passage beginning "Finland, Estonia . . ." is omitted from the Soviet version published in 1951.)

Reference: Pavel I. Pestel', *Russkaia Pravda*, ed. and introd. P. Shchegolev (St. Petersburg: Izd. "Kul'tura," 1906), pp. 6, 14, 15-16, 21-24, 202-05 (omitting the "Constitution"). The same excerpts plus the "Constitution" are in I. Ia. Shchipanov, ed., *Izbrannye sotsial'no-politicheskie i filosofskie proizvedeniia dekabristov*, 3 vols. (Moscow: Gosudarstvennoe izdatel'stvo politicheskoi literatury, 1951), 2:80, 88-89, 90, 91-92, and (for the "Constitution") 161-62. See also M. V. Nechkina, ed., *Vosstanie dekabristov*, vol. 7 (Moscow: Gosudarstvennoe izdatel'stvo politicheskoi literatury, 1958), for a new edition of the *Russkaia Pravda*. Since the completion of the present translation there has appeared another which, while not complete, includes much more of the Russian Law than is given here. It is in Marc Raeff, comp., ed., and trans., *The Decembrist Movement* (Englewood Cliffs, N.J.: Prentice-Hall, 1966).

[From *Russkaia Pravda:*]

It is the immutable law of civil societies that every state consists of the people and the government. Hence, the people is not the government, and each of these has its own specific obligations and rights. However, the government exists for the good of the people and has no other reason for its existence and organization except the good of the people. On the other hand, the people exists for its own good and in order to fulfill the will of the All Highest, who has commanded man on earth to praise his name and to be virtuous and happy. This divine law was decreed for all men in equal measure, and consequently everyone has an equal right to its fulfillment. Therefore the Russian people is not the property of any one person or family. On the contrary, the government belongs to the people and has been established for the good of the people, and the people does not exist for the good of the government.

   · · ·

These two contradictory desires, one based on the national right of the subject peoples, and the other on the general welfare [*blagoudobstvo*] of the dominant people, are both quite natural. However, both have their limitations, and in their mutual relations there are instances when one should yield to the other. This shifting of the balance in favor of the national rights or of the general welfare should be determined by a third rule, or a third consideration: namely, that the general welfare should be invoked for the sake of security, and not for any vainglorious expansion of the boundaries of the state. Thus, peoples under the rule of a large state, who are incapable by reason of their weakness of enjoying political independence and who must therefore exist only under the rule or protection of one of the large neighboring states, cannot invoke their national right, since this right is for them fictitious and nonexistent. Moreover, the small peoples situated among larger ones always serve as a field for military action, ravage, and disasters of every kind. It will therefore be better and to their own greater benefit if they join a large state, both in spirit and social intercourse, and merge their nationality completely with the nationality of the dominant people, forming a single people with the latter and abandoning vain dreams of the impossible and un-

attainable. And the strong state, resting upon a great people, should always remember that its power has been granted to it by Providence, not in order to oppress its neighbors, but in order to act righteously and in accordance with pure justice; and that, although it has, of course, the unassailable right to establish strong boundaries, to join to itself, for the sake of the general welfare, peoples that are incapable of enjoying genuine nationality, and to undertake and arrange everything that is essential for its true security, it also has the obligation not to expand its boundaries merely for the satisfaction of its vanity; it must willingly admit into its own nationality the peoples it has joined to itself, so that they will not constitute within the state mere loosely associated appendages but will merge entirely into the general body of the state, forgetting their former feeble nationality and entering gladly into the new and greater nationality; finally, it must not oppose with hostile feelings and actions the rightful separate existence of peoples that are capable of enjoying full political independence.

   · · ·

Finland, Estonia, Livonia, Courland, Belorussia, Little Russia, New Russia [Novorossiia], Bessarabia, the Crimea, Georgia, the entire Caucasus, the lands of the Kirghiz, all the peoples of Siberia, and various other tribes that live within the [Russian] state have never enjoyed and never can enjoy their own independence; they have always belonged either to Russia or else, at certain times, to Sweden, Denmark, Prussia, Poland, Turkey, Persia, or in general to some strong state. Nor, because of their weakness, can they ever in the future constitute separate states; and therefore they must all subject themselves to the principle of the general welfare and in doing so must renounce the right of separate nationhood. In consequence of this, all the above-mentioned countries, with all the tribes inhabiting them, must submit to the general welfare for Russia, and must declare, in conformity with this and on the basis of this, that they shall remain component parts of the Russian state for all time to come.

   · · ·

Russia is a united and indivisible state. States can be either *indivisible* or *federative.*

   · · ·

The main difference . . . between indivisible and federative states is that the right to issue laws, form social institutions, and manage state affairs is vested in an indivisible state exclusively in the supreme authority, while in a federative state it is divided between the general supreme authority and the individual local powers. . . .

The general disadvantages of a federative form of government are, among many others, the following. . . . In a federative government, the supreme authority, in fact, does not issue laws but only recommendations; for it can carry its laws into effect only through the local powers, as it does not have its own compulsory means.

. . .

As for Russia in particular, in order fully to realize to what degree a federative form of government would be fatal to her, one need only remember how many heterogeneous parts make up this enormous state. Its oblasti not only are governed by different institutions and administer justice under different laws but also speak completely different languages and confess completely different faiths; their inhabitants are of different origins, having once belonged to different powers. . . . She would once again, then, experience all the calamities and ineffable harm brought on Russia by the system of independent principalities, which was also nothing but a kind of federative structure of government.

. . .

There has been much discussion about this civil distribution of land, with the arguments falling into two main bodies of opinion. According to the first opinion, man lives on land, can live only on land, and can obtain his sustenance only from land. The Almighty has created the human race on earth and has given the earth into its possession, so that the earth may feed it. Nature itself produces everything that may serve as food for man. Consequently, the land is the common property of all mankind and not of private individuals, and it cannot be divided among a few, with the exclusion of the rest. As long as there is even a single person who owns no land, the will of the Almighty and the law of nature are completely violated, and the natural rights of man are set aside by force and evil rule. . . . The second opinion, on the contrary, argues that work and labor are the sources of property and that he who has made the land

fertile and capable of producing various crops must have the sole right of its possession. Still another consideration is added to this view, namely, that the flourishing of agriculture requires many expenditures, and only those who hold the land in their full possession will be willing to make these expenditures; and that the uncertainty of possession inherent in the frequent transfer of land from hand to hand will never permit the improvement of agriculture. Hence all land should be the property of a few individuals, even if such a rule should exclude the majority from possession of land. These two opinions are in complete contradiction to one another, and yet each contains a good deal of truth and justice. . . .

The [best] method consists of the division of the land of each volost' into two halves. . . . One half will be known as public land, and the other half, as private land. The public land will belong in common to the people of the entire volost', as their inalienable property; it can be neither sold nor mortgaged. It will be used to supply necessities to all citizens without exception and will belong to each and all. The private lands will belong to the treasury or to private individuals, who will own them freely, with the full right to do with them as they please. These lands, intended for the formation of private property, will serve to provide abundance. The public land will satisfy the justifiable opinions of one segment of the public, and the private lands, the opinions of the other.

[From Pestel's *Konstitutsiia:*]

8. . . . Supreme authority shall be divided into legislative and supreme executive. The first shall be entrusted to the National Veche [assembly]; the second to the Supreme Duma. In addition a supervisory authority is also needed, so that these two shall not exceed their limits. Supervisory authority shall be entrusted to a Supreme Council [sobor].

9. The National Veche shall consist of representatives of the people, elected by the people for five years. Each year a fifth [of the representatives] shall leave office and be replaced through new elections. Representatives may be reelected. . . . The National Veche shall be a single body and shall not be divided into chambers. It shall possess all legislative authority. It shall declare war and conclude peace. . . .

. . . No one shall have the right to dissolve the National Veche. It shall embody the will of the state and the spirit of the people.

10. The Supreme Duma shall consist of five members, elected by the people for five years. Each year one member of the Duma shall leave office and be replaced through a new election. The chairman shall be that member who is holding office for his last, or fifth, year. Each year every guberniia shall nominate a candidate. From among these candidates the National Veche shall make the final selection. The Supreme Duma shall have all final executive authority, shall conduct wars and carry on negotiations, but shall not declare war or conclude peace. All ministries and government offices in general shall be under the jurisdiction and direction of the Supreme Duma. . . .

11. The Supreme Council shall consist of 120 members, called boyars. Boyars shall be appointed for life and may not participate in either legislative or executive functions. Candidates shall be nominated by the guberniias, and the National Veche shall then fill the vacancies among the boyars. The chairman shall be elected for a year by the Council itself. The Council shall have complete supervisory authority. To it the National Veche shall transmit its laws for confirmation. The Council shall not discuss matters as to their substance but shall merely examine their forms to see that due legality is being observed; [only] after such confirmation shall a law go into effect.

XIII:40. THE CONSTITUTION DRAFTED BY NIKITA MURAV'EV, 1824

The constitution prepared by Nikita Mikhailovich Murav'ev (1796-1843) for the Northern Society reveals another facet of Decembrist thinking, significantly different from that of the Southern Society under Pestel'. Murav'ev came from a prominent noble family; his father had tutored Alexander I in history, literature, and moral philosophy. The first version of Murav'ev's constitution was drafted in 1821-22. The second, from which these excerpts are taken, was a more polished product reflecting the advice of many of Murav'ev's co-believers. It dates from about the autumn of 1824.

Reference: Shchipanov, *Izbrannye proizvedeniia dekabristov*, 1:299-305, 308, 310-11, 313, 316-17, 321. Since the completion of the present translation there has appeared another which, while not complete, includes more of this document than is given here. It is in Raeff, *Decembrist Movement*, pp. 104-18.

CHAPTER I. Concerning the Russian people and the government.

1. The Russian people, free and independent, is not and cannot be the property of any person or family.

2. The people is the source of supreme power; it enjoys the sole right to legislate *basic laws* for itself. . . .

CHAP. II. Concerning the citizens.

3. Citizenship is the right to participate, in the manner defined in the present statute, in public government, *indirectly,* i.e. by electing an official or his electors, or *directly,* i.e. by being elected to some public position in the *legislative, executive,* or *judicial* branch of government. . . .

CHAP. III. On the status, personal rights, and duties of Russians.

10. All Russians are equal before the law.
. . .

13. Serfdom and slavery are abolished; a slave, having stepped on Russian soil, becomes a free man. The distinction between the well-born and the simple people is rejected as contrary to our faith, which tells us that all men are *brothers,* all are born *well* by the will of God, all were born *for good,* and all are *simple people,* for all are weak and imperfect. . . .

23. The right to property, pertaining *only to things,* is sacred and inviolable.

24. The lands of the landowners remain in their possession. The houses and gardens of the villagers are declared to be their property, along with all the agricultural implements and livestock belonging to them. . . .

28. The *military settlements* are to be immediately abolished. The settled battalions and squadrons and the relatives of the men in the ranks are to enter the category of general [property] *owners* [*obshchikh vladel'tsev*]. . . .

32. Citizens have the right to form any type of society or association without asking anyone's permission or approval, provided their activities are not contrary to the law. . . .

40. The present police officials are to be dismissed and replaced through election by the people. . . .

CHAP. IV. Concerning Russia.

43. With respect to legislative and executive functions, Russia is divided into 13 *derzhavy* [states], 2 oblasti, and 569 uezdy or *povety* [districts].

The entire population is estimated at 22,630,000 persons of the male sex, and its representation is computed accordingly. . . .

CHAP. V. Concerning the internal organization of the volost' and uezd or povet.

44. In each uezd those citizens who own real property with a value of [at least] five hundred rubles in silver, or movable property with a value of [at least] a thousand rubles in silver, shall assemble in the capital city of the uezd and elect a tysiatskii [thousand-man] for a one-year term.

45. Those who own property in common [referring here to the communal peasants] shall not have the right to participate individually in the election of the tysiatskii, national representatives, and other officials; instead, the entire commune in assembly shall have the right to appoint *one elector* for every five hundred male inhabitants, and these electors, appointed by those who own property in common, shall have equal voting rights with the other citizens, as *deputies from the entire commune.* . . .

CHAP. VI. Concerning the people's veche.

59. The People's Veche, consisting of the Supreme [Verkhovnaia] Duma and the Chamber of People's Representatives [Palata Narodnykh Predstavitelei], is vested with all the legislative power.

CHAP. VII. Concerning the Chamber of Representatives and the number and election of representatives.

60. The Chamber of People's Representatives consists of members elected for two years by the citizens of the derzhavy. . . .

CHAP. VIII. Concerning the Supreme Duma.

73. The Supreme Duma consists of three citizens from each derzhava, two citizens from the Moscow oblast', and one citizen from the Don oblast'—altogether, forty-two members. These members of the Supreme Duma are elected by the governing institutions of the derzhavy and oblasti [states and regions], i.e. by both the chamber of the electors and the dumas of the derzhavy, meeting together in one place. . . .

75. The requisite conditions for becoming a member of the Supreme Duma are: age— thirty; nine years of citizenship in Russia for foreigners, and residence, at the time of election, in the derzhava to be represented by the member; real estate worth 1,500 pounds of pure silver, or movable property worth 3,000 pounds of pure silver. . . .

77. . . . The Duma acts together with the emperor in concluding peace, in appointing judges of the higher courts, commanders in chief of land and marine forces, corps commanders, chiefs of squadrons, and the supreme guardian [*verkhovnyi bliustitel'*, apparently a procurator-general]. This requires a two-thirds majority of the members of the Duma.

CHAP. IX. Concerning the powers and privileges of the People's Veche and the promulgation of laws. . . .

89. Every proposal ratified by the [Supreme] Duma and the Chamber of People's Representatives must further be submitted to the *emperor* before it becomes *law*. If the emperor approves the proposal, he signs it; if he does not approve it, he returns it, with his comment, to that chamber [division of the Veche] where it was first presented. The chamber enters into its records all the emperor's remarks against the given proposal and reopens discussion concerning it. If two-thirds of the members remain in favor of the proposal after the second debate, it is transmitted, with the emperor's remarks, to the other chamber, which also reopens debate about it. Then, if the *majority* of the second chamber approves it, it thereby becomes *law*. . . .

CHAP. X. Concerning supreme executive power. . . .

101. The emperor is the chief official of the Russian government. His rights and privileges are:

a. His power is hereditary in a direct line from father to son, but from the father-in-law it passes to the son-in-law.

b. He unites in his person all executive powers.

c. He has the authority to halt the action of the legislative branch and to compel it to reexamine legislation for a second time. . . .

g. He conducts negotiations with foreign powers and concludes peace treaties, with the advice and consent of the Supreme Duma, contingent on the approval of two-thirds of the members present. . . .

j. He appoints judges to the higher courts, with the advice and consent of the Supreme Duma. . . .

CHAP. XI. Concerning the internal powers and the governments of the derzhavy.

115. The government of each derzhava consists of three separate and independent branches, cooperating toward a single objective, namely, the administrative, the executive, and the judicial branches.

XIII:41. THE DECEMBRIST MANIFESTO OF DECEMBER 13, 1825

This document, intended for proclamation by the Senate after the fall of the autocracy, was hastily drafted by Sergei Trubetskoi, "dictator" of the Decembrists. It contains elements illustrating their views of the present and their goals for the future.

Reference: Mikhail N. Pokrovskii, ed., *Vosstanie dekabristov*, 11 vols. (Moscow: Gosizdat, 1925-54), 1:107-08. The translation is based largely on that in Anatole G. Mazour, *The First Russian Revolution, 1825: The Decembrist Movement* (Berkeley: University of California Press, 1937), pp. 283-84. See also Raeff, *Decembrist Movement*, pp. 101-03.

There will be proclaimed in the Manifesto of the Senate:

1. The abolition of the former government.

2. The establishment of a provisional government until a permanent one is set up by elected representatives.

3. Freedom of the press, hence abolition of censorship.

4. Religious tolerance for all faiths.

5. The abolition of rights of possession that apply to human beings.

6. Equality of all estates [*sosloviia*] before the law and, therefore, the abolition of military courts and every type of judicial commission, which shall give over all their judicial functions to the appropriate civil courts.

7. The announcement of the right of every citizen to engage in whatever occupation he wishes. . . .

8. The cancellation of the poll tax and the arrears that have accumulated on it.

9. The abolition of the monopolies on salt, the sale of alcohol, and the like, and, consequently, free distillation and free salt mining with payment of an industrial tax according to the respective amounts of salt and alcohol produced.

10. The abolition of conscription and military colonies.

11. Reduction of the term of military service for the lower ranks, the determination of which will follow after all classes are equalized with respect to military service.

12. The retirement without exception of all of the lower ranks who have served fifteen years.

13. The establishment of volost', uezd, guberniia, and oblast' administrations, and the substitution in these administrations of elected members for all officials appointed up to now by the civil government.

14. Public trials.

15. The introduction of a jury system in criminal and civil courts.

A board [*pravlenie*] of two or three persons shall be established to which all sections of the upper administration shall be subordinated, such as all ministries, the Council, the committee of ministers, the army and navy: in a word, the entire supreme executive power, but by no means the legislative or the judicial. . . .

The provisional government is instructed to carry out the following:

1. The equalization of the rights of all estates.

2. The formation of local, volost', uezd, guberniia, and oblast' administrations.

3. The formation of a national guard.

4. The formation of a judicial branch with a jury system.

5. The equalization of military recruiting obligations among all classes.

6. The abolition of the standing army.

7. The establishment of a system for electing the representatives to the Chamber of National Deputies which must set up, in the future, state statutes and a permanent system of government.

XIII:42. TESTIMONY OF DECEMBRISTS P. G. KAKHOVSKII, A. A. BESTUZHEV, V. I. SHTEINGEIL', P. I. PESTEL', AND P. I. BORISOV, 1826

The new tsar personally supervised a commission that inquired into the revolt. More than five hundred persons were investigated. Of them, 121 were brought to trial before a special Supreme

Criminal Court upon which Speranskii played an active role. Much of what is known about the Decembrists comes from the records of the investigation and trial. Here are a few excerpts.

Reference: Aleksandr K. Borozdin, ed., *Iz pisem i pokazanii dekabristov* (St. Petersburg: M. V. Pirozhkov, 1906), pp. 3-18 [Kakhovskii's letter], 35-40 [Bestuzhev], 69-70 [Shteingeil']; Pokrovskii, *Vosstanie dekabristov,* 4:86, 91, 105 [Pestel']; 5:28, 30 [Borisov]. Most of the passages are included in Mazour, *First Russian Revolution,* pp. 273-80, in which cases the translation is based largely on that of Mazour. See also Raeff, *Decembrist Movement,* pp. 44-57.

[From a letter of Petr Grigor'evich Kakhovskii to General Levashev, February 24, 1826:]

One must seek the origin and the roots of the [Secret, in this case Northern] Society in the spirit of the time and in our state of mind. I know a few belonging to the Secret Society but am inclined to think the membership is not very large. However, among my many acquaintances who do not adhere to any secret societies, very few are opposed to my opinions. Frankly I can state that among thousands of young men there are hardly a hundred who do not passionately long for freedom. These youths, inflamed with a strong, pure passion for the welfare of their fatherland and for true enlightenment, are growing mature.

The peoples of the world have conceived a sacred truth—that they do not exist for governments, but that governments must be organized for them. This is the cause of struggle in all countries; people, after tasting the sweetness of enlightenment and freedom, strive toward them; and governments, entrenched behind millions of bayonets, attempt to repel these peoples back into the darkness of ignorance. But all these efforts will prove in vain; impressions once received can never be erased. Liberty, that torch of intellect and warmth of life, has always and everywhere been the attribute of peoples emerged from primitive ignorance. We are unable to live like our ancestors, like barbarians or slaves.

But even our ancestors, though less educated, enjoyed extensive civil liberties. During the time of Tsar Aleksei Mikhailovich, the great assemblies, including representatives of various classes of the state, still functioned and participated in important affairs of state.
. . .

Emperor Alexander promised us much; it could be said that, like a giant, he stirred the minds of the people toward the sacred rights of humanity. Later he altered his principles and intentions. The people became frightened,

but the seed had sprouted and the roots had grown deep. The latter half of the past century and the events of our own time are so full of various revolutions that we have no need to refer to more distant eras. We are witnesses to great events. The discovery of the New World, and the United States of America, by virtue of its form of government, have forced Europe into rivalry with her. The United States will shine as an example even to distant generations. The name of Washington, the friend and benefactor of the people, will be passed on from generation to generation; the memory of his devotion to the welfare of the fatherland will stir the hearts of citizens.

[From a letter from Aleksandr Aleksandrovich Bestuzhev to Nicholas I, undated:]
Your Imperial Majesty!

Convinced that you, Sovereign, love the truth, I dare to lay before you the historical development of free thinking in Russia and in general of many ideas which constitute the moral and political basis of the enterprise of December 14. . . .

The beginning of the reign of Emperor Alexander was marked by the brightest hopes for Russia's prosperity. The gentry had recuperated, the merchant class did not complain about credit, military service was not burdensome, scholars studied what they wished, all spoke what they thought, and everyone expected still better days. Unfortunately, circumstances did not permit it, and hopes aged without fulfillment. . . . Napoleon invaded Russia and only then did the Russian people for the first time become aware of their strength; only then awakened in all our hearts a feeling of at first political and later national independence. That was the beginning of free thinking in Russia. The government itself spoke the words "liberty, emancipation." . . . The army, from generals to privates, upon its return, did nothing but discuss how good things were abroad. A comparison with their own country naturally led to the question, "Why is it not so in our own country?"

. . . The ray of hope that the emperor would grant a constitution, as he himself had mentioned at the opening of the Diet [Seim] in Warsaw, and the attempt of some generals to free their serfs [raby] also encouraged many. But after 1817 everything changed. Those who recognized evils or who wished improvement were forced, because of the mass of spies, to hold their conversations secretly, and this was the beginning of the secret societies. The oppression of deserving officers by officialdom irritated men's minds. Then the military men began to talk: "Did we free Europe in order to be ourselves placed in chains? Did we grant a constitution to France in order that we dare not talk about it, and did we buy with our blood primacy among nations in order that we might be humiliated at home?" The abolition of normal schools and the persecution of education forced people to consider, in utter despair, serious measures. And since the grumbling of the people, caused by exhaustion and the abuse of local and civil powers, threatened a bloody revolution, the societies intended to prevent a greater evil by a lesser one and to begin their activities at the first suitable occasion.

· · ·

Extortions [by Russian judges] rose to an unheard-of degree of shamelessness. . . .

. . . Lucrative positions were sold at a fixed price and placed on obrok. The centralization of the judicial system, bringing every trifle to the higher courts, was conducive to appeals, inquiries, and retrials, and tens of years passed before a decision, meaning the ruin of both parties. In a word, in the treasury, in the courts, in the commissariats, among the governors, among the governor generals, everywhere where self-interest was involved, he who could, plundered, while he who did not dare to do that, pilfered. Everywhere, honest people suffered and slanderers and scoundrels rejoiced.

[From a letter of Vladimir Ivanovich Shteingeil' to Nicholas I, January 11, 1826:]

No matter how many members there may be found of the Secret Society or persons who had only known of it, no matter how

many may be deprived of freedom through this prosecution, there will still remain a great many more people who share those ideas and sentiments. Russia is already so educated that even shopkeepers read newspapers and newspapers report what is said in the Chamber of Deputies in Paris. Is not the first thought to occur in everyone's mind, "Why can we not discuss our rights?" The greatest number of professors, literary men, and journalists have to agree wholeheartedly with those who desire a constitutional government, for freedom of the press is to their personal advantage. So do booksellers and merchants. Finally, all those who have been in foreign countries, and some who were educated there, and all those who have served or who now serve in the Guards hold the same opinions. Who of the young men, even somewhat educated, have not read and been fascinated by the works of Pushkin, which breathe freedom? . . . Sovereign! In order to eradicate free thinking, there is no other means than to destroy an entire generation, born and educated in the last reign. But if this is impossible there remains one thing—to win hearts by kindness and attract minds by decisive and evident action toward the future prosperity of the state.

[Extracts from the testimony of Pestel' before Nicholas I, January 1826:]

A large part of the members did not like Nikita Murav'ev's constitution at all, since its two chief underlying elements seemed utterly ruinous. He proposed a federative system of government, such as in the United States of America. This resembled the old appanage system and thus seemed pernicious. The second element was that the right to hold administrative office and participate in public and state affairs was based on wealth, so that to hold office even in the uezd administration some wealth was necessary, and increasingly so the higher the office. This terrible aristocracy of wealth compelled many people, myself among them, to argue strongly against this constitution.

· · ·

From my original idea of a constitutional monarchy I turned to think in terms of a republic, chiefly because of the following subjects and considerations. The works of Destutt de Tracy in French had a very strong effect upon me. He demonstrates that any government where the head of state is a single person, particularly when this dignity is hereditary, inevitably ends in despotism. All the newspapers and political works so strongly extolled the growth of prosperity in the United States of North America, ascribing this to their system of government, that this seemed to me a clear proof of the superiority of republican government. . . . It seemed to me that the chief tendency of the present age is the struggle between the masses of the people and aristocracies of every kind, founded both on wealth and on hereditary right. I judged that the aristocracies would in the end become stronger than the monarch himself, as in England, and that they present the greatest obstacle to national prosperity and moreover that they may be eliminated only under a republican form of government. The events in Naples, Spain, and Portugal also had a great effect upon me at the time. In them I found what seemed to me indubitable proof of the instability of constitutional monarchies and full and sufficient reason to mistrust the sincerity of the consent of monarchs to constitutions they have accepted. These latter considerations greatly strengthened my republican and revolutionary train of thought. . . . What this did was to make me a republican in spirit, one who could visualize no greater prosperity and no greater blessings for Russia than in a republican form of government.

· · ·

[Question 6: How did the revolutionary ideas and principles grow and become implanted in men's minds? Who first conceived these ideas and continued to preach and spread them throughout the state?]

[Answer 6:] . . . A survey of the events of 1812, 1813, 1814, and 1815, as well as of the preceding and following periods, reveals how many thrones have been toppled, how many others set up, how many kingdoms have been destroyed, and how many new ones created; how many sovereigns have been expelled, how many returned or invited to return and then again driven out; how many revolutions have been accomplished; how many coups d'état carried out. All these events have familiarized the minds of men with the idea of revolutions, of their possibilities and the favorable conditions under which to execute them. Besides that, every century has its peculiar characteristic. Ours is marked by revolutionary ideas. From one end of Europe to the other one finds the same thing—from Portugal to Russia, without excepting a single state, not even those two opposites, England and Turkey. The whole of America presents the same spectacle. The spirit of reform causes minds everywhere to seethe (*faire bouillir les esprits*). Here, I maintain, are the causes that gave rise to revolutionary ideas and principles and implanted them in the peoples' minds.

As to the cause of the spread of this spirit of reform throughout the [Russian] state, this cannot be ascribed to the society, for the organization was still too small to have any popular influence of this sort; but, if, indeed, there occurred a dissemination of these ideas, then, I maintain, it must be attributed to the above-mentioned factors which influenced the minds of the ordinary populace as well as those of the members of the society.

[From the testimony of Petr Ivanovich Borisov, spring 1826:]

Inflamed by such dreams [of serving mankind] and having met, in 1823, the Pole Liublinskii, who seemed to me at the beginning an experienced man, I proposed to my brother [Andrei] that we form a secret society whose goal would be the overthrow of the government—in the distant future and without serious upset—and that we invite the above-mentioned Pole, as a man with valuable knowledge, to join. After some thought, we revealed this to Liublinskii, who gave me his word, in response to my urging, to assist in the organization of such a society. To unite all the Slavic peoples and to make them free appeared to me a magnificent undertaking, for I thought thereby to bring happiness not only to my compatriots but even to other peoples as well. The principles and the solemn oath I had drawn up were translated into Polish by Liublinskii, which was his only action in assisting the establishment of a Slavic Union.

· · ·

The objective of the United Slavs [founded by Borisov] was to unite the Slavic peoples in a federative union and to build a city in the center of the union to which the Slavic peoples would send their deputies and which would be the seat of the chief administration of the federative union. On the coasts of the seas adjoining Slavic lands, we hoped to found commercial ports. We had no reliable means toward the achievement of this objective. Our sole activities were to increase our members and educate ourselves in the sciences and arts. I could do nothing more than draw up an outline of the goals of this society. It was left to time and fate to bring it into realization.

XIII:43. EXPLAINING THE DECEMBRISTS: IAKUSHKIN ON THE MILITARY SETTLEMENTS

Another valuable source on the ideas and activities of the Decembrists is the "Notes" of Ivan Dmitrievich Iakushkin (1793-1857), one of the founders of the Union of Salvation and a member of the Northern Society. Iakushkin's "Notes" were dictated by him to his sons in Siberia in 1853-55. In this brief excerpt he deals with one policy that influenced the attitudes of many of the Decembrists. (For Alexander's orders on the military settlements, see Item 32 in this chapter.)

Reference: Shchipanov, *Izbrannye proizvedeniia dekabristov,* 1:105.

A new evil was added to all that already plagued Russia: Emperor Alexander, who had long planned to establish military settlements, began now [ca. 1818] to carry out his plans. Count Arakcheev was entrusted with the execution of the projects for the military settlements, which had been drawn up by the tsar himself. Always proud of being merely the faithful tool of the autocracy, Count Arakcheev did not fail himself on this occasion. In the Novgorod guberniia, the state peasants of those volosti destined for the first military settlements sensed trouble for themselves and, warned by the quick instinct of the Russian people, broke out in rebellion. Count Arakcheev sent out the cavalry and artillery against them. The peasants were shot at and cut down by swords; many were forced to run the gauntlet; and in the end the poor people had to submit. . . . The news of the events in Novgorod horrified everybody.

The emperor Alexander, in Europe the patron and practically the leader of the liberals, was in Russia not only a cruel, but still worse a senseless, despot.

Changings of the guard, parades, and military reviews were almost his only occupations; he concerned himself solely with the military settlements and the construction of great highways throughout Russia, sparing in the process neither the money, nor the sweat, nor the blood of his subjects.

XIII:44. THE MEMOIRS OF M. A. FONVIZIN ON THE DECEMBRIST MOVEMENT

These retrospective observations on the Decembrist movement were made by Mikhail Aleksandrovich Fonvizin (1788-1854), leader of the Decembrists in Moscow, in the form of notes on a history of Russia published in France in 1835.

Reference: Mikhail A. Fonvizin, "Obozrenie proiavlenii politicheskoi zhizni v Rossii," in *Obshchestvennye dvizheniia v Rossii v pervuiu polovinu XIX veka,* vol. 1 (St. Petersburg: Tipolitografiia Gerol'd, 1905), pp. 102, 180-85, 193, 194, 197, 198.

Our forebears, the Slavs, were, like their Germanic neighbors, a half-savage but free people, and the democratic—the communal—element was predominant in their social life.

In the Middle Ages the Western Slavic tribes, disunited from time immemorial, were unable to resist the onslaught of the more warlike Germanic peoples [from the time of Charlemagne] and were subjugated by them. The eastern half of the Slavic world, Poland and Russia, remained independent. The former, a neighbor of the Germanic states, adopted their feudal, aristocratic order, which favored, if not the majority of the people, at least estates and individuals; and this order, guaranteeing their rights and freedoms, contained the seeds of future political development. Russia remained true to its indigenous Slavic element, the free communal order, based on purely democratic foundations.

The ancient free communities of Novgorod, Pskov, and Khlynov (Viatka), in which the Slavic element followed its own unique development, furnish incontrovertible proof of this.

Under the protection of this political and civil freedom, these popular states developed democratic institutions under which they lived an independent and prosperous life.

·   ·   ·

After the overthrow of Napoleon, the principal aim of all political actions of Emperor Alexander was the suppression of the spirit of freedom emerging everywhere and the strengthening of monarchic principles which were threatened by secret societies. All Alexander's government and diplomatic acts, beginning with the Holy Triple Alliance between Russia, Austria, and Prussia, concluded on September 14, 1815, attest to this.

. . .

In 1821 the emperors Alexander and Francis and the kings of Prussia and Naples, with their ministers and diplomats, met in Laibach [Ljubljana]. The congress resolved: to suppress the revolution in Naples, as a result of which the king adopted the proposed constitution and took an oath to observe it scrupulously; and to prevent by force the uprising in Piedmont against the king of Sardinia. The Austrian army was entrusted with the task of carrying out the resolution of the congress concerning Naples and Piedmont. Word of the insurrection of the Greeks reached Laibach, and Alexander, who had hitherto not only favored their liberation but had, through secret agents, incited them to rebellion, now blamed the Greek uprising on the demagogic schemes of European revolutionaries, expressed a readiness to suppress it by force, and sent assurances of this to the sultan himself.

The Verona Congress of 1822 confirmed Alexander in this cruel policy against his fellow believers. At Verona he, together with his allies, the emperor of Austria and the kings of Prussia and France, agreed to go to war against Spain, which had liberated itself from the despotic rule of Frederick VII, in order to restore absolute power to Frederick, and to make peace with the Sultan of Turkey, to whom the Congress of Verona betrayed the Greeks. This latter action provoked among Russians general indignation against Alexander for his inhuman indifference to the sufferings of their fellow believers, the Greeks, who had the right to expect of him not only sympathy but also active assistance, especially since Russia had from ancient times incited the Greeks against their oppressors and promised them independence.

But the spirit of freedom, which the governments of all European states acting in unison sought in every way to suppress, blew over autocratic Russia as well. Its younger generation, which entered public life during the first ten years of Alexander's reign and was reared under the influence of the freedom-loving principles he then proclaimed, fully realized how far Russia, as a truly civilized state, lagged behind Europe. However, loving and respecting Alexander and zealously preparing to assist him, it calmly awaited a beneficent transformation [of the state] at his hands.

The two unsuccessful wars with Napoleon, and the third, which threatened Russia's independence in 1812, compelled [the young] Russian patriots to devote themselves exclusively to the military calling in defense of the fatherland. The nobility, distressed as patriots over the decline of our military glory in the wars with France in 1805 and 1807, and foreseeing an imminent rupture with her, hastened to enter the ranks of the army, ready to meet Napoleon. All honorable and educated young men [of the nobility], disdaining civilian service, entered only the military. On the eve of 1812 young privy councillors and actual state councillors eagerly transferred into the army as lieutenant colonels and majors. The great events of that year [1812], the famous expulsion from Russia of the hitherto unconquerable emperor of France and the annihilation of his countless hosts, the subsequent campaigns of 1813 and 1814 and the taking of Paris in which our army played such an active part—all this raised extraordinarily the spirit of our troops and especially of our young officers.

. . .

It was in this mood, with a sense of their own worth and heightened devotion to the fatherland, that the greater part of our Guards officers and of the general staff returned to Petersburg in 1815. During the campaigns in Germany and France our young men had become acquainted with European civilization, which impressed them all the more since they were able to compare everything they saw abroad with what they encountered at every step at home—the slavery of the vast majority of Russians, the cruel treatment of subordinates by their superiors, every kind of abuse of power, and the arbitrariness that reigned everywhere. All this aroused the indignation of educated Russians and outraged their patriotic feelings. During the campaign many of them had met German officers and French liberals, members of the Prussian secret society (the Tugendbund), which had so successfully prepared the uprising in Prussia and furthered its liberation. In frank discussions with them our young men, ashamed of a Russia that was so greatly debased by autocracy, imperceptibly adopted their free manner of thinking and desire for constitutional government.

Returning to Petersburg, our liberals could not remain content with the trivial regimental life and the tedious petty tasks and details of army drill which were strictly demanded of them by their superiors, who sought in this way to please the innate fondness of Alexander and his brothers for drill, men at attention, individual training, and so forth, although the experience of two years of bitter warfare against a most skillful enemy might have convinced Alexander, it seems, that victory did not depend on these trifles. Moreover, the Russians were offended by the obvious preference the emperor showed, in general, to all foreigners over his own subjects, whom he openly treated with disrespect; he granted annexed Poland constitutional rights of which he considered Russia unworthy.

· · ·

However, nothing at the end of the war provoked as much public indignation against Alexander, not only among liberals but throughout Russia, as the compulsory establishment of military settlements. . . .

Of all the actions of the emperor Alexander after the change in his point of view, the establishment of military settlements was the most despotic and hateful.

· · ·

At that time many officers of the Guards and the general staff studied and read avidly political works and especially journals, as well as foreign newspapers, which reflected so dramatically the conflict of the opposition with the government in constitutional states. Those who engaged in the study of bold political systems and theories quite naturally wished to see them applied in their fatherland. And this was the main aim of the activities of the secret political societies which had spread throughout Europe, and whose members devoted themselves exclusively to politics. The statutes of some of these associations in France and Germany were brought to Russia, and they suggested to our liberals the idea of

organizing a secret political society in our country, aimed at limiting the autocracy. At the end of 1816 this plan was realized.

· · ·

[In December 1825:] The secret society was convinced that the Guards regiments, which had so many reasons for disliking Grand Duke Nicholas—because of his cruel treatment of officers and soldiers, and because of his endless petty fault-finding during drill—would act as one with the secret society, especially since persons who held the same views as its members were scattered throughout the Guards. The plan called for the Guards to oppose Grand Duke Nicholas's accession to the throne; power would then remain in the hands of the secret society, which would compel the Senate, together with the Synod, to appoint a provisional government which would be formed by two universally respected dignitaries, known for their free thinking and patriotism: Admiral N. S. Mordvinov and M. M. Speranskii. Both knew of the existence of the secret society and of its secret objectives; they were personally acquainted with some of its members and were well disposed toward them. The first act of the provisional government was to have been the convocation of representatives of all the free estates [*sosloviia*] in Russia, who would decide Russia's future destiny and form of government.

· · ·

That same night [December 13], the grand duke summoned to the palace the commanders of the Guards regiments (including one member of the secret society, General Shipov) and won them to his side by flattering persuasions, by promising rewards, and so forth. The generals of the Guards hastened to their regiments and had time even before daybreak to administer the oath of allegiance to the Emperor Nicholas I, knowing that they would bind the conscience of their soldiers thereby. By this happy stratagem, Nikolai Pavlovich succeeded in averting the danger threatening him.

· · ·

If the detachments that came out on Senate Square had had an enterprising and audacious leader, and if instead of remaining inactive on Senate Square he had boldly led it to the palace before the Guards regiments arrived, he could easily have taken prisoner the entire imperial family. With such hostages in its hands, final victory might well have come to the secret society.

· · ·

The investigating committee began its work. Many people were arrested in Saint Petersburg on suspicion of membership in the secret societies; others were sent from all corners of Russia to the fortress of Saints Peter and Paul. At first the emperor conducted some interrogations himself in the palace; the accused were brought to him with hands tied behind their backs with ropes, as if into a police station rather than a tsar's chambers. The sovereign of Russia, forgetting his dignity, allowed himself to hurl abuse upon defenseless men who were completely in his power and threatened them with cruel punishment. The secret investigating committee, composed of servile courtiers,

acted in the same inquisitional spirit.

. . . Those who failed to give the desired answers, either through ignorance of the events about which they were asked or from fear of bringing ruin to the innocent by some incautious word, were transferred to a dark and damp prison cell, were given nothing but bread and water to eat, and were burdened with heavy arm and leg irons.

· · ·

By the last weeks of the sessions of the investigation committee, the number of persons suspected of participation in the secret societies had risen so high that the government itself ordered the committee to limit its investigations to those persons whom it deemed the most guilty and to exclude the rest from investigation. In the course of six months about two thousand people were arrested on suspicion in various places.

XIII:45. THE MEMOIRS OF A. E. ROZEN ON THE DECEMBRIST MOVEMENT

These excerpts are from the memoirs of Andrei Evgen'evich Rozen (1799-1884), one of the Decembrists who was exiled to Siberia.

Reference: A. E. Rozen, *Zapiski dekabrista* (St. Petersburg: Obshchestvennaia Pol'za, 1907), pp. 57, 63, 66, 70, 71, 122.

For the young Russian nobles serving in the Guards regiments, the campaigns [of 1813-15] in Germany and France were like an entrance into a new cultural world which heretofore only single individuals or private persons had had any conception of. . . . The struggle of the numerous political parties then existing in France found its most avid and intelligent spectators and listeners among the young foreigners.

It was precisely the most talented and active of the young Russian guardsmen who enthusiastically imbibed the ideas of civic consciousness, freedom, and constitutional rights and attentively and admiringly entered into the life of the nation they had come from the remote east to pacify. Many began to consider the possibility of transmitting to their homeland the best of the constructive reforms, and with the fiery enthusiasm of youth they leaped across the wide chasm separating the levels of Russian and French cultural development.

When the final hour of their sojourn in France had struck, the flower of the Guards officer corps returned home with the intention of transplanting France in Russia. Thus

in most of the best regiments Masonic lodges of a purely political cast were formed. When these lodges were closed and abolished, their members came together in secret societies which had the goal of obtaining a constitutional regime for Russia. They all knew that the emperor Alexander had himself formed this intention, and they thought they would be acting in his spirit by undertaking preparatory measures. But Alexander, frightened by the liberal movements in Germany, changed the course of his policy, and the young nobles in the regiments were left in a position clearly at variance with the dominant system. Various restraining measures proved fruitless, since some of the soldiers had been infected with the French poison and desired the same sort of treatment to which they had become accustomed in France. The most ardent of the conspirators finally turned to a republican ideal.

· · ·

On the evening of December 12 [1825], I was invited to the homes of Ryleev and Prince Obolenskii for conferences; there I found the chief participants in [the events of] December 14. It was decided to gather in Senate Square on the day appointed for taking the new oath of allegiance, to lead there as many of the troops as possible under the pretense of supporting the rights of Constantine, [and] to entrust command to Prince Trubetskoi, unless [General] M. F. Orlov should arrive from Moscow by that time. If our side should be stronger, we would proclaim the abolition of the monarchy and immediately establish a provisional government consisting of five persons, chosen by the members of the State Council and Senate. Among the five, the names of I. S. Mordvinov, M. M. Speranskii, and P. I. Pestel' were proposed in advance. The provisional government would direct all affairs of state with the assistance of the Council and Senate, until such time as elected representatives from the entire Russian land could gather and lay the foundation for a new government. . . . The measures adopted for the uprising were unclear and indefinite, and thus to certain of my objections and remarks Prince Obolenskii and Bulatov replied ironically: "After all, we can't very well stage rehearsals!" All of those present were ready to act; all were full of enthusiasm; all hoped for success; and only one in the entire group surprised me by his spirit of utter self-sacrifice. He asked me privately if the assistance of the first and second battalions of our regiment [the Finland Guards Regiment] could be relied upon; and when I described to him all the obstacles and difficulties, and the near impossibility [of success], he said to me with a singular expression on his face and in his voice, "Yes, there is not much chance of success, but we must make a start all the same, we must do this all the same. Our initiative and example will bear fruit." I still hear those sounds, that tone of voice: "We must do this all the same." It was Kondratii Fedorovich Ryleev who said this to me.

· · ·

There were altogether more than two thousand soldiers in Senate Square taking part in the uprising. Under the command of a single leader this strength, in view of the thousands of people gathered around and ready to give help, might have been decisive, the more so since in the event of an attack many battalions would have joined the rebels, who stood without their overcoats in a cold of −10 degrees [Centigrade], in newly fallen snow and with a sharp wind from the east,

remained passive, and kept warm only by continual shouts of "Hurrah!" The dictator [Prince S. P. Trubetskoi] was nowhere to be seen, nor were his assistants on the spot. Command was offered to Bulatov: he refused; then to N. A. Bestuzhev: he refused on the grounds that he was a naval officer; finally command was thrust upon Prince E. P. Obolenskii, not as a tactician but as an officer whom the soldiers knew and liked. There was anarchy in the full meaning of the word; in the absence of any instructions everyone could give commands, everyone was waiting for something, and while waiting they jointly repelled attacks, stubbornly refused to surrender, and proudly rejected any offer of pardon.

· · ·

But the success of the intended venture was possible, taking all factors into consideration. Two thousand soldiers, and ten times that many onlookers, were ready for anything at a leader's beckoning. . . . Meanwhile time was passing; there was no unity of command: thus instead of acting our forces remained purely passive. The troops of the Moscow [Guards] Regiment stood firm and repelled five attacks by the Horse Guards. The soldiers yielded neither to threats nor to inducements. They did not waver in the presence of the metropolitan [Serafim of Saint Petersburg], who came out in full vestments and with a cross, imploring them in the name of the Lord. This force stood motionless in the cold and without overcoats for several hours, at a time when it could have seized the cannon loaded against it. The cannon stood nearby under cover of a platoon of the Chevalier Guards, commanded by a member of the secret society, I. A. Annenkov.

· · ·

The investigating committee did not wish to understand the difference between an actual uprising, on one hand, and, on the other, an intention of staging an uprising or an intention of assassinating the tsar; it not only condemned the rebels for their actions but also viewed as crimes their criminal words and phrases which had nothing to do with the uprising or even opposed an uprising. The investigating committee imposed shameful sentences of death and exile not only upon the participants in the uprising but also upon those who had desired an uprising or had merely discussed an uprising without taking any actual part in it. It found equally guilty those who had rebelled and those who had merely discussed rebellion.

XIII:46. THE MEMOIRS OF I. I. GORBACHEVSKII ON THE SOCIETY OF UNITED SLAVS

An organization of young, idealistic nobles, the United Slavs were drawn into the orbit of the Southern Society late in 1825. Their political philosophy differed somewhat from that of their colleagues in revolution, as is illustrated in these excerpts from a valuable source on the Society of the United Slavs, the memoirs of Ivan Ivanovich Gorbachevskii (1800-69). This work, the product of the author's long Siberian exile, was based not only on his personal recollections but also on extensive consultations with his fellow revolutionaries; hence it approaches the status of a research monograph.

Reference: I. I. Gorbachevskii, *Zapiski i pis'ma dekabrista,* ed. B. E. Syroechkovskii (Moscow: Gosizdat, 1925), pp. 56-57, 58-59, 83. See also (for the oath): Pokrovskii, *Vosstanie dekabristov,* 5:17-18.

[Gorbachevskii is telling about a meeting of the United Slavs in September 1825 for the purpose of electing an intermediary with the Southern Society:]

Wishing to acquaint the readers with the spirit of the Society of United Slavs, we shall ... set forth in a few words the society's objectives and principles.

The main objective of the society was the liberation of all Slavic peoples from absolutism, the eradication of the national enmities existing among some of them, and the bringing of all the lands they inhabited into a federative union. It advocated the exact delineation of the boundaries of each state, the introduction of a form of democratic representative government for all the peoples, and the establishment of a congress to administer the union's affairs and to make necessary changes in the fundamental general laws, while allowing each state to concern itself with its own internal organization and to establish its own laws independently.

. . .

Their faith in these principles induced the Slavs to draw the following conclusions:

1. No revolution can succeed without the consent and cooperation of the entire nation; therefore, it is necessary first of all to prepare the people for a new type of civic life and only afterward should it be given them.

2. The people can be free only if it becomes moral, enlightened, and industrial [*promyshlennyi*]. Although military revolutions attain the goal more rapidly, their results are dangerous: they may become, not the cradle, but the grave of freedom, in whose name they were carried out.

Convinced that their hopes could not be realized as quickly as they would wish, the [United] Slavs did not want to waste time in futile and impossible efforts but resolved to do everything that was within their power and that led, though slowly, to their goal. To fulfill these intentions, they decided to allot a certain portion of their funds to buy serfs their freedom; to attempt to organize or aid in the organization of small village and rural schools; to instill in peasants and soldiers a feeling for the necessity of knowing justice and a love for the fulfillment of a citizen's duties, thereby arousing in them the desire to alter the degrading condition of slavery, and so forth.

However, despite these gradual and peaceful methods, the Slavic Union bore the imprint of a certain militancy. The solemn oath, which bound the members to dedicate all their thoughts and actions to the welfare and freedom of their fellow Slavs, and to give up their entire lives to the attainment of this goal, was taken under arms. The Slavs relied only on their friends and on arms for the fulfillment of their desires. The idea that freedom is bought, not by tears nor by gold, but by blood was rooted in their hearts, and the words of the famous republican who said, "When you bare the sword against your sovereign, you must cast the scabbard as far away as possible," were to serve as a guide for their future conduct. [Gorbachevskii adds a footnote: "These resolutions and principles of the Slavic Union were examined solely in order to transmit them to the Southern Society without error, so that the latter might find in them the precepts that had received the approval of all (United) Slav members, a pledge of their future conduct, and the basic ideas of the society."]

. . .

[At another meeting a few days later, September 15, Gorbachevskii records himself as saying:] "In addition . . . every commander has so many methods at his disposal that if the soldiers do not follow him at the time of the uprising, this would certainly be the commander's own fault and should be ascribed only to his unwillingness or simple negligence."

S. Murav'ev replied that in his opinion the best means of influencing Russian soldiers was through religion, that fanaticism must be aroused in them, and that the reading of the Bible could inspire them with hatred toward the government.

. . .

[Gorbachevskii quotes the membership oath of the United Slavs:]

Upon joining the United Slavs for the liberation of myself from tyranny and for the restoration of freedom, which is so precious to the human race, I solemnly pledge on these arms mutual brotherly love, which is to me divine and from which I expect the fulfillment of all my desires. I swear to be always virtuous, always loyal to our aim, and to observe the deepest secrecy. Hell itself with all its horrors will not be able to

compel me to reveal to the tyrants my friends and their aims. I swear that only when a man proves undoubted desire to become a participant will my lips reveal the name of this society; I swear, to the last drop of my blood, to my last breath, to assist you, my friends, from this sacred moment. Special activities will be my first virtue, and mutual love and aid my sacred duty. I swear that nothing in the world will be able to move me. With sword in hand I will attain the aim designated by us. I will pass through a thousand deaths, a thousand obstacles—I will pass through, and dedicate my last breath to freedom and the fraternal union of the noble Slavs. Should I violate this oath, then let remorse be the first vengeance for my oath-breaking, let the point of this sword turn against my heart and fill it with hellish torment; let the moment of my life that is injurious to my friends be the last one; let my existence be transformed into a chain of unprecedented misfortunes from the fatal moment that I forget my pledge. May I see all that is dear to my heart perish by this weapon and in horrible suffering, and may this weapon, reaching me, the criminal, cover me with wounds and infamy. . . .

XIII:47. NICHOLAS I'S OWN ACCOUNT OF THE EVENTS OF DECEMBER 14, 1825

This account is valuable for what it tells both about the uprising and about the personality and viewpoint of Nicholas himself.

Reference: *Mezhdutsarstvie 1825 goda i vosstanie dekabristov v memuarakh i perepiske chlenov tsarskoi sem'i* (Moscow: Gosizdat, 1926), pp. 24-27.

The insurgents were standing in formation in a close irregular column, with their backs to the old Senate building. At that time there was still only the one Moscow [Guards] regiment. Suddenly, several shots rang out: they were firing, but without success, at General Voinov as he approached, wishing to talk to the men. . . .

. . . With Adjutant General Benkendorf, who had joined me, [I] rode out upon the square to examine the position of the rebels. They greeted me with shots.

. . .

At this time I learned that in the Izmailovskii Regiment there were disorders and a reluctance to swear the oath of allegiance. As grieved as I was by this, I definitely did not consider it authentic, but attributed it to

those same plots; therefore, I ordered Adjutant General Levashov, who had reported to me, to proceed to the regiment and, if at all possible, to move it—even, if need be, against me—but by all means to bring it out of the barracks. Meanwhile, realizing that the situation was becoming quite serious and still not foreseeing how it would end, I sent Adlerberg with orders to my equerry Prince Dolgorukov to prepare traveling carriages for my mother and my wife. I intended, in an emergency, to send them and the children to Tsarskoe Selo under the protection of the Horse Guards. I myself, having sent for the artillery, set out for Palace Square in order to secure the palace, to which two sapper battalions—a guards and a training battalion—had been ordered to proceed directly. Before I reached the general staff building, I saw the regiment of Guards Grenadiers, in complete disorder, walking in a body with their colors but without officers. Suspecting nothing, I approached them, wanting to stop the men and place them in formation, but when I called out "Halt!" they replied: "We're for Constantine!"

I indicated to them Senate Square and said: "In that case, that's your way."

And the entire throng walked past me, through all the troops, and joined without hindrance their equally misguided comrades. This was fortunate, for otherwise bloodshed would have begun under the windows of the palace, and our fate would have been more than doubtful. . . .

God's mercy was even more striking on the same occasion, when a throng of Guards Grenadiers, led by officer Panov, set out with the intention of taking the palace and killing our entire family, if they met with resistance. They reached the main gates of the palace in some semblance of a formation, so that the commandant mistook them for a unit sent by me to occupy the palace. Suddenly, Panov, walking at the head [of the detachment], noticed the Guards sapper battalion, which had only just had time to run in and form a column in the courtyard. Shouting, "But these are not our men!" he began to turn around the detachments which were entering and together with them fled back to the square. Had the sapper battalion been only a few minutes late, the palace and our entire family would have fallen into the hands of the insurgents, while I, occupied with the events in Senate Square and completely unaware of this grave danger threatening in the rear, would have been deprived of any possibility of preventing it.

· · ·

Returning to the troops, I found the artillery had arrived, but, unfortunately, without shells, which were stored at the arsenal. While they were being sent for, the rebellion was growing. The entire Guards equipage [sailors of the Guards] entered on the Galernaia [a street running into Senate Square] side and joined the initial group. The Moscow regiment and a crowd of Grenadiers posted themselves on the other side. The noise and shouting became incessant, and frequent shots were fired over the heads of the crowd. Finally, the people, too,

began to waver, and many deserted to the rebels, in front of whom we could see civilians. In a word, it was clear that misgiving concerning the oath of allegiance was not the real cause of the uprising; the existence of another, most serious conspiracy was growing obvious.

· · ·

The weather, which had been damp, was turning colder. There was very little snow; hence it was quite slippery. It began to grow darker, for it was already three in the afternoon. The noise and shouting grew more and more insistent, and the frequent rifle shots wounded many in the Horse Guards and flew over the heads of the troops; most of the soldiers on the side of the insurgents shot in the air.

I rode out into the square, wishing to determine whether it would be possible, by surrounding the crowd, to force it to surrender without bloodshed. The rebels fired a volley at me; bullets whistled over my head, but fortunately none of us was wounded. The workmen of the Cathedral of Saint Isaac began to throw logs at us from behind the fences. One had to decide to end this quickly; otherwise the rebellion could spread to the mob, and then the troops surrounded by it would be in a most difficult situation.

I agreed to try a cavalry attack. The Horse Guards attacked first by squadrons but could not accomplish anything because of the lack of room, because of the ice-covered ground, and particularly because their broadswords had not been sharpened. The enemy, drawn up in a tight column, had all the advantage on its side, and many of our men were seriously wounded, including Captain Velio, who lost a hand. The Kavalergardskii Regiment likewise attacked, but without much success.

Then Adjutant General Vasil'chikov turned to me and said:

"Sire, il n'y a pas un moment à perdre; l'on n'y peut rien maintenant; il faut de la mitraille!" ["Sire, there's not a moment to lose; there is nothing else to do now. We must use grapeshot!"]

I had foreseen the necessity of this, but, I confess, when the time came, I could not make up my mind to such a measure. I was terror stricken.

"Vous voulez que je verse le sang de mes sujets le premier jour de mon règne?" ["Do you wish me to spill the blood of my subjects on the first day of my reign?"] I replied to Vasil'chikov.

"Pour sauver votre Empire" ["In order to save your empire"], he answered me.

These words brought me back to myself; coming to my senses, I saw that I must either take it upon myself to spill the blood of a few and almost surely save everything, or *spare myself* at the cost of definitely sacrificing the state.

Sending one gun of the First Light Unmounted Battery to Mikhail Pavlovich in order to reinforce his side, the sole path of retreat for the insurgents, I took three other guns, placed them before the Preobrazhenskii Regiment, and ordered them loaded with

grapeshot; the guns were under the command of Staff Captain Bakunin.

All my hopes were that the mutineers would be intimidated by these preparations and, seeing no other way of saving themselves, would surrender. But they remained firm; their shouting continued still more persistently. At last, I sent Major General Sukhozanet to announce to them that, unless they put down their arms at once, I would give the order to fire. They replied with shouts of "Hurrah" and the same exclamations as before, and after that with a volley.

At that point, seeing no other alternative, I ordered: "Fire!"

XIII:48. THE COURT REPORT ON THE PUNISHMENT OF THE DECEMBRISTS, JULY 13, 1826

This is an excerpt from the report of the Supreme Criminal Court to the tsar. The effect of the sentences on the public was heightened because capital punishment had not been used as a legal penalty in Russia for fifty years, since the time of Pugachev.

Reference: *PSZRI,* 2d ser., 1:759, 772. Since the completion of the present translation there has appeared another which, while not complete, includes much more of this document than is given here. It is in Raeff, *Decembrist Movement,* pp. 169-75.

From this list, Your Imperial Majesty will graciously observe:

1. That, of the 121 defendants sentenced by the Supreme Criminal Court [Verkhovnyi Ugolovnyi Sud], 5 persons designated outside the categories are condemned to death by quartering; 31 persons, in the first category, are condemned to death by beheading; 17 persons, in the second category, are sentenced to civil death, exiled for life at hard labor [*katorzhnaia rabota*]; 2 persons, in the third category, are exiled to hard labor for life; 38 persons, in the fourth, fifth, sixth, and seventh categories, are sentenced to hard labor for specified terms, and then to penal settlement [*poselenie*]; 15 persons, in the eighth category, upon divestment of their rank and nobility, are sentenced to penal settlement for life; 3 persons, in the ninth category, upon divestment of their rank and nobility, are sentenced to banishment to Siberia for life; 1 person, in the tenth category, upon divestment of his rank and nobility,

is sentenced to service as a common soldier until he earns promotion; 8 persons, in the eleventh category, upon divestment of their rank, are sentenced to service as soldiers with the right to earn promotion.

· · ·

Extract from the Protocol of the Supreme Criminal Court, of July 11, 1826:

· · ·

In accordance with the powers vested in it by imperial authority, the Supreme Criminal Court has decreed: instead of the painful execution by quartering, to which the court sentenced Pavel Pestel', Kondratii Ryleev, Sergei Murav'ev-Apostol, Mikhail Bestuzhev-Riumin, and Petr Kakhovskii, these criminals are to hang for their grave crimes.

[Note: The sentence of the 31 in the "first category" (above) was commuted from death to hard labor either "for life" or for twenty years. Actually by 1839 all sentences to hard labor had been commuted to lesser punishments.]

CHAPTER XIV

Nicholas I,
1825-1855

A. POLITICAL DEVELOPMENTS

XIV:1. THE DECREE ESTABLISHING THE THIRD SECTION, JULY 3, 1826

Six months after the Decembrist uprising, Nicholas I created the Third Section. The scope of its activities is barely suggested by the formal enumeration contained in the decree, but some points are noteworthy for their elasticity. (See the comments of Vigel', in Item XIII:38.)

Reference: *PSZRI*, 2d ser., 1:666. The translation is largely based on that in Sidney Monas, *The Third Section: Police and Society in Russia under Nicholas I* (Cambridge: Harvard University Press, 1961), pp. 62-63.

Deeming it necessary to establish a Third Section in my own chancery, to be headed by Adjutant General Benkendorf, I command that the Special Chancery of the Ministry of Internal Affairs be abolished. . . .

The matters to occupy this Third Section of my own chancery shall be as follows:

1. All instructions and announcements of the higher police on all matters.

2. Intelligence concerning the number of various sects and schismatic [religious] groups existing with the state.

3. Information concerning the discovery of counterfeit banknotes, coins, stamps, documents, and so on, the investigation and further prosecution of which remains under the jurisdiction of the Ministries of Finance and Internal Affairs.

4. Detailed intelligence concerning all persons under police surveillance, as well as all orders bearing on this matter.

5. The exile and placement of suspicious and harmful persons.

6. Supervisory and economic management of all places of internment where state criminals are kept.

7. All edicts and instructions concerning foreigners residing in Russia, arriving within its borders, and leaving it.

8. Reports on all events, without exception.

9. Statistical information relevant to the police.

XIV:2. THE STATUTE ON CENSORSHIP, APRIL 22, 1828

The wording suggests the potential scope of censorship under Nicholas I, and provides a standard against which to measure the actuality.

Reference: *PSZRI*, 2d ser., 3:460.

Duties and Principal Divisions of the Censorship

1. It is the duty of the censorship to examine works of literature, science, and art intended for publication within the country by printing, engraving, or lithography, as well as those works brought in from abroad, and to permit the publication or sale of only those works that are not at variance, either wholly or in part, with general rules stated in section 3 below.

2. The expression "works of literature, science, and art" is understood to include books of every kind and in all languages, prints, drawings, sketches, plans, maps, and also music with lyrics.

3. Works of literature, science, and art are to be banned by the censorship: (a) if they contain anything that tends to undermine the teachings of the Orthodox Greco-Russian church, its traditions and rituals, or in general the truths and dogmas of the Christian faith; (b) if they contain anything infringing upon the inviolability of the supreme autocratic power or upon the respect for the imperial house, or anything contradicting basic government legislation; (c) if they offend good morals and decency; and (d) if they offend the honor of any person especially by slander and by indecent expressions or injurious dissemination of that which concerns his morals or domestic life.

4. The censorship is set up under the Ministry of Public Education and is divided into internal and foreign sections. The former examines works of literature, science, and art intended for publication inside the country. The latter permits or forbids the sale of books, prints, and so forth, brought from abroad.

5. A Chief Censorship Administration is to

be formed for general supervision over the activities of the censorship, both internal and foreign, and over the accurate execution of everything that is contained in the present statute.

XIV:3. THE DECLARATION OF THE REVOLUTION BY THE POLISH SEIM, DECEMBER 20, 1830

The Seim here explains its reasons. A few weeks later it voted to dethrone Nicholas.

Reference: Bronislaw Pawlowski, comp., *Krolestwo kongresow i powstanie listopadowe,* Teksty zrodlowe do nauki historji w szkole sredniej, part 49 (Krakow: Nakladem Krakowskiej Spolki Wydawniczej, 1923), pp. 20-21.

When a nation once free and powerful is forced, because of excessive suffering, to have recourse to its last right, that of opposing by force, it owes it to itself and to the world to make public the reasons that have led it to support its holy cause by arms. The chambers of the Diet [Seim] have felt this duty and, being in sympathy with the revolution that took place in the capital on November 29 [N.S., 17 O.S, 1830] . . . [have] determined to justify this step in the eyes of Europe. . . .

. . . Finally, the last consolation with which the Poles had alleviated their sufferings under Alexander—the hope of uniting with their brethren—was crushed by Emperor Nicholas. All ties were finally broken; the holy fires laid on the altars of the fatherland were not to be lighted except in our secret hearts. One feeling was common to all: that such humiliation was no longer to be endured; but our rulers precipitated the moment of explosion. On the heels of constantly increasing rumors of a war to be undertaken against the liberty of [other] peoples, orders arrived to put the Polish army on a war footing for the purpose of marching out of the country; in its place Russian troops were to occupy our land. We were ordered to use large sums of money, to be raised by the mortgage or sale of national lands and deposited in the banks, to defray the costs of this war to kill freedom. Imprisonments were begun again. We had no time to lose. It was a question involving the army, the treasury, our resources, and the honor of a nation that was unable to impose on others the chains it abhorred itself, or to fight against freedom and old comrades-in-arms. Everyone felt this, but the heart of the nation, the burning fire of enthusiasm, our courageous young army and our academic youth, together with the greater part of the capital's garrison and its citizens, was most strongly moved and gave the signal for the uprising. An electric spark ignited in one moment the army, the capital, the whole land. . . .

The Polish nation has risen from degradation and dependence with the manly determination not to return to the bonds it has broken, not to lay down the arms of its ancestors, until it has gained assurances of freedom, until it has secured those liberties it has a double right to demand as an honorable inheritance from its forefathers and as a pressing need in these times. . . .

We have not been moved by national hatred of the Russians, who, like ourselves, are a great branch of the Slavic family. We believe that our condition of freedom and independence, as it was formerly never aggressive toward neighboring nations but on the contrary established the balance and defense of the European peoples, now even more than at other times may be helpful to them. We stand before the powers and nations with the conviction that the voice of political expediency as well as that of humanity will speak for us.

XIV:4. NICHOLAS'S MANIFESTO ANNOUNCING THE CODE OF LAWS OF THE RUSSIAN EMPIRE, JANUARY 31, 1833

The manifesto properly suggests the profound importance of Nicholas's (and Speranskii's) codification for many of the developments of the decades that followed.

Reference: *PSZRI*, 2d ser., vol. 8, pt. 1, p. 68.

Having recognized the necessity of bringing clarity and a fixed order to our country's laws, we had at the very outset of our reign commanded, first, that they be collected and published in a body; and, second, that the laws currently effective in our empire be selected from this general collection, compiled into a correct and uniform code, and set forth exactly, without any essential change, upon the same foundation that was laid by Peter the Great in 1700.

The first of these intentions was fulfilled in 1830.

Now, with divine help, after seven years of uninterrupted labor under our personal supervision, the second has also been completed. All the laws promulgated in the course of 183 years, from the Ulozhenie of 1649 up to January 1, 1832, which have preserved their force and effectiveness to this day, despite the varied changes of the times, have been arranged according to kind and separated from all that had been abrogated by subsequent enactments. These laws, with the exception of military, naval, and certain other decrees enumerated below, have been brought together in a single uniform corpus, divided into books according to the main headings of governmental and judicial affairs. All legislation that has been enacted since January 1832, or that will be enacted in the future, shall be published in annual supplements to the code, classified according to the order of the books and with reference to their articles. And thus the Code of Laws, once established, shall be preserved forever in its entirety and unity.

The primary and essential needs of the state—justice and orderly administration—demanded this [code]. It confirms the force and effectiveness of present-day laws and lays a firm foundation for their gradual improvement in the future. Hereby are fulfilled the wishes our forebears have cherished almost uninterruptedly for 126 years.

XIV:5. THE CONVENTION OF BERLIN, OCTOBER 3 (15, N.S.), 1833

Under this agreement, Nicholas I had special responsibility for Poland, Hungary, and the Balkan region.

Reference: Fedor F. Martens, *Recueil des traités et conventions conclus par la Russie avec les puissances étrangères,* 15 vols. in 8 (St. Petersburg, 1874-1909), vol. 4, pt. 1, pp. 460-62.

In the name of the most holy and indivisible Trinity.

Their Majesties the emperor of Austria, the king of Prussia, and the emperor of all the Russias, having given mature consideration to the dangers that continue to threaten the order which has been established in Europe by public law and treaties, particularly by the treaties of 1815, having unanimously resolved to strengthen the conservative system which constitutes the unalterable basis of their policy, and having been sincerely convinced that mutual support among the governments is essential for the preservation of the independence of the states and the rights stemming therefrom, in the interests of European peace, have jointly agreed to set forth in a formal statement the resolutions adopted by the exalted parties to the treaty for the attainment of this salutary end.

ARTICLE I. The Austrian, Prussian, and Russian courts declare that each independent sovereign has the right, in time of internal troubles or external danger, to request assistance from any other independent sovereign whom he regards as most useful for the purpose of rendering such aid; and that the latter has the right to comply or to refuse his assistance, in accordance with his own interests and circumstances. They also declare that, in the event such aid is extended, no power—whether recognized or unrecognized by the threatened state—has the right to interfere, either to obstruct the assistance requested and rendered or to counteract it.

ART. II. In the event that material assistance is requested from one of the three courts—the Austrian, Prussian, or Russian—and any other power decides to oppose this by force of arms, these three courts shall regard any hostile action to this end as directed against them all. In such a case they will undertake the most swift and effective measures to repulse such an attack.

. . .

SEPARATE ARTICLE. The three exalted contracting powers mutually undertake to preserve secrecy regarding the articles signed on this date and to make no use of them until such a moment when events demand their application, and when the three courts decide in common to make them known where necessary.

XIV:6. NICHOLAS'S DIRECTIVE TO THE GOVERNORS, JUNE 3, 1837

This excerpt indicates some of the functions Nicholas expected his governors to perform.

Reference: *PSZRI*, 2d ser., vol. 12, pt. 1, pp. 362, 370.

SECTION I. Duties of civil governors in general.

1. Civil governors, being the direct heads of the guberniias entrusted to them by the supreme will of His Majesty the emperor, are the chief guardians there of the inviolability of the sovereign rights of the autocracy, of the well-being of the state, and of the universal and exact observance of all laws, statutes, imperial edicts, decrees of the Governing Senate, and directives of higher authority. Being constantly and conscientiously concerned for the welfare of the inhabitants of all classes of the region under their administration, and thoroughly investigating its true condition and needs, they are duty bound, through the power invested in them, to preserve everywhere the public tranquillity, the safety of all and sundry, and the observance of established law, order, and decorum. They are also instructed to take measures to maintain public health and to assure the food supply in the guberniia; to provide proper care for the afflicted and the helpless; and to exercise supreme supervision over the speedy discharge of justice and the immediate execution of all legal ordinances and claims. . . .

35. Civil governors, having as their duty the constant and conscientious concern for the welfare of the inhabitants of the territory entrusted to them, see to it that all those who live under the general protection and safeguard of the law enjoy inviolably, each according to his rank, the rights and privileges most graciously granted to the different classes and categories, in exact conformity with imperial edicts and other decrees. At the same time, they must also exercise vigilant supervision so that no one should usurp privileges not granted to him personally, nor to the category or class to which he belongs, and so that each man should always act in conformity with prescribed order and according to the rights given him.

36. Civil governors in any case pay special attention to protecting the privileges granted to the honorable Russian nobility by the Charter of April 21, 1785, confirmed and extended by the Imperial Manifesto of December 6, 1831, and by the decree of the same date concerning the assemblies of the nobility, and service by those elected by these Assemblies.

XIV:7. THE CRIMINAL LAW CODE, AUGUST 15, 1845

The Criminal Law Code of 1845, though by itself inadequate in curbing crime or combatting the then widespread disorder and venality in the Russian judiciary, does serve as a mirror of Russia's new as well as continuing social problems and of her economic development at mid-century.

Reference: *PSZRI*, 2d ser., vol. 20, pt. 1, pp. 917-18, 935-36.

Concerning the insubordination of mill and factory workers.

. . .

1792. For collusion among workers of any plant, factory, or manufacturing establishment to stop work before the expiration of the time agreed upon with the owners of these establishments, in order to compel the owners to raise their wages, the culprits are subject to the following penalties: the ringleaders, to imprisonment for terms of from three weeks to three months; and others, from seven days to three weeks.

III. Concerning illegal actions by directors of factories in regard to factory workers. . . .

1794. If the owners of factories, plants, and manufacturing establishments should willfully lower their workers' wages before the expiration of the time agreed upon with

these workers, or if they compel them to accept their wages in goods, bread, or any other articles, instead of the wages due them in money, they are subject to a monetary penalty of from one to three hundred rubles, and they are obligated, moreover, to compensate their workers for the losses suffered as a result of their action. . . .

Concerning the abuse of landlord [pomeshchik] power.

1900. When it is the fault of the landlord that, through the levying of excessive taxes or other such exorbitant burdens, a populated estate is brought to ruin, then this and any other populated estate of his is taken under trusteeship and the landlord is prohibited from personally residing on any settled estate belonging to him, as well as from transferring these estates to anyone else's management or ownership, except through a legally transacted sale. . . .

1901. Besides the establishment of a trusteeship over them and all their settled estates, landlords convicted of cruel treatment of their serfs [*krepostnye liudi*] are deprived of the right to have their serfs in service and are subject to: imprisonment in a house of correction for a period of from two to three years, with the loss of certain special rights and privileges, according to article 53 of the present code; or, without the loss of these rights and privileges, imprisonment in a house of correction for from six months to one year, depending on the circumstances more or less augmenting or mitigating their guilt. . . .

Concerning crimes committed by serfs against their masters [*gospoda*].

1907. For rebellion against their masters or persons to whom the landlords have legally transferred their authority, in full or with limitations, serfs are subject to penalties defined in articles 283-90 of the present code for rebellion against authorities established

by the government. [Note: Rebellion against authorities established by the government was punishable by sentences of exile and hard labor of from four to twenty years for the principals, and of exile to Siberia or imprisonment for from six months to six years for other participants.]

1908. For all persistent insubordination, even without open rebellion, to their masters or persons to whom the landlords have legally transferred their authority in full or with limitations, serfs—in cases when the owner, unwilling himself to apply the domestic corrective measures granted him by law, reports the matter to the proper authorities—are subject, depending on circumstances augmenting or mitigating their guilt, to punishment by flogging up to fifty strokes. The sole exception to this shall be in cases when they have refused to obey unlawful commands which, if carried out, would have made them accomplices in a crime.

1909. For submitting complaints against their landlords, which are forbidden by law, serfs are subject to flogging up to fifty strokes.

XIV:8. THE TREATY OF ADRIANOPLE, SEPTEMBER 2 (14, N.S.), 1829

This item and those that follow illustrate aspects of the Eastern Question, which loomed large during Nicholas's reign.

Reference: *PSZRI*, 2d ser., 4:624-27. Translation based largely on that in Edward Hertslet, ed., *The Map of Europe by Treaty since the General Peace of 1814*, 4 vols. (London, 1875-91), 2:813-31.

ARTICLE III. The Pruth shall, as formerly, form the boundary of the two empires, from the point where that river touches the territory of Moldavia to its confluence with the Danube. From this place the frontier line shall follow the course of the Danube to where the estuary of Saint George flows into the sea, so that all the islands formed by the different branches of this river will belong to Russia, but the right bank will remain, as heretofore, in the possession of the Ottoman Porte. . . .

ART. IV. . . . The whole Black Sea coast from the mouth of the Kuban' as far as the port of Saint Nicholas inclusively, shall remain in perpetuity under the dominion of the Empire of Russia. . . .

ART. V. Inasmuch as the Principalities of Moldavia and Wallachia by special capitulations [agreements] have placed themselves under the suzerainty of the Sublime Porte,

and inasmuch as Russia has guaranteed their well-being, it is understood that they shall preserve all the rights, privileges, and benefits that have been granted to them either by their capitulations, or by the treaties concluded between the two empires, or by the hatti-sherifs [sultan's edicts] promulgated at different times. In consequence whereof, they shall enjoy freedom of public worship, complete security, an independent national government, and the right of free trade. . . .

ART. VI. . . . The Sublime Porte undertakes in the most solemn manner . . . to restore immediately the six districts detached from Serbia and in this way to guarantee forever the tranquillity and welfare of that faithful and devoted nation. . . .

ART. VII. Russian subjects shall enjoy, throughout the whole extent of the Ottoman Empire, both on land and at sea, full and absolute freedom of trade. . . .

The Sublime Porte engages, moreover, to take special care that the trade and in particular the navigation of the Black Sea shall be impeded in no manner whatsoever. . . .

ART. IX. Inasmuch as the prolongation of the war, to which the present treaty of peace puts a satisfactory end, has occasioned the Russian imperial court considerable expenses, the Sublime Porte acknowledges the necessity of offering it a suitable indemnification. . . .

ART. X. In declaring its complete agreement with the stipulations of the treaty concluded at London on June 24 (July 6, N.S.), 1827, between Russia, Great Britain, and France [concerning the granting of political autonomy to Greece], the Sublime Porte equally accedes to the act entered into on March 10 (22, N.S.), 1829 [establishing the boundaries of the Greek state].

XIV:9. THE TREATY OF UNKIAR-SKELESSI, JUNE 26 (JULY 8, N.S.), 1833

This treaty between Russia and Turkey, concluded at a time when the sultan was threatened by the Egyptian revolt, proved to be a major factor in the subsequent development of tensions in the Balkans and Near East.

Reference: T. Iuzefovich, ed., *Dogovory Rossii s vostokom: politicheskie i torgovye* (St. Petersburg, 1869), pp. 90-92; translation based largely on Hertslet, *Map of Europe by Treaty*, 2:926-28.

ARTICLE I. There shall be forever peace, amity, and alliance between His Majesty the emperor of all the Russias and His Majesty the emperor of the Ottomans, their empires and their subjects, both on land and at sea. Inasmuch as this alliance has as its sole object the common defense of their dominions against all attack, Their Majesties engage to come to an unreserved understanding with each other upon all the matters that concern their respective tranquillity and security, and to afford to each other mutually for this purpose substantial aid and the most efficacious assistance. . . .

ART. III. In conformity with the principle of protection and mutual defense, which is the basis of the present treaty of alliance, and in consequence of a most sincere desire to secure the permanence, maintenance, and full independence of the Sublime Porte, His Majesty the emperor of all the Russias, in the event of circumstances occurring which should again determine the Sublime Porte to call for the naval and military assistance of Russia . . . engages to furnish, by land and by sea, as many troops and forces as the two High Con-

tracting Parties may deem necessary. . . .

ART. V. Although the two High Contracting Parties sincerely intend to maintain this engagement to the most distant period of time, yet, as it is possible that in the course of time circumstances may require that some changes should be made in this treaty, it has been agreed to fix its duration at eight years. . . .

Separate and Secret Article

. . . His Majesty the emperor of all the Russias, wishing to spare the Sublime Ottoman Porte the expense and inconvenience that might be occasioned to it by affording substantial aid, will not ask for that aid if circumstances should place the Sublime Porte under the obligation of furnishing it. The Sublime Ottoman Porte, in place of the aid it is bound to furnish in case of need, according to the principle of reciprocity of the Patent Treaty, shall confine its action in favor of the imperial court of Russia to closing the Strait of the Dardanelles, that is to say, to not allowing any foreign vessels of war to enter therein under any pretext whatsoever.

XIV:10. THE RUSSIAN DECLARATION OF WAR AGAINST TURKEY, OCTOBER 20 (NOVEMBER 1, N.S.), 1853

The complex struggle of the European powers over the Eastern Question led to the Porte's refusal of Russia's peremptory demands concerning the Orthodox in Turkey (June 1853), Russia's reoccupation of Moldavia and Wallachia (July, N.S.), the Turkish declaration of war against Russia (October 4, N.S.), and, on November 1 (N.S.), Russia's own declaration. It contained the following justification for the war that came to be known as the Crimean.

Reference: *PSZRI*, 2d ser., 28:490-91; translation based on Hertslet, *Map of Europe by Treaty*, 2:1177-78, slightly modified.

To no purpose have the principal powers of Europe sought by their exhortations to shake the blind obstinacy of the Ottoman government. It has replied to the pacific efforts made by Europe, as well as to our forbearance, by a declaration of war. . . . Finally, embodying in the ranks of its army the revolutionists of all countries, the Porte has commenced hostilities on the Danube. Russia is challenged to the fight; nothing, therefore, remains for her, but . . . to have recourse to arms in order to compel the Ottoman government to respect treaties, and to obtain from it reparation for the manner in which it has responded to our most moderate demands and to our legitimate solicitude for the defense of the Orthodox faith in the East.

XIV:11. THE MANIFESTO ON WAR AGAINST GREAT BRITAIN, FRANCE, AND TURKEY, APRIL 11 (23, N.S.), 1854

A manifesto of the following spring supplied further justification of Russia's actions in waging the Crimean War. Here is part of it.

Reference: *PSZRI*, 2d ser., vol. 29, pt. 1, pp. 176-77; translation based on Hertslet, *Map of Europe by Treaty*, 2:1205-06, slightly modified.

From the very beginning of our dispute with the Turkish government, we solemnly announced to our faithful subjects that a feeling of justice had alone induced us to reestablish the violated rights of the Orthodox Christian subjects of the Ottoman Porte. We have not sought, we do not seek, to make conquests nor to exercise in Turkey any supremacy, beyond that which is authorized by existing treaties.

At the outset we met with mistrust, and soon after with secret hostility on the part of the governments of France and England, which strove to mislead the Porte by misinterpreting our intentions. At last, England and France, now discarding every mask, have announced that our disagreement with Turkey is only a secondary affair in their common aim to weaken Russia, to snatch from her a part of her possessions, and to make our country fall from the powerful position to which the hand of the Almighty has elevated her.

Is Orthodox Russia to fear such threats? Ready to confound the audacity of the enemy, shall she deviate from the sacred aim assigned to her by almighty Providence? No! Russia has not forgotten God! It is not for worldly interests that she has taken up arms; she fights for the Christian faith, and for the defence of her co-religionists oppressed by implacable enemies.

XIV:12. THE BRITISH PARLIAMENT VIEWS RUSSIA'S INVOLVEMENT IN THE CRIMEAN WAR, MARCH 19 (31, N.S.), 1854

These excerpts from debates in the British Parliament shed additional light on the reasons for Russia's war with Turkey in 1853 and on Anglo-Russian relations at this period.

Reference: *Hansard's Parliamentary Debates*, 3d ser., vol. 132 (London, 1854), pp. 145, 148, 150 [Clarendon]; 212 [Russell]; 245-48, 253 [Bright]; 277-78 [Palmerston].

[In the House of Lords; the Earl of Clarendon, foreign secretary, is speaking:]

The Emperor of Russia has endeavored by a treaty, or by an engagement which should have the force of treaty, to obtain that right of interference between the Sultan and many millions of his subjects which would have extended not only to a virtual protectorate, but have conferred actual government upon him. Had the Sultan entered into the engagements which were required from him, the Greek Christians, who are the subjects of the Porte, would have been placed in the same position as the subjects of the Emperor of Russia. No question, however small and however trifling, connected with the control of the affairs of the Greek subjects of the Sultan could have arisen which would not have had to be determined by the Russian Ambassador at Constantinople. We should then have seen the enlightenment, the intelligence, and the progress of the Greek subjects of Turkey, as well as the free exercize of their religion, brought down to the same low level as those of the subjects of the Emperor of Russia; and any demur upon the part of the Sultan to submit to the government of the Russian Ambassador would have been an infraction

of treaty and a legitimate cause of quarrel.
Under these circumstances, my Lords, Russia
would have been enabled at any moment,
and upon any pretext, with her powerful
fleet in the Black Sea, to render herself
mistress of Constantinople. . . .

. . . Could we, under such circumstances—
could France and England—allow the virtual
supremacy over millions of the subjects of
the Sultan to be handed over to the Emperor
of Russia? Could France and England submit
to the degradation of allowing Russia to take
up a position as regards Turkey which would
be the means of inflicting death upon that
country, either by slow poison or by sudden
death? for that is the alternative which Russia
offers. There could be but one answer to that
question, and that answer has already been
given by the generous and high-minded
people of this country, who detest aggression,
whatever form it may assume, and who are
always ready to protect the weak against the
strong. . . .

. . . I believe there is not a man in the
dominions of the Czar who does not expect
that Constantinople will ultimately belong to
Russia. It will be our duty, as far as we possibly can, to prevent the realization of that
expectation, and to take care that a Russian
occupation may never begin there. Were it to
succeed, and were Russia to be in possession
of Constantinople, commanding, as she
would do then, the Black Sea and its shores,
being enabled, as she would, to occupy Cir-
cassia and Georgia, and convert the population of those frontier countries into one
mighty army, having access to the Mediter-
ranean and a vast naval fleet in the Baltic,
and determined, as she now is, to increase her
naval power by all those facilities which
steam and modern invention have offered
for the transport of troops—with all these
advantages, were Russia in possession of
Constantinople, it would not be too much
to anticipate that more than one Western
Power would have to undergo the fate of
Poland. The wealth, and the intelligence, and
the civilization of Europe would be no more
a barrier against encroachments upon the
part of Russia than were the intelligence and
civilization of ancient Rome against the en-
croachment of the Huns and Vandals. And,
my Lords, the more we examine this question,
the more gigantic is the aspect it assumes. It

is not merely the protection of Turkey against
the aggressions of Russia that is concerned in
the Eastern question, as it is commonly called,
but it is the battle of civilization against barbarism, for the maintenance of the independence
of Europe. . . .

[In the House of Commons; Lord John Russell,
member of the cabinet without portfolio:]

[The Governments of France and England]
considered that, after having given . . . an
implied promise of assistance to the Sultan
in his resistance to the unjust demands of Russia, they would be wanting in honour if they
did not fulfill that implied promise of material
aid. They considered that the safety of Europe
depended upon the maintenance of the equi-
librium of which the integrity and independence
of Turkey form a part. They considered that it
would be impossible to hope to maintain that
integrity and independence if Russia was allowed unchecked and uninterrupted to impose
her own terms upon Turkey. It was therefore
decided by Her Majesty's Government at once
to address this House—to advise Her Majesty
to send down a message to the Houses of
Parliament, and at the same time to issue a
declaration of war. That declaration of war
has been issued.

[Mr. J. Bright, a Liberal from Manchester:]

The Turkish empire is falling, or has fallen,
into a state of decay, and into anarchy so
permanent as to have assumed a chronic character. The noble Lord surely has not forgotten
that Turkey has lost the Crimea and Bessarabia,
and its control over the Danubian Principalities; that the Kingdom of Greece has been
carved out of it; that it has lost its authority
over Algiers, and has run great risk of being
conquered by its own vassal the Pasha of
Egypt; and from this he might have drawn the
conclusion that that empire was gradually
falling into decay, and that to pledge ourselves to effect its recovery and sustentation,
is to undertake what no human power will be
able to accomplish. . . .

. . . And . . . what is the position of Russia?
It is a powerful country, under a strong Executive Government; it is adjacent to a weak
and falling people; it has in its history the evi-
dences of a succession of triumphs over Turkey;
it has religious affinities with a majority of the
population of European Turkey which make

it absolutely impossible that its Government should not, more or less, interfere, or have a strong interest, in the internal policy of the Ottoman empire. . . .

. . . Russia had reason to complain, that she has certain rights and duties by treaty, and by tradition, with regard to the protection of the Christians in Turkey. Russia asserted these rights, and wished to have them defined in a particular form. . . .

. . . Now, if Russia made certain demands on Turkey, this country insisted that Turkey should not consent to them . . . I defy any one to read the despatches of Lord Stratford de Redcliffe without coming to the conclusion that, from the beginning to the end of the negotiations, the English Ambassador had insisted, in the strongest manner, that Turkey should refuse to make the slightest concession on the real point at issue in the demands of the Russian Government. . . . The Turk was advised to resist, first the treaty, then the convention, and then the note or memorandums; and an armed force was promised on behalf of this country; at the same time he knew that he would incur the high displeasure of England and France, and especially of England, if he made the slightest concession to Russia. . . .

. . . [Since I] suppose that Turkey is not a growing Power, but that the Ottoman rule in Europe is tottering to its fall, I come to the conclusion that, whatever advantages were afforded to the Christian population of Turkey would have enabled them more rapidly to grow in number, in industry, in wealth, in intelligence, and in political power; and that, as they thus increased in influence, they would have become more able, in case any accident, which might not be far distant, occurred, to supplant the Mahomedan rule, and to establish themselves in Constantinople as a Christian State, which, I think every man who hears me will admit is infinitely more to be desired than that the Mahomedan power should be permanently sustained by the bayonets of France and the fleets of England. . . .

[Viscount Palmerston, secretary for the Home Department:]

There is a settled intention on the part of Russia to overrun and overthrow the Turkish empire for the purpose of establishing in the territory of Turkey the ascendancy and domination of Russia.

. . . But the real question is, not what you would wish to see established in the Turkish empire, but that which you are determined shall not be established—it is not what might be, but what for the interests of all Europe ought not to be. And that which ought not to be, and that which I trust Europe will take care shall not be, is the transfer of those countries to the sceptre of the Emperor of Russia.

B. SOCIAL AND ECONOMIC DEVELOPMENTS

XIV:13. TWO ORDERS CONCERNING PEASANT DISTURBANCES, MAY 12 AND AUGUST 9, 1826

These documents illuminate one aspect of the peasant problem as Nicholas faced it near the beginning of his reign.

Reference: *PSZRI*, 2d ser., 1:455, 843.

[From a manifesto of May 12, 1826:]

We proclaim to all the people: It has come to our attention, in the reports of the heads of the guberniias, that in some of the villages state peasants, and those of the private landowners, deceived by false rumors and ill-intentioned pronouncements, are abandoning proper order. The former, that is, the state peasants, assume that they will be released from payment of taxes, and the latter, that is, the landowners' peasants, that they will be released from the obligation of obeying their masters.

Regretting the error of these peasants, and wishing to set them on the right path by gentle measures, commensurate with our paternal clemency, we command that it be proclaimed everywhere:

1. That all rumors about the freeing of state peasants from payment of taxes, and of the latter, i.e. the landowners' peasants and household serfs [*dvorovye liudi*], from the obligation of obeying their masters, are false rumors, invented and spread about by ill-intentioned persons, whose sole aim is to enrich themselves through these rumors at the expense of the trusting peasants.

2. All classes [*sostoianiia*] in the state, including state peasants as well as the landlords' peasants and the household serfs, must fulfill exactly all their duties as prescribed by the law and must unquestioningly obey the authorities established over them.

3. If, despite our present command, there should still be some disorders . . . the culprits will draw upon themselves our just anger and shall be punished without delay to the full extent of the law.

4. The heads of the guberniias are enjoined to maintain steadfast vigilance so that disseminators of such rumors or false reports be brought to trial without delay, to be dealt with according to the full severity of the law.

5. And, since we already receive unjustified petitions from peasants, based on the above rumors, we command, in order to put an end to this evil and to preserve peace, that the authors or writers of such petitions be brought to trial as disturbers of the general tranquillity and be punished to the full extent of the law.

The Governing Senate shall immediately issue appropriate orders for the nationwide publication of the present edict, with instructions that the reading of this edict on Sundays and holidays in churches, markets, and fairs be continued for six months from the day of its receipt . . . in the guberniias.

[From an order of August 9, 1826:]

His Imperial Majesty notes from reports submitted to His Majesty's attention that, even subsequent to the publication of the imperial manifesto of May 12 of the current year, commanding the peasants to obey, in accordance with the law, their landowners and the authorities, some of those guilty of insubordination, persisting in their rank error, paying no heed either to the imperial manifesto or the urging and persuasion of the authorities, and, even scorning the punishment imposed upon them by the court verdict, continue this criminal disobedience of authority. His Imperial Majesty has therefore deigned to command that the Committee of Ministers be advised of the following: In cases where it is necessary to employ military force after the proclamation of the above imperial manifesto in order to restore to obedience peasants who persist in causing disorders, His Imperial Majesty deems it advisable to issue orders that the culprits be brought to trial at once before a military court, which shall consist of available officers of the military unit assigned to the area and of members of the uezd courts, represented in equal numbers. As for the execution of the sentences imposed by this court, His Majesty suggests that direct ratification of the sentence by the civil governor should be sufficient in cases where corporal punishment is imposed on not more than nine persons. Where more than nine persons are involved, the sentence should be submitted through the governor general, or, where there is none, directly to the acting head of the Ministry of Internal Affairs, for consideration at the earliest meeting of the Committee of Ministers and submission for imperial ratification by special report.

XIV:14. SPERANSKII'S MEMORANDUM OF DECEMBER 1826

This is from a copy of a memorandum submitted by Michael Speranskii in December 1826 to the "secret" committee which was established December 6, 1826, to consider various proposals for reform. This copy, like some others in this section, comes from the work of Petr Ivanovich Bartenev (1829-1912), a historian, who edited *Russkii arkhiv* from 1863 until his death, and who devoted himself to the editing and publishing of many volumes of documents from public and private archives.

Reference: P. Bartenev, ed., *Deviatnadtsatyi vek,* 2 vols. (Moscow, 1872), 2:160-61.

Thanks to the unlimited freedom to turn peasants into household serfs, the houses of the gentry have been flooded with crowds of idle servants; there has been an increase in capricious and often licentious activities, as well as insane luxury and ruinous vanity; new needs have appeared along with new taxes upon the peasants and irredeemable debts; the condition of the peasants has been further aggravated by the fact that the village often must supply the poll tax and recruits for this idle mob which is registered on the village rolls.

Because of the establishment and dispersion of handicrafts in the villages, our cities remain empty: for where are the lesser townspeople [*meshchane,* includes tradesmen and artisans] to find consumers to work for, when every landowner produces at home all his necessities and even the objects of his fancy, no matter how poorly and unprofitably, and even offers some for sale? How can trades be improved in the cities without competition among the artisans? And what competition can there be among artisans when they are scattered and in slavery? Assuredly it may be said that, under such conditions, we shall have neither cities nor a stable urban life.

Thanks to the [estate owner's] right to sell peasants without land and to send them away as recruits out of turn, the person of the peasant has become chattel, a piece of property which the owner can dispose of at will; that this arbitrariness has often been and still is at times today cruel and abusive is shown by fact and experience.

XIV:15. THE MANIFESTO ON THE ASSEMBLIES OF THE NOBILITY, DECEMBER 6, 1831

This statute redefined in part Catherine II's Charter of the Nobility (1785). (See also the manifesto of June 11, 1845, Item 28 in this chapter.)

Reference: *PSZRI,* 2d ser., vol. 6, pt. 2, pp. 248-52.

The State Council has considered the draft of a new "Regulation concerning the Ordering of Assemblies of the Nobility, and of the Elections and Service in These," prepared in accordance with principles stated by us. Affirming this regulation as fully consonant with the general weal of the state and with the privileges granted to the nobility, we have resolved to show this estate [*soslovie*] further signs of our special favor. Henceforth, not only some members but even the chairmen of the guberniia courts [*predsedateli gubernskikh sudebnykh palat*] shall be elected by the nobility, and the confirmation of those whom it honors with election to the post of guberniia marshal of the nobility [*gubernskii predvoditel'*] shall be left to our personal discretion. We do not doubt that the honorable Russian nobility, which has never betrayed its lofty calling of being the prime mainstay of the throne, both on the field of honor and in other areas of state service, will now in full measure justify our trust.

. . .

SECTION II. Concerning affairs of the guberniia assemblies of the nobility.

I. Affairs of regular guberniia assemblies.

7. The principal business of the regular guberniia assemblies is the election of officials to various posts. Moreover, at the assemblies the nobility may discuss its needs and benefits and make representations concerning these through the guberniia marshal of the nobility to the head of the guberniia and to the Ministry of Internal Affairs; but in important cases, it may submit its . . . petitions to His Imperial Majesty. . . .

SEC. III. Concerning the membership of the assemblies of the nobility.

14. The assemblies of the nobility shall be composed solely of the hereditary nobility of the guberniia or uezd. Of these, some *have the right to vote* on the affairs of the assembly, while others *do not have such a right.*

15. The right to participate in the affairs of the assembly or to vote on its decisions belongs to the noble who fulfills the following conditions: (1) if he is honest and blameless in conduct and is not openly guilty of or under suspicion of iniquity; (2) if he is registered in the genealogical records of the guberniia in whose assemblies he wishes to participate, and if he owns land in this guberniia; (3) if he has reached his majority according to the general law, i.e. if he is not less than twenty-one years of age. . . . (4) if he holds at least the rank of the fourteenth class, received during active service, and not at the time of entering such service or at retirement; or if he has already served three years as an official elected by the nobility. . . .

17. Attendance at the assembly, *without participation in its resolutions,* is permitted to hereditary nobles who hold no rank, who have not served as elected officials, and who own no land.

18. *The right to vote* on the affairs of the assembly is of two kinds: (1) a right to vote in all the decisions of the assembly, except elections; and (2) a right to vote in the elections as well.

19. The former right belongs to all hereditary nobles who meet the conditions stated in [article] 15. . . .

I. Concerning the right of direct election.

21. The right of electing directly to office belongs to the noble who owns no fewer than one hundred male peasants, or who has no fewer than one hundred settlers [*poseliane*] living on his land under agreement with him; and also to the noble who owns not less than 3,000 desiatinas of land, which may be uninhabited, but must be in one guberniia. . . .

II. Concerning the right to elect through authorized deputies.

31. Nobles who do not own as much property as indicated above but who have no fewer than five settled peasants [*poselennykh krestian*] or not less than 150 desiatinas of arable land, even if unsettled, may vote in

elections for office through authorized deputies whom they select from among themselves.

32. The number of such deputies is determined by the number of peasants or desiatinas of arable land, even if unpopulated or unsettled, belonging to all these nobles: there is to be one deputy for every 100 souls or every 3,000 desiatinas of land. Thus, for example: if this group of nobles includes two owners of 75 souls each; two of 50 souls each; five of 30 each; four of 25 each; ten of 10 each; and twenty of 5 each; then the total number of souls is 700, and the above forty-three owners may send seven deputies to represent them at the elections.

XIV:16. VASIL CHIKOV'S MEMORANDUM ON THE PEASANT QUESTION, 1835

This document and others that follow give some measure of the thought devoted to the problem of serfdom under Nicholas I. Prince I. V. Vasil'chikov was chairman of the Committee for Investigating Ways and Means of Improving the Condition of Peasants of Various Classification. This excerpt is from his memorandum of 1835, which dealt with the definition of peasant wages and duties. It was addressed to the tsar.

Reference: Andrei P. Zablotskii-Desiatovskii, *Graf P. D. Kiselev i ego vremia*, 4 vols. (St. Petersburg, 1882), 4:149.

The fundamental principles of this work should be the following:

a. The dissemination and affirmation on every suitable occasion of the basic rule that the land is the inalienable and inviolable property of the landlord (the state treasury or the private individual), and that the peasants cannot use it in any other way except with the consent of the landlord and in ex-

change for a specified amount of labor. The unfortunate idea harbored almost universally by the peasants of the pomeshchiki that they themselves belong to the master, but that the land belongs to them, is one of the main obstacles to the achievement of the desired goal in the introduction of the proposed improvements in the lot of the peasants: it can excite the mind and give rise to serious disorders.

XIV:17. P. D. KISELEV'S REPORT ON STATE PEASANTS, MAY 17, 1837

This excerpt is from a program for the reorganization of the administration of state domains and the state peasants, submitted by Count (and General) Pavel Dmitrievich Kiselev (1788-1872), in his report to the tsar. When, a few months later, a separate Ministry of State Domains was established, Nicholas appointed Kiselev as its head, and he kept him there through the rest of his reign.

Reference: Zablotskii-Desiatovskii, *Graf P. D. Kiselev*, 2:55-56.

The volosti [to be organized] should be larger than those existing at the time, and the volost' board should be retained *for the time being*.

In conformity with indigenous popular custom, mir assemblies and village boards [*upravleniia*] should be established in the village communities to take charge of public affairs.

The okrug and volost' authorities have supervisory powers; the village authorities have executive powers.

The village community is considered the basic administrative and land unit; each may consist of either a single village or several villages; but a village whose boundaries were fixed separately [*otdel'no zamezhevannoe*] should constitute a single community, however large it may be; villages with small populations, but holding land in common, should constitute a single community.

Lands and properties should be left in the permanent use of the communities, which are granted the right to distribute the lands among the householders in whatever manner they may find most suitable.

Villages with little land should either be allotted land from free state holdings [*kazennye uchastki*], or their peasants should be resettled on free state lands, according to special regulations.

Separate family plots in the form of separate farmsteads [*khutory*] should be set up in the places of new settlement, with the right of permanent hereditary use and without being parceled out among family members.

XIV:18. THE LAWS REFORMING THE ADMINISTRATION OF THE STATE PEASANTS, DECEMBER 26, 1837, AND APRIL 30, 1838

The important measures taken under Nicholas I to improve the condition of the state peasants, who constituted approximately half of the peasants of Russia, were largely carried out by Count Kiselev. The first excerpt below is from the law of late 1837 establishing a special ministry which Kiselev ran until 1856; the remaining excerpts are from various portions of the voluminous law of April 1838 providing for the administration of his ministry and the peasants within its jurisdiction at the level of the okrug, volost', and village.

Reference: *PSZRI*, 2d ser., vol. 12, pt. 2, p. 1041 [law of 1837]; 13:504, 507, 552, 553, 563-65, 601, 604-06, 650 [law of April 1838].

[From the law of December 26, 1837:]

1. The Ministry of State Domains [*Ministerstvo Gosudarstvennykh Imushchestv*] is established to administer state domains, to superintend free rural inhabitants, and to supervise agriculture.

2. Under this ministry's authority are: (1) state [i.e. treasury] lands, populated, unpopulated, and uncultivated; (2) state obrok holdings [*kazennye obrochnye stat'i*, i.e. treasury lands granted on lease]; (3) forests of the State Forestry Department, except those exempted from the supervision of the forestry authorities. . . .

3. Under the charge of the Ministry of State Domains are: (1) state [*gosudarstvennye*] peasants of all designations, except those attached to special departments; (2) all free farmers [*svobodnye khlebopashtsy*] . . . [including both those who have fulfilled their obligations to their lords and those who have not yet fulfilled their obligations]; (3) foreign settlers, installed: (a) on state lands, (b) on lands acquired in possession, and (c) on private lands, under contract with their owners; (4) nomadic peoples: (a) the Kalmyks of the Astrakhan' guberniia and the Caucasus oblast'; (b) Siberian tribes [*inorodsty*] settled, nomadic, and itinerant, and (c) the Samoyeds.

4. Under the management of the Ministry of State Domains are matters of rural economy specified in the Code of Laws concerning Urban and Rural Economies, such as: (1) measures to encourage and improve agriculture; (2) tillage and market gardening; (3) cultivation of crops for commercial, industrial, and medicinal purposes; (4) horticulture and viticulture; (5) wine-making; (6) sericulture; (7) cattle- and sheep-raising; (8) marine fisheries and sealing, as well as hunting and trapping; (9) all associations and companies concerned with these matters and especially those established in the field of forestry, the Forestry Corps, the Lisinsk Forestry Training School, the Schools of Agriculture, Horticulture, Viticulture, and Sericulture, model farms, state orchards, and silkworm farms; the editing of agricultural and forestry journals, and funds for the encouragement of rural industries in Russia's southern region.

[From the law of April 30, 1838:]
[Part II, concerning okrug administration:]

120. The okrug administrator [*nachal'nik*] must see to it that the volost' administrations and the village authorities under their jurisdiction faithfully fulfill the obligations placed upon them, as set forth in the statute establishing the village and volost' administrations, and that no one exceeds the limits of his position and authority.

121. Apart from supervising current developments and accounts, the okrug administrator carries out annually general and special inspections in his okrug. . . .

150. The okrug administrator must protect and defend the volosti in his charge, their village communities and their peasants, from all oppression, false claims, and abuse, averting and suppressing such actions by legal measures.

151. The okrug administrator must listen patiently and with particular attention to all complaints brought before him by state peasants; he must not make it difficult for them to have access to him nor send off the aggrieved petitioners to other places and authorities under the pretext that their complaints do not belong to the sphere of the okrug administrator. However, should these complaints indeed be outside the competence of his department, he must explain to the petitioner to whom he may apply to obtain satisfaction. . . .

[Part III, concerning the establishment of volost' administration:]

2. Every volost' is to consist of several adjacent village communities with a population of up to 6,000 male souls registered under the census. . . .

9. In every volost' there shall be established: (1) a volost' board [*volostnoe pravlenie*] to administer the affairs of the volost'; (2) a volost' assembly [skhod] to hold volost' elections; (3) a volost' court [*rasprava*] to deal with the judicial affairs of the state peasants. . . .

12. . . . For transcribing and copying, the volost' board employs, prior to their assignment to positions, candidates for the posts of village clerks from among peasant children who have gone to school and have completed their training in secretarial work in the office of the okrug administrator.

13. During their training at the offices of the okrug administrators and as clerks at the volost' boards, the peasant children are maintained with funds assigned from a public levy [*obshchestvennyi sbor*] or, until this is instituted, from the levy for mir expenses, according to the special ruling by the Ministry of State Domains on this matter. . . .

21. The volost' chief [*golova*] is elected for a three-year term by the volost' assembly; he is confirmed in this post and dismissed from it, at the suggestion of the okrug administrator, by the Ministry of State Domains, with the authorization of the head [nachal'nik] of the guberniia. However, the volost' chief may remain in his post for an indefinite period after the expiration of his three-year term until he himself requests to be discharged, or until his superiors deem it necessary to elect another man in his stead because of peasants' complaints, [his] incompetence, or any other valid reason.

22. The assessors [*zasedateli*] are elected for three-year terms by the volost' assembly; they are confirmed in their posts or dismissed from them by the Ministry of State Domains at the suggestion of the okrug administrator.

23. The volost' clerk is appointed for an indefinite term by the okrug administrator, with the approval of the Ministry of State Domains, from among the state peasants of the same volost'; if no competent person is to be found there, he may be chosen from another volost', or from among the meshchane, retired military officers of the lower ranks, civil officials, or office employees. . . .

98. The volost' assembly comprises, in addition to the volost' chief, delegates from the village communities of the volost', elected on the basis of one delegate for every four men appointed to the village assembly, which means one delegate for every twenty households. . . .

CHAP. V. Concerning mir elections.

101. There are three types of mir elections: (1) special village elections [*chastnye sel'skie*]; (2) general village elections; (3) volost' elections. . . .

103. Those elected must not be under twenty-five years of age or without their own house; they must be of good character and industrious farmers. . . .

105. In localities where there are residents of the Orthodox Christian faith, no Dukhobors ["spirit-wrestlers"], Molokane ["milk-drinkers"], iconoclasts, Jews, or persons of other heresies deemed particularly harmful may be elected to public offices entailing powers or authority.

106. In villages, communities, and volosti where Christians reside together with idolaters, the latter cannot be elected as village or volost' chiefs; and where Mohammedans live together with Christians, the head official shall be elected from among the Christians, but his subordinates may be elected from among the Mohammedans.

107. No one can shun elected office without legitimate reasons, which must be submitted to the volost' assembly for discussion and consideration.

108. The legitimate reasons for which a state peasant may, at his request, be excused by the volost' assembly from election to a post are as follows: (a) if he has already served three three-year terms; (b) if there are no other adult workers in his family except him; (c) if he is more than sixty years of age; (d) if he suffers from a serious physical illness. . . .

111. Special village elections are held to select delegates to the village and volost' assemblies.

112. Two delegates for every ten households are appointed by adult householders from among the peasants belonging to these households. . . .

113. The village chief [*starshina*], having assembled all the householders, summons them separately and in proper order, beginning with number one, in groups of ten heads of households, inquires whom they wish to appoint as their delegate, and records in a list the names of those chosen. . . .

120. The village assembly elects the following officials for three-year terms: (1) a village chief; (2) village elders [starosty], their number being determined by article 42 of the Enactment concerning Village Administration; (3) a tax collector and, where required, his assistants; (4) an overseer [*smotritel'*] of the village granary; (5) arbiters [*dobrosovestnye*] of the village court; (6) foresters for public and state forest districts; (7) fire wardens for state districts; (8) village policemen [*sotskie*], their numbers being determined by the Enactment Establishing the Okrug Administration; (9) three candidates for each [volost'] post. . . .

[Section III, concerning the volost' court (rasprava):]

464. In connection with the volost' board, there shall be established a second-instance domestic court, to be known as the volost' court.

465. The volost' court shall consist of two volost' arbiters [dobrosovestnye], one senior and one junior, under the chairmanship of the volost' chief. . . .

470. The volost' court examines the same cases as the village court, but only on appeal by those who are dissatisfied with the verdict of the latter, in cases specified by the Rural Judicial Statute. The only exceptions to this are cases concerning wills of state peasants that were registered with the volost' board. Cases of this type are subject to direct and immediate examination by the volost' board. . . .

[Part IV, concerning the establishment of village administration:]

16. In every village community there shall be established: (1) a village assembly to deal with village affairs; (2) a village authority [nachal'stvo] to administer the community;

(3) a village court to deal with the judicial affairs of state peasants. . . .

18. The village assembly consists of the village chief, the elders, the tax collector, the overseer of the village granary, and elected delegates.

19. The delegates are appointed from among state peasants belonging to the village community, two from every ten households, in the manner specified for village elections.

20. The matters dealt with by the village assembly are: (1) village elections; (2) appointment of candidates for posts in the volost' administration; (3) designation of peasant children to be trained for the posts of village and volost' clerks and smallpox vaccinators; (4) releases allowing state peasants to join other village communities, enter other categories [sostoianie, status], or emigrate; (5) admission into the village community of persons of other categories; (6) appointment of guardians for orphans who are minors; (7) annual accounts of such guardians of all the income and expenditure connected with their guardianship; (8) division of the lands of the village community among the state peasants; (9) conferences and decisions concerning the mir's obrok holdings, the allotment of community lands to various institutions connected with agriculture and industry, and the allotment of poor lands to private use on condition that they be fertilized. . . . (13) allotment of money levies for the mir's expenditures; (14) apportionment among state peasants of taxes, obligations, and levies for which the village community is responsible; (15) measures for collecting arrears in money and grain levies; (16) consideration of the reports of the tax collector and the overseer of the village grain reserves; (17) matters connected with the fulfillment of recruit obligations, such as: (a) the dividing up of [large] families [semeinye razdely], (b) the designation of men from these families as recruits and substitutes [podstavnye], (c) the determination of the money levy required for the fulfillment of the recruit obligation, (d) the appointment of the recruiting agents [otdatchiki], (e) the verification of their accounts, and (f) grants of permission to state peasants to hire recruits [naem v rekruty] and to transfer recruitment out of turn for settlement if unfit for military service; (18) grants of power of attorney in the prosecution of community lawsuits [khozhdenie po delam obshchestvennym]. . . .

30. No one is admitted to the [village] assembly except those called to it.

31. Officials of the Ministry of State Domains and of the okrug administration are not permitted to participate in the deliberations of state peasants in the village assembly.

32. The village assembly can pass resolutions only when not less than two-thirds of all state peasants who have the right to attend are present. . . .

35. If there is disagreement at the assembly, the opinion of the majority of those present determines the final decision, even if the majority is decided by only one vote. In the event of a tie at the village assembly, the village chief casts the deciding ballot. . . .

SEC. III.

CHAP. I. Concerning composition of the village court.

397. In every village community there shall be established a village court, in the form of a first-instance domestic court, to deal with affairs of state peasants. . . .

398. The village court under the chairmanship of the village chief consists of two village arbiters, one senior and one junior, elected for three-year terms from among the state peasants known for their good character and moral conduct. [According to articles 419 and 420, the village court issued final judgments in disputes concerning property valued at not more than five silver rubles and could sentence offenders to fines up to one silver ruble, to arrest and public works up to six days, and/or to flogging up to twenty strokes.]

XIV;19. KISELEV'S MEMORANDUM OF 1839

This is Bartenev's copy of the memorandum submitted by Count Kiselev to the "secret" committee established November 16, 1839, to consider the proposals that led to the law of April 2, 1842, on "obligated peasants" (concerning which, see below). (On Bartenev, see the introduction to Speranskii's memorandum of December 1826, Item 14 in this chapter.)

Reference: Bartenev, *Deviatnadtsatyi vek*, 2:179.

It is, of course, impossible to question the great benefit to the state to be derived from the emancipation of the serfs. But state interest also demands the greatest caution in choosing how to organize the life of a class that embraces up to twenty-five million souls of both sexes and which, because of its moral condition, demands the closest supervision and tutelage. In general, it cannot be denied that it is impossible and unadvisable suddenly to transfer half-educated people from total slavery to total freedom. Between the aforesaid two extreme and equally dangerous measures of peasant emancipation—in the one case, turning them into landless peasants [*bobyli*], and, in the other, equating them with the upper classes in the right to own land—there is a middle way, a measure which, placing the peasants at a decent level as free or obligated farmers, legally guarantees their way of life without introducing them to rights that belong only to the gentry.

XIV:20. THE MARQUIS DE CUSTINE'S IMPRESSIONS OF RUSSIA IN 1839

These comments are a few of the many made by Custine after a three-month journey through European Russia in 1839. They may serve to illustrate why his travel journal remains a much debated document to this day.

Reference: *Journey for our Time: The Journals of the Marquis de Custine*, ed. and trans. Phyllis P. Kohler (New York: Pellegrini and Cudahy, 1951), pp. 73, 75, 98, 137, 161, 169, 185, 191, 229, 245, 249, 250.

People and government—here all is harmony. The Russians would not give up the miracles of will of which they are witnesses, accomplices, and victims, if it were a question of bringing back to life all the slaves they have cost. All the same, the thing that surprises me is not that a man, steeped in self-idolatry, a man ascribed as all-powerful by sixty million men, or so-called men, undertakes and brings to conclusion such things; it is that among the voices which recount these accomplishments to the glory of this one man, not one separates itself from the chorus to protest in the name of humanity against the miracles of autocracy. It can be said of the Russians, great and small—they are intoxicated with slavery.

This population of automatons is like half a game of checkers, for a single man makes all the plays and the invisible adversary is humanity. One does not die, one does not breathe here except by permission or by imperial order; therefore, everything is gloomy and constrained. Silence presides over life and paralyzes it. Officers, coachmen, Cossacks, serfs, courtiers, all are servants, of different rank, of the same master and blindly obeying an idea that they do not understand. It is a masterpiece of military mechanics; but the sight of this beautiful order does not satisfy me at all, as so much regularity cannot be obtained except through the complete absence of independence. I seem to see the shadow of death hovering over this part of the globe.

Among these People deprived of leisure and of will one sees only bodies without souls, and one trembles in thinking that for such a great multitude of arms and legs there is only one head.

. . .

The political system of Russia could not withstand twenty years of free communication with Western Europe. Do not listen to the boasts of Russians; they take pomp for elegance, luxury for politeness, police and fear for the foundations of society. In their minds, to be disciplined is to be civilized. They forget that there are savages with gentle manners who are very cruel soldiers. In spite of all their pretensions to good manners, in spite of their superficial education and their profound and premature corruption, in spite of their facility in recognizing and understanding the realities of life, the Russians are not yet civilized. They are regimented Tartars, nothing more.

. . .

The Russian people are mocking, like the slave who consoles himself for his yoke by quietly making fun of it; they are superstitious, boastful, brave, and lazy, like the soldier; they are poetic, musical, and thoughtful, like the shepherd; for the customs of the nomadic races will prevail for a long time among the Slavs. All of this is in keeping neither with the style of the buildings nor with the plan of the streets in Petersburg; there is obvious dissension between the architect and the inhabitant. European engineers came to tell the Muscovites how they should build and embellish a capital worthy of the admiration of Europe; and they, with their military submission, ceded to the force of command. . . .

Happily for the painter and for the poet, the Russians are essentially religious—their churches, at least, are their own.

. . .

The slave fears the bad humor of his master and applies himself with all his might to keeping him in a protected cheerfulness. The chains, the cell, the knout, Siberia are indeed close to an irritated Czar, or at the very least the Caucasus—this temperate Siberia for the use of a despotism which is softening every day according to the progress of the century.

Russia is a nation of mutes; some magician has changed sixty million men into automatons who await the wand of another magician to be reborn and to live. Nothing is lacking in Russia . . . except liberty, that is to say life.

. . .

The morals of a people are produced slowly by the reciprocal action of laws on customs and customs on laws; they do not change at the wave of a wand.

. . . Russians, despite all the pretensions of these half-savages, are cruel and will remain so for a long time yet. It is scarcely more than a century since they were real Tartars; it was only Peter the Great who began to force men to introduce women into gatherings. Beneath their modern elegance, many of these newcomers to civilization are still bears; they have turned their skins inside out, but one has only to scratch a little to find the bristling fur.

. . .

Such a social organization produces a fever of envy so violent, a straining of minds toward ambition so constant, that by now the Russian people must be inept in everything except the conquest of the world. I always come back to this term because such a goal is the only thing that can explain the excessive sacrifices imposed here on the individual by society. . . . Without this ulterior design, admitted or not, which many men obey, perhaps in ignorance, the history of Russia seems to me an inexplicable enigma.

. . .

They wish to rule the world by conquest; they mean to seize by armed force the countries accessible to them, and thence to oppress the rest of the world by terror. The extension of power they dream of is in no way either intelligent or moral; and if God grants it to them, it will be for the woe of the world.

The spectacle of this society, all the springs of which are taut like the trigger of a weapon that one is about to fire, frightens me to the point of dizziness.

. . .

The first thing that struck me in the streets of Moscow was that the population is more lively and more openly gay than in Petersburg. Here one breathes an air of liberty unknown in the rest of the Empire. This explains to me the secret aversion the sovereigns have for this city.

. . .

Be completely convinced that the Kremlin of Moscow is not all what they say it is. This is not a palace; it is not a national sanctuary where the historical treasures of the Empire are conserved; it is not the boulevard of Russia, the revered sanctuary where sleep the saints, the protectors of the fatherland; it is less and it is more than all that—it is quite simply the citadel of specters. . . .

Heritage of the fabulous times when falsehood was king without control: jail, palace, sanctuary, bulwark against the foreigner, fortress against the nation, support of tyrants, prison of peoples—that is the Kremlin!

. . .

The Kremlin is, without contradiction, the work of a superhuman being, but a malevolent being. Glory in slavery, such is the allegory featured in this satanic monument, as extraordinary in architecture as the visions of St. John are extraordinary in poetry—it is a habitation suitable for the personages of the Apocalypse.

XIV:21. ZABLOTSKII-DESIATOVSKII'S MEMORANDUM OF 1841

This is from a memorandum of Andrei Parfen'evich Zablotskii-Desiatovskii (1808-81), an economist and high official of the Ministry of State Domains.
Reference: Zablotskii-Desiatovskii, *Graf P. D. Kiselev,* 4:276, 296, 336.

THE PRESENT CONDITION OF THE SERFS
A. Economic Condition

In examining the present condition of the peasants of the pomeshchiki, we must note first of all that the law does not absolutely determine the status of this estate [soslovie] but leaves it almost entirely to the discretion of the owner. But this arbitrary rule has become consolidated by custom and, sustained by various economic needs, has established the main distinct divisions in the functions of this estate, which have a powerful effect on the position of the peasants.

In accordance with their economic functions, the peasants are divided into:
1. *Izdel'nye* peasants [i.e. *barshchinnye, on corvée*]
2. Obrok [quitrent] peasants
3. Factory and workshop peasants
4. Household peasants

Izdel'nye Peasants

The izdel'nyi peasant is obligated to work the land for the pomeshchik, in exchange for which he receives some land for his own cultivation.

Usually according to custom, all calculations in this arrangement are based on the peasant tiaglo, [a labor unit] consisting of a full-grown male worker and a female worker, who receive an allotment of land.

. . .

B. Administration of the Peasants

As to the manner of administration of the estates of the pomeshchiki, one must distinguish between estates on which the owners never reside and those on which they do.

In the former case, if it is an obrok estate, it is managed most frequently by the peasants, through a bailiff or elder whom they themselves elect, with the consent of the landowner.

On large estates, under barshchina, management is entrusted in most cases to free, hired stewards. . . . On the same estates there are often assistants, or overseers, from among the serfs on the estate.

On middle-sized estates there may also be occasional stewards from the free classes. But, generally, the pomeshchiki complain of the inefficiency and greed of these men and most often prefer to entrust management of the estate to their own serfs. . . .

Finally, the owners themselves in most cases manage directly those estates on which they reside.

· · ·

The talk among the gentry has had nothing to do with the rumors spread among the peasantry. These latter have a special source and their own form. They are important because they spring up spontaneously, subside, and then arise with new strength, especially in connection with various state occasions. During the sovereign's last sojourn in Moscow, there was incessant talk of freedom, especially among the household serfs. Many of them left their masters' houses, disappeared for days, and wandered about under the windows of the Kremlin palace expecting the sovereign himself or his heir to proclaim their freedom.

The gentry themselves believe that these rumors have never spread as rapidly or revived as often as under the present reign. The majority are convinced that this talk, these rumors, are the product of nothing else but the *spirit of the time,* against which no human force can prevail.

Despite the differences in interpretation of the causes of the rumors rife among the serfs, the gentry agrees on one thing—its *fear of peasant rebellion.* It is difficult to decide to what degree these apprehensions are justified, but it is indubitable that they are not without foundation.

XIV:22. NICHOLAS'S DECREE ON RAILROAD CONSTRUCTION, FEBRUARY 1, 1842

Although it was the second railroad to be constructed in Russia, the line from Moscow to Saint Petersburg was the first one of major importance. (For one sequel, see the decree of 1857 in the next chapter, Item XV:20.)

Reference: *PSZRI,* 2d ser., vol. 17, pt. 1, p. 74.

In our unceasing concern to improve communications in our empire, and cognizant of the benefits produced by the construction of railroads in many foreign lands, several years ago we commanded the Committee of Ministers to examine proposals regarding this matter. As a result of this investigation, the Chief Administrations [Glavnye Upravleniia] of Communications and of Mining Engineers were instructed to collect further information about foreign railroads, so that, upon determining the degree of merit of such roads for Russia, their best application in our country, and their most efficient technical execution, we might avail ourselves, without excessive sacrifices, of all the advantages of this new means of communication.

Accordingly, individuals chosen by both the departments were sent to study closely and at firsthand the best foreign railroads. After investigating in this manner almost all such roads in Europe and America, these

persons were instructed to prepare, jointly with some of the first originators of railroads in Russia, their recommendations concerning the construction of a similar line between Saint Petersburg and Moscow.

Now, after consideration and extensive discussion of these recommendations in our personal presence, and deeming it beneficial to grant our fatherland a means of communication which, despite its considerable expense, nevertheless promises the country various advantages and will in a manner of speaking unite the two capitals as if they were one, we have decreed the construction of a railroad from Saint Petersburg to Moscow, to be built— according to the example of other powers— at the expense of the treasury, for the general welfare and in order to retain permanently in the hands of the government a means of transportation of such great importance for the entire industrial and active life of the country.

XIV:23. THE DECREE ON THE EXPANSION OF POTATO PLANTING, FEBRUARY 16, 1842

Here is an example of one of the steps taken in Russia's attempt to alleviate the recurring crises faced by Russian agriculture in the mid-nineteenth century. It was addressed by Nicholas to the minister of imperial domains. (For an earlier decree on potatoes, see Item XII:37, above.)

Reference: *PSZRI,* 2d ser., vol. 17, pt. 1, p. 93.

Mindful of the repeated failures of grain crops in certain guberniias in 1829 and 1840, we turned our attention to the improvement of methods

for assuring the nation's food supply. Recalling that the edicts of May 31, 1765, and April 5, 1797, addressed to this purpose, ordered the introduction of potato planting everywhere, we deemed it beneficial, for the attainment of this salutary end, to instruct you— since the Ministry of State Domains has principal charge of agricultural matters—to take measures to extend the planting of potatoes, as a product of great help in years of bad harvest. Now, from the reports of the civil governors of thirty-eight guberniias, which you have submitted concerning the results of this ordinance, we learn with particular pleasure that in 1841 the planting of potatoes, in accordance with our will, was increased as compared with the past and that, with the general willingness of the peasants to increase their planting of this product, even more success may be expected in its general dissemination. Wishing to assist the utmost development of this branch of agriculture, which bears so closely upon the assurance of the national food supply, the constant object of our concern, we command that:

1. In all guberniias where state peasants are already planting potatoes, the measures hitherto adopted are to continue in effect, under the supervision of the local authorities. In those guberniias where the volost' boards set up special plots for growing potatoes and for supplying seed to the peasants, such plots are to be set up in all village communities and potatoes are to be cultivated on them until potato growing becomes sufficiently widespread among the state peasants.

2. State peasants who distinguish themselves by particularly successful cultivation of potatoes are to be presented for awards of gold and silver medals, according to the established manner. Moreover, to stimulate them to general competition in this matter, special money prizes shall be assigned from the funds placed at the disposal of the Ministry of State Domains. You shall issue the proper instructions for the execution of the above and shall submit to us a report on the results of these measures at the end of each year, together with the reports that will be submitted to you annually by the heads of the guberniias concerning the planting and yield of potatoes on privately owned lands and on those belonging to various departments, in accordance with our special decree of December 3, 1840. We shall be pleased to see successes in this matter, both among the landowners and among all who engage in agriculture, and to reward all useful initiative in extending potato planting, which—apart from the direct purpose of assuring the nation's food supply—may lead to the introduction of a fourth vegetable field [i.e. to a four-field instead of a three-field system of crop rotation].

XIV:24. NICHOLAS'S SPEECH IN THE STATE COUNCIL ON THE PEASANT PROBLEM, MARCH 30, 1842

This is a partial paraphrase of the tsar's remarks to the State Council on March 30, 1842, during the discussion of the draft of the law concerning "obligated" (*obiazannye*) peasants (see below). Reference: Zablotskii-Desiatovskii, *Graf P. D. Kiselev*, 2:254-55.

Arriving at [the meeting of] the State Council, the emperor declared that he deems it necessary, before consideration of the subject, to acquaint the members with his ideas concerning agreements between landowners and peasants, and the motives that prompted His Majesty in this matter. There is no question that serfdom in its present state in our country is an evil, palpable and obvious to everyone. However, to attack it now would be, of course, an even more disastrous evil. Emperor Alexander I, of blessed memory, who had intended at the beginning of his reign to grant freedom to the serfs, later, himself, abandoned this idea as still entirely premature and impossible to fulfill. His Majesty, likewise, will never venture to do it, feeling that, since the time when it can be undertaken is still quite distant, any thought of it at the present period would merely be a criminal infringement upon the public peace and welfare of the state. The Pugachev rebellion showed how far mob violence can go. Fortunately, later occurrences and ventures of this kind have always, until now, been suppressed, and this, of course, will continue to be the object of the government's special and, with the help of God, successful concern. But we must not conceal from ourselves the fact that current ideas are not the same as those that existed previously, and it is clear to every reasonable observer that the present situation cannot last *forever.* The most important reasons for this change in ideas and the ever more frequent unrest in recent times must be attributed in the main: first, to the imprudence of the landowners themselves, who give their serfs more education than is appropriate for their status, thereby developing in them a new range of ideas and making their position still more burdensome; and, second, to the fact that certain landowners—although, thank God, only a small minority of them—employ their power evilly, forgetting their noble duty. And the marshals of the nobility, as many of them have reported to His Majesty, can find no way of halting these abuses under the law, which places virtually no restrictions upon the power of the landowners. But, since the present situation is such that it cannot continue, and since decisive measures to end it are impossible without a general disturbance, it is essential at least to prepare ways and means for a gradual transition to a different order and calmly to discuss its benefits and consequences, without growing frightened at every change. There must be no emancipation, but it is necessary to open a path to another, transitional state, linking with it the inviolable preservation of patrimonial [*votchinnaia*] ownership of the land.

XIV:25. THE LAW ESTABLISHING THE CATEGORY OF "OBLIGATED" PEASANTS, APRIL 2, 1842

With this law Nicholas I sought to protect his noble landowners and yet to indicate his interest in loosening the bonds of serfdom. He felt this law to be a decided improvement over the Free Farmers Law of 1803. Three landowners took advantage of its provisions, and 24,708 peasants thus received the status of "obligated."

Reference: *PSZRI,* 2d ser., vol. 17, pt. 1, pp. 261-62.

Articles 440 and 457 of the Code of Laws concerning status [sostoianie] set forth the rules under which landowners are permitted to convert their serfs into free farmers [*svobodnye khlebopashtsy*], conceding them the possession of landowner's land in exchange for a specified compensation, mutually agreed upon. Desiring, for the sake of the state's interests, that the lands belonging to the landowners, as the patrimonial property of the gentry, be protected against expropriation of gentry possessions during the conclusion of such contracts, we have deemed it beneficial . . . to allow landowners who wish to do so to conclude by mutual consent contracts with their peasants, on such a basis that the landowners, not restricted by the edict concerning free farmers, would retain their full right of patrimonial ownership of the land, with all its resources [*ugod'ia*] and wealth, both on the surface and underground, while the peasant would receive from them allotments of land for cultivation in exchange for specified obligations. In drawing up such contracts, the landowners may fix the subsequent conditions with the peasants, according to mutual agreement, on the basis of the following principal rules, considered by the State Council and approved by us:

1. The peasants' obligations to the landowners may be defined in the contracts in the form of money dues [obrok], produce, the cultivation of the landowner's fields, or other work.

2. In the event the peasants fail to fulfill the obligations assumed under the contract, they are compelled to do so by the rural [*zemskaia*] police, under the direction of the uezd marshals of the nobility and under the higher control of the guberniia administration.

3. After due confirmation of the contracts between them and the landowners, the peasants assume the designation of obligated peasants. . . .

6. The landowner shall establish a patrimonial board [*votchinnoe upravlenie*] in the villages of the obligated peasants and shall exercise supervision over the village police and the observance of laws assuring rural order and well-being. They shall also possess the right of trial and judgment of misdemeanors and minor offenses on the part of obligated peasants, as well as the right of initial examination of litigations and disputes among them.

XIV:26. BARON VON HAXTHAUSEN ON RUSSIA IN 1843-1844

The German writer and economist August Franz Ludwig Maria, Freiherr von Haxthausen-Abben-burg (1792-1866), visited European Russia in 1843-44, seeing much and studying many aspects of Russian life. In 1847-52 he published his famous three-volume *Studien ueber die innern Zustaende . . . Russlands*. He became known to the English-speaking world largely through a two-volume version published in London in 1856—a version that was in part a translation but in places more an abridgment of the German original. The following excerpts, selected from the original German edition, are illustrative of Haxthausen's views concerning several subjects that were of special interest to him, such as the national character of the Russian people, their economy, their government, and the institution of the mir or peasant commune, of which many Europeans first learned through this observant German.

Reference: August Freiherr von Haxthausen-Abbenburg, *Studien ueber die innern Zustaende, das Volksleben und insbesondere die laendlichen Einrichtungen Russlands,* 3 vols. (Hanover, 1847-52), 1:xii, xiii, 124-25, 129-30; 2:120-21, 129-30, 549-50; 3:121-22, 122-23, 145, 147-48, 150-51, 197, 201, 213, 216-17, 221, 238, 504, 505, 514. The English version (Baron von Haxthausen, *The Russian Empire: Its People, Institutions, and Resources,* trans. Robert Farie, 2 vols. [London, 1856]) has been checked and used in those cases where it contains the passages included above, but Farie's translation has been somewhat revised. (This English version has recently been reprinted—New York: Da Capo, 1968.)

As every Russian belongs to a commune [*Gemeinde*], and all the members are entitled to equal shares in the land, there are no born proletarians in Russia.

. . .

In recent years Russia has made remarkable progress in the modern system of manufacturing, and a large number of the nobles have engaged in it. Moscow, the center of industrial activity, has been transformed from the residence of the nobility into a manufacturing city. It is very doubtful whether the result can be considered altogether advantageous. The wages of labor, partly on this account, have risen immensely in Russia and, in fact, taking everything into consideration, there is no country where they are so high.

. . .

The following information was given to us concerning the division of land in the village communes. The principle is that the whole of the land (tillage, meadows, pasture, woods, streams, and so on) belongs to the population of a village community [*Dorfgemeinde*] regarded as a whole, and in using these communal possessions every male inhabitant has a right to an equal share. This share is therefore constantly changing; for the birth of every boy creates a new claim, and the shares of those who die revert to the commune. The woods, pastures, hunting grounds, and fisheries remain undivided and free to all the inhabitants; but the arable land and meadows are divided equally, according to their value,

among the males. This equal division is of course very difficult, as the soil differs in quality, and portions of it may be distant or inconveniently situated. The difficulties are great; nevertheless the Russians overcome them easily. There are in each commune skillful land surveyors, who, competently, with insight acquired from the traditional habits of the place, execute the work to the satisfaction of all. The land is first divided, according to its quality, position, or general value, into sections, each possessing on the whole equal advantages. The sections are then divided into as many portions, in long strips, as there are shares required, and these are taken by lot. This is the usual plan, but each region, and frequently each commune, has its local customs.

. . .

The facts here described constitute the basis of the Russian communal system, one of the most remarkable and interesting political institutions in existence, and one that undeniably possesses great advantages for the social condition of the country. The Russian communes evince an organic coherence and compact social strength that can be found nowhere else and yield the incalculable advantage that no proletariat can be formed so long as they exist with their present structure. A man may lose or squander all he possesses, but his children do not inherit his poverty. They still retain their claim upon the land, by a right derived, not from him, but from their birth as members of the commune. On the other hand, it must be admitted that this fundamental basis of the communal system, the equal division of the land, is not favorable to the progress of agriculture, which . . . under this system could for a long time remain at a low level.

. . .

[Haxthausen describes Khar'kov, then an important university city and guberniia capital of about 30,000 inhabitants:]

It is elegantly built, and we were told that no house in the modern part of the town was older than thirty years; the more detestable were the streets! We were here on the black humus soil, two or three feet deep. Dry weather had prevailed for a long time, and the dust in the streets was so terrible that the houses could not be seen across them. It is said to be still worse after rainy weather. The ground then becomes soft, the feet of the horses and pedestrians and the wheels of the carriages tread it into a morass, and at last it is impossible to cross the street. From six to eight horses are attached to the lightest carriages. Some years ago even the carriage of the empress stuck fast in the middle of the street. Generally speaking, paving is one of Russia's weak points.

. . .

The students are placed under strict discipline and close observation. . . . All the more remarkable, therefore, are the political sentiments manifested wherever the students believe themselves unobserved and uncontrolled. These sentiments are generally of the most destructive character, although literature is strictly controlled, and the students never hear in the professors' lectures the slightest hints of such doctrines and opinions. . . . The chief cause may be the French and Swiss—butlers, tutors, and governesses—who came in large numbers to Russia, and to whose influence on political opinion little attention was formerly paid, so that such doctrines could be spread inside all families. The conspiracies that broke out afterward under the Emperor Alexander handed them down as traditions to the youth of the country. These doctrines prevail widely among the students even in the gymnasiums and seminaries, but more especially in the cadet academies, in the educational institutions of the capitals [Saint Petersburg and Moscow],

and among the young people in the civil and military service, especially the young officers of the Guards.

. . .

The workers in Russian factories are rather interesting to observe. In various respects they present a different picture than do factory workers in western European countries. Since they are nearly all country people or peasants and generally work in factories only temporarily and intermittently, we find characteristics of Russian country folk in them, that is, really of the Russian common people . . . for the lower classes of the cities are barely differentiated from the country people. Furthermore, in general they are distinguished from the factory workers of other countries by their better living conditions and physical health. Their situation is such that they do not become proletarians, and therefore it follows that the pay for the work cannot be too low, because workers are not forced by necessity to allow their wages to be determined at the discretion of the master. Furthermore, there is usually no abundance of those seeking work. Wages for work are therefore generally ample, and indeed with weavers in wool and silk factories wages are so high that they can save a considerable amount. Thus the factory owners must allow the workers to go home for several weeks, twice a year. This occurs at harvest time and at Easter.

. . .

I can recollect no German or Romanic proverb in which the power, rights, and sacredness of the commune are recognized. The Russian language has a great number:
>   God alone directs the mir.
>   The mir is great.
>   The mir is the surging billow.
>   The neck and shoulders of the mir are
>   broad.
>   Throw everything upon the mir; it will
>   carry it all.
>   The tear of the mir is liquid but sharp.
>   The mir sighs, and the rock is rent asunder.
>   The mir sighs, and it reechoes in the
>   forest.
>   Trees are felled in the forest, and
>   splinters fly in the mir.
>   A thread from the mir becomes a shirt
>   for the naked.
>   No one in the world can separate from
>   the mir.

What belongs to the mir belongs also to
  the mother's little son.
What is decided by the mir must come
  to pass.
The mir is answerable for the country's
  defence.

. . .

We are convinced that the mir or Russian
community is the real, true basis of the whole
national constitution. . . .

To know the nature of the mir or the Russian community, one must inspect closely
the basic character of the Slavic nationality
in general and that of the Russian specifically.
The Slavic people are generally very sociable,
but the Russian is the most sociable of them
all. If ten Russians, common people, meet at
some place such as Riga or Mitau, they immediately form an association, a society with
members, choose a head, and so forth.

Nowhere does the unity of blood, of the
family and its further development into the
community, stand out so decisively and
strongly as with the Russian people. Family
unity and communal ownership of property
were original characteristics of the Slavic
nations, but these characteristics were not so
clearly preserved among the Western Slavic
peoples as among the Russians.

The family, however, found unity in its
head, the father. Without a father it cannot
exist at all. Furthermore, full equality is the
rule among all family members; therefore
anarchy would break out immediately if there
were no common head. Thus, if there were
no more real father, his oldest brother or son
would take his place, with the total power of
the father. If the natural succession of paternal
power was interrupted, for example by the
insanity of the eldest son, by his becoming a
monk, or the like, then the family head, the
father, was chosen by the remaining members
of the family. The choice could fall on the
youngest, perhaps, who would thus become
the "father," who would be unconditionally
obeyed.

. . .

Let us now take an overall view of the
general character of the Russian people.

The complete feeling of *national unity,* of
communal unity, and of *family unity* is the
basis of all the social life of the Russian
people. All the individuality of the people is
absorbed into each of these three units, and

with it nearly every kind of individual property, especially private ownership of the land.
Nowhere is there true, genuine, private property. It all belongs to the nation and its chief
representative, i.e. the tsar, and on a smaller
scale to the communities or the families.
Ownership is only temporary, not permanent.
Always and under all conditions of life the
thought of community ownership prevails. It
is the basic principle of the Russian people.

. . .

There is a peculiar lightness and mobility
in the Russian character. No fixed forms
prevail. The Russian does not like rules or a
regulated existence. He desires no settled
position in the world or in business but demands the utmost freedom, with liberty to
go where he pleases or to remain at home,
according to his own convenience. He cannot
stand being bound down to regular habits and
thrift: he is hospitable and lavish in his expenditures for food and drink, does not save
his supplies, is fond of risk, and is addicted
to play and speculation. . . .

Against this restless character of the
people and these variable tendencies which
endanger the stability of all social relations,
the government, since the time of Peter I,
has imposed the most elaborate formalism in
all governmental organization and activity.
The forms, checks, laws, and decrees introduced are innumerable and have no parallel
in all of Europe. To all outward appearances
a degree of perfect order, uniformity, and
security prevails . . . but in truth the best
elements in the different government organs
lie beyond these forms.

. . .

Among the Russians there is no national
or family relationship that does not have a
center, a unity, a chief, a father, or a master.
A master is required by the Russian, who
cannot exist and live without a superior. If
God has removed his natural father, the Russian will create one. The commune elects the
starosta [elder] and then obeys him without
question. He is not an elected delegate but a
father with the authority of a father. One
must keep this in mind if one seeks to understand the position of the tsar. The Russian
people are very similar to a beehive, for which
the kingship is a natural necessity; it cannot
exist without the queen bee, and such is the
tsar to the Russian people. The tsar in Russia

is neither the delegate of a sovereign people, nor the first servant of the state, nor even the legitimate owner of all land, nor sovereign by the grace of God. He is the personified unity, the head, the temporal father of the people. . . . The constitution of the Russian commune, described above in its principal features, is politically of the greatest value for Russia, especially today. All western states suffer from the same illness, which threatens them with death and which they do not yet know how to cure: pauperism and proletarianism. Russia, being saved from it by the communal constitution, does not have this illness. Every Russian has a home and a communal share of the land, and even if he loses or relinquishes it his children may claim it again. There is in Russia no proletarian *mob,* but simply *people,* and this condition will continue unless by some new antinational regulations an indigent mob is created.

· · ·

In Russia . . . we find an extremely compact nationality: the thirty-six million Great Russians have a community of language found among no other people; the dialect of the higher classes is the same as that of the common people; the emperor and muzhik (peasant) speak the same language and have even the same modes of expression.

The language of the White Russians and of the seven million Little Russians differs from that of the Great Russians, but not nearly so much as the language of the inhabitants of the Harz Mountains differs from that of the people of Brunswick.

· · ·

When half-culture touches the Russian he is ruined; it is said that when he shaves off his beard, lays aside the caftan, and puts on a European coat, he becomes a knave. The Russians who have acquired the usual western-European education are called lacquered barbarians; this is inaccurate: they are not barbarians but a healthy, vigorous, ingenious people, of noble race, religious and moral. If, however, they receive the taint of modern culture, their national virtues vanish, their religion and morals, simplicity, and honesty are destroyed, and nothing remains but the animal nature common to every man.

· · ·

The Russian people proper retains all the characteristics of a healthy, vigorous, unspoiled nature and a blooming youthfulness, such as deep family feelings, a strong communal life, hospitality, generosity, compassion, a spirit of self-sacrifice and patience, together with a physical strength—increased by a severe climate and privations of all kinds—which enables them easily to endure fatigue and hardships, and finally a firm, religious, and almost childlike attachment to their church and nation, a fervent love of country, and an unshakable conviction of their own greatness and strength.

· · ·

The Romans appear in all times of history as a conquering race. In the Russians there is no trace of this. On the contrary, they are a peaceable and industrious people—brave, but not at all warlike. The Russian soldier is one of the best soldiers in the world, but he becomes one very unwillingly.

· · ·

Conquest for its own sake alone—the simple lust of conquest—has gone out of fashion since the time of Napoleon. No trace of this exists in the Russian people, and the government, at least for the last twenty-five years, has shown a moderation in this respect that Europe did not anticipate.

· · ·

Russia's love of conquest is decried throughout Europe; nevertheless in the last twenty years she has not conquered a single village. England's conquests rarely meet the censure of the world, but in one century she has conquered territories and subjugated nations four times her own extent, and hardly a year passes in which she does not make new conquests.

· · ·

I have here given a survey of the reorganization of the crown estates and their population [i.e. Kiselev's reform of 1837-38] in order to show that much can be effected in Russia by decision and energy. . . . The knot was not cut through, nor the whole organization arbitrarily formed upon an artificial model, nor the natural relations of the people interfered with; but it was laid down as a principle that the popular manners and customs and the law of the country . . . must be respected.

· · ·

The entire organization rests on just principles—I would say on truly liberal principles, were it not that this beautiful expression has become so misused and hackneyed! They have acted with calm benevolence but also with firmness and understanding.

· · ·

The establishment of a ministry for the management of the crown lands, and the organization thereby effected of that half of the peasantry which belongs to the crown; the granting of firm institutions and forms for governmental as well as for communal administration; but above all the solemn expression and acknowledgment of the great national principle of law, the freedom and independence of the Russian commune, as the real basis of the entire national constitution—these constitute the greatest event that has occurred in Russia since the time of Peter I.

XIV:27. COUNT KISELEV'S CIRCULAR OF NOVEMBER 30, 1843

This is an excerpt from a circular sent by Count Kiselev to the heads of departments of state domains in the various guberniias.
Reference: Zablotskii-Desiatovskii, *Graf P. D. Kiselev*, 4:172.

In all of their orders, the administrative or executive authorities do not act arbitrarily but are guided by the *law*. . . .

The judgment of disputes and litigations between state peasants as well as corrective punishment for offenses are left to the jurisdiction of the village and volost' courts, without interference by administrative officials.

The religious education of the rural class is introduced as the prime foundation of the well-being of its future generations.

And so, *legality* for the present and *education* for the future are the bases of the entire reorganization—wise foundations, prescribed by the highest solicitude of our most august monarch. Hence, our principal efforts should consist, in accordance with the purpose of the enactment, in furthering the development among the peasants of their own mir administration and in seeing to the fulfillment of the rules given to them and to the proper ordering of the composition of the assemblies. We must not, however, interfere with decisions on affairs within the competence of the village administration and courts, nor with the resolutions adopted by the mir assemblies when they act on their affairs according to their rights as provided by law. Furthermore, we must protect the peasants from outside oppression, help them by defense and intercession, not deprive them of advice, and, most of all, listen to their petitions patiently and attentively, offering a clear and just decision and answer to each. Finally, in all matters concerning the betterment of peasant conditions, we must not act with force and severity but must stimulate competition among the peasants as we have said above, by inviting and encouraging those householders who, in following directions, will attract others by their example.

These, in main outline, are the duties of guardianship to be exercised by the local administration and the methods for gaining the confidence of the peasants and winning the right to my respect and gratitude.

XIV:28. THE MANIFESTO ON THE HOLDING OF NOBLE STATUS, JUNE 11, 1845

Nicholas I never ceased in his efforts to get Russia's nobility (*dvorianstvo*) to take seriously the idea of a service obligation to the state (see Item XIV:15, above). Nor did he cease to protect the privileges of this group. The law quoted here, by making it more difficult for the *raznochintsy* to achieve nobility, altered the sociological function of the Table of Ranks as conceived by Peter the Great. (See the Table of Ranks of January 24, 1722, Item X:25, above, and that of 1901, Item XVI:78, below.)
Reference: *PSZRI*, 2d ser., vol. 20, pt. 1, pp. 450-51.

Since ancient times, nobility in Russia has been acquired by service; but the conditions of acquiring it have been changed from time to time, with the change of the order of military and civil service. . . .

Having as our constant aim to maintain the nobility, which has rendered so much service to the throne, at the level to which it has been raised by state enactments, yet at the same time desiring that no one be barred from attaining the privileges of nobility through hard work and talent, we have deemed it beneficial—without depriving anyone of rank that is already his, according to laws hitherto in force—

to transfer the acquisition of hereditary nobility to the higher ranks, which provide a genuine opportunity to render services worthy of so high a reward.

In accordance with this, we decree that in the future:

1. A non-noble in military service, upon promotion while in actual service to the first officer's rank, shall receive the rights of personal nobility; having risen to the rank of field officer [i.e. to the rank of major], he shall acquire hereditary nobility.

. . .

Non-nobles who enter the civil service shall, upon promotion to a rank of the fourteenth class, receive the right of personal honorary citizenship, and upon promotion to the ninth class they shall acquire the rights of personal nobility; having risen to a rank of the fifth class, they shall acquire hereditary nobility.

XIV:29. THE MEMORANDUM OF COUNT L. A. PEROVSKII, 1846

This is Bartenev's (see Item XIV:14, above) copy of the memorandum submitted to the tsar (and thence to the "secret" committee of 1846) by Count L. A. Perovskii, minister of internal affairs from 1841 to 1852, and of the record of the committee's subsequent deliberations.

Reference: Bartenev, *Deviatnadtsatyi vek,* 2:185-88 [Perovskii's memorandum], 189-92 [committee report].

[Memorandum from Count L. A. Perovskii to the tsar:]

The question of the abolition of serfdom not only claims the attention of the highest government circles but has even become a topic of frank discussion among educated classes and has finally reached the lowest classes in the form of obscure and distorted rumors.

The government evidently has not yet evolved any positive plan of action.

There is no doubt that the emancipation of the peasants or the abolition of serfdom is highly desirable. But first of all it is necessary to define the meaning of freedom for serfs in the present day.

This freedom must, of course, consist of equalizing the rights and duties of the landlords' peasants with the rights and duties of state peasants.

This, however, is not the view of the common people, who do not consider the state peasants free, and who see freedom or liberty only in complete anarchy and disobedience— a senseless and terrible concept. A single stroke of the sovereign emperor's pen can turn serfs into freemen; but no foresight can predict the consequences of such a sudden change, and no powers will be sufficient to restore order and security amidst general anarchy.

. . .

Under the present conditions, the land is the property of the landlord, but he is also master over his peasant, whom he must look after, both for the sake of his own advantage and in accord with the special edicts of the government.

From this it clearly follows that the peasants cannot be freed unconditionally, either without land or even with land.

Assuming the former, we may ask what will the twenty-four million landless peasants of both sexes do, and how will their livelihood be guaranteed? The Baltic guberniias provide a contemporary example of how onerous personal freedom is for the peasants when they are in no way protected against the arbitrary rule of the landlords.

Assuming the latter, i.e. the distribution of land to peasants according to the number of souls, it would become necessary to continue, as the population increases, the distribution to the last scrap of landlords' land. . . .

And so, on the one hand, the peasant should, to a certain extent, be bound to the land by laws themselves; and, on the other, the law should invest the landowner with a certain degree of police power. Otherwise, it would be impossible to compel the peasant to fulfill his duties even toward the government.

And if it is necessary to limit considerably the proposed freedom for peasants, and if the granting of limited freedom will in fact be the same as a limitation of serfdom, it is clear that this reverse method, so to speak [i.e. a limitation of serfdom], will achieve the very same end far more surely and safely, and in a manner imperceptible to the peasants.

Apart from the fact that the ancient, absolute power of the lord over his slave has long since ceased to exist, it is important to note the gradual limitations of serfdom which, in their aggregate, have unquestionably reduced it to less than half of what it was fifty years ago.

If we continue to act cautiously on the same basis, we can move a step forward with each prudent measure and finally reach our goal imperceptibly without uttering the dangerous words "liberty" or "freedom."

[Report of the secret committee of 1846:]

After a discussion of the proposals and explanations of the minister of internal affairs, the committee has fully approved his basic idea: that the emancipation of the serfs should be achieved by the gradual limitation of serfdom, in a manner imperceptible to the serfs, without arousing dangerous rumors among the people and without even pronouncing the words, "liberty" or "freedom."

.   .   .

The future of Russia is in the hands of the Almighty, and man's foreknowledge is limited by his will. As long as Russia, according to its foreseeable destiny, does not lose its unity and might, other nations cannot serve as an example for her. This colossus calls for other principles and other concepts of freedom, relating not only to the peasants but also to all other classes. The fundamental principle of Russia has been and must be autocracy;

without it she cannot exist in her true greatness. Freedom in Russia should consist in the protection of both the persons and the property of each from the oppression of another, and in everyone's obedience to the laws that emanate from a single supreme source. All the actions of the government should be an expression of this idea, and the generations that inhabit Russia should be brought up on these concepts. Under any other conditions, her well-being is insecure. The power of the gentry, as the owners of the land, is the instrument and bulwark of autocratic power. They are the immediate overseer of a population of twenty-four million souls of both sexes, and they bear the responsibility before the autocracy for the peace and welfare of this vast portion of its subjects. The power of the landowner must not, however, be unrestricted, and the peasant must be protected by law from abuse of this power.

.   .   .

And so, in the opinion of this committee, the first actions of the government in this important matter should be: first, exact definition of the power of the landowner over the person of the peasant to the extent required for the preservation of peace and order within the boundaries of his possessions; second, protection of the peasant's property against arbitrary claims by the landowner; third, granting the peasants the right to complain against abuses of the landowner's power.

XIV:30. NICHOLAS'S ADDRESS TO A DELEGATION OF NOBLES, CA. JUNE 4, 1847

The tsar's address to a delegation of local nobles is quoted as follows in a letter of June 4, 1847, from the marshal of the nobility of Roslavl' (south of Smolensk) to the marshal of the nobility of the Smolensk guberniia (see the decree of April 2, 1842, Item XIV:25, above).
Reference: Zablotskii-Desiatovskii, *Graf P. D. Kiselev*, 2:278.

"Gentlemen, I mainly want to talk to you *confidentially* about the obligated [*obiazannye*] peasants. In my decree concerning this subject I clearly expressed my idea that the land earned by us of the nobility, or by our forebears, is our land. Note that I am speaking to you in my capacity as the first nobleman of the state. But the peasant who is today living in a condition of serfdom which became consolidated in our country almost not at all by law, but by custom over a long period of time,

cannot be considered as property, and even less as a chattel. Consequently, my wish when I published the well-known decree was, and remains today, that the nobility should help me in this matter of such great importance for the development of our country's well-being, by the gradual transfer of peasants from the status of serfs to that of obligated peasants—if need be, on various conditions, according to the locality. For I am convinced that such a transfer should forestall a drastic change."

XIV:31. THE REPORT OF THE MINISTRY OF INTERNAL AFFAIRS CONCERNING PEASANT
DISTURBANCES, 1847

Reference: Zablotskii-Desiatovskii, *Graf P. D. Kiselev,* 2:275.

The disorders on the estates of the pomeshchiki were more persistent and serious than
those of preceding years, although the number
of instances was somewhat smaller. In 1845
insubordination occurred on twenty-six
estates, in 1846, on twenty-five, and in 1847,
on twenty-three estates in sixteen guberniias.
The causes of these disorders were: oppression
of the peasants and overburdening them with
work on the part of the owners . . . but the
main reason for the insubordination among
the peasants of the pomeshchiki was the
desire for freedom. . . . The aspiration to acquire freedom, aroused by various absurd
rumors, resulted in persistent insubordination
and violence among the peasants of the pomeshchiki on fifteen estates and prompted more
than 11,000 peasants to flee.

XIV:32. PRINCE DRUTSKOI-SOKOLINSKII ON THE PEASANT QUESTION, 1848

This excerpt summarizes the views of Prince Drutskoi-Sokolinskii, marshal of the nobility of
Smolensk, on the serf problem during the revolutionary year 1848. The text is Bartenev's (see
Item XIV:14, above) copy of the account prepared by the secretary of the "secret" committee
of 1848, before which the prince spoke.
Reference: Bartenev, *Deviatnadtsatyi vek,* 2:204-06.

Enumerating the factors that raised the current question of the reform of serfdom, Prince
Drutskoi-Sokolinskii explained:

1. The idea prevailing in the West that the
serfs in Russia are a class of slaves is unjust.
Our serfdom is based on laws that firmly and
substantially protect the serfs.

2. In a state of freedom, intelligence,
strength, and quick wit will rapidly make
their way. But, on the other hand, laziness
and other vices, once freed from the supervision of the pomeshchiki, will develop as
rapidly. Many people will grow richer, but
still more will become poor, and there will
come into being in our country a hitherto
unknown class of proletarians, which will
bring more than enough harm to make up
for the benefits to be expected from free
labor.

3. The proposed change will not end the
abuse of power. Only the people involved
will change: instead of the bad landlord, there
will be a bad official. There was a time when
the majority of the landowners interpreted
their rights according to ancient traditions
and customs, when slavery still had significance in a legal sense. But the development
and improvement of our legislation, accompanied by the rapid extension of education,
have shown the landowners their true rights,
and they have quickly entered the confines
set by law. The ideas of the present younger
generation are developing within these boundaries, and if contrary ideas still appear here and
there today, they are immediately suppressed
by law and punished by general contempt.

4. The aspiration for freedom is found
everywhere and always, and there are no
limits to this aspiration. On the contrary, the
more sweeping the rights of the class that is
seeking freedom, and the wider its field of
action, the more boundless become its desires
and the more forceful the measures required
to curb them. In our country, the autocracy
can suppress the disastrous idea of all-corrupt-
ing freedom, and the gentry, true to its duty,
will, with its present influence upon the
peasants, serve as the most reliable support
of the throne. However, with a change in the
present system of governing the serfs, there
is no guarantee that the development of the
new system might not demand changes in
the government of the country as well.

Everything stated above, according to
Prince Drutskoi-Sokolinskii, attests to the
superiority of the present system of pomeshchik administration, which does not cost
either the government or the people anything;
while to appoint, in place of the landowners,
officials, who are also subject to human weaknesses, would require vast sums for their
maintenance. Furthermore, the landowners,

who realize that their own welfare is closely bound up with that of the peasants, strive for the best possible conditions for their peasants.

But these important motives for the care of the peasants cannot exist under any other system of administration.

C. EDUCATION AND INTELLECTUAL TRENDS

XIV:33. THE DECREE OF NICHOLAS I LIMITING FOREIGN EDUCATION, FEBRUARY 18, 1831

Reference: *PSZRI*, 2d ser., 6:167.

With the means of education currently existing in our fatherland, and with our firm resolve to extend and strengthen these still further, we note with regret certain instances of a desire to educate youth outside the country, and the harmful consequences for those who receive such foreign schooling. Young men sometimes return to Russia with the most spurious ideas about it. Ignorant of its true needs, laws, customs, and order, and often of its language, they are strangers in their native land.

To avert such serious inconveniences, we have deemed it necessary to decree the following:

1. Russian youth from ten to eighteen years of age should preferably be educated in native public institutions, or even in their own homes under the supervision of parents and guardians, but always in Russia.

2. Exceptions from this rule may be made solely for certain important reasons, and never otherwise than with our permission.

3. Youths under eighteen years of age cannot be sent to foreign countries for study.

4. Those whose education does not adhere to the above rules shall be deprived of the right to enter the military or any other government service.

XIV:34. THE STATUTE FOR THE RUSSIAN UNIVERSITIES, JULY 26, 1835

This charter altered considerably the organization, administration, and curricula of the universities from the pattern set by Alexander I.

Reference: *PSZRI*, 2d ser., 10:842–44, 846–48, 852.

1. A university is composed of: (1) a definite number of faculties; (2) a council [*sovet*]; and (3) an executive board [*pravlenie*].

2. In its full composition, a university should contain three faculties: philosophy, law, and medicine. . . .

5. The university council, under the chairmanship of the rector, shall be composed of the professors and associate professors [*ordinarnye i ekstraordinarnye professory*].

6. The executive board of the university shall consist of the deans and the syndic, under the chairmanship of the rector.

7. All the Russian universities are under the special patronage of His Imperial Majesty, and therefore bear the name of "imperial."

8. Each university, under the chief jurisdiction of the minister of education, shall be entrusted to the special authority of a superintendent [*popechitel'*]. . . .

11. The faculty of philosophy, consisting of two departments, shall cover the following subjects of study:

First department: (1) philosophy; (2) Greek literature and antiquities; (3) Roman literature and antiquities; (4) Russian literature and the history of Russian letters; (5) the history and literature of the Slavic dialects; (6) world history; (7) Russian history; (8) political economy and statistics; (9) oriental literature, including (a) the Arabic, Turkish, and Persian languages, and (b) the Mongolian and Tatar languages.

Second department: (1) pure and applied mathematics; (2) astronomy; (3) physics and physical geography; (4) chemistry; (5) mineralogy and geognosy; (6) botany; (7) zoology; (8) technology, agriculture, forestry, and architecture. Note: The instructor in architecture shall also serve as university architect.

12. The subjects taught in the faculty of law shall be: (1) the encyclopedia, or a general survey of the system of jurisprudence, Russian state law, i.e. fundamental laws, laws pertaining to the legal status of social classes, and state institutions; (2) Roman legislation and its history; (3) civil law, general, special, and local; (4) laws relating to public law and order; (5) laws concerning state obligations

and finances; (6) police and criminal law; (7) principles of international law (*ius gentium*). . . .

14. A special chair, not belonging to any faculty and for the benefit of all students of the Greco-Russian faith, shall be established for [the teaching of] dogmatic and moral theology, church history, and ecclesiastical law.

15. Each university should have lecturers [*lektory*] in the [following] languages: (1) German, (2) French, (3) English, and (4) Italian.

16. In addition to a teacher of drawing, teachers may be appointed for the [following] arts: (1) fencing, (2) music, and (3) dancing; and, in the Universities of Khar'kov and Kazan', (4) teachers of horseback riding.

17. The professors and associate professors of a faculty, under the chairmanship of the dean, shall constitute the faculty meeting, at which one of the assistant professors [*ad"iunkty*] shall serve as secretary.

18. In the illness or absence of the dean, the senior member of the faculty shall serve in his place.

19. Every faculty member shall be accorded the right, at the meeting, to offer suggestions related to scholarly matters and the curriculum, but this must be done in writing.

20. The subjects dealt with at the faculty meetings shall be: the semiannual distribution and scheduling of courses in the disciplines pertaining to each faculty; review of teaching methods and texts selected by the professors; examination of students and others wishing to receive academic degrees or the right to enter the civil service in the first category [*pervyi razriad*] of officials; examination of candidates for teaching positions in the gymnasiums and uezd schools [*uezdnye uchilishcha*] of the [school] district, if they do not possess the proper academic attestations or certificates; consideration of treatises proposed for publication with the approval of the university and at its expense; censorship of treatises and translations of scholarly content, published by the professors and assistants; selection of annual topics [for prize essays] and judgment of the papers submitted; action on recommendations of the council, and discussion of proposals made by the dean or members of the faculty.

21. Everything said in this chapter concern-ing the faculties also applies to each of the [two] departments of the faculty of philosophy.

Note: The subjects of instruction in each of the faculties, as indicated above, may be increased or temporarily reduced, at the discretion of the minister of education, depending on local conditions and the availability of competent instructors. . . .

30. Subjects dealt with by the council shall include: (1) the election of a rector, honorary members, and correspondents; (2) the election of professors and assistants; their assignment to various positions in the university; the appointment and discharge of lecturers and teachers in the university; (3) consideration of proposals from the faculties concerning measures for the improvement of instruction within the university; (4) the general arrangement of the distribution and scheduling of courses in the university. . . .

47. The superintendent of the university shall be appointed by supreme sovereign decree.

48. The superintendent shall use every means to bring the university into a flourishing state, keeping strict watch that the institutions and personnel connected with it perform their duties vigilantly. He shall pay heed to the ability, diligence, and moral character of the professors, assistants, teachers, and officials of the university, shall reprimand the negligent, and shall take legitimate measures to remove the unreliable. . . .

61. The rector shall be elected for four years from among the full professors by a majority of the votes of the council, and he shall be confirmed in this post by supreme authority [i.e. by the emperor]. . . .

68. The deans shall be chosen for four years from among the full professors by their faculties and shall be confirmed in their posts by the minister [of education]. . . .

71. Particular and direct supervision over the moral character of all students of the university shall be entrusted to the inspector.

72. The inspector shall be under the direct authority of the superintendent. . . .

80. Professors, instructors, and honorary members of the university shall be confirmed in their posts by the minister of education, to whom shall also be accorded the right to appoint at his own discretion, as professors and assistants to vacant chairs, men of outstanding

scholarship and pedagogical gifts, having the academic degree required for these posts. . . .

120. The universities shall maintain their own censorship for theses, dissertations, and other treatises of a scholarly character, whether published by the universities or by their professors. This censorship shall be guided by the regulations of the general statute on censorship.

121. The universities shall be accorded the right to order any kind of educational mate-

rials from abroad, without restriction or payment of duties. . . .

134. Books, manuscripts, and periodicals ordered by professors for their own use shall be allowed to enter from abroad duty free and shall not be subject to examination by the censorship; if, however, any such works of impermissible content are furnished for others to read, responsibility shall be placed upon those who ordered them.

XIV:35. S. S. UVAROV'S PRONOUNCEMENTS ON AUTOCRACY, ORTHODOXY, AND OFFICIAL NATIONALITY, CA. 1833-1843

Count Uvarov, when minister of education under Nicholas I, expounded what became the core of the official philosophy of that regime. The expression "official nationality" has become standard only since the late-nineteenth century as the designation for what Uvarov and his contemporaries called simply *narodnost'* ("nationality").

Reference: *Zhurnal Ministerstva Narodnogo Prosveshcheniia*, pt. 1, no. 1 (1834), pp. XLIX-L [Mar. 21, 1833]; pt. 18, no. 4 (April 1838), pp. CXLV-CLI [General Report for 1837]; *Desiatiletie Ministerstva Narodnogo Prosveshcheniia, 1833-1843* (St. Petersburg, 1864), pp. 2-3 [1843 report]. The translation of the last selection is taken from Nicholas V. Riasanovsky, *Nicholas I and Official Nationality in Russia, 1825-1855* (Berkeley and Los Angeles: University of California Press, 1959), pp. 74-75.

[From Uvarov's instruction to the staff of the Ministry of Public Education, March 21, 1833:]

Our general duty consists of this: that the education of the people be conducted in conformity with the *supreme* intention of our *august monarch* in the united spirit of Orthodoxy, autocracy, and [official] nationality.

[From Uvarov's General Report for 1837, submitted to His Imperial Majesty by the Ministry of Public Education, April 1838:]
General Conclusion

In concluding this brief review, I make bold to add that the feeling of gratification with which I hope this picture of successes will be received by the well-intentioned can find its origin not only in the harmonious development of mental powers, nor only in the unexpected increase in the statistics, nor even in the awakening of a common aspiration in men's minds for a goal set forth by the government. Other aspects and a higher purpose were envisaged at the same time by the ministry, renovated to its very foundations and uplifted by the unceasing concern of Your Imperial Majesty.

To enliven all intellectual powers, but yet to keep their tendencies within the limits of

a secure order; to inspire youth with the knowledge that at all levels of public life mental improvement without moral improvement is but a dream, and a pernicious one; to eradicate the antagonism between so-called European education and our needs and requirements; to cure our newest generation of blind and unthinking predilection toward the superficial and the foreign, instilling in its youthful minds a cordial respect for things of their own country and a full conviction that only the adaptation of general, universal education to our national way of life and to our national spirit can bring forth genuine benefits for each and all; then, to encompass with a sure glance the vast sphere of action opened before our beloved fatherland, to appraise precisely all the contradictory elements of our civil education, all the historical facts that converge in the vast structure of our empire; to direct these developing elements and awakened energies insofar as possible toward a common denominator; and, finally, to seek this denominator in the tripartite concept of Orthodoxy, autocracy and [official] nationality—such, in brief outline, is the direction given to the Ministry of Public Education by Your Majesty from the time when Your Most Gracious Majesty deigned to entrust me with the difficult, but at the same time important and flattering, task of serving as the instrument of your high purpose in this transformation. . . .

Soon after assuming this post, I set forth before Your Imperial Majesty with most loyal frankness and in the following manner the dangers that at the time seemed, to my mind, to beset this road: "Fortunately, Russia has preserved her warm faith in certain religious, moral, and political ideas which belong exclusively to her. . . . But these principles [Orthodoxy, autocracy, nationality], dispelled by premature and superficial education, by fanciful and unsuccessful experiments—. . . principles that for the past thirty years have continuously faced a prolonged and stubborn struggle—how can they be reconciled with the contemporary frame of mind? Shall we have time to include them in the system of general education, which would combine the advantages of our time with the traditions of the past and the hopes of the future? How can we establish popular education appropriate to our way of life and not alien to the European spirit? Whose hand, both experienced and strong, can contain the aspirations of intellects within the bounds of order and tranquillity and repulse anything that may violate the general order?" . . .

Everything in public institutions seethes with new life; everything flows toward the goal of superior and most proper education. Having lost none of the advantages of European education inherited from our forebears, we shun its errors; we are becoming less receptive to its blandishments; language, the true promoter of national spirit, is already gradually bringing together the center of the empire and territories where heretofore its sound has evoked either hatred or indifference. But, on the other hand, it would be futile to subject everything indiscriminately to a single fixed form throughout the vast expanse of Russia, with all its diverse sections, without regard for the local needs and the special situation in each separate section. Today, according to the will of Your Majesty, the eastern regions of the empire enjoy a system of education that is gradually acquainting itself with Asiatic life, pays particular attention to the languages and literatures of Asia, and attracts to our schools inhabitants of the remote Asiatic steppes. With the further

development of this plan, which is to encompass the territory of the Caucasus and the Trans-Caucasian regions, the University of Kazan' should one day constitute an important link connecting two peoples and, so to speak, two parts of the world, at least in an intellectual sense. At the other end of the empire, in what is known as the Baltic [Ostzeiskie] guberniias, the ministry, prompted by your instructions, has made every endeavor to inculcate knowledge of the Russian language and Russian education, without, however, impeding the development of knowledge in subjects related to the special position of these guberniias. But nowhere has the success been as striking as in the guberniias restored from Poland.

[From Uvarov's report on ten years of the Ministry of Education, 1843:]

In the midst of the rapid collapse in Europe of religious and civil institutions, at the time of a general spread of destructive ideas, at the sight of grievous phenomena surrounding us on all sides, it was necessary to establish our fatherland on firm foundations upon which is based the well-being, strength, and life of a people. It was necessary to find the principles which form the distinctive character of Russia, and which belong only to Russia; it was necessary to gather into one whole the sacred remnants of Russian nationality and to fasten to them the anchor of our salvation. Fortunately, Russia has retained a warm faith in the sacred principles without which she cannot prosper, gain in strength, live. Sincerely and deeply attached to the church of his fathers, the Russian has of old considered it the guarantee of social and family happiness. Without a love for the faith of its ancestors a people, as well as an individual, must perish. A Russian, devoted to his fatherland, will agree as little to the loss of a single dogma of our *Orthodoxy* as to the theft of a single pearl from the tsar's crown. *Autocracy* constitutes the main condition of the political existence of Russia. The Russian giant stands on it as on the cornerstone of his greatness. An innumerable majority of the subjects of *Your Majesty* feel this truth: they feel it in full measure, although they are placed in different rungs of civil life and although they vary in education and in their relations to the government. The saving conviction that Russia lives and is protected by the spirit of a strong, humane, and enlightened autocracy must permeate popular education and must develop with it. Together with these two national principles there is a third, no less important, no less powerful: *nationality*.

XIV:36. THE "FIRST PHILOSOPHICAL LETTER" OF PETER CHAADAEV, 1836

This "Letter" by Petr Iakovlevich Chaadaev (1793-1856) was originally written in French in 1829. Its publication in Russian in 1836 by the journal *Teleskop* led not only to the banning of the journal but also to the tsar's decision that Chaadaev was "officially" insane. Through this *cause célèbre* Chaadaev gained great prestige and popularity among the Russian intelligentsia. The following excerpts help to explain the divergent reactions to his views.

Reference: *Sochineniia i pis'ma P. Ia. Chaadaeva,* ed. M. O. Gershenzon, 2 vols. (Moscow: A. I. Mamontov, 1913-14), 1:78-86; 2:109-19. The English translation in Eugene A. Moskoff, *The Russian Philosopher Chaadayev: His Ideas and His Epoch* (New York: Colonial Printing and Publishing Co., 1937), pp. 29-46, has been used with considerable revision. Recently there have appeared several other translations of this document: James M. Edie, James P. Scanlan, and Mary-Barbara Zeldin, eds., *Russian Philosophy,* 2 vols. (Chicago: Quadrangle Books, 1965), 1: 106-25; Marc Raeff, ed., *Russian Intellectual History: An Anthology* (New York: Harcourt, Brace and World, 1966), pp. 160-73; *The Major Works of Peter Chaadaev,* trans. and commentary Raymond T. McNally (Notre Dame, Ind.: University of Notre Dame Press, 1969), pp. 23-51; and *Peter Yakovlevich Chaadayev: Philosophical Letters and Apology of a Madman,* trans. and introduction Mary-Barbara Zeldin (Knoxville: University of Tennessee Press, 1969), pp. 31-51. Portions are included in Hans Kohn, ed., *The Mind of Modern Russia: Historical and Political Thought of Russia's Great Age* (New Brunswick, N.J.: Rutgers University Press, 1955), pp. 38-46. (Kohn's book also gives translated excerpts from the writings of Belinskii, Chernyshevskii, Herzen, and others.)

Every people has its period of violent agitation, passionate uneasiness, of activity without any deliberate motive. During that period men become wanderers about the world, both in body and in spirit. It is the age of great excitement, vast enterprise, strong national passions. People then toss in excitement, without any apparent reason, but not without benefit for future generations. All societies have passed through these periods which have provided them with their most vivid memories, their marvels, their poetry, and all their greatest and most fertile concepts. Such periods are the essential bases of any society; otherwise, societies would have nothing in their soil. This fascinating phase in the history of nations is the period of adolescence, a moment when their faculties are at the highest stage of development, a moment whose memory is a joy and a lesson for their maturity. We [Russians] have nothing like this. Savage barbarism, first, immense superstition next, then cruel and debasing foreign domination whose spirit our national government later inherited. Such is the sad history of our youth. We have had nothing similar to that age of exuberant activity, of the impassioned play of the moral forces of nations. The epoch of our social life corresponding to this period has been dull and somber, without vigor or energy, enlivened only by crime and mitigated only by servitude. No charming souvenirs, no pleasing images in the memory; no mighty lessons in our national tradition. Cast your eye over all the centuries we have traversed, over all the territory we occupy, and you will discover no arresting memory, no venerable memorial which speaks with force about the past, and vividly and picturesquely recreates it for you. We live only in the most confined present, without a past or a future, in the midst of a dead calm.

   · · ·

If we wish to occupy a position similar to that of other civilized peoples, we must, somehow, retrace the entire education of mankind for ourselves. The history of nations and the results of the passage of centuries will serve as aids. . . .

Peoples live only by the strong impressions which the preceding ages have left in their spirit and by their contact with other peoples. In this way each individual feels himself in harmony with all of humanity. . . . Having come into the world as illegitimate children, without a heritage, without any links with the men who preceded us on the earth, we possess in our hearts none of the lessons which preceded our own existence. . . . This is the natural consequence of an entirely imported and imitative culture. We have had no internal development, no natural progress. New ideas sweep away the old because they do not come from the latter but rather appear from God knows where. Since we merely acquire ideas already completely formed, the indelible mark which a consistent movement of ideas engraves on the mind and which gives it strength leaves no trace on our brain. We grow but do not mature; we advance but along a devious line, that is to say along one which leads to no goal. We are like those children who have not been made to think for themselves. Having become men, they have nothing of their own; all their knowledge lies on the surface of their being; their whole soul is on the outside. This is precisely the case with us.

. . .

And I ask you, where are our sages or our thinkers? . . . Nevertheless, situated between the two great world divisions, the Orient and the Occident, with one elbow touching China and the other, Germany, we should unite in ourselves the two great principles of an intelligent nature, imagination and reason, and combine in our civilization the histories of the entire world. This is not the role assigned us by Providence. Far from it; it seems to be in no way concerned with our destiny. . . . The historical experience does not exist for us. Epochs and generations have passed without any benefit to us. Looking at us one could say that the general law of mankind has been revoked in our case. Alone in the world, we have given it nothing, we have taught it nothing; we have added not a single idea to the multitude of man's ideas; we have contributed nothing to the progress of the human mind and we have disfigured everything we have gained from this process. Nothing, since the very first moment of our social existence, has issued from us for the general good of man; no useful thought has sprouted from the sterile soil of our fatherland; no great

truth has sprung forth from our midst. We have not taken the trouble to invent anything ourselves and we have borrowed from the inventions of others only deceptive externals and useless luxury. . . . In order to attract attention, it was necessary for us to stretch from the Bering Strait to the Oder. Once a great man wished to civilize us and he threw the mantle of civilization to us to give us a foretaste of enlightenment; we picked up the mantle but did not meddle with the civilization. Later, another great prince, associating us with his glorious mission, led us victoriously from one end of Europe to the other. Returning from this triumphant march across the most civilized countries of the world, we brought back only ideas and aspirations the result of which was an immense calamity which set us back a half century. We have a certain indefinable something in our blood which repulses any genuine progress. In the end, we have lived and still live only to serve as some great lesson for distant generations who will understand it. Today, whatever one says, we are a blank spot in the intellectual order. I cannot wonder enough at this emptiness and astonishing isolation of our social existence. . . .

While the edifice of modern civilization was arising from the struggle between the energetic barbarism of the peoples of the North and the lofty concepts of religion, what were we doing? Driven by a fatal destiny, we went to seek in miserable Byzantium, greatly despised by these people, a moral code which should shape our education.

. . .

Although we bore the name of Christians, we did not budge while Christianity advanced majestically along the route traced for it by its divine maker and carried along generations after it. While the world completely rebuilt itself, nothing was constructed in our country; we remained huddled in our hovels of logs and straw. In a word, the new destinies of the human race achieved nothing for us. Though we were Christians, the fruits of Christianity did not ripen for us.

XIV:37. THE WESTERNIZERS: BELINSKII IN THE 1840s

Vissarion Grigorievich Belinskii (1811–48), a colorful young literary critic, was a changeable but influential voice in the debates over Russia's relationship with the West. These excerpts touch upon only a few of his many opinions.

Reference: V. G. Belinskii, *Polnoe sobranie sochinenii,* 13 vols. (Moscow: AN SSSR, 1953-59), 5:91, 93, 105, 121, 136, 137, 144, 145 [on Golikov's work]; 10:8, 17-18, 19, 21, 29, 30 [on 1846]; 10:198, 202, 213 [1847]; 12:23-24, 66 [letters of 1841]. Vissarion G. Belinsky, *Selected Philosophical Works* (Moscow: Foreign Languages Publishing House, 1948) contains translations of the last four excerpts from the article on Golikov's work and the three letters to Botkin and Gogol; those translations have been used here with considerable revision. The letter to Gogol is also translated in Raeff, *Russian Intellectual History,* pp. 253-61, and in Ralph E. Matlaw, ed. and introduction, *Belinsky, Chernyshevsky, and Dobrolyubov: Selected Criticism* (New York: E. P. Dutton, 1962), pp. 83-92.

[From his article "On I. I. Golikov's Work, *The Deeds of Peter the Great*" (1841):]

What is love for one's own without love for what belongs to all? What is love for that which is of one's native land without love for that which belongs to mankind in general? Do the Russians exist by themselves, and mankind by itself? God forbid! Only some Chinese can be separate and independent in their relations with mankind. But this is why they are a caricature, a parody on mankind.

. . .

Peter the Great was the greatest phenomenon not only in our history, but in the history of all mankind. He was a god who called us back to life, who blew a living soul into the body of ancient Russia, colossal, but sunk in a deadly torpor.

. . .

Everything great, noble, human, and spiritual came up, grew, burst into splendid bloom, and brought forth sumptuous fruit on European soil. The diversity of life, the noble relations between the sexes, the refinement of customs, art, science, the subjugation of the unconscious forces of nature, the victory over matter, the triumph of the spirit, the respect for the human personality, the sacredness of human rights—in short, everything that makes one proud of being a man . . . all this is the result of the development of European life. Everything human is European, and everything European is human. . . .

Russia never belonged and never could belong, in the basic elements of its life, to Asia: it represented a singular, isolated phenomenon. The Tatars, perhaps, should have brought her into closer kinship with Asia. They did, indeed, manage mechanically to bind her with external ties to Asia for a time, but they could not accomplish this spiritually, because Russia is a Christian country. And so, Peter acted entirely within the national spirit when he brought his native land into closer contact with Europe and sought to eradicate the temporary Asiatic elements introduced by the Tatars.

. . .

Peter the Great's reforms and the Europeanism he introduced in no way changed, nor could they change, our national character but only reanimated it with the spirit of a new and richer life and provided it with a boundless sphere for development and activity.

. . .

The nation was the same and Peter did not recreate it (no one but God could perform such a feat), but merely led it out of crooked trite paths onto the high road of a universal-historical life.

. . .

And, therefore, gentlemen, defenders of our barbarous ancient custom, say what you will, but the equestrian statue to Peter the Great on Saint Isaac's Square is not enough: altars should be put up to him in all the squares and streets of the great kingdom of Russia!

. . .

If we are destined to become European Russians and Russian Europeans, we should not reproach Peter but rather should wonder how he could have accomplished such a gigantic task, a task without precedent since the beginning of the world. And so the crux of the matter consists in the words "Shall we be?" And we can answer firmly and freely that we not only *shall be,* but are already *becoming* European Russians and Russian Europeans, that we have been becoming so since the reign of Catherine II, and that we are making progress therein day by day right up to the present time.

. . .

Peter carried out in thirty years a task that provides work for whole centuries. That is why he is a giant among giants, a genius among geniuses, a tsar among tsars.

[From his article "A View on Russian Literature in 1846":]

Like everything else in contemporary Russia that is alive, beautiful, and rational, our literature is the product of Peter the Great's reforms. True, he gave no attention to literature and did nothing for its inception, but he turned his attention to education and cast the seed of learning and enlightenment on the fertile soil of the Russian spirit—and literature eventually appeared of its own accord, without his knowledge, as a natural result of his own activity.

.   .   .

[About the Slavophiles:] The fact of the matter is that the positive side of their doctrine consists of some sort of nebulous, mystical presentiments of the victory of the East over the West, the fallacy of which is all too clearly exposed by the facts of reality. . . . The negative side of their teaching, however, deserves much more attention, not because it speaks out against the allegedly decaying West (the Slavophiles are absolutely unable to understand the West because they measure it with an oriental yardstick) but because they speak out against Russian Europeanism, about which they have a good deal to say that is pertinent and which one cannot help at least half-agreeing with, such as, e.g., that there is a sort of duality in Russian life and, consequently, a lack of moral unity; that this deprives us of a clearly defined national character such as distinguishes, to their credit, almost all European nations; that this makes us some sort of intellectual straddlers well able to think in French, German, and English but unable to think in Russian.

.   .   .

Are the Slavophiles right, and have the reforms of Peter the Great merely deprived us of nationality and made us intellectual straddlers? . . .

No, this [the partial validity of Slavophile accusations] indicates something quite different, namely, that Russia has fully spent and gotten over the epoch of reform, that the reforms have completed their work, have done for her everything they could have and are supposed to have done, and that the time has come for Russia to develop independently and in accordance with her own essence.

.   .   .

It is time for us to cease admiring everything European simply because it is not Asiatic and to admire, respect, and seek it simply because it is *human* [*chelovecheskoe*], rejecting on those grounds everything European that is not human as vigorously as we would reject everything Asiatic that is not human.

.   .   .

It is impossible to define yet exactly what this Russian nationality comprises: we are content for the time being that the elements of it are beginning to come to light and break through the colorless imitative gloom into which Peter the Great's reforms had plunged us.

.   .   .

Nationalities are the personalities of humanity. Without nationalities humanity would be a dead logical abstraction, a word without meaning, a sound without tenor. On this subject I would sooner side with the Slavophiles than remain on the side of the humanist cosmopolitans, because, if the former do err, they err as living human beings, whereas the latter, if they speak the truth, sound like some sort of book of logic. . . . But, fortunately, I hope to remain where I am without taking sides.

.   .   .

No single man can by himself substitute for all men . . . each and all are indispensable to all and each. On this is based the unity and fraternity of the human race. Man is strong and secure only in society; but in order that society in its turn might be strong and secure it needs an inner, direct, organic bond—nationality [*natsional'nost'*].

.   .   .

Strictly speaking, the conflict of the human with the national is nothing more than a rhetorical figure of speech, and in reality it does not exist. Even when the progress of one nation is accomplished by borrowing from another, it is nevertheless accomplished nationally. Otherwise there is no progress. . . . A nation without nationality is like a man without personality. This is evidenced by the fact that all nations that have been playing and still play leading roles in the history of mankind have been distinguished and are still distinguished by clearly defined nationality. Remember the Jews, the Greeks, and the Romans; look at the French, the English, the

Germans. In our times national feuds and antipathies have entirely died out.

[From his review article "The *Moscow Literary and Scientific Anthology* for 1847" (1847):]

Loving Russia above all else, and wishing her, first of all, all the best, we also desire every good both for all the Slavic and for all other *human* tribes. Nevertheless, only Russia will remain the exclusive object of our love; but then we are also concerned and interested in those nations and peoples of Europe from which the light of education and enlightenment came pouring into Russia. We understand even the warmest and most exclusive love of the Russian for Russia, but we do not understand Slavophilism and consider it something bookish, literary, spurious, and artificial. All the European nations are kin to one another. . . . Russia has so far outdistanced all the [other] Slavic peoples in enlightenment and education, with her political and state power; she is so rich in the promise of life and a splendid future, that she has nothing whatsoever to learn or borrow from the [other] Slavic peoples. Study of the Slavic tribes can only be of purely scholarly or literary interest to us, important chiefly from a philological point of view.

. . .

[But] Mr. Khomiakov wants to bring society [*obshchestvo*] down to the level of the people [narod] at any cost, rather than to elevate the people to the level of society, which would be a much more natural desire. . . . The supposed cleavage between society and the people will be eliminated in time by the achievements of civilization, which will raise the people to the level of society. But this cleavage, I repeat, is more apparent than real: it is more a matter of the style of clothing than of ideas or even habits. The Russian is Russian everywhere. . . . The Russian soldier, just like the French, the English, and the German soldier, has his special character, his special physiognomy. The Russian soldier is altogether a Russian, both in his virtues and in his faults. His ideas, ways of thinking, speech, proverbs, jests, and songs—all are purely Russian, national, despite the fact that he dresses, marches, and fights in wars in completely European fashion.

[From Belinskii's letter to N. V. Gogol, July 3, 1847:]

You did not notice that Russia sees her salvation not in mysticism, nor in asceticism, nor in pietism, but in the successes of civilization, enlightenment, and humanity. What she needs is not sermons (she has heard enough of them!) or prayers (she has repeated them enough!), but the awakening in the people of a sense of their human dignity lost for so many centuries amid the dirt and refuse; she needs rights and laws conforming, not with the teachings of the church, but with common sense and justice, and the strictest possible observance of them. But, instead, she presents the dire spectacle of a country where men traffic in men, without even having the excuse so insidiously exploited by American plantation owners who claim that the Negro is not a man; . . . of a country where there are not only no guarantees for individuality, honor, and property, but even no police order, and where there is nothing but vast corporations of official thieves and robbers of various descriptions!

[From a letter to fellow-critic V. P. Botkin, March 1, 1841:]

A fine Prussian government in which we fancied to see the ideal of rational government! Scoundrels, tyrants of mankind! A member of the triple alliance of executioners of liberty and reason. So that's Hegel for you! . . . The most rational government is that of the North American States, followed by England and France.

[From a letter to Botkin, September 8, 1841:]

You know my nature: it is always at extremes and never strikes the center of an idea. I part with an old idea with difficulty and a pang, renounce it completely, and take up a new one with all the fanaticism of a proselyte. And so, I am now at a new extreme, the idea of *socialism,* which has become for me the idea of ideas, the being of beings, the question of questions, the alpha and omega of belief and knowledge. It is the be-all and end-all. It is the question and its solution. It has (for me) engulfed history and religion and philosophy.

XIV:38. PETRASHEVSKII'S TESTIMONY, MAY-JUNE 1849

Mikhail Vasil'evich Butashevich-Petrashevskii (1821-66), a minor bureaucrat, formed a circle of young intellectuals in Saint Petersburg in 1845 to discuss socialism and reforms in Russia. The group came to be known as the *Petrashevtsy;* one member was Fedor Dostoevskii. In April 1849, in the wake of the European revolution of 1848, the Third Section arrested most of them for treason and subversion. Their military trial brought fifteen death sentences, which however were at the last minute commuted to lesser punishments, including various terms of exile at hard labor. These are excerpts from the testimony given by Butashevich-Petrashevskii in May and June 1849.

Reference: V. Desnitskii, ed., *Delo petrashevtsev,* Pamiatniki obshchestvennoi mysli no. 1 (Moscow: AN SSSR, 1937), pp. 28-30, 71, 73-74, 86, 88-89, 91, 92, 95-96, 127, 138.

My prison companions—those whom I know—and I are not fanatics, nor wild zealots, nor heretics. . . . We are people convinced of the truth and usefulness of many ideas in the system of Fourier. We are philosophers, and we value truth above all. If I, who am perhaps the chief and the oldest propagator of Fourierist ideas, am still only twenty-eight years old, the rest are younger and have been acquainted with this system for less time. We are not hardened criminals nor enemies of public tranquillity, but rather the friends of peaceful development. If there is anything erroneous and wrong in our thinking, show us the truth and we shall renounce our ideas. In the meantime, allow us to remain what we are.

Let a learned commission be appointed . . . to include professors of universities and academies, and educated men from various ministries. Let the commission itself elect its own chairman. But allow us also some time to get ready. This will not be an answer to a criminal charge; it will be something more important. Allow us to gather our resources. Let this commission meet three or four months hence. If you consider us harmful, keep us confined until then. But return our books to us, and permit us to confer with each other. Permit us also to form a committee for the defense of our convictions.

· · ·

I beg you, Messrs. Interrogators, also to inform His Imperial Majesty that here, in the silence of imprisonment, while analyzing the accusation itself—this black calumny, this fantastic design imputed to me—I have become even more strongly convinced than before that the greatest need of the Russian land is for justice; here is the surest bulwark of the social order. What Russia needs—and

needs greatly—is the introduction of advocates and trial by jury.

· · ·

I deny any intent to revolt—I am too intelligent to think of such nonsense, much less to prepare it. The slip of paper cited as evidence is an introduction to a plan for the emancipation of the peasants, a general sketch of all the reforms, everything that can influence the development of society. I confess that much more I wished to see a full and complete reform of our social life, and I regarded the phalanstery as the key, the touchstone of such a reform.

· · ·

I declared that I confess to regarding Fourier's system the best of all the social theories I have heretofore known and that I have spoken about those of Fourier's ideas that I consider true. In addition to this, I have the honor to declare that I consider those ideas true and just that do not run counter to the fundamental principles of social life.

· · ·

Fourier's system is nothing other than a philosophy of social life (almost the same as an encyclopedia of jurisprudence, or natural law—only more sensible than either), one of the component parts of the philosophy of nature or of philosophy in general. I do not know of any law that forbids men to occupy themselves with philosophy in general, or with the philosophy of nature, or any of its parts, or even to evince their preference for any philosopher, such as Kant, Hegel, Plato, and so on, and to endeavor to convince others of the justice of such esteem. In replying to this clause in the accusation, one might ask: "Can science flourish in Russia after this?" And you ask yourself: "Are you indeed living in Europe, in the mid-nineteenth century, a member of the Caucasian race?" Such an accusation in our century is more absurd than the charge of black magic and sorcery leveled in former times against all who concerned themselves with the natural sciences.

If we take all these circumstances into account, it becomes clear that the attempt by the prosecutors to treat the acceptance of these ideas and the dissemination of those that are not contrary to the fundamental principles of society as a crime is an action directly counter to the law.

Those who cite belief in Fourier's ideas as proof of intent to revolt simply reveal by this accusation their total ignorance of Fourier's system. Not only is this system openly anti-revolutionary—i.e. opposed to every upheaval produced by violence—but also it generally attributes almost no significance to political reforms, i.e. shifts in power of any form; for the mere shift in power cannot in itself raise low levels of public prosperity. We might cite many passages from Fourier's works as proof of its antirevolutionary nature, and hence of its desire to preserve every existing order. . . .

Thus, the entering of approval of many of Fourier's ideas as evidence of criminal intent is, on the one hand, unlawful, and, on the other, clear proof of the absolute ignorance of the accuser.

. . .

Since I know more about socialism than the other prisoners (of whom many would declare themselves socialists), I consider it my duty to offer the clearest possible explanation of this subject, in order that the false prejudices, which may be assumed to exist to the detriment of socialism, may vanish entirely, and everything relating to this matter may become properly comprehensible. . . .

By the term *socialism* is generally understood the theories concerning society, and *socialists* are all those who are occupied with the problems of social life. . . . What living member of society, I ask you, is not a socialist in some sense, without knowing it himself?

Socialism is not an invention of modern times, a cunning innovation of the nineteenth century like the steamship, locomotive, or photography. It has always existed in the nature of man and will continue to exist there until mankind loses its capacity to develop and perfect itself.

. . .

Read the Acts of the Apostles; you will be convinced yourselves that the first Christians were socialists in feeling (les socialistes par le sentiment)—that is, communists. You will see that in practice communism existed among them, as among the Essenes, one of the Jewish sects preceding them in time. At first, the basic tenet of communism—communal property— was strictly observed by them, as corroborated by the story of Ananias and his wife, who were put to death for concealing a small sum of money, even after they surrendered the entire value of their possessions. However, the communism of the first centuries of Christianity was only a burst of noble feelings. It consisted of gifts from the rich for the benefit of their poor brethren, but this did not take the form of correct economic institutions and did not embrace all the areas of social life. This is why it remained a phenomenon or trend of primitive Christianity that has received little notice until recent years.

It does not require unusual intellectual power or an extraordinarily fertile imagination to arrive at the idea of communism once you embrace the dogma "Love thy neighbor as thyself." This will occur by itself if only you desire to follow this dogma faithfully. . . . If I come to love my neighbor as myself, can I deny him the right to equal use of my goods, my possessions, my property? . . . Those who attack communism as a doctrine are attacking the basic tenet of Christianity and prohibiting its external manifestation. . . . In condemning it, you deprive man of the right to do good . . . you introduce into society the deadening company of egotism.

. . .

Socialism generally is not the whimsical invention of a few eccentrics but the result of mankind's development; it is the tenet of Christian love, seeking its practical realization in contemporary life . . . "Honi soit qui mal y pense."

. . .

Socialism, despite the beneficence of its aims and aspirations, has been and still is in Europe subjected to so much misinterpretation and even cheap abuse and ridicule, chiefly because it is a theory (a principle) *directly contrary to liberalism;* and also because, in opposing the abuses and the robbery which the Rothschilds and other owners of monetary capital are still permitted by law to perpetrate in society by means of *cornering the market* (*accaparage*) and stock market speculation (*agiotage*), it presents such immoral activities in their true light and thus interferes with the success of speculations of this sort. The liberals and the bankers are today the rulers (the feudal lords) of western Europe. The former rule through their influence upon public opinion; the latter, through the stock exchange and industry, ordering the phenomena of social life according to their own arbitrary will.

. . .

Socialism . . . is the vital creative force within society, the spirit of betterment, the dogma of Christianity, taking root in practical life. The higher and more complete the development of a society, the more you will find in it objects of communal *use, of communal ownership* (communist institutions), or the cheaper will be their use because *of pooled resources* (*par Association* . . .). Take a look at the churches of God, where everyone prays free of charge, at public promenades, shelters, monasteries, barracks, at public institutions for education, and so forth. Wherever there are comforts and services accessible to many, you will find the spirit of socialism. Take a look at your villages, at your peasant who has not, despite his lack of industry, descended to a degree of poverty in any way commensurate with his laziness. Look for the reasons, and you will find that the system of repartition of fields, the common use of land, is responsible for this.

If I have succeeded in fully explaining this, I flatter myself with the hope that you will tell those who may attack socialism in the future that to do so is to attack everything that is alive and vital in society, to break social bonds, to deprive everyone of the right to perform good, to introduce deadening egotism into society—and to plunge it into the silence of the grave and the stillness of the cemetery!

. . .

I have often said to my acquaintances—it was probably well known to everyone that the secret police kept a close eye on me for a long time—that, guilty or innocent, I would be the first to be seized, and that they too might share this fate. But the need for intelligent conversation was so strong that it compelled people to overlook the danger . . . and now they share with me the unpleasantness of imprisonment. . . . Such is the triumph of the spirit over matter. . . . None of them was willing to believe that it is possible for a man to find himself in a dungeon only because there are a couple of consistent ideas in his head. . . . Yet this turned out to be true. . . . Oh, men! . . . Oh, times! . . .

Had we a public "Literary-Scientific Society," where all scholars and writers could meet, dine, and talk about subjects of interest to them, without playing cards, then everyone would have preferred such discourse to discussions in a private home. . . . The Russian public has a pressing need for such a society.

. . .

You see before you, Messrs. Interrogators, the moral and intellectual flower of Petersburg, and perhaps of Russian youth. . . . Do not permit a hostile hand to inflict a heavy blow against our public life, meager as it is; . . . do not bring upon society the stillness of the grave and the silence of the cemetery. . . . Crowds of moral cripples are not a sight to gladden the eye, and social cretinism is not a heavenly blessing. . . . But this cretinism will install itself among us if science is destroyed in society, and if all free development of the personality is stopped. . . .

Do not seek to indict us for concern with the problem of social organization; do not quarrel with every rash and careless word, but look into the moral sentiment that moved each of us.

XIV:39. THE DIRECTIVE TO TIGHTEN STATE CONTROL OVER HIGHER EDUCATION, JANUARY 23, 1851

Other consequences of the unrest of 1848 in Europe and European universities are reflected in this directive.
Reference: *PSZRI*, 2d ser., vol. 26, pt. 1, pp. 82-84.

Instruction to the Rector of the University and to the Deans of the Faculties:

1. . . . The present instruction applies to the Universities of Saint Petersburg, Moscow, Saint Vladimir [Kiev], Khar'kov, and Kazan'.

2. The special purpose of the present instruction is to strengthen control over university teaching. All other duties of the rector and the deans remain unchanged.

3. The rector shall have supervision over university courses and over the performance of instructors. . . . The deans, as chairmen of the faculties, are the rector's closest assistants, sharing with him direct supervision over the successful conduct, the appropriate progress, and particularly over the spirit and direction of instruction.

4. Before the beginning of his lectures, every professor must submit to his dean a detailed syllabus of his subject, explaining the scope, sequence, and method of instruction, and giving complete information about the works to be used as texts, either in full or in part. . . . The syllabus thus prepared must be reviewed and confirmed at the faculty meeting, with all members participating, and consequently must serve as the chief basis for the professor's lectures. . . .

7. No lectures may be delivered prior to the faculty's ratification of the syllabus and the rector's approval. The only exceptions to this rule are theological and philosophical subjects (logic and experimental psychology), whose syllabi are approved by the Ministry of Public Education in consultation with the authorities of the Orthodox church. . . .

11. In reviewing each syllabus, the following must be kept constantly in mind: (a) that the subject must be presented fully, in accordance with the requirements of university study; (b) that the general outlines as well as the specific points of the syllabus must strictly conform to a scholarly and moral purpose; (c) that the contents of the syllabus should not cover anything at variance with the doctrine of the Orthodox church or with our system of government and the spirit of our national institutions; and (d) that, on the contrary, reverence for everything holy, devotion to the sovereign, and love of the fatherland should be given clear and positive expression wherever reasonably applicable.

12. The dean shall see to the proper fulfillment of the syllabi by the professors of his faculty, attending their lectures for this purpose as often as possible.

13. If he notices that a professor permits himself to deviate somewhat, no matter how harmlessly, from the curriculum, or injects into his lectures remarks having no direct connection with the subject and therefore useless to the students, the dean shall immediately notify the rector of this fact.

14. If the rector and dean establish that this infraction of the predetermined order was without any reprehensible intention, they shall make the proper admonition to the professor in private and shall intensify their joint surveillance over his lectures.

15. If, contrary to expectation, the professor should not heed this private admonition, or if he should permit himself harmful utterances to the students during his lectures, the rector and dean must report this without delay to the district superintendent and the latter must, upon proper verification of the soundness of their information and the immediate adoption of the requisite measures to halt the evil, report the matter to the minister of public education.

16. The dean has the right at any time to demand of the professor the manuscripts of his lectures, or to collect from the students their lecture notes, compiled from the professor's words, for closer comparison of the actual teaching with the syllabus.

XIV:40. THE WESTERNIZERS: GRANOVSKII'S WRITINGS OF CA. 1840-1855

Timofei Nikolaevich Granovskii (1813-55), professor of European history at the University of Moscow from 1839 to 1855, was extremely influential in fostering a wide understanding of Western culture among his students. The first selection below, intended as part of the introduction to his textbook, was found among his notes after his death and was first published in the third edition of his works, in 1892.

Reference: *Sochineniia T. N. Granovskogo*, 3d ed., 2 vols. (Moscow, 1892, 2:457-62 [from his textbook]; *T. N. Granovskii i ego perepiska*, 2 vols. (Moscow, 1897), 2:381, 448, 453, 456.

[From Granovskii's textbook on universal history:]

Universal history presupposes the concept of the unity of mankind, which did not and could not exist in a pagan world—which presented the spectacle of people divided by countless, mutually hostile religions. Only Christianity, which proclaimed that all men are the children of one Father and united them into a single spiritual family, has brought into man's life those ideas that ultimately made possible the development of our discipline.

. . .

Above all the laws of historical development discovered by science, there is one supreme law, the moral law, the fulfillment of which constitutes humanity's ultimate purpose on earth. The highest benefit of history, therefore, is that it imparts to us a rational conviction of the inevitable triumph of good over evil. . . .

. . . Mankind, which is to be merged by Christianity into one spiritual family, already constitutes a natural family, united by its common forefather Adam. If we admit this kinship as existing among all the inhabitants of the earth, we must also necessarily accept its logical corollary that all races of men possess equal capacity for education and perfectibility.

[From Granovskii's correspondence: a letter to N. V. Stankevich, February 1840:]

I know very well the weaknesses of the Kireevskiis. Their convictions differ from mine; I even consider these convictions harmful and fight against them within my own sphere of activity. As a teacher, I shall always attack like views. As a writer (if I should write), I will do the same. But as a private individual I enjoy visiting them. Whatever one might say, they are educated people: they think (even if their ideas are awry); they have profound interests and high integrity.

[From a letter to A. I. Herzen, 1854:]

Why did you cast a stone at Peter [the Great], who by no means deserved your accusations, since your facts are incorrect? The more we live, the more colossal does Peter's image loom before us. To you, who have been cut off from Russia and have lost touch with it, he cannot be as near and as comprehensible. Seeing the faults of the West, you lean toward the Slavs and are prepared to extend your hand to them. But if you lived here for awhile, you would speak differently. One must have much faith and love to preserve any hope for the future of even the strongest and sturdiest of the Slavic peoples. Our soldiers and sailors are dying gloriously in the Crimea. But no one here knows how to live.

[From a letter to the historian K. D. Kavelin, January 1855:]

I have never seen such beauty. . . . All evening I looked at this portrait of the man [Peter the Great] who gave us the right to history, who was perhaps the only one to proclaim our historic mission. All evening my mind was filled with thoughts of him. He was the sole topic of our conversation with Pogodin and Samarin. It will be a shame and a sin, Kavelin, if you do not contribute something toward a history of Petrine institutions. It seems to me that you alone among us can accomplish such a work with honor. Peter has waited a hundred and thirty years for someone who can truly appreciate him.

[From a letter to Kavelin, October 2, 1855:]

Not only would Peter the Great be useful now, but even his stick, which taught the Russian fool some sense. There is misfortune on all sides. Things are bad within and without, yet neither society nor literature reacts to the situation with a single sensible word. . . . In general, the public is more afraid of publicity than of the Third Section. . . . Samarin, having joined the militia, argues that the present events are important because after the war is over officers who served with the militia will be permitted to wear beards. Hence the blood of the defenders of Sevastopol' was not spilled in vain, having helped to embellish the countenance of the Aksakovs, Samarins, and their ilk. These men are as repugnant to me as graves. They exude the odor of putrefaction. Not a single enlightened idea, not a single noble view. Their opposition is sterile, because it is based solely on the negation of everything that has been accomplished in our country during the past century and a half. I am delighted that they have started a journal. . . . I am delighted because this philosophy should be given ultimate expression; it should emerge into the open in all its glory. They will perforce have to divest themselves of all the liberal adornments with which they have succeeded in deceiving such children as you. It will be necessary to say the last word of the system. And this last word is Orthodox patriarchy, which is incompatible with any form of forward movement.

XIV:41. THE SLAVOPHILES: KIREEVSKII IN 1852

Trained at German universities, where he studied under Hegel, among others, Ivan Vasilievich Kireevskii (1806-56) is sometimes referred to as the father of the Slavophile movement. His famous article of 1852 in the Slavophile journal *Moskovskii sbornik*, "The Character of European Education and Its Relation to Russian Education," from which this excerpt is taken, was said by Chernyshevskii to be the best single summary of Slavophile thought. It must be noted, however, that Kireevskii came to this position very late, having been strongly pro-Westernizer during the 1830s and early 1840s.

Reference: *Polnoe sobranie sochinenii I. V. Kireevskogo*, ed. M. Gershenzon, 2 vols. (Moscow: Tipografiia Imperatorskogo Moskovskogo Universiteta, 1911), 1:184, 217-18, 220.

These three elements of the West—the Roman church, ancient Roman civilization, and state organization born of violent conquest—were entirely unknown to ancient Russia.

· · ·

Christianity penetrated the minds of Western peoples only through the teaching of the Roman church. In Russia it was kindled in the tapers of the whole Orthodox church. Theology in the West assumed the character of rational abstractness; in the Orthodox world it retained an inner wholeness of spirit. . . . There, the church became merged with the state, combining the spiritual power with the temporal power, and fusing church and secular values into a single system of mixed character. In Russia, the church remained apart from secular purposes and organizations. In the West, there were universities for scholasticism and law; in ancient Russia—monasteries for prayer, concentrating within themselves all higher knowledge. There, the rational and scholastic study of higher truths; here, the striving toward an active and complete understanding of them. There, the mutual growth of pagan and Christian civilization; here, a perpetual effort to purify truth. There, a state organization based on violent conquest; here, one based on the natural development of the people's way of life, permeated with the unity of a fundamental belief. There, a hostile division of classes; in ancient Russia, their harmonious association in all their natural variety. There, the artificial bond between knights' castles and their properties led to the formation of separate states; here, the common consent of the whole country expressed spiritually its indivisible unity. There, ownership of land was the prime basis of civil relationships; here, property was only an accidental expression of personal relationships. There, a formally logical system; here, one arising

from custom. There, a propensity in the law toward the appearance of justice; here, a preference for the essence of justice. There, jurisprudence strives for a logical code; here, instead of formal connections, it seeks the intrinsic bond between legal principles and the principles of faith and custom. There, laws stem artificially from prevailing opinion; here, they are born naturally from life itself. There, improvements were always accomplished by forcible changes; here, by harmonious natural growth. There, the tumult of partisan spirit; here, the stability of fundamental convictions. There, the whims of fashion; here, the steadfastness of a way of life. There, the precariousness of each individual regulating himself; here, the firmness of family and social bonds. There, the foppery of luxury and the artificiality of life; here, the simplicity of basic needs and the courage of moral fortitude. . . . In short, there, the splitting of the spirit, the splitting of thought, the splitting of knowledge, the splitting of the state, the splitting of classes, the splitting of society, the splitting of family rights and duties, the splitting of morals and emotions, the splitting of the totality and of all the separate forms of human existence, both social and individual; in Russia, on the contrary, the primary aspiration toward the oneness of existence, both internal and external, social and individual, intellectual and worldly, artificial and moral. Therefore, if what we have said above is correct, then *splitting* and *wholeness, rationality* and *wisdom* will be, respectively, the ultimate expression of western European and ancient Russian civilization.

· · ·

The root of Russia's civilization still lives in her people and, most important of all, it lives in her Holy Orthodox church. Hence, it is only on this foundation, and on no other, that must be erected the firm edifice of

Russian education, which has until now been built out of mixed and largely foreign materials and must therefore be rebuilt with pure materials of our own.

XIV:42. THE SLAVOPHILES: KONSTANTIN AKSAKOV IN THE 1850s

Known in Moscow as "the Slavophile Belinskii," Konstantin Sergeevich Aksakov (1817-60) was an ebullient and vigorous publicist with a deep interest in history. These excerpts suggest some of his views on the character and fate of what he saw as two worlds—the western European and the Slavic-Russian.

Reference: *Polnoe sobranie sochinenii K. S. Aksakova*, ed. I. S. Aksakov, 2 vols. (Moscow, 1861-71), 1:7-9, 13, 19, 49, 52, 53, 150, 154, 251, 291-92, 296-97, 300, 301; K. S. Aksakov, *Zamechaniia na novoe administrativnoe ustroistvo krest'ian v Rossii* (Leipzig, 1861), pp. 5, 10, 52. For a recent translation of other excerpts giving Aksakov's views on Russian history see Raeff, *Russian Intellectual History*, pp. 231-51.

[From his manuscript "Concerning the Fundamental Principles of Russian History," probably written about 1850:]

Russia is a completely original [*samobytnaia*] country, entirely unlike European states and nations.

· · ·

The history of our native land is so original that it was different from its very first moments. It was there, in its very origins, that the Russian way diverged from the western European, until the moment when, strangely and forcibly, they were brought together, when Russia took a terrible detour, abandoned its own way and joined the Western.

· · ·

All European states are formed by conquest. Their fundamental principle is enmity. Government appeared there as a hostile and armed power and established itself *by force* over subjugated peoples. One people, or more accurately a single armed band, would conquer a people and form a state whose fundamental principle was enmity, which has lasted throughout their history. . . .

The Russian state, on the contrary, was founded, not by conquest, but by a *voluntary invitation* to govern. Hence, its basis is not hatred but peace and harmony. Our government came as a desirable, not as a hostile, authority, as a defender, and was established with the consent of the people.

· · ·

And so, the Western state rests upon a foundation of *coercion, slavery, and hostility.* The Russian state is founded on *free will, liberty, and peace.* These principles represent an important and decisive difference between Russia and western Europe and determine the history of each.

Their paths are entirely different, so different that they can never converge, and the peoples following them can never agree in their attitudes. The West, turning from slavery to rebellion, mistakes rebellion for freedom, boasts of it, and sees slavery in Russia. Russia, on the other hand, has always kept the government she has herself acknowledged, has maintained it voluntarily and *freely,* and therefore regards the rebel merely as the reverse side of the slave.

· · ·

And these paths diverged still further when a question of utmost importance to mankind was added—the question of faith. Bliss descended on Russia. She adopted the Orthodox faith. The West took the road of Catholicism.

· · ·

The land [*zemlia*] or people [*narod*] tilled the soil and engaged in its various occupations and commerce. It supported the state with money and, in case of need, it rallied to the banners. It constituted a vast entity, which needed the state to enable it to live its own life and to preserve serenely and without interference its religion and its traditional way of life. The tsar [in the Muscovite period], the first champion and protector of the land, supported the communal principle, and the people governed itself, under the supreme authority of the sovereign. The village communes elected their own elders, sworn assistants, and other officials. From time to time the tsar summoned the land for council and made it a participant in political affairs.

· · ·

The Russian people . . . is a Christian people in the true sense of the word, always aware of its sinfulness. *The history of the Russian people is unique in the world. It is the history of a people that is Christian, not only in profession, but also in its life—at any rate, in the aspirations of its life.*

[From his manuscript "Concerning Volume I of the History of Russia, by Solov'ev," written ca. 1851:]

The Petersburg Period. The state carried out a revolution, broke its alliance with the land, and subjected it to the state, instituting a new order. It hastened to build a new capital, *its own,* having nothing in common with Russia and no Russian memories. Betraying the Russian land, the people, the state also betrayed its national character [*narodnost'*] and organized itself according to the example of the West, where statism [*gosudarstvennost'*] had developed to its utmost and introduced imitativeness to foreign lands, to western Europe. Everything Russian was subjected to persecution. State officials and service people went over to the side of the state. But the people, strictly speaking the common people, retained its former principles. . . . Russia was divided in two, with two capitals. On the one hand, there was the state with its foreign capital Saint Petersburg; on the other, the land, the people, with its Russian capital, Moscow.

.   .   .

The West is the victim of formal law. Formal law demands only obedience to its rules and fulfillment of its dictates, without caring or appealing to man's conscience, and thus it relieves man of the need for an inner moral voice. It is obvious that the prevalence of formal law in society weakens man's moral fiber, teaching him to act without inner moral reasons, and in such a way as to be right only before the (formal) law. But the purpose of mankind is to realize the moral law on earth.

.   .   .

Wherever we look, especially among contemporary Western states, we see worship of the state. Everywhere we see that its ideal, the ideal of *order,* of outward harmony, of an adroitly adjusted, so to speak, mechanical organization, has captured men's minds. Some hope to achieve this ideal through monarchy; others, through a constitution; still others, through a republic, or through communist institutions. But belief in the state, in external truth, is strong everywhere in the West and has resulted everywhere in the impoverishment of

the inner man, of the free man, of himself. This is least true of England. For England is supported, not by the strength of its law, but by the strength of custom, not by the state, but by national character.

[From his article "Concerning Volume VI of the History of Russia, by Solov'ev," published in *Russkaia Beseda* in 1856:]

As soon as there was a single state over a single Russian land; as soon as the state began to sense its wholeness; as soon as the grand prince of Moscow became the tsar, then the united state turned to the united Russian land and summoned it to hold council. The first tsar convoked the first zemskii sobor. At this sobor the land and the state met and established a free union. The relations between the tsar and the people were defined: to the government went the power of authority; to the land, the power of opinion. These two powers were solemnly recognized at the zemskii sobor as the two harmonious forces governing Russia: state authority and public opinion.

. . . The assembly of the entire land, the zemskii sobor, was not an accidental phenomenon, but a fundamental, basic, and organic phenomenon of ancient Russia.

[From his article "Concerning Volume VII of the History of Russia, by Solov'ev," published in *Russkaia beseda* in 1858:]

The state [during the Moscow period] was always considered by the land as something outside, something necessary for its external defense. The state always recognized the land's independent existence and moral right of opinion, thought, counsel, and custom. Of course, under these conditions, the land was the prime factor. It was clearly understood that the land did not exist for the state, but the state for the land. The source of life, of moral achievement, of the spirit lies unquestionably in the commune [*obshchina*], in the people. The state is secondary and, by its very idea, cannot instill a soul in the people, but can at best impart to it only mechanical motion.

[From his manuscript "Short Historical Sketch of the Zemskii Sobor," written ca. 1859:]

The commune is the supreme, the true, principle which can no longer discover anything higher than itself but need only flourish, purify, and elevate itself. . . .

The commune is an association of people who have renounced their egoism, their individuality, and who manifest their common accord: this is an act of love, a noble Christian act. . . . The commune thus represents a moral choir; and just as in a choir a voice is not lost but, subject to the general pattern, is heard in the harmony of all voices, so, in the commune, the individual is not lost but, renouncing his exclusiveness for the sake of general accord, he finds himself in a higher, purified state, in harmony with equally selfless individualities. . . . The commune is the triumph of the human spirit.

· · ·

Formal truth belongs to the state, intrinsic truth, to the land; unlimited power, to the tsar, complete freedom of life and spirit, to the people; freedom of action and of law, to the tsar, freedom of opinion and expression, to the people.

· · ·

The right to spiritual freedom—in other words, freedom of thought and expression— is the inalienable right of the land; but with this right it wants no political rights, leaving unrestricted political power to the state. Moral force—this freedom of thought and expression—is the element in which the land lives and moves, and when it possesses this it renounces all political power. But, besides living always in moral freedom, the land is summoned to council by the state whenever the latter deems it necessary. Then, at the call of the sovereign, men elected from all estates gather from every corner of Russia, and this convocation of elected representatives is called a zemskii sobor or a *zemskaia duma.*

· · ·

Recognizing the state as a necessary, unavoidable evil, regarding it merely as an extraneous means, and not the goal, not the ideal of their national existence, the Slavs (in Russia) did not transform themselves into a state, did not draw up its structure from their own midst, but summoned the state

from overseas, from outside, from an alien place, as an alien phenomenon. Having summoned the state, the Slavs placed it alongside the people's life, the life of the land, and preserved their council, their veche.

· · ·

Thus, there were now two elements in Russia: the land and the sovereign. These two elements, different in essence, did not intermix, and because of this, perhaps, the business of each was carried on in amity and harmony. . . . The state . . . protected the land, but did not overstep its limits. The land did not infringe upon the rights of the state, nor did the state infringe upon the rights of the land. These two elements—the land and the state—lived in amity under a system of mutual noninterference, or better, mutual nonencroachment, and the state was useful for the land.

[From his book *Zamechaniia* . . . ("Comments on the New Administrative Organization of the Russian Peasants"), 1861:]
    Letter to A. S. Khomiakov, 1857:
    . . . Can Petersburg—our governing city— do anything good while it governs? The best and most beneficial thing that Petersburg could do for Russia would be to drown itself in the sea that is so conveniently near. But such magnanimity is not to be expected of it.

· · ·

    Letter to N. N. (Member of the Editorial Commissions), 1859:
    After all, you are dealing not with cattle, but with the people, which has much more understanding of social matters than you, the members of the noble assembly of the gentry, with your right of voting in the celebrated gentry elections.

· · ·

    [*Comment on the Mir:*]
    In its essence, the mir is a self-regulating [*samozakonnoe*], supreme manifestation of the people, fully satisfying all the demands of legality, social truth, and social justice—in short, the social will. The mir, as a higher phenomenon, combines within itself all powers, since it is the source of every power.

XIV:43. THE SLAVOPHILES: KHOMIAKOV IN THE 1840s AND 1850s

Aleksei Stepanovich Khomiakov (1804-60), a philosopher and layman theologian (like Vladimir Solov'ev; see Items XVI:50 and 51, below), wrote on a wide range of topics. His two main ideas were those of *sobornost'* ("togetherness in spirit") as the basis of the church and *obshchinnost'* ("communality") as the basis of society.

Reference: *Polnoe sobranie sochinenii A. S. Khomiakova*, 8 vols. (Moscow: Tip. Imperator-skogo Universiteta, 1900-07), 1:4 [1845 essay], 96-97 [1847], 259 [1852]; 2:235, 248 [1853]; 3:198-99, 433 [1856, 1859]; 4:255-56 [1854]. For the last item, see also Aleksei Khomiakov, *Izbrannye Sochineniia* (New York: Chekhov, 1955), pp. 70-71.

[From his essay "On the Opinion of Foreigners about Russia," 1845:]

We are always warmly concerned with the fate of our foreign brethren, both with their sufferings and with their achievements, hopes, and glory. But we never find a response to this friendly impulse, this sympathy—never a word of affection or fraternal feeling, almost never a word of truth or impartiality. We encounter only one response—ridicule and abuse; only one feeling—a mixture of fear and contempt. This is not what one man wants from another.

It is difficult to explain these hostile feelings on the part of the Western peoples, who have nurtured so many good seeds and brought mankind so far along the road of intelligent enlightenment. Europe has often showed sympathy even for savage tribes, entirely alien to her and lacking any ties of blood or spiritual kinship. Of course, even this sympathy contained an element of contempt, of an aristocratic pride of blood . . . of course, the European, despite his constant talk of humanity, has never quite attained the idea of man; nevertheless, he has manifested, though rarely, sympathy and some capacity for love. It is strange that Russia alone appears privileged to evoke the worst emotions in the European heart. It would seem that we have the same Indo-European blood as our Western neighbors, the same Indo-European skin (and the skin, as we know, is a matter of great importance, which entirely alters all moral relations among men), and an Indo-European language—and what a language! The purest, almost Indian! And yet our neighbors do not consider us brothers.

The hostility of other peoples toward us is evidently based on two factors: a deep awareness of the difference in all the fundamental principles underlying the spiritual and social development of Russia and western Europe; and an involuntary annoyance with this independent force which has demanded and taken all the rights of equality in the community of European nations. They cannot deny us these rights—we are too strong. But neither can they admit that we deserve them.

[From his essay "On the Possibility of the Existence of a Russian School of Art," 1847:]

Certain journals mockingly refer to us as Slavophiles, a word of foreign cast, but which would mean in Russian translation, *Lovers of Slavs*. For my part, I am willing to accept this designation and will readily admit that I love the Slavs. . . . I love them because there is no Russian who does not love them, no Russian who is not aware of his fraternity with the Slav, and particularly with the Orthodox Christian Slav. Whoever wishes may inquire about this from the Russian soldier who took part in the Turkish campaign, or at the Moscow bazaar where the Frenchman, the German, and the Italian are treated as foreigners, while Serbs, Dalmatians, and Bulgarians are welcomed like brothers. Therefore, I accept the ridicule of our love for the Slavs as willingly as the ridicule of the fact that we are Russians.

[From his manuscript "On I. V. Kireevskii's Article 'About the Nature of European Education,'" 1852:]

It would be unreasonable not to value the wealth of useful knowledge we have drawn and are still drawing from the tireless labors of the Western world. And to use this knowledge while speaking of it with ungrateful disdain would be not only unreasonable but also dishonest. Let us leave to the despair of certain Westerners, who are frightened at the suicidal development of rationalism, their dull and partly feigned contempt for science. We must accept, preserve, and develop science with all the intellectual scope it requires. But at the same time we must constantly subject it to our own criticism, enlightened by those high principles that were bequeathed to us from olden times from the Orthodox Christianity of our forebears. This is the only way in which we can elevate science itself, impart to it the integrity and completeness it still lacks, and repay in full, or even with interest, our debt to our Western teachers.

[From his essay "A Few Words by A Russian Orthodox Christian about Western Denominations," 1853:]

A surface unity which denies freedom and

hence is unreal—such is Romanism. A surface
freedom, which brings no unity and is therefore also nugatory—such is Reform. But we
know that the mystery of Christ's unity with
his elect, a union realized by his human freedom, is open within the church to the actual
unity and actual freedom of the faithful. . . .
The church is given both, because its unity
is nothing else but the consent of personal
freedoms.

. . .

Three voices are heard most loudly in
Europe. "Obey and believe in my edicts,"
says Rome. "Be free and try to create some
sort of faith for yourselves," says Protestant-
ism. But our church calls to its own: "Let us
love one another and in harmony profess our
faith in the Father, the Son, and the Holy
Ghost."

[From his foreword to the new Slavophile
journal *Russkaia beseda* (Russian discussion),
1856:]

When Russian society stood face to face
with Western learning, astonished and dazzled
by the newly discovered treasures, it embraced them with all the passion of which its
somewhat indolent nature was capable. It
seemed that only now was intellectual and
spiritual life beginning for Russia, that formerly Russia either had not lived at all, or, at any
rate, had not created anything worth remembering by mankind. But actually this was
quite untrue. The Russian spirit had created
the Russian land itself in all its vastness, for
this was not the work of the flesh but of the
spirit. The Russian spirit had founded forever the mir community, the best form of
communal living within close, confined areas.
The Russian spirit had grasped the sacredness
of the family and made it the purest and
most steadfast foundation of the entire edifice
of society. It had nurtured in the people all
its moral strength, its faith in the holy truth,
its indomitable patience, and its profound
humility. Such were its accomplishments, the
fruits of God's grace, which illumined it with
the full radiance of Orthodox Christianity.
Today, when thought has gained strength in
knowledge, when the very course of history,
which reveals the secret principles of social
phenomena, has exposed in many respects
the falseness of the Western world, and when
we are conscious of the value of . . . the

strength and beauty of the primordial principles of our life, we should once more reexamine all the postulates, all the conclusions
reached by Western science, in which we believed so absolutely. We should subject the
whole shaky edifice of our education to the
impassive criticism of our own spiritual principles and thus give it unshatterable strength.
At the same time, it is our duty wisely to
adopt every new product of Western thought,
still so rich and worthy of study, in order that
we may not find ourselves lagging at the time
when the wealth of our gifts imposes upon us
the obligation to strive for first place in the
ranks of enlightened mankind.

[From his speech before the Society of
Friends of Russian Letters, April 26, 1859:]

Holy and noble is the vocation of the state,
which protects and makes possible social life.
It embraces this life like a living organic in-
tegument, fortifying and protecting it against
all external adversities, growing with it, changing, expanding, and adapting itself to the
development and inner transformation of social
life. The wiser the state and the better it knows
its own interests and its own significance, the
more keenly it will sense and the more clearly
it will see the full diversity of social life, and
the more flexible it will be in adapting itself
to the forms and historical growth of this life,
enveloping it, as it were, in a living coat of
armor and constantly drawing strength from
its natural energies. Such is the relation of a
state—a state with a normal and healthy
development—to social life.

[From his poem "To Russia," March 1854,
at the start of the Crimean War:]

Chosen for holy struggle,
Beloved of God,
Who gave thee fateful power
To crush the evil will
Of blind, insane, and savage forces.

Arise, my native land!
Fight for thy brothers! God is calling thee
Across the angry Danube's waves—
Where, circling round the shore,
Aegean currents sing.

Remember, though: to be the tool
of God
Is hard for earthly creatures.

He sits in stern judgment of His slaves—
And thou, alas! art burdened
By multitudes of dreadful sins!

Thy courts are black with black
     injustice,
The yoke of slavery thy brand;
With Godless flattery and lies corrupted,
Inert with dead and shameful sloth,
With vile abominations overrun!

Oh, though unworthy of His choice,
Thou art His chosen! Purify
Thyself in the cool stream of penitence,
Lest the thunder of double punishment
Come down on thy head!

With kneeling soul,
With head bowed low in dust,
Pray in humility,
And heal the wounds of thy corrupted
     conscience
With the balm of tears!

Then rise, and true to thy vocation
Plunge into the fire of battle!
Fight for thy brothers, firm in combat,
Hold up God's banner with a steadfast
     hand,
Strike with thy sword—it is the sword
     of God!

XIV:44. HERZEN ON RUSSIA AND EUROPE IN THE 1830s AND 1840s

Alexander Ivanovich Herzen (Gertsen) (1812-70), an émigré from 1847 on, wrote freely on many topics and was widely read in Russia, especially through his journal *Kolokol* (The Bell, 1857-67). The following excerpts from Herzen's memoirs concern various aspects of Russia and Europe in the 1830s and 1840s and help to illustrate why Herzen was regarded as neither Slavophile nor Westernizer. (For the views of Herzen on the 1850s and 1860s, see Item XV:44.)

Reference: Aleksandr I. Gertsen, *Byloe i dumy* (Moscow: OGIZ, 1946), pp. 57, 87, 217, 283, 293, 413, 414; translation based on Constance Garnett's in *My Past and Thoughts: The Memoirs of Alexander Herzen*, 6 vols. (London: Chatto and Windus, 1924-27), 1:120, 190; 2:117-18, 252-53, 274; 3: 140-41, 142, 143, considerably revised.

[On Moscow University in the 1830s:] The youthful strength of Russia streamed into it from all sides, from all classes of society, as into a common reservoir; in its halls they were purified from the prejudices they had picked up at the domestic hearth, attained a common level, became like brothers, and dispersed again to all parts of Russia and among all classes of its people.

Until 1848 the organization of our universities was entirely democratic. Their doors were open to everyone who could pass the [entrance] examination, unless he were . . . a serf.

· · ·

[In the 1830s:] A new world was pushing at the door, and our hearts and souls opened wide to meet it. Saint-Simonism became the foundation of our convictions and remained unalterably so in its essentials.

· · ·

[On the influence of German philosophy:] Our young philosophers corrupted not only their language but their understanding; their attitude toward life, toward reality, became scholastic, bookish; it was that learned con-

ception of simple things which Goethe mocks with such genius in the conversation of Mephistopheles with the students. Everything that *in reality* was immediate, every simple feeling, was raised into some abstract category and emerged without a drop of living blood, a pale, algebraic shadow. In all of this there was a naïveté of a sort, because it was all perfectly sincere. The man who went for a walk in Sokol'niki [a park in Moscow] went in order to give himself up to the pantheistic feeling of his unity with the cosmos; and if on the way he happened to meet a drunken soldier or a peasant woman who got into conversation with him, the philosopher did not simply talk to them, but tried to define the essential substance of the common people in its immediate and phenomenal manifestation.

· · ·

[On the Moscow professors of the 1830s and 1840s:] Granovskii was not alone; he was one of a group of young professors who came back from Germany while we were in exile. They did a great deal for the advancement of the University of Moscow. History will not forget them. . . .

Our professors brought with them these cherished dreams [that the dialectical approach could solve contemporary historical problems], and an ardent faith in learning and in men; they preserved all the fervor of youth, and the professorial chair was for them a sacred pulpit from which they had been called to preach the truth. They came to the lecture room, not as mere professional savants, but as missionaries of the religion of humanity.

. . .

The mistake of the Slavophiles lies in their imagining that Russia once had a culture peculiar to itself, which was eclipsed by various events and finally by the Petersburg period. Russia never had, and could never have had, such a culture. That which is now reaching our consciousness, that which begins to glimmer in our thoughts as a presentiment, that which existed unconsciously in the peasant hut and in the open field, is *only now* beginning to sprout in the pastures of history, fertilized by the blood, tears, and sweat of twenty generations.

These are the foundations of our life, not memories; these are living elements, existing not in chronicles but in the actual present; but they have merely *survived* under the hard historical process of building up a unified state, and under the yoke of the state they have only been preserved but not developed. I doubt, indeed, whether the inner strength for their development would have been found without the Petrine period, without a period of European education.

The primitive foundations of our life are insufficient. In India there has existed for ages and exists to this day a village commune very similar to our own and based upon the division of fields; yet the people of India have not gone very far with it.

Only the mighty thought of the West, with which all its long history is permeated, is able to fertilize the seeds slumbering in the patriarchal mode of life of the Slavs. The *artel'* [workers' cooperative] and the village commune, the sharing of profits and the division of fields, the communal assembly and the union of villages into self-governing volosti— all these are the cornerstones on which the temple of our future free, communal existence will be built. But still, these cornerstones are only stones—and without Western thought our future cathedral will not rise above its foundations.

. . .

After spending a year or two in Europe, we see with surprise that in general the men of the West do not correspond to our conception of them, that they are *greatly inferior* to it.

Elements of truth enter into the ideals we have formed, but either these elements no longer exist or they have completely changed their character. Knightly valor, the elegance of aristocratic manners, the strict decorum of the Protestants, the proud independence of the English, the luxurious life of the Italian artists, the sparkling wit of the Encyclopedists, and the saturnine energy of the terrorists—all this has been melted down and transmuted into a whole conjunction of universally predominant *petty bourgeois manners.* They make up a complete whole—that is, a finished, self-contained outlook upon life, with its traditions and rules, with its own good and evil, with its own ways and its own morality *of a lower order.*

As the knight was the prototype of the feudal world, so has the merchant become the prototype of the new world; lords are replaced by *employers.*

. . .

Under the influence of the petty bourgeois, everything in Europe has changed. Knightly honor is replaced by a bookkeeper's honesty, elegant manners by propriety, courtesy by affection, pride by touchiness, parks by kitchen gardens, palaces by hotels open to *all* (that is, to all who have money).

. . .

All morality has been reduced to this: in every way possible the indigent must acquire property, while the rich must preserve and increase what they have; the flag which is run up in the marketplace when trading begins has become the banner of a new society. Man has de facto become the appurtenance of property; life has been reduced to a perpetual struggle for money.

. . . Life has been reduced to speculating on the stock exchange; everything—editorial offices of magazines, electoral colleges, legislative chambers—all have turned into money changers' shops and markets. The English are so used to putting everything into shop language that they call their old Anglican church the Old Shop.

All parties and shades of opinion in the petty bourgois world have gradually divided into two main camps: on the one hand, the petty bourgois property owners who obstinately refuse to abandon their monopolies; on the other, the petty bourgeois who have nothing, who want to tear the wealth out of the others' hands but have not the power—that is, on the one hand, *avarice,* and on the other hand, *envy.*

BIBLIOGRAPHY

Note: This bibliography is limited to those works that were used in the preparation of the Source Book and
does not include all of the collections mentioned in the reference notes as supplementary material. In
general, the publisher is given only for works published since 1900.

Adrianova-Peretts, V. P., ed. *Vremennik Ivana Timofeeva.* Moscow: AN SSSR, 1951.
————, and D. S. Likhachev, eds. *Povest' vremennykh let.* Moscow: AN SSSR, 1950.
Aksakov, Ivan S. *Polnoe sobranie sochinenii I. S. Aksakova.* 7 vols. Moscow, 1886-87.
Aksakov, Konstantin S. *Polnoe sobranie sochinenii K. S. Aksakova.* Ed. I. S. Aksakov. 2 vols.
Moscow, 1861-71.
————. *Zamechaniia na novoe administrativnoe ustroistvo krest'ian v Rossii.* Leipzig, 1861.
*Akty sobrannye v bibliotekakh i arkhivakh Rossiiskoi Imperii arkheograficheskoiu ekspeditsieiu
Imperatorskoi Akademii Nauk.* 4 vols. St. Petersburg, 1836.
Akty sotsial'no-ekonomicheskoi istorii severovostochnoi Rusi. 3 vols. Ed. B. D. Grekov (vol. 1),
L. V. Cherepnin (vols. 2 and 3). Moscow: AN SSSR, 1952-64.
Aleksandra Fedorovna: see *Letters of the Tsaritsa to the Tsar;* see also Tsentral'nyi Gosudarstvennyi
Istoricheskii Arkhiv v Moskve, ed., *Perepiska . . .*
Annales Bertiniani. Ed. G. Waitz. Hanover, 1883.
Antonovich, Vladimir B. *Monografii po istorii zapadnoi i iugozapadnoi Rossii.* Vol. 1. Kiev, 1885.
Arkheograficheskaia Komissiia, ed. *Akty istoricheskie.* 5 vols. St. Petersburg, 1841-42.
————. *Akty otnosiashchiesia do iuridicheskogo byta drevnei Rossii.* Ed. Nikolai Kalachev. 3 vols.
St. Petersburg, 1857, 1864, 1884.
————. *Akty otnosiashchiesia k istorii iuzhnoi i zapadnoi Rossii.* 15 vols. St. Petersburg, 1863-
92.
————. *Akty otnosiashchiesia k istorii zapadnoi Rossii.* 5 vols. St. Petersburg, 1846-51.
————. *Dnevnik Liublinskogo seima 1569 g.* St. Petersburg, 1869.
————. *Dokumenty ob"iasniaiushchie istoriiu zapadno-russkogo kraia i ego otnosheniia k Rossii
i Pol'she.* St. Petersburg, 1865.
————. *Dopolneniia k aktam istoricheskim.* 12 vols. St. Petersburg, 1846-72.
————. *Letopis' po Ipatskomu spisku.* St. Petersburg, 1871.
————. *Letopis' po Lavrent'evskomu spisku.* St. Petersburg, 1897.
————. *Novgorodskie letopisi (Novgorodskaia vtoraia i Novgorodskaia tret'ia letopisi).* St. Peters-
burg, 1879.
————. *Polnoe Sobranie Russkikh Letopisei.* 31 vols. St. Petersburg, 1841-1968.
————. *Russkaia istoricheskaia biblioteka.* 39 vols. St. Petersburg: Arkheograficheskaia Komissiia,
1872-1927.
————. *Sibirskie letopisi.* St. Petersburg: I. N. Skorokhodov, 1907.
Arkhiv iugo-zapadnoi Rossii. 35 vols. Kiev: Tip. G. T. Korchak-Novitskogo, 1859-1914.
Arkhiv russkoi revoliutsii. Ed. I. V. Gessen. 22 vols. Berlin: Slovo, 1921-27.
Avvakum, *The Life of Archpriest Avvakum, by Himself.* Trans. Jane Harrison and Hope Mirrlees.
London: L. and V. Woolf at the Hogarth Press, 1924.

Bakunin, Mikhail A. *Izbrannye sochineniia.* 5 vols. Petrograd: Golos Truda, 1920-22. See also
Maximoff.
Bartenev, Petr I., ed. *Deviatnadtsatyi vek.* 2 vols. Moscow, 1872. See also *Russkii arkhiv.*
Bazilevskii, B. [Vasilii Ia. Iakovlev], ed. *Literatura partii Narodnoi Voli.* Paris: Société nouvelle
de librairie et d'édition, 1905.
————. *Revoliutsionnaia zhurnalistika semidesiatykh godov . . .* Paris [?], 1906.
Belinskii, Vissarion G. *Polnoe sobranie sochinenii.* 13 vols. Moscow: AN SSSR, 1953-59.
Belinsky, Vissarion G. *Selected Philosophical Works.* Moscow: Foreign Languages Publishing
House, 1948.

Benedetto, L. F. *The Travels of Marco Polo.* Trans. Aldo Ricci. London: G. Routledge and Sons, 1931.

Berry, Lloyd E., and Robert O. Crummey, eds. *Rude and Barbarous Kingdom: Russia in the Accounts of Sixteenth-Century English Voyagers.* Madison: University of Wisconsin Press, 1968.

Bodemann, Eduard, ed. *Briefe der Kurfuerstin Sophie von Hannover an die Raugraefinnen und Raugrafen zu Pfalz.* Publicationen aus den K. Preussischen Staatsarchiven, vol. 37. Leipzig, 1888.

Bogoiavlenskii, S. K., and I. S. Riabinin, eds. *Akty vremeni mezhdutsarstviia (1610-1613),* Moscow: Izd. Imperatorskogo Obshchestva Istorii i Drevnostei Rossiiskikh pri Moskovskom Universitete, 1915.

Bogucharskii: See Iakovlev, V. Ia.

Bolotov, Andrei T. "Nakaz dlia derevenskogo upravitelia." In Vol'noe Ekonomicheskoe Obshchestvo, *Trudy Vol'nogo Ekonomicheskogo Obshchestva,* Vol. 16, pp. 69-230. St. Petersburg, 1770.

Borozdin, Aleksandr K., ed. *Iz pisem i pokazanii dekabristov.* St. Petersburg: M. V. Pirozhkov, 1906.

Browder, Robert Paul, and Alexander F. Kerensky, eds. *The Russian Provisional Government, 1917: Documents.* 3 vols. Stanford: Stanford University Press, 1961.

Bruce, Peter H. *Memoirs of Peter Henry Bruce, Esq.* Dublin, 1783. Reprint. New York: Da Capo, 1968.

Bubnoff: see *The Russian Co-operator.*

Buchanan, George W. *My Mission to Russia and Other Diplomatic Memories.* 2 vols. Boston: Little, Brown, 1923.

Burtsev, Vladimir L., comp. and ed. *Za sto let, 1800-1896: Sbornik po istorii politicheskikh i obshchestvennykh dvizhenii v Rossii.* London, 1897. Reprint. The Hague: Europe Printing, 1965.

Buryshkin, Pavel A. *Moskva kupecheskaia.* New York: Chekhov, 1954.

Burzhuaziia nakanune fevral'skoi revoliutsii: see Tsentral'nyi Gosudarstvennyi Istoricheskii Arkhiv v Moskve.

Butashevich-Petrashevskii, Mikhail V. *Delo Petrashevtsev.* 3 vols. Moscow: AN SSSR, 1937-51.

Carpini, Giovanni de Plano. *The Mongol Mission.* Ed. and intro. Christopher Dawson. New York: Sheed and Ward, 1955.

Catherine II. *Memoirs of Catherine the Great.* Trans. Katherine Anthony. New York: Knopf, 1927. See also Reddaway; Chechulin.

————. *The Memoirs of Catherine the Great.* Ed. Dominique Maroger, intro. G. P. Gooch, trans. Moura Budberg. New York: Macmillan [1955].

————. *Pis'ma Imperatritsy Ekateriny II k Grimmu. Sbornik Imperatorskogo Russkogo Istoricheskogo Obshchestva,* vol. 23. St. Petersburg, 1878.

Chaadaev, Petr Ia. *The Major Works of Peter Chaadaev.* Trans. and commentary Raymond T. McNally. Notre Dame, Ind.: University of Notre Dame Press, 1969.

————. *Peter Yakovlevich Chaadayev: Philosophical Letters and Apology of a Madman.* Trans. and intro. Mary-Barbara Zeldin. Knoxville: University of Tennessee Press, 1969.

————. *Sochineniia i pis'ma P. Ia. Chaadaeva.* Ed. M. O. Gershenzon. 2 vols. Moscow: A. I. Mamontov, 1913-14. *See also* Moskoff.

Chancellor, Richard. "A Letter of Richard Chancellor . . . Touching His Discoverie of Moscovia." In *Hakluytus Posthumus or Purchas His Pilgrimes,* ed. Samuel Purchas. Vol. 11. Glasgow: J. MacLehose and Sons, 1906.

Chechulin, Nikolai D., ed. *Nakaz Imperatritsy Ekateriny II, dannyi Komissii o sochinenii proekta novogo Ulozheniia.* St. Petersburg: Tip. Imperatorskoi Akademii Nauk, 1907.

Cherepnin, Lev V., ed. *Akty feodal'nogo zemlevladeniia i khoziaistva XIV-XVI vekov.* Pt. 1. Moscow: AN SSSR, 1951.

————. *Pamiatniki prava perioda obrazovaniia russkogo tsentralizovannogo gosudarstva. Pamiatniki russkogo prava,* vol. 3. Moscow: Gosiurizdat, 1955.

Cherepnin, Lev V., and S. V. Bakhrushin, eds. *Dukhovnye i dogovornye gramoty velikikh i udel'nykh kniazei XIV-XVI vv.* Moscow: AN SSSR, 1950.

Cherniavsky, Michael, ed. *Prologue to Revolution: Notes of A. N. Iakhontov on the Secret Meetings of the Council of Ministers, 1915.* Englewood Cliffs, N.J.: Prentice-Hall, 1967.

Chernov, Viktor M. *Konstruktivnyi sotsializm.* Prague: Volia Rossii, 1925.

[Chernov, Viktor M.] *Ocherednoi vopros revoliutsionnogo dela.* London: Agrarian Socialist League, 1900.

Chernyshevskii, Nikolai G. *Polnoe sobranie sochinenii N. G. Chernyshevskogo.* 10 vols. St. Petersburg: I. Kraig, 1905-06.

———. *Selected Philosophical Essays.* Moscow: Foreign Languages Publishing House, 1953.

Chertkov, Vladimir G., ed. *Studencheskoe dvizhenie 1899 goda.* Purleigh, Eng.: Svobodnoe slovo, 1900.

Chronicle of Novgorod: see Michell.

Chteniia v Imperatorskom Obshchestve Istorii i Drevnostei Rossiiskikh pri Moskovskom Universitete: see Obshchestvo Istorii i Drevnostei Rossiiskikh.

Collins, Samuel. *The Present State of Russia.* London, 1671.

Constantine Porphyrogenitus. *De administrando imperio.* Greek text ed. Gy. Moravcsik, Eng. trans. R. J. H. Jenkins. Budapest: Institute of Greek Philology of Peter Pazmany University, 1949.

Coxe, William. *Travels into Poland, Russia, Sweden, and Denmark.* 3 vols. London: T. Cadell, 1784-90.

Cross, Samuel H., and Olgerd P. Sherbowitz-Wetzor, eds. and trans. *The Russian Primary Chronicle. Laurentian Text.* Cambridge, Mass.: Mediaeval Academy of America, 1953.

Custine, Astolphe, Marquis de. *Journey for Our Time: The Journals of the Marquis de Custine.* Ed. and trans. Phyllis P. Kohler. New York: Pellegrini and Cudahy, 1951.

Czartoryski, Adam J. *Memoirs of Prince Adam Czartoryski and His Correspondence with Alexander I.* Ed. Adam Gielgud. 2d ed. 2 vols. London, 1888.

Desiatiletie Ministerstva Narodnogo Prosveshcheniia, 1833-1843, St. Petersburg, 1864.

Desnitskii, V., ed. *Delo petrashevtsev. Pamiatniki obshchestvennoi mysli,* vol. 1. Moscow: AN SSSR, 1937.

Dewey, Horace W., comp., trans., and ed. *Muscovite Judicial Texts, 1488-1556.* Michigan Slavic Materials No. 7. Ann Arbor: Department of Slavic Languages and Literatures, University of Michigan, 1966.

———. *The Sudebnik of 1497.* Ann Arbor: University Microfilms, 1955.

———. "The White Lake Charter: A Mediaeval Russian Administrative Statute." *Speculum,* 32 (1957): 74-84.

D'iakonov, Mikhail A., ed. *Akty otnosiashchiesia k istorii tiaglogo naseleniia v Moskovskom gosudarstve.* 2 vols. St. Petersburg, 1895-97.

Dmitrieva, R. P. *Skazanie o kniaziakh vladimirskikh.* Moscow: AN SSSR, 1955.

Dmytryshyn, Basil, ed. *Imperial Russia: A Source Book, 1700-1917.* New York: Holt, Rinehart and Winston, 1967.

———, ed. *Medieval Russia: A Source Book, 900-1700.* New York: Holt, Rinehart and Winston, 1967.

Documents diplomatiques français, 1871-1914. Ser. 1 (1871-1900), 16 vols. Paris: Imprimerie Nationale, Alfred Costes, L'Europe Nouvelle, 1929-56.

Domostroi, intro. I. E. Zabelin. In *Chteniia v Imperatorskom Obshchestve Istorii i Drevnostei Rossiiskikh pri Moskovskom Universitete.* Moscow, 1881, bk. 2.

Domostroi po Konshinskomu spisku i podobnym. Ed. A. S. Orlov. 2 vols. Moscow: Sinodal'naia Tipografiia, 1908-10. Reprint. The Hague: Mouton, 1967.

Dostoevskii, Fedor M. *The Diary of a Writer: F. M. Dostoevsky.* Trans. Boris Brasol. 2 vols. New York: Charles Scribner's Sons, 1949.

———. *Polnoe sobranie sochinenii F. M. Dostoevskogo.* 12 vols. St. Petersburg: A. F. Marks, 1894-95.

Dovnar-Zapol'skii, Mitrofan V., ed. *Akty Litovsko-Russkogo Gosudarstva, vypusk I (1390-1529 gg.).* In *Chteniia v Imperatorskom Obshchestve Istorii i Drevnostei Rossiiskikh pri Moskovskom Universitete,* vol. 191, Moscow, 1899, bk. 4.

———. "Materialy dlia istorii votchinnogo upravleniia v Rossii," *Kievskie Universitetskie Izvestiia* (Kiev), 1903, no. 12; 1904, no. 6; 1909, no. 7; 1910, no. 11.

Druzhinin, Vasilii G., ed. *Pamiatniki pervykh let russkogo staroobriadchestva.* 3 vols. St. Petersburg: M. A. Aleksandrov, 1912-14.

Dubel't, M. L. "Iz epokhi osvobozhdeniia krest'ian, rasskaz gen.-leit. M. L. Dubel'ta, 1861." *Russkaia starina,* 69 (February 1891): 469-74.

Dubiecki, Marjan, comp. *Powstanie styczniowe w swietle zrodel.* Teksty zrodlowe do nauki historji w szkole sredniej, pt. 54. Krakow: Nakladem Krakowskiej Spolki Wydawniczej, 1924.

Dubrovin, Nikolai F., comp. *Sbornik istoricheskikh materialov izvlechennykh iz arkhiva Pervogo Otdeleniia Sobstvennoi Ego Imperatorskogo Velichestva Kantselarii.* 16 vols. St. Petersburg: Pervoe Otd. S. E. I. V. Kantseliarii, 1876-1917.

Dukhovnye i dogovornye gramoty velikikh i udel'nykh kniazei XIV-XVI vv. Moscow: AN SSSR, 1950.

Duma: see Gosudarstvennaia Duma.

Dumont, Jean. *Corps universel diplomatique du droit des gens.* 8 vols. bound in 16. Amsterdam, 1726-31.

Durnovo, P. N. "Zapiska." *Krasnaia nov',* no. 10 (November-December 1922). pp. 178-99.

Dzhivelegov, A. K., S. P. Mel'gunov, and V. I. Picheta, eds. *Velikaia reforma.* 6 vols. Moscow: Sytin, 1911.

Edie, James M., James P. Scanlan, and Mary-Barbara Zeldin, eds.; collab. George L. Kline. *Russian Philosophy.* 2 vols. Chicago: Quadrangle Books, 1965.

Entsiklopedicheskii Slovar'. 41 vols. St. Petersburg: Brokgauz and Efron, 1890-1904.

Fennell, John L. I., ed. and trans. *The Correspondence between Prince A. M. Kurbsky and Tsar Ivan IV of Russia, 1564-1579.* Cambridge: At the University Press, 1955.

Fennell, John L. I., and Dimitri Obolensky, eds. *A Historical Russian Reader: A Selection of Texts from the Eleventh to the Sixteenth Centuries.* Oxford: Clarendon Press, 1969.

"Fevral'skaia revolutsiia 1917 goda." *Krasnyi arkhiv,* 21 (1927 no. 2): 3-78; 22 (1927 no. 3): 3-70.

Filipowicz, Tytus, ed. *Confidential Correspondence of the British Government respecting the Insurrection in Poland: 1863.* Paris: Soudier, 1914.

Fischer, George. *Russian Liberalism.* Cambridge: Harvard University Press, 1958.

Fletcher, Giles. *Of the Rus Commonwealth.* Ed. Albert J. Schmidt. Ithaca, N.Y.: Cornell University Press, 1966. See also Berry.

———. *Of the Russe Commonwealth: Facsimile Edition with Variants.* Ed. John V. A. Fine, Jr., intro. Richard Pipes. Cambridge: Harvard University Press, 1966.

———. *Russia at the Close of the Sixteenth Century, Comprising the Treatise "Of the Russe Common Wealth" by Dr. Giles Fletcher and "The Travels of Jerome Horsey, Knt."* Ed. Edward A. Bond. London: Hakluyt Society, 1856.

Fonvizin, Mikhail A. "Obozrenie proiavlenii politicheskoi zhizni v Rossii." In *Obshchestvennye dvizheniia v Rossii v pervuiu polovinu XIX veka,* comp. V. I. Semevskii, V. Bogucharskii, and P. E. Shchegolev, vol. 1, pp. 97-202. St. Petersburg: Tipo-litografiia Gerol'd, 1905.

Garkavi, Avraam Ia. *Skazaniia musul'manskikh pisatelei o slavianakh i russkikh* (VII-X vv.). St. Petersburg, 1870. Reprint. The Hague: Mouton, 1969.

Ger'e, Vladimir [Guerrier, W.], ed. *Sbornik pisem i memorialov Leibnitsa otnosiashchikhsia k Rossii i Petru Velikomu.* St. Petersburg: Tip. Imperatorskoi Akademii Nauk, 1873. See also Guerrier.

Gertsen, Aleksandr I. *Byloe i dumy.* Moscow: OGIZ, 1946.

———. *Izbrannye filosofskie proizvedeniia.* 2 vols. Moscow: OGIZ, 1946.

———. *My Past and Thoughts: The Memoirs of Alexander Herzen.* Trans. Constance Garnett. 6 vols. London: Chatto and Windus, 1924-27. Rev. ed. by Humphrey Higgens. 4 vols.

(London: Chatto and Windus, 1968).

——. *Polnoe sobranie sochinenii i pisem.* Ed. M. K. Lemke. 22 vols. Petrograd-Leningrad-Moscow: Gosizdat and others, 1917-25.

——. *Sochineniia A. I. Gertsena.* 7 vols. bound in 3. St. Petersburg: F. Pavlenkov, 1905.

Giovanni de Plano Carpini: see Carpini.

Glinskii, Boris B. *Revoliutsionnyi period russkoi istorii (1861-1881).* 2 vols. St. Petersburg: A. S. Suvorin, 1913.

Gnevushev, A. M., comp. and ed. *Akty vremeni pravleniia tsaria Vasiliia Shuiskogo (19 maia 1606 g.-17 iiulia 1610 g.).* Moscow: Izd. Imperatorskogo Obshchestva Istorii i Drevnostei Rossiiskikh pri Moskovskom Universitete, 1914.

Goetz, Leopold K. *Deutsch-Russische Handelsvertraege des Mittelalters.* Hamburg: L. Friederichsen, 1916.

Golder, Frank A., ed. *Documents of Russian History 1914-1917.* Trans. Emanuel Aronsberg. New York: Century, 1927. Reprint. Gloucester, Mass.: Peter Smith, 1964.

Golovin, Nikolai N. *The Russian Army in the World War.* New Haven: Yale University Press, 1931.

Gorbachevskii, Ivan I. *Zapiski i pis'ma dekabrista.* Ed. B. E. Syroechkovskii. Moscow: Gosizdat, 1925.

Gosudarstvennaia Duma. *Stenograficheskie otchety Gosudarstvennoi Dumy I, II, III, i IV sozyvov.* 36 vols. St. Petersburg: Gosudarstvennaia Tipografiia, 1906-17.

Gosudarstvennyi Sovet: see *Otchet po . . .*

Got'e, Iu. V., ed. *Akty otnosiashchiesia k istorii zemskikh soborov. Pamiatniki russkoi istorii,* vol. 3. Moscow: N. N. Klochkov, 1909.

Granovskii, Timofei N. *Sochineniia T. N. Granovskogo.* 3d ed. 2 vols. Moscow, 1892.

——. *T. N. Granovskii i ego perepiska.* 2 vols. Moscow, 1897.

Grekov, Boris D., ed. *Pravda Russkaia.* 2 vols. Moscow: AN SSSR, 1940-47.

Grushevskii: see Hrushevsky.

Gudzii, Nikolai K., ed., and L. B. Lekhtblau, comp. *Russkie satiricheskie zhurnaly XVIII veka.* Moscow: Uchpedgiz, 1940.

Guerrier, W. *Leibniz in seinen Beziehungen zu Russland und Peter dem Grossen.* Leipzig, 1873. See also Ger'e.

Gurko, Vladimir I. *Features and Figures of the Past: Government and Opinion in the Reign of Nicholas II.* Palo Alto: Stanford University Press, 1939.

Hansard's Parliamentary Debates. 3d ser., vol. 132. London, 1854.

Hanway, Jonas. *An Historical Account of the British Trade over the Caspian Sea, with a Journal of Travels from London through Russia into Persia and Back.* 2 vols. London, 1753.

Harkavy: see Garkavi.

Haxthausen, Baron August von. *The Russian Empire, Its People, Institutions, and Resources.* Trans. Robert Farie. 2 vols. London, 1856.

——. *Studien ueber die innern Zustaende, das Volksleben und insbesondere die laendlichen Einrichtungen Russlands.* 3 vols. Hanover, 1847-52.

Hellie, Richard, trans. and ed. *Readings for Introduction to Russian Civilization: Muscovite Society.* Chicago: University of Chicago Syllabus Division, 1967.

Herberstein, Sigismund von. *Commentaries on Muscovite Affairs.* Ed. and trans. Oswald P. Backus III. Lawrence: University of Kansas Bookstore, 1956.

——. *Description of Moscow and Muscovy 1557.* Ed. Bertold Picard, trans. J. B. C. Grundy. London: J. M. Dent, 1969.

Herrmann, Ernst, ed. *Russland unter Peter dem Grossen: Nach den handschriftlichen Berichten Johann Gotthilf Vockerodt's und Otto Pleyer's.* Leipzig, 1872. See also *Rossiia pri Petre . . .*

Hertslet, Edward, ed. *The Map of Europe by Treaty since the General Peace of 1814.* 4 vols. London, 1875-91.

Herzen: See Gertsen.

Howes, Robert C., trans. and ed. *The Testaments of the Grand Princes of Moscow*. Ithaca, N.Y.: Cornell University Press, 1967.

Hrushevsky, Michael S. *Istoriia Ukraini-Rusi*. 10 vols. in 11 pts. New York: Knigospilka, 1954-58 (facsimile reprint of original edition of 1905-36).

Iablonskis, K. I., ed. *Statut velikogo kniazhestva litovskogo 1529 goda*. Minsk: AN BSSR, 1960.

Iakhontov, A. N. "Tiazhelye dni." *Arkhiv russkoi revoliutsii*, 18 (Berlin: Slovo, 1926): 5-136.

Iakovlev, A. I., ed. *Akty khoziaistva boiarina B. I. Morozova*. 2 pts. Moscow: AN SSSR, 1940-45.

———. *Pamiatniki istorii Smutnogo vremeni. Pamiatniki russkoi istorii*, vol. 4. Moscow: N. N. Klochkov, 1909.

Iakovlev, Vasilii Ia. [pseudonyms: B. Bazilevskii, V. Bogucharskii], ed. *Gosudarstvennye prestupleniia v Rossii v XIX veke, sbornik izvlechennykh iz ofitsial'nykh izdanii pravitel'stvennykh soobshchenii*. 3 vols. St. Petersburg: Russkaia Skoropechatnia, 1906. See also Bazilevskii.

Intelligentsiia v Rossii: Sbornik statei. St. Petersburg: Knigoizdat. "Zemlia," 1910.

Iosif Volotskii: see Sanin.

Iswolsky [Izvol'skii], Alexander P. *The Memoirs of Alexander Iswolsky*. Ed. and trans. C. I. Seeger. London: Hutchinson, 1920.

Iushkov, Serafim V., ed. *Pamiatniki prava feodal'no-razdroblennoi Rusi XII-XV vv. Pamiatniki russkogo prava*, vol. 2. Moscow: Gosiurizdat, 1953.

———. *Pamiatniki prava Kievskogo gosudarstva. Pamiatniki russkogo prava*, vol. 1. Moscow: Gosiurizdat, 1952.

Iuzefovich, T., ed. *Dogovory Rossii s vostokom: politicheskie i torgovye*. St. Petersburg, 1869.

Izveshchenie o III s"ezde Rossiiskoi Sotsial'-demokraticheskoi Rabochei Partii. Geneva: Izd. RSDRP, 1905.

Izveshchenie o vtorom ocherednom s"ezde Rossiiskoi Sotsial'-demokraticheskoi Rabochei Partii. Geneva: Izd. RSDRP, 1903.

Izvol'skii: see Iswolsky.

"Iz zapisnoi knizhki arkhivista: Dva dokumenta iz istorii Zubatovshchiny." *Krasnyi arkhiv*, 19 (1926, no. 6): 210-11.

Jakobson, Roman. "Saint Constantine's Prologue to the Gospels." *Saint Vladimir's Seminary Quarterly*, vol. 7, N.S., 1963.

Jordanes. *The Gothic History*. Trans. C. C. Mierow. Princeton: Princeton University Press, 1915. Photographically reprinted, Cambridge, Eng., and New York, 1960.

Kalachev, Nikolai V., ed. *Doklady i prigovory v . . . Senate v tsarstvovanie Petra Velikogo*. 6 vols. St. Petersburg: Tip. Imperatorskoi Akademii Nauk, 1880-1901.

Kalinychev, F. I., comp. *Gosudarstvennaia Duma v Rossii v dokumentakh i materialakh*. Moscow: Gosiurizdat, 1957.

Kapterev, Nikolai F. *Patriarkh Nikon i Tsar' Aleksei Mikhailovich*. 2 vols. Sergiev Posad: Tip. Sviato-Troitskoi Sergievoi Lavry, 1909-12.

Karamzin, Nikolai M. *Zapiska o drevnei i novoi Rossii*. Ed. Richard Pipes. Cambridge: Harvard University Press, 1959. See also Pipes.

Katkov, Mikhail N. *Sobranie peredovykh statei "Moskovskikh Vedomostei" s 1863 po 1887 god*. 24 vols. Moscow, 1897-98.

Kennan, George. *Siberia and the Exile System*. 2 vols. New York, 1891.

Khomiakov, Aleksei S. *Izbrannye sochineniia*. New York: Chekhov, 1955.

———. *Polnoe sobranie sochinenii A. S. Khomiakova*. 8 vols. Moscow: Tip. Imperatorskogo Moskovskogo Universiteta, 1900-07.

Khrestomatiia po istorii SSSR. Moscow: Gosudarstvennoe Uchebno-Pedagogicheskoe Izdatel'stvo Ministerstva Prosveshcheniia RSFSR. Vol. 1, *S drevneishikh vremen do kontsa XVII veka*. Comp. V. I. Lebedev, M. N. Tikhomirov, V. E. Syroechkovskii. 4th ed., 1951. Vol. 2, *1682-1856*. Comp. S. S. Dmitriev and M. V. Nechkina. 3d ed., 1953. Vol. 3, *1857-1894*. Comp. S. S.

Dmitriev. 2d ed., 1952.

Kireevskii, Ivan V. *Polnoe sobranie sochinenii I. V. Kireevskogo*. Ed. M. O. Gershenzon. 2 vols. Moscow: Tip. Imperatorskogo Moskovskogo Universiteta, 1911.

"K istorii Loris-Melikovskoi 'Konstitutsii.'" *Krasnyi arkhiv* 8 (1925, no. 1): 132-50.

Knox, Alfred. *With the Russian Army 1914-1917: Being Chiefly Extracts from the Diary of a Military Attaché*. 2 vols. New York: E. P. Dutton, 1921.

Kohn, Hans, ed. *The Mind of Modern Russia: Historical and Political Thought of Russia's Great Age*. New Brunswick, N.J.: Rutgers University Press, 1955.

Kokovtsov, Vladimir N. *Iz moego proshlogo: Vospominaniia, 1903-1919*. 2 vols. Paris: Illiustri-rovannaia Rossiia, 1933.

———. *The Memoirs of Count Kokovtsov: Out of My Past*. Ed. Harold H. Fisher, trans. Laura Matveev. Palo Alto: Stanford University Press, 1935.

Korb, Johann G. *Diarium itineris in Moscoviam* . . . Vienna, 1700 or 1701.

———. *Diary of an Austrian Secretary of Legation at the Court of Peter the Great*. Trans. and ed. Count Macdonnell. 2 vols. London, 1863. Reprint. New York: Da Capo, 1968.

———. *Dnevnik puteshestviia v Moscoviiu (1698-1699 gg.)*. Trans. and commentary, A. I. Malein. St. Petersburg: A. S. Suvorin, 1906.

Kormchaia Kniga. Republished from the edition of 1653 (under Patriarch Nikon). 2 pts. Moscow, 1787.

Korobkov, Nikolai M., ed. *Fel'dmarshal Kutuzov, sbornik dokumentov i materialov*. Moscow: OGIZ, 1947.

Korsakov, Dimitri A. *Votsarenie Imperatritsy Anny Ioannovny*. Kazan', 1880.

Kotoshikhin, Grigorii. *O Rossii v tsarstvovanie Aleksiia Mikhailovicha*. 3d ed. St. Petersburg: Arkheograficheskaia Komissiia, 1884. See also Uroff.

Krachkovskii, Ignatii Iu., ed. *Puteshestvie Ibn-Fadlana na Volgu*. Moscow: AN SSSR, 1939.

Krasnyi arkhiv. 106 vols. bound in 35. Moscow, 1922-41.

Kravchinskii [Stepniak], Sergei M. *The Russian Peasantry: Their Agrarian Condition, Social Life, and Religion*. New York: Harper and Brothers, 1905.

Krizhanich, Iurii. *Russkoe gosudarstvo v polovine XVII veka*. ed. P. Bezsonov. Moscow, 1859.

Kropotkin, Peter. *Memoirs of a Revolutionist*. Boston: Houghton Mifflin, 1930.

———. *Modern Science and Anarchism*. 2d ed. London: Freedom Press, 1923.

———. *Mutual Aid: A Factor of Evolution*. New York: MacLure Phillips, 1902.

Kurakin: see Semevskii.

Kurbskii, Prince Andrei M. *Sochineniia kniazia Kurbskogo. Russkaia istoricheskaia biblioteka*, vol. 31. St. Petersburg: Arkheograficheskaia Komissiia, 1914.

Kutrzeba, Stanislaw, and W. Semikowicz, eds. *Akta unji Polski z Litwa, 1385-1791*. Krakow: Nakladem Polskiej Akademji Umiejetnosci i Towarzystwa Naukowego Warszawskiego, 1932.

Kutuzov: see Korobkov.

Lamzdorf [Lamsdorff], Vladimir N. *Dnevnik 1891-1892*. Moscow: AN SSSR, 1934.

Langer, William L. *The Franco-Russian Alliance 1890-1894*. Cambridge: Harvard University Press, 1929.

Lannoy, Ghillebert de. *Oeuvres de Ghillebert de Lannoy, voyageur, diplomate, et moraliste*. Louvain, 1878.

Lantzeff, George V. *Siberia in the Seventeenth Century: A Study of the Colonial Administration*. Berkeley: University of California Press, 1943.

Lassota von Steblau, Erich. *Tagebuch des Erich Lassota von Steblau*. Ed. Reinhold Schottin. Halle, 1866.

Laue, T. H. von: See Von Laue.

Lavrov, Petr L. ["Mirtov"]. *Historical Letters*. Ed. and trans. James P. Scanlan. Berkeley: University of California Press, 1967.

———. *Istoricheskie pis'ma*. St. Petersburg, 1870.

Lazarevskii, N. I., ed. *Zakonodatel'nye akty perekhodnogo vremeni 1904-1908*. St. Petersburg: Izd. Pravo, 1909.

Lemke, Mikhail K., ed. *Politicheskie protsessy v Rossii 1860-kh gg.* 2d ed. Moscow: Gosizdat, 1923. Reprint. The Hague: Mouton, 1969. See also Gertsen.

Lenin, Vladimir I. *The Essential of Lenin in Two Volumes.* London: Lawrence and Wishart, 1947.

——. *Sochineniia.* 2d ed. 30 vols. Moscow: Gosizdat, 1926-30.

——. *What Is to Be Done?* Trans. Sergei V. and Patricia Utechin. New York: Oxford University Press, 1963.

Letters of the Tsar to the Tsaritsa: see Vulliamy.

Letters of the Tsaritsa to the Tsar, 1914-1916. Intro. Bernard Pares. London: Duckworth, 1923.

Levshin, A. I. "Dostopamiatnye minuty v moei zhizni, zapiska A. I. Levshina." *Russkii arkhiv,* 1885, no. 8, pp. 475-557.

Lewicki, Tadeusz, ed. *Zrodla arabskie do dziejow slowianszczyzny.* Vol. 1. Wroclaw and Krakow: Wyd. Polskiej Akademii Nauk, 1956.

Liubavskii, Matvei K. *Ocherk istorii litovsko-russkogo gosudarstva.* 2d ed. Moscow: Moskovskaia Khudozhestvennaia Pechatnia, 1915.

Loubat, J. F. *Narrative of the Mission to Russia, in 1866, of the Honorable Gustavus Vasa Fox, Assistant-Secretary of the Navy, from the Journal and Notes of J. F. Loubat.* New York, 1874.

Loukomsky [Lukomskii], Alexander S. *Memoirs of the Russian Revolution.* London: T. F. Unwin, 1922.

——. *Vospominaniia Generala A. S. Lukomskogo.* 2 vols. Berlin: Otto Kirchner, 1922.

Macartney, Carlile A. *The Magyars in the Ninth Century.* Cambridge: At the University Press, 1930.

Maklakov, Vasilii A. *The First Duma: Contemporary Reminiscences.* Trans. Mary Belkin. Bloomington: Indiana University Press, 1964.

——. *Iz vospominanii.* New York: Chekhov, 1954.

——. *Pervaia Gosudarstvennaia Duma: Vospominaniia sovremennika.* Paris: Dom Knigi, 1939.

——. *Vlast' i obshchestvennost' na zakate staroi Rossii: Vospominaniia sovremennika.* Paris: Illiustrirovannaia Rossiia, 1939.

——. *Vtoraia Gosudarstvennaia Duma: Vospominaniia sovremennika.* Paris [1946].

Malinin, Vasilii N. *Starets Eleazarova monastyria Filofei i ego poslaniia.* Kiev: Tip. Kievo-Pecherskoi Uspenskoi Lavry, 1901.

Manifest Rossiiskoi Sotsial'-demokraticheskoi Rabochei Partii, 1898 g. Geneva: T. A. Kuklin, 1903.

Manstein, Christopher Hermann von. *Mémoires historiques, politiques et militaires sur la Russie depuis l'Année 1727 jusqu'à 1744, par le Général de Manstein.* 2 vols. Paris, 1860.

——. *Memoirs of Russia from the Year 1727 to 1744.* Ed. David Hume. London, 1770.

——. "Zapiski Manshteina o Rossii, 1727-1744." *Russkaia starina,* 1875, no. 12, suppl.

Martens, Fedor F. *Recueil des traités et conventions conclus par la Russie avec les puissances étrangères.* 15 vols. bound in 8. St. Petersburg: A. Böhnke, 1874-1909.

Materialy po istorii SSSR. Vol. 2. Moscow: AN SSSR, 1955.

Matlaw, Ralph E., ed. and intro. *Belinsky, Chernyshevsky, and Dobrolyubov: Selected Criticism.* New York: E. P. Dutton, 1962.

Maximoff, G. P., comp. and ed. *The Political Philosophy of Bakunin: Scientific Anarchism.* Glencoe, Ill.: Free Press, 1953.

Mazour, Anatole G. *The First Russian Revolution, 1825: The Decembrist Movement.* Berkeley: University of California Press, 1937.

Memoirs of Catherine . . .: see Catherine II, *Memoirs . . .*

Metternich, Prince Richard, ed. *Memoirs of Prince Metternich.* Arr. M. A. Klinkowström, trans. Mrs. Alexander Napier. 5 vols. New York, 1880-82.

Mezhdutsarstvie 1825 goda i vosstanie dekabristov v memuarakh i perepiske chlenov tsarskoi sem'i. Moscow: Gosizdat, 1926.

Michell, Robert, and Nevill Forbes, eds. and trans. *The Chronicle of Novgorod.* Intro. C. Raymond Beazley, commentary by A. A. Shakhmatov. London: Royal Historical Society, 1914 (Camden, 3d ser., vol. 25).

Mikhailovskii, Nikolai K. *Poslednie sochineniia N. K. Mikhailovskogo*. 2 vols. St. Petersburg: Russkoe Bogatstvo, 1905.

——. *Sochineniia N. K. Mikhailovskogo*. Vols. 1-3 (of 6), 4th ed. St. Petersburg: Russkoe Bogatstvo, 1906-09. Vols. 4-6, St. Petersburg: Russkoe Bogatstvo, 1897.

Miliukov, Pavel N. *God bor'by, 1905-06*. St. Petersburg: Obshchestvennaia Pol'za, 1907.

——. *Russia and Its Crisis*. London: T. F. Unwin, 1905.

——. *Vospominaniia 1859-1917*. 2 vols. New York: Chekhov, 1955.

Miliutin, Dmitrii A. *Dnevnik D. A. Miliutina, 1873-1882*. Ed. Petr A. Zaionchkovskii. 4 vols. Moscow [Bibl. Lenina], 1947-50.

Miliutina, Mariia A. "Iz zapisok Marii Aggeevny Miliutinoi." *Russkaia starina*, 98 (April 1899): 105-27.

Miller [Mueller], G. F. *Istoriia Sibiri*. 2 vols. Moscow: AN SSSR, 1937-41.

Mishulin, A. V. "Drevnie slaviane v otryvkakh greko-rimskikh i vizantiiskikh pisatelei po VII v. n. e." *Vestnik drevnei istorii*, 14 (1941, no. 1), suppl.

Monas, Sidney. *The Third Section: Police and Society in Russia under Nicholas I*. Cambridge: Harvard University Press, 1961.

Moskoff, Eugene A. *The Russian Philosopher Chaadayev: His Ideas and His Epoch*. New York: Colonial Printing and Publishing, 1937.

Mukhanov, Pavel A., ed. *Zapiski getmana Zholkevskogo o Moskovskoi voine*. 2d ed. St. Petersburg, 1871.

Naumov, Aleksandr N. *Iz utselevshikh vospominanii 1868-1917*. 2 vols. New York: A. K. Naumova and O. A. Kusevitskaia, 1954-55.

Nevskii, Vladimir I., comp. *1905: Sovetskaia pechat' i literatura o sovetakh: Materialy i dokumenty*. Vol. 3. Moscow: Gosizdat, 1925.

Nolde, Boris. *L'Alliance Franco-Russe*. Paris: Librarie Droz, 1936.

Nomad, Max. *Apostles of Revolution*. Boston: Little, Brown, 1939.

Novgorodskaia pervaia letopis'. Ed. A. N. Nasonov. Moscow: AN SSSR, 1950.

Novikov, Nikolai I., ed. *Drevniaia rossiiskaia vivliofika*. 2d ed. 12 vols. Moscow, 1788-91. Vol. 6, 1788.

——. *Satiricheskie zhurnaly N. I. Novikova*. Ed. P. N. Berkov. Moscow: AN SSSR, 1951.

Novosil'tsev, N. N. "N. N. Novosil'tsev's Project for a Constitutional Charter for the Russian Empire." Ed. David Urquhart. *The Portfolio*, 5 (1837): 512-22, 610-39; 6 (1837): 72-83.

Obshchestvo Istorii i Drevnostei Rossiiskikh. *Chteniia v Imperatorskom Obshchestve Istorii i Drevnostei Rossiiskikh pri Moskovskom Universitete*. 264 vols. Moscow: Universitetskaia Tipografiia, 1846-1918.

Obshchestvo Istorii i Drevnostei Rossiiskikh. *Vremennik Imperatorskogo Moskovskogo Obshchestva Istorii i Drevnostei Rossiiskikh*. 25 vols. Moscow, 1849-57.

Olearius, Adam. *Der Welt-beruehmten Adami Olearii Reise-Beschreibungen . . . nach Musskau und Persien*. 4th ed. Hamburg, 1696.

——. *The Travels of Olearius in Seventeenth-Century Russia*. Trans. and ed. Samuel H. Baron. Stanford: Stanford University Press, 1967.

Osvobozhdenie. Ed. and publ. P. B. Struve. Stuttgart, 1902-04; Paris, 1904-05.

Otchet po Gosudarstvennomu Sovetu za 1886 god. St. Petersburg, 1888.

Page, Stanley W., ed. *Russia in Revolution: Selected Readings in Russian Domestic History since 1855*. Princeton: Van Nostrand, 1965.

Paléologue, [Georges] Maurice. *An Ambassador's Memoirs*. Trans. F. A. Holt. 4th ed. 3 vols. New York: George H. Doran, 1924-25.

——. *La Russie des tsars pendant la grande guerre*. 6th ed. 3 vols. Paris: Plon-Nourrit, 1922.

Palitsyn, Avraamii. *Skazanie Avraamiia Palitsyna*. Commentary by O. A. Derzhavina and E. V. Kolosova, ed. L. V. Cherepnin. Moscow: AN SSSR, 1955.

Palmer, W. *The Patriarch and the Tsar*. 6 vols. London, 1871-76.

Pamiatniki russkogo prava. 8 vols. Moscow: Gosiurizdat, 1952-61. See also Cherepnin; Iushkov.
Pamiatniki russkoi istorii. Ed. members of the history faculty of Moscow University. 8 vols.
   Moscow: N. N. Klochkov, 1909-11. See also Got'e; Iakovlev; Pososhkov.
Pares, Bernard. *Day by Day with the Russian Army, 1914-15.* London: Constable, 1915.
———. *The Fall of the Russian Monarchy: A Study of the Evidence.* New York: Alfred A. Knopf,
   1939.
Pawlowski, Bronislaw, comp. *Krolestwo kongresowe i powstanie listopadowe.* Teksty zrodlowe
   do nauki historji w szkole sredniej, pt. 49. Krakow: Nakladem Krakowskiej Spolki Wydawniczej,
   1923.
Perepiska Nikolaia i Aleksandry Romanovykh 1914-1917: see Tsentral'nyi Gosudarstvennyi
   Istoricheskii Arkhiv v Moskve.
Peresvetov, Ivan. *Sochineniia I. Peresvetova.* Ed. A. A. Zimin and D. S. Likhachev. Moscow: AN
   SSSR, 1956.
———. *Sochineniia Ivana Peresvetova.* Ed. V. F. Rzhiga. In *Chteniia v Obshchestve Istorii i
   Drevnostei Rossiiskikh pri Moskovskom Universitete.* Moscow, 1908, no. I.
Perry, John. *The State of Russia under the Present Czar, By Captain John Perry.* London, 1716.
Pestel', Pavel I. *Russkaia Pravda.* Ed. and intro. P. Shchegolev. St. Petersburg: Izd. "Kul'tura,"
   1906.
"Petr Mikhailovich Bestuzhev-Riumin i ego pomest'e." *Russkii arkhiv.* vol. 42 (1904, no. 1),
   pp. 5-42.
Pipes, Richard. *Karamzin's Memoir on Ancient and Modern Russia: A Translation and Analysis.*
   Cambridge: Harvard University Press, 1959.
Pisarev, Dmitrii I. *Izbrannye sochineniia.* Vol. 1. Moscow: Gosudarstvennoe Izd. Khudozhest-
   vennoi Literatury, 1935.
———. *Selected Philosophical, Social, and Political Essays.* Moscow: Foreign Languages Publish-
   ing House, 1958.
———. *Sochineniia.* 4 vols. Moscow: Gosudarstvennoe Izd. Khudozhestvennoi Literatury, 1955-56.
Pis'ma i bumagi Imperatora Petra Velikogo. 11 vols. Vols. 1-7, St. Petersburg: Gosudarstvennaia
   Tipografiia, 1887-1918. Vols. 8-11, Moscow: AN SSSR, 1948-64.
Plekhanov, Georgii V. *Dnevnik sotsial-demokrata.* Vol. 1. Petrograd: M. V. Popov, 1916.
———. *Nashi raznoglasiia.* St. Petersburg: Novyi Mir, 1906.
———. *Selected Philosophical Works.* 2 vols. Moscow: Foreign Languages Publishing House, 1959.
———. *Sochineniia.* 24 vols. Moscow: Gosizdat, 1923-27.
Pobedonostsev, Konstantin P. *Moskovskii sbornik.* Moscow, 1896.
———. *Pis'ma Pobedonostseva k Aleksandru III.* 2 vols. Moscow: Novaia Moskva, 1925-26.
———. *Reflexions of a Russian Statesman.* Trans. Robert C. Long. London, 1898.
Pokrovskii, Mikhail N., et al., eds. *Vosstanie dekabristov.* 11 vols. Moscow: Gosizdat, 1925-54.
"Politicheskoe polozhenie Rossii nakanune fevral'skoi revoliutsii v zhandarmskom osveshchenii."
   Krasnyi arkhiv, 17 (1926, no. 4): 3-35.
Polner, Tikhon J. *Russian Local Government during the War and the Union of Zemstvos.* Russian
   Series, "Economic and Social History of the World War," no. 9. New Haven: Yale University
   Press, 1930.
Polnoe Sobranie Zakonov Rossiiskoi Imperii . . . 1649-1913. 134 vols. St. Petersburg, 1830-1916
   (1st ser., 46 vols., containing laws of 1649-1825; 2d ser., 55 vols., covering 1825-81; 3d ser.,
   33 vols., covering 1881-1913).
Polnyi sbornik platform vsekh russkikh politicheskikh partii. 4th ed. St. Petersburg, 1907.
Polovtsev, Aleksandr A. "Dnevnik A. A. Polovtseva, 1901-1908." *Krasnyi arkhiv,* 3 (1923): 75-
   172; 4 (1923): 63-128.
Ponomarev, A. I. *Pamiatniki drevnerusskoi tserkovno-uchitel'noi literatury.* Pt. 1. St. Petersburg:
   Izd. zhurnala "Strannik," 1894.
Pososhkov, Ivan T. "Donesenie boiarinu F. A. Golovinu o ratnom povedenii." In *Pamiatniki
   russkoi istorii,* vol. 8. Moscow: N. N. Klochkov, 1911.
———. *Kniga o skudosti i bogatstve.* Moscow: AN SSSR, 1937.

Po voprosam programmy i taktiki: Sbornik statei iz "Revoliutsionnoi Rossii." [Paris:] Tip. Sotsialistov-Revoliutsionerov, 1903.

Pravitel'stvennyi vestnik. St. Petersburg, 1869-1917.

Pravo (weekly legal journal). 1898-1917.

Priselkov, Mikhail D. *Khanskie iarlyki russkim mitropolitam.* St. Petersburg: Nauchnoe Delo, 1916.

Procopius. *History of the Wars.* Trans. H. B. Dewing. Loeb Classical Library, vol. 4. Cambridge: Harvard University Press, 1924.

Programma i organizatsionnyi ustav Partii Sotsialistov-Revoliutsionerov. Paris: Izd. TsK PS-R, 1906.

Programma i ustav Rossiiskoi Sotsial'-Demokraticheskoi Rabochei Partii, Paris: *Sotsial'demokrat,* 1909.

Protokoly ob"edinitel'nogo s"ezda Rossiiskoi Sotsial'-demokraticheskoi Rabochei Partii, sostoiavshegosia v Stokgol'me v 1906 g. Moscow: TsK RSDRP, 1907.

Protokoly pervoi obshchepartiinoi konferentsii P.S-R. 1908 g. Paris: Izd. TsK PS-R, 1908.

Protokoly zasedanii soveshchaniia . . . po peresmotru osnovnykh gosudarstvennykh zakonov. St. Petersburg: Gosudarstvennaia Tipografiia, 1906.

Pskovskie letopisi. Ed. A. N. Nasonov. Moscow: AN SSSR, 1941.

Pugachevshchina: see Tsentral'nyi Gosudarstvennyi Istoricheskii Arkhiv v Moskve.

Purchas, Samuel: see Chancellor.

Putnam, Peter, ed. *Seven Britons in Imperial Russia.* Princeton: Princeton University Press, 1952.

Radishchev, Aleksandr N. *A Journey from St. Petersburg to Moscow, by A. N. Radishchev.* Ed. Roderick Page Thaler, trans. Leo Wiener. Cambridge: Harvard University Press, 1958.

———. *Puteshestvie iz Peterburga v Moskvu.* Moscow: AN SSSR, 1935 (reprint of ed. of 1790).

Raeff, Marc. *The Decembrist Movement.* Englewood Cliffs, N.J.: Prentice-Hall, 1966.

———. *Plans for Political Reform in Imperial Russia, 1730-1905.* Englewood Cliffs, N.J.: Prentice-Hall, 1966.

———, ed. *Russian Intellectual History, an Anthology.* New York: Harcourt, Brace and World, 1966.

Reddaway, W. F., ed. *Documents of Catherine the Great: The Correspondence with Voltaire and the Instructions of 1767.* Cambridge: At the University Press, 1931.

Riasanovsky, Nicholas V. *Nicholas I and Official Nationality in Russia, 1825-1855.* Berkeley: University of California Press, 1959.

Riha, Thomas, ed. *Readings in Russian Civilization.* 3 vols. Chicago: University of Chicago Press, 1964. 2d ed. 1969.

Rittikh, Aleksandr A., ed. *Krest'ianskoe zemlepol'zovanie.* St. Petersburg: V. F. Kirsbaum, 1903.

Rockhill, William W., ed. *Journey of William of Rubruck to the Eastern Parts of the World, 1253-1255, as Narrated by Himself.* London: Hakluyt Society, 1900.

Rodzianko, Mikhail V. "Ekonomicheskoe polozhenie Rossii pered revoliutsiei: Zapiska M. V. Rodzianki." *Krasnyi arkhiv,* 10 (1925, no. 3): 69-86.

———. "Gosudarstvennaia Duma i fevral'skaia 1917 g. revoliutsiia." *Arkhiv russkoi revoliutsii,* 6 (1922): 5-80.

———. "Krushenie Imperii." *Arkhiv russkoi revoliutsii,* 17 (1926): 1-169.

Rossiia pri Petre Velikom, po rukopisnomu izvestiiu I. G. Vokerodta i O. Pleiera. Trans. A. N. Shemiakin. *Chteniia v Imperatorskom Obshchestve Istorii i Drevnostei Rossiiskikh pri Moskovskom Universitete,* vol. 89, pt. 4. Moscow, 1874, bk. 2.

Rousset de Missy, Jean. *Recueil historique d'actes . . . et traitez de paix depuis la Paix d'Utrect.* 21 vols. The Hague, 1728-55.

Rozen, Andrei E. *Zapiski dekabrista.* St. Petersburg: Obshchestvennaia Pol'za, 1907.

The Russian Co-operator: A Journal of Co-operative Unity. Ed. J. V. Bubnoff and A. N. Balakshin. London, 1916-21.

Russian Primary Chronicle: See Cross.

Russkaia istoricheskaia biblioteka: see Arkheograficheskaia Komissiia.

Russkaia starina. Ed. M. I. Semevskii. St. Petersburg, 1870-1918.

Russkii arkhiv. Ed. P. Bartenev. Moscow, 1863-1917.

Rychkov, Petr I. "Nakaz dlia derevenskogo upravitelia . . ." *Trudy Vol'nogo Ekonomicheskogo Obshchestva,* 16: 9-68. St. Petersburg, 1770.

Sanin [Volotskii], Iosif. *Prosvetitel' ili oblichenie eresi zhidovstvuiushchikh.* Kazan', 1855.

Sazonov, Sergei D. *Fateful Years 1909-1916: The Reminiscences of Serge Sazonov.* London: J. Cape, 1928.

Sbornik dogovorov i diplomaticheskikh dokumentov po delam Dal'nego Vostoka 1895-1905 gg.. St. Petersburg: Ministerstvo Inostrannykh Del, 1906.

Sbornik Imperatorskogo Russkogo Istoricheskogo Obshchestva. 148 vols. St. Petersburg: Tip. Imperatorskogo Russkogo Istoricheskogo Obshchestva, 1867-1916.

Segel, Harold B., ed. and trans. *The Literature of Eighteenth-Century Russia.* 2 vols. New York: E. P. Dutton, 1967.

Semennikov, Vladimir P., ed. *Monarkhiia pered krusheniem, 1914-1917: Bumagi Nikolaia II i drugie dokumenty.* Moscow: Gosizdat, 1927.

———. *Politika Romanovykh nakanune revoliutsii.* Moscow: Gosizdat, 1926.

Semenov, Nikolai P. *Osvobozhdenie krest'ian v tsarstvovanie Imperatora Aleksandra II: Khronika deiatel'nosti komissii po krest'ianskomu delu.* 3 vols. St. Petersburg, 1889-92.

Semevskii, M. I., ed. *Arkhiv kniazia F. A. Kurakina.* Vol. 1. St. Petersburg, 1890. (Contains "Zhizn' kniazia Borisa Ivanovicha Kurakina.")

Senn, Alfred E., ed. *Readings in Russian Political and Diplomatic History.* 2 vols. Homewood, Ill.: Dorsey Press, 1966.

Sergeev, A. A. "Pervaia Gosudarstvennaia Duma v Vyborge." *Krasnyi arkhiv,* 4 (1923, no. 2): 85-99.

Sergeevskii, Nikolai D., ed. *Konstitutsionnaia khartiia 1815 g. i nekotorye drugie akty byvshego Tsarstva Pol'skogo (1814-1881). Biblioteka Okrain Rossii,* vol. 5. St. Petersburg: Izd. Sergeevskogo, 1907.

Shavel'skii, Georgii. *Vospominaniia poslednego protopresvitera russkoi armii i flota.* 2 vols. New York: Chekhov, 1954.

Shcherbatov, Mikhail M. *On the Corruption of Morals in Russia.* Ed. and trans. A. Lentin. Cambridge: At the University Press, 1969.

———. *Sochineniia Kniazia M. M. Shcherbatova.* Ed. I. P. Khrushchov and A. G. Voronov. St. Petersburg, 1898.

Shchipanov, I. Ia., ed. *Izbrannye sotsial'no-politicheskie i filosofskie proizvedeniia dekabristov.* 3 vols. Moscow: Gosudarstvennoe izdatel'stvo politicheskoi literatury, 1951.

Shil'der, N. K. *Imperator Aleksandr Pervyi, ego zhizn' i tsarstvovanie.* 4 vols. St. Petersburg: A. S. Suvorin, 1897-98.

Shilovskii, Petr P. *Akty otnosiashchiesia k politicheskomu polozheniiu Finliandii.* St. Petersburg: M. M. Stasiulevich, 1903.

Shul'gin, Vasilii V. *Dni.* Belgrade: Novoe Vremia, 1925.

Skarga, Piotr. *Kazania sejmowe.* Ed. Stanislaw Kot. Krakow: Nakladem Krakowskiej Spolki Wydawniczej, 1925.

Smirnov, Ivan I. *Vosstanie Bolotnikova 1606-1607.* Moscow: AN SSSR, 1951.

Smith, Robert E. F. *The Enserfment of the Russian Peasantry.* Cambridge: At the University Press, 1968.

Solov'ev, Ia. A. "Zapiski Senatora Ia. A. Solov'eva." *Russkaia starina,* 27 (1880): 319-62; 30 (1881): 211-46, 721-56, 903-05.

Solov'ev, Sergei M. "Istoriia padeniia Pol'shi." *Sobranie sochinenii S. M. Solov'eva.* St. Petersburg: Obshchestvennaia Pol'za, 1900.

Solov'ev [Solovyof], Vladimir S. *The Justification of the Good.* Trans. Nathalie A. Duddington, note by Stephen Graham. London: Constable, 1918.

——. *Opravdanie dobra: Nravstvennaia filosofiia Vladimira Solov'eva.* 2d ed. Moscow, 1899.

——. *Sobranie sochinenii Vladimira Sergeevicha Solov'eva.* 9 vols. St. Petersburg: Obshchestvennaia Pol'za, [1901]-07.

Sovremennoe polozhenie i zadachi partii: Platforma, vyrabotannaia gruppoi Bol'shevikov. Paris: Izd. Gruppy "Vpered," 1910.

Spector, Ivar and Marion, eds. *Readings in Russian History and Culture.* Palo Alto: Pacific Books, 1968.

Speranskii, Mikhail M. *Plan gosudarstvennogo preobrazovaniia, vvedenie k "Ulozheniiu Gosudarstvennykh Zakonov" 1809 g.* Moscow: Izd. Russkoi Mysli, 1905.

Staden, Heinrich von. *Aufzeichnungen ueber den Moskauer Staat.* Ed. Fritz Epstein. Hamburg: Friederichsen, de Gruyter, 1930.

——. *The Land and Government of Muscovy: A Sixteenth-Century Account.* Trans. and ed. Thomas Esper. Stanford: Stanford University Press, 1967.

Staehlin-Storcksburg, Jacob von. *Original Anecdotes of Peter the Great.* London, 1788.

Statut velikogo kniazhestva litovskogo 1529 goda. Ed. K. I. Iablonskis. Minsk: An BSSR, 1960.

Steblau: see Lassota.

Stoglav: Tsarskie voprosy i sobornye otvety. Moscow, 1890.

Stroev, Pavel M. *Obstoiatel'noe opisanie staropechatnykh knig slavianskikh i rossiiskikh, khraniashchikhsia v biblioteke grafa F. A. Tolstova.* Moscow, 1829.

Struys, John. *The Voiages and Travels of John Struys.* Trans. John Morrison. London, 1684.

"Studencheskie volneniia v. 1901-1902 gg. Vvodnaia stat'ia A. Syromiatnikova." *Krasnyi arkhiv,* 89-90 (1938, nos. 4-5): 258-308.

"Studencheskoe dvizhenie v 1901 g., s predisloviem V. Orlova." *Krasnyi arkhiv,* 75 (1936, no. 2): 83-112.

"Sudebnik 1497 g." *Pamiatniki russkogo prava,* 3: 346-57. Moscow: Gosizdat, 1955.

"Sudebnik 1550 g." *Pamiatniki russkogo prava,* 4: 233-61. Moscow: Gosizdat, 1956.

Sudebniki XV-XVI vekov. Ed. B. D. Grekov. Moscow: AN SSSR, 1952.

Svod Zakonov Rossiiskoi Imperii. 3d ed. 16 vols. St. Petersburg: Gosudarstvennaia Tipografiia, 1857-1916.

Tatishchev, Sergei S. *Imperator Aleksandr II.* 2 vols. St. Petersburg: A. S. Suvorin, 1911.

Tolstoi, Iurii K., ed. *Pervye sorok let snoshenii mezhdu Rossiei i Angliei 1553-1593.* St. Petersburg, 1875. Reprinted by Burt Franklin. New York: 1963.

Tolstoi, Lev N. *Polnoe sobranie sochinenii.* 90 vols. Moscow: Gosudarstvennoe Izd. Khudozhestvennoi Literatury, 1928-58.

——. *Sochineniia grafa L. N. Tolstogo.* 12th ed. 20 vols. Moscow: T. and I. N. Kushnerev, 1911.

——. *The Works of Leo Tolstoy: Tolstoy Centenary Edition.* 21 vols. London: Oxford University Press, 1928-37.

Tooke, William. *The Life of Catharine II, Empress of Russia.* 2d ed. 3 vols. London, 1800.

——. *View of the Russian Empire during the Reign of Catherine the Second and to the Close of the Eighteenth Century.* 2d ed. 3 vols. London, 1800.

Traités et conventions entre L'Empire du Japon et les puissances étrangères. Tokyo: Z. P. Maruya, 1908.

Trudy Vol'nogo . . . : see Vol'noe Ekonomicheskoe Obshchestvo.

Tsentral'nyi Gosudarstvennyi Istoricheskii Arkhiv v Moskve, ed. *Burzhuaziia nakanune fevral'skoi revolutsii.* Moscow: Gosizdat, 1927.

——. *Perepiska Nikolaia i Aleksandry Romanovykh 1914-1917.* Vols. 3-5. Moscow: Gosizdat, 1923.

——. *Pugachevshchina.* 2 vols. Moscow: Gosizdat, 1926-29.

Tsentral'nyi Statisticheskii Komitet. *Ezhegodnik Rossii 1906 g.* St. Petersburg: Ministerstvo Vnutrennikh Del, 1907.

——. *Ezhegodnik Rossii 1910.* St. Petersburg: Ministerstvo Vnutrennikh Del, 1911.

——. *Statisticheskii Ezhegodnik Rossii 1914.* St. Petersburg: Ministerstvo Vnutrennikh Del, 1915.

Ulozhenie gosudaria tsaria i velikogo kniazia Alekseia Mikhailovicha. St. Petersburg: Gosudarst-vennaia Tipografiia, 1913.

Uroff, Benjamin Phillip. "Grigorii Karpovich Kotoshikhin, *On Russia in the Reign of Alexis Mikhailovich:* An Annotated Translation." 2 vols. Ph.D. dissertation, Columbia University, 1970.

Urusov [Urussov] , Sergei D. *Memoirs of a Russian Governor, Prince S. D. Urussov.* Trans. Hermann Rosenthal. New York: Harper and Brothers, 1908.

Ustrialov, Nikolai G. *Istoriia tsarstvovaniia Petra Velikogo.* 5 vols. (nos. 1-4, 6) St. Petersburg, 1858-63.

Valk, Sigizmunt N., ed. *Gramoty velikogo Novgoroda i Pskova.* Moscow: AN SSSR, 1949.

Vashkevich, Vladislav V., comp. *Sbornik uzakonenii kasaiushchikhsia evreev.* St. Petersburg, 1884.

Vasiliev, A. A. *The Russian Attack on Constantinople in 860.* Cambridge: Harvard University Press, 1946.

"Vekhi," kak znamenie vremeni: Sbornik statei. Moscow: "Zveno," 1910.

Vekhi: Sbornik statei o russkoi intelligentsii. 4th ed. Moscow: T. and I. N. Kushnerev, 1909. Reprint. Frankfurt-am-Main: Posev, 1967.

Vernadsky, George. *Bohdan, Hetman of Ukraine.* New Haven: Yale University Press, 1941.

———. *La Charte Constitutionelle de l'Empire russe de l'an 1820.* Paris: Librairie du Recueil Sirey, 1933.

———. "Juwaini's Version of Chingis-Khan's Yasa." *Annales de l'Institut Kondakov,* 11 (1939): 39, 42-44.

———. *Medieval Russian Laws.* New York: Columbia University Press, 1947. Reprint. New York: Octagon Books, 1955; New York: W. W. Norton, 1969.

———. *The Mongols and Russia.* George Vernadsky and Michael Karpovich, *A History of Russia,* vol. 3. New Haven: Yale University Press, 1953.

———. *The Origins of Russia.* Oxford: Clarendon Press, 1959.

Vigel', Filipp F. *Vospominaniia F. F. Vigelia.* 7 vols. in 3. Moscow, 1864-65.

———. *Zapiski.* Ed. S. Ia. Shtraikh. 2 vols. Moscow: Artel' Pisatelei Krug, 1928.

Vitte: See Witte.

Vol'noe Ekonomicheskoe Obshchestvo. *Istoriia Imperatorskogo Vol'nogo Ekonomicheskogo Obshchestva s 1765 do 1865.* Comp. A. I. Khodnev. St. Petersburg, 1865.

Vol'noe Ekonomicheskoe Obshchestvo. *Trudy Vol'nogo Ekonomicheskogo Obshchestva k pooshchreniiu v Rossii zemledeliia i domostroitel'stva.* 280 vols. St. Petersburg, various pub-lishers, 1765-1915. See also Bolotov, Rychkov.

Von Laue, Theodore H. "A Secret Memorandum of Sergei Witte on the Industrialization of Imperial Russia." *Journal of Modern History,* 26 (March 1954): 60-74.

Voskresenskaia letopis'. Polnoe Sobranie Russkikh Letopisei, vols. 7-8. St. Petersburg, 1853.

Vossoedinenie Ukrainy s Rossiei: Dokumenty i materialy. 3 vols. Moscow: AN SSSR, 1954.

Vulliamy, C. E., ed. *The Letters of the Tsar to the Tsaritsa, 1914-1917.* Trans. A. L. Hynes. London: J. Lane, 1929.

Wallace, Donald Mackenzie. *Russia.* Rev. and enlarged ed. London: Cassell, 1912.

Walsh, Warren B., ed. *Readings in Russian History.* 3 vols. 4th ed. Syracuse, N.Y.: Syracuse University Press, 1963.

Weber, Friedrich Christian. *The Present State of Russia.* 2 vols. London, 1722-23.

Whitworth, Charles. *An Account of Russia As It Was in the Year 1710.* London, 1758.

Wiener, Leo, ed. *Anthology of Russian Literature from the Earliest Period to the Present Time.* 2 vols. New York: G. P. Putnam's Sons, 1902.

Wilhelm II. *The Kaiser's Letters to the Tsar.* Ed. N. F. Grant. London: Hodder and Stoughton, 1920.

Witte [Vitte], Sergei Iu. *Vospominaniia: Tsarstvovanie Nikolaia II.* 2 vols. Berlin: Slovo, 1922. See also: Yarmolinsky; Von Laue.

Wolf, L., ed. *The Legal Sufferings of the Jews in Russia.* London: T. F. Unwin, 1912.

Wormeley, Katherine Prescott, ed. and trans. *Prince de Ligne: His Memoirs, Letters and Miscellaneous Papers.* 2 vols. Boston: Hardy, Pratt, 1899.

Yarmolinsky, Abraham, ed. and trans. *The Memoirs of Count Witte.* Garden City, N.Y.: Doubleday, Page, 1921.

Zablotskii-Desiatovskii, Andrei P. *Graf P. D. Kiselev i ego vremia.* 4 vols. St. Petersburg, 1882.

Zaionchkovskii, A. M., comp. "Iz zapisnoi knizhki arkhivista v gody reaktsii." *Krasnyi arkhiv,* 8 (1925, no. 1): 240-43.

Zapadnorusskie letopisi. Polnoe Sobranie Russkikh Letopisei, vol. 17. St. Petersburg: Arkheograficheskaia Kommissiia, 1907.

Zemskii s"ezd 6-go i sl. noiabria 1904 g. Paris: Izd. Red. "Osvobozhdenie," 1905.

Zenkovsky, Serge A., ed. and trans. *Medieval Russia's Epics, Chronicles, and Tales.* New York: E. P. Dutton, 1963.

Zhurnal Ministerstva Iustitsii, 1917, nos. 2-3 (February-March), pp. 1-7.

Zhurnal Ministerstva Narodnogo Prosveshcheniia. 362 vols. St. Petersburg, 1834-1905; n.s. 72 vols., 1906-17.

Zisserman, Arnold L. *Fel'dmarshal Kniaz A. I. Bariatinskii, 1815-1877.* 3 vols. Moscow, 1888-91.

Zolkiewski, Stanislas. *Expedition to Moscow: A Memoir by Hetman Stanislas Zolkiewski.* Trans. M. W. Stephan. Intro. and notes by Jedrzej Giertych. Preface by Robert Bruce Lockhart. Polonica Series no. 1. London: Polonica Publications, 1959. See also Mukhanov.

PERMISSIONS